FORD
CROWN VICTORIA/GRAND MARQUIS
1989-94 REPAIR MANUAL

CHILTON'S

President	Dean F. Morgantini, S.A.E.
Vice President–Finance	Barry L. Beck
Vice President–Sales	Glenn D. Potere
Executive Editor	Kevin M. G. Maher, A.S.E.
Manager–Consumer	Richard Schwartz, A.S.E.
Manager–Professional	George B. Heinrich III, A.S.E., S.A.E.
Manager–Marine/Recreation	James R. Marotta, A.S.E., S.T.S.
Manager–Production	Ben Greisler, S.A.E.
Production Assistant	Melinda Possinger
Project Managers	Will Kessler, A.S.E., S.A.E., Todd W. Stidham, A.S.E., Ron Webb
Schematics Editor	Christopher G. Ritchie, A.S.E.
Editor	Michael L. Grady

CHILTON Automotive Books

PUBLISHED BY **W. G. NICHOLS, INC.**

Manufactured in USA
© 1999 W. G. Nichols
1020 Andrew Drive
West Chester, PA 19380
ISBN 0-8019-9129-3
Library of Congress Catalog Card No. 99-072475
1234567890 8765432109

www.Chiltononline.com

Contents

Contents

See last page for information on additional titles

SAFETY NOTICE

Proper service and repair procedures are vital to the safe, reliable operation of all motor vehicles, as well as the personal safety of those performing repairs. This manual outlines procedures for servicing and repairing vehicles using safe, effective methods. The procedures contain many NOTES, CAUTIONS and WARNINGS which should be followed, along with standard procedures to eliminate the possibility of personal injury or improper service which could damage the vehicle or compromise its safety.

It is important to note that repair procedures and techniques, tools and parts for servicing motor vehicles, as well as the skill and experience of the individual performing the work vary widely. It is not possible to anticipate all of the conceivable ways or conditions under which vehicles may be serviced, or to provide cautions as to all possible hazards that may result. Standard and accepted safety precautions and equipment should be used when handling toxic or flammable fluids, and safety goggles or other protection should be used during cutting, grinding, chiseling, prying, or any other process that can cause material removal or projectiles.

Some procedures require the use of tools specially designed for a specific purpose. Before substituting another tool or procedure, you must be completely satisfied that neither your personal safety, nor the performance of the vehicle will be endangered.

Although information in this manual is based on industry sources and is complete as possible at the time of publication, the possibility exists that some car manufacturers made later changes which could not be included here. While striving for total accuracy, NP/Chilton cannot assume responsibility for any errors, changes or omissions that may occur in the compilation of this data.

PART NUMBERS

Part numbers listed in this reference are not recommendations by Chilton for any product brand name. They are references that can be used with interchange manuals and aftermarket supplier catalogs to locate each brand supplier's discrete part number.

SPECIAL TOOLS

Special tools are recommended by the vehicle manufacturer to perform their specific job. Use has been kept to a minimum, but where absolutely necessary, they are referred to in the text by the part number of the tool manufacturer. These tools can be purchased, under the appropriate part number, from your local dealer or regional distributor, or an equivalent tool can be purchased locally from a tool supplier or parts outlet. Before substituting any tool for the one recommended, read the SAFETY NOTICE at the top of this page.

ACKNOWLEDGMENTS

NP/Chilton expresses appreciation to Ford Motor Co. for their generous assistance.

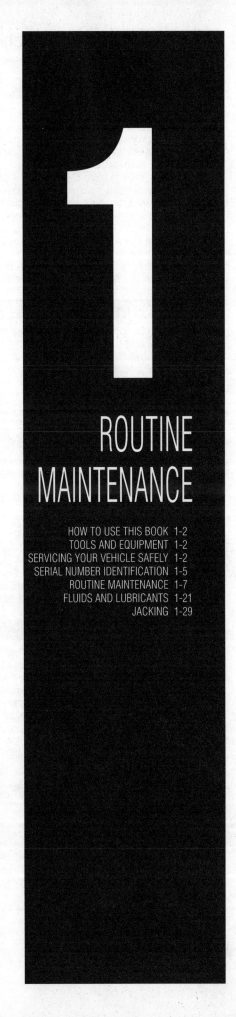

1

ROUTINE MAINTENANCE

HOW TO USE THIS BOOK

Chilton's Total Car Care Manual for the Ford Crown Victoria and Mercury Grand Marquis is intended to help you learn more about the inner workings of your vehicle and save you money on its upkeep and operation.

The beginning of the book will likely be referred to the most, since that is where you will find information for maintenance and tune-up. The other sections deal with the more complex systems of your vehicle. Systems (from engine through brakes) are covered to the extent that the average do-it-yourselfer can attempt. This book will not explain such things as rebuilding a differential because the expertise required and the special tools necessary make this uneconomical. It will, however, give you detailed instructions to help you change your own brake pads and shoes, replace spark plugs, and perform many more jobs that can save you money and help avoid expensive problems.

A secondary purpose of this book is a reference for owners who want to understand their vehicle and/or their mechanics better.

Where to Begin

Before removing any bolts, read through the entire procedure. This will give you the overall view of what tools and supplies will be required. So read ahead and plan ahead. Each operation should be approached logically and all procedures thoroughly understood before attempting any work.

If repair of a component is not considered practical, we tell you how to remove the part and then how to install the new or rebuilt replacement. In this way, you at least save labor costs.

Avoiding Trouble

Many procedures in this book require you to "label and disconnect . . ." a group of lines, hoses or wires. Don't be think you can remember where everything goes—you won't. If you hook up vacuum or fuel lines incorrectly, the vehicle may run poorly, if at all. If you hook up electrical wiring incorrectly, you may instantly learn a very expensive lesson.

You don't need to know the proper name for each hose or line. A piece of masking tape on the hose and a piece on its fitting will allow you to assign your own label. As long as you remember your own code, the lines can be reconnected by matching your tags. Remember that tape will dissolve in gasoline or solvents; if a part is to be washed or cleaned, use another method of identification. A permanent felt-tipped marker or a metal scribe can be very handy for marking metal parts. Remove any tape or paper labels after assembly.

Maintenance or Repair?

Maintenance includes routine inspections, adjustments, and replacement of parts which show signs of normal wear. Maintenance compensates for wear or deterioration. Repair implies that something has broken or is not working. A need for a repair is often caused by lack of maintenance. for example: draining and refilling automatic transmission fluid is maintenance recommended at specific intervals. Failure to do this can shorten the life of the transmission/transaxle, requiring very expensive repairs. While no maintenance program can prevent items from eventually breaking or wearing out, a general rule is true: MAINTENANCE IS CHEAPER THAN REPAIR.

Two basic mechanic's rules should be mentioned here. First, whenever the left side of the vehicle or engine is referred to, it means the driver's side. Conversely, the right side of the vehicle means the passenger's side. Second, screws and bolts are removed by turning counterclockwise, and tightened by turning clockwise unless specifically noted.

Safety is always the most important rule. Constantly be aware of the dangers involved in working on an automobile and take the proper precautions. Please refer to the information in this section regarding SERVICING YOUR VEHICLE SAFELY and the SAFETY NOTICE on the acknowledgment page.

Avoiding the Most Common Mistakes

Pay attention to the instructions provided. There are 3 common mistakes in mechanical work:

1. Incorrect order of assembly, disassembly or adjustment. When taking something apart or putting it together, performing steps in the wrong order usually just costs you extra time; however, it CAN break something. Read the entire procedure before beginning. Perform everything in the order in which the instructions say you should, even if you can't see a reason for it. When you're taking apart something that is very intricate, you might want to draw a picture of how it looks when assembled in order to make sure you get everything back in its proper position. When making adjustments, perform them in the proper order. One adjustment possibly will affect another.

2. Overtorquing (or undertorquing). While it is more common for overtorquing to cause damage, undertorquing may allow a fastener to vibrate loose causing serious damage. Especially when dealing with aluminum parts, pay attention to torque specifications and utilize a torque wrench in assembly. If a torque figure is not available, remember that if you are using the right tool to perform the job, you will probably not have to strain yourself to get a fastener tight enough. The pitch of most threads is so slight that the tension you put on the wrench will be multiplied many times in actual force on what you are tightening.

There are many commercial products available for ensuring that fasteners won't come loose, even if they are not torqued just right (a very common brand is Loctite®). If you're worried about getting something together tight enough to hold, but loose enough to avoid mechanical damage during assembly, one of these products might offer substantial insurance. Before choosing a threadlocking compound, read the label on the package and make sure the product is compatible with the materials, fluids, etc. involved.

3. Crossthreading. This occurs when a part such as a bolt is screwed into a nut or casting at the wrong angle and forced. Crossthreading is more likely to occur if access is difficult. It helps to clean and lubricate fasteners, then to start threading the bolt, spark plug, etc. with your fingers. If you encounter resistance, unscrew the part and start over again at a different angle until it can be inserted and turned several times without much effort. Keep in mind that many parts have tapered threads, so that gentle turning will automatically bring the part you're threading to the proper angle. Don't put a wrench on the part until it's been tightened a couple of turns by hand. If you suddenly encounter resistance, and the part has not seated fully, don't force it. Pull it back out to make sure it's clean and threading properly.

Be sure to take your time and be patient, and always plan ahead. Allow yourself ample time to perform repairs and maintenance.

TOOLS AND EQUIPMENT

▶ **See Figures 1 thru 15**

Without the proper tools and equipment it is impossible to properly service your vehicle. It would be virtually impossible to catalog every tool that you would need to perform all of the operations in this book. It would be unwise for the amateur to rush out and buy an expensive set of tools on the theory that he/she may need one or more of them at some time.

The best approach is to proceed slowly, gathering a good quality set of those tools that are used most frequently. Don't be misled by the low cost of bargain tools. It is far better to spend a little more for better quality. Forged wrenches, 6 or 12-point sockets and fine tooth ratchets are by far preferable to their less expensive counterparts. As any good mechanic can tell you, there are few worse

experiences than trying to work on a vehicle with bad tools. Your monetary savings will be far outweighed by frustration and mangled knuckles.

Begin accumulating those tools that are used most frequently: those associated with routine maintenance and tune-up. In addition to the normal assortment of screwdrivers and pliers, you should have the following tools:

• Wrenches/sockets and combination open end/box end wrenches in sizes from ⅛ –¾ in. or 3–19mm, as well as a ¹³⁄₁₆ in. or ⅝ in. spark plug socket (depending on plug type).

➥ **If possible, buy various length socket drive extensions. Universal-joint and wobble extensions can be extremely useful, but be careful when using them, as they can change the amount of torque applied to the socket.**

Fig. 1 All but the most basic procedures will require an assortment of ratchets and sockets

TCCS1200

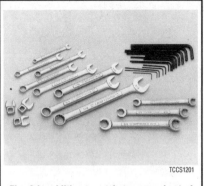

Fig. 2 In addition to ratchets, a good set of wrenches and hex keys will be necessary

TCCS1201

Fig. 3 A hydraulic floor jack and a set of jackstands are essential for lifting and supporting the vehicle

TCCS1202

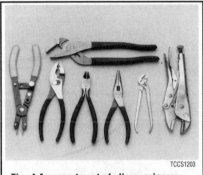

Fig. 4 An assortment of pliers, grippers and cutters will be handy for old rusted parts and stripped bolt heads

TCCS1203

Fig. 5 Various drivers, chisels and prybars are great tools to have in your toolbox

TCCS1204

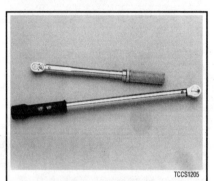

Fig. 6 Many repairs will require the use of a torque wrench to assure the components are properly fastened

TCCS1205

Fig. 7 Although not always necessary, using specialized brake tools will save time

TCCS1209

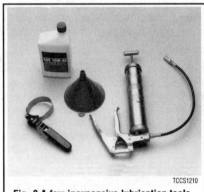

Fig. 8 A few inexpensive lubrication tools will make maintenance easier

TCCS1210

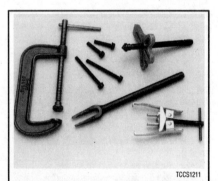

Fig. 9 Various pullers, clamps and separator tools are needed for many larger, more complicated repairs

TCCS1211

Fig. 10 A variety of tools and gauges should be used for spark plug gapping and installation

TCCS1212

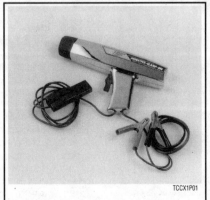

Fig. 11 Inductive type timing light

TCCX1P01

Fig. 12 A screw-in type compression gauge is recommended for compression testing

TCCX1P02

Fig. 13 A vacuum/pressure tester is necessary for many testing procedures

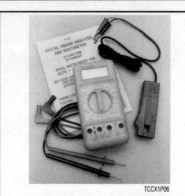

Fig. 14 Most modern automotive multimeters incorporate many helpful features

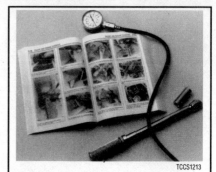

Fig. 15 Proper information is vital, so always have a Chilton Total Car Care manual handy

- Jackstands for support.
- Oil filter wrench.
- Spout or funnel for pouring fluids.
- Grease gun for chassis lubrication (unless your vehicle is not equipped with any grease fittings)
- Hydrometer for checking the battery (unless equipped with a sealed, maintenance-free battery).
- A container for draining oil and other fluids.
- Rags for wiping up the inevitable mess.

In addition to the above items there are several others that are not absolutely necessary, but handy to have around. These include an equivalent oil absorbent gravel, like cat litter, and the usual supply of lubricants, antifreeze and fluids. This is a basic list for routine maintenance, but only your personal needs and desire can accurately determine your list of tools.

After performing a few projects on the vehicle, you'll be amazed at the other tools and non-tools on your workbench. Some useful household items are: a large turkey baster or siphon, empty coffee cans and ice trays (to store parts), a ball of twine, electrical tape for wiring, small rolls of colored tape for tagging lines or hoses, markers and pens, a note pad, golf tees (for plugging vacuum lines), metal coat hangers or a roll of mechanic's wire (to hold things out of the way), dental pick or similar long, pointed probe, a strong magnet, and a small mirror (to see into recesses and under manifolds).

A more advanced set of tools, suitable for tune-up work, can be drawn up easily. While the tools are slightly more sophisticated, they need not be outrageously expensive. There are several inexpensive tach/dwell meters on the market that are every bit as good for the average mechanic as a professional model. Just be sure that it goes to a least 1200–1500 rpm on the tach scale and that it works on 4, 6 and 8-cylinder engines. The key to these purchases is to make them with an eye towards adaptability and wide range. A basic list of tune-up tools could include:

- Tach/dwell meter.
- Spark plug wrench and gapping tool.
- Feeler gauges for valve adjustment.
- Timing light.

The choice of a timing light should be made carefully. A light which works on the DC current supplied by the vehicle's battery is the best choice; it should have a xenon tube for brightness. On any vehicle with an electronic ignition system, a timing light with an inductive pickup that clamps around the No. 1 spark plug cable is preferred.

In addition to these basic tools, there are several other tools and gauges you may find useful. These include:

- Compression gauge. The screw-in type is slower to use, but eliminates the possibility of a faulty reading due to escaping pressure.
- Manifold vacuum gauge.
- 12V test light.
- A combination volt/ohmmeter
- Induction Ammeter. This is used for determining whether or not there is current in a wire. These are handy for use if a wire is broken somewhere in a wiring harness.

As a final note, you will probably find a torque wrench necessary for all but the most basic work. The beam type models are perfectly adequate, although the newer click types (breakaway) are easier to use. The click type torque wrenches tend to be more expensive. Also keep in mind that all types of torque wrenches should be periodically checked and/or recalibrated. You will have to decide for yourself which better fits your pocketbook, and purpose.

Special Tools

Normally, the use of special factory tools is avoided for repair procedures, since these are not readily available for the do-it-yourself mechanic. When it is possible to perform the job with more commonly available tools, it will be pointed out, but occasionally, a special tool was designed to perform a specific function and should be used. Before substituting another tool, you should be convinced that neither your safety nor the performance of the vehicle will be compromised.

Special tools can usually be purchased from an automotive parts store or from your dealer. In some cases special tools may be available directly from the tool manufacturer.

SERVICING YOUR VEHICLE SAFELY

◢ See Figures 16, 17 and 18

It is virtually impossible to anticipate all of the hazards involved with automotive maintenance and service, but care and common sense will prevent most accidents.

The rules of safety for mechanics range from "don't smoke around gasoline," to "use the proper tool(s) for the job." The trick to avoiding injuries is to develop safe work habits and to take every possible precaution.

Do's

- Do keep a fire extinguisher and first aid kit handy.
- Do wear safety glasses or goggles when cutting, drilling, grinding or prying, even if you have 20–20 vision. If you wear glasses for the sake of vision, wear safety goggles over your regular glasses.

- Do shield your eyes whenever you work around the battery. Batteries contain sulfuric acid. In case of contact with, flush the area with water or a mixture of water and baking soda, then seek immediate medical attention.
- Do use safety stands (jackstands) for any undervehicle service. Jacks are for raising vehicles; jackstands are for making sure the vehicle stays raised until you want it to come down.
- Do use adequate ventilation when working with any chemicals or hazardous materials. Like carbon monoxide, the asbestos dust resulting from some brake lining wear can be hazardous in sufficient quantities.
- Do disconnect the negative battery cable when working on the electrical system. The secondary ignition system contains EXTREMELY HIGH VOLTAGE. In some cases it can even exceed 50,000 volts.
- Do follow manufacturer's directions whenever working with potentially hazardous materials. Most chemicals and fluids are poisonous.
- Do properly maintain your tools. Loose hammerheads, mushroomed

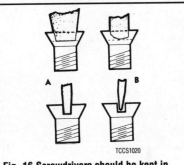

Fig. 16 Screwdrivers should be kept in good condition to prevent injury or damage which could result if the blade slips from the screw

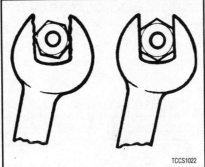

Fig. 17 Using the correct size wrench will help prevent the possibility of rounding off a nut

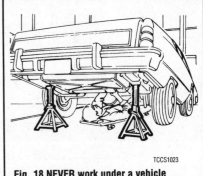

Fig. 18 NEVER work under a vehicle unless it is supported using safety stands (jackstands)

punches and chisels, frayed or poorly grounded electrical cords, excessively worn screwdrivers, spread wrenches (open end), cracked sockets, slipping ratchets, or faulty droplight sockets can cause accidents.

• Likewise, keep your tools clean; a greasy wrench can slip off a bolt head, ruining the bolt and often harming your knuckles in the process.

• Do use the proper size and type of tool for the job at hand. Do select a wrench or socket that fits the nut or bolt. The wrench or socket should sit straight, not cocked.

• Do, when possible, pull on a wrench handle rather than push on it, and adjust your stance to prevent a fall.

• Do be sure that adjustable wrenches are tightly closed on the nut or bolt and pulled so that the force is on the side of the fixed jaw.

• Do strike squarely with a hammer; avoid glancing blows.

• Do set the parking brake and block the drive wheels if the work requires a running engine.

Don'ts

• Don't run the engine in a garage or anywhere else without proper ventilation—EVER! Carbon monoxide is poisonous; it takes a long time to leave the human body and you can build up a deadly supply of it in your system by simply breathing in a little at a time. You may not realize you are slowly poisoning yourself. Always use power vents, windows, fans and/or open the garage door.

• Don't work around moving parts while wearing loose clothing. Short sleeves are much safer than long, loose sleeves. Hard-toed shoes with neoprene soles protect your toes and give a better grip on slippery surfaces. Watches and jewelry is not safe working around a vehicle. Long hair should be tied back under a hat or cap.

• Don't use pockets for toolboxes. A fall or bump can drive a screwdriver deep into your body. Even a rag hanging from your back pocket can wrap around a spinning shaft or fan.

• Don't smoke when working around gasoline, cleaning solvent or other flammable material.

• Don't smoke when working around the battery. When the battery is being charged, it gives off explosive hydrogen gas.

• Don't use gasoline to wash your hands; there are excellent soaps available. Gasoline contains dangerous additives which can enter the body through a cut or through your pores. Gasoline also removes all the natural oils from the skin so that bone dry hands will suck up oil and grease.

• Don't service the air conditioning system unless you are equipped with the necessary tools and training. When liquid or compressed gas refrigerant is released to atmospheric pressure it will absorb heat from whatever it contacts. This will chill or freeze anything it touches.

• Don't use screwdrivers for anything other than driving screws! A screwdriver used as an prying tool can snap when you least expect it, causing injuries. At the very least, you'll ruin a good screwdriver.

• Don't use an emergency jack (that little ratchet, scissors, or pantograph jack supplied with the vehicle) for anything other than changing a flat! These jacks are only intended for emergency use out on the road; they are NOT designed as a maintenance tool. If you are serious about maintaining your vehicle yourself, invest in a hydraulic floor jack of at least a 1½ ton capacity, and at least two sturdy jackstands.

SERIAL NUMBER IDENTIFICATION

Vehicle

▶ See Figure 19

The Vehicle Identification Number (VIN) is stamped on a metal plate that is fastened to the instrument panel adjacent to the windshield. It can be seen by looking through the lower corner of the windshield on the driver's side.

The VIN is a 17 digit combination of numbers and letters. The first 3 digits represent the world manufacturer identifier. Using the example in the figure, the number and letter combination 2FA signifies Ford Motor Company of Canada, Ltd. The 4th digit indicates the type of passenger restraint system; in the example the letter C stands for active belts and a driver's side air bag. The 5th digit is a constant, the letter P signifying passenger car. The 6th and 7th digits indicate the body style, in this case 74 for a Crown Victoria LX. The 8th digit is the engine code: F for the 5.0L engine, G for the 5.8L engine or in this case W for the 4.6L engine. The 9th digit is a check digit for all vehicles. The 10th digit indicates the model year: K for 1989, L for 1990, M for 1991, N for 1992, P for 1993 or R for 1994. The 11th digit is the assembly plant code, the letter X represents St. Thomas, Ontario, Canada. The 12th through 17th digits indicate the production sequence number.

The Vehicle Certification Label is attached to the left front door lock panel. The upper half of the label contains the name of the manufacturer, month and year of manufacture, Gross Vehicle Weight Rating (GVWR), Gross Axle Weight Rating (GAWR), and the certification statement. The lower half of the label contains the VIN and a series of codes indicating exterior color, body type, interior trim type and color, radio type, sun roof type (if any), as well as axle, transmission, spring, district and special order codes.

Fig. 19 Vehicle Identification Number (VIN) location

VEHICLE IDENTIFICATION CHART

It is important for servicing and ordering parts to be certain of the vehicle and engine identification. The VIN (vehicle identification number) is a 17 digit number visible through the windshield on the driver's side of the dash and contains the vehicle and engine identification codes. The tenth digit indicates model year and the eighth digit indicates engine code. It can be interpreted as follows:

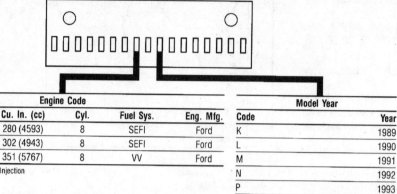

Engine Code

Code	Liters	Cu. In. (cc)	Cyl.	Fuel Sys.	Eng. Mfg.
W	4.6	280 (4593)	8	SEFI	Ford
F	5.0	302 (4943)	8	SEFI	Ford
G	5.8	351 (5767)	8	VV	Ford

SEFI—Sequential Electronic Fuel Injection
VV—Variable Venturi carburetor

Model Year

Code	Year
K	1989
L	1990
M	1991
N	1992
P	1993
R	1994

84171R10

Engine

♦ See Figure 20

The engine identification code is located in the VIN at the 8th digit. The VIN can be found on the Vehicle Certification Label and on the VIN plate attached to the instrument panel. See the Engine Identification chart for engine VIN codes.

There is also an engine code information label located on the engine. This label contains the engine calibration number, engine build date and engine plant code. On the 5.0L and 5.8L engines, the label is located on the side of the right rocker arm cover. On the 4.6L engine, the label is located on the front of the engine.

Fig. 20 Sample engine code information label

ENGINE IDENTIFICATION

Year	Model	Engine Displacement Liters (cc)	Engine Series (ID/VIN)	Fuel System	No. of Cylinders	Engine Type
1989	Crown Victoria	5.0 (4943)	F	SEFI	8	OHV
	Crown Victoria	5.8 (5767)	G	VV	8	OHV
	Grand Marquis	5.0 (4943)	F	SEFI	8	OHV
	Grand Marquis	5.8 (5767)	G	VV	8	OHV
1990	Crown Victoria	5.0 (4943)	F	SEFI	8	OHV
	Crown Victoria	5.8 (5767)	G	VV	8	OHV
	Grand Marquis	5.0 (4943)	F	SEFI	8	OHV
	Grand Marquis	5.8 (5767)	G	VV	8	OHV
1991	Crown Victoria	5.0 (4943)	F	SEFI	8	OHV
	Crown Victoria	5.8 (5767)	G	VV	8	OHV
	Grand Marquis	5.0 (4943)	F	SEFI	8	OHV
	Grand Marquis	5.8 (5767)	G	VV	8	OHV
1992	Crown Victoria	4.6 (4593)	W	SEFI	8	OHC
	Grand Marquis	4.6 (4593)	W	SEFI	8	OHC
1993-94	Crown Victoria	4.6 (4593)	W	SEFI	8	OHC
	Grand Marquis	4.6 (4593)	W	SEFI	8	OHC

SEFI—Sequential electronic fuel injection
VV—Variable Venturi carburetor
OHV—Overhead valve
OHC—Overhead camshaft

8417R111

Transmission

♦ **See Figures 21 and 22**

The transmission identification code can be found in the space marked TR on the Vehicle Certification Label. There is also an identification tag located on the transmission case which contains the transmission model code, build date code, serial number and assembly part number prefix and suffix.

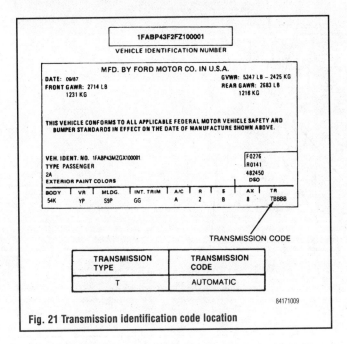

Fig. 21 Transmission identification code location

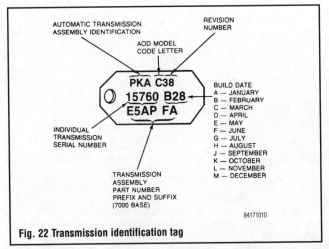

Fig. 22 Transmission identification tag

All 1989–92½ vehicles are equipped with a 4-speed Automatic Overdrive (AOD) transmission. Beginning in February 1992, an electronically controlled Automatic Overdrive (AODE) transmission replaced the AOD transmission.

Drive Axle

♦ **See Figures 23 and 24**

The drive axle identification code can be found in the space marked AX on the Vehicle Certification Label. There is also an identification tag located on the axle.

The plant code on the identification tag is the official service identifier. The plant code for a particular axle assembly will not be duplicated. As long as that particular axle assembly never undergoes an external design change, the plant code will not change. However, if an internal design change takes place in the same axle during the production life of the axle, and the change affects service parts interchangeability, a dash and numerical suffix is added to the plant code.

CODE CONVENTIONAL	RATIO
8 (M*)	2.73:1
G	2.26:1
Y (Z*)	3.08:1
F (R*)	3.45:1
B	2.47:1

*TRACTION LOK

84171013

Fig. 23 Drive axle ratios—1989 vehicles

CODE CONVENTIONAL	RATIO
8 (M*)	2.73:1
Y (Z*)	3.08:1
5 (E*)	3.27:1
2 (K*)	3.55:1

*TRACTION LOK

84171014

Fig. 24 Drive axle ratios—1990–94 vehicles

ROUTINE MAINTENANCE

♦ **See Figures 25, 26 and 27**

Air Cleaner

The air cleaner prevents dirt or other foreign material from entering the engine. The air cleaner is a paper element contained in a sealed housing. On vehicles equipped with 4.6L or 5.0L engines, the air cleaner housing is located on the left side of the engine compartment. On vehicles equipped with the 5.8L engine, the air cleaner housing is located directly on top of the carburetor.

The air cleaner should be serviced at the intervals recommended in the Maintenance Intervals Chart at the end of this Section. However, the air cleaner should be checked more often if the vehicle is operated in severely dusty conditions. A dirty air cleaner can cause engine performance problems such as lack of power, rough idling and stalling.

➡ **The air cleaner housing on the 5.8L engine also contains the crankcase emission filter. Service this filter at the intervals recommended in the Maintenance Intervals Chart at the end of this Section, more often if the vehicle is operated in severely dusty conditions.**

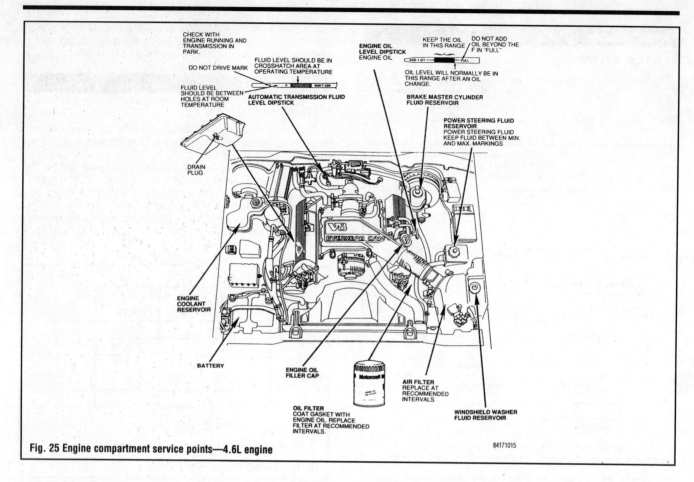

Fig. 25 Engine compartment service points—4.6L engine

84171015

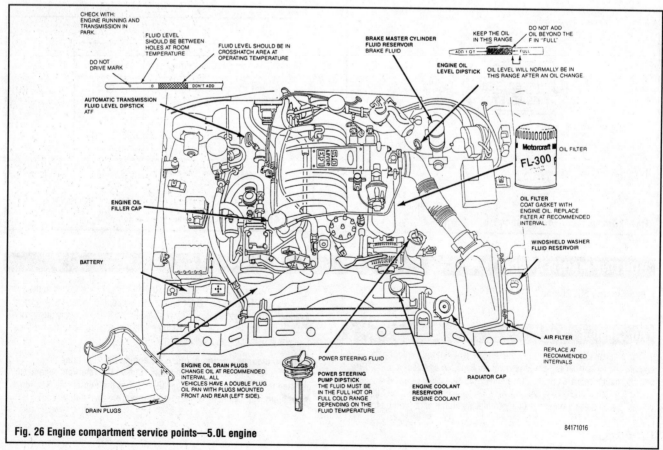

Fig. 26 Engine compartment service points—5.0L engine

84171016

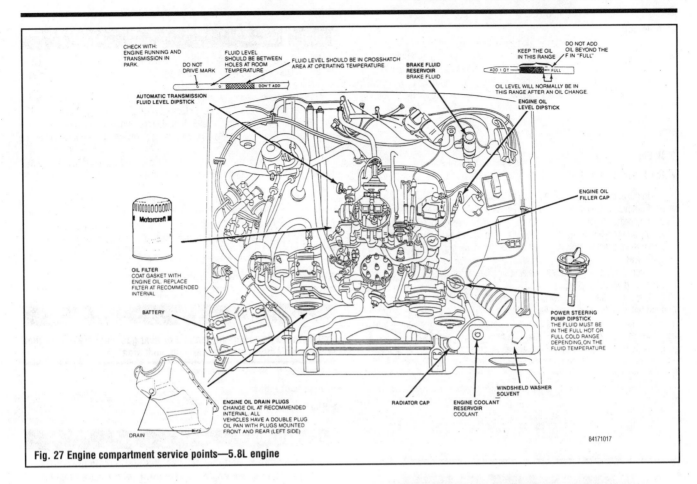

Fig. 27 Engine compartment service points—5.8L engine

REMOVAL & INSTALLATION

Except 5.8L Engine

⬥ **See Figures 28, 29 and 30**

1. Release the spring clips retaining the air cleaner cover to the air cleaner tray.

2. Lift the cover and remove the air cleaner element.

Fig. 29 Removing the air cleaner element—4.6L engine

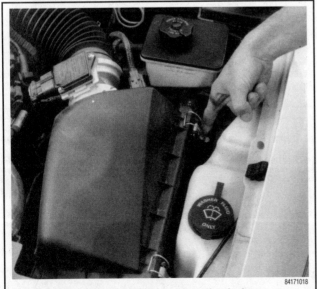

Fig. 28 Releasing the spring clips to remove the air cleaner cover—4.6L engine

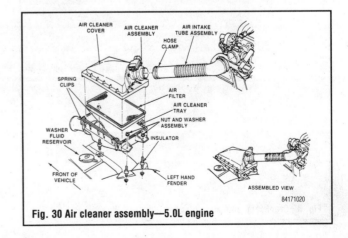

Fig. 30 Air cleaner assembly—5.0L engine

To install:

3. Inspect the air cleaner, cover and tray for signs of dust or dirt leaking through holes in the filter element or past the sealing edges. Shine a light on the bottom (clean side) of the filter element and look through the filter at the light. If any holes can be seen, no matter how small, the filter must be replaced.

4. Wipe all the inside surfaces of the air cleaner tray and cover. Install the air cleaner element.

5. Place the air cleaner cover on the air cleaner tray and secure with the clips.

5.8L Engine

♦ See Figures 31 and 32

1. Remove the wing nut retaining the air cleaner cover.
2. Remove the air cleaner cover and remove the air cleaner element.
3. If necessary, remove the retaining clip from the crankcase emission filter assembly and remove the assembly from the air cleaner tray. Remove the filter pad from the crankcase emission filter container and discard.

To install:

4. If removed, clean the crankcase emission filter container. Lightly oil a new filter pad with clean engine oil and install it in the container.

5. Inspect the air cleaner, cover and tray for signs of dust or dirt leaking through holes in the filter element or past the sealing edges. Shine a light on the clean side of the filter element and look through the filter at the light. If any holes can be seen, no matter how small, the filter must be replaced.

6. Wipe the inside surfaces of the air cleaner cover and tray.
7. If removed, install the crankcase emission filter assembly and secure with the retaining clip. Make sure the filter container is fully secured to the elbow; the retaining clip must engage the inner ring of the elbow, not between the rings.

8. Install the air cleaner element.
9. Install the air cleaner cover and secure with the wing nut.

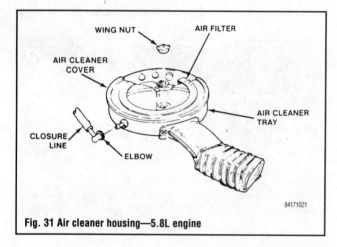

Fig. 31 Air cleaner housing—5.8L engine

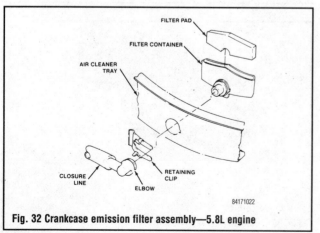

Fig. 32 Crankcase emission filter assembly—5.8L engine

Fuel Filter

The fuel filter prevents small particles from entering the fuel injectors or carburetor. A clogged or dirty fuel filter will restrict the flow of fuel, seriously affecting engine performance.

On fuel injected vehicles, fuel is filtered at 3 locations. A nylon filter element is mounted on the electric fuel pump located inside the fuel tank. An in-line filter is located downstream of the electric fuel pump and is mounted to the frame on the underside of the vehicle. There is also a small screen filter located at the top of each fuel injector.

On carbureted vehicles, fuel is filtered with a nylon filter element attached to the fuel gauge sending unit inside the fuel tank and with a filter element located inside the carburetor.

Only the in-line fuel filter on fuel injected vehicles and the carburetor fuel inlet filter on carbureted vehicles are normally serviced. Ford does not list a recommended change interval for the fuel filter, however, if you would like to replace the filter, follow the removal and installation procedure that applies to your car.

REMOVAL & INSTALLATION

✱✱ CAUTION

Never smoke when working around or near gasoline! Make sure that there is no ignition source near your work area!

In-Line Fuel Filter

♦ See Figures 33, 34, 35 and 36

✱✱ CAUTION

Fuel supply lines on fuel injected vehicles will remain pressurized for some time after the engine is shut off. Fuel pressure must be relieved before servicing the fuel system.

1. Disconnect the negative battery cable.
2. Relieve the fuel system pressure as follows:
   a. Remove the fuel tank cap to relieve the pressure in the fuel tank.
   b. Remove the cap from the Schrader valve located on the fuel injection supply manifold.
   c. Attach fuel pressure gauge T80L–9974–A or equivalent, to the Schrader valve and drain the fuel through the drain tube into a suitable container.
   d. After the fuel system pressure is relieved, remove the fuel pressure gauge and install the cap on the Schrader valve.
3. Raise and safely support the vehicle.
4. Remove the hairpin clip push connect fittings from both ends of the fuel filter as follows:
   a. Inspect the visible internal portion of the fitting for dirt accumulation. If more than a light coating of dust is present, clean the fitting before disassembly.

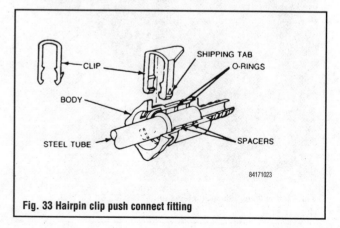

Fig. 33 Hairpin clip push connect fitting

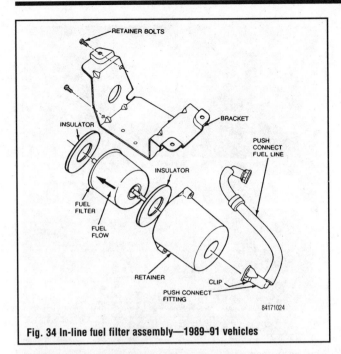

Fig. 34 In-line fuel filter assembly—1989–91 vehicles

Fig. 35 In-line fuel filter location—1992–94 vehicles

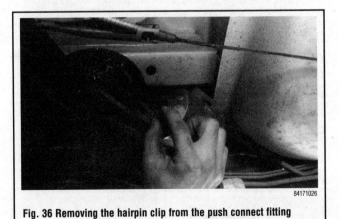

Fig. 36 Removing the hairpin clip from the push connect fitting

b. Some adhesion between the seals in the fitting and the filter will occur with time. To separate, twist the fitting on the filter, then push and pull the fitting until it moves freely on the filter.

c. Remove the hairpin clip from the fitting by first bending and breaking the shipping tab. Next, spread the 2 clip legs by hand about 1/8 in. each to disengage the body and push the legs into the fitting. Lightly pull the triangular end of the clip and work it clear of the filter and fitting.

➡ Do not use hand tools to complete this operation.

d. Grasp the fitting and pull in an axial direction to remove the fitting from the filter. Be careful on 90 degree elbow connectors, as excessive side loading could break the connector body.

e. After disassembly, inspect the inside of the fitting for any internal parts such as O-rings and spacers that may have been dislodged from the fitting. Replace any damaged connector.

5. On 1989–91 vehicles, remove the filter retainer bolts and remove the filter and retainer from the mounting bracket. Remove the filter from the retainer. Note that the direction of the flow arrow points to the open end of the retainer. Remove the rubber insulator rings.

6. On 1992–94 vehicles, loosen the filter retaining clamp and remove the fuel filter. Note the direction of the flow arrow on the filter, so the replacement filter can be reinstalled in the same position.

To install:

7. On 1992–94 vehicles, install the fuel filter with the flow arrow facing the proper direction and tighten the filter retaining clamp.

8. On 1989–91 vehicles, install the rubber insulator rings on the new filter (replace the insulator rings if the filter moves freely after the retainer is installed). Install the filter into the retainer with the flow arrow pointing out the open end of the retainer. Install the retainer on the bracket and tighten the mounting bolts to 27–44 inch lbs. (3–5 Nm).

9. Install the hairpin clip push connect fittings at both ends of the fuel filter as follows:

a. Install a new connector if damage was found. Insert a new clip into any 2 adjacent openings with the triangular portion pointing away from the fitting opening. Install the clip until the legs of the clip are locked on the outside of the body. Piloting with an index finger is necessary.

b. Before installing the fitting on the filter, wipe the filter end with a clean cloth. Inspect the inside of the fitting to make sure it is free of dirt and/or obstructions.

c. Apply a light coating of engine oil to the filter end. Align the fitting and filter axially and push the fitting onto the filter end. When the fitting is engaged, a definite click will be heard. Pull on the fitting to make sure it is fully engaged.

10. Lower the vehicle and connect the negative battery cable. Start the engine and check for leaks.

Carburetor Fuel Inlet Filter

▶ See Figures 37 and 38

1. Disconnect the negative battery cable.

2. Remove the air cleaner filter element as detailed in this Section.

3. Disconnect the fresh air inlet tube and hot air inlet tube from the air cleaner housing duct.

4. Disconnect the crankcase emission filter hose and the necessary vacuum hoses. Label the vacuum hoses prior to removal so they can be reinstalled in their proper locations. Remove the air cleaner housing.

5. Place a rag under the carburetor inlet fitting to catch fuel spillage.

6. Hold the carburetor inlet fitting with a backup wrench and unscrew the fuel line tube nut from the fitting.

7. Unscrew the fuel inlet fitting and remove the gasket, filter and spring. Discard the gasket and filter.

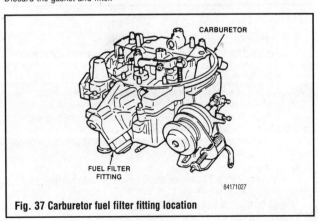

Fig. 37 Carburetor fuel filter fitting location

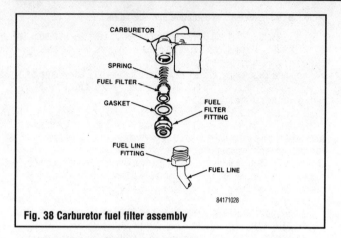

Fig. 38 Carburetor fuel filter assembly

To install:

8. Install the spring, new filter and gasket.

9. Hand start the fuel inlet fitting into the carburetor. Tighten to 90–125 inch lbs. (10–14 Nm).

10. Apply clean engine oil to the fuel tube nut threads and tube flare. Hand start the fuel line tube nut into the fuel inlet fitting, approximately 2 threads.

11. Use a backup wrench on the fuel inlet fitting while tightening the fuel line tube nut to 15–18 ft. lbs. (20–24 Nm).

12. Start the engine and check for leaks. Install the air cleaner housing assembly.

PCV Valve

The Positive Crankcase Ventilation (PCV) system prevents harmful pollutants from escaping the engine crankcase into the atmosphere. The system draws clean filtered air into the crankcase, where it mixes with the crankcase vapors, passes through the PCV valve and into the intake manifold. In the intake manifold, the crankcase vapors mix with the incoming air/fuel mixture and then are drawn into the combustion chamber and burned. The PCV valve regulates the flow of crankcase vapors to the intake manifold.

The PCV valve is located in a grommet attached to the rocker arm cover on the 4.6L engine or at the rear of the intake manifold on the 5.0L engine. On 5.8L engines, the PCV valve is located in an elbow attached to the oil filler on the rocker arm cover. The valve should be serviced at the intervals recommended in the Maintenance Intervals Chart at the end of this Section. For a more detailed discussion of the PCV system as well as testing procedures, refer to Section 4.

➡ On the 5.0L engine, the crankcase emission filter is located under the PCV valve grommet. Service this filter at the intervals recommended in the Maintenance Intervals Chart at the end of this Section, more often if the vehicle is operated in severely dusty conditions.

REMOVAL & INSTALLATION

♦ See Figure 39

1. Remove the PCV valve from the grommet or elbow.

2. Disconnect the hose(s) from the PCV valve and remove it from the vehicle.

3. Check the PCV valve for deposits and clogging. If the valve rattles when shaken, it is okay. If the valve does not rattle, clean the valve with solvent until the plunger is free, or replace it.

4. Check the PCV hose(s) and the grommet or elbow for clogging and signs of wear or deterioration. Clean or replace parts, as necessary.

5. If necessary, on the 5.0L engine remove the grommet and remove the crankcase emission filter.

To install:

6. If removed, on the 5.0L engine install a new crankcase emission filter element and install the grommet.

7. Connect the PCV hose(s) to the PCV valve.

8. Install the PCV valve in the grommet or elbow.

Fig. 39 The PCV valve is mounted in a rubber grommet on the top of the motor

Evaporative Canister

♦ See Figure 40

The vapor, or carbon canister is located in the right front of the engine compartment and is part of the evaporative emission control system. This system prevents the emission of harmful fuel vapors into the atmosphere. The canister contains activated charcoal which absorbs the fuel vapors from the fuel tank and carburetor float bowl, if equipped. The fuel vapors are stored in the canister until the engine is started. Then the vapors are drawn into the engine for burning through a vacuum operated purge valve or solenoid purge valve.

SERVICING

Servicing the evaporative canister is only necessary if it is clogged or contains liquid fuel. If replacement is necessary, the canister must be replaced as a unit; it cannot be disassembled. For more detailed information on the evaporative emission control system as well as testing procedures, refer to Section 4.

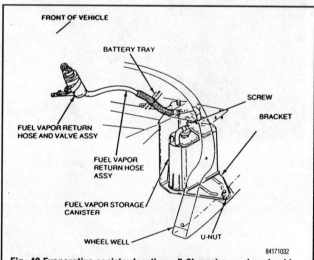

Fig. 40 Evaporative canister location—5.0L engine equipped vehicles

Battery

PRECAUTIONS

Always use caution when working on or near the battery. Never allow a tool to bridge the gap between the negative and positive battery terminals. Also, be careful not to allow a tool to provide a ground between the positive cable/terminal and any metal component on the vehicle. Either of these conditions will cause a short circuit, leading to sparks and possible personal injury.

Do not smoke or all open flames/sparks near a battery; the gases contained in the battery are very explosive and, if ignited, could cause severe injury or death.

All batteries, regardless of type, should be carefully secured by a battery hold-down device. If not, the terminals or casing may crack from stress during vehicle operation. A battery which is not secured may allow acid to leak, making it discharge faster. The acid can also eat away at components under the hood.

Always inspect the battery case for cracks, leakage and corrosion. A white corrosive substance on the battery case or on nearby components would indicate a leaking or cracked battery. If the battery is cracked, it should be replaced immediately.

GENERAL MAINTENANCE

Always keep the battery cables and terminals free of corrosion. Check and clean these components about once a year.

Keep the top of the battery clean, as a film of dirt can help discharge a battery that is not used for long periods. A solution of baking soda and water may be used for cleaning, but be careful to flush this off with clear water. DO NOT let any of the solution into the filler holes. Baking soda neutralizes battery acid and will de-activate a battery cell.

Batteries in vehicles which are not operated on a regular basis can fall victim to parasitic loads (small current drains which are constantly drawing current from the battery). Normal parasitic loads may drain a battery on a vehicle that is in storage and not used for 6–8 weeks. Vehicles that have additional accessories such as a phone or an alarm system may discharge a battery sooner. If the vehicle is to be stored for longer periods in a secure area and the alarm system is not necessary, the negative battery cable should be disconnected to protect the battery.

Remember that constantly deep cycling a battery (completely discharging and recharging it) will shorten battery life.

BATTERY FLUID

♦ See Figure 41

Check the battery electrolyte level at least once a month, or more often in hot weather or during periods of extended vehicle operation. On non-sealed batteries, the level can be checked either through the case (if translucent) or by removing the cell caps. The electrolyte level in each cell should be kept filled to the split ring inside each cell, or the line marked on the outside of the case.

If the level is low, add only distilled water through the opening until the level is correct. Each cell must be checked and filled individually. Distilled water

should be used, because the chemicals and minerals found in most drinking water are harmful to the battery and could significantly shorten its life.

If water is added in freezing weather, the vehicle should be driven several miles to allow the water to mix with the electrolyte. Otherwise, the battery could freeze.

Although some maintenance-free batteries have removable cell caps, the electrolyte condition and level on all sealed maintenance-free batteries must be checked using the built-in hydrometer "eye." The exact type of eye will vary. But, most battery manufacturers, apply a sticker to the battery itself explaining the readings.

➡Although the readings from built-in hydrometers will vary, a green eye usually indicates a properly charged battery with sufficient fluid level. A dark eye is normally an indicator of a battery with sufficient fluid, but which is low in charge. A light or yellow eye usually indicates that electrolyte has dropped below the necessary level. In this last case, sealed batteries with an insufficient electrolyte must usually be discarded.

Checking the Specific Gravity

♦ See Figures 42, 43 and 44

A hydrometer is required to check the specific gravity on all batteries that are not maintenance-free. On batteries that are maintenance-free, the specific gravity is checked by observing the built-in hydrometer "eye" on the top of the battery case.

✳✳ CAUTION

Battery electrolyte contains sulfuric acid. If you should splash any on your skin or in your eyes, flush the affected area with plenty of clear water. If it lands in your eyes, get medical help immediately.

The fluid (sulfuric acid solution) contained in the battery cells will tell you many things about the condition of the battery. Because the cell plates must be kept submerged below the fluid level in order to operate, the fluid level is

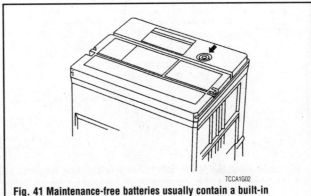

TCCA1G02

Fig. 41 Maintenance-free batteries usually contain a built-in hydrometer to check fluid level

TCCA1P07

Fig. 42 On non-sealed batteries, the fluid level can be checked by removing the cell caps

TCCA1P08

Fig. 43 If the fluid level is low, add only distilled water until the level is correct

TCCA1P09

Fig. 44 Check the specific gravity of the battery's electrolyte with a hydrometer

extremely important. And, because the specific gravity of the acid is an indication of electrical charge, testing the fluid can be an aid in determining if the battery must be replaced. A battery in a vehicle with a properly operating charging system should require little maintenance, but careful, periodic inspection should reveal problems before they leave you stranded.

At least once a year, check the specific gravity of the battery. It should be between 1.20 and 1.26 on the gravity scale. Most auto stores carry a variety of inexpensive battery hydrometers. These can be used on any non-sealed battery to test the specific gravity in each cell.

The battery testing hydrometer has a squeeze bulb at one end and a nozzle at the other. Battery electrolyte is sucked into the hydrometer until the float is lifted from its seat. The specific gravity is then read by noting the position of the float. If gravity is low in one or more cells, the battery should be slowly charged and checked again to see if the gravity has come up. Generally, if after charging, the specific gravity between any two cells varies more than 50 points (0.50), the battery should be replaced, as it can no longer produce sufficient voltage to guarantee proper operation.

CABLES

▶ **See Figures 45, 46, 47 and 48**

Once a year (or as necessary), the battery terminals and the cable clamps should be cleaned. Loosen the clamps and remove the cables, negative cable first. On top post batteries, the use of a puller specially made for this purpose is recommended. These are inexpensive and available in most parts stores. Side terminal battery cables are secured with a small bolt.

Clean the cable clamps and the battery terminal with a wire brush, until all corrosion, grease, etc., is removed and the metal is shiny. It is especially important to clean the inside of the clamp thoroughly (an old knife is useful here), since a small deposit of oxidation there will prevent a sound connection and inhibit starting or charging. Special tools are available for cleaning these parts, one type for conventional top post batteries and another type for side terminal

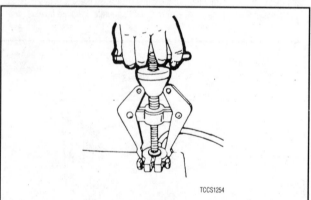

Fig. 45 A special tool is available to pull the clamp from the post

batteries. It is also a good idea to apply some dielectric grease to the terminal, as this will aid in the prevention of corrosion.

After the clamps and terminals are clean, reinstall the cables, negative cable last; DO NOT hammer the clamps onto battery posts. Tighten the clamps securely, but do not distort them. Give the clamps and terminals a thin external coating of grease after installation, to retard corrosion.

Check the cables at the same time that the terminals are cleaned. If the cable insulation is cracked or broken, or if the ends are frayed, the cable should be replaced with a new cable of the same length and gauge.

CHARGING

✳✳ CAUTION

The chemical reaction which takes place in all batteries generates explosive hydrogen gas. A spark can cause the battery to explode and splash acid. To avoid personal injury, be sure there is proper ventilation and take appropriate fire safety precautions when working with or near a battery.

A battery should be charged at a slow rate to keep the plates inside from getting too hot. However, if some maintenance-free batteries are allowed to discharge until they are almost "dead," they may have to be charged at a high rate to bring them back to "life." Always follow the charger manufacturer's instructions on charging the battery.

REPLACEMENT

When it becomes necessary to replace the battery, select one with an amperage rating equal to or greater than the battery originally installed. Deterioration and just plain aging of the battery cables, starter motor, and associated wires makes the battery's job harder in successive years. This makes it prudent to install a new battery with a greater capacity than the old.

Belts

▶ **See Figure 49**

The cooling fan, water pump, alternator, power steering pump, air conditioner compressor and air pump, if equipped, are belt driven by the crankshaft.

Vehicles equipped with the 5.0L engine or the 5.8L engine and air conditioning, use 2 V-ribbed belts, one for the cooling fan, water pump, alternator and power steering pump and another for the air conditioner compressor and air pump. Vehicles equipped with the 5.8L engine without air conditioning, use 1 V-ribbed belt to drive the cooling fan, water pump, alternator and power steering pump, and a conventional V-belt to drive the air pump.

The 4.6L engine is equipped with 1 serpentine V-ribbed belt to drive all engine accessories.

Fig. 46 The underside of this special battery tool has a wire brush to clean post terminals

Fig. 47 Place the tool over the battery posts and twist to clean until the metal is shiny

Fig. 48 The cable ends should be cleaned as well

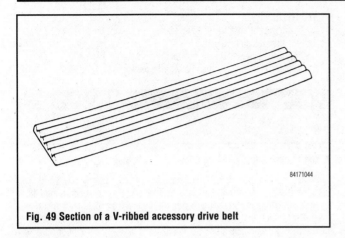

Fig. 49 Section of a V-ribbed accessory drive belt

INSPECTION

▶ **See Figures 50 and 51**

The accessory drive belt(s) should be inspected at the intervals specified in the Maintenance Intervals Chart at the end of this Section. Inspect the belt(s) for signs of glazing, cracking or chunking, and oil or grease contamination.

Glazed belts with hard surfaces can cause overheating and slippage. Engine oil or grease can rot the belt. A conventional V-belt should be replaced if it shows signs of cracking. However, cracking on a V-ribbed belt, providing the cracks are across the backing, is not cause for concern. Cracking is not acceptable on a V-ribbed belt, and is cause for replacement, only if the cracks run with the backing. Belt chunking, where a portion of the belt is missing, is cause for replacement on both V and V-ribbed belts.

ADJUSTING

Proper belt tension is important and should be checked periodically, where adjustment is possible. A loose belt will result in slippage, which may cause noise or improper accessory operation (alternator not charging, etc.). A belt that is too tight will overload the accessory bearings, shortening their life.

The alternator and air conditioner compressor drive belts on the 5.0L and 5.8L engines are adjustable. The serpentine drive belt on the 4.6L engine is kept in proper adjustment with an automatic tensioner; no adjustment is necessary or possible.

Alternator Belt

▶ **See Figures 52 and 53**

1. Loosen the alternator pivot and adjustment bolts.
2. Position a suitable belt tension gauge at the point indicated in the figure. Install an open end wrench over the alternator adjustment boss, then apply tension to the belt, using the wrench.
3. Set the tension on a new belt to 170 lbs. or a used belt to 140 lbs. While maintaining the tension, tighten the alternator adjustment bolt to 29 ft. lbs. (39 Nm).
4. Remove the belt tension gauge, start the engine and let it idle for 5 minutes.
5. Shut off the engine and install the tension gauge. Apply tension with the open end wrench and slowly loosen the adjustment bolt to allow belt tension to increase to the used belt specification, 140 lbs. Tighten the adjustment bolt to 29 ft. lbs. (39 Nm).
6. Tighten the pivot bolt to 50 ft. lbs. (68 Nm).

Air Conditioner Compressor Belt

▶ **See Figures 52 and 53**

1. Loosen the idler pulley bracket adjustment and pivot bolts.
2. Position a suitable belt tension gauge at the point indicated in the figure.
3. Install a ½ in. breaker bar in the hole in the idler pulley bracket as shown in the figure. Apply tension to the belt using the breaker bar.
4. Set the tension on a new belt to 170 lbs. or a used belt to 140 lbs. While maintaining the tension, tighten the adjustment bolt to 30 ft. lbs. (40 Nm).
5. Remove the belt tension gauge and the breaker bar. Start the engine and let it idle for 5 minutes.
6. Shut the engine off, then reinstall the belt tension gauge and breaker bar. Apply tension with the breaker bar and slowly loosen the adjustment bolt to allow belt tension to increase to the used belt specification, 140 lbs. Tighten the adjustment bolt to 30 ft. lbs. (40 Nm).
7. Tighten the pivot bolt to 50 ft. lbs. (68 Nm).

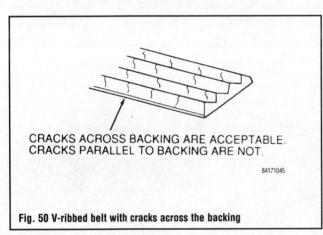

CRACKS ACROSS BACKING ARE ACCEPTABLE.
CRACKS PARALLEL TO BACKING ARE NOT.

Fig. 50 V-ribbed belt with cracks across the backing

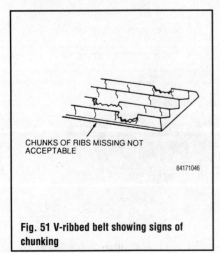

CHUNKS OF RIBS MISSING NOT ACCEPTABLE

Fig. 51 V-ribbed belt showing signs of chunking

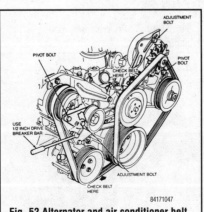

Fig. 52 Alternator and air conditioner belt tension adjustment—5.0L and 5.8L engines

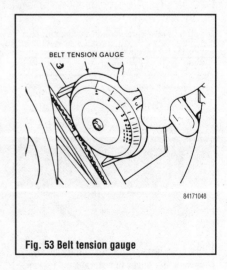

Fig. 53 Belt tension gauge

REMOVAL & INSTALLATION

4.6L Engine

▶ **See Figures 54 and 55**

1. Install a breaker bar in the ½ in. square hole in the automatic tensioner arm.
2. Rotate the tensioner away from the belt with the breaker bar.
3. Lift the old belt over the alternator pulley flange and remove it.

To install:

4. Install the new belt over the pulleys, making sure it is routed properly. Refer to the belt routing illustration on the sticker located at the front of the engine compartment. Make sure the ribs on the belt properly contact the grooves on the pulleys.
5. Rotate the tensioner toward the belt and remove the breaker bar.

5.0L and 5.8L Engines

▶ **See Figure 54**

ALTERNATOR BELT

1. Loosen the alternator adjustment and pivot bolts.
2. Rotate the alternator towards the engine until the belt is slack enough to remove from the pulleys.

To install:

3. Install the belt over the pulleys. Make sure the ribs on the belt properly contact the grooves on the pulleys.
4. Adjust the belt tension as described earlier in this Section.

AIR CONDITIONER COMPRESSOR BELT

1. Remove the alternator belt.
2. Loosen the idler bracket adjustment and pivot bolts.
3. Rotate the idler bracket away from the belt until the belt is slack enough to remove from the pulleys.

To install:

4. Install the belt over the pulleys. Make sure the ribs on the belt properly contact the grooves on the pulleys.
5. Adjust the belt tension as described earlier in this Section.
6. Install the alternator belt and adjust the tension.

Hoses

INSPECTION

▶ **See Figures 56, 57, 58 and 59**

Inspect the condition of the radiator and heater hoses periodically. Early spring and at the beginning of the fall or winter, when you are performing other maintenance, are good times. Make sure the engine and cooling system are cold. Visually inspect for cracking, rotting or collapsed hoses, and replace as necessary. Run your hand along the length of the hose. If a weak or swollen spot is noted when squeezing the hose wall, replace the hose.

REMOVAL & INSTALLATION

1. Remove the radiator cap.

✳✳ CAUTION

Never remove the radiator cap while the engine is running or personal injury from scalding hot coolant or steam may result. If possible, wait until the engine has cooled to remove the radiator cap. If this is not possible, wrap a thick cloth around the radiator cap and turn it slowly to the first stop. Step back while the pressure is released from the cooling system. When you are sure all the pressure has been released, press down on the cap, still with the cloth, and turn and remove it.

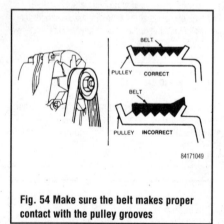

Fig. 54 Make sure the belt makes proper contact with the pulley grooves

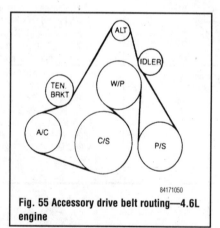

Fig. 55 Accessory drive belt routing—4.6L engine

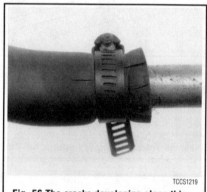

Fig. 56 The cracks developing along this hose are a result of age-related hardening

Fig. 57 A hose clamp that is too tight can cause older hoses to separate and tear on either side of the clamp

Fig. 58 A soft spongy hose (identifiable by the swollen section) will eventually burst and should be replaced

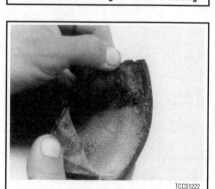

Fig. 59 Hoses are likely to deteriorate from the inside if the cooling system is not periodically flushed

2. Position a suitable container under the radiator and open the draincock to drain the radiator.

❊❊ CAUTION

When draining the coolant, keep in mind that cats and dogs are attracted by the ethylene glycol antifreeze, and are quite likely to drink any that is left in an uncovered container or in puddles on the ground. This will prove fatal in sufficient quantity. Always drain the coolant into a sealable container. Coolant should be reused unless it is contaminated or several years old.

3. Loosen the hose clamps at each end of the hose requiring replacement. Pull the clamps back on the hose away from the connection.

4. Twist, pull and slide the hose off the radiator, water pump, thermostat or heater connection.

➡**If the hose is stuck at the connection, do not try to insert a screwdriver or other sharp tool under the hose end in an effort to free it, as the connection and/or hose may become damaged. Heater connections especially are easily damaged. If the hose is not to be reused, make a slice at the end of the hose with a single edge razor blade, perpendicular to the end of the hose. Do not cut deep so as not to damage the connection. The hose can then be peeled from the connection.**

5. Clean both hose mounting connections. Inspect the condition of the hose clamps and replace them, if necessary.

To install:

6. Coat the connection surfaces with a water resistant sealer.

7. Slide the hose clamps over the replacement hose and slide the hose ends over the connections into position.

8. Position the hose clamps at least ⅛ in. from each end of the hose. Make sure they are located beyond the raised bead of the connector, if equipped, and centered in the clamping area of the connection.

9. If the clamps are the screw type, tighten them to 22–31 inch lbs. (2.5–3.5 Nm). Do not overtighten.

10. Close the radiator draincock and fill the cooling system.

11. Start the engine and allow it to reach normal operating temperature. Check for leaks.

Air Conditioning System

SYSTEM SERVICE & REPAIR

➡**It is recommended that the A/C system be serviced by an EPA Section 609 certified automotive technician utilizing a refrigerant recovery/recycling machine.**

The do-it-yourselfer should not service his/her own vehicle's A/C system for many reasons, including legal concerns, personal injury, environmental damage and cost.

According to the U.S. Clean Air Act, it is a federal crime to service or repair (involving the refrigerant) a Motor Vehicle Air Conditioning (MVAC) system for money without being EPA certified. It is also illegal to vent R-12 and R-134a refrigerants into the atmosphere. State and/or local laws may be more strict than the federal regulations, so be sure to check with your state and/or local authorities for further information.

➡**Federal law dictates that a fine of up to $25,000 may be levied on people convicted of venting refrigerant into the atmosphere.**

When servicing an A/C system you run the risk of handling or coming in contact with refrigerant, which may result in skin or eye irritation or frostbite. Although low in toxicity (due to chemical stability), inhalation of concentrated refrigerant fumes is dangerous and can result in death; cases of fatal cardiac arrhythmia have been reported in people accidentally subjected to high levels of refrigerant. Some early symptoms include loss of concentration and drowsiness.

➡**Generally, the limit for exposure is lower for R-134a than it is for R-12. Exceptional care must be practiced when handling R-134a.**

Also, some refrigerants can decompose at high temperatures (near gas heaters or open flame), which may result in hydrofluoric acid, hydrochloric acid and phosgene (a fatal nerve gas).

It is usually more economically feasible to have a certified MVAC automotive technician perform A/C system service on your vehicle.

R-12 Refrigerant Conversion

If your vehicle still uses R-12 refrigerant, one way to save A/C system costs down the road is to investigate the possibility of having your system converted to R-134a. The older R-12 systems can be easily converted to R-134a refrigerant by a certified automotive technician by installing a few new components and changing the system oil.

The cost of R-12 is steadily rising and will continue to increase, because it is no longer imported or manufactured in the United States. Therefore, it is often possible to have an R-12 system converted to R-134a and recharged for less than it would cost to just charge the system with R-12.

If you are interested in having your system converted, contact local automotive service stations for more details and information.

PREVENTIVE MAINTENANCE

Although the A/C system should not be serviced by the do-it-yourselfer, preventive maintenance should be practiced to help maintain the efficiency of the vehicle's A/C system. Be sure to perform the following:

• The easiest and most important preventive maintenance for your A/C system is to be sure that it is used on a regular basis. Running the system for five minutes each month (no matter what the season) will help ensure that the seals and all internal components remain lubricated.

➡**Some vehicles automatically operate the A/C system compressor whenever the windshield defroster is activated. Therefore, the A/C system would not need to be operated each month if the defroster was used.**

• In order to prevent heater core freeze-up during A/C operation, it is necessary to maintain proper antifreeze protection. Be sure to properly maintain the engine cooling system.

• Any obstruction of or damage to the condenser configuration will restrict air flow which is essential to its efficient operation. Keep this unit clean and in proper physical shape.

➡**Bug screens which are mounted in front of the condenser (unless they are original equipment) are regarded as obstructions.**

• The condensation drain tube expels any water which accumulates on the bottom of the evaporator housing into the engine compartment. If this tube is obstructed, the air conditioning performance can be restricted and condensation buildup can spill over onto the vehicle's floor.

SYSTEM INSPECTION

Although the A/C system should not be serviced by the do-it-yourselfer, system inspections should be performed to help maintain the efficiency of the vehicle's A/C system. Be sure to perform the following:

The easiest and often most important check for the air conditioning system consists of a visual inspection of the system components. Visually inspect the system for refrigerant leaks, damaged compressor clutch, abnormal compressor drive belt tension and/or condition, plugged evaporator drain tube, blocked condenser fins, disconnected or broken wires, blown fuses, corroded connections and poor insulation.

A refrigerant leak will usually appear as an oily residue at the leakage point in the system. The oily residue soon picks up dust or dirt particles from the surrounding air and appears greasy. Through time, this will build up and appear to be a heavy dirt impregnated grease.

For a thorough visual and operational inspection, check the following:

• Check the surface of the radiator and condenser for dirt, leaves or other material which might block air flow.

• Check for kinks in hoses and lines. Check the system for leaks.

• Make sure the drive belt is properly tensioned. During operation, make sure the belt is free of noise or slippage.

• Make sure the blower motor operates at all appropriate positions, then check for distribution of the air from all outlets.

➡Remember that in high humidity, air discharged from the vents may not feel as cold as expected, even if the system is working properly. This is because moisture in humid air retains heat more effectively than dry air, thereby making humid air more difficult to cool.

Windshield Wipers

ELEMENT (REFILL) CARE & REPLACEMENT

▶ **See Figures 60, 61 and 62**

For maximum effectiveness and longest element life, the windshield and wiper blades should be kept clean. Dirt, tree sap, road tar and so on will cause

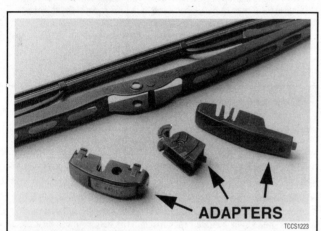

Fig. 60 Most aftermarket blades are available with multiple adapters to fit different vehicles

streaking, smearing and blade deterioration if left on the glass. It is advisable to wash the windshield carefully with a commercial glass cleaner at least once a month. Wipe off the rubber blades with the wet rag afterwards. Do not attempt to move wipers across the windshield by hand; damage to the motor and drive mechanism will result.

To inspect and/or replace the wiper blade elements, place the wiper switch in the **LOW** speed position and the ignition switch in the **ACC** position. When the wiper blades are approximately vertical on the windshield, turn the ignition switch to **OFF**.

Examine the wiper blade elements. If they are found to be cracked, broken or torn, they should be replaced immediately. Replacement intervals will vary with usage, although ozone deterioration usually limits element life to about one year. If the wiper pattern is smeared or streaked, or if the blade chatters across the glass, the elements should be replaced. It is easiest and most sensible to replace the elements in pairs.

If your vehicle is equipped with aftermarket blades, there are several different types of refills and your vehicle might have any kind. Aftermarket blades and arms rarely use the exact same type blade or refill as the original equipment.

Regardless of the type of refill used, be sure to follow the part manufacturer's instructions closely. Make sure that all of the frame jaws are engaged as the refill is pushed into place and locked. If the metal blade holder and frame are allowed to touch the glass during wiper operation, the glass will be scratched.

Installing Original Equipment Refills

▶ **See Figures 63, 64, 65, 66 and 67**

1. Position the wiper blades on the windshield as explained earlier.
2. Insert a small screwdriver in the slot, as shown in the figure, push down on the spring lock and pull the blade assembly from the wiper arm pin.
3. Insert a small screwdriver as shown in the figure and twist it slowly until the element clears 1 side of the jaws. Slide the element out of the jaws.
4. Slide the element into the jaws, starting with the second set from either end of the blade assembly. Slide the element into all the jaws to the element stop.
5. Insert the element into 1 side of the end jaws and with a rocking motion, push the element upward until it snaps in.

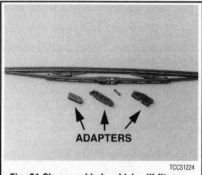

Fig. 61 Choose a blade which will fit your vehicle, and that will be readily available next time you need blades

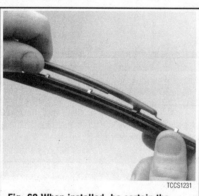

Fig. 62 When installed, be certain the blade is fully inserted into the backing

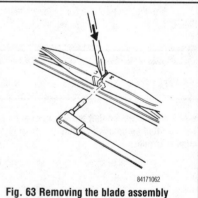

Fig. 63 Removing the blade assembly from the wiper arm

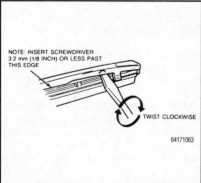

Fig. 64 Removing the element from the frame

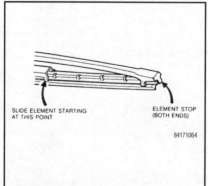

Fig. 65 Slide the element into the frame jaws to the stop

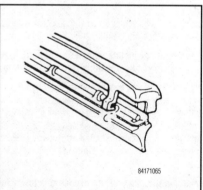

Fig. 66 Insert the element into one side of the end jaws

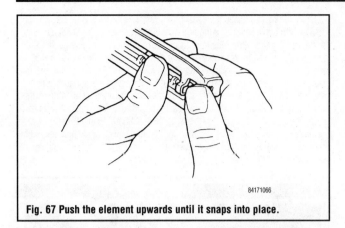

84171066

Fig. 67 Push the element upwards until it snaps into place.

6. Push the blade assembly on the wiper arm pin so the spring lock engages the pin. Make sure the blade assembly is securely attached to the pin.

Tires and Wheels

Common sense and good driving habits will afford maximum tire life. Make sure that you don't overload the vehicle or run with incorrect pressure in the tires. Either of these will increase tread wear. Fast starts, sudden stops and sharp cornering are hard on tires and will shorten their useful life span.

➡**For optimum tire life, keep the tires properly inflated, rotate them often and have the wheel alignment checked periodically.**

Inspect your tires frequently. Be especially careful to watch for bubbles in the tread or sidewall, deep cuts or underinflation. Replace any tires with bubbles in the sidewall. If cuts are so deep that they penetrate to the cords, discard the tire. Any cut in the sidewall of a radial tire renders it unsafe. Also look for uneven tread wear patterns that may indicate the front end is out of alignment or that the tires are out of balance.

TIRE ROTATION

◆ **See Figure 68**

Tires must be rotated periodically to equalize wear patterns that vary with a tire's position on the vehicle. Tires will also wear in an uneven way as the front steering/suspension system wears to the point where the alignment should be reset.

Rotating the tires will ensure maximum life for the tires as a set, so you will not have to discard a tire early due to wear on only part of the tread. Regular rotation is required to equalize wear.

When rotating "unidirectional tires," make sure that they always roll in the same direction. This means that a tire used on the left side of the vehicle must not be switched to the right side and vice-versa. Such tires should only be rotated front-to-rear or rear-to-front, while always remaining on the same side of the vehicle. These tires are marked on the sidewall as to the direction of rotation; observe the marks when reinstalling the tire(s).

Some styled or "mag" wheels may have different offsets front to rear. In these cases, the rear wheels must not be used up front and vice-versa. Furthermore, if these wheels are equipped with unidirectional tires, they cannot be rotated unless the tire is remounted for the proper direction of rotation.

➡**The compact or space-saver spare is strictly for emergency use. It must never be included in the tire rotation or placed on the vehicle for everyday use.**

TIRE DESIGN

◆ **See Figure 69**

For maximum satisfaction, tires should be used in sets of four. Mixing of different brands or types (radial, bias-belted, fiberglass belted) should be avoided. In most cases, the vehicle manufacturer has designated a type of tire on which the vehicle will perform best. Your first choice when replacing tires should be to use the same type of tire that the manufacturer recommends.

When radial tires are used, tire sizes and wheel diameters should be selected to maintain ground clearance and tire load capacity equivalent to the original specified tire. Radial tires should always be used in sets of four.

✳✳ CAUTION

Radial tires should never be used on only the front axle.

When selecting tires, pay attention to the original size as marked on the tire. Most tires are described using an industry size code sometimes referred to as P-Metric. This allows the exact identification of the tire specifications, regardless of the manufacturer. If selecting a different tire size or brand, remember to check the installed tire for any sign of interference with the body or suspension while the vehicle is stopping, turning sharply or heavily loaded.

Snow Tires

Good radial tires can produce a big advantage in slippery weather, but in snow, a street radial tire does not have sufficient tread to provide traction and control. The small grooves of a street tire quickly pack with snow and the tire behaves like a billiard ball on a marble floor. The more open, chunky tread of a snow tire will self-clean as the tire turns, providing much better grip on snowy surfaces.

To satisfy municipalities requiring snow tires during weather emergencies, most snow tires carry either an M + S designation after the tire size stamped on the sidewall, or the designation "all-season." In general, no change in tire size is necessary when buying snow tires.

Most manufacturers strongly recommend the use of 4 snow tires on their vehicles for reasons of stability. If snow tires are fitted only to the drive wheels, the opposite end of the vehicle may become very unstable when braking or turning on slippery surfaces. This instability can lead to unpleasant endings if the driver can't counteract the slide in time.

Note that snow tires, whether 2 or 4, will affect vehicle handling in all non-snow situations. The stiffer, heavier snow tires will noticeably change the turning and braking characteristics of the vehicle. Once the snow tires are installed, you must re-learn the behavior of the vehicle and drive accordingly.

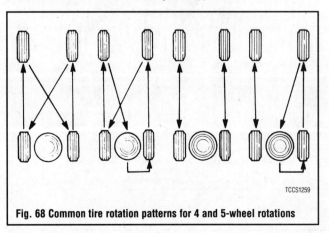

TCCS1259

Fig. 68 Common tire rotation patterns for 4 and 5-wheel rotations

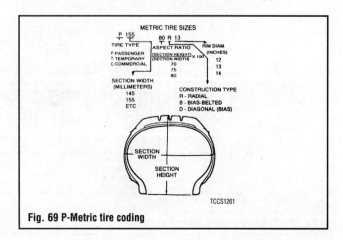

TCCS1261

Fig. 69 P-Metric tire coding

➥Consider buying extra wheels on which to mount the snow tires. Once done, the "snow wheels" can be installed and removed as needed. This eliminates the potential damage to tires or wheels from seasonal removal and installation. Even if your vehicle has styled wheels, see if inexpensive steel wheels are available. Although the look of the vehicle will change, the expensive wheels will be protected from salt, curb hits and pothole damage.

TIRE STORAGE

If they are mounted on wheels, store the tires at proper inflation pressure. All tires should be kept in a cool, dry place. If they are stored in the garage or basement, do not let them stand on a concrete floor; set them on strips of wood, a mat or a large stack of newspaper. Keeping them away from direct moisture is of paramount importance. Tires should not be stored upright, but in a flat position.

INFLATION & INSPECTION

♦ See Figures 70 thru 75

The importance of proper tire inflation cannot be overemphasized. A tire employs air as part of its structure. It is designed around the supporting strength of the air at a specified pressure. For this reason, improper inflation drastically reduces the tire's ability to perform as intended. A tire will lose some air in day-to-day use; having to add a few pounds of air periodically is not necessarily a sign of a leaking tire.

Two items should be a permanent fixture in every glove compartment: an accurate tire pressure gauge and a tread depth gauge. Check the tire pressure (including the spare) regularly with a pocket type gauge. Too often, the gauge on the end of the air hose at your corner garage is not accurate because it suffers too much abuse. Always check tire pressure when the tires are cold, as pressure increases with temperature. If you must move the vehicle to check the tire inflation, do not drive more than a mile before checking. A cold tire is generally one that has not been driven for more than three hours.

A plate or sticker is normally provided somewhere in the vehicle (door post, hood, tailgate or trunk lid) which shows the proper pressure for the tires. Never counteract excessive pressure build-up by bleeding off air pressure (letting some air out). This will cause the tire to run hotter and wear quicker.

❊❊ CAUTION

Never exceed the maximum tire pressure embossed on the tire! This is the pressure to be used when the tire is at maximum loading, but it is rarely the correct pressure for everyday driving. Consult the owner's manual or the tire pressure sticker for the correct tire pressure.

Once you've maintained the correct tire pressures for several weeks, you'll be familiar with the vehicle's braking and handling personality. Slight adjustments in tire pressures can fine-tune these characteristics, but never change the cold pressure specification by more than 2 psi. A slightly softer tire pressure will give a softer ride but also yield lower fuel mileage. A slightly harder tire will give crisper dry road handling but can cause skidding on wet surfaces. Unless you're fully attuned to the vehicle, stick to the recommended inflation pressures.

All automotive tires have built-in tread wear indicator bars that show up as ½ in. (13mm) wide smooth bands across the tire when 1/16 in. (1.5mm) of tread remains. The appearance of tread wear indicators means that the tires should be replaced. In fact, many states have laws prohibiting the use of tires with less than this amount of tread.

TCCS1095

Fig. 70 Tires with deep cuts, or cuts which bulge, should be replaced immediately

PROPERLY INFLATED   IMPROPERLY INFLATED

RADIAL TIRE

TCCS1263

Fig. 71 Radial tires have a characteristic sidewall bulge; don't try to measure pressure by looking at the tire. Use a quality air pressure gauge

CONDITION	RAPID WEAR AT SHOULDERS	RAPID WEAR AT CENTER	CRACKED TREADS	WEAR ON ONE SIDE	FEATHERED EDGE	BALD SPOTS	SCALLOPED WEAR
EFFECT							
CAUSE	UNDER-INFLATION OR LACK OF ROTATION	OVER-INFLATION OR LACK OF ROTATION	UNDER-INFLATION OR EXCESSIVE SPEED*	EXCESSIVE CAMBER	INCORRECT TOE	UNBALANCED WHEEL OR TIRE DEFECT*	LACK OF ROTATION OF TIRES OR WORN OR OUT-OF-ALIGNMENT SUSPENSION.
CORRECTION	ADJUST PRESSURE TO SPECIFICATIONS WHEN TIRES ARE COOL ROTATE TIRES			ADJUST CAMBER TO SPECIFICATIONS	ADJUST TOE-IN TO SPECIFICATIONS	DYNAMIC OR STATIC BALANCE WHEELS	ROTATE TIRES AND INSPECT SUSPENSION

*HAVE TIRE INSPECTED FOR FURTHER USE.

Fig. 72 Common tire wear patterns and causes

TCCS1267

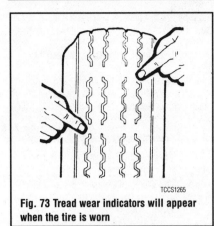

Fig. 73 Tread wear indicators will appear when the tire is worn

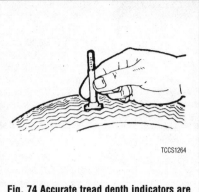

Fig. 74 Accurate tread depth indicators are inexpensive and handy

Fig. 75 A penny works well for a quick check of tread depth

You can check your own tread depth with an inexpensive gauge or by using a Lincoln head penny. Slip the Lincoln penny (with Lincoln's head upside-down) into several tread grooves. If you can see the top of Lincoln's head in 2 adjacent grooves, the tire has less than ¹⁄₁₆ in. (1.5mm) tread left and should be replaced. You can measure snow tires in the same manner by using the "tails" side of the Lincoln penny. If you can see the top of the Lincoln memorial, it's time to replace the snow tire(s).

FLUIDS AND LUBRICANTS

Fluid Disposal

Used fluids such as engine oil, transmission fluid, antifreeze and brake fluid are hazardous wastes and must be disposed of properly. Before draining any fluids, consult with the local authorities; in many areas, waste oil, etc. is being accepted as a part of recycling programs. A number of service stations and auto parts stores are also accepting waste fluids for recycling.

Be sure of the recycling center's policies before draining any fluids, as many will not accept different fluids that have been mixed together.

Fuel and Engine Oil Recommendations

FUEL

Depending on the year produced, your vehicle may be equipped with a catalytic converter as a part of its emission control system, necessitating the use of unleaded gasoline. Using leaded fuel will damage the catalytic converter, resulting in poor vehicle performance and excessive exhaust emissions.

If your car is equipped with a converter, the engine is designed to use gasoline with a minimum octane rating of 87, which in most areas means regular unleaded gasoline. Always use a high quality fuel containing detergent additives, to keep fuel injectors and intake valves clean.

If the engine occasionally knocks lightly under acceleration, or when going up a hill, do not be concerned. However, if the engine knocks heavily under all driving conditions, or knocks lightly at cruising speeds, try switching to another brand or higher grade of gasoline. If knocking persists, the cause should be investigated or serious engine damage could result.

OIL

▶ See Figure 76

Always use a high quality detergent motor oil. To determine an oil's quality and viscosity, look for the American Petroleum Institute (API) symbol on the oil container label. The highest quality oil currently available carries the API Service rating "SG". Look for the letters "SG" alone or in combination with other letters such as "SG/CC" or "SG/CD". An oil rated "SC", "SD", "SE" or "SF" is not acceptable for use in your car's engine.

For maximum fuel economy, look for an oil that carries the words "Energy Conserving II" in the API symbol. This means that the oil contains friction reducing additives that help reduce the amount of fuel burned to overcome engine friction.

The Society of Automotive Engineers (SAE) viscosity rating indicates an oil's ability to flow at a given temperature. The number designation indicates the thickness or "weight" of the oil. An SAE 5 weight oil is a thin, light oil; it allows the engine to crank over easily even when it is very cold, and quickly provides lubrication for all parts of the engine. However, as the engine temperature increases, the 5 weight oil becomes too thin, resulting in metal-to-metal contact and damage to internal engine parts. A heavier SAE 50 weight oil can lubricate and protect internal engine parts even under extremely high operating temperatures, but would not be able to flow quickly enough to provide internal engine protection during cold weather start-up, one of the most critical periods for lubrication protection in an engine.

The answer to the temperature extremes problem is the multi-grade or multi-viscosity oil. Multi-viscosity oils carry multiple number designations, such as SAE 10W-40 or SAE 20W-50 (the "W" in the designation stands for winter). A 10W-40 oil has the flow characteristics of the thin 10 weight oil in cold weather, providing rapid lubrication and allowing easy engine cranking. When the engine warms up, the oil acts like a straight 40 weight oil, providing internal engine protection under higher temperatures.

Ford Motor Company recommends using either SAE 5W-30 or SAE 10W-30 oil. SAE 5W-30 should be used if you anticipate the ambient temperature in which you'll be driving to fall below 0°F (−18°C) but not go higher than 100°F (38°C) during the period before your next oil change. SAE 10W-30 should be used if you anticipate the temperature in which you'll be driving to be between 0°F (−18°C) and 100°F (38°C) and above, during the period before your next oil change.

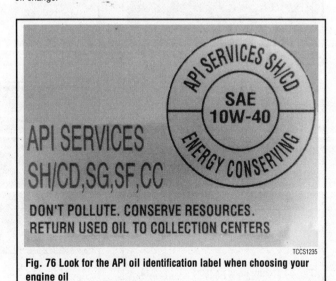

API SERVICES
SH/CD,SG,SF,CC

API SERVICES SH/CD

SAE
10W-40

ENERGY CONSERVING

DON'T POLLUTE. CONSERVE RESOURCES.
RETURN USED OIL TO COLLECTION CENTERS

Fig. 76 Look for the API oil identification label when choosing your engine oil

Engine

OIL LEVEL CHECK

♦ **See Figures 77, 78, 79 and 80**

Check the engine oil level every time you fill the gas tank. Make sure the oil level is between the FULL and ADD marks on the engine oil level dipstick. The engine and oil must be warm and the vehicle parked on level ground to get an accurate reading. Also, allow a few minutes after turning off the engine for the oil to drain back into the pan before checking, or an inaccurate reading will result. Check the engine oil level as follows:

1. Open the hood and locate the engine oil dipstick.
2. If the engine is hot, you may want to wrap a rag around the dipstick handle before removing it.

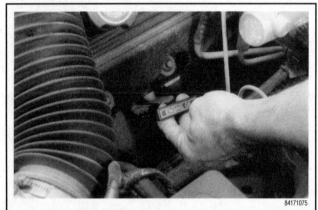

Fig. 77 Engine oil level dipstick location—4.6L engine

3. Remove the dipstick and wipe it with a clean, lint-free rag, then reinsert it into the dipstick tube. Make sure it is inserted all the way or an inaccurate reading will result.
4. Pull out the dipstick and note the oil level. It should be between the marks, as stated above.
5. If the oil level is below the ADD mark, remove the oil filler cap from the rocker arm cover and add fresh oil to bring the level within the proper range. Do not overfill; approximately 1 quart of oil is required to raise the oil level from the ADD mark to the FULL mark.

➡ **Using a funnel when adding oil prevents spillage.**

6. Wait a few minutes for the oil to drain into the pan and recheck the oil level. Add more oil only if required.
7. Install the oil filler cap. Install the dipstick, making sure it is fully inserted into the dipstick tube. Close the hood.

OIL AND FILTER CHANGE

♦ **See Figures 81 thru 86**

The engine oil and oil filter should be changed at the same time, at the recommended interval on the Maintenance Intervals chart. The oil should be changed more frequently if the vehicle is being operated in very dusty areas. Before draining the oil, make sure the engine is at operating temperature. Hot oil will hold more impurities in suspension and will flow better, allowing the removal of more oil and dirt.

Change the oil and filter as follows:

1. Apply the parking brake and block the drive wheels.
2. Run the engine until it reaches the normal operating temperature, then turn the engine OFF.
3. Raise and safely support the front of the car on jackstands.
4. Slide a drain pan under the oil pan drain plug. Vehicles equipped with 5.0L or 5.8L engines, have 2 oil drain plugs on the oil pan; both must be removed.

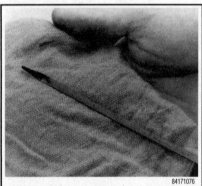

Fig. 78 Wipe the dipstick with a clean cloth before replacing it in the tube

Fig. 79 The oil level is correct in this engine

Fig. 80 Add oil through the filler hole in the rocker arm cover

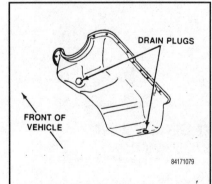

Fig. 81 The oil pans on the 5.0L and 5.8L engines have 2 drain plugs

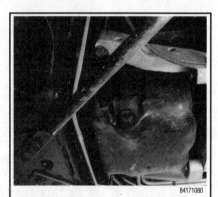

Fig. 82 Oil pan drain plug location—4.6L engine

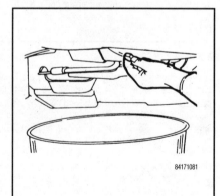

Fig. 83 Removing the oil pan drain plug

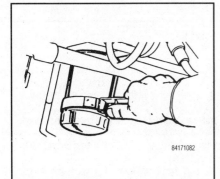

Fig. 84 Removing the oil filter with an oil filter wrench

Fig. 85 Oil filter location—4.6L engine

Fig. 86 Before installing a new oil filter, lightly coat the rubber gasket with clean oil

✳✳ CAUTION

The EPA warns that prolonged contact with used engine oil may cause a number of skin disorders, including cancer! You should make every effort to minimize your exposure to used engine oil. Protective gloves should be worn when changing the oil. Wash your hands and any other exposed skin areas as soon as possible after exposure to used engine oil. Soap and water, or waterless hand cleaner should be used.

5. Wipe the drain plug and the surrounding area clean. Loosen the drain plug with a socket or box wrench, and then remove it by hand, using a rag to shield your fingers from the heat. Push in on the plug as you turn it out, so that no oil escapes until the plug is completely removed.

6. Allow the oil to drain into the pan. Be careful; if the engine is at operating temperature, the oil is hot enough to burn you.

7. Clean and install the drain plug, making sure that the gasket is still on the plug. If the gasket is missing or damaged, install a new one. Tighten the drain plugs on 5.0L and 5.8L engines to 15–25 ft. lbs. (20–34 Nm). Tighten the drain plug on the 4.6L and all otherengines engines to 8–12 ft. lbs. (11–16 Nm).

8. Slide the drain pan under the oil filter. Slip an oil filter wrench onto the filter and turn it counterclockwise to loosen it. Wrap a rag around the filter and unscrew it the rest of the way. Be careful of oil running down the side of the filter.

9. Make sure the old oil filter gasket is not stuck on the cylinder block or oil filter adapter. Thoroughly clean the sealing surface and mounting threads on the cylinder block or adapter.

10. Coat the rubber gasket on the replacement filter with clean engine oil. Place the filter in position and screw it on clockwise by hand. After the rubber gasket contacts the sealing surface, tighten the filter according to the specifications supplied with the filter.

11. Pull the drain pan from under the vehicle and lower the vehicle to the ground.

12. Remove the oil filler cap from the rocker arm cover and place a funnel in the oil filler hole. Fill the crankcase with the quantity of oil specified in the Capacities chart at the end of this Section.

13. Remove the funnel and install the oil filler cap. Be sure to wipe away any spilled oil.

14. Start the engine and let it run until it reaches normal operating temperature.

15. Turn the engine OFF. Check for oil leaks at the drain plug(s) and oil filter. Check the oil level as explained earlier.

Automatic Transmission

FLUID RECOMMENDATIONS

Motorcraft MERCON® (DEXRON®II) automatic transmission fluid is required.

LEVEL CHECK

♦ **See Figures 87 and 88**

The automatic transmission fluid level should be checked when the fluid is at an operating temperature of 150–170°F (66–77°C). This fluid temperature can be obtained by driving the car for 15–20 miles of city type driving with an ambient air temperature of 50°F (10°C) or higher. When the fluid is checked at this temperature, the fluid level should be within the cross-hatched area on the dipstick.

If the vehicle has not been driven recently and the engine is cold, perform a preliminary fluid check before driving the vehicle to warm the fluid. With the transmission fluid at room temperature, 70–95°F (21–35°C), the fluid level should be between the holes on the dipstick. If the fluid level is below the bot-

Fig. 87 Removing the transmission fluid dipstick

Fig. 88 Detail of the transmission fluid dipstick. The fluid level should be between the holes at room temperature and within the cross-hatched area at operating temperature

tom hole, do not drive the vehicle. Add enough fluid to just bring the level to between the holes on the dipstick, before driving.

Never bring the fluid level to between the cross-hatched area on the dipstick when the fluid is at room temperature. The transmission will be overfilled when the fluid reaches operating temperature.

Check the transmission fluid level as follows:

1. Make sure the vehicle is parked on a level surface. Place the transmission selector lever in P and start the engine.

2. Apply the foot brake and move the transmission selector lever to each position, pausing for a moment while the transmission is in each position.

3. Place the transmission selector lever in P and apply the parking brake. Leave the engine running.

4. Clean any dirt from the transmission fluid dipstick cap.

5. Remove the dipstick from the tube. You may want to wrap a rag around the dipstick handle; if the transmission fluid is at operating temperature, it will be hot. Wipe the fluid from the dipstick using a clean lint-free rag and reinsert the dipstick into the tube. Make sure the dipstick is fully seated.

6. Pull the dipstick from the tube and check the fluid level. It should be within the cross-hatched area on the dipstick when the fluid is at operating temperature, or between the holes on the dipstick if the fluid is at room temperature, as explained earlier.

➡In order to obtain an accurate reading, if the vehicle has been operated for an extended period at high speed, in city traffic, in hot weather, or has been pulling a trailer, allow the fluid to cool for at least ½ hour after the vehicle is shut off.

7. If the fluid level is okay, reinstall the dipstick in the tube, making sure it is fully seated.

8. If the fluid level is low, install a suitable funnel in the dipstick tube. Add only enough fluid through the funnel to bring the fluid to the correct level.

❊❊ WARNING

Do not overfill the transmission. Overfilling can result in foaming, fluid loss through the vent, or possible transmission malfunction. If the transmission is overfilled, the excess fluid must be removed.

9. When the transmission fluid level is correct, reinstall the dipstick in the tube, making sure it is fully seated.

DRAIN AND REFILL

The transmission fluid should be changed at the intervals specified in the Maintenance Intervals chart at the end of this Section.

To drain the transmission fluid, the transmission fluid pan must be removed; only the torque converter is equipped with a drain plug. Any time the transmission pan is removed, the transmission filter should be replaced. Refer to the procedure that follows.

PAN AND FILTER SERVICE

◆ **See Figures 89, 90, 91 and 92**

1. Raise and safely support the vehicle on jackstands.

2. Remove the torque converter dust cover from the transmission housing.

3. If the torque converter drain plug is inaccessible, install a socket and breaker bar on the crankshaft damper bolt. Turn the crankshaft until the torque converter drain plug can be seen.

4. Position a suitable drain pan under the torque converter. Remove the torque converter drain plug and allow the fluid to drain.

5. After the torque converter has drained, install the drain plug and tighten to 21–23 ft. lbs. (28–30 Nm). Install the dust cover.

6. Position the drain pan under the transmission fluid pan. Remove all but two of the retaining bolts. Loosen the 2 remaining retaining bolts and allow the fluid to drain. If the pan is stuck to the transmission, tap it lightly with a plastic mallet. Do not attempt to pry the pan away from the transmission housing.

7. When the fluid has drained, remove the remaining retaining bolts. Allow the pan to drop and slowly drain the remaining fluid.

8. When all the fluid has drained, remove the pan. Remove and discard the pan gasket.

9. If equipped with automatic overdrive transmission, remove the 3 filter retaining bolts and remove the filter, grommet and gasket.

10. If equipped with electronic automatic overdrive transmission, use both hands to remove the filter by pulling downward. If the grommet stays in the main control bore, pry it out using a small prybar. Be careful not to damage the main control bore.

11. Remove the magnet from the transmission fluid pan, if equipped. Thoroughly clean the pan and magnet. Clean all old pan gasket material from the transmission housing.

Fig. 89 Transmission fluid pan

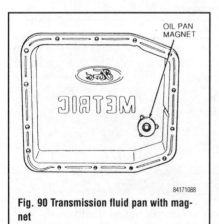

Fig. 90 Transmission fluid pan with magnet

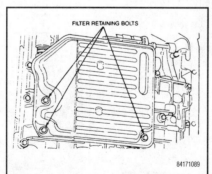

Fig. 91 Transmission filter retaining bolt locations—automatic overdrive transmission

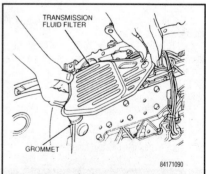

Fig. 92 Removing the transmission filter—electronic automatic overdrive transmission

➡The magnet is installed to collect any metal shavings from the transmission fluid. A small amount of shavings clinging to the magnet are not cause for concern; they are caused by normal wear of internal components during transmission operation. However, you should consult a reputable transmission shop if any large pieces of metal are found on the magnet, especially if the transmission is not operating properly.

12. If equipped with automatic overdrive transmission, install a new filter on the transmission valve body, using a new gasket. Install the retaining bolts and tighten to 80–120 inch lbs. (9–14 Nm).

13. If equipped with electronic automatic overdrive transmission, install a new filter and grommet.

14. Place the magnet, if equipped, in the fluid pan in its original location. Install a new gasket on the fluid pan.

15. Install the fluid pan with the retaining bolts. Tighten the retaining bolts, evenly, to 107–119 inch lbs. (12–13.5 Nm).

16. Lower the vehicle.

17. Fill the transmission with the proper quantity of fluid. Refer to the Capacities chart at the end of this Section. Check the fluid level according to the procedure described earlier.

Rear Drive Axle

FLUID RECOMMENDATIONS

SAE 90 weight hypoid gear oil is required. If equipped with Traction-Lok differential, the addition of friction modifier additive C8AZ–19B546–A or equivalent, is also required when draining and refilling.

LEVEL CHECK

♦ **See Figure 93**

Checking the differential fluid level is generally unnecessary unless a leak is suspected.

1. Raise and safely support the vehicle on jackstands.

2. Remove the oil fill plug from the differential housing. The hex drive on a ⅜ in. drive ratchet, breaker bar or extension works well on some applications.

3. Insert a finger into the fill hole; be careful as the threads can be sharp. The oil level should be about ¼ in. below the bottom of the fill hole with the axle in normal running position.

4. If the oil level feels low, add oil through the fill hole. Most hypoid gear oil comes in squeeze bottles equipped with small fill nozzles, designed for this purpose.

5. When the oil level is correct, install the oil fill plug and tighten to 15–30 ft. lbs. (20–41 Nm).

DRAIN AND REFILL

♦ **See Figure 94**

The differential should be drained and refilled every 100,000 miles or if the axle has been submerged in water.

1. Raise and safely support the vehicle on jackstands.

2. Clean all dirt from the area of the differential cover.

3. Position a drain pan under the differential.

4. Remove all but 2 cover retaining bolts and allow the fluid to drain from the differential. Once the fluid has drained, remove the remaining bolts to free the cover.

5. Thoroughly clean the differential cover. Cover the differential carrier with a clean rag to prevent axle contamination, then clean all the old sealant from the machined surface of the differential housing.

6. Make sure the machined surfaces of the cover and differential are clean and free of oil. Apply a ¼ in. wide bead of silicone sealer around the circumference of the cover, going inside the bolt holes.

7. Install the cover with the retaining bolts. Tighten the bolts, evenly, to 25–35 ft. lbs. (34–47 Nm) in a crisscross pattern.

8. Remove the oil fill plug and add the required amount of hypoid gear oil through the oil fill hole. Refer to the Capacities chart at the end of this Section.

➡**If equipped with Traction-Lok differential, 4 oz. of friction modifier additive C8AZ–19B546–A or equivalent, must be included in the refill.**

9. Install the oil fill plug and tighten to 15–30 ft. lbs. (20–41 Nm). Lower the vehicle.

10. Road test the vehicle to warm the fluid. Check for leaks.

Cooling System

♦ **See Figure 95**

Check the cooling system at the interval specified in the Maintenance Intervals chart at the end of this section.

Hose clamps should be tightened, and soft or cracked hoses replaced. Damp spots, or accumulations of rust or dye near hoses, water pump or other areas, indicate areas of possible leakage. Check the radiator cap for a worn or cracked gasket. If the cap doesn't seal properly, fluid will be lost and the engine will overheat. A worn cap should be replaced with a new one.

Periodically clean any debris such as leaves, paper, insects, etc. from the radiator fins. Pick the large pieces off by hand. The smaller pieces can be washed away with water pressure from a hose.

Carefully straighten any bent radiator fins with a pair of needle nose pliers. Be careful—the fins are very soft. Don't wiggle the fins back and forth too much. Straighten them once and try not to move them again.

FLUID RECOMMENDATIONS

The recommended fluid is a 50/50 mixture of ethylene glycol antifreeze and water for year round use. Use a good quality antifreeze with water pump lubricants, rust inhibitors and other corrosion inhibitors along with acid neutralizers. Use only antifreeze that is SAFE FOR USE WITH AN ALUMINUM RADIATOR.

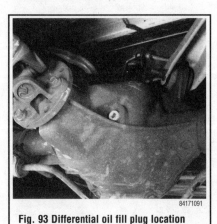

Fig. 93 Differential oil fill plug location

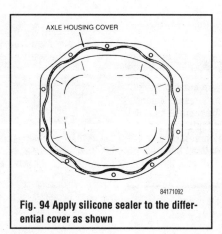

Fig. 94 Apply silicone sealer to the differential cover as shown

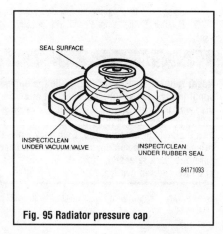

Fig. 95 Radiator pressure cap

LEVEL CHECK

♦ See Figures 96 and 97

The coolant level should be checked at least once a month. With the engine cold, the coolant level should be at or above the FULL COLD mark on the coolant reservoir.

Check the appearance of the coolant. If it is dirty or rusty, it should be replaced in order to protect the cooling system from corrosion damage.

Check the coolant concentration using an antifreeze tester. The protection level should be at least −20°F (−30°C) to maintain proper engine operating temperature and for maximum anti-rust corrosion protection.

Fig. 96 Engine coolant reservoir—1992–94 vehicles

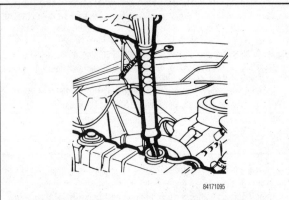

Fig. 97 Checking coolant concentration with an antifreeze tester

DRAIN AND REFILL

♦ See Figure 98

1. Raise and safely support the vehicle on jackstands.
2. Position a suitable drain pan under the radiator draincock. Remove the radiator cap.

❋❋ CAUTION

Never remove the radiator cap while the engine is running or personal injury from scalding hot coolant or steam may result. If possible, wait until the engine has cooled to remove the radiator cap. If this is not possible, wrap a thick cloth around the radiator cap and turn it slowly to the first stop. Step back while the pressure is released from the cooling system. When it is certain all the pressure has been released, press down on the cap, still with the cloth, and turn and remove it.

3. Open the radiator draincock and allow the coolant to drain.

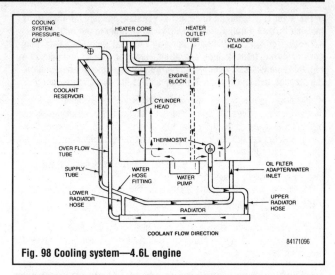

Fig. 98 Cooling system—4.6L engine

➡The cylinder block drain plugs, located on the sides of the engine block, must be removed to completely drain the system.

❋❋ CAUTION

When draining the coolant, keep in mind that cats and dogs are attracted to ethylene glycol antifreeze, and could drink any that is left in an uncovered container or in puddles on the ground. This will prove fatal in sufficient quantity. Always drain the coolant into a sealable container.

4. After the coolant has drained, close the radiator draincock and install the cylinder block drain plugs, if removed. Flush the system, if necessary.
5. Fill the cooling system with a 50/50 mixture of water and ethylene glycol antifreeze. Fill to the level of the radiator filler neck seat on vehicles equipped with 5.0L or 5.8L engines, or to the reservoir filler neck seat if equipped with 4.6L or other engines.
6. Install the radiator cap to the first notch to keep spillage to a minimum.
7. Place the heater temperature selector in the maximum heat position.
8. Start the engine and let it idle until the upper radiator hose is warm. This indicates that the thermostat is open and coolant is flowing through the entire system.
9. Stop the engine and carefully remove the radiator cap. If equipped with 5.0L or 5.8L engines, top off the radiator with the 50/50 water/anti-freeze mixture. If equipped with the 4.6L or other engines, fill the reservoir to the minimum level with the coolant mixture. Install the pressure cap securely.
10. On vehicles with 5.0L or 5.8L engine, fill the coolant recovery reservoir to the FULL HOT mark with the coolant mixture and install the reservoir cap.

FLUSHING AND CLEANING THE SYSTEM

To remove rust, sludge and any other foreign matter from the cooling system, it should be flushed whenever the coolant is replaced. Flushing the system restores cooling efficiency and helps avoid engine overheating.

The easiest way to flush the system is to use a can of liquid cooling system flush, available at most auto parts stores. Proceed as follows:

1. After draining the cooling system, close the draincock(s) and add water and the radiator flush to the cooling system.
2. Run the engine until the upper radiator hose gets hot, then drain the system.
3. Repeat the process using plain water until the drained water is clear and free of scale.

➡These are general radiator flushing instructions. Always follow the directions on the radiator flush container label. Make sure the flush is SAFE FOR USE WITH AN ALUMINUM RADIATOR.

4. Disconnect the coolant reservoir from the system and flush it with clean water. Reconnect the reservoir to the system.
5. Refill the cooling system, as described earlier.

In some cases, where a cleaning solvent is not enough to clean the system, it will be necessary to pressure flush the system. The thermostat should always be removed prior to pressure flushing; see Section 3. Various types of pressure flushing equipment are available; consult your auto parts store.

Regardless of the type of engine cooling system flush used, the heater core must be flushed separately to prevent engine cooling system particles from clogging the heater core tubes and reducing coolant flow through the heater core. Flush the heater core as follows:

6. Disconnect the heater core outlet heater hose from the water pump fitting on 5.0L or 5.8L engines, or from the return fitting on 4.6L or other engines. Install a female garden hose end fitting adapter in the end of the outlet heater hose and secure with a hose clamp.

7. Connect the female garden hose end of the outlet heater hose to the male end of a water supply garden hose.

8. Disconnect the heater core inlet heater hose from the engine block on 5.0L or 5.8L engines, or the intake manifold fitting on 4.6L or other engines. Allow the hose to drain into a suitable container.

9. If a water valve is installed in the heater core inlet heater hose, make sure the valve is open (no vacuum).

10. Turn the water supply valve on and off several times so the surge action will help to dislodge larger stubborn particles from the heater core tubes. Allow full water pressure to flow for about 5 minutes.

11. If a water valve is installed in the heater core inlet hose, apply vacuum to the valve vacuum motor, using a vacuum tester, to make sure the valve is operating properly. When the valve is closed there should be no water leakage. Replace the valve, if required.

12. Remove the hose clamp and female garden hose end adapter from the end of the outlet heater hose and reconnect the hose to the water pump fitting or heater return fitting, as required.

13. Connect the inlet heater hose to the engine block fitting or intake manifold fitting, as required.

14. Fill the cooling system, as described earlier. Check the heating system for proper operation.

Master Cylinder

FLUID RECOMMENDATIONS

The brake master cylinder requires brake fluid that meets or exceeds DOT 3 standards.

LEVEL CHECK

▶ **See Figure 99**

If it is necessary to add fluid, first wipe away any accumulated dirt or grease from the reservoir. Then remove the reservoir cap by using a screwdriver to pry the clip off the top of the resevoir. Add fluid to the proper level. Avoid spilling brake fluid on any painted surface as it will harm the finish. Replace the reservoir cap.

Power Steering Pump

FLUID RECOMMENDATIONS

Ford power steering fluid part number E6AZ–19582–AA or equivalent, or Type F automatic transmission fluid should be used.

LEVEL CHECK

▶ **See Figure 100**

1. Run the engine until the fluid reaches a normal operating temperature of 165–175°F (74–79°C).

2. Turn the steering wheel all the way to the left and right, several times.

3. Shut the engine OFF.

4. On vehicles with engine type other than 5.0L or 5.8L, check the fluid level in the power steering fluid reservoir. The reservoir is translucent, enabling the fluid level to be checked without removing the reservoir cap. The fluid level should be between the MIN and MAX marks on the side of the reservoir.

5. On vehicles with 5.0L or 5.8L engines, wipe away any accumulated dirt or grease, then remove the dipstick from the power steering fluid reservoir. Wipe the dipstick with a clean cloth, reinsert it fully into the reservoir, then remove it. The fluid level should be within the FULL HOT range on the dipstick if the fluid is at normal operating temperature, within the FULL COLD range if it is not.

6. If the fluid level is low, add the specified fluid, being careful not to overfill. Be sure to wipe away any accumulated dirt or grease before removing the reservoir cap.

Chassis Greasing

▶ **See Figures 101 and 102**

Lubrication of steering and suspension parts requires the use of a pressure-type grease gun, in order to force the lubricant through the grease fitting. A premium long life chassis grease should be used.

There are grease fittings located on the inner and outer tie rod ends, pitman arm and lower ball joints on all vehicles. In addition, some vehicles are equipped with grease fittings on the upper ball joints. These should be lubricated as indicated in the Maintenance Intervals chart at the end of this Section.

Wipe away any dirt or accumulated grease from the fitting. Attach the grease gun to the fitting and pump lubricant into the joint. Be careful not to pump in so much lubricant that the joint boot splits.

Use a brush to apply grease to the steering stop pads, located on the lower control arms.

In addition to the steering and suspension components, the cable guides, levers and linkage of the parking brake should be lubricated periodically, using multi-purpose spray grease.

Fig. 99 Brake master cylinder fluid reservoir

Fig. 100 Power steering fluid reservoir—1992–94 vehicles

Fig. 101 View of the pitman arm and inner tie rod end grease fittings

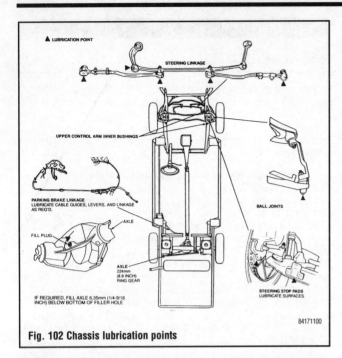

Fig. 102 Chassis lubrication points

Body Lubrication and Maintenance

Regular body maintenance will preserve your car's appearance. A great looking car instills pride of ownership and helps resale value. All the maintenance records in the world mean little to a prospective buyer if the car appears ill-kept.

Exterior

Your car should be washed frequently. Never try to wipe dirt from the car with a dry cloth, as this will only tend to rub the dust and dirt into the surface, scratching the finish. Wash the car with a clean sponge or cloth, using a mild soap and cold water solution. There are many types of car wash cleaning concentrates on the market; these can be found at your local auto parts store.

Wash one section of the car at a time, starting at the top, and rinse frequently with cold water. Never wash your car with hot water, in direct sunlight, or if the sheet metal is hot.

➡Rinsing the car is a good time to check for water leaks at the doors, trunk and hood. If a leak is found, it can be cured by repair or replacement of the weather-strips, or adjustment of the body part.

If you live in an area where the roads are frequently salted for snow and ice removal, the underside of the car should be flushed frequently with clean water, especially after driving on salt covered roads. Pay particular attention to cleaning out underbody members and drain holes where dirt and other foreign material have collected.

After the car has been completely washed, wipe the surfaces dry with a clean lint-free cloth. This will prevent water spotting, which results if the car is merely allowed to air dry. However, the car must be absolutely clean before it is wiped dry, to prevent scratching the paint.

The paint and bright metal on your car should be polished and/or waxed periodically to remove harmful deposits and provide added protection. There are many specialized products available at your local auto parts store to care for the appearance of painted metal surfaces, plastic, chrome, wheels and tires. Be sure to follow the manufacturer's instructions before using them.

Touch-up paint should be applied to any chipped or scratched areas. Consult your Ford or Lincoln-Mercury dealer for the correct color match.

There are drain holes on the underside of each rocker panel, quarter panel and door. These should be cleared periodically.

Interior

The interior of your car should be vacuumed thoroughly on a regular basis. Clean the carpeting, seats, trim panels, instrument panel and headliner. There are many specialized products available at your local auto parts store for clean-

ing and preserving interior components; be sure to follow the manufacturer's instructions before using them.

Check all weather-stripping. Replace any pieces that are cracked or broken and no longer usable; use weatherstrip cement to attach any pieces that are usable but loose. Apply silicone lubricant to the weather-stripping to preserve it and to prevent squeaks.

Lubricate all hinges, pivots and latches with multi-purpose spray grease. Apply lock lubricant to all lock cylinders.

Front Wheel Bearings

REMOVAL, PACKING AND INSTALLATION

1989–91

▶ **See Figures 103, 104, 105, 106 and 107**

1. Raise and support the vehicle safely on jackstands.
2. Remove the wheel and tire assembly and the disc brake caliper. Suspend the caliper with a length of wire; do not let it hang from the brake hose.
3. Pry off the dust cap. Tap out and discard the cotter pin. Remove the nut retainer.
4. Being careful not to drop the outer bearing, pull off the brake disc and wheel hub assembly.
5. Remove the inner grease seal using a prybar. Remove the inner wheel bearing.
6. Clean the wheel bearings with solvent and inspect them for pits, scratches and excessive wear. Wipe all the old grease from the hub and inspect the bearing races (cups). If either bearings or races are damaged, the bearing races must be removed and the bearings and races replaced as an assembly.
7. If the bearings are to be replaced, drive out the races (cups) from the hub using a brass drift, or pull them from the hub using a puller.
8. Make sure the spindle, hub and bearing assemblies are clean prior to installation.

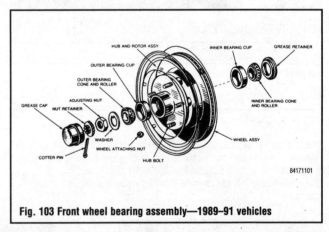

Fig. 103 Front wheel bearing assembly—1989–91 vehicles

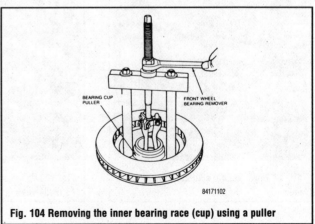

Fig. 104 Removing the inner bearing race (cup) using a puller

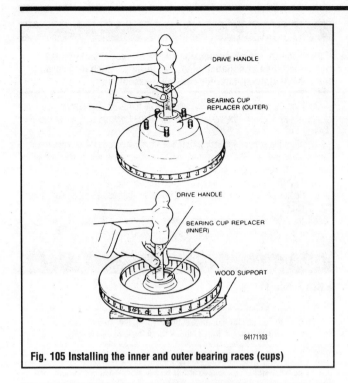

Fig. 105 Installing the inner and outer bearing races (cups)

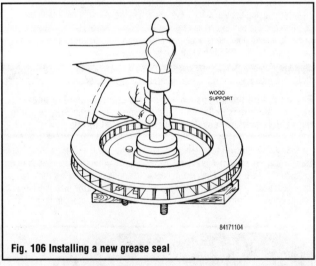

Fig. 106 Installing a new grease seal

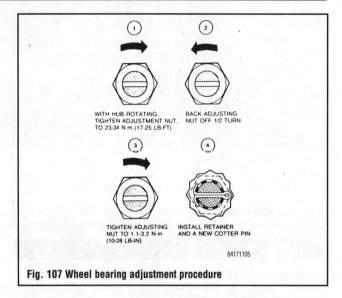

Fig. 107 Wheel bearing adjustment procedure

To install:

9. If the bearing races (cups) were removed, install new ones using a suitable bearing race installer. Pack the bearings with high-temperature wheel bearing grease using a bearing packer. If a packer is not available, work as much grease as possible between the rollers and cages using your hands.

10. Coat the inner surface of the hub and bearing races (cups) with grease.

11. Install the inner bearing in the hub. Using a seal installer, install a new grease seal into the hub. Lubricate the lip of the seal with grease.

12. Install the hub/disc assembly on the spindle, being careful not to damage the oil seal.

13. Install the outer bearing, washer and spindle nut. Install the caliper and the wheel and tire assembly. Adjust the bearings as follows:

 a. Loosen the adjusting nut 3 turns and rock the wheel in and out a few times to release the brake pads from the rotor.

 b. While rotating the wheel and hub assembly in a counterclockwise direction, tighten the adjusting nut to 17–25 ft. lbs. (23–34 Nm).

 c. Back off the adjusting nut ½ turn, then retighten to 10–28 inch lbs. (1.1–3.2 Nm).

 d. Install the nut retainer and a new cotter pin. Replace the grease cap.

14. Lower the vehicle. Before driving the vehicle, pump the brake pedal several times to restore normal brake pedal travel.

1992–94

The front wheel bearings are of a hub unit design and are pregreased, sealed and require no maintenance. The bearings are preset and cannot be adjusted. For bearing hub removal and installation, see Section 8.

JACKING

The service jack that comes with your car should ONLY be used for changing a flat tire. It should NEVER be used to raise the car for any other purpose.

Hydraulic, screw or scissors jacks of adequate lifting capacity are satisfactory for raising the vehicle; jackstands should then be used to support it. Drive-on trestles or ramps are also a handy and safe way to both raise and support the car.

Service Jack

1989–91

♦ **See Figures 108 and 109**

1. Place the gearshift lever in **P** and apply the parking brake. Block the wheel diagonally opposite the wheel to be removed.

2. If your car is equipped with air suspension, turn **OFF** the air suspension switch, located in the trunk on the right-hand trim panel.

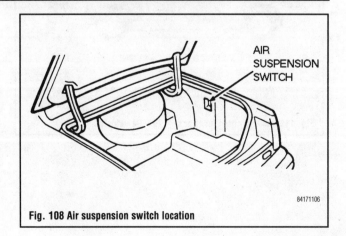

Fig. 108 Air suspension switch location

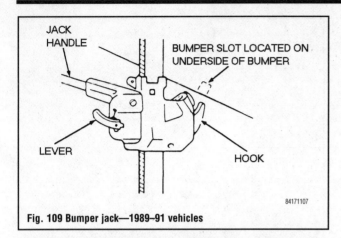

Fig. 109 Bumper jack—1989–91 vehicles

✸✸ CAUTION

Failure to turn the air suspension switch off may result in unexpected inflation or deflation of the air springs, which may result in the vehicle shifting, possibly causing personal injury.

3. Insert the bottom of the jack post into the base. Pull up on the small lever near the jack handle socket. Insert the jack hook into the slot in the bumper, making sure it fits snugly.

4. Position the jack so the bottom of the post is slightly angled in toward the vehicle.

5. Put the jack handle into the jack handle socket. Push up and down on the handle until the vehicle is raised.

6. Remove and install the wheel and tire assembly, as described earlier in this Section.

7. To lower the vehicle, place the small lever near the jack handle socket in the down position. Move the handle up and down to lower the vehicle, keeping a firm grasp on the jack handle.

8. If equipped, turn the air suspension switch **ON**.

1992–94

♦ See Figure 110

1. Place the gearshift lever in **P** and apply the parking brake. Block the wheel diagonally opposite the wheel to be removed.

2. If your car is equipped with air suspension, turn **OFF** the air suspension switch, located in the trunk on the right-hand trim panel.

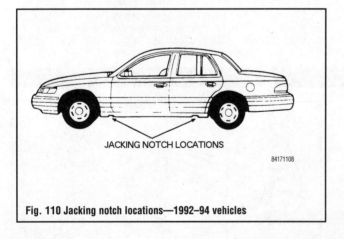

Fig. 110 Jacking notch locations—1992–94 vehicles

✸✸ CAUTION

Failure to turn the air suspension switch off may result in unexpected inflation or deflation of the air springs, which may result in the vehicle shifting, possibly causing personal injury.

3. Find the jacking notch for the wheel to be removed. The notches are located on each side of the vehicle, one behind the front tire and one ahead of the rear tire.

4. Align the tabs on the jack with the rectangular notch on the sheet metal. Slowly push the jack straight until the tabs are against the side of the frame. Make sure the jack is properly positioned.

5. Turn the handle of the jack clockwise to raise the vehicle.

6. Remove and install the wheel and tire assembly, as described earlier in this Section.

7. Turn the jack handle counterclockwise to lower the vehicle.

8. If equipped, turn the air suspension switch **ON**.

Floor Jack

♦ See Figure 111

When using a floor jack, either side of the front of the vehicle can be raised by positioning the jack on the lower control arm, at the spindle connection. However, it is usually easier to raise the front of the vehicle at the front cross-member.

At the rear of the vehicle, the jack can be positioned under the rear axle housing tubes, between the suspension arm brackets and the differential housing. Do not raise the rear of the vehicle using the differential housing as a lift point.

Before raising the vehicle, always make sure the gearshift lever is in the **P** position and the parking brake is applied. Block the wheels at the opposite end of the vehicle. If your car is equipped with air suspension, always turn the air suspension switch **OFF** before raising the vehicle.

✸✸ CAUTION

Failure to turn the air suspension switch off may result in unexpected inflation or deflation of the air springs, which may result in the vehicle shifting, possibly causing personal injury.

After the vehicle has been raised, it must be supported with jackstands, especially if you will be working under it. Never use cinder blocks or stacks of wood to support the car, even if you're only going to be under it for a few minutes. Jackstands can be positioned under the frame rails, under the rear axle tubes, and/or under the front lower control arms, at the spindle connections.

Fig. 111 Lifting the front of the vehicle using a floor jack

Follow this Schedule if your driving habits MAINLY include one or more of the following conditions:

- Short trips of less than 16 km (10 miles) when outside temperatures remain below freezing.
- Operating during HOT WEATHER
  — Driving in stop-and-go "rush hour" traffic.
- Towing a trailer, using a car-top carrier.
- Operating in severe dust conditions.
- Extensive idling, such as police, taxi or door-to-door delivery service.

SERVICE INTERVAL Perform at the months or distances shown, whichever comes first. Miles × 1000	3	6	9	12	15	18	21	24	27	30	33	36	39	42	45	48	51	54	57	60
Kilometers × 1000	4.8	9.6	14.4	19.2	24	28.8	33.6	38.4	43.2	48	52.8	57.6	62.4	67.2	72	76.8	81.6	86.4	91.2	96
EMISSION CONTROL SERVICE																				
Replace Engine Oil and Oil Filter Every 3 Months OR	X	X	X	X	X	X	X	X	X	X	X	X	X	X	X	X	X	X	X	X
Replace Spark Plugs										X										X
Inspect Accessory Drive Belt(s)										X										X
Replace PCV Valve and Crankcase Emission Filter (5.0L Engine)					(X)					(X)					(X)					X
Replace Air Cleaner Filter①										X										X
Replace Crankcase Emission Filter① (5.8L Engine)										X										X
Check/Clean Choke Linkage (5.8L Engine)										X										X
Replace Engine Coolant, EVERY 36 Months OR										X										X
Check Engine Coolant Protection, Hoses and Clamps	ANNUALLY																			
GENERAL MAINTENANCE																				
Inspect Exhaust Heat Shields										X										X
Change Automatic Transmission Fluid②										X										X
Lubricate Suspension										X										X
Lubricate Steering Linkage					X					X					X					X
Inspect Disc Brake Pads and Rotors③										X										X
Inspect Brake Linings and Drums (Rear)③										X										X
Inspect and Repack Front Wheel Bearings										X										X
Rotate Tires		X				X						X				X				

① If operating in severe dust, more frequent intervals may be required.
② Change automatic transmission fluid if your driving habits frequently include one or more of the following conditions:
- Operation during hot weather (above 32°C (90°F)) carrying heavy loads and in hilly terrain.
- Towing a trailer or using a car top carrier.
- Police, taxi or door to door delivery service.
③ If your driving includes continuous stop-and-go driving or driving in mountainous areas. more frequent intervals may be required.
X All items designated by an X must be performed in all states.
(X) This item not required to be performed, however, Ford recommends that you also perform maintenance on items designated by an (X) in order to achieve best vehicle operation. Failure to perform this recommended maintenance will not invalidate the vehicle emissions warranty or manufacturer recall liability.

84171117

Fig. 112 Maintenance interval chart applicable to most driving conditions (usually called Severe)—5.0L and 5.8L engines

Follow Maintenance Schedule B if, generally, you drive your vehicle on a daily basis for more than 16 km (10 miles) and NONE OF THE UNIQUE DRIVING CONDITIONS SHOWN IN SCHEDULE A APPLY TO YOUR DRIVING HABITS.

SERVICE INTERVALS Perform at the months or distances shown, whichever comes first. Miles x 1000	7.5	15	22.5	30	37.5	45	52.5	60
Kilometers x 1000	12	24	36	48	60	72	84	96
EMISSIONS CONTROL SERVICE								
Replace Engine Oil and Filter (Every 6 Months) OR 7,500 Miles Whichever Occurs First	X	X	X	X	X	X	X	X
Replace Spark Plugs				X				X
Replace Crankcase Emission Filter①				X				X
Inspect Accessory Drive Belt(s)				X				X
Replace Air Cleaner Filter①				X				X
Replace PCV Valve and Crankcase Emission Filter — 5.0L Engine		(X)		(X)		(X)		X
Check/Clean Choke Linkage (5.8L only)				X				X
Change Engine Coolant Every 36 Months OR				X				X
Check Engine Coolant Protection, Hoses and Clamps				ANNUALLY				
GENERAL MAINTENANCE								
Check Exhaust Heat Shields				X				X
Lube Suspension		X		X		X		X
Lubricate Steering Linkage		X		X		X		X
Inspect Disc Brake Pads and Rotors (Front)②				X				X
Inspect Brake Linings and Drums (Rear)②				X				X
Inspect and Repack Front Wheel Bearings				X				X
Rotate Tires	X		X		X		X	

① If operating in severe dust, more frequent intervals may be required.
② If your driving includes continuous stop-and-go driving or driving in mountainous areas, more frequent intervals may be required.

X All items designated by an X must be performed in all states.
(X) This item not required to be performed, however, Ford recommends that you also perform maintenance on items designated by an (X) in order to achieve best vehicle operation. Failure to perform this recommended maintenance will not invalidate the vehicle emissions warranty or manufacturer recall liability.

84171118

Fig. 113 Maintenance interval chart for low stress/highway mileages (usually called Normal)—5.0L and 5.8L engines

Follow this Schedule if your driving habits MAINLY include one or more of the following conditions:
- Short trips of less than 16 km (10 miles) when outside temperatures remain below freezing.
- Operating during HOT WEATHER
  — Driving in stop-and-go "rush hour" traffic.
- Towing a trailer, using a car-top carrier.
- Operating in severe dust conditions.
- Extensive idling, such as police, taxi or door-to-door delivery service.

SERVICE INTERVALS Perform at the months or distances shown, whichever comes first	Miles x 1000	3	6	9	12	15	18	21	24	27	30	33	36	39	42	45	48	51	54	57	60
	Kilometers x 1000	4.8	9.6	14.4	19.2	24	28.8	33.6	38.4	43.2	48	52.8	57.6	62.4	67.2	72	76.8	81.6	86.4	91.2	96
EMISSION CONTROL SERVICE																					
Replace Engine Oil and Oil Filter Every 3 Months OR		X	X	X	X	X	X	X	X	X	X	X	X	X	X	X	X	X	X	X	X
Replace Spark Plugs											X										X
Replace PCV Valve					(X)						(X)					(X)					X
Replace Air Cleaner Filter ①											X										X
Replace Engine Coolant, EVERY 36 Months OR													X								X
GENERAL MAINTENANCE																					
Inspect Engine Coolant Protection, Hoses and Clamps		ANNUALLY																			
Inspect Exhaust Heat Shields											X										X
Replace Automatic Transmission Fluid ②											X										X
Lubricate Suspension/Ball Joints											X										X
Lubricate Steering Linkage (Inner-outer tie rod ends both sides, pitman arm socket)						X					X					X					X
Inspect Disc Brake Pads and Rotors (Front and Rear)③											X										X
Rotate Tires			X					X					X					X			

① If operating in severe dust, more frequent intervals may be required.

② Change automatic transmission fluid if your driving habits frequently include one or more of the following conditions:
- Operation during hot weather (above 32°C (90°F)) carrying heavy loads and in hilly terrain.
- Towing a trailer or using a car top carrier.
- Police, taxi or door to door delivery service.

③ If your driving includes continuous stop-and-go driving in mountainous areas, more frequent intervals may be required.

(X) This item not required to be performed, however, Ford recommends that you also perform maintenance on items designated by an (X) in order to achieve best vehicle operation. Failure to perform this recommended maintenance will not invalidate the vehicle emissions warranty or manufacturer recall liability.

84171119

Fig. 114 Maintenance interval chart applicable to most driving conditions (usually called Severe)—4.6L engines

---

Follow Maintenance Schedule B if, generally, you drive your vehicle on a daily basis for more than 16 km (10 miles) and NONE OF THE UNIQUE DRIVING CONDITIONS SHOWN IN SCHEDULE A APPLY TO YOUR DRIVING HABITS.

SERVICE INTERVALS Perform at the months or distances shown, whichever comes first.	Miles x 1000	7.5	15	22.5	30	37.5	45	52.5	60
	Kilometers x 1000	12	24	36	48	60	72	84	96
EMISSION CONTROL SERVICE									
Replace Engine Oil and Filter (Every 6 Months) OR 7,500 Miles Whichever Occurs First		X	X	X	X	X	X	X	X
Replace Spark Plugs					X				X
Replace Air Cleaner Filter ①					X				X
Replace PCV Valve			(X)		(X)		(X)		X
Replace Engine Coolant Every 36 Months OR					X				X
GENERAL MAINTENANCE									
Inspect Engine Coolant Protection, Hoses and Clamps					ANNUALLY				
Inspect Exhaust Heat Shields					X				X
Lubricate Suspension/Ball Joints			X		X		X		X
Lubricate Steering Linkage (Inner-outer tie rod ends both sides, pitman arm socket)			X		X		X		X
Inspect Disc Brake Pads and Rotors (Front and Rear)②					X				X
Rotate Tires		X		X		X		X	

① If operating in severe dust, more frequent intervals may be required.

② If your driving includes continuous stop-and-go driving or driving in mountainous areas, more frequent intervals may be required.

(X) This item not required to be performed, however, Ford recommends that you also perform maintenance on items designated by an (X) in order to achieve best vehicle operation. Failure to perform this recommended maintenance will not invalidate the vehicle emissions warranty or manufacturer recall liability.

84171120

Fig. 115 Maintenance interval chart for low stress/highway mileages(usually called Normal)—4.6L engines

CAPACITIES

Year	Model	Engine ID/VIN	Engine Displacement Liters (cc)	Engine Crankcase with Filter	Transmission (pts.) 4-Spd	5-Spd	Auto.	Transfer case (pts.)	Drive Axle Front (pts.)	Rear (pts.)	Fuel Tank (gal.)	Cooling System (qts.)
1989	Crown Victoria	F	5.0 (4943)	5	—	—	24.6	—	—	4.0	18.0	14.1
	Crown Victoria	G	5.8 (5767)	5	—	—	24.6	—	—	4.0	20.0	14.1
	Grand Marquis	F	5.0 (4943)	5	—	—	24.6	—	—	4.0	18.0	14.1
	Grand Marquis	G	5.8 (5767)	5	—	—	24.6	—	—	4.0	20.0	14.1
1990	Crown Victoria	F	5.0 (4943)	5	—	—	24.6	—	—	4.0	18.0	14.1
	Crown Victoria	G	5.8 (5767)	5	—	—	24.6	—	—	4.0	20.0	14.1
	Grand Marquis	F	5.0 (4943)	5	—	—	24.6	—	—	4.0	18.0	14.1
	Grand Marquis	G	5.8 (5767)	5	—	—	24.6	—	—	4.0	20.0	14.1
1991	Crown Victoria	F	5.0 (4943)	5	—	—	24.6	—	—	4.0	18.0	14.1
	Crown Victoria	G	5.8 (5767)	5	—	—	24.6	—	—	4.0	20.0	14.1
	Grand Marquis	F	5.0 (4943)	5	—	—	24.6	—	—	4.0	18.0	14.1
	Grand Marquis	G	5.8 (5767)	5	—	—	24.6	—	—	4.0	20.0	14.1
1992	Crown Victoria	W	4.6 (4593)	5	—	—	24.6	—	—	4.0	20.0	14.1
	Grand Marquis	W	4.6 (4593)	5	—	—	24.6	—	—	4.0	20.0	14.1
1993 -94	Crown Victoria	W	4.6 (4593)	5	—	—	27.2	—	—	4.0	20.0	14.1
	Grand Marquis	W	4.6 (4593)	5	—	—	27.2	—	—	4.0	20.0	14.1

84171R21

TORQUE SPECIFICATIONS

Component	U.S.	Metric
Air conditioner compressor adjustment bolt	30 ft. lbs.	40 Nm
Air conditioner compressor pivot bolt	50 ft. lbs.	68 Nm
Alternator adjustment bolt	29 ft. lbs.	39 Nm
Alternator pivot bolt	50 ft. lbs.	68 Nm
Differential cover bolts	25–35 ft. lbs.	34–47 Nm
Differential oil fill plug	15–30 ft. lbs.	20–41 Nm

Fuel filter retainer bolts
  5.0L engine
    1989–91
	27–44 inch lbs.	3–5 Nm

Fuel inlet fitting 5.8L engine	90–125 inch lbs.	10–14 Nm
Fuel line tube nut 5.8L engine	15–18 ft. lbs.	20–24 Nm
Hose screw clamps	22–31 inch lbs.	2.5–3.5 Nm

Oil pan drain plug
  4.6L engine
  5.0L and 5.8L engines
	8–12 ft. lbs.
	15–25 ft. lbs.
		11–16 Nm
		20–34 Nm

Torque converter drain plug	21–23 ft. lbs.	28–30 Nm
Transmission filter bolts	80–120 inch lbs.	9–14 Nm
Transmission pan bolts	107–119 inch lbs.	12–13.5 Nm
Wheel lug nuts	85–105 ft. lbs.	115–142 Nm

84171122

ENGLISH TO METRIC CONVERSION: MASS (WEIGHT)

Current **mass** measurement is expressed in pounds and ounces (lbs. & ozs.). The metric unit of mass (or weight) is the kilogram (kg). Even although this table does not show conversion of masses (weights) larger than 15 lbs, it is easy to calculate larger units by following the data immediately below.

To convert ounces (oz.) to grams (g): multiply th number of ozs. by 28
To convert grams (g) to ounces (oz.): multiply the number of grams by .035

To convert pounds (lbs.) to kilograms (kg): multiply the number of lbs. by .45
To convert kilograms (kg) to pounds (lbs.): multiply the number of kilograms by 2.2

lbs	kg	lbs	kg	oz	kg	oz	kg
0.1	0.04	0.9	0.41	0.1	0.003	0.9	0.024
0.2	0.09	1	0.4	0.2	0.005	1	0.03
0.3	0.14	2	0.9	0.3	0.008	2	0.06
0.4	0.18	3	1.4	0.4	0.011	3	0.08
0.5	0.23	4	1.8	0.5	0.014	4	0.11
0.6	0.27	5	2.3	0.6	0.017	5	0.14
0.7	0.32	10	4.5	0.7	0.020	10	0.28
0.8	0.36	15	6.8	0.8	0.023	15	0.42

ENGLISH TO METRIC CONVERSION: TEMPERATURE

To convert Fahrenheit (°F) to Celsius (°C): take number of °F and subtract 32; multiply result by 5; divide result by 9

To convert Celsius (°C) to Fahrenheit (°F): take number of °C and multiply by 9; divide result by 5; add 32 to total

Fahrenheit (F)	Celsius (C)			Fahrenheit (F)	Celsius (C)			Fahrenheit (F)	Celsius (C)		
°F	°C	°C	°F	°F	°C	°C	°F	°F	°C	°C	°F
−40	−40	−38	−36.4	80	26.7	18	64.4	215	101.7	80	176
−35	−37.2	−36	−32.8	85	29.4	20	68	220	104.4	85	185
−30	−34.4	−34	−29.2	90	32.2	22	71.6	225	107.2	90	194
−25	−31.7	−32	−25.6	95	35.0	24	75.2	230	110.0	95	202
−20	−28.9	−30	−22	100	37.8	26	78.8	235	112.8	100	212
−15	−26.1	−28	−18.4	105	40.6	28	82.4	240	115.6	105	221
−10	−23.3	−26	−14.8	110	43.3	30	86	245	118.3	110	230
−5	−20.6	−24	−11.2	115	46.1	32	89.6	250	121.1	115	239
0	−17.8	−22	−7.6	120	48.9	34	93.2	255	123.9	120	248
1	−17.2	−20	−4	125	51.7	36	96.8	260	126.6	125	257
2	−16.7	−18	−0.4	130	54.4	38	100.4	265	129.4	130	266
3	−16.1	−16	3.2	135	57.2	40	104	270	132.2	135	275
4	−15.6	−14	6.8	140	60.0	42	107.6	275	135.0	140	284
5	−15.0	−12	10.4	145	62.8	44	112.2	280	137.8	145	293
10	−12.2	−10	14	150	65.6	46	114.8	285	140.6	150	302
15	−9.4	−8	17.6	155	68.3	48	118.4	290	143.3	155	311
20	−6.7	−6	21.2	160	71.1	50	122	295	146.1	160	320
25	−3.9	−4	24.8	165	73.9	52	125.6	300	148.9	165	329
30	−1.1	−2	28.4	170	76.7	54	129.2	305	151.7	170	338
35	1.7	0	32	175	79.4	56	132.8	310	154.4	175	347
40	4.4	2	35.6	180	82.2	58	136.4	315	157.2	180	356
45	7.2	4	39.2	185	85.0	60	140	320	160.0	185	365
50	10.0	6	42.8	190	87.8	62	143.6	325	162.8	190	374
55	12.8	8	46.4	195	90.6	64	147.2	330	165.6	195	383
60	15.6	10	50	200	93.3	66	150.8	335	168.3	200	392
65	18.3	12	53.6	205	96.1	68	154.4	340	171.1	205	401
70	21.1	14	57.2	210	98.9	70	158	345	173.9	210	410
75	23.9	16	60.8	212	100.0	75	167	350	176.7	215	414

TCCS1C01

ENGLISH TO METRIC CONVERSION: LENGTH

To convert inches (ins.) to millimeters (mm): multiply number of inches by 25.4

To convert millimeters (mm) to inches (ins.): multiply number of millimeters by .04

Inches	Decimals	Milli-meters	Inches to millimeters — inches	mm		Inches	Decimals	Milli-meters	Inches to millimeters — inches	mm
1/64	0.051625	0.3969	0.0001	0.00254		33/64	0.515625	13.0969	0.6	15.24
1/32	0.03125	0.7937	0.0002	0.00508		17/32	0.53125	13.4937	0.7	17.78
3/64	0.046875	1.1906	0.0003	0.00762		35/64	0.546875	13.8906	0.8	20.32
1/16	0.0625	1.5875	0.0004	0.01016		9/16	0.5625	14.2875	0.9	22.86
5/64	0.078125	1.9844	0.0005	0.01270		37/64	0.578125	14.6844	1	25.4
3/32	0.09375	2.3812	0.0006	0.01524		19/32	0.59375	15.0812	2	50.8
7/64	0.109375	2.7781	0.0007	0.01778		39/64	0.609375	15.4781	3	76.2
1/8	0.125	3.1750	0.0008	0.02032		5/8	0.625	15.8750	4	101.6
9/64	0.140625	3.5719	0.0009	0.02286		41/64	0.640625	16.2719	5	127.0
5/32	0.15625	3.9687	0.001	0.0254		21/32	0.65625	16.6687	6	152.4
11/64	0.171875	4.3656	0.002	0.0508		43/64	0.671875	17.0656	7	177.8
3/16	0.1875	4.7625	0.003	0.0762		11/16	0.6875	17.4625	8	203.2
13/64	0.203125	5.1594	0.004	0.1016		45/64	0.703125	17.8594	9	228.6
7/32	0.21875	5.5562	0.005	0.1270		23/32	0.71875	18.2562	10	254.0
15/64	0.234375	5.9531	0.006	0.1524		47/64	0.734375	18.6531	11	279.4
1/4	0.25	6.3500	0.007	0.1778		3/4	0.75	19.0500	12	304.8
17/64	0.265625	6.7469	0.008	0.2032		49/64	0.765625	19.4469	13	330.2
9/32	0.28125	7.1437	0.009	0.2286		25/32	0.78125	19.8437	14	355.6
19/64	0.296875	7.5406	0.01	0.254		51/64	0.796875	20.2406	15	381.0
5/16	0.3125	7.9375	0.02	0.508		13/16	0.8125	20.6375	16	406.4
21/64	0.328125	8.3344	0.03	0.762		53/64	0.828125	21.0344	17	431.8
11/32	0.34375	8.7312	0.04	1.016		27/32	0.84375	21.4312	18	457.2
23/64	0.359375	9.1281	0.05	1.270		55/64	0.859375	21.8281	19	482.6
3/8	0.375	9.5250	0.06	1.524		7/8	0.875	22.2250	20	508.0
25/64	0.390625	9.9219	0.07	1.778		57/64	0.890625	22.6219	21	533.4
13/32	0.40625	10.3187	0.08	2.032		29/32	0.90625	23.0187	22	558.8
27/64	0.421875	10.7156	0.09	2.286		59/64	0.921875	23.4156	23	584.2
7/16	0.4375	11.1125	0.1	2.54		15/16	0.9375	23.8125	24	609.6
29/64	0.453125	11.5094	0.2	5.08		61/64	0.953125	24.2094	25	635.0
15/32	0.46875	11.9062	0.3	7.62		31/32	0.96875	24.6062	26	660.4
31/64	0.484375	12.3031	0.4	10.16		63/64	0.984375	25.0031	27	690.6
1/2	0.5	12.7000	0.5	12.70						

ENGLISH TO METRIC CONVERSION: TORQUE

To convert foot-pounds (ft. lbs.) to Newton-meters: multiply the number of ft. lbs. by 1.3

To convert inch-pounds (in. lbs.) to Newton-meters: multiply the number of in. lbs. by .11

in lbs	N-m	in lbs	N-m	in lbs	N-m	in lbs	N-m	in lbs	N-m
0.1	0.01	1	0.11	10	1.13	19	2.15	28	3.16
0.2	0.02	2	0.23	11	1.24	20	2.26	29	3.28
0.3	0.03	3	0.34	12	1.36	21	2.37	30	3.39
0.4	0.04	4	0.45	13	1.47	22	2.49	31	3.50
0.5	0.06	5	0.56	14	1.58	23	2.60	32	3.62
0.6	0.07	6	0.68	15	1.70	24	2.71	33	3.73
0.7	0.08	7	0.78	16	1.81	25	2.82	34	3.84
0.8	0.09	8	0.90	17	1.92	26	2.94	35	3.95
0.9	0.10	9	1.02	18	2.03	27	3.05	36	4.0

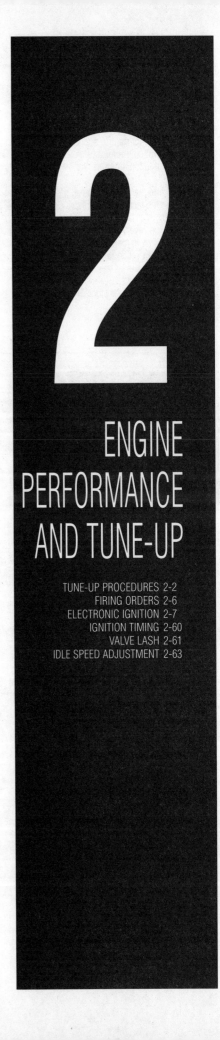

2

ENGINE PERFORMANCE AND TUNE-UP

TUNE-UP PROCEDURES

♦ **See Figure 1**

Your car does not require a regular tune-up in the traditional sense. The advent of electronic ignition systems, electronic fuel injection and computer controlled engine functions has obviated the need for the annual tune-up ritual.

The most important thing you can do to ensure that your car performs optimally is to do the recommended service described in Section 1 at the intervals specified in the Maintenance Intervals chart. Ford recommends that the spark plugs be replaced every 30,000 miles, and although not specifically required, this is a good time to make the checks and adjustments (where possible) traditionally associated with a tune-up.

If the specifications on the Vehicle Emission Control Information label in the engine compartment disagree with the Tune-Up Specification chart in this Section, use the figures on the label. The label often includes changes made during the model year.

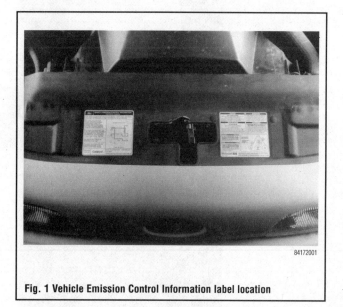

84172001

Fig. 1 Vehicle Emission Control Information label location

Spark Plugs

♦ **See Figures 2 and 3**

A typical spark plug consists of a metal shell surrounding a ceramic insulator. A metal electrode extends downward through the center of the insulator and protrudes a small distance. Located at the end of the plug and attached to the side of the outer metal shell is the side electrode. The side electrode bends in at a 90⁻ angle so that its tip is just past and parallel to the tip of the center electrode. The distance between these two electrodes (measured in thousandths of an inch or hundredths of a millimeter) is called the spark plug gap.

The spark plug does not produce a spark, but instead provides a gap across which the current can arc. The coil produces anywhere from 20,000 to 50,000 volts (depending on the type and application) which travels through the wires to the spark plugs. The current passes along the center electrode and jumps the gap to the side electrode, and in doing so, ignites the air/fuel mixture in the combustion chamber.

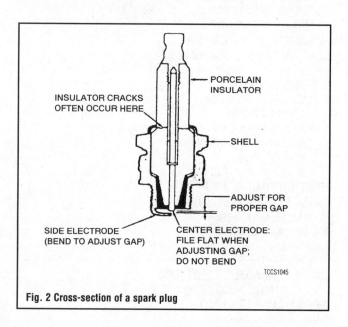

TCCS1045

Fig. 2 Cross-section of a spark plug

GASOLINE ENGINE TUNE-UP SPECIFICATIONS

Year	Engine ID/VIN	Engine Displacement Liters (cc)	Spark Plugs Gap (in.)	Ignition Timing (deg.) MT	AT	Fuel Pump (psi)	Idle Speed (rpm) MT	AT	Valve Clearance In.	Ex.
1989	F	5.0 (4943)	0.050	—	10B	35–40 ③	—	①	Hyd.	Hyd.
	G	5.8 (5767)	0.044	—	14B	6–8	—	①	Hyd.	Hyd.
1990	F	5.0 (4943)	0.050	—	10B	35–40 ③	—	①	Hyd.	Hyd.
	G	5.8 (5767)	0.044	—	14B	6–8	—	①	Hyd.	Hyd.
1991	F	5.0 (4943)	0.050	—	10B	35–40 ③	—	①	Hyd.	Hyd.
	G	5.8 (5767)	0.044	—	14B	6–8	—	①	Hyd.	Hyd.
1992	W	4.6 (4593)	0.054	—	10B	35–40 ③	—	560 ②	Hyd.	Hyd.
1993-94	W	4.6 (4593)	0.054	—	10B	35–40 ③	—	560 ②	Hyd.	Hyd.

NOTE: If these specifications differ from those on the vehicle emission control information label, follow the specifications on the label.
Hyd.—Hydraulic
B—Before top dead center
① Refer to the vehicle emission control information label
② Transmission in drive
③ Key on, engine off

84172R39

Fig. 3 A variety of tools and gauges are needed for spark plug service

Fig. 5 Opening the spark plug wire separator—4.6L engine shown

SPARK PLUG HEAT RANGE

▶ See Figure 4

Spark plug heat range is the ability of the plug to dissipate heat. The longer the insulator (or the farther it extends into the engine), the hotter the plug will operate; the shorter the insulator (the closer the electrode is to the block's cooling passages) the cooler it will operate. A plug that absorbs little heat and remains too cool will quickly accumulate deposits of oil and carbon since it is not hot enough to burn them off. This leads to plug fouling and consequently to misfiring. A plug that absorbs too much heat will have no deposits but, due to the excessive heat, the electrodes will burn away quickly and might possibly lead to preignition or other ignition problems. Preignition takes place when plug tips get so hot that they glow sufficiently to ignite the air/fuel mixture before the actual spark occurs. This early ignition will usually cause a pinging during low speeds and heavy loads.

The general rule of thumb for choosing the correct heat range when picking a spark plug is: if most of your driving is long distance, high speed travel, use a colder plug; if most of your driving is stop and go, use a hotter plug. Original equipment plugs are generally a good compromise between the 2 styles and most people never have the need to change their plugs from the factory-recommended heat range.

REMOVAL & INSTALLATION

▶ See Figures 5, 6, 7, 8 and 9

Remove the spark plugs one at a time. If you remove all the spark plug wires and spark plugs at the same time, the wires may get mixed up. The original equipment spark plug wires should already be numbered. However, if the wires have been replaced and are not numbered, take a minute before you begin and number the wires with tape. The best location for numbering is near where the wires are attached to the distributor cap (ignition coils on 4.6L engine). Refer to the Firing Order diagrams for the cylinder and corresponding distributor cap or ignition coil numbers.

1. Open the wire separator to remove the spark plug wire, if necessary.
2. Grasp each wire by the rubber boot. Twist and pull the boot and wire from the spark plug. Never pull on the plug wire directly, or it may become separated from the connector inside the boot.
3. Using a spark plug socket, loosen the plugs slightly by turning counterclockwise. Wipe or blow all dirt away from around the plug base.
4. Unscrew and remove the spark plugs from the engine. Check the condition of the plugs using the Spark Plug Diagnosis chart.
5. Before installing a spark plug, new or used, use a round wire feeler gauge to check the plug gap. The correct size gauge should pass through the electrode gap with a slight drag. If you're in doubt, try the next size larger and next size smaller gauges. The smaller gauge should pass through easily while

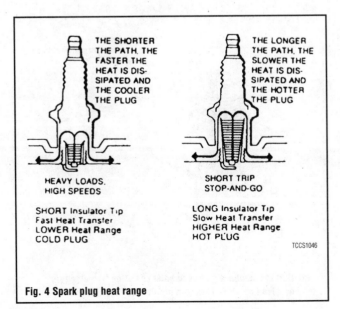

Fig. 4 Spark plug heat range

THE SHORTER THE PATH, THE FASTER THE HEAT IS DISSIPATED AND THE COOLER THE PLUG

THE LONGER THE PATH, THE SLOWER THE HEAT IS DISSIPATED AND THE HOTTER THE PLUG

HEAVY LOADS, HIGH SPEEDS

SHORT Insulator Tip
Fast Heat Transfer
LOWER Heat Range
COLD PLUG

SHORT TRIP
STOP-AND-GO

LONG Insulator Tip
Slow Heat Transfer
HIGHER Heat Range
HOT PLUG

Fig. 6 Twist the spark plug wire boot while pulling it from the spark plug

Fig. 7 Always use a spark plug socket to remove spark plugs. The use of a regular socket could break the spark plug

Fig. 8 Loosening the spark plug

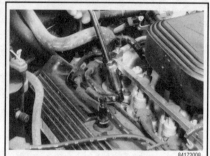

Fig. 9 Removing a spark plug from the 4.6L engine. The spark plug socket has an insulator that grips the spark plug, aiding removal and installation

the larger gauge should not pass through at all. If the gap is incorrect, use the electrode bending tool on the gauge to adjust the gap. Only the side electrode is adjustable.

To install:

6. Put a drop of penetrating oil on the base threads of the plug. Start the spark plug into the cylinder head by hand and turn until it is snug. Tighten the plug to 7 ft. lbs. (10 Nm) on the 4.6L engine, 10 ft. lbs. (14 Nm) on the 5.0L engine or 15 ft. lbs. (20 Nm) on the 5.8L engine.

7. Apply a small amount of silicone dielectric compound D7AZ–19A331–A or equivalent, to the entire inside surface of the spark plug wire boot and connect the wire to the spark plug. If you did not number the wires, refer to the Firing Order diagrams to make sure the wires are connected properly.

INSPECTION & GAPPING

▶ **See Figures 10, 11, 12 and 13**

Check the plugs for deposits and wear. If they are not going to be replaced, clean the plugs thoroughly. Remember that any kind of deposit will decrease the efficiency of the plug. Plugs can be cleaned on a spark plug cleaning machine, which can sometimes be found in service stations, or you can do an acceptable job of cleaning with a stiff brush. If the plugs are cleaned, the electrodes must be filed flat. Use an ignition points file, not an emery board or the like, which will leave deposits. The electrodes must be filed perfectly flat with sharp edges; rounded edges reduce the spark plug voltage by as much as 50%.

Check spark plug gap before installation. The ground electrode (the L-shaped one connected to the body of the plug) must be parallel to the center electrode and the specified size wire gauge (please refer to the Tune-Up Specifications chart for details) must pass between the electrodes with a slight drag.

➥**NEVER adjust the gap on a used platinum type spark plug.**

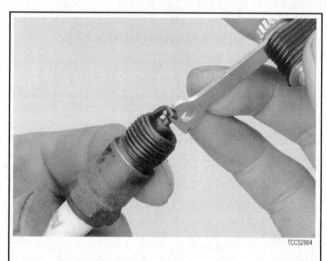

Fig. 11 Adjusting the spark plug gap

Always check the gap on new plugs as they are not always set correctly at the factory. Do not use a flat feeler gauge when measuring the gap on a used plug, because the reading may be inaccurate. A round-wire type gapping tool is the best way to check the gap. The correct gauge should pass through the electrode gap with a slight drag. If you're in doubt, try one size smaller and one larger. The smaller gauge should go through easily, while the larger one shouldn't go through at all. Wire gapping tools usually have a bending tool attached. Use that to adjust the side electrode until the proper distance is obtained. Absolutely never attempt to bend the center electrode. Also, be careful not to bend the side

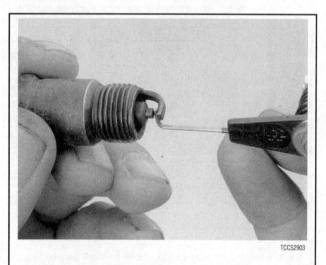

Fig. 10 Checking the spark plug gap with a feeler gauge

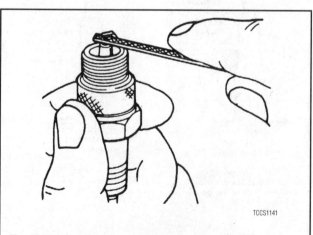

Fig. 12 If the standard plug is in good condition, the electrode may be filed flat—WARNING: do not file platinum plugs

A **normally worn** spark plug should have light tan or gray deposits on the firing tip.

A **carbon fouled** plug, identified by soft, sooty, black deposits, may indicate an improperly tuned vehicle. Check the air cleaner, ignition components and engine control system.

This spark plug has been **left in the engine too long,** as evidenced by the extreme gap- Plugs with such an extreme gap can cause misfiring and stumbling accompanied by a noticeable lack of power.

An oil fouled spark plug indicates an engine with worn poston rings and/or bad valve seals allowing excessive oil to enter the chamber.

A **physically damaged** spark plug may be evidence of severe detonation in that cylinder. Watch that cylinder carefully between services, as a continued detonation will not only damage the plug, but could also damage the engine.

A **bridged or almost bridged** spark plug, identified by a build-up between the electrodes caused by excessive carbon or oil build-up on the plug.

TCCA1P40

Fig. 13 Inspect the spark plug to determine engine running conditions

electrode too far or too often as it may weaken and break off within the engine, requiring removal of the cylinder head to retrieve it.

Spark Plug Wires

Visually inspect the spark plug wires for burns, cuts, or breaks in the insulation. Check the spark plug boots and the nipples on the distributor cap and/or coil(s). Replace any damaged wiring. If no physical damage is obvious, the wires can be checked with an ohmmeter for excessive resistance and continuity. Resistance should be at least 7000 ohms per 1 ft. (30.5cm) of cable. On 5.0L and 5.8L engines, measure the resistance with the plug wire still attached to the distributor cap.

REMOVAL & INSTALLATION

▶ **See Figures 14 and 15**

When installing a new set of spark plug wires, replace the wires one at a time so there will be no mixup. Start by replacing the longest wire first. Route the wire exactly the same as the original.

84172011

Fig. 14 Removing the spark plug wire from the spark plug on the 4.6L engine. Note the cylinder number markings on the wire

Fig. 15 Spark plug wires connected to the right-hand ignition coil—4.6L engine

1. Grasp the wire by the rubber boot. Twist and pull the boot and wire from the spark plug. Never pull on the plug wire directly, or it may become separated from the connector inside the boot.

2. On 5.0L and 5.8L engines, disconnect the spark plug wire from the distributor cap in the same manner as the wire was disconnected from the spark plug. On the 4.6L engine, squeeze the locking tabs and twist the boot, while pulling upward from the coil.

3. Remove the necessary wire retainer clips and separators and remove the spark plug wire.

To install:

4. Apply a small amount of silicone dielectric compound D7AZ–19A331–A or equivalent, to the entire inside surface of the spark plug wire boots.

5. Install the wire to the proper distributor cap or ignition coil terminal, making sure the boot is firmly seated. On the 4.6L engine, make sure the coil boot locking tabs are engaged.

❄❄ WARNING

On the 4.6L engine, it is critical to vehicle operation that the spark plug wires be properly installed at the spark plugs and ignition coils. If one spark plug wire is not properly installed, both spark plugs connected to that ignition coil may not fire under load.

6. Route the wire through the necessary retainer clips and separators.
7. Connect the spark plug wire to the spark plug.

➡On the 4.6L engine, the spark plug boot must be positioned 45 degrees from crankshaft centerline (outboard and forward) to make sure the boot seal is fully seated.

FIRING ORDERS

▶ **See Figures 16, 17 and 18**

➡**To avoid confusion, remove and tag the spark plug wires one at a time, for replacement.**

If a distributor is not keyed for installation with only one orientation, it could have been removed previously and rewired. The resultant wiring would hold the correct firing order, but could change the relative placement of the plug towers in relation to the engine. For this reason it is imperative that you label all wires before disconnecting any of them. Also, before removal, compare the current wiring with the accompanying illustrations. If the current wiring does not match, make notes in your book to reflect how your engine is wired.

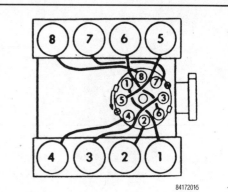

Fig. 17 5.0L Engine
Engine Firing Order: 1–5–4–2–6–3–7–8
Distributor Rotation: Counterclockwise

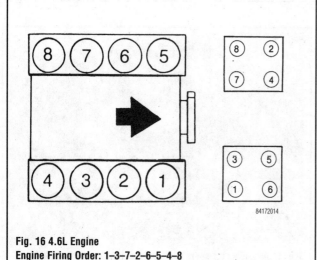

Fig. 16 4.6L Engine
Engine Firing Order: 1–3–7–2–6–5–4–8
Distributorless Ignition System

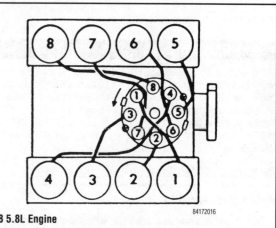

Fig. 18 5.8L Engine
Engine Firing Order: 1–3–7–2–6–5–4–8
Distributor Rotation: Counterclockwise

ELECTRONIC IGNITION

Description and Operation

Your car is equipped with one of 3 different electronic ignition systems, depending on engine application. Vehicles with the 5.0L engine are equipped with the Thick Film Integrated (TFI-IV) ignition system, vehicles with the 5.8L engine are equipped with the Duraspark II ignition system and vehicles with the 4.6L engine are equipped with the Electronic Distributorless Ignition System (EDIS).

THICK FILM INTEGRATED (TFI-IV) IGNITION SYSTEM

▶ **See Figures 19, 20, 21 and 22**

The Thick Film Integrated (TFI-IV) ignition system uses a camshaft driven distributor with no centrifugal or vacuum advance. The distributor has a diecast base, incorporating a Hall effect stator assembly. The TFI-IV system module is mounted on the distributor base, it has 6 pins and uses an E-Core ignition coil, named after the shape of the laminations making up the core.

The TFI-IV module supplies voltage to the Profile Ignition Pick-up (PIP) sensor, which sends the crankshaft position information to the TFI-IV module. The TFI-IV module then sends this information to the EEC-IV module, which determines the spark timing and sends an electronic signal to the TFI-IV ignition module to turn off the coil and produce a spark to fire the spark plug.

The operation of the universal distributor is accomplished through the Hall effect stator assembly, causing the ignition coil to be switched off and on by the ECC-IV computer and TFI-IV modules. The vane switch is an encapsulated package consisting of a Hall sensor on one side and a permanent magnet on the other side.

A rotary vane cup, made of ferrous metal, is used to trigger the Hall effect switch. When the window of the vane cup is between the magnet and the Hall effect device, a magnetic flux field is completed from the magnet through the Hall effect device back to the magnet. As the vane passes through the opening,

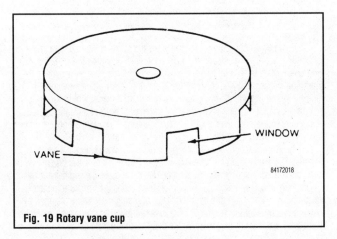

Fig. 19 Rotary vane cup

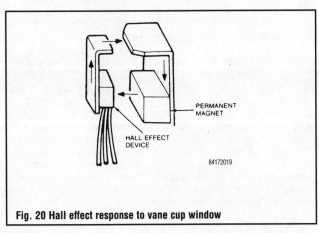

Fig. 20 Hall effect response to vane cup window

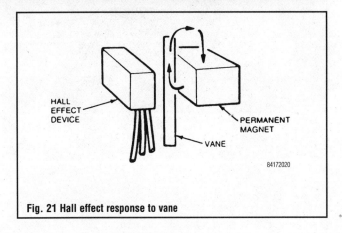

Fig. 21 Hall effect response to vane

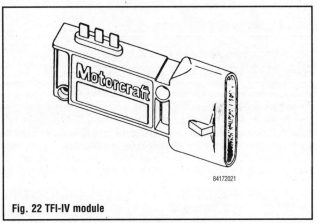

Fig. 22 TFI-IV module

the flux lines are shunted through the vane and back to the magnet. A voltage is produced while the vane passes through the opening. When the vane clears the opening, the window causes the signal to go to 0 volts. The signal is then used by the EEC-IV system for crankshaft position sensing and the computation of the desired spark advance based on the engine demand and calibration. The voltage distribution is accomplished through a conventional rotor, cap and ignition wires.

DURASPARK II IGNITION SYSTEM

▶ **See Figures 23 and 24**

The Duraspark II ignition system consists of the typical electronic primary and conventional secondary circuits, designed to carry higher voltages. The primary and secondary circuits consists of the following components:

Primary Circuit

- Battery
- Ignition switch
- Ballast resistor start bypass (wires)
- Ignition coil primary winding
- Ignition module
- Distributor stator assembly

Secondary Circuit

- Battery
- Ignition coil secondary winding
- Distributor rotor
- Distributor cap
- Ignition wires
- Spark plugs

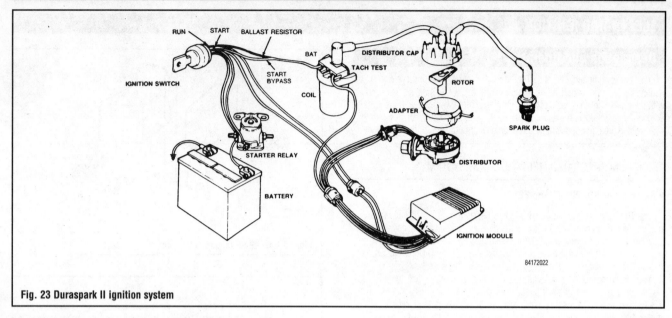

Fig. 23 Duraspark II ignition system

With the ignition switch in the **RUN** position, the primary circuit current is directed from the battery, through the ignition switch, the ballast resistor, the ignition coil (in the positive side, out the negative side), the ignition module and back to the battery through the ignition system ground in the distributor. This current flow causes a magnetic field to be built up in the ignition coil. When the poles on the armature and the stator assembly align, the ignition module turns the primary current flow off, collapsing the magnetic field in the ignition coil. The collapsing field induces a high voltage in the ignition coil secondary windings. The ignition coil wire then conducts the high voltage to the distributor where the cap and rotor distributes it to the appropriate spark plug.

A timing device in the ignition module turns the primary current back on after a very short period of time. High voltage is produced each time the magnetic field is built up and collapsed.

The red ignition module wire provides operating voltage for the ignition module electronic components in the run mode. The white ignition module wire and start bypass provide increased voltage for the ignition module and ignition coil, respectively, during start mode.

The distributor provides a signal to the ignition module, which controls the timing of the spark at the spark plugs. This signal is generated as the armature, attached to the distributor shaft, rotates past the stator assembly. The rotating armature causes fluctuations in a magnetic field produced by the stator assembly magnet. These fluctuations induce a voltage in the stator assembly pick-up coil. The signal is connected to the ignition module by the vehicle wiring harness.

The occurrence of the signal to the ignition module, in relation to the initial spark timing, is controlled by centrifugal and vacuum advance mechanisms. The centrifugal advance mechanism controls spark timing in response to engine rpm. The vacuum advance mechanism controls spark timing in response to engine load.

The centrifugal advance mechanism varies the relationship of the armature to the stator assembly. The sleeve and plate assembly, on which the armature is mounted, rotates in relation to the distributor shaft. This rotation is caused by centrifugal weights moving in response to the engine rpm. The movement of the centrifugal weights change the initial relationship of the armature to the stator assembly by rotating the sleeve and plate assembly ahead of its static position on the distributor shaft. This results in spark advance. The rate of movement of the centrifugal weights is controlled by calibrated springs.

The vacuum spark control mechanism can provide spark advance if a single diaphragm assembly is used or spark advance and retard if a dual diaphragm assembly is used. The diaphragm assembly used depends on the engine calibration.

The single vacuum diaphragm assembly also varies the armature to stator assembly relationship. In this case the stator assembly position is changed by means of vacuum applied to the diaphragm assembly. The diaphragm assembly is attached to the stator assembly by the diaphragm rod. The stator assembly is mounted on the upper plate assembly. The vacuum applied to the diaphragm assembly causes the diaphragm and attached diaphragm rod to move, compressing the advance spring, which controls the rate of spark advance. The rate of spark advance is controlled by a calibrated spring.

Spark advance is obtained with a dual diaphragm assembly in the same manner as with a single diaphragm assembly. In this case, vacuum applied to the vacuum advance port cause the advance diaphragm rod to move, otherwise the action is the same. Spark retard is obtained by applying vacuum to the vacuum retard port. This causes the retard diaphragm to move, compressing the retard spring, which controls the rate of spark retard. Compressing the retard spring allows the diaphragm rod stop to move due to force applied by an advance spring pushing against it by means of a diaphragm rod. The result is the diaphragm rod moves, causing the attached stator assembly to change position with respect to the armature. In this instance, the direction of the stator assembly movement is opposite that occurring during vacuum advance, resulting in spark retard. It should be noted that vacuum applied to the advance port overrides any spark retard caused by vacuum applied to the retard port.

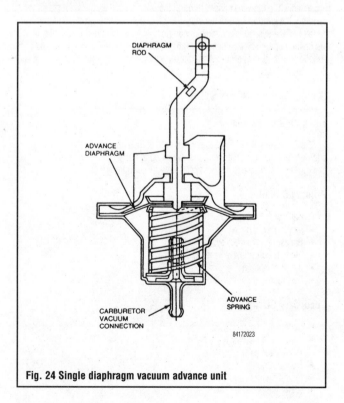

Fig. 24 Single diaphragm vacuum advance unit

ELECTRONIC DISTRIBUTORLESS IGNITION SYSTEM (EDIS)

♦ See Figure 25

The EDIS consists of the following components: crankshaft sensor, ignition module, ignition coil pack, the spark angle portion of the Powertrain Control Module (PCM) and the related wiring.

The EDIS eliminates the need for a distributor by using multiple ignition coils. Each coil fires 2 spark plugs at the same time. The plugs are paired so as one fires during the compression cycle, the other fires during the exhaust stroke. The next time the coil is fired, the plug that was on exhaust will be on compression and the one that was on compression will be on exhaust. The spark in the exhaust cylinder is wasted but little of the coil energy is lost. The ignition coils are mounted together in coil packs. There are 2 coil packs used, each containing 2 ignition coils.

The crankshaft sensor is a variable reluctance-type sensor triggered by a 36-minus-1 tooth trigger wheel configuration pressed onto the rear of the crankshaft damper. The signal generated by this sensor is called a Variable Reluctance Sensor (VRS) signal. The VRS signal provides engine position and rpm information to the ignition module.

The ignition module is a microprocessor that receives input from the crankshaft sensor in regards to engine position, base timing and engine speed and input from the PCM pertaining to spark advance. The ignition module uses this information to direct which coil to fire and to calculate the turn and turn off times of the coils required to achieve the correct dwell and spark advance.

Diagnosis and Testing

SERVICE PRECAUTIONS

- Always turn the key **OFF** and isolate both ends of a circuit whenever testing for short or continuity.
- Never measure voltage voltage or resistance directly at the processor connector.

- Never connect the positive lead of the EDIS diagnostic cable or VRS tee until directed to do so.
- On vehicles with the 4.6L engine, be careful not to bring a fluorescent trouble lamp to close to the vehicle's wiring. If the key is **ON** and the VR sensor is disconnected, the EDIS module may fire the coil.
- Always disconnect solenoids and switches from the harness before measuring for continuity, resistance or energizing by way of a 12 volts source.
- When disconnecting connectors, inspect for damaged or pushed-out pins, corrosion, loose wires, etc. Perform service, if required.

SYSTEM INSPECTION

1. Visually inspect the components of the ignition system. Check for the following:
- Discharged battery
- Damaged or loose connections
- Damaged electrical insulation
- Poor coil, distributor and spark plug connections
- Ignition module connections
- Blown fuses
- Damaged vacuum hoses
- Damaged or worn rotor and distributor cap
- Damaged spark plugs
- Distributor cap, rotor and spark plug wires are properly seated

2. Check the vehicle's maintenance schedule to ensure spark plugs have been properly maintained.

3. Check spark plug wires and boots for signs of poor insulation that could cause cross firing.

4. A worn timing chain can cause symptoms that appear to be ignition timing related.

5. Make certain the engine idle speed is within specification.

6. Be certain that the battery is fully charged and that all accessories should be **OFF** during the diagnosis.

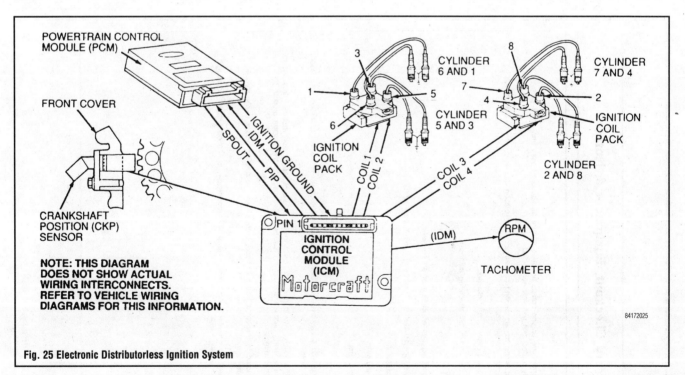

Fig. 25 Electronic Distributorless Ignition System

Start Circuits

DS II	Part 2 Test 1

TEST STEP	RESULT	▲	ACTION TO TAKE
1. Connect spark tester between ignition coil wire and engine ground.	Yes	▲	GO to Part 2, Test 2.
2. Crank engine using ignition switch.	No	▲	MEASURE resistance of ignition coil wire. REPLACE if greater than 7,000 ohms per foot.
3. **Were sparks present?**			INSPECT ignition coil for damage, carbon tracking.
			CRANK engine to verify distributor rotation.
			GO to Part 2, Test 5.

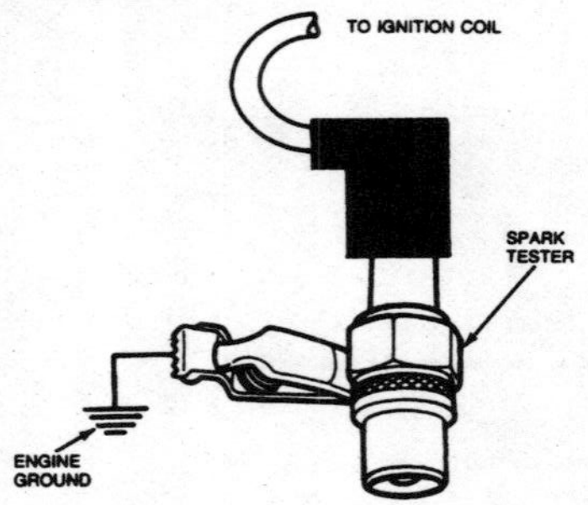

SPARK TESTER
TO IGNITION COIL
ENGINE GROUND

Fig. 27 Duraspark II ignition system testing

Preliminary Checkout, Equipment & Notes

CHECKOUT

- Visually inspect the engine compartment to ensure all vacuum hoses and spark plug wires are properly routed and securely connected.
- Examine all wiring harnesses and connectors for insulation damage, burned, overheated, loose or broken conditions.
- Be certain the battery is fully charged.
- All accessories should be off during diagnosis.

EQUIPMENT

Obtain the following test equipment or an equivalent:

- Spark Tester, Special Service Tool D81P-6666-A. See **NOTE**.
- Volt/Ohm Meter Rotunda 014-00407.
- 12 Volt Test Lamp.
- Small straight pins (2).

NOTES

- A spark plug with a broken side electrode **is not** sufficient to check for spark and may lead to incorrect results.
- All wire colors referred to in this part relate to the colors of the ignition module wires. When working with a wiring harness, the wires must be traced back to the ignition module for proper color identification.
- When instructed to inspect a wiring harness, both a visual inspection and a continuity test should be performed.
- When making measurements on a wiring harness or connector, it is good practice to wiggle the wires while measuring.

Fig. 26 Duraspark II ignition system testing

Module Voltage		DS II	Part 2 Test 3

TEST STEP	RESULT	▲	ACTION TO TAKE
• Turn ignition switch off.			
1. Carefully insert small straight pin in RED module wire.	Yes	▲	GO to Part 2, Test 4.
CAUTION	No	▲	REFER to vehicle wiring diagram. INSPECT wiring harness between module and ignition switch.
Do not allow straight pin to contact electrical ground.			
2. Attach negative (−) VOM lead to distributor base.			Damaged or worn ignition switch.
3. Measure battery voltage.			
4. Measure voltage at straight pin with ignition switch in RUN position.			
5. Turn ignition switch to OFF position.			
6. Remove straight pin.			
7. **Is voltage 90 percent of battery voltage or greater?**			

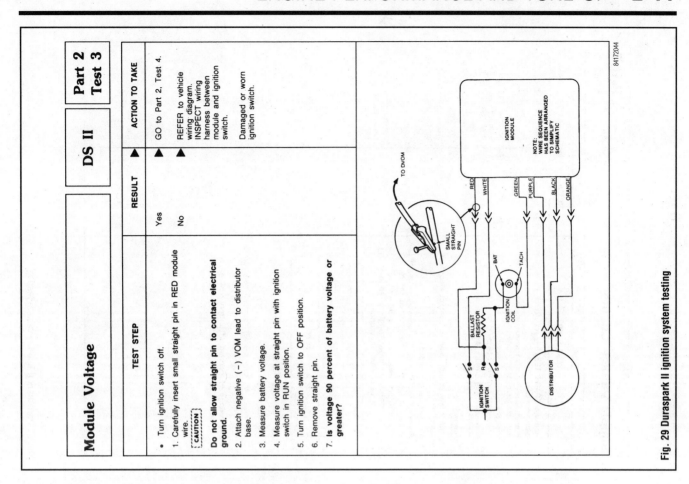

84172044

Fig. 29 Duraspark II ignition system testing

Run Circuits		DS II	Part 2 Test 2

TEST STEP	RESULT	▲	ACTION TO TAKE
1. Turn ignition switch from OFF to RUN to OFF position several times.	Yes	▲	INSPECT distributor cap, adapter, rotor for cracks, carbon tracking.
2. Spark should occur each time switch goes from RUN to OFF position.			CHECK for roll pin securing armature to sleeve in distributor.
3. Remove spark tester, reconnect coil wire to distributor cap.			CHECK that ORANGE and PURPLE wires not crossed between distributor and ignition module.
4. **Were sparks present?**			If ignition module has Basic Part No. (-12A244-), GO to Spark Timing Advance to check spark retard operation.
	No	▲	GO to Part 2, Test 3.

84172043

Fig. 28 Duraspark II ignition system testing

Supply Voltage Circuits

DS II	Part 2 Test 5

TEST STEP	RESULT	▲ ACTION TO TAKE
1. Remove SPARK TESTER, reconnect coil wire to distributor cap. 2. If starter relay has I terminal, disconnect cable from starter relay to starter motor. 3. If starter relay does not have I terminal, disconnect wire to S terminal of starter relay. 4. Carefully insert small straight pins in RED and WHITE module wires. **CAUTION** **Do not allow straight pins to contact electrical ground.** 5. Measure battery voltage. 6. Following table below, measure voltage at points listed with ignition switch in position shown. **NOTE: Attach negative (–) VOM lead to distributor base. Wiggle wires in wiring harness when measuring.**	Yes	▲ Test result OK. GO to Part 2, Test 6.
	No	▲ REFER to vehicle wiring diagram. INSPECT wiring harness and connector(s) in faulty circuit(s). Damaged or worn ignition switch. Radio interference capacitor on ignition coil.

Wire/ Terminal	Circuit	Ignition Switch Test Position	
		Run	Start
Red	Run	Run	
White	Start		Start
'Bat' Terminal Ignition Coil	Ballast Resistor Bypass		Start

7. Turn ignition switch to OFF position.
8. Remove straight pins.
9. Reconnect any cables/wires removed from starter relay.
10. **Is voltage 90 percent of battery voltage or greater?**

Fig. 31 Duraspark II ignition system testing

Ballast Resistor

DS II	Part 2 Test 4

TEST STEP	RESULT	▲ ACTION TO TAKE
1. Separate and inspect ignition module two wire connector with RED and WHITE wires. 2. Disconnect and inspect ignition coil connector. 3. Measure ballast resistor between BAT terminal of ignition coil connector and wiring harness connector mating with RED module wire. 4. Reconnect all connectors. 5. **Was the resistance 0.8 to 1.6 ohms?**	Yes	▲ REPLACE ignition module.
	No	▲ REPLACE ballast resistor.

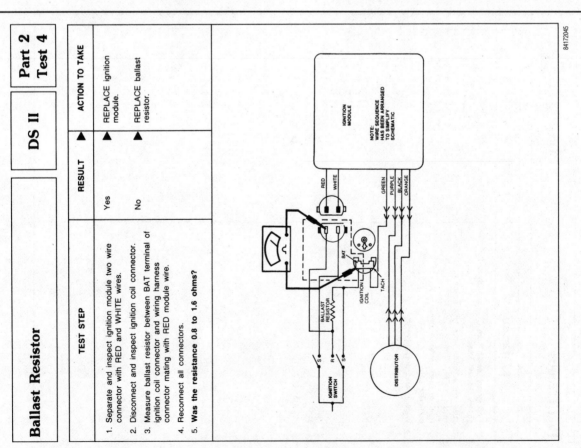

Fig. 30 Duraspark II ignition system testing

Ignition Coil Supply Voltage

	DS II	Part 2 Test 6

TEST STEP	RESULT	ACTION TO TAKE
1. Attach negative (–) lead of VOM to distributor base.		
2. Turn ignition switch to RUN position.	Yes ▲	GO to Part 2, Test 7.
3. Measure voltage at BAT terminal of ignition coil.	No ▲	GO to Part 2, Test 12.
4. Turn ignition switch to OFF position.		
5. **Was the voltage 6 to 8 volts?**		

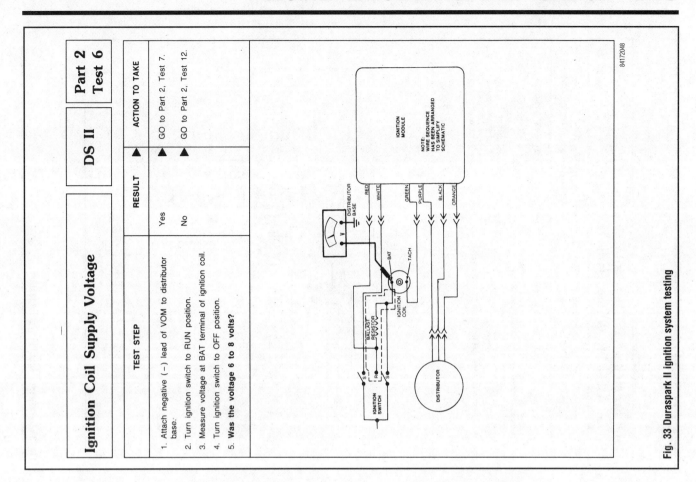

Fig. 33 Duraspark II ignition system testing

Supply Voltage Circuits— Continued

	DS II	Part 2 Test 5

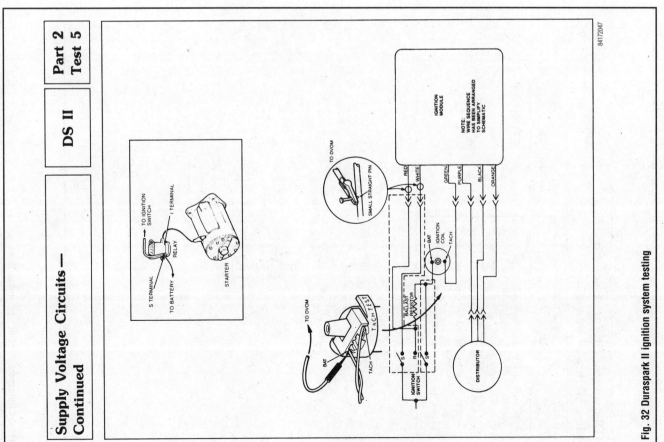

Fig. 32 Duraspark II ignition system testing

Ignition Module to Distributor Stator Assembly Wiring Harness

DS II		Part 2 Test 8

TEST STEP	RESULT	▲	ACTION TO TAKE
1. Attach one VOM lead to distributor base.			
2. Alternately measure resistance between wiring harness terminals mating with ORANGE and PURPLE module wires and ground.	▲ Yes		TEST result OK. GO to Part 2, Test 9.
3. Reconnect four wire connector.	▲ No		INSPECT wiring harness between module connector and distributor, including distributor grommet.
4. **Was the resistance greater than 70,000 ohms?**			

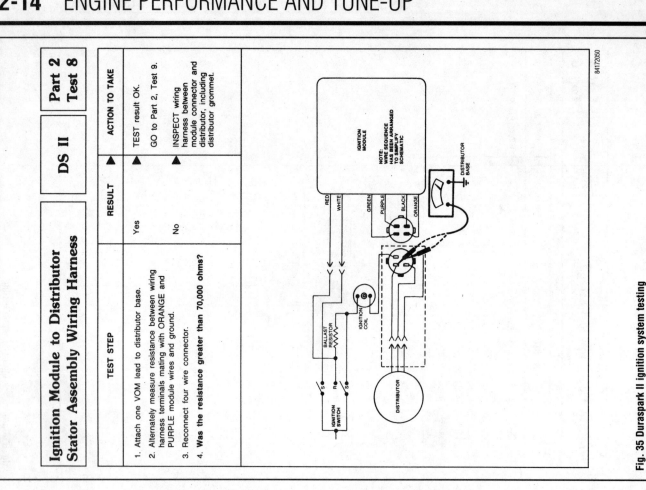

84172050

Fig. 35 Duraspark II ignition system testing

Distributor Stator Assembly and Wiring Harness

DS II		Part 2 Test 7

TEST STEP	RESULT	▲	ACTION TO TAKE
1. Separate ignition module four wire connector. Inspect for dirt, corrosion, and damage.	▲ Yes		Test result OK. GO to Part 2, Test 8.
2. Measure stator assembly and wiring harness resistance between wiring harness terminals mating with ORANGE and PURPLE module wires.	▲ No		GO to Part 2, Test 11.
NOTE: Wiggle wires in wiring harness when measuring.			
3. **Was the resistance 400 to 1,300 ohms?**			

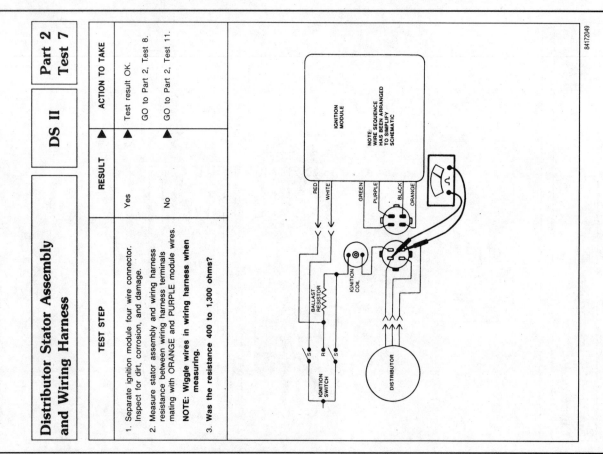

84172049

Fig. 34 Duraspark II ignition system testing

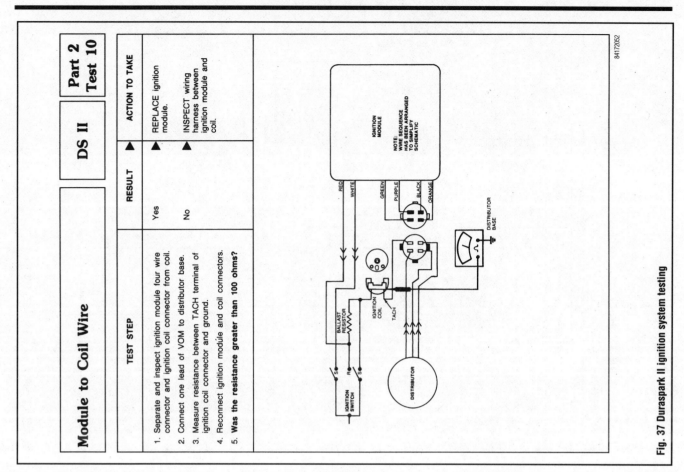

Module to Coil Wire | DS II | Part 2 Test 10

TEST STEP	RESULT	ACTION TO TAKE
1. Separate and inspect ignition module four wire connector and ignition coil connector from coil.		►
2. Connect one lead of VOM to distributor base.	► Yes	► REPLACE ignition module.
3. Measure resistance between TACH terminal of ignition coil connector and ground.	No	► INSPECT wiring harness between ignition module and coil.
4. Reconnect ignition module and coil connectors.		
5. **Was the resistance greater than 100 ohms?**		

Fig. 37 Duraspark II ignition system testing

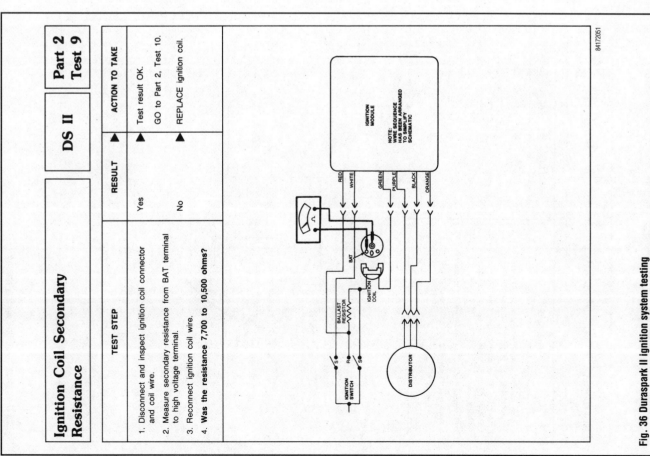

Ignition Coil Secondary Resistance | DS II | Part 2 Test 9

TEST STEP	RESULT	ACTION TO TAKE
1. Disconnect and inspect ignition coil connector and coil wire.	►	►
2. Measure secondary resistance from BAT terminal to high voltage terminal.	► Yes	► Test result OK.
3. Reconnect ignition coil wire.		GO to Part 2, Test 10.
4. **Was the resistance 7,700 to 10,500 ohms?**	No	► REPLACE ignition coil.

Fig. 36 Duraspark II ignition system testing

Ignition Coil Primary Resistance

| | DS II | Part 2 Test 12 |

TEST STEP	RESULT		ACTION TO TAKE
1. Disconnect ignition coil connector.			
2. Measure primary resistance from BAT to TACH terminal.			
3. Reconnect ignition coil connector.			
4. **Was resistance 0.8 to 1.6 ohms?**	Yes	▲	Test result OK. GO to Part 2, Test 13.
	No	▲	REPLACE ignition coil.

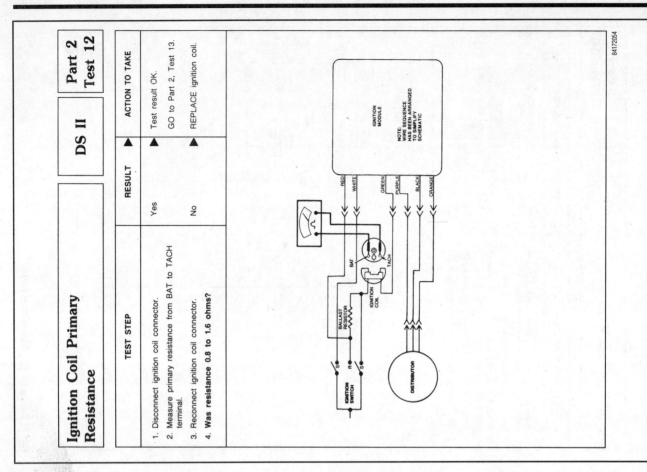

Fig. 39 Duraspark II ignition system testing

Distributor Stator Assembly

| | DS II | Part 2 Test 11 |

TEST STEP	RESULT		ACTION TO TAKE
1. Separate distributor connector from harness. Inspect for dirt, corrosion, and damage.			
2. Measure stator assembly resistance across ORANGE and PURPLE wires at distributor connector.			
3. Reconnect distributor and module connectors.			
4. **Was resistance 400 to 1,300 ohms?**	Yes	▲	Test result OK. INSPECT wiring harness between distributor and ignition module.
	No	▲	REPLACE stator assembly.

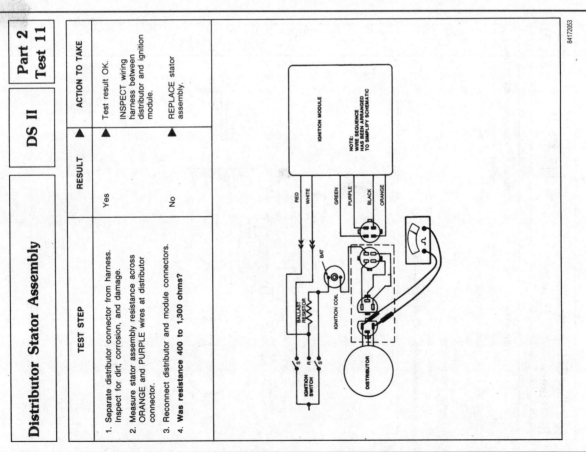

Fig. 38 Duraspark II ignition system testing

Primary Circuit Continuity		DS II		Part 2 Test 13
TEST STEP		**RESULT**	▲	**ACTION TO TAKE**
1. Carefully insert small straight pin in module GREEN wire.		Yes	▲	GO to Part 2, Test 14.
[CAUTION]		No	▲	INSPECT wiring harness and connectors between ignition module and coil.
Do not allow straight pin to contact electrical ground.				
2. Attach negative (–) VOM lead to distributor base.				
3. Turn ignition switch to RUN position.				
4. Measure voltage at GREEN module wire.				
5. Turn ignition switch to OFF position.				
6. Remove straight pin.				
7. **Was voltage greater than 1.5 volts?**				

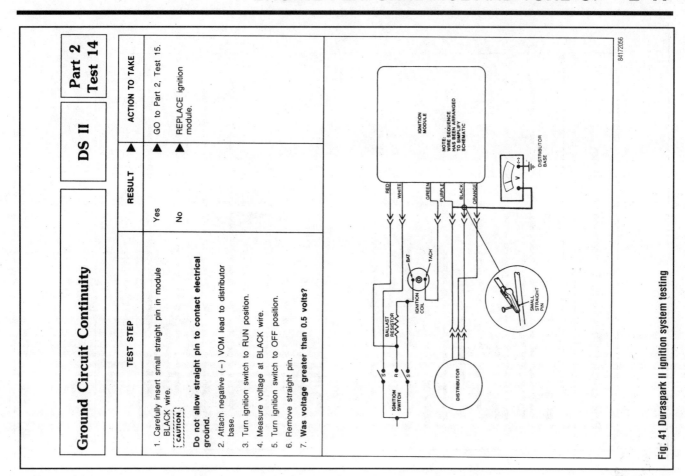

Fig. 40 Duraspark II ignition system testing

Ground Circuit Continuity		DS II		Part 2 Test 14
TEST STEP		**RESULT**	▲	**ACTION TO TAKE**
1. Carefully insert small straight pin in module BLACK wire.		Yes	▲	GO to Part 2, Test 15.
[CAUTION]		No	▲	REPLACE ignition module.
Do not allow straight pin to contact electrical ground.				
2. Attach negative (–) VOM lead to distributor base.				
3. Turn ignition switch to RUN position.				
4. Measure voltage at BLACK wire.				
5. Turn ignition switch to OFF position.				
6. Remove straight pin.				
7. **Was voltage greater than 0.5 volts?**				

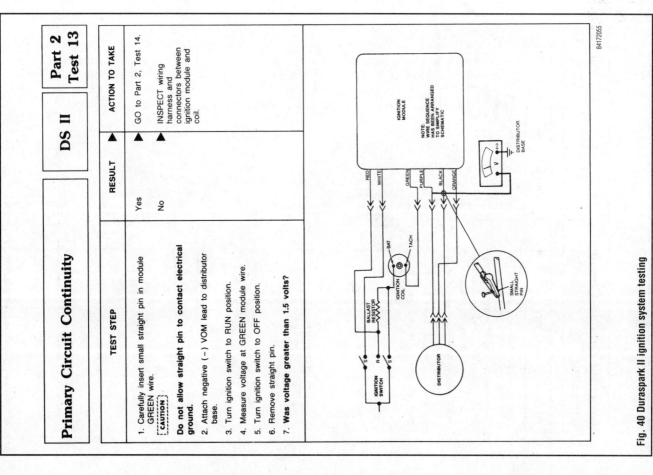

Fig. 41 Duraspark II ignition system testing

Preliminary Checkout, Equipment & Notes

CHECKOUT
- Visually inspect the engine compartment to ensure all vacuum hoses and spark plug wires are properly routed and securely connected.
- Examine all wiring harnesses and connectors for insulation damage, and burned, overheated, loose or broken conditions.
- Check that the TFI module is securely fastened to the distributor base.
- Be certain the battery is fully charged.
- All accessories should be off during diagnosis.

EQUIPMENT

Obtain the following test equipment or an equivalent:
- Spark Tester, Special Service Tool D81P-6666-A. See **NOTES.**
- Volt/Ohm Meter Rotunda 014-00407 or 007-00001.
- 12 Volt Test Lamp.
- Small straight pin.
- Remote Starter Switch.
- TFI Ignition Tester, Rotunda 105-00002.
- E-core Ignition Coil E73F-12029-AB.
- Ignition coil secondary wire E43E-12A012-AB.

NOTES
- A spark plug with a broken side electrode **is not** sufficient to check for spark and may lead to incorrect results.
- When instructed to inspect a wiring harness, both a visual inspection and a continuity test should be performed.
- When making measurements on a wiring harness or connector, it is good practice to wiggle the wires while measuring.
- References to pin-in-line connector apply to a shorting bar type connector used to set base timing.

Fig. 43 TFI-IV ignition system testing

Distributor Ground Circuit Continuity

DS II — **Part 2 Test 15**

TEST STEP	RESULT	ACTION TO TAKE
1. Separate distributor connector from harness. Inspect for dirt, corrosion, and damage.		
2. Attach one lead of VOM to distributor base.		
3. Measure resistance by attaching other VOM lead to BLACK wire in distributor connector.		
NOTE: Wiggle distributor grommet when measuring.		
4. Reconnect distributor connector.		
5. **Was resistance less than 1 ohm?**	Yes	Test result OK.
		INSPECT wiring harness and connectors between distributor and ignition module.
	No	INSPECT ground screw in distributor.

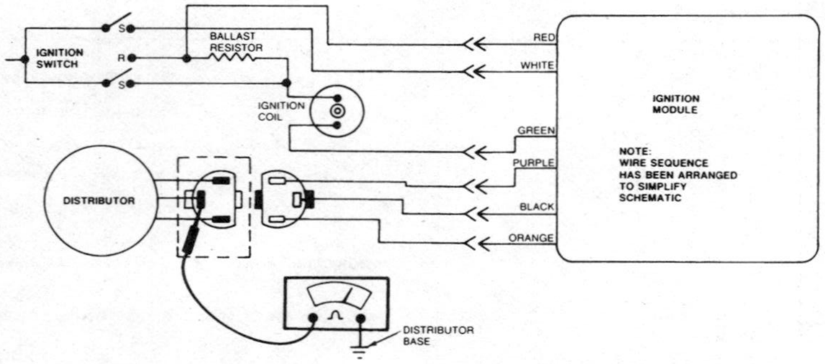

Fig. 42 Duraspark II ignition system testing

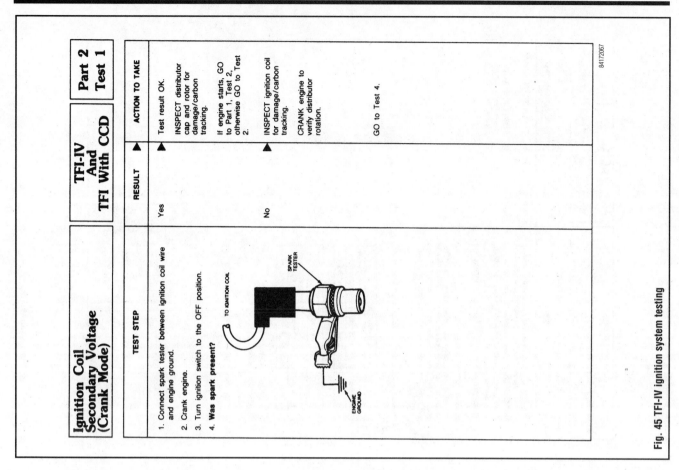

Ignition Coil Secondary Voltage (Crank Mode)	TFI-IV And TFI With CCD	Part 2 Test 1
TEST STEP	**RESULT** ▲	**ACTION TO TAKE**
1. Connect spark tester between ignition coil wire and engine ground. 2. Crank engine. 3. Turn ignition switch to the OFF position. **4. Was spark present?**	Yes ▲	Test result OK. INSPECT distributor cap and rotor for damage/carbon tracking. If engine starts, GO to Part 1, Test 2, otherwise GO to Test 2.
	No ▲	INSPECT ignition coil for damage/carbon tracking. CRANK engine to verify distributor rotation. GO to Test 4.

Fig. 45 TFI-IV ignition system testing

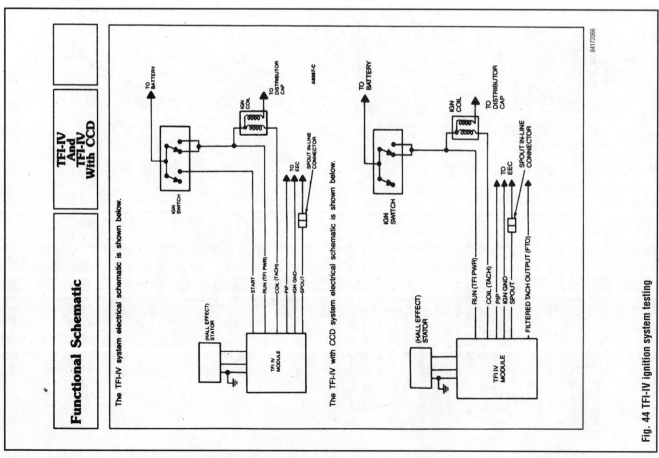

Functional Schematic	TFI-IV And TFI-IV With CCD

The TFI-IV system electrical schematic is shown below.

The TFI-IV with CCD system electrical schematic is shown below.

Fig. 44 TFI-IV ignition system testing

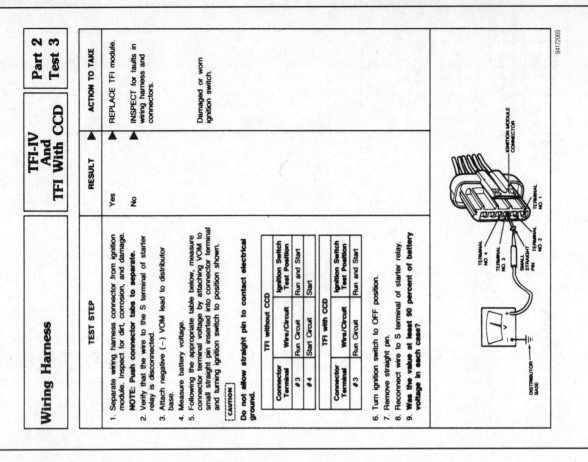

Wiring Harness

TFI-IV And TFI With CCD — Part 2 Test 3

TEST STEP	RESULT	ACTION TO TAKE
1. Separate wiring harness connector from ignition module. Inspect for dirt, corrosion, and damage. NOTE: Push connector tabs to separate.	Yes	REPLACE TFI module.
2. Verify that the wire to the S terminal of starter relay is disconnected.	No	INSPECT for faults in wiring harness and connectors.
3. Attach negative (−) VOM lead to distributor base.		Damaged or worn ignition switch.
4. Measure battery voltage.		
5. Following the appropriate table below, measure connector terminal voltage by attaching VOM to small straight pin inserted into connector terminal and turning ignition switch to position shown.		

> **CAUTION**
> Do not allow straight pin to contact electrical ground.

TFI without CCD

Connector Terminal	Wire/Circuit	Ignition Switch Test Position
#3	Run Circuit	Run and Start
#4	Start Circuit	Start

TFI with CCD

Connector Terminal	Wire/Circuit	Ignition Switch Test Position
#3	Run Circuit	Run and Start

TEST STEP	RESULT	ACTION TO TAKE
6. Turn ignition switch to OFF position.		
7. Remove straight pin.		
8. Reconnect wire to S terminal of starter relay.		
9. Was the value at least 90 percent of battery voltage in each case?		

Fig. 47 TFI-IV ignition system testing

84172069

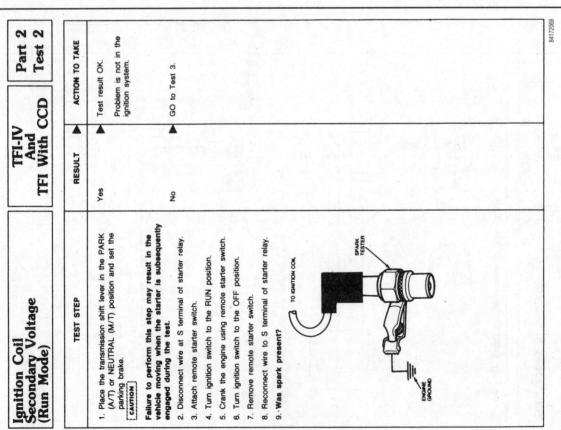

Ignition Coil Secondary Voltage (Run Mode)

TFI-IV And TFI With CCD — Part 2 Test 2

TEST STEP	RESULT	ACTION TO TAKE
1. Place the transmission shift lever in the PARK (A/T) or NEUTRAL (M/T) position and set the parking brake.	Yes	Test result OK. Problem is not in the ignition system.
CAUTION **Failure to perform this step may result in the vehicle moving when the starter is subsequently engaged during the test.**	No	GO to Test 3.
2. Disconnect wire at S terminal of starter relay.		
3. Attach remote starter switch.		
4. Turn ignition switch to the RUN position.		
5. Crank the engine using remote starter switch.		
6. Turn ignition switch to the OFF position.		
7. Remove remote starter switch.		
8. Reconnect wire to S terminal of starter relay.		
9. Was spark present?		

Fig. 46 TFI-IV ignition system testing

84172068

Stator — TFI-IV

	TFI-IV And TFI With CCD	Part 2 Test 5

TEST STEP	RESULT	ACTION TO TAKE
1. Remove the distributor from the engine and the TFI module from the distributor.		
2. Measure resistance between TFI module terminals as shown below.		
	Yes	Replace stator.
	No	Replace TFI.
3. Are all these readings as specified?		

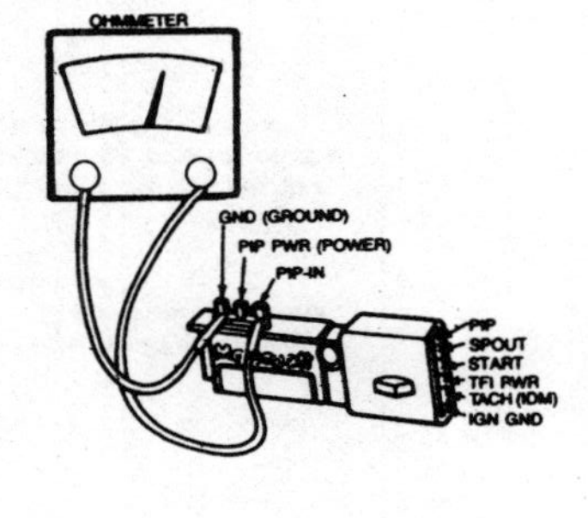

Measure Between These Terminals	Resistance Should Be
GND — PIP In	Greater than 500 Ohms
PIP PWR — PIP IN	Less than 2K Ohms
PIP PWR — TFI PWR	Less than 200 Ohms
GND — IGN GND	Less than 2 Ohms
PIP In — PIP	Less than 200 Ohms

Fig. 49 TFI-IV ignition system testing

84172071

Stator — TFI

	TFI-IV And TFI With CCD	Part 2 Test 4

TEST STEP	RESULT	ACTION TO TAKE
1. Place the transmission shift lever in the PARK (A/T) or NEUTRAL (M/T) position and set the parking brake.	Yes	GO to Test 6.
	No	REMOVE distributor cap and VERIFY rotation. If OK, GO to Test 5.
CAUTION		
Failure to perform this step may result in the vehicle moving when the starter is subsequently engaged during the test.		
2. Disconnect the harness connector from the TFI module and connect the TFI tester.		
3. Connect the red lead from the tester to the positive (+) side of the battery.		
4. Disconnect the wire at the S terminal of the starter relay, and attach remote starter switch.		
5. Crank the engine using the remote starter switch and note the status of the two LED lamps.		
6. Remove the tester and remote starter switch.		
7. Reconnect the wire to the starter relay and the connector to the TFI.		
8. Did the PIP light blink?		

84172070

Fig. 48 TFI-IV ignition system testing

Ignition Coil and Secondary Wire — TFI-IV And TFI With CCD — Part 2 Test 7

TEST STEP	RESULT	ACTION TO TAKE
1. Disconnect ignition coil connector. Inspect for dirt, corrosion and damage.	Yes	MEASURE resistance of the ignition coil wire (from vehicle). REPLACE if greater than 7,000 ohms per foot.
2. Connect the ignition coil connector to a known good ignition coil.		If OK, REPLACE ignition coil.
3. Connect one end of a known good secondary wire to the spark tester. Connect the other end to the known good ignition coil.	No	RECONNECT coil connector to the vehicle coil and spark tester to vehicle secondary wire and GO to Test 8.
CAUTION DO NOT HOLD THE COIL while performing this test. Dangerous voltages may be present on the metal laminations as well as the high voltage tower.		
4. Crank engine.		
5. Turn ignition switch to OFF position.		
6. **Was spark present?**		

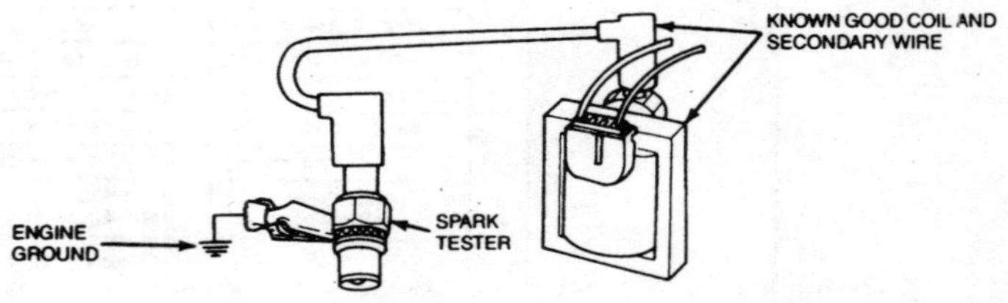

Fig. 51 TFI-IV ignition system testing

TFI Module — TFI-IV And TFI-IV With CCD — Part 2 Test 6

TEST STEP	RESULT	ACTION TO TAKE
1. Use status of Tach light from Test 4.	Yes	GO to Test 7.
2. **Did the Tach light blink?**	No	REPLACE TFI module and CHECK for spark using the method described in Test 1. If spark was not present REPLACE the coil also.

Fig. 50 TFI-IV ignition system testing

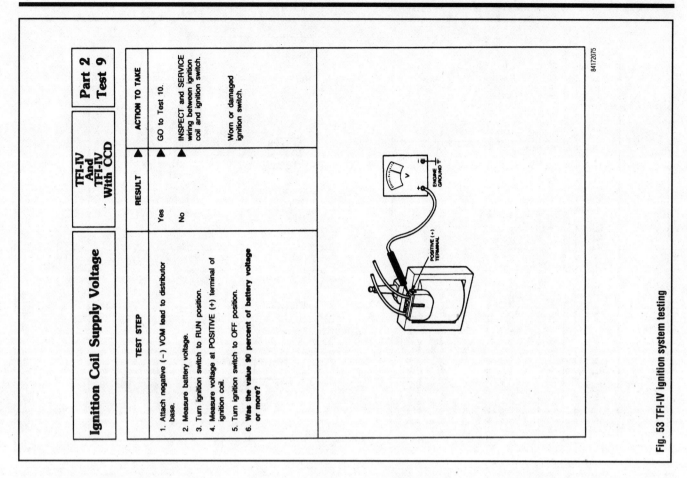

Ignition Coil Supply Voltage

	TFI-IV And TFI-IV With CCD	Part 2 Test 9

TEST STEP	RESULT	ACTION TO TAKE
1. Attach negative (–) VOM lead to distributor base.	Yes	GO to Test 10.
2. Measure battery voltage.	No	INSPECT and SERVICE wiring between ignition coil and ignition switch.
3. Turn ignition switch to RUN position.		
4. Measure voltage at POSITIVE (+) terminal of ignition coil.		Worn or damaged ignition switch.
5. Turn ignition switch to OFF position.		
6. Was the value 90 percent of battery voltage or more?		

84172075

Fig. 53 TFI-IV ignition system testing

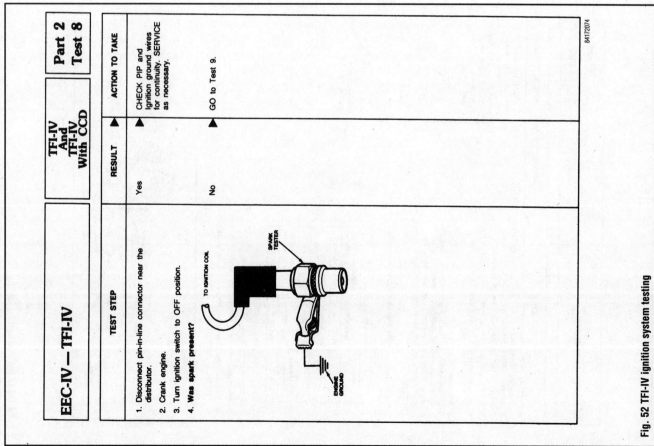

EEC-IV—TFI-IV

	TFI-IV And TFI-IV With CCD	Part 2 Test 8

TEST STEP	RESULT	ACTION TO TAKE
1. Disconnect pin-in-line connector near the distributor.	Yes	CHECK PIP and ignition ground wires for continuity. SERVICE as necessary.
2. Crank engine.	No	GO to Test 9.
3. Turn ignition switch to OFF position.		
4. Was spark present?		

84172074

Fig. 52 TFI-IV ignition system testing

Spark Timing Advance—EEC

Test 1

TEST STEP	RESULT	ACTION TO TAKE
1. Key in OFF position. 2. Disconnect the pin in-line connector near the TFI module (SPOUT). 3. Attach the negative (–) VOM lead to the distributor base. 4. Start the engine and measure the battery voltage at idle. 5. Measure the voltage on the TFI module side of the pin in-line connector. 6. **Is the result between 30 percent and 60 percent of battery voltage?**	Yes No	TFI is OK. GO to Test 2.

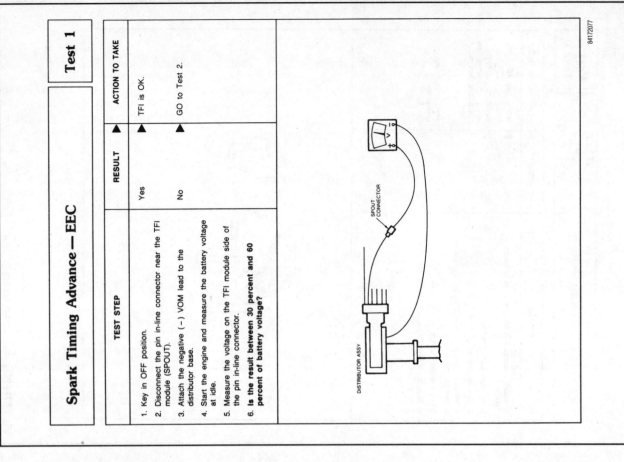

SPOUT CONNECTOR

DISTRIBUTOR ASSY

Fig. 55 TFI-IV ignition system testing

84172077

Wiring Harness

TFI-IV **Part 2 Test 10**

TEST STEP	RESULT	ACTION TO TAKE
1. Separate wiring harness connector from ignition module. Inspect for dirt, corrosion, and damage. **NOTE: Push connector tabs to separate.** 2. Disconnect the wire at S terminal of starter relay. 3. Attach negative (–) VOM lead to distributor base. 4. Measure battery voltage. 5. Following the appropriate table below, measure connector terminal voltage by attaching VOM to small straight pin inserted into connector terminal and turning ignition switch to position shown. **CAUTION** **Do not allow straight pin to contact electrical ground.**	Yes No	INSPECT for faults in wiring between the coil and TFI module terminal No. 2 or any additional wiring or components connected to that circuit. INSPECT for faults in wiring harness and connectors.

TFI without CCD

Connector Terminal	Wire/Circuit	Ignition Switch Test Position
#3	Run Circuit	Run and Start
#4	Start Circuit	Start

TFI with CCD

Connector Terminal	Wire/Circuit	Ignition Switch Test Position
#3	Run Circuit	Run and Start

| 6. Turn ignition switch to OFF position.
7. Remove straight pin.
8. Reconnect wire to S terminal of starter relay.
9. **Was the value at least 90 percent of battery voltage in each case?** | | Damaged or worn ignition switch. |

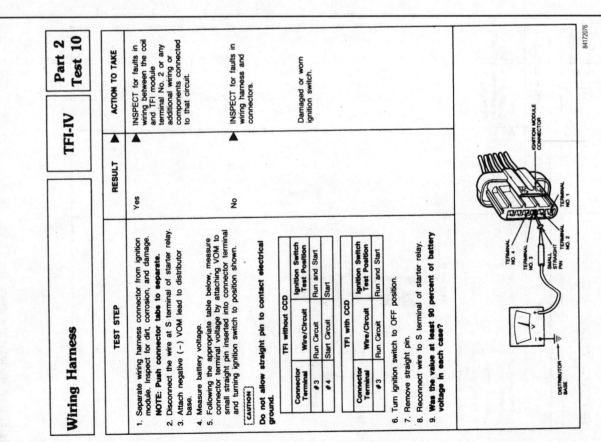

IGNITION MODULE CONNECTOR

TERMINAL NO. 1

TERMINAL NO. 4
TERMINAL NO. 3
SMALL STRAIGHT PIN
TERMINAL NO. 2

DISTRIBUTOR BASE

Fig. 54 TFI-IV ignition system testing

84172076

Preliminary Checkout, Equipment and Notes

Checkout

- Visually inspect the engine compartment to ensure all vacuum hoses and spark plug wires are properly and securely connected.
- Examine all wiring harnesses and connectors for damaged insulation, burned, overheated, damaged pins, loose or broken conditions. **Check sensor shield connector.** Make sure EDIS module mounting screw is tight.
- Be certain the battery is fully charged.
- All accessories should be off during diagnosis.

Equipment (Required)

Obtain the following test equipment or an equivalent

- EDIS Diagnostic Cable (Rotunda 007-00059)
- Spark Tester, Neon bulb type (Special Service Tool D89P-6666-A).
- Volt-Ohmmeter (Rotunda 007-00001).
- Remote starter switch.
- EEC-IV Breakout Box (Rotunda T83L-50-EEC-IV).
- Spark Tester, Gap type (Special Service Tool D81P-6666-A). A spark plug with a broken side electrode is not sufficient to check for spark and may lead to incorrect results.
- Inductive Timing Light (Rotunda 059-00006).

Fig. 57 EDIS testing—1992 vehicles

Spark Timing Advance—EEC   Test 2

TEST STEP	RESULT	ACTION TO TAKE
1. Separate wiring harness connector from ignition module. Inspect for dirt, corrosion and damage. **NOTE: PUSH connector tabs to separate.** 2. Using small straight pin inserted into connector terminal 5, measure resistance between the terminal and the TFI module side of the pin in-line connector. 3. **Is the result less than 5 ohms?**	▲ Yes ▲ No	▲ REPLACE the TFI module. ▲ SERVICE the wiring between the pin in-line connector and the TFI connector.

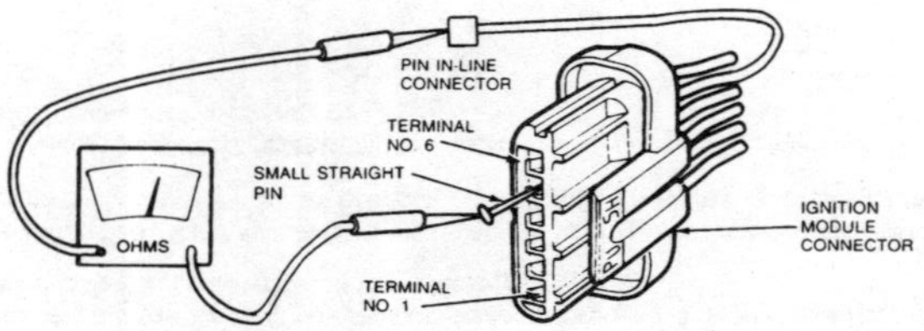

Fig. 56 TFI-IV ignition system testing

Preliminary Checkout, Equipment and Notes

Notes

- When making measurements on a wiring harness, both a visual inspection and a continuity test should be performed. Inspect the connector pins for damage (corrosion, bent or spread pins, etc.) when directed to remove a connector.

- Spark timing adjustments are not possible.

- When making voltage checks a GROUND reading means any value within a range of zero to 1 volt. Also VBAT readings mean any value that falls within a range of VBAT to 2 volts less than VBAT.

- When making voltage checks and a reference to ground is made use either the negative battery lead or cast iron on the engine. BAT+ means the positive battery cable at the battery.

- When using the spark plug firing indicator, place the grooved end as close as possible to the plug boot. Very weak or no flashing may be caused by a fouled plug.

- LED test lamp. A 12 volt test lamp should not be used to test circuit signals. It will load the circuit and may cause erroneous measurements or improper EDIS/EEC-IV operation. (i.e. engine stall).

- Do not use an incandescent test lamp to check the VRS-, VRS+, PIP, IDM, or SAW circuits. The lamp will prevent the circuit from operating.

Fig. 58 EDIS testing—1992 vehicles

EDIS Breakout Box Overlay Acronyms

EDIS Acronyms

There is a logic to the names on the Schematic and Overlays for the EDIS DIAGNOSTIC HARNESS that will help you.

Acronym	Definition
PIP	Profile Ignition Pickup (EDIS output signal).
IDM	Ignition Diagnostic Monitor (Diagnostic signal to EEC-IV).
SAW	Spark Angle Word (EEC spark control signal).
IGN GND	Ignition Ground (Low current ground reference).
VRS-	Variable Reluctance Sensor Negative.
VRS+	Variable Reluctance Sensor Positive.
VRS Shield	Variable Reluctance Sensor Shield.
BAT+	Battery Positive.
GND or BAT-	Battery Negative.
VBAT	Ignition Power to component.
C1, C2, C3, C4	Coil Drive (For Coils 1, 2, 3 and 4).
vPWR	Vehicle Power

Overlay Designators

On the Schematic and Overlays, each of these signals is identified along with a suffix letter that tells you where the measurement is being taken. The key to these letters is:

Prefix/Suffix	Measurement Location
Prefix	"J" is a Breakout Box jack.
Suffix	"E" is at the EDIS Module.
Suffix	"S" is at the sensor.
Suffix	"C" is at the coil.

A couple of examples:

Acronym	Definition
VBAT C	VBAT at the Coil.
VBAT E	VBAT at the EDIS Module.

Fig. 59 EDIS testing—1992 vehicles

4.6L—2V Car EDIS No Start — Pinpoint Test A

	TEST STEP	RESULT		ACTION TO TAKE
A1	PERFORM EEC-IV QUICK TEST			
	• Was Quick Test performed according to procedures	Yes	▶	GO to **A2**.
		No	▶	PERFORM Quick Test.
	NOTE: These diagnostic procedures are designed to correct one ignition failure at a time. When a component is replaced or a service is completed, remove all test equipment, reconnect all components and rerun Quick Test.			
A2	CHECK FOR SPARK DURING CRANK			
	• Using a Neon Bulb Spark Tester (Special Service Tool D89P-6666-A) or Air Gap Spark Tester (Special Service Tool D81P-6666-A), check for spark at all spark plug wires while cranking.	Yes	▶	GO to **A13**.
		No	▶	GO to **A3**.
	• Was spark consistent on ALL spark plug wires (one spark per crankshaft revolution)?			
A3	CHECK PLUGS AND WIRES			
	• Check spark plug wires for insulation damage, looseness, shorting or other damage.	Yes	▶	REINSTALL plugs and wires. GO to **A4**.
	• Remove and check spark plugs for damage, wear, carbon deposits and proper plug gap.	No	▶	SERVICE or REPLACE damaged component. REMOVE all test equipment. RECONNECT all components. CLEAR Continuous Memory. RERUN Quick Test.
	• Are spark plugs and wires OK?			
A4	CHECK VEHICLE PERFORMANCE WITH EDIS DIAGNOSTIC CABLE INSTALLED			
	WARNING: NEVER CONNECT THE EEC-IV PROCESSOR TO THE EEC-IV BREAKOUT BOX WHEN PERFORMING EDIS DIAGNOSTICS.	Yes	▶	GO to **A32**.
		No	▶	GO to **A5**.
	• Key off.			
	• Install EDIS diagnostic cable to breakout box and EDIS module.			
	• Do not connect VRS tee or coil tee.			
	• Use EDIS 8 overlay.			
	• Connect EDIS diagnostic cable negative lead to battery, leave positive lead disconnected.			
	• Set EDIS diagnostic cable box switch to ''8 cylinder'' position.			
	• Will vehicle start and run?			

Fig. 61 EDIS testing—1992 vehicles

84172083

4.6L—2V Car EDIS Diagnostics — Pinpoint Test — Typical Values

The Following Voltage Readings are Typical for a Normal Vehicle:

First Pin	Second Pin	Key On Engine Off (Volts)	Engine Cranking (Volts AC)	Engine Running (Volts AC)
VRS+S (J31)	VRS-S (J32)	0	0.5-1.5	2-5
VRS+E (J48)	VRS-E (J47)	0	0.5-1.5	2-5
PIPE (J43)	PWR GND (J53)	0	—	5-7
C1E (J51)	PWR GND (J53)	VBAT VDC	1-1.5	1.2-1.6
C2E (J27)	PWR GND (J53)	VBAT VDC	1-1.5	1.2-1.6
C3E (J54)	PWR GND (J53)	VBAT VDC	1-1.5	1.2-1.6
C4E (J55)	PWR GND (J53)	VBAT VDC	1-1.5	1.2-1.6
C1C (J3)	PWR GND (J53)	0	0.1-0.8	0.2-0.4
C2C (J6)	PWR GND (J53)	0	0.1-0.8	0.2-0.4
C3C (J10)	PWR GND (J53)	0	0.1-0.8	0.2-0.4
C4C (J18)	PWR GND (J53)	0	0.1-0.8	0.2-0.4
SAW (J45)	PWR GND (J53)	0	0.01-0.3	0.5-3
IDME (J41)	PWR GND (J53)	0	0.1-0.5	0.22-2.0
VRS+E (J48)	PWR GND (J53)	0	0.1-0.9	1.5-1.9
VRS-E (J47)	PWR GND (J53)	0	0.1-0.9	1.5-1.9

NOTE:
- Do not connect the positive lead of the EDIS diagnostic cable or VRS tee until directed to do so.
- The SAW and IDM detectors in the EDIS diagnostic will not work unless the positive and negative leads of the cable are connected.
- The vehicle battery voltage must be at least 12 volts DC.
- Be careful not to bring a fluorescent trouble lamp close to the vehicle wiring. If the key is on and the VRS is disconnected, the EDIS module may fire the coil.
- When using a DVOM to measure DC voltage readings, connect the positive lead to the jack identified with A (+) sign and the negative lead to the jack with A (-) sign.

Fig. 60 EDIS testing—1992 vehicles

84172082

4.6L—2V Car EDIS No Start — Pinpoint Test A

TEST STEP	RESULT		ACTION TO TAKE
A5 CHECK PWR GND TO EDIS MODULE • Key off. • DVOM on 200 ohm scale. • Measure resistance between J53 (PWR GND) and J7 (BAT-) at breakout box. • **Is the resistance less than 5.0 ohms?**	Yes No	▶ ▶	GO to **A6**. CHECK connectors, SERVICE or REPLACE harness. Power ground is open. REMOVE all test equipment. RECONNECT all components. CLEAR Continuous Memory. RERUN Quick Test.
A6 CHECK FOR VBAT TO EDIS MODULE • Key off. • DVOM on 20 volt DC scale. • Key on, engine off. • Measure voltage between (+)J35 (VPWR E) and (-)J7 (BAT-) at breakout box. • **Is DC voltage greater than 10.5 volts?**	Yes No	▶ ▶	GO to **A7**. CHECK connectors, SERVICE or REPLACE harness. VPWR to EDIS module is open. REMOVE all test equipment. RECONNECT all components. CLEAR Continuous Memory. RERUN Quick Test.
A7 CHECK VRS + BIAS AT EDIS MODULE • Key off. • DVOM on 20 volt DC scale. • Key on, engine off. • Measure voltage between (+)J48 (VRS+ E) and (-)J7 (BAT-) at breakout box. • **Is DC voltage between 1.0 and 2.0 volts?**	Yes No	▶ ▶	GO to **A21**. GO to **A8**.
A8 CHECK VRS + BIAS —BIAS FAULT—VRS • Key off. • Disconnect VRS from vehicle harness connector. • DVOM on 20 volt DC scale. • Key on, engine off. • Measure voltage between (+)J48 (VRS+ E) and (-)J7 (BAT-) at breakout box. • **Is DC voltage greater than 1.0 volt but less than 2.0 volts?**	Yes No	▶ ▶	GO to **A9**. GO to **A29**.

Fig. 62 EDIS testing—1992 vehicles

4.6L—2V Car EDIS No Start — Pinpoint Test A

TEST STEP	RESULT		ACTION TO TAKE
A9 CHECK VRS — BIAS—VRS DISCONNECTED • Key off. • DVOM on 20 volt DC scale. • Key on, engine off. • Measure voltage between (+)J47 (VRS-E) and (-)J7 (BAT-) at breakout box. • **Is DC voltage between 1.0 and 2.0 volts?**	Yes No	▶ ▶	REPLACE VR sensor. Short to ground in VR sensor. REMOVE all test equipment. RECONNECT all components. CLEAR Continuous Memory. RERUN Quick Test. GO to **A10**.
A10 CHECK VRS — HIGH or LOW BIAS—BIAS FAULT • **Was bias voltage reading in Step A9 less than 1.0 volt?**	Yes No	▶ ▶	GO to **A11**. GO to **A12**.
A11 CHECK VRS — FOR SHORT TO GROUND—BIAS LOW FAULT — VR SENSOR AND EDIS MODULE DISCONNECTED • Key off. • Disconnect EDIS module from EDIS module tee, leave EDIS diagnostic cable connected to vehicle harness connector. • DVOM on 20K ohm scale. • Measure resistance between J47 (VRS-E) and J7 (BAT-) at breakout box. • **Is the resistance greater than 10K ohms?**	Yes No	▶	REPLACE EDIS module. VRS is shorted low. REMOVE all test equipment. RECONNECT all components. CLEAR Continuous Memory. RERUN Quick Test. CHECK connectors, SERVICE or REPLACE harness. VRS is shorted low. REMOVE all test equipment. RECONNECT all components. CLEAR Continuous Memory. RERUN Quick Test.

Fig. 63 EDIS testing—1992 vehicles

4.6L—2V Car EDIS No Start — Pinpoint Test A

	TEST STEP	RESULT		ACTION TO TAKE
A14	CHECK FOR PIP OPEN TO PROCESSOR—PROCESSOR DISCONNECTED			
	• Key off.			
	• DVOM on 200 ohm scale.			
	• Install a second breakout box to processor vehicle harness connector.			
	• Measure resistance between J43 (PIP E) at the breakout box and Pin 56 (PIP) at the second breakout box.			
	Is resistance less than 5.0 ohms?	Yes	▲	GO to A15.
		No	▲	CHECK connectors, SERVICE or REPLACE harness. PIP is open. REMOVE all test equipment. RECONNECT all components. CLEAR Continuous Memory. RERUN Quick Test.
A15	CHECK IGN GND AT EDIS MODULE—PROCESSOR DISCONNECTED			
	• Key off.			
	• DVOM on 2K ohm scale.			
	• Measure resistance between J50 (IGN GND E) and J7 (BAT-) at breakout box.			
	Is resistance less than 1025 ohms?	Yes	▲	GO to A16.
		No	▲	GO to A17.
A16	CHECK FOR IGN GND OPEN TO PROCESSOR—PROCESSOR DISCONNECTED			
	• Key off.			
	• DVOM on 2K ohm scale.			
	• Measure resistance between J50 (IGN GND E) at the breakout box and Pin 16 (IGN GND) at the second breakout box.			
	Is resistance less than 1025 ohms?	Yes	▲	Ignition system is OK. REMOVE all test equipment. RECONNECT all components. CLEAR Continuous Memory. RERUN Quick Test.
		No	▲	CHECK connectors, SERVICE or REPLACE harness. IGN GND is open. REMOVE all test equipment. RECONNECT all components. CLEAR Continuous Memory. RERUN Quick Test.

Fig. 65 EDIS testing—1992 vehicles

4.6L—2V Car EDIS No Start — Pinpoint Test A

	TEST STEP	RESULT		ACTION TO TAKE
A12	CHECK VRS FOR SHORT HIGH—BIAS HIGH FAULT—VRS AND EDIS MODULE DISCONNECTED			
	• Key off.			
	• Disconnect EDIS module from EDIS module tee; leave EDIS diagnostic cable connected to vehicle harness connector.			
	• DVOM 20 volt DC scale.			
	• Key on, engine off.			
	• Measure voltage between (+)J47 (VRS- E) and (-)J7 (BAT-) at the breakout box.			
	Is DC voltage less than 0.5 volts?	Yes	▲	REPLACE EDIS module. VRS- shorted high. REMOVE all test equipment. RECONNECT all components. CLEAR Continuous Memory. RERUN Quick Test.
		No	▲	CHECK connectors, SERVICE or REPLACE harness. VRS- is shorted high. REMOVE all test equipment. RECONNECT all components. CLEAR Continuous Memory. RERUN Quick Test.
A13	CHECK PIP AT EDIS MODULE			
	WARNING: NEVER CONNECT THE EEC-IV PROCESSOR TO THE EEC-IV BREAKOUT BOX WHEN PERFORMING EDIS DIAGNOSTICS.			
	• Key off.			
	• Install EDIS diagnostic cable to the breakout box and EDIS module.			
	Do not connect VR sensor tee or coil tee.			
	• Use EDIS 8 overlay.			
	• Connect EDIS diagnostic cable negative lead to battery, leave positive lead disconnected.			
	• Set EDIS diagnostic cable box switch to "8 cylinder" position.			
	• DVOM on 20 volt AC scale.			
	• Crank engine and measure voltage between J43 (PIP E) and J7 (BAT-) at the breakout box.			
	Is the settled AC voltage reading greater than 3.5 volts?	Yes	▲	GO to A14.
		No	▲	GO to A18.

Fig. 64 EDIS testing—1992 vehicles

4.6L—2V Car EDIS No Start — Pinpoint Test A

TEST STEP	RESULT	ACTION TO TAKE
A17 CHECK PWR GND TO EDIS MODULE—PWR GND FAULT • Key off. • DVOM on 200 ohm scale. • Measure resistance between J53 (PWR GND) and J7 (BAT-) at breakout box. • **Is resistance less than 5.0 ohms?**	Yes	▶ REPLACE EDIS module. REMOVE all test equipment. RECONNECT all components. CLEAR Continuous Memory. RERUN Quick Test.
	No	▶ CHECK connectors, SERVICE or REPLACE harness. Power ground to EDIS module is open. REMOVE all test equipment. RECONNECT all components. CLEAR Continuous Memory. RERUN Quick Test.
A18 CHECK PIP AT EDIS MODULE—PIP FAULT—PIP CIRCUIT DISCONNECTED • Key off. • DVOM on 20 volt AC scale. • Push and hold EDIS diagnostic cable PIP push button down (opens PIP circuit to processor). • Crank engine and measure voltage between J43 (PIP E) and J7 (BAT-) at breakout box. • **Is settled AC voltage reading greater than 3.5 volts?**	Yes	▶ GO to A19.
	No	▶ REPLACE EDIS module. No PIP output from EDIS. REMOVE all test equipment. RECONNECT all components. CLEAR Continuous Memory. RERUN Quick Test.
A19 CHECK FOR PIP SHORT TO GROUND IN HARNESS—EDIS MODULE AND PROCESSOR DISCONNECTED • Key off. • Disconnect EEC processor. • Disconnect EDIS module from EDIS module tee. Leave EDIS diagnostic cable connected to EDIS vehicle harness connector. • Disconnect EDIS diagnostic cable positive lead to battery. • DVOM on 20K ohm scale. • Measure resistance between J43 (PIP E) and J7 (BAT-) at breakout box. • **Is resistance greater than 10K ohms?**	Yes	▶ GO to A20.
	No	▶ CHECK connectors, SERVICE or REPLACE harness. PIP is shorted low. REMOVE all test equipment. RECONNECT all components. CLEAR Continuous Memory. RERUN Quick Test.

Fig. 67 EDIS testing—1992 vehicles

4.6L—2V Car EDIS No Start — Pinpoint Test A

TEST STEP	RESULT	ACTION TO TAKE
A20 CHECK FOR PIP SHORT HIGH—EDIS MODULE AND PROCESSOR DISCONNECTED • Key off. • DVOM on 20 volt DC scale. • Key on, engine off. • Measure voltage between J43 (PIP E) and J7 (BAT-) at breakout box. • **Is DC voltage less than 0.5 volts?**	Yes	▶ REPLACE processor. PIP is shorted in processor. REMOVE all test equipment. RECONNECT all components. CLEAR Continuous Memory. RERUN Quick Test.
	No	▶ CHECK connectors, SERVICE or REPLACE harness. PIP is shorted high. REMOVE all test equipment. RECONNECT all components. CLEAR Continuous Memory. RERUN Quick Test.
A21 CHECK VRS AMPLITUDE AT EDIS MODULE • Key off. • DVOM on 20 volt AC scale. • Crank engine and measure voltage between J48 (VRS+ E) and J47 (VRS- E) at breakout box. • **Is settled AC voltage reading greater than 0.4 volts?**	Yes	▶ GO to Pinpoint Test Step D1.
	No	▶ GO to A22.
A22 CHECK VRS AMPLITUDE AT EDIS MODULE—AMPLITUDE FAULT—EDIS MODULE DISCONNECTED • Key off. • Disconnect EDIS module from EDIS module tee, leave EDIS diagnostic cable connected to vehicle harness connector. • DVOM 20 volt AC scale. • Crank engine and measure voltage between J48 (VRS+ E) and J47 (VRS- E) at breakout box. • **Is settled AC voltage reading greater than 0.4 volts?**	Yes	▶ REPLACE EDIS module. VRS is shorted in EDIS module. REMOVE all test equipment. RECONNECT all components. CLEAR Continuous Memory. RERUN Quick Test.
	No	▶ GO to A23.

Fig. 67 EDIS testing—1992 vehicles

4.6L—2V Car EDIS No Start | **Pinpoint Test** | **A**

TEST STEP	RESULT	ACTION TO TAKE
A27 CHECK VRS AIR GAP AND TRIGGER WHEEL • Key off. • Check trigger wheel for damage. • Check VRS air gap. • **Are air gap and trigger data wheel OK?**	Yes ▲	REPLACE VR sensor. No output from sensor. REMOVE all test equipment. RECONNECT all components. CLEAR Continuous Memory. RERUN Quick Test.
	No ▲	SERVICE or REPLACE bad parts. REMOVE all test equipment. RECONNECT all components. CLEAR Continuous Memory. RERUN Quick Test.
A28 CHECK VRS + SHORTED TO VRS—RESISTANCE LOW FAULT—VRS DISCONNECTED • Key off. • Disconnect VR sensor from the vehicle harness connector. • DVOM on 20K ohm scale. • Measure resistance between J48 (VRS+E) and J47 (VRS-E) at the breakout box. • **Is resistance greater than 3K ohms?**	Yes ▲	REPLACE VR sensor. Shorted sensor windings. REMOVE all test equipment. RECONNECT all components. CLEAR Continuous Memory. RERUN Quick Test.
	No ▲	CHECK connectors, SERVICE or REPLACE harness. VRS+ shorted to VRS- in harness. REMOVE all test equipment. RECONNECT all components. CLEAR Continuous Memory. RERUN Quick Test.
A29 CHECK VRS + HIGH or LOW—VR SENSOR DISCONNECTED • **Was bias voltage reading in Step A8 less than 1.0 volts?**	Yes ▲	GO to A30.
	No ▲	GO to A31.

Fig. 69 EDIS testing—1992 vehicles

84172091

4.6L—2V Car EDIS No Start | **Pinpoint Test** | **A**

TEST STEP	RESULT	ACTION TO TAKE
A23 CHECK VRS RESISTANCE • Key off. • DVOM on 20K ohm scale. • Measure resistance between J47 (VRS-E) and J48 (VRS+E) at the breakout box. • **Is resistance between 2300 and 2500 ohms?**	Yes ▲	GO to A27.
	No ▲	GO to A24.
A24 CHECK VRS HIGH OR LOW RESISTANCE—RESISTANCE FAULT • Key off. • DVOM on 20K ohm scale. • Measure resistance between J47 (VRS-E) and J48 (VRS+E) at breakout box. • **Is resistance less than 2550 ohms?**	Yes ▲	GO to A28.
	No ▲	GO to A25.
A25 CHECK VRS + OPEN—RESISTANCE HIGH FAULT • Key off. • Connect VR sensor tee to VR sensor and vehicle harness connector. • DVOM on 20K ohm scale. • Measure resistance between J31 (VRS+S) and J48 (VRS+E) at the breakout box. • **Is resistance less than 2025 ohms?**	Yes ▲	GO to A26.
	No ▲	CHECK connectors, SERVICE or REPLACE harness. VRS+ open. REMOVE all test equipment. RECONNECT all components. CLEAR Continuous Memory. RERUN Quick Test.
A26 CHECK VRS — OPEN FAULT • Key off. • DVOM on 20K ohm scale. • Measure resistance between J32 (VRS-S) and J47 (VRS-E) at the breakout box. • **Is resistance less than 2025 ohms?**	Yes ▲	REPLACE VR sensor. High resistance. REMOVE all test equipment. RECONNECT all components. CLEAR Continuous Memory. RERUN Quick Test.
	No ▲	CHECK connectors, SERVICE or REPLACE harness. VRS— open. REMOVE all test equipment. RECONNECT all components. CLEAR Continuous Memory. RERUN Quick Test.

Fig. 68 EDIS testing—1992 vehicles

84172090

4.6L—2V Car EDIS No Start — Pinpoint Test A

	TEST STEP	RESULT	ACTION TO TAKE
A30	CHECK VRS + FOR SHORT TO GROUND—VRS AND EDIS MODULE DISCONNECTED • Key off. • Disconnect the EDIS module from EDIS module tee, leave EDIS diagnostic cable connected to vehicle harness connector. • DVOM on 20K ohm scale. • Measure resistance between J48 (VRS+) and J7 (BAT-) at breakout box. • **Is resistance greater than 10K ohms?**	Yes ▲ No ▲	REPLACE EDIS module. REMOVE all test equipment. RECONNECT all components. CLEAR Continuous Memory. RERUN Quick Test. CHECK connectors, SERVICE or REPLACE harness. VRS+ is shorted low. REMOVE all test equipment. RECONNECT all components. CLEAR Continuous Memory. RERUN Quick Test.
A31	CHECK VRS + FOR SHORT HIGH—BIAS HIGH FAULT—VRS AND EDIS MODULE DISCONNECTED • Key off. • Disconnect EDIS module from EDIS module tee, leave EDIS diagnostic cable connected to vehicle harness connector. • DVOM on 20 volt DC scale. • Key on, engine off. • Measure voltage between +J48 (VRS+ E) and -J7 (BAT-) at breakout box. • **Is DC voltage less than 0.5 volts?**	Yes ▲ No ▲	REPLACE EDIS module. REMOVE all test equipment. RECONNECT all components. CLEAR Continuous Memory. RERUN Quick Test. CHECK connectors, SERVICE or REPLACE harness. VRS+ is shorted high. REMOVE all test equipment. RECONNECT all components. CLEAR Continuous Memory. RERUN Quick Test.
A32	CHECK VRS RESISTANCE • Key off. • Disconnect EDIS module from EDIS module tee. Leave EDIS diagnostic cable connected to vehicle harness connector. • DVOM on 20K ohm scale. • Measure resistance between J47 (VRS- E) and J48 (VRS+ E) at breakout box. • **Is resistance between 2300 and 2500 ohms?**	Yes ▲ No ▲	REPLACE EDIS module. REMOVE all test equipment. RECONNECT all components. CLEAR Continuous Memory. RERUN Quick Test. GO to A24.

Fig. 70 EDIS testing—1992 vehicles

4.6L—2V Car EDIS Code 212 IDM Failure — Pinpoint Test B

	TEST STEP	RESULT	ACTION TO TAKE
B1	CHECK FOR IDM AT EDIS MODULE **WARNING: NEVER CONNECT THE EEC-IV PROCESSOR TO EEC-IV BREAKOUT BOX WHEN PERFORMING EDIS DIAGNOSTICS.** • Key off. • Install EDIS diagnostic cable to breakout box, and EDIS module. **Do not connect VR sensor tee or coil tees.** • Use EDIS 8 overlay. • Connect EDIS diagnostic cable negative and positive leads to battery. • Set EDIS diagnostic cable box switch to "8 cylinder" position. • DVOM on 20 volt AC scale. • Start engine and measure voltage between (+)J30 (EDIS diagnostic cable IDM detector) and (-)J7 (BAT-) at breakout box. NOTE: If pulses are present, the IDM detector output will be between 5.0 and 7.0 volts AC. • **Is AC voltage between 5.0 and 7.0 volts?**	Yes ▲ No ▲	GO to B2. GO to B3.
B2	CHECK FOR IDM OPEN TO PROCESSOR—IDM FAULT—EDIS MODULE AND PROCESSOR DISCONNECTED • Key off. • Disconnect processor. • Disconnect EDIS module from EDIS module tee, leave EDIS diagnostic cable connected to vehicle harness connector. • DVOM on 200 ohm scale. • Install a second breakout box to processor vehicle harness connector. • Measure resistance between J41 (IDM E) at breakout box and Pin 4 at second breakout box. • **Is resistance less than 5.0 ohms?**	Yes ▲ No ▲	REPLACE processor. Processor does not respond to IDM input. REMOVE all test equipment. RECONNECT all components. CLEAR Continuous Memory. RERUN Quick Test. CHECK connectors, SERVICE or REPLACE harness. IDM is open. REMOVE all test equipment. RECONNECT all components. CLEAR Continuous Memory. RERUN Quick Test.

Fig. 71 EDIS testing—1992 vehicles

4.6L—2V Car EDIS Code 212 IDM Failure	Pinpoint Test	B

	TEST STEP	RESULT	ACTION TO TAKE
B3	CHECK IDM OUTPUT FROM EDIS MODULE—IDM FAULT—IDM CIRCUIT DISCONNECTED • Key off. • DVOM on 20 volt AC scale. • Push and hold EDIS diagnostic cable IDM button down (opens IDM circuit to processor). • Start engine and measure voltage between J30 (EDIS diagnostic cable IDM detector) and J7 (BAT-) at breakout box. • Is AC voltage greater than 5.0 volts?	Yes No	▲ GO to B4. ▲ REPLACE EDIS module. No IDM output from module. REMOVE all test equipment. RECONNECT all components. CLEAR Continuous Memory. RERUN Quick Test.
B4	CHECK FOR IDM SHORT IN PROCESSOR—PROCESSOR DISCONNECTED • Key off. • Disconnect processor. • DVOM on 20 volt AC scale. • Crank engine and measure voltage between J30 (EDIS diagnostic cable IDM detector) and (-)J7 (BAT-) at breakout box. • Is AC voltage greater than 5.0 volts?	Yes No	▲ REPLACE processor. Processor is loading IDM signal. REMOVE all test equipment. RECONNECT all components. CLEAR Continuous Memory. RERUN Quick Test. ▲ GO to B5.
B5	CHECK FOR IDM SHORT TO GROUND IN HARNESS—EDIS MODULE AND PROCESSOR DISCONNECTED • Key off. • Disconnect EDIS module from EDIS module tee, leave EDIS diagnostic cable connected to vehicle harness connector. • DVOM on 20K ohm scale. • Measure resistance between J41 (IDM E) and (-)J7 (BAT-) at breakout box. • Is resistance greater than 10K ohms?	Yes No	▲ GO to B6. ▲ CHECK connectors, SERVICE or REPLACE harness. IDM is shorted low. REMOVE all test equipment. RECONNECT all components. CLEAR Continuous Memory. RERUN Quick Test.

Fig. 72 EDIS testing—1992 vehicles

4.6L—2V Car EDIS Code 212 IDM Failure	Pinpoint Test	B

	TEST STEP	RESULT	ACTION TO TAKE
B6	CHECK FOR IDM SHORT HIGH IN HARNESS—EDIS MODULE AND PROCESSOR DISCONNECTED • Key off. • DVOM on 20 volt DC scale. • Key on, engine off. • Measure voltage between (+)J41 (IDM E) and (-)J7 (BAT-) at breakout box. • Is DC voltage less than 0.5 volts?	Yes No	▲ CHECK connectors, SERVICE or REPLACE harness. IDM is shorted to another wire between EDIS module and processor. REMOVE all test equipment. RECONNECT all components. CLEAR Continuous Memory. RERUN Quick Test. ▲ CHECK connectors, SERVICE or REPLACE harness. IDM is shorted high. REMOVE all test equipment. RECONNECT all components. CLEAR Continuous Memory. RERUN Quick Test.

Fig. 73 EDIS testing—1992 vehicles

4.6L—2V Car EDIS Code 213 Or Lack Of Power Or Poor Fuel Economy — Pinpoint Test C

TEST STEP	RESULT	ACTION TO TAKE
C1 CHECK BASE TIMING **WARNING: NEVER CONNECT EEC-IV PROCESSOR TO EEC-IV BREAKOUT BOX WHEN PERFORMING EDIS DIAGNOSTICS.** • Key off. • Install EDIS diagnostic cable to breakout box and EDIS module. **Do not connect the VR sensor tee or coil tees.** • Use EDIS 8 overlay. • Connect EDIS diagnostic cable negative and positive leads to battery. • Set EDIS diagnostic cable switch to to "8 cylinder" position. • Connect timing light (must be EDIS/DIS compatible). • Start engine and allow it to warm up. • Is timing 10 ± 2 degrees BTDC when the EDIS diagnostic cable SAW detector button is pushed?	Yes No	▶ GO to C2 ▶ GO to C8
C2 CHECK FOR SPARK ANGLE ADVANCE • Is engine timing greater than 15 degrees BTDC when the EDIS diagnostic cable SAW detector button is released?	Yes No	▶ EDIS Ignition System is OK. ▶ GO to C3
C3 CHECK SAW AT EDIS MODULE • Key off. • DVOM on 20 volt AC scale. • Start engine and measure voltage between J21 (EDIS diagnostic cable SAW detector) and (-)J7 (BAT-) at breakout box. • Is AC voltage reading greater than 5.0 volts?	Yes No	▶ REPLACE EDIS module. SAW input to EDIS module is OK, but no spark advance is present. REMOVE all test equipment. RECONNECT all components. CLEAR Continuous Memory. RERUN Quick Test. ▶ GO to C4

Fig. 74 EDIS testing—1992 vehicles

4.6L—2V Car EDIS Code 213 Or Lack Of Power Or Poor Fuel Economy — Pinpoint Test C

TEST STEP	RESULT	ACTION TO TAKE
C4 CHECK FOR SAW SHORT IN EDIS MODULE—SAW FAULT—SAW CIRCUIT DISCONNECTED • Key off. • DVOM on 20 volt AC scale. • Push and hold EDIS diagnostic cable SAW button down (open SAW circuit to EDIS module). • Start engine and measure voltage between (+)J21 (EDIS diagnostic cable SAW detector) and (-)J7 (BAT-) at breakout box. • Is AC voltage reading greater than 5.0 volts?	Yes No	▶ REPLACE EDIS module. SAW is shorted in EDIS module. REMOVE all test equipment. RECONNECT all components. CLEAR Continuous Memory. RERUN Quick Test. ▶ GO to C5
C5 CHECK FOR SAW SHORT TO GROUND IN HARNESS—EDIS MODULE AND PROCESSOR DISCONNECTED • Key off. • Disconnect processor. • Disconnect the EDIS module from EDIS module tee, leave EDIS diagnostic cable connected to vehicle harness connector. • DVOM on 20K ohm scale. • Disconnect EDIS diagnostic cable positive lead to battery. • Measure resistance between J45 (SAW E) and J7 (BAT-) at breakout box. • Is the resistance greater than 10K ohms?	Yes No	▶ GO to C6 ▶ CHECK connectors, SERVICE or REPLACE harness. SAW is shorted low. REMOVE all test equipment. RECONNECT all components. CLEAR Continuous Memory. RERUN Quick Test.
C6 CHECK FOR SAW SHORT HIGH IN HARNESS—EDIS MODULE AND PROCESSOR DISCONNECTED • Key off. • DVOM on 20 volt DC scale. • Key on, engine off. • Measure voltage between J45 (SAW E) and J7 (BAT-) at the breakout box. • Is DC voltage reading less than 0.5 volts?	Yes No	▶ GO to C7 ▶ CHECK connectors, SERVICE or REPLACE harness. SAW is shorted high. REMOVE all test equipment. RECONNECT all components. CLEAR Continuous Memory. RERUN Quick Test.

Fig. 75 EDIS testing—1992 vehicles

4.6L—2V Car EDIS No Start or Code 217 or 238 and/or Coil Failure — Pinpoint Test D

	TEST STEP	RESULT	ACTION TO TAKE
D1	CHECK FOR SPARK DURING CRANK • Using a Neon Bulb Spark Tester (Special Service Tool D89P-6666-A) or Air Gap Spark Tester (D81P-6666-A), check for spark at all spark plug wires while cranking. • Was spark consistent on ALL spark plug wires (one spark per crankshaft revolution?)	Yes No	▲ The ignition system is OK. ▲ GO to D2.
D2	CHECK FOR SPARK AT RIGHT SPARK PLUG WIRES DURING CRANK • Was spark consistent on all right spark plug wires (one spark per crankshaft revolution)? NOTE: Check spark at spark plugs.	Yes No	▲ GO to D3. ▲ GO to D19.
D3	CHECK LEFT SPARK PLUGS AND WIRES • Check left side coil pack spark plug wires for insulation damage, looseness, shorting or other damage. • Remove and check left side spark plugs for damage, wear, carbon deposits and proper plug gap. • Left coil plugs and wires are attached to the left coil pack. • Are spark plugs and wires OK?	Yes No	▲ REINSTALL plugs and wires. GO to D4. ▲ SERVICE or REPLACE damaged component. REMOVE all test equipment. RECONNECT all components. CLEAR Continuous Memory. RERUN Quick Test.
D4	CHECK FOR VBAT TO LEFT COIL FAULT WARNING: NEVER CONNECT EEC-IV PROCESSOR TO THE EEC-IV BREAKOUT BOX WHEN PERFORMING EDIS DIAGNOSTICS. • Key off. • Install EDIS diagnostic cable to breakout box. • Install the left coil tee. • Connect EDIS diagnostic cable negative lead to battery. • Use 4.6L EDIS 8 overlay. • Set EDIS cable box switch to 8 cylinder position. • DVOM on 20 volt DC scale. • Key on, engine off. • Measure voltage between (+)J11 (VBAT L) and (-)J7 (BAT) at breakout box. • Is DC voltage greater than 10.0 volts?	Yes No	▲ GO to D5. ▲ CHECK connectors, SERVICE or REPLACE harness. VBAT is open to left coil. REMOVE all test equipment. RECONNECT all components. CLEAR Continuous Memory. RERUN Quick Test.

Fig. 77 EDIS testing—1992 vehicles

4.6L—2V Car EDIS Code 213 Or Lack Of Power Or Poor Fuel Economy — Pinpoint Test C

	TEST STEP	RESULT	ACTION TO TAKE
C7	CHECK FOR SAW OPEN TO EDIS MODULE—EDIS MODULE AND PROCESSOR DISCONNECTED • Key off. • DVOM on 200 ohm scale. • Install a second breakout box to the vehicle harness connector. • Measure resistance between J45 (SAW E) at breakout box and Pin 36 at the second breakout box. • Is resistance less than 5.0 ohms?	Yes No	▲ REPLACE processor. SAW is not being transmitted by the processor. REMOVE all test equipment. RECONNECT all components. CLEAR Continuous Memory. RERUN Quick Test. ▲ CHECK connectors, SERVICE or REPLACE harness. SAW is open. REMOVE all test equipment. RECONNECT all components. CLEAR Continuous Memory. RERUN Quick Test.
C8	INSPECT VRS / TRIGGER WHEEL—TIMING FAULT • Is the VR sensor or Trigger Wheel damaged, i.e., loose or misaligned?	Yes No	▲ REPLACE or SERVICE as required. REMOVE all test equipment. RECONNECT all components. CLEAR Continuous Memory. RERUN Quick Test. ▲ REPLACE EDIS module. Incorrect output from EDIS module. REMOVE all test equipment. RECONNECT all components. CLEAR Continuous Memory. RERUN Quick Test.

Fig. 76 EDIS testing—1992 vehicles

4.6L—2V Car EDIS No Start or Code 217 or 238 and/or Coil Failure — Pinpoint Test D

	TEST STEP	RESULT	ACTION TO TAKE
D10	CHECK FOR C4 HIGH AT COIL CONNECTOR—COIL DISCONNECTED • Key on, engine off. • Measure voltage between (+)J18 (LC4C) and (-)J7 (BAT-) at breakout box. • Is DC voltage reading less than 0.5 volts?	Yes No	▲ GO to D11. ▲ GO to D18.
D11	CHECK C3 AT COIL CONNECTOR WHILE CRANKING—COIL DISCONNECTED • Connect EDIS diagnostic cable positive lead to battery. • Connect an incandescent test lamp between J1 (BAT+) and J10 (LC3C). • Crank engine. • **Does lamp blink consistently and brightly (one blink per engine revolution)?**	Yes No	▲ GO to D12. ▲ REPLACE EDIS module. C3 open in EDIS. REMOVE all test equipment. RECONNECT all components. CLEAR Continuous Memory. RERUN Quick Test.
D12	CHECK C4 AT COIL CONNECTOR WHILE CRANKING—COIL DISCONNECTED • Connect an incandescent test lamp between J1 (BAT+) and J18 (LC4C). • Crank engine. • **Does lamp blink consistently and brightly (one blink per engine revolution)?**	Yes No	▲ REPLACE left coil pack. Input to coil pack is OK, but no high voltage output. REMOVE all test equipment. RECONNECT all components. CLEAR Continuous Memory. RERUN Quick Test. ▲ REPLACE EDIS module. C4 open in EDIS module. REMOVE all test equipment. RECONNECT all components. CLEAR Continuous Memory. RERUN Quick Test.

Fig. 79 EDIS testing—1992 vehicles

4.6L—2V Car EDIS No Start or Code 217 or 238 and/or Coil Failure — Pinpoint Test D

	TEST STEP	RESULT	ACTION TO TAKE
D5	CHECK FOR C3 HIGH AT COIL PACK • Key on, engine off. • Measure voltage between (+)J10 (LC3C) and (-)J7 (BAT-) at breakout box. • Is DC voltage reading greater than 10.0 volts?	Yes No	▲ GO to D6. ▲ GO to D13.
D6	CHECK FOR C4 HIGH AT COIL PACK • Key on, engine off. • Measure voltage between (+)J18 (LC4C) and (-)J7 (BAT-) at the breakout box. • Is DC voltage reading greater than 10.0 volts?	Yes No	▲ GO to D7. ▲ GO to D15.
D7	CHECK FOR C3 HIGH AT EDIS MODULE • Key off. • Connect EDIS module tee to the EDIS module and vehicle harness connector. • DVOM on 20 volt DC scale. • Key on, engine off. • Measure voltage between (+)J54 (LC3E) and (-)J7 (BAT-) at the breakout box. • Is DC voltage reading greater than 10.0 volts?	Yes No	▲ GO to D8. ▲ CHECK connectors, SERVICE or REPLACE harness. C3 is open. REMOVE all test equipment. RECONNECT all components. CLEAR Continuous Memory. RERUN Quick Test.
D8	CHECK FOR C4 HIGH AT EDIS MODULE • Key on, engine off. • Measure voltage between (+)J55 (LC4E) and (-)J7 (BAT-) at breakout box. • Is DC voltage reading greater than 10.0 volts?	Yes No	▲ GO to D9. ▲ CHECK connectors, SERVICE or REPLACE harness. C4 is open.REMOVE all test equipment. RECONNECT all components. CLEAR Continuous Memory. RERUN Quick Test.
D9	CHECK FOR C3 HIGH AT COIL CONNECTOR—COIL DISCONNECTED • Key off. • Disconnect left coil pack from coil tee, leave EDIS diagnostic cable connected to vehicle harness left coil connector. • DVOM on 20 volt DC scale. • Key on, engine off. • Measure voltage between (+)J10 (LC3C) and (-)J7 (BAT-) at breakout box. • Is DC voltage reading less than 0.5 volts?	Yes No	▲ GO to D10. ▲ GO to D17.

Fig. 78 EDIS testing—1992 vehicles

4.6L—2V Car EDIS No Start or Code 217 or 238 and/or Coil Failure — Pinpoint Test D

TEST STEP	RESULT	ACTION TO TAKE
D13 CHECK FOR C3 SHORT LOW—COIL DISCONNECTED • Key off. • DVOM on 20K ohm scale. • Disconnect coil from coil tee, leave EDIS diagnostic cable connected to vehicle harness coil connector. • Measure resistance between J7 (BAT-) and J10 (C3C) at breakout box. • **Is resistance reading greater than 2K ohms?**	Yes No	▸ REPLACE Left Coil Pack. C3 open in coil. REMOVE all test equipment. RECONNECT all components. CLEAR Continuous Memory. RERUN Quick Test. ▸ GO to D14.
D14 CHECK FOR C3 SHORT LOW—EDIS MODULE AND COIL DISCONNECTED • Key off. • Disconnect EDIS module from vehicle harness. • DVOM on 20K ohm scale. • Measure resistance between J7 (BAT-) and J10 (C3C) at breakout box. • **Is resistance greater than 10K ohms?**	Yes No	▸ REPLACE EDIS module. C3 is shorted low. REMOVE all test equipment. RECONNECT all components. CLEAR Continuous Memory. RERUN Quick Test. ▸ CHECK connectors, SERVICE or REPLACE harness. C3 is shorted low. REMOVE all test equipment. RECONNECT all components. CLEAR Continuous Memory. RERUN Quick Test.
D15 CHECK FOR C4 SHORT LOW—COIL DISCONNECTED • Key off. • DVOM on 20K ohm scale. • Disconnect coil from coil tee, leave EDIS diagnostic cable connected to vehicle harness coil connector. • Measure resistance between J7 (BAT-) and J18 (LC4C) at breakout box. • **Is resistance reading greater than 2K ohms?**	Yes No	▸ REPLACE left coil pack. C4 open in coil. REMOVE all test equipment. RECONNECT all components. CLEAR Continuous Memory. RERUN Quick Test. ▸ GO to D16.

Fig. 80 EDIS testing—1992 vehicles

4.6L-2V Car EDIS No Start or Code 215 or 216 and/or Coil Failure — Pinpoint Test D

TEST STEP	RESULT	ACTION TO TAKE
D32 CHECK FOR C2 SHORT LOW—EDIS MODULE AND COIL DISCONNECTED • Key off. • Disconnect EDIS module from vehicle harness. • DVOM on 20K ohm scale. • Measure resistance between J6 (RC2C) and J7 (BAT-) at breakout box. • **Is resistance reading greater than 10K ohms?**	Yes No	▸ REPLACE EDIS module. C2 is shorted low. REMOVE all test equipment. RECONNECT all components. CLEAR Continuous Memory. RERUN Quick Test. ▸ CHECK connectors, SERVICE or REPLACE harness. C2 is shorted low. REMOVE all test equipment. RECONNECT all components. CLEAR Continuous Memory. RERUN Quick Test.
D33 CHECK FOR C1 HIGH—EDIS MODULE AND COIL DISCONNECTED • Key off. • Disconnect EDIS module from EDIS module tee, leave EDIS diagnostic cable connected to vehicle harness connector. • DVOM on 20 volt DC scale. • Key on, engine off. • Measure voltage between (+)J3 (RC1C) and (-)J7 (BAT-) at breakout box. • **Is DC voltage reading less than 0.5 volts?**	Yes No	▸ REPLACE EDIS module. REMOVE all test equipment. RECONNECT all components. CLEAR Continuous Memory. RERUN Quick Test. ▸ CHECK connectors, SERVICE or REPLACE harness. C1 is shorted high. REMOVE all test equipment. RECONNECT all components. CLEAR Continuous Memory. RERUN Quick Test.

Fig. 81 EDIS testing—1992 vehicles

4.6L—2V Car EDIS No Start or Code 217 or 238 and/or Coil Failure

Pinpoint Test		D

TEST STEP	RESULT	ACTION TO TAKE
D18 CHECK FOR C4 HIGH—EDIS MODULE AND COIL DISCONNECTED • Key off. • Disconnect EDIS module from EDIS module tee, leave EDIS diagnostic cable connected to vehicle harness connector. • DVOM on 20 volt DC scale. • Key on, engine off. • Measure voltage between (+)J18 (LC4C) and (-)J7 (BAT-) at breakout box. • Is DC voltage reading less than 0.5 volts?	Yes No	▲ REPLACE EDIS module. C4 is shorted high in EDIS module. REMOVE all test equipment. RECONNECT all components. CLEAR Continuous Memory. RERUN Quick Test. ▲ CHECK connectors, SERVICE or REPLACE harness. C4 is shorted high. REMOVE all test equipment. RECONNECT all components. CLEAR Continuous Memory. RERUN Quick Test.

Fig. 82 EDIS testing—1992 vehicles

84172104

4.6L-2V Car EDIS No Start or Code 215 or 216 and/or Coil Failure

Pinpoint Test		D

TEST STEP	RESULT	ACTION TO TAKE
D19 CHECK RIGHT PLUGS AND WIRES • Check right side coil pack spark plug wires for insulation damage, looseness, shorting or other damage. • Remove and check right spark plugs for damage, wear, carbon deposits and proper plug gap. NOTE: Right coil plugs and wires are attached to the right coil. • Are spark plugs and wires OK?	Yes No	▲ REINSTALL plugs and wires. GO to D20. ▲ SERVICE or REPLACE damaged component. REMOVE all test equipment. RECONNECT all components. CLEAR Continuous Memory. RERUN Quick Test.
D20 CHECK FOR VBAT OPEN TO RIGHT COIL WARNING: NEVER CONNECT EEC-IV PROCESSOR TO THE EEC-IV BREAKOUT BOX WHEN PERFORMING EDIS DIAGNOSTICS. • Key off. • Install EDIS diagnostic cable to the breakout box. • Connect EDIS diagnostic cable negative lead to battery. • Install the right coil tee. • Use 4.6L EDIS 8 overlay. • DVOM on 20 volt DC scale. • Set EDIS cable box switch to 8 cylinder position. • Key on, engine off. • Measure voltage between (+)J5 (VBAT R) and (-)J7 (BAT-) at breakout box. • Is DC voltage greater than 10.0 volts?	Yes No	▲ GO to D21. ▲ CHECK connectors, SERVICE or REPLACE harness. VBAT is open to right coil. REMOVE all test equipment. RECONNECT all components. CLEAR Continuous Memory. RERUN Quick Test.
D21 CHECK FOR C1 HIGH AT COIL PACK • DVOM on 20 volt DC scale. • Key on, engine off. • Measure voltage between (+)J3 (RC1C) and (-)J7 (BAT-) at breakout box. • Is DC voltage reading greater than 10.0 volts?	Yes No	▲ GO to D22. ▲ GO to D29.
D22 CHECK FOR C2 HIGH AT COIL PACK • DVOM on 20 volt DC scale. • Key on, engine off. • Measure voltage between (+)J6 (RC2C) and (-)J7 (BAT-) at breakout box. • Is DC voltage reading greater than 10.0 volts?	Yes No	▲ GO to D23. ▲ GO to D31.

Fig. 83 EDIS testing—1992 vehicles

84172105

4.6L-2V Car EDIS No Start or Code 215 or 216 and/or Coil Failure — Pinpoint Test — D

	TEST STEP	RESULT	ACTION TO TAKE
D27	CHECK C1 AT COIL CONNECTOR WHILE CRANKING ENGINE—COIL DISCONNECTED • Connect EDIS diagnostic cable positive lead to battery. • Connect an incandescent test lamp between J1 (BAT+) and J3 (RC1C). • Crank engine. • **Does lamp blink consistently and brightly (one blink per engine revolution)?**	Yes No	GO to D28. REPLACE EDIS module. C1 is open in EDIS module. REMOVE all test equipment. RECONNECT all components. CLEAR Continuous Memory. RERUN Quick Test.
D28	CHECK C2 AT COIL CONNECTOR WHILE CRANKING ENGINE—COIL DISCONNECTED • Connect an incandescent test lamp between J1 (BAT+) and J6 (RC2C). • Crank engine. • **Does lamp blink consistently and brightly (one blink per engine revolution)?**	Yes No	REPLACE Right Coil Pack. Input to coil pack is OK, but no high voltage output. REMOVE all test equipment. RECONNECT all components. CLEAR Continuous Memory. RERUN Quick Test. REPLACE EDIS module. C2 is open in EDIS module. REMOVE all test equipment. RECONNECT all components. CLEAR Continuous Memory. RERUN Quick Test.
D29	CHECK FOR C1 SHORT LOW—COIL DISCONNECTED • Key off. • DVOM on 20K ohm scale. • Disconnect coil from coil tee, leave EDIS diagnostic cable connected to vehicle harness coil connector. • Measure resistance between J7 (BAT-) and J3 (RC1C) at breakout box. • **Is resistance reading greater than 2K ohms?**	Yes No	REPLACE Right Coil Pack. C1 is open in coil. RECONNECT all components. CLEAR Continuous Memory. RERUN Quick Test. GO to D30.

Fig. 85 EDIS testing—1992 vehicles

4.6L-2V Car EDIS No Start or Code 215 or 216 and/or Coil Failure — Pinpoint Test — D

	TEST STEP	RESULT	ACTION TO TAKE
D23	CHECK FOR C1 HIGH AT EDIS MODULE • Key off. • Connect EDIS module tee to the EDIS module and vehicle harness connector. • DVOM on 20 volt DC scale. • Key on, engine off. • Measure voltage between (+)J51 (RC1E) and (-)J7 (BAT-) at breakout box. • **Is DC voltage reading greater than 10.0 volts?**	Yes No	GO to D24. CHECK connectors, SERVICE or REPLACE harness. C1 is open. REMOVE all test equipment. RECONNECT all components. CLEAR Continuous Memory. RERUN Quick Test.
D24	CHECK FOR C2 HIGH AT EDIS MODULE • Key on, engine off. • Measure voltage between (+)J27 (RC2E) and (-)J7 (BAT-) at breakout box. • **Is DC voltage reading greater than 10.0 volts?**	Yes No	GO to D25. CHECK connectors, SERVICE or REPLACE harness. C2 is open. REMOVE all test equipment. RECONNECT all components. CLEAR Continuous Memory. RERUN Quick Test.
D25	CHECK C1 HIGH AT COIL CONNECTOR—COIL DISCONNECTED • Key off. • Disconnect right coil from coil tee, leave EDIS diagnostic cable connected to vehicle harness right coil connector. • DVOM on 20 volt DC scale. • Key on, engine off. • Measure voltage between (+)J3 (RC1C) and (-)J7 (BAT-) at breakout box. • **Is DC voltage reading less than 0.5 volts?**	Yes No	GO to D26. GO to D33.
D26	CHECK FOR C2 HIGH AT COIL CONNECTOR—COIL DISCONNECTED • Key on, engine off. • Measure voltage between (+)J6 (RC2C) and (-)J7 (BAT-) at breakout box. • **Is DC voltage reading less than 0.5 volts?**	Yes No	GO to D27. GO to D34.

Fig. 84 EDIS testing—1992 vehicles

4.6L-2V Car EDIS No Start or Code 215 or 216 and/or Coil Failure — Pinpoint Test D

	TEST STEP	RESULT		ACTION TO TAKE
D32	CHECK FOR C2 SHORT LOW—EDIS MODULE AND COIL DISCONNECTED • Key off. • Disconnect EDIS module from vehicle harness. • DVOM on 20K ohm scale. • Measure resistance between J6 (RC2C) and J7 (BAT-) at breakout box. • Is resistance reading greater than 10K ohms?	Yes	▲	REPLACE EDIS module. C2 is shorted low. REMOVE all test equipment. RECONNECT all components. CLEAR Continuous Memory. RERUN Quick Test.
		No	▲	CHECK connectors, SERVICE or REPLACE harness. C2 is shorted low. REMOVE all test equipment. RECONNECT all components. CLEAR Continuous Memory. RERUN Quick Test.
D33	CHECK FOR C1 HIGH—EDIS MODULE AND COIL DISCONNECTED • Key off. • Disconnect EDIS module from EDIS module tee, leave EDIS diagnostic cable connected to vehicle harness connector. • DVOM on 20 volt DC scale. • Key on, engine off. • Measure voltage between (+)J3 (RC1C) and (-)J7 (BAT-) at breakout box. • Is DC voltage reading less than 0.5 volts?	Yes	▲	REPLACE EDIS module. REMOVE all test equipment. RECONNECT all components. CLEAR Continuous Memory. RERUN Quick Test.
		No	▲	CHECK connectors, SERVICE or REPLACE harness. C1 is shorted high. REMOVE all test equipment. RECONNECT all components. CLEAR Continuous Memory. RERUN Quick Test.

84172109

Fig. 87 EDIS testing—1992 vehicles

4.6L-2V Car EDIS No Start or Code 215 or 216 and/or Coil Failure — Pinpoint Test D

	TEST STEP	RESULT		ACTION TO TAKE
D30	CHECK FOR C1 SHORT LOW—EDIS MODULE AND COIL DISCONNECTED • Key off. • Disconnect EDIS module from vehicle harness. • DVOM on 20K ohm scale. • Measure resistance between J7 (BAT-) and J3 (RC1C) at breakout box. • Is resistance reading greater than 10K ohms?	Yes	▲	REPLACE EDIS module. C1 is shorted low in EDIS module. REMOVE all test equipment. RECONNECT all components. CLEAR Continuous Memory. RERUN Quick Test.
		No	▲	CHECK connectors, SERVICE or REPLACE harness. C1 is shorted to low. REMOVE all test equipment. RECONNECT all components. CLEAR Continuous Memory. RERUN Quick Test.
D31	CHECK FOR C2 SHORT LOW—COIL DISCONNECTED • Key off. • Disconnect coil from coil tee, leave EDIS diagnostic cable connected to vehicle harness coil connector. • DVOM on 20K ohm scale. • Measure resistance between J7 (BAT-) and J6 (RC2C) at breakout box. • Is resistance reading greater than 2K ohms?	Yes	▲	REPLACE Right Coil Pack. C2 open in coil. REMOVE all test equipment. RECONNECT all components. CLEAR Continuous Memory. RERUN Quick Test.
		No	▲	GO to D32.

84172108

Fig. 86 EDIS testing—1992 vehicles

Preliminary Checkout, Equipment and Notes

Checkout

- Visually inspect the engine compartment to ensure all vacuum hoses and spark plug wires are properly and securely connected.
- Examine all wiring harnesses and connectors for damaged insulation, burned, overheated, damaged pins, loose or broken conditions. **Check sensor shield connector.**
- Be certain the battery is fully charged.
- All accessories should be off during diagnosis.

Equipment (Required)

Obtain the following test equipment or an equivalent

- EI (High Data Rate) Diagnostic Harness (Rotunda 007-00059)
- Spark Tester, Neon bulb type (Special Service Tool D89P-6666-A).
- Volt-Ohmmeter (Rotunda 007-00001, 105-00050, 105-00051, 105-00052, 105-00053, or Scan Tool).
- Remote starter switch.
- EEC Breakout Box (Rotunda T83L-50-EEC-IV).
- Spark Tester, Gap type (Special Service Tool D81P-6666-A). A spark plug with a broken side electrode is not sufficient to check for spark and may lead to incorrect results.
- Inductive Timing Light (Rotunda 059-00006).

Fig. 89 EDIS testing—1993–94 vehicles

4.6L-2V Car EDIS No Start or Code 215 or 216 and/or Coil Failure

Pinpoint Test D

TEST STEP	RESULT	▶	ACTION TO TAKE
D34 CHECK FOR C2 HIGH—EDIS MODULE AND COIL DISCONNECTED • Key off. • Disconnect EDIS module from EDIS module tee, leave EDIS diagnostic cable connected to vehicle harness connector. • DVOM on 20 volt DC scale. • Key on, engine off. • Measure voltage between (+)J6 (RC2C) and (–)J7 (BAT–) at breakout box. • **Is DC voltage reading less than 0.5 volts?**	Yes ▶		REPLACE EDIS module. REMOVE all test equipment. RECONNECT all components. CLEAR Continuous Memory. RERUN Quick Test.
	No ▶		CHECK connectors, SERVICE or REPLACE harness. C2 is shorted high. REMOVE all test equipment. RECONNECT all components. CLEAR Continuous Memory. RERUN Quick Test.

Fig. 88 EDIS testing—1992 vehicles

Preliminary Checkout, Equipment and Notes

Notes

- When making measurements on a wiring harness, both a visual inspection and a continuity test should be performed. Inspect the connector pins for damage (corrosion, bent or spread pins, etc.) when directed to remove a connector.

- Spark timing adjustments are not possible.

- When making voltage checks a GROUND reading means any value within a range of zero to 1 volt. Also VPWR or COIL PWR readings mean any value that falls within a range of B+ to 2 volts less than B+.

- When making voltage checks and a reference to ground is made use either the negative battery lead or cast iron on the engine. B+ means the positive battery cable at the battery.

- When using the spark plug firing indicator, place the grooved end as close as possible to the plug boot. Very weak or no flashing may be caused by a fouled plug.

- Do not use an incandescent test lamp to check the CKP-, CKP+, PIP, IDM, or SPOUT circuits. The lamp will prevent the circuit from operating.

Fig. 90 EDIS testing—1993–94 vehicles

EI (High Data Rate) Breakout Box Overlay Acronyms

EI Acronyms

There is a logic to the names on the Schematic and Overlays for the EI (High Data Rate) DIAGNOSTIC HARNESS that will help you.

Acronym	Definition
PIP	Profile Ignition Pickup (ICM output signal).
IDM	Ignition Diagnostic Monitor (Diagnostic signal to PCM).
SPOUT	SPark OUTput (PCM spark control signal).
IGN GND	Ignition Ground (Low current ground reference).
CKP-	Crankshaft Position Sensor Negative.
CKP+	Crankshaft Position Sensor Positive.
CKP Shield	Crankshaft Position Sensor Shield.
B+	Battery Positive.
GND or B-	Battery Negative.
COIL PWR	Vehicle power to coils.
C1, C2, C3, C4	Coil Drive (For Coils 1, 2, 3 and 4).
VPWR	Vehicle Power

Overlay Designators

On the Schematic and Overlays, each of these signals is identified along with a suffix letter that tells you where the measurement is being taken. The key to these letters is:

Prefix/Suffix	Measurement Location
Prefix	"J" is a Breakout Box jack.
Suffix	"I" is at the Ignition Control Module (ICM).
Suffix	"S" is at the crankshaft position (CKP) sensor.
Suffix	"C" is at the coil.

A couple of examples:

Acronym	Definition
COIL PWR	Battery voltage at the Coil.
VPWR	Battery voltage at the ICM.

Fig. 91 EDIS testing—1993–94 vehicles

4.6L—2V, 4V Car EI (High Data Rate) Diagnostics — Pinpoint Test — Typical Values

The Following Voltage Readings are Typical for a Normal Vehicle:

Measure Between Pins		Key On Engine Off (Volts)	Engine Cranking (Volts AC)	Engine Idling (Volts AC)
First Pin	Second Pin			
CKPS+S (J31)	CKPS-S(J32)	0	0.5-1.5	2-5
CKPS+I (J48)	CKPS-I(J47)	0	0.5-1.5	2-5
PIPI (J43)	PWR GND (J53)	0	—	5-7
C11 (J51)	PWR GND (J53)	B+ DC	1-1.5	1.2-1.6
C21 (J27)	PWR GND (J53)	B+ DC	1-1.5	1.2-1.6
C31 (J54)	PWR GND (J53)	B+ DC	1-1.5	1.2-1.6
C41 (J55)	PWR GND (J53)	B+ DC	1-1.5	1.2-1.6
C1C (J3)	PWR GND (J53)	0	0.1-0.8	0.2-0.4
C2C (J6)	PWR GND (J53)	0	0.1-0.8	0.2-0.4
C3C (J10)	PWR GND (J53)	0	0.1-0.8	0.2-0.4
C4C (J18)	PWR GND (J53)	0	0.1-0.8	0.2-0.4
SPOUT (J45)	PWR GND (J53)	0	0.01-0.3	0.5-3
IDMI (J41)	PWR GND (J53)	0	0.1-0.5	0.2-2.0
CKPS+H (J48)	PWR GND (J53)	0	0.1-0.9	1.5-1.9
CKPS-I (J47)	PWR GND (J53)	0	0.1-0.9	1.5-1.9

NOTE:
- Do not connect the positive lead of the EI (High Data Rate) diagnostic harness or CKP sensor tee until directed to do so.
- The SPOUT and IDM detectors in the EI (High Data Rate) diagnostic harness will not work unless the positive and negative leads of the harness are connected.
- The vehicle battery voltage must be at least 12 volts DC.
- Be careful not to bring a fluorescent trouble lamp close to the vehicle wiring. If the key is on and the CKP sensor is disconnected, the ICM may fire the coil.
- When using a DVOM to measure DC voltage readings, connect the positive lead to the jack identified with a (+) sign and the negative lead to the jack with a (-) sign.

Fig. 92 EDIS testing—1993-94 vehicles

4.6L—2V, 4V Car EI (High Data Rate) No Start — Pinpoint Test — A

	TEST STEP	RESULT	ACTION TO TAKE
A1	**PERFORM EEC QUICK TEST**		
	• Was Quick Test performed according to procedures	Yes	▶ GO to A2.
		No	▶ PERFORM Quick Test.
	NOTE: These diagnostic procedures are designed to correct one ignition failure at a time. When a component is replaced or a service is completed, remove all test equipment, reconnect all components and rerun Quick Test.		
A2	**CHECK FOR SPARK DURING CRANK—KOEC**		
	• Using a Neon Bulb Spark Tester (Special Service Tool D89P-6666-A) or Air Gap Spark Tester (Special Service Tool D81P-6666-A), check for spark at all spark plug wires while cranking.	Yes	▶ GO to A13.
	• Was spark consistent on ALL spark plug wires (one spark per crankshaft revolution)?	No	▶ GO to A3. Spark fault.
A3	**CHECK PLUGS AND WIRES—KEY OFF**		
	• Check spark plug wires for insulation damage, looseness, shorting or other damage.	Yes	▶ REINSTALL plugs and wires. GO to A4.
	• Remove and check spark plugs for damage, wear, carbon deposits and proper plug gap.	No	▶ SERVICE or REPLACE damaged component. REMOVE all test equipment. RECONNECT all components. CLEAR Continuous Memory. RERUN Quick Test.
	• Are spark plugs and wires OK?		
A4	**CHECK FOR VEHICLE START WITH DIAGNOSTIC HARNESS INSTALLED**		
	WARNING: NEVER CONNECT THE PCM TO THE EEC BREAKOUT BOX WHEN PERFORMING EI DIAGNOSTICS.	Yes	▶ GO to A32.
	• Key off.	No	▶ GO to A5.
	• Install EI diagnostic harness to breakout box and to both the ICM and vehicle harness.		
	• Do not connect CKP sensor tee or coil tee.		
	• Use EI (High Data Rate) 8 overlay.		
	• Connect EI diagnostic harness negative lead to battery, leave positive lead disconnected.		
	• Set EI diagnostic harness box type switch to "8 cylinder" position.		
	• Will vehicle start and run?		

Fig. 93 EDIS testing—1993-94 vehicles

4.6L—2V, 4V Car EI (High Data Rate) No Start — Pinpoint Test A

	TEST STEP	RESULT	ACTION TO TAKE
A9	CHECK CKP- SENSOR — BIAS FAULT — CKP SENSOR DISCONNECTED—KOEO • Key off. • DVOM on 20 volt DC scale. • Key on, engine off. • Measure voltage between (+)J47 (CKP-I) and (-)J7 (B-) at breakout box. • **Is DC voltage between 1.0 and 2.0 volts?**	Yes ▲ No ▲	REPLACE CKP sensor. Short to ground. REMOVE all test equipment. RECONNECT all components. CLEAR Continuous Memory. RERUN Quick Test. GO to [A10]. Bias fault.
A10	DETERMINE IF BIAS HIGH OR BIAS LOW FAULT—KEY OFF • **Was bias voltage reading in Step [A9] less than 1.0 volt?**	Yes ▲ No ▲	GO to [A11] Bias low fault. GO to [A12] Bias high fault.
A11	CHECK CKP SENSOR — FOR SHORT TO GROUND—BIAS LOW FAULT—CKP SENSOR AND ICM DISCONNECTED—KEY OFF • Key off. • Disconnect ICM from ICM tee, leave EI diagnostic harness connected to vehicle harness connector. • DVOM on 20K ohm scale. • Measure resistance between J47 (CKP-I) and J7 (B-) at breakout box. • **Is the resistance greater than 10K ohms?**	Yes ▲ No ▲	REPLACE ICM. CKP- is shorted low. REMOVE all test equipment. RECONNECT all components. CLEAR Continuous Memory. RERUN Quick Test. CHECK connectors, SERVICE or REPLACE harness. CKP- is shorted low. REMOVE all test equipment. RECONNECT all components. CLEAR Continuous Memory. RERUN Quick Test.

Fig. 95 EDIS testing—1993-94 vehicles

4.6L—2V, 4V Car EI (High Data Rate) No Start — Pinpoint Test A

	TEST STEP	RESULT	ACTION TO TAKE
A5	CHECK PWR GND TO ICM—KEY OFF • Key off. • Install EI diagnostic harness breakout box and ICM. • Do not connect CKP sensor or coil tees at this time. • Use EI (High Data Rate) 8 overlay. • Connect only the EI diagnostic harness negative lead. Do not connect positive lead. Set diagnostic harness switch to the 8 position. • DVOM on 200 ohm scale. • Measure resistance between J53 (PWR GND) and J7 (B-) at breakout box. • **Is the resistance less than 5.0 ohms?**	Yes ▲ No ▲	GO to [A6]. CHECK connectors, SERVICE or REPLACE harness. Power ground is open. REMOVE all test equipment. RECONNECT all components. CLEAR Continuous Memory. RERUN Quick Test.
A6	CHECK FOR VPWR TO ICM—KOEO • Key off. • DVOM on 20 volt DC scale. • Key on, engine off. • Measure voltage between (+)J35 (VPWR I) and (-)J7 (B-) at breakout box. • **Is DC voltage greater than 10.5 volts?**	Yes ▲ No ▲	GO to [A7]. CHECK connectors, SERVICE or REPLACE harness. VPWR to ICM is open. REMOVE all test equipment. RECONNECT all components. CLEAR Continuous Memory. RERUN Quick Test.
A7	CHECK CKP+ BIAS AT ICM—KOEO • Key off. • DVOM on 20 volt DC scale. • Key on, engine off. • Measure voltage between (+)J48 (CKP+I) and (-)J7 (B-) at breakout box. • **Is DC voltage between 1.0 and 2.0 volts?**	Yes ▲ No ▲	GO to [A21]. GO to [A8]. Bias fault.
A8	CHECK CKP+ BIAS SENSOR DISCONNECTED—BIAS FAULT—KOEO • Key off. • Disconnect CKP sensor from vehicle harness connector. • DVOM on 20 volt DC scale. • Key on, engine off. • Measure voltage between (+)J48 (CKP+I) and (-)J7 (B-) at breakout box. • **Is DC voltage greater than 1.0 volt but less than 2.0 volts?**	Yes ▲ No ▲	GO to [A9]. GO to [A29]. Bias fault.

Fig. 94 EDIS testing—1993-94 vehicles

4.6L—2V, 4V Car EI (High Data Rate) No Start — Pinpoint Test A

TEST STEP	RESULT	ACTION TO TAKE
A12 CHECK CKP- SENSOR FOR SHORT HIGH—BIAS HIGH FAULT—CKP SENSOR AND ICM DISCONNECTED—KOEO • Key off. • Disconnect ICM from ICM tee; leave EI diagnostic harness connected to vehicle harness connector. • DVOM 20 volt DC scale. • Key on, engine off. • Measure voltage between (+)J47 (CKP- I) and (-)J7 (B-) at the breakout box. • **Is DC voltage less than 0.5 volts?**	Yes ▶ No ▶	REPLACE ICM. CKP- shorted high. REMOVE all test equipment. RECONNECT all components. CLEAR Continuous Memory. RERUN Quick Test. CHECK connectors, SERVICE or REPLACE harness. CKP- is shorted high. REMOVE all test equipment. RECONNECT all components. CLEAR Continuous Memory. RERUN Quick Test.
A13 CHECK PIP AT ICM—KOEO **WARNING: NEVER CONNECT THE PCM TO THE EEC BREAKOUT BOX WHEN PERFORMING EI DIAGNOSTICS.** • Key off. • Install EI diagnostic harness to the breakout box and to both the ICM and vehicle harness. **Do not connect CKP sensor tee or coil tee.** • Use EI (High Data Rate) 8 overlay. • Connect EI diagnostic harness negative lead to battery, leave positive lead disconnected. • Set EI diagnostic harness type switch to 8 position. • DVOM on 20 volt AC scale. • Crank engine and measure voltage between J43 (PIP I) and J7 (B-) at the breakout box. • **Is the settled AC voltage reading greater than 3.5 volts?**	Yes ▶ No ▶	GO to **A14**. GO to **A18**.
A14 CHECK FOR PIP OPEN TO PCM—PCM DISCONNECTED—KEY OFF • Key off. • DVOM on 200 ohm scale. • Install a second breakout box to PCM vehicle harness connector. • Measure resistance between J43 (PIP I) at the breakout box and Pin 56 (PIP) at the second breakout box. • **Is resistance less than 5.0 ohms?**	Yes ▶ No ▶	GO to **A15**. CHECK connectors, SERVICE or REPLACE harness. PIP is open. REMOVE all test equipment. RECONNECT all components. CLEAR Continuous Memory. RERUN Quick Test.

Fig. 96 EDIS testing—1993–94 vehicles

4.6L—2V, 4V Car EI (High Data Rate) No Start — Pinpoint Test A

TEST STEP	RESULT	ACTION TO TAKE
A15 CHECK IGN GND AT ICM—PCM DISCONNECTED • Key off. • DVOM on 2K ohm scale. • Measure resistance between J50 (IGN GND I) and J7 (B-) at breakout box. • **Is resistance less than 1050 ohms?**	Yes ▶ No ▶	GO to **A16**. GO to **A17**. Ground fault.
A16 CHECK FOR IGN GND OPEN TO PCM—PCM DISCONNECTED —KEY OFF • Key off. • DVOM on 2K ohm scale. • Measure resistance between J50 (IGN GND I) and Pin 16 (IGN GND) at the second breakout box. • **Is resistance less than 1050 ohms?**	Yes ▶ No ▶	Ignition system is OK. REMOVE all test equipment. RECONNECT all components. CLEAR Continuous Memory. RERUN Quick Test. CHECK connectors, SERVICE or REPLACE harness. IGN GND is open. REMOVE all test equipment. RECONNECT all components. CLEAR Continuous Memory. RERUN Quick Test.
A17 CHECK PWR GND TO ICM—PWR GND FAULT—KEY OFF • Key off. • DVOM on 200 ohm scale. • Measure resistance between J53 (PWR GND) and J7 (B-) at breakout box. • **Is resistance less than 5.0 ohms?**	Yes ▶ No ▶	REPLACE ICM. Ground open. REMOVE all test equipment. RECONNECT all components. CLEAR Continuous Memory. RERUN Quick Test. CHECK connectors, SERVICE or REPLACE harness. Power ground to ICM is open. REMOVE all test equipment. RECONNECT all components. CLEAR Continuous Memory. RERUN Quick Test.

Fig. 97 EDIS testing—1993–94 vehicles

4.6L—2V, 4V Car EI (High Data Rate) No Start — Pinpoint Test A

	TEST STEP	RESULT	ACTION TO TAKE
A22	CHECK CKP AMPLITUDE AT ICM—AMPLITUDE FAULT—ICM DISCONNECTED—KOEC • Key off. • Disconnect ICM from ICM tee, leave EI diagnostic harness connected to vehicle harness connector. • DVOM 20 volt AC scale. • Crank engine and measure voltage between J48 (PIP I) and J47 (CKP-I) at breakout box. • **Is settled AC voltage reading greater than 0.4 volts?**	Yes No	▶ REPLACE ICM. CKP is shorted in ICM. REMOVE all test equipment. RECONNECT all components. CLEAR Continuous Memory. RERUN Quick Test. ▶ GO to A23.
A23	CHECK CIRCUIT RESISTANCE—AMPLITUDE FAULT—KEY OFF • Key off. • DVOM on 20K ohm scale. • Measure resistance between J47 (CKP-I) and J48 (CKP+I) at the breakout box. • **Is resistance between 2300 and 2500 ohms?**	Yes No	▶ GO to A27. ▶ GO to A24. CKP- circuit resistance fault.
A24	DETERMINE IF RESISTANCE HIGH OR RESISTANCE LOW FAULT • **Was the resistance reading from Step A23 less than 2300 ohms?**	Yes No	▶ GO to A28. Low resistance fault. ▶ GO to A25. High resistance fault.
A25	CHECK CKP+ SENSOR OPEN—RESISTANCE HIGH FAULT—KEY OFF • Key off. • Connect CKP sensor tee to CKP sensor and vehicle harness connector. • DVOM on 20K ohm scale. • Measure resistance between J31 (CKP+ S) and J48 (CKP+I) at the breakout box. • **Is resistance less than 2050 ohms?**	Yes No	▶ GO to A26. ▶ CHECK connectors, SERVICE or REPLACE harness. CKP+ open. REMOVE all test equipment. RECONNECT all components. CLEAR Continuous Memory. RERUN Quick Test.

Fig. 99 EDIS testing—1993–94 vehicles

4.6L—2V, 4V Car EI (High Data Rate) No Start — Pinpoint Test A

	TEST STEP	RESULT	ACTION TO TAKE
A18	CHECK PIP AT ICM—PIP FAULT—PIP CIRCUIT OPEN—KOEC • Key off. • DVOM 20 volt AC scale. • Push and hold EI diagnostic harness PIP push button down (opens PIP circuit to PCM). • Crank engine and measure voltage between J43 (PIP I) and J7 (B-) at breakout box. • **Is settled AC voltage reading greater than 3.5 volts?**	Yes No	▶ GO to A19. ▶ REPLACE ICM. No PIP output. REMOVE all test equipment. RECONNECT all components. CLEAR Continuous Memory. RERUN Quick Test.
A19	CHECK FOR PIP SHORT HIGH—ICM AND PCM DISCONNECTED—KOEO • Key off. • DVOM on 20 volt DC scale. • Key on, engine off. • Measure voltage between J43 (PIP I) and J7 (B-) at breakout box. • **Is DC voltage less than 0.5 volts?**	Yes No	▶ GO to A20. ▶ CHECK connectors, SERVICE or REPLACE harness. PIP is shorted high. REMOVE all test equipment. RECONNECT all components. CLEAR Continuous Memory. RERUN Quick Test.
A20	CHECK FOR PIP SHORT TO GROUND—ICM AND PCM DISCONNECTED—KEY OFF • Key off. • Disconnect PCM. • Disconnect ICM from ICM tee, leave EI diagnostic harness connected to vehicle harness connector. • Disconnect EI diagnostic harness positive lead to battery. • DVOM on 20K ohm scale. • Measure resistance between J43 (PIP I) and J7 (B-) at breakout box. • **Is resistance greater than 10K ohms?**	Yes No	▶ REPLACE PCM. PIP is shorted. REMOVE all test equipment. RECONNECT all components. CLEAR Continuous Memory. RERUN Quick Test. ▶ CHECK connectors, SERVICE or REPLACE harness. PIP is shorted low. REMOVE all test equipment. RECONNECT all components. CLEAR Continuous Memory. RERUN Quick Test.
A21	CHECK CKP SENSOR AMPLITUDE AT ICM—KOEC • Key off. • DVOM on 20 volt AC scale. • Crank engine and measure voltage between J48 (CKP+I) and J47 (CKP-I) at breakout box. • **Is settled AC voltage reading greater than 0.4 volts?**	Yes No	▶ GO to Pinpoint Test Step D1. ▶ GO to A22. Amplitude fault.

Fig. 98 EDIS testing—1993–94 vehicles

4.6L—2V, 4V Car EI (High Data Rate) No Start — Pinpoint Test A

	TEST STEP	RESULT		ACTION TO TAKE
A28	**CHECK FOR CKP+ SHORTED TO CKP- —RESISTANCE LOW FAULT—CKP SENSOR DISCONNECTED—KEY OFF** • Key off. • Disconnect CKP sensor from the vehicle harness connector. • DVOM on 20K ohm scale. • Measure resistance between J48 (CKP+) and J47 (CKP-) at the breakout box. • **Is resistance greater than 3K ohms?**	Yes	▶	REPLACE CKP sensor. Shorted sensor windings. REMOVE all test equipment. RECONNECT all components. CLEAR Continuous Memory. RERUN Quick Test.
		No	▶	CHECK connectors, SERVICE or REPLACE harness. CKP+ shorted to CKP- in harness. REMOVE all test equipment. RECONNECT all components. CLEAR Continuous Memory. RERUN Quick Test.
A29	**DETERMINE IF BIAS VOLTAGE HIGH OR BIAS VOLTAGE LOW FAULT** • **Was bias voltage reading in Step [A8] less than 1.0 volts?**	Yes	▶	GO to [A30]. Low bias voltage fault.
		No	▶	GO to [A31]. High bias voltage fault.
A30	**CHECK CKP+ SENSOR FOR SHORT TO GROUND—CKP SENSOR AND ICM DISCONNECTED—LOW BIAS VOLTAGE FAULT—KEY OFF** • Key off. • Disconnect the ICM from ICM tee, leave EI diagnostic harness connected to vehicle harness connector. • DVOM on 20K ohm scale. • Measure resistance between J48 (CKP+) and J7 (B-) at breakout box. • **Is resistance greater than 10K ohms?**	Yes	▶	REPLACE ICM. CKP+ shorted low. REMOVE all test equipment. RECONNECT all components. CLEAR Continuous Memory. RERUN Quick Test.
		No	▶	CHECK connectors, SERVICE or REPLACE harness. CKP+ is shorted low. REMOVE all test equipment. RECONNECT all components. CLEAR Continuous Memory. RERUN Quick Test.

Fig. 101 EDIS testing—1993–94 vehicles

4.6L—2V, 4V Car EI (High Data Rate) No Start — Pinpoint Test A

	TEST STEP	RESULT		ACTION TO TAKE
A26	**CHECK FOR CKP OPEN—RESISTANCE HIGH FAULT—KEY OFF** • Key off. • DVOM on 20K ohm scale. • Measure resistance between J32 (CKP-S) and J47 (CKP-) at the breakout box. • **Is resistance less than 2050 ohms?**	Yes	▶	REPLACE CKP sensor. High resistance. REMOVE all test equipment. RECONNECT all components. CLEAR Continuous Memory. RERUN Quick Test.
		No	▶	CHECK connectors, SERVICE or REPLACE harness. CKP- open. REMOVE all test equipment. RECONNECT all components. CLEAR Continuous Memory. RERUN Quick Test.
A27	**CHECK CKP SENSOR AND TRIGGER WHEEL** • Key off. • Check trigger wheel and CKP sensor for damage. • **Is CKP sensor and trigger data wheel OK?**	Yes	▶	REPLACE CKP sensor. No output from sensor. REMOVE all test equipment. RECONNECT all components. CLEAR Continuous Memory. RERUN Quick Test.
		No	▶	SERVICE or REPLACE bad parts. REMOVE all test equipment. RECONNECT all components. CLEAR Continuous Memory. RERUN Quick Test.

Fig. 100 EDIS testing—1993–94 vehicles

4.6L—2V, 4V Car EI (High Data Rate) Code 212 IDM Failure — Pinpoint Test B

TEST STEP	RESULT	ACTION TO TAKE
B1 CHECK FOR IDM AT ICM—KOER **WARNING: NEVER CONNECT THE PCM TO EEC BREAKOUT BOX WHEN PERFORMING EI DIAGNOSTICS.** • Key off. • Install EI diagnostic harness to breakout box, and to both the ICM and vehicle harness. • **Do not connect CKP sensor tee or coil tees.** • Use EI (High Data Rate) 8 overlay. • Connect EI diagnostic harness negative and positive leads to battery. • Set EI diagnostic harness type switch to "8" position. • DVOM on 20 volt AC scale. • Start engine and measure voltage between (+)J30 (EI diagnostic harness IDM detector) and (-)J7 (B-) at breakout box. **NOTE: If pulses are present, the IDM detector output will be between 5.0 and 7.0 volts AC.** • **Is AC voltage between 5.0 and 7.0 volts?**	Yes No	▲ GO to **B2**. ▲ GO to **B3**. IDM fault.
B2 CHECK FOR IDM OPEN TO PCM—IDM FAULT—ICM AND PCM DISCONNECTED—KEY OFF • Key off. • Disconnect PCM. • Disconnect ICM from ICM tee, leave EI diagnostic harness connected to vehicle harness connector. • DVOM on 200 ohm scale. • Install a second breakout box to PCM vehicle harness connector. • Measure resistance between J41 (IDM I) at breakout box and Pin 4 at second breakout box. • **Is resistance less than 5.0 ohms?**	Yes No	▲ REPLACE PCM. PCM does not respond to IDM input. REMOVE all test equipment. RECONNECT all components. CLEAR Continuous Memory. RERUN Quick Test. ▲ CHECK connectors, SERVICE or REPLACE harness. IDM is open. REMOVE all test equipment. RECONNECT all components. CLEAR Continuous Memory. RERUN Quick Test.

Fig. 103 EDIS testing—1993-94 vehicles

4.6L—2V, 4V Car EI (High Data Rate) No Start — Pinpoint Test A

TEST STEP	RESULT	ACTION TO TAKE
A31 CHECK CKP+ SENSOR FOR SHORT HIGH—BIAS VOLTAGE HIGH FAULT—CKP SENSOR AND ICM DISCONNECTED—KEOO • Key off. • Disconnect ICM from ICM tee, leave EI diagnostic harness connected to vehicle harness connector. • DVOM on 20 volt DC scale. • Key on, engine off. • Measure voltage between +J48 (CKP+ I) and -J7 (B-) at breakout box. • **Is DC voltage less than 0.5 volts?**	Yes No	▲ REPLACE ICM. CKPS+ shorted high. REMOVE all test equipment. RECONNECT all components. CLEAR Continuous Memory. RERUN Quick Test. ▲ CHECK connectors, SERVICE or REPLACE harness. CKP+ is shorted high. REMOVE all test equipment. RECONNECT all components. CLEAR Continuous Memory. RERUN Quick Test.
A32 CHECK CKP SENSOR RESISTANCE—CKP CIRCUIT FAULT—KEY OFF • Key off. • Disconnect ICM from ICM tee, leave EI diagnostic harness connected to vehicle harness connector. • DVOM on 20K ohm scale. • Measure resistance between J47 (CKP- I) and J48 (CKP+ I) at breakout box. • **Is resistance between 2300 and 2500 ohms?**	Yes No	▲ REPLACE ICM. REMOVE all test equipment. RECONNECT all components. CLEAR Continuous Memory. RERUN Quick Test. ▲ GO to **A24**. Resistance fault.

Fig. 102 EDIS testing—1993-94 vehicles

4.6L—2V, 4V Car EI (High Data Rate) Code 212 IDM Failure | **Pinpoint Test** | **B**

	TEST STEP	RESULT	ACTION TO TAKE
B6	CHECK FOR IDM SHORT TO GROUND IN HARNESS—ICM AND PCM DISCONNECTED—KEY OFF • Key off. • Disconnect ICM from ICM tee, leave EI diagnostic harness connected to vehicle harness connector. • DVOM on 20K ohm scale. • Measure resistance between J41 (IDM1) and (-)J7 (B-) at breakout box. • **Is resistance greater than 10K ohms?**	Yes ▲ No ▲	▲ CHECK connectors, SERVICE or REPLACE harness. IDM is shorted to another wire between the ICM and PCM. REMOVE all test equipment. RECONNECT all components. CLEAR Continuous Memory. RERUN Quick Test. ▲ CHECK connectors, SERVICE or REPLACE harness. IDM is shorted low. REMOVE all test equipment. RECONNECT all components. CLEAR Continuous Memory. RERUN Quick Test.

Fig. 105 EDIS testing—1993–94 vehicles

4.6L—2V, 4V Car EI (High Data Rate) Code 212 IDM Failure | **Pinpoint Test** | **B**

	TEST STEP	RESULT	ACTION TO TAKE
B3	CHECK IDM OUTPUT FROM ICM—IDM FAULT—IDM CIRCUIT OPEN—KOER • Key off. • DVOM on 20 volt AC scale. • Push and hold EI diagnostic harness IDM button down (opens IDM circuit to PCM). • Start engine and measure voltage between J30 (EI diagnostic harness IDM detector) and J7 (B-) at breakout box. • **Is AC voltage greater than 5.0 volts?**	Yes ▲ No ▲	▲ GO to **B4**. ▲ REPLACE ICM. No IDM output from module. REMOVE all test equipment. RECONNECT all components. CLEAR Continuous Memory. RERUN Quick Test.
B4	CHECK FOR IDM SHORT IN PCM—PCM DISCONNECTED—KOEC • Key off. • Disconnect PCM. • DVOM on 20 volt AC scale. • Crank engine and measure voltage between J30 (EI diagnostic harness IDM detector) and (-)J7 (B-) at breakout box. • **Is AC voltage less than 5.0 volts?**	Yes ▲ No ▲	▲ GO to **B5**. ▲ REPLACE PCM. PCM is loading IDM signal. REMOVE all test equipment. RECONNECT all components. CLEAR Continuous Memory. RERUN Quick Test.
B5	CHECK FOR IDM SHORT HIGH IN HARNESS—ICM AND PCM DISCONNECTED—KOEO • Key off. • DVOM on 20 volt DC scale. • Key on, engine off. • Measure voltage between (+)J41 (IDM1) and (-)J7 (B-) at breakout box. • **Is DC voltage less than 0.5 volts?**	Yes ▲ No ▲	▲ GO to **B6**. ▲ CHECK connectors, SERVICE or REPLACE harness. IDM is shorted high. REMOVE all test equipment. RECONNECT all components. CLEAR Continuous Memory. RERUN Quick Test.

Fig. 104 EDIS testing—1993–94 vehicles

4.6L—2V, 4V Car EI (High Data Rate) Code 213 Or Lack Of Power Or Poor Fuel Economy

Pinpoint Test C

TEST STEP	RESULT	ACTION TO TAKE
C1 CHECK BASE TIMING—KOER **WARNING: NEVER CONNECT PCM TO EEC BREAKOUT BOX WHEN PERFORMING EI DIAGNOSTICS.** • Key off. • Install EI diagnostic harness to breakout box and to both the ICM and vehicle harness. **Do not connect the CKP sensor tee or coil tees.** • Use EI (High Data Rate) 8 overlay. • Connect EI diagnostic harness negative and positive leads to battery. • Set EI diagnostic harness type switch to "8" position. • Connect timing light (must be EI compatible). • Start engine and allow it to warm up. • Is timing 10 ± 2 degrees BTDC when the diagnostic harness SPOUT button is pushed?	Yes No	► GO to C2. ► GO to C8. Base timing fault.
C2 CHECK FOR SPARK ANGLE ADVANCE—KOER • Is engine timing greater than 15 degrees BTDC when the diagnostic harness SPOUT button is released?	Yes No	► Ignition System is OK. ► GO to C3. Advance spark fault.
C3 CHECK SPOUT AT ICM—KOER • Key off. • DVOM on 20 volt AC scale. • Start engine and measure voltage between J21 (EI diagnostic harness SPOUT detector) and (-)J7 (B-) at breakout box. • Is AC voltage reading greater than 5.0 volts?	Yes No	► REPLACE ICM. SPOUT input to ICM is OK, but no spark advance is present. REMOVE all test equipment. RECONNECT all components. CLEAR Continuous Memory. RERUN Quick Test. ► GO to C4. SPOUT fault.

84172128

Fig. 106 EDIS testing—1993–94 vehicles

4.6L—2V, 4V Car EI (High Data Rate) Code 213 Or Lack Of Power Or Poor Fuel Economy

Pinpoint Test C

TEST STEP	RESULT	ACTION TO TAKE
C4 CHECK FOR SPOUT SHORT IN ICM—SPOUT FAULT—SPOUT CIRCUIT OPEN—KOER • Key off. • DVOM on 20 volt AC scale. • Push and hold EI diagnostic harness SPOUT button down (opens SPOUT circuit to ICM). • Start engine and measure voltage between (+)J21 (EI diagnostic harness SPOUT detector) and (-)J7 (B-) at breakout box. • Is AC voltage reading greater than 5.0 volts?	Yes No	► REPLACE ICM. SPOUT is shorted in ICM. REMOVE all test equipment. RECONNECT all components. CLEAR Continuous Memory. RERUN Quick Test. ► GO to C5.
C5 CHECK FOR SPOUT SHORT HIGH IN HARNESS—ICM AND PCM DISCONNECTED—KOEO • Key off. • Disconnect PCM. • Disconnect the ICM tee from the ICM, but leave the vehicle harness connected to module tee. • DVOM on 20 volt DC scale. • Key on, engine off. • Measure voltage between J45 (SPOUT I) and J7 (B-) at the breakout box. • Is DC voltage reading less than 0.5 volts?	Yes No	► GO to C6. ► CHECK connectors, SERVICE or REPLACE harness. SPOUT is shorted high. REMOVE all test equipment. RECONNECT all components. CLEAR Continuous Memory. RERUN Quick Test.
C6 CHECK FOR SPOUT SHORT TO GROUND IN HARNESS—ICM AND PCM DISCONNECTED—KEY OFF • Key off. • DVOM on 20K ohm scale. • Disconnect EI diagnostic harness positive lead to battery. • Measure resistance between J45 (SPOUT I) and J7 (B-) at breakout box. • Is the resistance greater than 10K ohms?	Yes No	► GO to C7. ► CHECK connectors, SERVICE or REPLACE harness. SPOUT is shorted low. REMOVE all test equipment. RECONNECT all components. CLEAR Continuous Memory. RERUN Quick Test.

84172129

Fig. 107 EDIS testing—1993–94 vehicles

4.6L—2V, 4V Car EI (High Data Rate) Code 213 Or Lack Of Power Or Poor Fuel Economy

Pinpoint Test C

	TEST STEP	RESULT		ACTION TO TAKE
C7	CHECK FOR SPOUT OPEN TO ICM—ICM AND PCM DISCONNECTED—KEY OFF • Key off. • DVOM on 200 ohm scale. • Install a second breakout box to the vehicle harness connector. • Measure resistance between J45 (SPOUT I) at breakout box and Pin 36 at the second breakout box. • **Is resistance less than 5.0 ohms?**	Yes	▲	REPLACE PCM. SPOUT is not being transmitted by the PCM. REMOVE all test equipment. RECONNECT all components. CLEAR Continuous Memory. RERUN Quick Test.
		No	▲	CHECK connectors, SERVICE or REPLACE harness. SPOUT is open. REMOVE all test equipment. RECONNECT all components. CLEAR Continuous Memory. RERUN Quick Test.
C8	INSPECT CKP SENSOR AND TRIGGER WHEEL—TIMING FAULT • **Is the CKP sensor or Trigger Wheel damaged, i.e., loose or misaligned?**	Yes	▲	REPLACE or SERVICE as required. REMOVE all test equipment. RECONNECT all components. CLEAR Continuous Memory. RERUN Quick Test.
		No	▲	REPLACE ICM. Incorrect output. REMOVE all test equipment. RECONNECT all components. CLEAR Continuous Memory. RERUN Quick Test.

Fig. 108 EDIS testing—1993–94 vehicles

4.6L—2V, 4V Car EI (High Data Rate) No Start or Code 217 or 238 and/or Coil Failure

Pinpoint Test D

	TEST STEP	RESULT		ACTION TO TAKE
D1	CHECK FOR SPARK DURING CRANK—KOEC • Using a Neon Bulb Spark Tester (Special Service Tool D89P-6666-A) or Air Gap Spark Tester (D81P-6666-A), check for spark at all spark plug wires while cranking. • **Was spark consistent on all spark plug wires (one spark per crankshaft revolution)?**	Yes	▲	The ignition system is OK.
		No	▲	GO to D2. Spark fault.
D2	CHECK FOR SPARK AT ALL RIGHT SPARK PLUG WIRES DURING CRANK—KOEC • **Was spark consistent on all right spark plug wires (one spark per crankshaft revolution)?** NOTE: Check spark at spark plugs.	Yes	▲	GO to D3.
		No	▲	GO to D19.
D3	CHECK LEFT SPARK PLUGS AND WIRES—KEY OFF • Check left side coil pack spark plug wires for insulation damage, looseness, shorting or other damage. • Remove and check left side spark plugs for damage, wear, carbon deposits and proper plug gap. • Left coil plugs and wires are attached to the left coil pack. • **Are spark plugs and wires OK?**	Yes	▲	REINSTALL plugs and wires. GO to D4.
		No	▲	SERVICE or REPLACE damaged component. REMOVE all test equipment. RECONNECT all components. CLEAR Continuous Memory. RERUN Quick Test.
D4	CHECK FOR COIL PWR TO LEFT COIL FAULT—KOEO **WARNING: NEVER CONNECT PCM TO THE EEC BREAKOUT BOX WHEN PERFORMING EI DIAGNOSTICS.** • Key off. • Install EI (High Data Rate) diagnostic harness to breakout box. • Install the left coil tee. The tee is yellow (left coil). • Connect EI diagnostic harness negative lead to battery. • Use 4.6L EI (High Data Rate) 8 overlay. • Set EI harness type switch to "8" position. • DVOM on 20 volt DC scale. • Key on, engine off. • Measure voltage between (+)J11 (COIL PWR L) and (-)J7 (B-) at breakout box. • **Is DC voltage greater than 10.0 volts?**	Yes	▲	GO to D5.
		No	▲	CHECK connectors, SERVICE or REPLACE harness. COIL PWR is open to left coil. REMOVE all test equipment. RECONNECT all components. CLEAR Continuous Memory. RERUN Quick Test.

Fig. 109 EDIS testing—1993–94 vehicles

4.6L—2V, 4V Car EI (High Data Rate) No Start or Code 217 or 238 and/or Coil Failure — Pinpoint Test D

	TEST STEP	RESULT	ACTION TO TAKE
D10	CHECK FOR C4 LOW AT COIL CONNECTOR—COIL DISCONNECTED—KOEO • Key on, engine off. • Measure voltage between (+)J18 (LC4C) and (-)J7 (B-) at breakout box. • **Is DC voltage reading less than 0.5 volts?**	Yes No	▲ GO to D11. ▲ GO to D18. C4 high fault.
D11	CHECK C3 AT COIL CONNECTOR WHILE CRANKING—COIL DISCONNECTED—KOEC • Connect EI diagnostic harness positive lead to battery. • Connect an incandescent test lamp between J1 (B+) and J10 (LC3C). • Crank engine. • **Does lamp blink consistently and brightly (one blink per engine revolution?**	Yes No	▲ GO to D12. ▲ REPLACE ICM. C3 open. REMOVE all test equipment. RECONNECT all components. CLEAR Continuous Memory. RERUN Quick Test.
D12	CHECK C4 AT COIL CONNECTOR WHILE CRANKING—COIL DISCONNECTED—KOEC • Connect an incandescent test lamp between J1 (B+) and J18 (LC4C). • Crank engine. • **Does lamp blink consistently and brightly (one blink per engine revolution)?**	Yes No	▲ REPLACE left coil pack. Input to coil pack is OK, but no high voltage output. REMOVE all test equipment. RECONNECT all components. CLEAR Continuous Memory. RERUN Quick Test. ▲ REPLACE ICM. C4 open in ICM. REMOVE all test equipment. RECONNECT all components. CLEAR Continuous Memory. RERUN Quick Test.
D13	CHECK FOR C3 SHORT LOW—COIL DISCONNECTED—KEY OFF • Key off. • DVOM on 20K ohm scale. • Disconnect coil from coil tee, leave EI diagnostic harness connected to vehicle harness coil connector. • Measure resistance between J7 (B-) and J10 (C3C) at breakout box. • **Is resistance reading less than 2K ohms?**	Yes No	▲ GO to D14. ▲ REPLACE Left Coil Pack. C3 open in coil. REMOVE all test equipment. RECONNECT all components. CLEAR Continuous Memory. RERUN Quick Test.

Fig. 111 EDIS testing—1993-94 vehicles

4.6L—2V, 4V Car EI (High Data Rate) No Start or Code 217 or 238 and/or Coil Failure — Pinpoint Test D

	TEST STEP	RESULT	ACTION TO TAKE
D5	CHECK FOR C3 HIGH AT COIL PACK—KOEO • Key on, engine off. • Measure voltage between (+)J10 (LC3C) and (-)J7 (B-) at breakout box. • **Is DC voltage reading greater than 10.0 volts?**	Yes No	▲ GO to D6. ▲ GO to D13. C3 low fault.
D6	CHECK FOR C4 HIGH AT COIL PACK—KOEO • Key on, engine off. • Measure voltage between (+)J18 (LC4C) and (-)J7 (B-) at breakout box. • **Is DC voltage reading greater than 10.0 volts?**	Yes No	▲ GO to D7. ▲ GO to D15. C4 low fault.
D7	CHECK FOR C3 HIGH AT ICM—KOEO • Key off. • Connect ICM tee to the ICM and vehicle harness connector. • DVOM on 20 volt DC scale. • Key on, engine off. • Measure voltage between (+)J54 (LC3I) and (-)J7 (B-) at the breakout box. • **Is DC voltage reading greater than 10.0 volts?**	Yes No	▲ GO to D8. ▲ CHECK connectors, SERVICE or REPLACE harness. C3 is open. REMOVE all test equipment. RECONNECT all components. CLEAR Continuous Memory. RERUN Quick Test.
D8	CHECK FOR C4 HIGH AT ICM—KOEO • Key on, engine off. • Measure voltage between (+)J55 (LC4I) and (-)J7 (B-) at breakout box. • **Is DC voltage reading greater than 10.0 volts?**	Yes No	▲ GO to D9. ▲ CHECK connectors, SERVICE or REPLACE harness. C4 is open.REMOVE all test equipment. RECONNECT all components. CLEAR Continuous Memory. RERUN Quick Test.
D9	CHECK FOR C3 LOW AT COIL CONNECTOR—COIL DISCONNECTED—KOEO • Key off. • Disconnect left coil pack from coil tee, leave EI diagnostic harness connected to vehicle harness coil connector. • DVOM on 20 volt DC scale. • Key on, engine off. • Measure voltage between (+)J10 (LC3C) and (-)J7 (B-) at breakout box. • **Is DC voltage reading less than 0.5 volts?**	Yes No	▲ GO to D10. ▲ GO to D17. C3 high fault.

Fig. 110 EDIS testing—1993-94 vehicles

4.6L—2V, 4V Car EI (High Data Rate) No Start or Code 217 or 238 and/or Coil Failure — Pinpoint Test — D

TEST STEP	RESULT	ACTION TO TAKE
D14 CHECK FOR C3 SHORT LOW—ICM AND COIL DISCONNECTED—KEY OFF • Key off. • Disconnect ICM from vehicle harness. • DVOM on 20K ohm scale. • Measure resistance between J7 (B-) and J10 (C3C) at breakout box. • **Is resistance greater than 10K ohms?**	Yes ▲ No ▲	REPLACE ICM. C3 is shorted low. REMOVE all test equipment. RECONNECT all components. CLEAR Continuous Memory. RERUN Quick Test. CHECK connectors, SERVICE or REPLACE harness. C3 is shorted low. REMOVE all test equipment. RECONNECT all components. CLEAR Continuous Memory. RERUN Quick Test.
D15 CHECK FOR C4 SHORT LOW—COIL DISCONNECTED—KEY OFF • Key off. • DVOM on 20K ohm scale. • Disconnect coil from coil tee, leave EI diagnostic harness connected to vehicle harness coil connector. • Measure resistance between J7 (B-) and J18 (LC4C) at breakout box. • **Is resistance reading less than 2K ohms?**	Yes ▲ No ▲	GO to D16. REPLACE left coil pack. C4 open in coil. REMOVE all test equipment. RECONNECT all components. CLEAR Continuous Memory. RERUN Quick Test.
D16 CHECK FOR C4 SHORT LOW—ICM AND COIL DISCONNECTED—KEY OFF • Key off. • Disconnect ICM from vehicle harness connector. • DVOM on 20K ohm scale. • Measure resistance between J7 (B-) and J18 (LC4C) at breakout box. • **Is resistance reading greater than 10K ohms?**	Yes ▲ No ▲	REPLACE ICM. C4 is shorted low. REMOVE all test equipment. RECONNECT all components. CLEAR Continuous Memory. RERUN Quick Test. CHECK connectors, SERVICE or REPLACE harness. C4 is shorted low. REMOVE all test equipment. RECONNECT all components. CLEAR Continuous Memory. RERUN Quick Test.

84172134

Fig. 112 EDIS testing—1993–94 vehicles

4.6L—2V, 4V Car EI (High Data Rate) No Start or Code 217 or 238 and/or Coil Failure — Pinpoint Test — D

TEST STEP	RESULT	ACTION TO TAKE
D17 CHECK FOR C3 LOW—ICM AND COIL DISCONNECTED—KOEO • Key off. • Disconnect ICM from the ICM tee, leave EI diagnostic harness connected to vehicle harness connector. • DVOM on 20 volt DC scale. • Key on, engine off. • Measure voltage between (+)J10 (LC3C) and (-)J7 (B-) at breakout box. • **Is DC voltage reading less than 0.5 volts?**	Yes ▲ No ▲	REPLACE ICM. C3 is shorted high. REMOVE all test equipment. RECONNECT all components. CLEAR Continuous Memory. RERUN Quick Test. CHECK connectors, SERVICE or REPLACE harness. C3 is shorted high. REMOVE all test equipment. RECONNECT all components. CLEAR Continuous Memory. RERUN Quick Test.
D18 CHECK FOR C4 LOW—ICM AND COIL DISCONNECTED—KOEO • Key off. • Disconnect ICM from ICM tee, leave EI diagnostic harness connected to vehicle harness connector. • DVOM on 20 volt DC scale. • Key on, engine off. • Measure voltage between (+)J18 (LC4C) and (-)J7 (B-) at breakout box. • **Is DC voltage reading less than 0.5 volts?**	Yes ▲ No ▲	REPLACE ICM. C4 is shorted high. REMOVE all test equipment. RECONNECT all components. CLEAR Continuous Memory. RERUN Quick Test. CHECK connectors, SERVICE or REPLACE harness. C4 is shorted high. REMOVE all test equipment. RECONNECT all components. CLEAR Continuous Memory. RERUN Quick Test.

84172135

Fig. 113 EDIS testing—1993–94 vehicles

4.6L-2V, 4V Car EI (High Data Rate) No Start or Code 215 or 216 and/or Coil Failure — Pinpoint Test D

TEST STEP	RESULT		ACTION TO TAKE
D19 CHECK RIGHT PLUGS AND WIRES—KEY OFF • Check right side coil pack spark plug wires for insulation damage, looseness, shorting or other damage. • Remove and check right spark plugs for damage, wear, carbon deposits and proper plug gap. NOTE: Right coil plugs and wires are attached to the right coil. • **Are spark plugs and wires OK?**	Yes No	▶ ▶	REINSTALL plugs and wires. GO to D20. SERVICE or REPLACE damaged component. REMOVE all test equipment. RECONNECT all components. CLEAR Continuous Memory. RERUN Quick Test.
D20 CHECK FOR RIGHT COIL PWR—KOEO WARNING: NEVER CONNECT PCM TO THE EEC BREAKOUT BOX WHEN PERFORMING EI DIAGNOSTICS. • Key off. • Install EI diagnostic harness to the breakout box. • Connect EI diagnostic harness negative lead to battery. • Install the right coil tee. • Use 4.6L EI (High Data Rate) 8 overlay. • DVOM on 20 volt DC scale. • Set EI harness box type switch to 8 cylinder position. • Key on, engine off. • Measure voltage between (+)JU5 (COIL PWR R) and (-)JU7 (B-) at breakout box. • **Is DC voltage greater than 10.0 volts?**	Yes No	▶ ▶	GO to D21. CHECK connectors, SERVICE or REPLACE harness. COIL PWR is open to right coil. REMOVE all test equipment. RECONNECT all components. CLEAR Continuous Memory. RERUN Quick Test.
D21 CHECK FOR C1 HIGH AT RIGHT COIL PACK—KOEO • DVOM on 20 volt DC scale. • Key on, engine off. • Measure voltage between (+)JJ3 (RC1C) and (-)JU7 (B-) at breakout box. • **Is DC voltage reading greater than 10.0 volts?**	Yes No	▶ ▶	GO to D22. D29. C1 low fault.
D22 CHECK FOR C2 HIGH AT RIGHT COIL PACK • Key on, engine off. • Measure voltage between (+)JU6 (RC2C) and (-)JU7 (B-) at breakout box. • **Is DC voltage reading greater than 10.0 volts?**	Yes No	▶ ▶	GO to D23. D31. C2 low fault.

Fig. 114 EDIS testing—1993-94 vehicles

4.6L-2V, 4V Car EI (High Data Rate) No Start or Code 215 or 216 and/or Coil Failure — Pinpoint Test D

TEST STEP	RESULT		ACTION TO TAKE
D23 CHECK FOR C1 HIGH AT ICM—KOEO • Key off. • Connect ICM tee to the ICM and vehicle harness connector. • DVOM on 20 volt DC scale. • Key on, engine off. • Measure voltage between (+)JU51 (RC1I) and (-)JU7 (B-) at breakout box. • **Is DC voltage reading greater than 10.0 volts?**	Yes No	▶ ▶	GO to D24. CHECK connectors, SERVICE or REPLACE harness. C1 is open. REMOVE all test equipment. RECONNECT all components. CLEAR Continuous Memory. RERUN Quick Test.
D24 CHECK FOR C2 HIGH AT ICM • Key on, engine off. • Measure voltage between (+)JU27 (RC2I) and (-)JU7 (B-) at breakout box. • **Is DC voltage reading greater than 10.0 volts?**	Yes No	▶ ▶	GO to D25. CHECK connectors, SERVICE or REPLACE harness. C2 is open. REMOVE all test equipment. RECONNECT all components. CLEAR Continuous Memory. RERUN Quick Test.
D25 CHECK C1 LOW AT COIL CONNECTOR—COIL DISCONNECTED • Key off. • Disconnect right coil from coil tee, leave EI diagnostic harness connected to vehicle harness right coil connector. • DVOM on 20 volt DC scale. • Key on, engine off. • Measure voltage between (+)JJ3 (RC1C) and (-)JU7 (B-) at breakout box. • **Is DC voltage reading less than 0.5 volts?**	Yes No	▶ ▶	GO to D26. D33. C1 high fault.
D26 CHECK FOR C2 LOW AT COIL CONNECTOR—COIL DISCONNECTED • Key on, engine off. • Measure voltage between (+)JU6 (RC2C) and (-)JU7 (B-) at breakout box. • **Is DC voltage reading less than 0.5 volts?**	Yes No	▶ ▶	GO to D27. D34. C2 high fault.

Fig. 115 EDIS testing—1993-94 vehicles

4.6L-2V, 4V Car EI (High Data Rate) No Start or Code 215 or 216 and/or Coil Failure — Pinpoint Test D

	TEST STEP	RESULT	ACTION TO TAKE
D30	CHECK FOR C1 SHORT LOW—ICM AND COIL DISCONNECTED • Key off. • Disconnect ICM from vehicle harness. • DVOM on 20K ohm scale. • Measure resistance between J7 (B-) and J3 (RC1C) at breakout box. • **Is resistance reading greater than 10K ohms?**	Yes ▲ No ▲	REPLACE ICM. C1 is shorted low. REMOVE all test equipment. RECONNECT all components. CLEAR Continuous Memory. RERUN Quick Test. CHECK connectors, SERVICE or REPLACE harness. C1 is shorted to low. REMOVE all test equipment. RECONNECT all components. CLEAR Continuous Memory. RERUN Quick Test.
D31	CHECK FOR C2 SHORT LOW—COIL DISCONNECTED • Key off. • DVOM on 20K ohm scale. • Disconnect coil from coil tee, leave EI diagnostic harness connected to vehicle harness coil connector. • Measure resistance between J7 (B-) and J6 (RC2C) at breakout box. • **Is resistance reading less than 2K ohms?**	Yes ▲ No ▲	GO to **D32**. REPLACE Right Coil Pack. C2 open in coil. REMOVE all test equipment. RECONNECT all components. CLEAR Continuous Memory. RERUN Quick Test.
D32	CHECK FOR C2 SHORT LOW—ICM AND COIL DISCONNECTED • Key off. • Disconnect ICM from vehicle harness. • DVOM on 20K ohm scale. • Measure resistance between J6 (RC2C) and J7 (B-) at breakout box. • **Is resistance reading greater than 10K ohms?**	Yes ▲ No ▲	REPLACE ICM. C2 is shorted low. REMOVE all test equipment. RECONNECT all components. CLEAR Continuous Memory. RERUN Quick Test. CHECK connectors, SERVICE or REPLACE harness. C2 is shorted low. REMOVE all test equipment. RECONNECT all components. CLEAR Continuous Memory. RERUN Quick Test.

Fig. 117 EDIS testing—1993–94 vehicles

4.6L-2V, 4V Car EI (High Data Rate) No Start or Code 215 or 216 and/or Coil Failure — Pinpoint Test D

	TEST STEP	RESULT	ACTION TO TAKE
D27	CHECK C1 AT COIL CONNECTOR WHILE CRANKING ENGINE—COIL DISCONNECTED • Connect EI diagnostic harness positive lead to battery. • Connect an incandescent test lamp between J1 (B+) and J3 (RC1C). • Crank engine. • **Does lamp blink consistently and brightly (one blink per engine revolution)?**	Yes ▲ No ▲	GO to **D28**. REPLACE ICM. C1 is open. REMOVE all test equipment. RECONNECT all components. CLEAR Continuous Memory. RERUN Quick Test.
D28	CHECK C2 AT COIL CONNECTOR WHILE CRANKING ENGINE—COIL DISCONNECTED • Connect an incandescent test lamp between J1 (B+) and J6 (RC2C). • Crank engine. • **Does lamp blink consistently and brightly (one blink per engine revolution)?**	Yes ▲ No ▲	REPLACE Right Coil Pack. Input to coil pack is OK, but no high voltage output. REMOVE all test equipment. RECONNECT all components. CLEAR Continuous Memory. RERUN Quick Test. REPLACE ICM. C2 is open in ICM. REMOVE all test equipment. RECONNECT all components. CLEAR Continuous Memory. RERUN Quick Test.
D29	CHECK FOR C1 SHORT LOW—COIL DISCONNECTED • Key off. • DVOM on 20K ohm scale. • Disconnect coil from coil tee, leave EI diagnostic harness connected to vehicle harness coil connector. • Measure resistance between J7 (B-) and J3 (RC1C) at breakout box. • **Is resistance reading less than 2K ohms?**	Yes ▲ No ▲	GO to **D30**. REPLACE Right Coil Pack. C1 is open in coil. REMOVE all test equipment. RECONNECT all components. CLEAR Continuous Memory. RERUN Quick Test.

Fig. 116 EDIS testing—1993–94 vehicles

4.6L-2V, 4V Car EI (High Data Rate) No Start or Code 215 or 216 and/or Coil Failure	Pinpoint Test	D

	TEST STEP	RESULT	▶	ACTION TO TAKE
D33	CHECK FOR C1 HIGH—ICM AND COIL DISCONNECTED			
	• Key off. • Disconnect ICM from ICM tee, leave EI diagnostic harness connected to vehicle harness connector. • DVOM on 20 volt DC scale. • Key on, engine off. • Measure voltage between (+)J3 (RC1C) and (-)J7 (B-) at breakout box. • **Is DC voltage reading less than 0.5 volts?**	Yes No	▶ ▶	REPLACE ICM. REMOVE all test equipment. RECONNECT all components. CLEAR Continuous Memory. RERUN Quick Test. CHECK connectors, SERVICE or REPLACE harness. C1 is shorted high. REMOVE all test equipment. RECONNECT all components. CLEAR Continuous Memory. RERUN Quick Test.
D34	CHECK FOR C2 LOW—ICM AND COIL DISCONNECTED—KOEO			
	• Key off. • Disconnect ICM from ICM tee, leave EI diagnostic harness connected to vehicle harness connector. • DVOM on 20 volt DC scale. • Key on, engine off. • Measure voltage between (+)J6 (RC2C) and (-)J7 (B-) at breakout box. • **Is DC voltage reading less than 0.5 volts?**	Yes No	▶ ▶	REPLACE ICM. REMOVE all test equipment. RECONNECT all components. CLEAR Continuous Memory. RERUN Quick Test. CHECK connectors, SERVICE or REPLACE harness. C2 is shorted high. REMOVE all test equipment. RECONNECT all components. CLEAR Continuous Memory. RERUN Quick Test.

84172140

Fig. 118 EDIS testing—1993–94 vehicles

Component Replacement

DISTRIBUTOR

Removal

1. Disconnect the negative battery cable.
2. Mark the position of the No. 1 cylinder wire tower on the distributor base.

➡**This reference is necessary in case the engine is disturbed while the distributor is removed.**

3. Remove the distributor cap and position the cap and ignition wires to the side. Disconnect the wiring harness plug from the distributor connector. Disconnect and plug the vacuum hoses from the vacuum diaphragm assembly, if equipped.
4. Scribe a mark on the distributor body to indicate the position of the rotor tip. Scribe a mark on the distributor housing and engine block to indicate the position of the distributor in the engine.
5. Remove the hold-down bolt and clamp located at the base of the distributor. Remove the distributor from the engine. Note the direction the rotor tip points if it moves from the No. 1 position when the drive gear disengages. For reinstallation purposes, the rotor should be at this point to insure proper gear mesh and timing.
6. Cover the distributor opening in the engine to prevent the entry of dirt or foreign material.
7. Avoid turning the engine, if possible, while the distributor is removed. If the engine is disturbed, the No. 1 cylinder piston will have to be brought to Top Dead Center (TDC) on the compression stroke before the distributor is installed.

Installation

➡**Before installing, visually inspect the distributor. The drive gear should be free of nicks, cracks and excessive wear. The distributor drive shaft should move freely, without binding. If equipped with an O-ring, it should fit tightly and be free of cuts.**

TIMING NOT DISTURBED

1. Position the distributor in the engine, aligning the rotor and distributor housing with the marks that were made during removal. If the distributor does not fully seat in the engine block or timing cover, it may be because the distributor is not engaging properly with the oil pump intermediate shaft. Remove the distributor and, using a screwdriver or similar tool, turn the intermediate shaft until the distributor will seat properly.
2. Install the hold-down clamp and bolt. Snug the mounting bolt so the distributor can be turned for ignition timing purposes.
3. Install the distributor cap and connect the distributor to the wiring harness.
4. Connect the negative battery cable. Check and, if necessary, set the ignition timing. Tighten the distributor hold-down clamp bolt to 17–25 ft. lbs. (23–34 Nm). Recheck the ignition timing after tightening the bolt.
5. If equipped, connect the vacuum diaphragm hoses.

TIMING DISTURBED

1. Disconnect the No. 1 cylinder spark plug wire and remove the No. 1 cylinder spark plug.
2. Place a finger over the spark plug hole and crank the engine slowly until compression is felt.
3. Align the TDC mark on the crankshaft pulley with the pointer on the timing cover. This places the piston in No. 1 cylinder at TDC on the compression stroke.
4. Turn the distributor shaft until the rotor points to the distributor cap No. 1 spark plug tower.
5. Install the distributor in the engine, aligning the rotor and distributor housing with the marks that were made during removal. If the distributor does not fully seat in the engine block or timing cover, it may be because the distributor is not engaging properly with the oil pump intermediate shaft. Remove the distributor and, using a screwdriver or similar tool, turn the intermediate shaft until the distributor will seat properly.

6. Install the hold-down clamp and bolt. Snug the mounting bolt so the distributor can be turned for ignition timing purposes.
7. Install the No. 1 cylinder spark plug and connect the spark plug wire. Install the distributor cap and connect the distributor to the wiring harness.
8. Connect the negative battery cable and set the ignition timing.
9. After the timing has been set, tighten the distributor hold-down clamp bolt to 17–25 ft. lbs. (23–34 Nm). Recheck the ignition timing after tightening the bolt.
10. If equipped, connect the vacuum diaphragm hoses.

STATOR ASSEMBLY

Removal & Installation

5.0L ENGINE

♦ See Figures 119 and 120

1. Remove the distributor assembly from the engine; refer to the procedure in this Section.
2. Remove the ignition rotor from the distributor shaft.

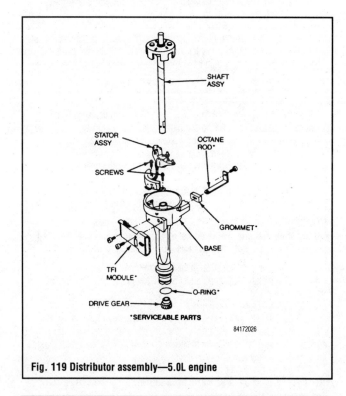

Fig. 119 Distributor assembly—5.0L engine

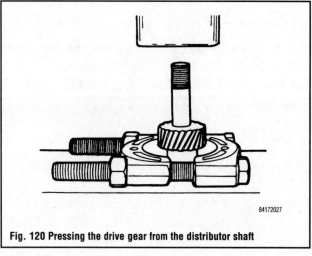

Fig. 120 Pressing the drive gear from the distributor shaft

3. Remove the 2 TFI-IV module retaining screws and remove the module. Wipe the grease from the distributor and module, keeping the surfaces free of dirt.

4. Mark the armature and distributor drive gear with a felt tip pen or equivalent, to note their orientation. While holding the distributor gear, loosen the 2 armature retaining screws and remove the armature.

➡**Do not hold the armature to loosen the screws.**

5. Use a suitable punch to remove the roll pin from the distributor drive gear; discard the roll pin.

6. Position the distributor upside down in a suitable press. Using a press plate and suitable driver, press off the distributor drive gear.

7. Use a file and/or emery paper to remove any burrs or deposits from the distributor shaft, that would keep the shaft from sliding freely from the distributor housing. Remove the shaft assembly.

8. Remove the 2 stator assembly retaining screws and remove the stator assembly.

9. Inspect the base bushing for wear or signs of excess heat concentration. If damage is evident, the entire distributor assembly must be replaced.

10. Inspect the base O-ring for cuts or damage and replace, as necessary.

11. Inspect the base for cracks and wear. Replace the entire distributor assembly if the base is damaged.

To install:

12. Position the stator assembly over the bushing and press down to seat.

13. Position the stator connector. The tab should fit in the notch on the base and the fastening eyelets should be aligned with the screw holes. Be sure the wires are positioned out of the way of moving parts.

14. Install the 2 stator retaining screws and tighten to 15–35 inch lbs. (1.7–4.0 Nm).

15. Apply a thin coat of clean engine oil to the distributor shaft below the armature. Insert the shaft into the distributor base.

16. Place a ½ in. deep well socket over the distributor shaft, invert the assembly and place on the press plate.

17. Position the distributor drive gear on the end of the distributor shaft, aligning the marks on the armature and gear. Make sure the holes in the shaft and drive gear are aligned, so the roll pin can be installed.

18. Place a ⅝ in. deep well socket over the shaft and gear and press the gear until the holes are aligned.

➡**If the shaft and gear holes do not align, the gear must be removed and repressed. Do not attempt to use a drift punch to align the holes.**

19. Drive a new roll pin through the gear and shaft.

20. Install the armature and tighten the screws to 25–35 inch lbs. (2.8–4.0 Nm).

21. Check that the distributor shaft moves freely over full rotation. If the armature contacts the stator, the entire distributor must be replaced.

22. Make sure the back of the TFI-IV module and and the distributor mounting face are clean. Apply silicone dielectric compound to the back of the module, spreading thinly and evenly.

23. Turn the distributor base upside down, so the stator connector is in full view. Install the module, watching to make sure the 3 module pins are fully inserted into the stator connector. Fully seat the module into the connector and against the base.

24. Install the 2 module retaining screws and tighten to 15–35 inch lbs. (1.7–4.0 Nm).

25. Install the ignition rotor onto the distributor shaft. Install the distributor, as described in this Section.

5.8L ENGINE

♦ **See Figure 121**

1. Disconnect the negative battery cable.

2. Remove the distributor cap, rotor and adapter.

3. Separate the distributor connector from the wiring harness.

4. Using a small gear puller or 2 small prybars, remove the armature from the sleeve and plate assembly. Use caution to avoid losing the roll pin.

5. Remove the C-clip securing the diaphragm rod to the stator assembly. Lift the diaphragm rod off the stator assembly pin.

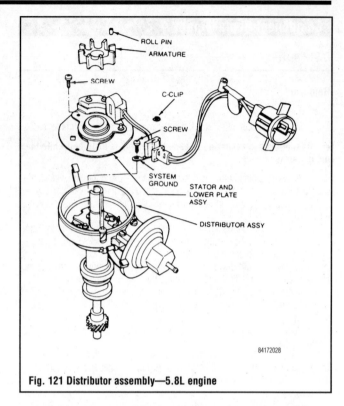

Fig. 121 Distributor assembly—5.8L engine

6. Remove the screw retaining the ground strap at the stator assembly grommet. Remove the wire retaining clip from the lower plate assembly.

7. Remove the ground from the distributor base and lift the stator assembly off the lower plate assembly.

To install:

8. Place the stator assembly on the lower plate assembly bushing and install the wire retaining clip.

9. Place the diaphragm rod over the pin on the stator assembly and install the C-clip.

10. Insert the stator assembly grommet in the distributor base slot. Install and tighten the ground strap retaining screw to 15 inch lbs. (1.7 Nm).

11. Note there are 2 locating notches in the armature and install it on the sleeve and plate assembly with the unused notch and new roll pin.

12. Connect the distributor wiring harness. Install the distributor adapter, rotor and cap. Install the ignition wires. Verify that the spark plug wires are securely connected to the distributor cap and spark plugs.

13. Connect the negative battery cable and check the ignition timing.

VACUUM DIAPHRAGM ASSEMBLY

Removal & Installation

5.8L ENGINE

1. Disconnect the diaphragm assembly vacuum hose(s).

2. Remove the C-clip securing the diaphragm rod to the stator assembly pin. Lift the diaphragm rod off the stator assembly pin.

3. Remove the 2 diaphragm assembly attaching screws and identification tag.

4. Remove the diaphragm assembly from the distributor base.

To install:

5. Adjust the new diaphragm assembly per manufacturer's instructions included with the new diaphragm.

6. Install the diaphragm to the distributor base. Attach the diaphragm assembly and identification tag to the distributor base with the 2 attaching screws and tighten to 15 inch lbs. (1.7 Nm).

7. Place diaphragm rod on the stator assembly pin and install the C-clip.

8. Reconnect the vacuum hoses.

IGNITION MODULE

Removal & Installation

4.6L ENGINE

♦ See Figure 122

1. Disconnect the negative battery cable.
2. Disconnect the electrical connectors at the module by pushing in on the connector finger ends while grasping the connector body and pulling away from the module.

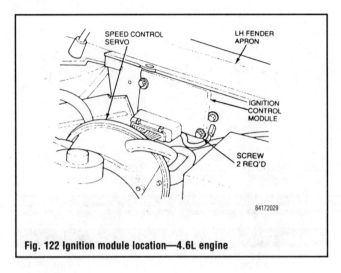

Fig. 122 Ignition module location—4.6L engine

3. Remove the module retaining screws and remove the module.

To install:

4. Install the module and the retaining screws. Tighten the screws to 24–35 inch lbs. (3–4 Nm).
5. Connect the electrical connectors to the module by pushing until the connector fingers are locked over the locking wedge feature on the module.

➡**Locking the connector is important to ensure sealing of the connector/module interface.**

6. Connect the negative battery cable.

5.0L ENGINE

1. Disconnect the negative battery cable.
2. Remove the distributor assembly from the engine, as described in this Section.
3. Place the distributor on a workbench and remove the the module retaining screws. Pull the right side of the module down the distributor mounting flange and back up to disengage the module terminals from the connector in the distributor base. The module may be pulled toward the flange and away from the distributor.

➡**Do not attempt to lift the module from the mounting surface except as explained in Step 3, as the pins will break at the distributor module connector.**

To install:

4. Coat the base plate of the TFI-IV ignition module uniformly with a ¹⁄₃₂ (0.79mm) thick film of silicone dielectric compound.
5. Position the module on the distributor base mounting flange. Carefully position the module toward the distributor bowl and engage the 3 connector pins securely.
6. Install the retaining screws. Tighten to 15–35 inch lbs. (1.7–4.0 Nm), starting with the upper right screw.
7. Install the distributor into the engine. Install the distributor cap and wires.
8. Connect the negative battery cable. Check the ignition timing.

CRANKSHAFT POSITION SENSOR

Removal & Installation

4.6L ENGINE

♦ See Figures 123 and 124

1. Disconnect the negative battery cable.
2. Remove the accessory drive belt (Refer to Section 1).
3. Raise and safely support the vehicle.
4. Disconnect the crankshaft position sensor and air conditioner compressor electrical connectors from the engine wiring harness.
5. Properly discharge the air conditioning system and remove the air conditioner compressor.
6. Remove the crankshaft position sensor retaining screw and remove the sensor.

To install:

7. Make sure the sensor mounting surface is clean and the sensor O-ring is in the proper location on the sensor assembly.
8. Position the sensor assembly and install the retaining screw. Tighten to 71–106 inch lbs. (8–12 Nm).

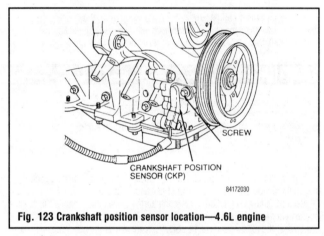

Fig. 123 Crankshaft position sensor location—4.6L engine

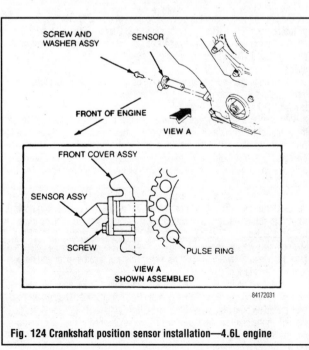

Fig. 124 Crankshaft position sensor installation—4.6L engine

Do not overtighten the screw.

9. Install the air conditioner compressor. Evacuate and recharge the system according to the proper procedure.
10. Properly route the engine wiring harness and connect the electrical connectors to the air conditioner compressor and crankshaft sensor.
11. Lower the vehicle.
12. Install the accessory belt and connect the negative battery cable.

IGNITION COIL PACK

Removal & Installation

4.6L ENGINE

▶ See Figure 125

1. Disconnect the negative battery cable.
2. Disconnect the electrical connectors from the coil pack and capacitor.
3. Disconnect the spark plug wires by squeezing the locking tabs and twisting while pulling upward.
4. Remove the 4 coil pack retaining bolts and remove the coil pack and capacitor. Save the capacitor for installation with the new coil pack.
5. Installation is the reverse of the removal procedure. Tighten the retaining

IGNITION TIMING

Ignition timing is the measurement, in degrees of crankshaft rotation, of the point at which the spark plugs fire in each of the cylinders. It is measured in degrees before or after Top Dead Center (TDC) of the compression stroke.

Ideally, the air/fuel mixture in the cylinder will be ignited by the spark plug just as the piston passes TDC of the compression stroke. If this happens, the piston will be beginning the power stroke just as the compressed and ignited air/fuel mixture starts to expand. The expansion of the air/fuel mixture then forces the piston down on the power stroke and turns the crankshaft.

Because it takes a fraction of a second for the spark plug to ignite the mixture in the cylinder, the spark plug must fire a little before the piston reaches TDC. Otherwise, the mixture will not be completely ignited as the piston passes TDC and the full power of the explosion will not be used by the engine.

The timing measurement is given in degrees of crankshaft rotation before the piston reaches TDC (BTDC, or Before Top Dead Center). If the setting for the ignition timing is 10 BTDC, each spark plug must fire 10 degrees before each piston reaches TDC. This only holds true, however, when the engine is at idle speed.

As the engine speed increases, the pistons go faster. The spark plugs have to ignite the fuel even sooner if it is to be completely ignited when the piston reaches TDC.

With the Duraspark II ignition system, the distributor has a means to advance the timing of the spark as the engine speed increases. This is accomplished by centrifugal weights within the distributor and a vacuum diaphragm mounted on the side of the distributor. With the TFI-IV and EDIS ignition systems, ignition timing is calculated at all phases of vehicle operation by the ignition control module.

If the ignition is set too far advanced (BTDC), the ignition and expansion of the fuel in the cylinder will occur too soon and tend to force the piston down while it is still traveling up. This causes engine ping. If the ignition spark is set too far retarded after TDC (ATDC), the piston will have already passed TDC and started on its way down when the fuel is ignited. This will cause the piston to be forced down for only a portion of its travel. This will result in poor engine performance and lack of power.

The ignition timing is checked with a timing light on 5.0L and 5.8L engines. This device is connected in series with the No. 1 spark plug. The current that fires the spark plug also causes the timing light to flash. The timing scale is located on the crankshaft pulley and a pointer is attached to the front timing cover. When the engine is running, the timing light is aimed at the mark on the crankshaft pulley and the scale. Timing adjustment is made at the distributor.

On the 4.6L engine, the base ignition timing is set from the factory at 10 degrees BTDC and is not adjustable.

bolts to 40–61 inch lbs. (5–7 Nm). Apply silicone dielectric compound to all spark plug wire boots prior to installation.

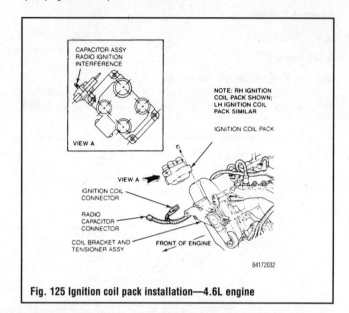

CAPACITOR ASSY
RADIO IGNITION
INTERFERENCE

NOTE: RH IGNITION
COIL PACK SHOWN;
LH IGNITION COIL
PACK SIMILAR

IGNITION COIL PACK

VIEW A

VIEW A

IGNITION COIL
CONNECTOR

RADIO
CAPACITOR
CONNECTOR

COIL BRACKET AND
TENSIONER ASSY

FRONT OF ENGINE

84172032

Fig. 125 Ignition coil pack installation—4.6L engine

Timing Procedures

ADJUSTMENT

5.0L Engine

▶ See Figure 126

1. Locate the timing marks and pointer on the crankshaft pulley and the timing cover. Clean the marks so they will be visible with a timing light. Apply chalk or bright-colored paint, if necessary.
2. Place the transaxle in **P** or **N**. The air conditioning and heater controls should be in the **OFF** position.
3. Connect a suitable tachometer and inductive timing light according to the manufacturer's instructions.

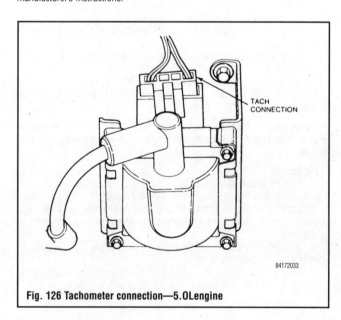

TACH
CONNECTION

84172033

Fig. 126 Tachometer connection—5.0L engine

➡The tachometer can be connected to the ignition coil without removing the coil connector. Insert an alligator clip into the back of the connector, onto the dark green/yellow dotted wire. Do not let the clip accidently ground to a metal surface as it may permanently damage the coil.

4. Disconnect the single wire in-line SPOUT connector or remove the shorting bar from the double wire SPOUT connector.

5. Start the engine and allow it to warm up to operating temperature.

➡To set timing correctly, a remote starter should not be used. Use the ignition key only to start the vehicle. Disconnecting the start wire at the starter relay will cause the TFI module to revert to start mode timing after the vehicle is started. Reconnecting the start wire after the vehicle is running will not correct the timing.

6. With the engine at the timing rpm specified, check the initial timing by aiming the timing light at the timing marks and pointer. Refer to the Vehicle Emission Control Information Label for specifications.

7. If the marks align, shut OFF the engine and proceed to Step 8. If the marks do not align, shut OFF the engine and loosen the distributor hold-down clamp bolt. Start the engine, aim the timing light and turn the distributor until the timing marks align. Shut off the engine and tighten the distributor hold-down clamp bolt to 17–25 ft. lbs. (23–34 Nm). Recheck the timing after the bolt has been tightened.

8. Reconnect the single wire in-line SPOUT connector or reinstall the shorting bar on the double wire SPOUT connector. Check the timing advance to verify the distributor is advancing beyond the initial setting.

9. Remove the inductive timing light and tachometer.

5.8L Engine

◆ See Figure 127

1. Locate the timing marks and pointer on the crankshaft pulley and the timing cover. Clean the marks so they will be visible with a timing light. Apply chalk or bright-colored paint, if necessary.

2. Place the transaxle in **P** or **N**. The air conditioning and heater controls should be in the **OFF** position.

3. Disconnect the vacuum hoses from the distributor vacuum advance connection at the distributor and plug the hoses.

4. Connect a suitable inductive timing light and a tachometer according to the manufacturer's instructions.

➡The tachometer can be connected to the ignition coil without removing the coil connector. Insert an alligator clip into the TACH TEST cavity and connect the tachometer lead to the alligator clip.

5. If equipped with a barometric pressure switch, disconnect it from the ignition module and place a jumper wire across the pins at the ignition module connector (yellow and black wires).

6. Start the engine and allow it to warm up to operating temperature.

7. With the engine at the timing rpm specified, check the initial timing by aiming the timing light at the timing marks and pointer. Refer to the Vehicle Emission Control Information Label for specifications.

8. If the marks align, proceed to Step 9. If the marks do not align, shut OFF the engine and loosen the distributor hold-down clamp bolt. Start the engine, aim the timing light and turn the distributor until the timing marks align. Shut OFF the engine and tighten the distributor hold-down clamp bolt to 17–25 ft. lbs. (23–34 Nm). Recheck the timing after the bolt has been tightened.

9. Remove the timing light and tachometer.

10. Unplug and reconnect the vacuum hoses. Remove the jumper wire from the ignition connector and reconnect, if applicable.

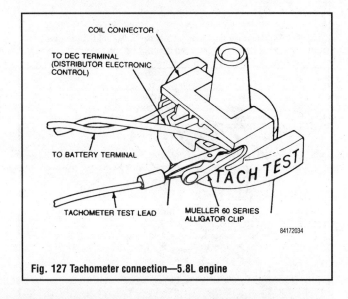

Fig. 127 Tachometer connection—5.8L engine

VALVE LASH

The 4.6L engine is equipped with hydraulic valve lash adjusters. The valve lash adjusters are mounted stationary in bores in the cylinder head. A roller follower is positioned between each lash adjuster and valve. When the camshaft turns, a lobe of the camshaft acts on the follower to open the valve. When the valve opening event is over and the base circle of the camshaft lobe contacts the follower, the valve spring pulls the valve closed. The function of the hydraulic lash adjuster is to maintain zero valve lash during the entire valve opening and closing process; any lash is instantaneously taken up by hydraulic action.

The 5.0L and 5.8L engines are equipped with hydraulic lifters. The lifters are located in bores in the cylinder block. As the camshaft turns, a camshaft lobe forces the lifter upwards in its bore. The lifter drives a pushrod upwards and acts on a pivoting rocker arm, which in turn opens the valve. When the valve opening event is over and the base circle of the camshaft lobe contacts the hydraulic lifter, the valve spring pulls the valve closed. The function of the hydraulic valve lifter is to maintain zero valve lash during the entire valve opening and closing process; any lash is instantaneously taken up by hydraulic action.

The hydraulic lash adjuster/lifter consists of 3 main parts: the body, the plunger and the valve. Oil under pressure from the engine lubricating system passes through the check valve and forces the plunger upwards in the body of the lash adjuster/lifter. The plunger contacts the roller follower in the case of the lash adjuster or the pushrod in the case of the lifter. The oil pressure removes all clearance between the 2 parts. The valve spring prevents the valve from being lifted off its seat.

During the valve opening event, the pressure from the valve spring forces the ball check valve onto its seat, preventing most of the oil from escaping from the

lash adjuster/lifter. The lash adjuster/lifter now acts as a solid link. Some oil is designed to escape from the lash adjuster/lifter to prevent the possibility of negative clearance, which would keep the valve open slightly.

When the valve is closing, any oil lost from the lash adjuster/lifter is replaced by the engine lubricating system. Once again, the oil pressure forces the plunger upwards to contact the follower or pushrod. The plunger constantly moves up and down a small amount within the bore of the lash adjuster/lifter, in this manner. On impact with the rocker arm or pushrod it moves downwards and, when relieved of the valve spring pressure, oil pressure forces it upwards.

The components of the hydraulic valve lash adjusters and valve lifters are manufactured to very close tolerances, so regular engine oil and filter changes are a must. Any dirt that gets into the lash adjuster/lifter can cause the check valve to malfunction and the plunger to wear, causing poor engine performance and noisy valve train operation.

Lash Procedures

CHECKING

◆ See Figures 128 and 129

Adjustment of the hydraulic lash adjusters or hydraulic lifters is neither possible or necessary. However, on the 4.6L engine, the collapsed hydraulic lash adjuster clearance can be checked and on the 5.0L and 5.8L engines, the collapsed hydraulic lifter clearance can be checked.

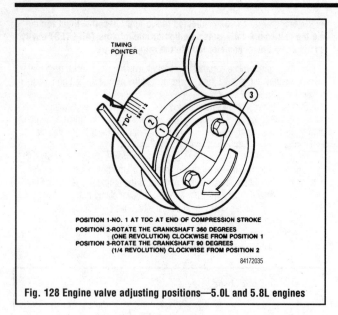

Fig. 128 Engine valve adjusting positions—5.0L and 5.8L engines

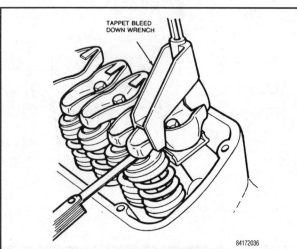

Fig. 129 Checking collapsed lifter valve clearance—5.0L and 5.8L engines

If the collapsed lash adjuster clearance is incorrect on the 4.6L engine, check the camshaft, roller follower and valve for wear or damage. If the collapsed lifter clearance is found to be incorrect on the 5.0L or 5.8L engines, there are replacement pushrods available to compensate for excessive or insufficient clearance.

4.6L Engine

1. Disconnect the negative battery cable.
2. Remove the camshaft covers. Refer to Section 3.
3. Rotate the crankshaft until the camshaft base circle is contacting the roller follower.
4. Use a suitable tool to bleed down the lash adjuster. Slowly compress the lash adjuster until the plunger is bottomed.
5. Use a feeler gauge to check the clearance between the roller follower and the valve stem tip. The clearance should be 0.018–0.033 in. (0.45–0.85mm).

5.0L Engine

1. Disconnect the negative battery cable.
2. Remove the rocker arm covers. Refer to Section 3.

3. Disconnect the spark plug wire from the No. 1 cylinder spark plug. Remove the spark plug.
4. Place a finger over the spark plug hole. Turn the crankshaft in the normal direction of engine rotation, using a socket and ratchet or breaker bar on the crankshaft bolt. Turn the crankshaft until compression is felt with your finger, indicating the piston is approaching Top Dead Center (TDC) on the compression stroke.
5. Continue turning the crankshaft until the mark on the crankshaft damper aligns with the pointer on the timing cover. The piston in No. 1 cylinder is now at TDC on the compression stroke.
6. With the crankshaft in the positions designated in Steps 8, 9 and 10, position lifter bleed down wrench tool T71P–6513–B or equivalent, on the rocker arm. Slowly apply pressure to bleed down the lifter until the plunger is completely bottomed. Hold the lifter in this position and check the available clearance between the rocker arm and the valve stem tip with a feeler gauge.
7. The clearance should be 0.071–0.171 in. If the clearance is less than specification, install a shorter pushrod. If the clearance is greater than specification, install a longer pushrod.
8. The following valves can be checked with the engine in position 1, No. 1 piston at TDC on the compression stroke.
   a. No. 1 intake—No. 1 exhaust
   b. No. 7 intake—No. 5 exhaust
   c. No. 8 intake—No. 4 exhaust
9. Rotate the crankshaft 360 degrees (1 revolution) from the 1st position and check the following valves:
   a. No. 5 intake—No. 2 exhaust
   b. No. 4 intake—No. 6 exhaust
10. Rotate the crankshaft 90 degrees (¼ revolution) from the 2nd position and check the following valves:
   a. No. 2 intake—No. 7 exhaust
   b. No. 3 intake—No. 3 exhaust
   c. No. 6 intake—No. 8 exhaust

5.8L Engine

1. Disconnect the negative battery cable.
2. Remove the rocker arm covers. Refer to Section 3.
3. Disconnect the spark plug wire from the No. 1 cylinder spark plug. Remove the spark plug.
4. Place a finger over the spark plug hole. Turn the crankshaft in the normal direction of engine rotation, using a socket and ratchet or breaker bar on the crankshaft bolt. Turn the crankshaft until compression is felt with your finger, indicating the piston is approaching Top Dead Center (TDC) on the compression stroke.
5. Continue turning the crankshaft until the **O** mark on the crankshaft damper aligns with the pointer on the timing cover. The piston in No. 1 cylinder is now at TDC on the compression stroke.
6. With the crankshaft in the positions designated in Steps 8, 9 and 10, position lifter bleed down wrench tool T71P–6513–B or equivalent, on the rocker arm. Slowly apply pressure to bleed down the lifter until the plunger is completely bottomed. Hold the lifter in this position and check the available clearance between the rocker arm and the valve stem tip with a feeler gauge.
7. The clearance should 0.092–0.192 in. If the clearance is less than specification, install a shorter pushrod. If the clearance is greater than specification, install a longer pushrod.
8. The following valves can be checked with the engine in position 1, No. 1 piston at TDC on the compression stroke.
   a. No. 1 intake—No. 1 exhaust
   b. No. 4 intake—No. 3 exhaust
   c. No. 8 intake—No. 7 exhaust
9. Rotate the crankshaft 360 degrees (1 revolution) from the 1st position and check the following valves:
   a. No. 3 intake—No. 2 exhaust
   b. No. 7 intake—No. 6 exhaust
10. Rotate the crankshaft 90 degrees (¼ revolution) from the 2nd position and check the following valves:
   a. No. 2 intake—No. 4 exhaust
   b. No. 5 intake—No. 5 exhaust
   c. No. 6 intake—No. 8 exhaust

IDLE SPEED ADJUSTMENT

On the 4.6L and 5.0L engines, the curb idle and fast idle speeds are controlled by the Powertrain Control Module (PCM) and the idle rpm control device. The idle rpm control device cannot be adjusted. The adjustment procedure should only be attempted if there is a change in idle speed and you have eliminated the following possible causes:

- Contamination within the throttle bore (check the throttle body, it may be identified with a yellow/black attention decal indicating it is of a sludge tolerant design).
- Contamination within the idle speed control device.
- Contaminated or defective oxygen sensor.
- Throttle sticking or binding.
- Engine not reaching operating temperature.
- Ignition timing out of specification.
- Clogged PCV system.
- Vacuum leaks at the intake manifold, vacuum hoses, vacuum reservoirs, power brake booster, etc.

ADJUSTMENT PROCEDURES

4.6L Engine

▶ See Figure 130

This procedure requires the use of the Ford SUPER STAR II tester, tool number 007–00028 or equivalent scan tool. Refer to Section 4 for further information.

1. Place the transaxle in **P** and apply the parking brake.
2. Start the engine and bring to normal operating temperature. Make sure the heater, air conditioning and all other accessories are OFF.
3. Check and if necessary, adjust the ignition timing.
4. Make sure the fuel pressure is correct. Any indicated vehicle malfunction service codes should be resolved before proceeding further.
5. Connect the SUPER STAR II tester or other suitable scan tool to the Self-Test connector. Activate the Key On Engine Running (KOER) Self-Test.
6. After Code 1 or 111 has been displayed, unlatch and within 4 seconds, latch the STI button.
7. A single pulse code indicates the entry mode, then observe the Self-Test Output (STO) on the tester for the following:

    a. A constant tone, solid light or **STO LO** readout means the base idle speed is within the correct range. To exit the test, unlatch the STI button, then wait 4 seconds for reinitialization. After 10 minutes, the tool will exit by itself.

    b. A beeping tone, flashing light or **STO LO** readout at 8 Hz indicates the Throttle Position Sensor (TPS) is out of range due to over adjustment. Adjustment may be required.

    c. A beeping tone, flashing light or **STO LO** readout at 4 Hz indicates the base idle speed is too fast and adjustment is required. Proceed to Step 9.

    d. A beeping tone, flashing light or **STO LO** readout at 1 Hz indicates the base idle speed is too low and adjustment is required. Proceed to Step 8.

8. If the idle speed is too low, do not clean the throttle body. Turn the air trim screw counterclockwise using offset Allen wrench T91P–9550–A or equivalent, until the conditions in Step 7a are satisfied.

9. If the idle speed is too high, do not clean the throttle body. Turn the air trim screw clockwise using offset Allen wrench T91P–9550–A or equivalent, until the conditions in Step 7a are satisfied.

5.0L Engine

1. Place the transmission in **N** or **P**. Apply the emergency brake and block the wheels. If equipped with automatic brake release, disconnect the vacuum hose and plug it.
2. Bring the engine to normal operating temperature. Place the air conditioner/heater selector to the **OFF** position. Check and, if necessary, adjust the ignition timing.
3. Disconnect the negative battery terminal for 5 minutes, then reconnect. Start the engine and stabilize for 2 minutes, then goose the engine and let it return to idle. Lightly depress and release the accelerator and let the engine idle. Check the engine idle.
4. If the engine does not idle properly, shut the engine OFF and proceed to Step 5.
5. Back out the throttle plate stop screw clear off the throttle lever pad. With a 0.010 in. feeler gauge between the throttle plate stop screw and the throttle lever pad, turn the screw in until contact is made, then turn an additional $1\frac{7}{8}$ turns.
6. Start the engine and stabilize for 2 minutes, then goose the engine and let it return to idle. Lightly depress and release the accelerator and let the engine idle.
7. Check the throttle valve cable adjustment; refer to Section 7.

5.8L Engine

▶ See Figure 131

1. Place the transmission in **N** or **P**. Apply the parking brake and block the wheels. If equipped with automatic brake release, disconnect the vacuum hose and plug it.
2. Bring the engine to normal operating temperature. Place the air conditioner/heater selector to the **OFF** position.
3. Disconnect the vacuum hose at the EGR valve and plug.
4. Place the fast idle adjustment on the second step of the fast idle cam. Check and/or adjust fast idle rpm to specification. Refer to the Vehicle Emission Control Information label.
5. Rev the engine momentarily and repeat Step 4. Remove the plug from the EGR vacuum hose and reconnect.
6. Disconnect and plug the vacuum hose at the throttle kicker and place

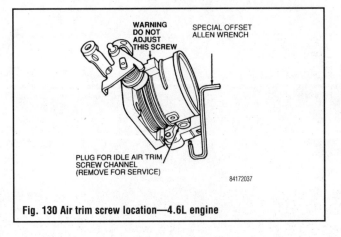

Fig. 130 Air trim screw location—4.6L engine

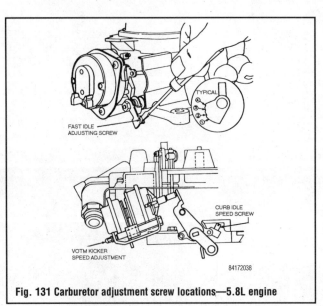

Fig. 131 Carburetor adjustment screw locations—5.8L engine

the transmission in the idle setting position specified on the Vehicle Emission Control Information label. If adjustment is required, turn the curb idle speed screw and set the idle to the speed specified on the label.

7. Put the transmission in **N** or **P**, increase the engine speed momentarily and recheck.

8. Apply a slight pressure on top of the nylon nut located on the accelerator pump to take up the linkage clearance. Turn the nut on the accelerator pump rod clockwise until a clearance of 0.010 in. plus or minus 0.005 in. is obtained between the top of the accelerator pump and the pump lever.

9. Turn the accelerator pump rod 1 turn counterclockwise to set the lever lash preload. Remove the plug from the throttle kicker vacuum hose and reconnect.

10. Disconnect and plug the vacuum hose at the Vacuum Operated Throttle Modulator (VOTM) kicker. Connect an external vacuum source providing a minimum of 10 in. Hg to the VOTM kicker. With the transmission in the specified position, check/adjust the VOTM kicker speed.

11. If adjustment is required, turn the VOTM kicker speed adjusting screw. Remove external vacuum source and reconnect VOTM kicker hose.

TORQUE SPECIFICATIONS

Component	U.S.	Metric
Armature retaining screws		
5.0L engine	25–35 inch lbs.	2.8–4.0 Nm
Crankshaft position sensor screw		
4.6L engine	71–106 inch lbs.	8–12 Nm
Distributor ground strap screw		
5.8L engine	15 inch lbs.	1.7 Nm
Distributor hold-down clamp bolt	17–25 ft. lbs.	23–34 Nm
Ignition coil pack bolts		
4.6L engine	40–61 inch lbs.	5–7 Nm
Ignition module retaining screws		
4.6L engine	24–35 inch lbs.	3–4 Nm
5.0L engine	15–35 inch lbs.	1.7–4.0 Nm
Spark plugs		
4.6L engine	7 ft. lbs.	10 Nm
5.0L engine	10 ft. lbs.	14 Nm
5.8L engine	15 ft. lbs.	20 Nm
Stator retaining screws		
5.0L engine	15–35 inch lbs.	1.7–4.0 Nm
Vacuum diaphragm screws		
5.8L engine	15 inch lbs.	1.7 Nm

CP84172141

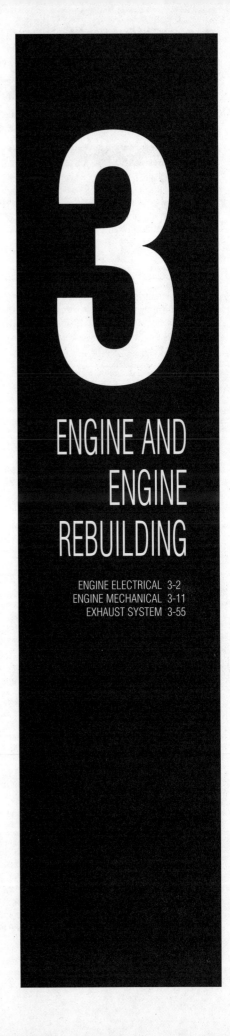

3

ENGINE AND ENGINE REBUILDING

ENGINE ELECTRICAL

➡For information on understanding electricity and troubleshooting electrical circuits, please refer to Section 6 of this manual.

Alternator

There are 2 different types of alternators used on 1989–91 vehicles. One is the side terminal alternator which uses an externally mounted voltage regulator. The other is an external fan alternator which has the voltage regulator mounted in the rear of the alternator housing (integral). All 1992–94 vehicles are equipped with an internal fan/integral voltage regulator type alternator.

PRECAUTIONS

Your car is equipped with an alternator. Unlike the direct current (DC) generators used on many old cars, there are several precautions which must be strictly observed in order to avoid damaging the unit. They are:

1. Always observe proper polarity of the battery connections: be especially careful when jump starting the car. (See Section 1 for jump starting procedures).
2. Never ground or short out the alternator or alternator regulator terminals.
3. Never operate the alternator with any of its or the battery's lead wires disconnected.
4. Always remove the battery or at least disconnect the ground cable while charging.
5. Always disconnect the battery ground cable while repairing or replacing an electrical component.
6. Never use a fast battery charger to jump start a dead battery.
7. Never attempt to polarize an alternator.
8. Never subject the alternator to excessive heat or dampness (for instance, steam cleaning the engine).
9. Never use arc welding equipment on the car with the alternator connected.

TESTING

▶ See Figure 1

When performing charging system tests, turn off all lights and electrical components. Place the transmission in **P** and apply the parking brake.

To ensure accurate meter indications, the battery terminal posts and battery cable clamps must be clean and tight.

✳✳ WARNING

Do not make jumper wire connections except as instructed. Incorrect jumper wire connections can damage the regulator or fuse links.

Preliminary Inspection

1. Make sure the battery cable connections are clean and tight.
2. Check all alternator and regulator wiring connections. Make sure all connections are clean and secure.
3. Check the alternator belt tension. Adjust, if necessary.
4. Check the fuse link between the starter relay and alternator. Replace if burned out.
5. Make sure the fuses/fuse links to the alternator are not burned or damaged. This could cause an open circuit or high resistance, resulting in erratic or intermittent charging problems.
6. If equipped with heated windshield, make sure the wiring connections to the alternator output control relay are correct and tight.
7. If equipped with heated windshield, make sure the connector to the heated windshield module is properly seated and there are no broken wires.

1989–91 Vehicles with External Regulator Alternator

CHARGING SYSTEM INDICATOR LIGHT TEST

▶ See Figure 2

1. If the charging system indicator light does not come on with the ignition key in the **RUN** position and the engine not running, check the ignition switch-to-regulator I terminal wiring for an open circuit or burned out charging system indicator light. Replace the light, if necessary.
2. If the charging system indicator light does not come on, disconnect the electrical connector at the regulator and connect a jumper wire between the I terminal of the connector and the negative battery cable clamp.
3. The charging system indicator light should go on with the ignition switch in the **RUN** position.
4. If the light does not go on, check the light for continuity and replace, if necessary.
5. If the light is not burned out, there is an open circuit between the ignition switch and the regulator.
6. Check the 500 ohm resistor across the indicator light.

BASE VOLTAGE TEST

▶ See Figure 3

1. Connect the negative and positive leads of a voltmeter to the negative and positive battery cable clamps.
2. Make sure the ignition switch is in the **OFF** position and all electrical loads (lights, radio, etc.) are OFF.
3. Record the battery voltage shown on the voltmeter; this is the base voltage.

NO-LOAD TEST

1. Connect a suitable tachometer to the engine.
2. Start the engine and bring the engine speed to 1500 rpm. With no other electrical loads (doors closed, foot off the brake pedal), the reading on the voltmeter should increase, but no more than 2.5 volts above the base voltage.

➡The voltage reading should be taken when the voltage stops rising. This may take a few minutes.

3. If the voltage increases as in Step 2, perform the Load Test.
4. If the voltage continues to rise, perform the Over Voltage Tests.
5. If the voltage does not rise to the proper level, perform the Under Voltage Tests.

LOAD TEST

1. With the engine running, turn the blower speed switch to the high speed position and turn the headlights on to high beam.
2. Raise the engine speed to approximately 2000 rpm. The voltmeter reading should be a minimum of 0.5 volts above the base voltage. If not, perform the Under Voltage Tests.

➡If the voltmeter readings in the No-Load Test and Load Test are as specified, the charging system is operating properly. Go to the following tests if one or more of the voltage readings differs, and also check for battery drain.

OVER VOLTAGE TESTS

▶ See Figure 4

1. If the voltmeter reading was more than 2.5 volts above the base voltage in the No-Load Test, connect a jumper wire between the voltage regulator base and the alternator frame or housing. Repeat the No-Load Test.
2. If the over voltage condition disappears, check the ground connections on the alternator, regulator and from the engine to the dash panel and to the battery. Clean and securely tighten the connections.
3. If the over voltage condition still exists, disconnect the voltage regulator wiring connector from the voltage regulator. Repeat the No-Load Test.

CONDITION	POSSIBLE SOURCE	ACTION
• Battery Does Not Stay Charged — Engine Starts OK	• Battery.	• Test battery, replace if necessary.
	• Loose or worn alternator belt.	• Adjust or replace belt.
	• Damaged or worn wiring or cables.	• Service as required.
	• Alternator.	• Test and/or replace components as required
	• Regulator.	• Test, replace if necessary
	• Other vehicle electrical systems.	• Check other systems for current draw. Service as required
• Alternator Noisy	• Loose or worn alternator belt.	• Adjust tension or replace belt.
	• Bent pulley flanges.	• Replace pulley.
	• Alternator.	• Service or replace alternator
• Lamps and/or Fuses Burn Out Frequently	• Damaged or worn wiring.	• Service as required.
	• Alternator/Regulator.	• Test, service, replace if necessary.
	• Battery.	• Test, replace if necessary.
• Charge Indicator Lamp Flickers After Engine Starts or Comes On While Vehicle Is Being Driven	• Loose or worn alternator belt.	• Adjust tension or replace.
	• Alternator.	• Service or replace
	• Field circuit ground.	• Service or replace wiring.
	• Regulator.	• Test, replace if necessary.
	• Lamp circuit wiring and connector.	• Service as required.
• Charge Indicator Lamp Flickers While Vehicle Is Being Driven	• Loose or worn alternator belt.	• Adjust tension or replace belt.
	• Loose or improper wiring connections.	• Service as required.
	• Alternator.	• Service or replace
	• Regulator.	• Test, replace if necessary
• Charge Indicator Gauge Shows Discharge	• Loose or worn alternator belt.	• Adjust tension or replace belt.
	• Damaged or worn wiring (battery to alternator for ground or open).	• Service or replace wiring.
	• Field circuit ground.	• Service or replace wiring.
	• Alternator.	• Service or replace
	• Regulator.	• Test, replace if necessary
	• Charge indicator gauge wiring and connections.	• Service as required.
	• Damaged or worn gauge.	• Replace gauge.
	• Other vehicle electrical system malfunction.	• Service as required.

84173195

Fig. 1 General charging system diagnosis

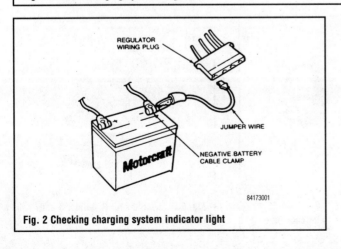

84173001

Fig. 2 Checking charging system indicator light

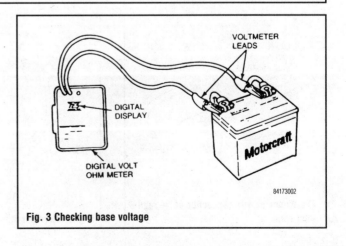

84173002

Fig. 3 Checking base voltage

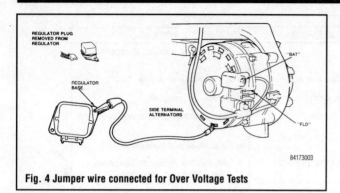

Fig. 4 Jumper wire connected for Over Voltage Tests

4. If the over voltage condition disappears (voltmeter reads base voltage), replace the voltage regulator.

5. If the over voltage condition still exists with the voltage regulator wiring connector disconnected, check for a short between circuits A and F in the wiring harness and service, as necessary. Then reconnect the voltage regulator wiring connector.

UNDER VOLTAGE TESTS

▶ **See Figures 5, 6 and 7**

1. If the voltage reading was not more than 0.5 volts above the base voltage, disconnect the wiring connector from the voltage regulator and connect an ohmmeter from the F terminal of the connector to ground. The ohmmeter should indicate more than 2.4 ohms.

2. If the ohmmeter reading is less than 2.4 ohms, service the grounded field circuit in the wiring harness or alternator and repeat the Load Test.

✳✳ WARNING

Do not replace the voltage regulator before a shorted rotor coil or field circuit has been serviced. Damage to the regulator could result.

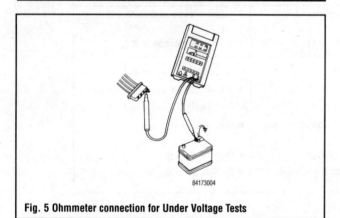

Fig. 5 Ohmmeter connection for Under Voltage Tests

3. If the ohmmeter reading is more than 2.4 ohms, connect a jumper wire from the A to F terminals of the wiring connector and repeat the Load Test. If the voltmeter now indicates more than 0.5 volts above the base voltage, the regulator or wiring is damaged or worn. Perform the S and I Circuit Tests and service the wiring or regulator, as required.

4. If the voltmeter still indicates an under voltage problem, remove the jumper wire from the voltage regulator connector and leave the connector disconnected from the regulator.

5. Disconnect the FLD terminal on the alternator and pull back the protective cover from the BAT terminal. Connect a jumper wire between the FLD and BAT terminals and repeat the Load Test.

6. If the voltmeter indicates a 0.5 volts or more increase above base voltage, perform the S and I Circuit Tests and service the wiring or regulator, as indicated.

7. If the voltmeter still indicates under voltage, shut the engine OFF and move the positive voltmeter lead to the BAT terminal of the alternator. If the voltmeter now indicates the base voltage, service the alternator. If the voltmeter indicates 0 volts, service the alternator-to-starter relay wire.

REGULATOR S AND I CIRCUIT TESTS

▶ **See Figure 8**

1. Disconnect the voltage regulator wiring connector and install a jumper wire between the A and F terminals.

2. With the engine idling and the negative voltmeter lead connected to the negative battery terminal, connect the positive voltmeter lead to the S terminal and then to the I terminal of the regulator wiring connector.

3. The S circuit voltage reading should be approximately ½ the I circuit reading. If the voltage readings are correct, remove the jumper wire. Replace the voltage regulator and repeat the Load Test.

4. If there is no voltage present, service the faulty wiring circuit. Connect the positive voltmeter lead to the positive battery terminal.

5. Remove the jumper wire from the regulator wiring connector and connect the connector to the regulator. Repeat the Load Test

FUSE LINK CONTINUITY

1. Make sure the battery is okay (See Section 1).

2. Turn on the headlights or any accessory. If the headlights or accessory do not operate, the fuse link is probably burned out.

3. On some vehicles there are several fuse links. Proceed as in Step 2 to test other fuse links.

4. To test the fuse link that protects the alternator, check for voltage at the BAT terminal of the alternator, using a voltmeter. If there is no voltage, the fuse link is probably burned out.

1989–91 Vehicles with Integral Regulator/External Fan Alternator

CHARGING SYSTEM INDICATOR LIGHT TEST

▶ **See Figure 9**

Two conditions can cause the charging system indicator light to come on when your car is running: no alternator output, caused by a damaged alternator, regulator or wiring, or an over voltage condition, caused by a shorted alternator rotor, regulator or wiring.

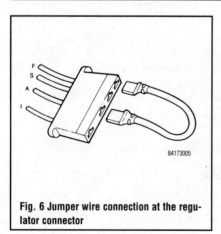

Fig. 6 Jumper wire connection at the regulator connector

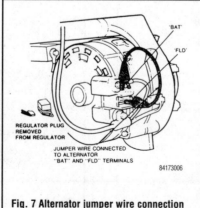

Fig. 7 Alternator jumper wire connection

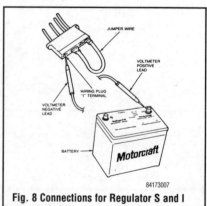

Fig. 8 Connections for Regulator S and I Circuit Tests

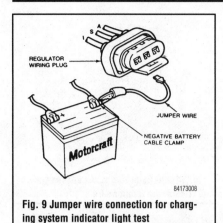

Fig. 9 Jumper wire connection for charging system indicator light test

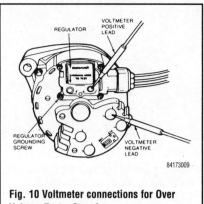
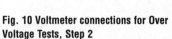

Fig. 10 Voltmeter connections for Over Voltage Tests, Step 2

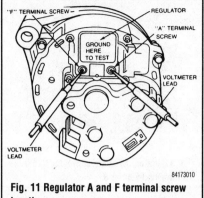

Fig. 11 Regulator A and F terminal screw locations

In a normally functioning system, the charging system indicator light will be OFF when the ignition switch is in the **OFF** position, ON when the ignition switch is in the **RUN** position and the engine not running, and OFF when the ignition switch is in the **RUN** position and the engine is running.

1. If the charging system indicator light does not come on, disconnect the wiring connector from the regulator.

2. Connect a jumper wire between the connector I terminal and the negative battery cable clamp.

3. Turn the ignition switch to the **RUN** position, but leave the engine OFF. If the charging system indicator light does not come on, check for a light socket resistor. If there is a resistor, check the contact of the light socket leads to the flexible printed circuit. If they are good, check the indicator light for continuity and replace if burned out. If the light checks out good, perform the Regulator I Circuit Test.

4. If the indicator light comes on, remove the jumper wire and reconnect the wiring connector to the regulator. Connect the negative voltmeter lead to the negative battery cable clamp and connect the positive voltmeter lead to the regulator A terminal screw. Battery voltage should be indicated. If battery voltage is not indicated, service the A circuit wiring.

5. If battery voltage is indicated, clean and tighten the ground connections to the engine, alternator and regulator. Tighten loose regulator mounting screws to 15–26 inch lbs. (1.7–2.8 Nm).

6. Turn the ignition switch to the **RUN** position with the engine OFF. If the charging system indicator light still does not come on, replace the regulator.

BASE VOLTAGE TEST

▶ **See Figure 3**

1. Connect the negative and positive leads of a voltmeter to the negative and positive battery cable clamps.

2. Make sure the ignition switch is in the **OFF** position and all electrical loads (lights, radio, etc.) are OFF.

3. Record the battery voltage shown on the voltmeter; this is the base voltage.

NO-LOAD TEST

1. Connect a suitable tachometer to the engine.

2. Start the engine and bring the engine speed to 1500 rpm. With no other electrical loads (doors closed, foot off the brake pedal), the reading on the voltmeter should increase, but no more than 2.5 volts above the base voltage.

➡**The voltage reading should be taken when the voltage stops rising. This may take a few minutes.**

3. If the voltage increases as in Step 2, perform the Load Test.

4. If the voltage continues to rise, perform the Over Voltage Tests.

5. If the voltage does not rise to the proper level, perform the Under Voltage Tests.

LOAD TEST

1. With the engine running, turn the blower speed switch to the high speed position and turn the headlights on to high beam.

2. Raise the engine speed to approximately 2000 rpm. The voltmeter reading should be a minimum of 0.5 volts above the base voltage. If not, perform the Under Voltage Tests.

➡**If the voltmeter readings in the No-Load Test and Load Test are as specified, the charging system is operating properly. Go to the following tests if one or more of the voltage readings differs, and also check for battery drain.**

OVER VOLTAGE TESTS

▶ **See Figures 10 and 11**

If the voltmeter reading was more than 2.5 volts above base voltage in the No-Load Test, proceed as follows:

1. Turn the ignition switch to the **RUN** position, but do not start the engine.

2. Connect the negative voltmeter lead to the alternator rear housing. Connect the positive voltmeter lead first to the alternator output connection at the starter solenoid and then to the regulator A screw head.

3. If there is greater than 0.5 volts difference between the 2 locations, service the A wiring circuit to eliminate the high resistance condition indicated by excessive voltage drop.

4. If the over voltage condition still exists, check for loose regulator and alternator grounding screws. Tighten loose regulator grounding screws to 15–26 inch lbs. (1.7–2.8 Nm).

5. If the over voltage condition still exists, connect the negative voltmeter lead to the alternator rear housing. With the ignition switch in the **OFF** position, connect the positive voltmeter lead first to the regulator A screw head and then to the regulator F screw head. If there are different voltage readings at the 2 screw heads, a malfunctioning grounded brush lead or a grounded rotor coil is indicated; service or replace the entire alternator/regulator unit.

6. If the same voltage is obtained at both screw heads in Step 5 and there is no high resistance in the ground of the A+ circuit, replace the regulator.

UNDER VOLTAGE TESTS

▶ **See Figures 12, 13 and 14**

If the voltmeter reading was not more than 0.5 volts above base voltage, proceed as follows:

1. Disconnect the electrical connector from the regulator. Connect an ohmmeter between the regulator A and F terminal screws. The ohmmeter reading should be more than 2.4 ohms. If it is less than 2.4 ohms, the regulator has failed. also check the alternator for a shorted rotor or field circuit. Perform the Load Test after servicing.

> ✳✳ **WARNING**
>
> **Do not replace the voltage regulator before a shorted rotor coil or field circuit has been serviced. Damage to the regulator could result.**

2. If the ohmmeter reading is greater than 2.4 ohms, connect the regulator wiring connector and connect the negative voltmeter lead to the alternator rear housing. Connect the positive voltmeter lead to the regulator A terminal screw. The voltmeter should indicate battery voltage. If there is no voltage, service the A wiring circuit and then perform the Load Test.

3. If the voltmeter indicates battery voltage, connect the negative voltmeter lead to the alternator rear housing. With the ignition switch in the **OFF** position, connect the positive voltmeter lead to the regulator F terminal screw. The volt-

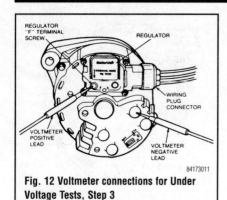

Fig. 12 Voltmeter connections for Under Voltage Tests, Step 3

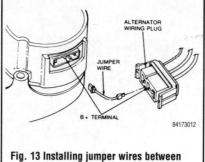

Fig. 13 Installing jumper wires between the B+ terminals

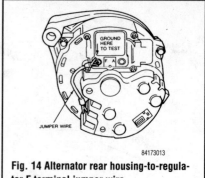

Fig. 14 Alternator rear housing-to-regulator F terminal jumper wire

meter should indicate battery voltage. If there is no voltage, there is an open field circuit in the alternator. Service or replace the alternator, then perform the Load Test after servicing.

4. If the voltmeter indicates battery voltage, connect the negative voltmeter lead to the alternator rear housing. Turn the ignition switch to the **RUN** position, leaving the engine off, and connect the positive voltmeter lead to the regulator F terminal screw. The voltmeter should read 1.5 volts or less. If more than 1.5 volts is indicated, perform the I circuit tests and service the I circuit if needed. If the I circuit is normal, replace the regulator, if needed, and perform the Load Test after servicing.

5. If 1.5 volts or less is indicated, disconnect the alternator wiring connector. Connect a set of 12 gauge jumper wires between the alternator B+ terminal blades and the mating wiring connector terminals. Perform the Load Test, but connect the positive voltmeter lead to one of the B+ jumper wire terminals. If the voltage increases more than 0.5 volts above base voltage, service the alternator-to-starter relay wiring. Repeat the Load Test, measuring voltage at the battery cable clamps after servicing.

6. If the voltage does not increase more than 0.5 volts above base voltage, connect a jumper wire from the alternator rear housing to the regulator F terminal. Repeat the Load Test with the positive voltmeter lead connected to one of the B+ jumper wire terminals. If the voltage increases more than 0.5 volts, replace the regulator. If the voltage does not increase more than 0.5 volts, service or replace the alternator.

REGULATOR S AND I CIRCUIT TEST

♦ **See Figure 15**

1. Disconnect the wiring connector from the regulator. Connect a jumper wire between the regulator A terminal and the wiring connector A lead and connect a jumper wire between the regulator F screw and the alternator rear housing.

2. With the engine idling and the negative voltmeter lead connected to the negative battery terminal, connect the positive voltmeter lead first to the S terminal and then to the I terminal of the regulator wiring connector.

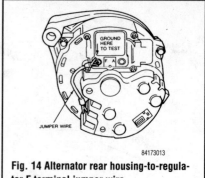

Fig. 15 Regulator wiring connector S and I terminal locations

3. The S circuit voltage should be approximately ½ that of the I circuit. If the voltage readings are correct, remove the jumper wire. Replace the regulator and connect the regulator wiring connector. Perform the Load Test.

4. If there is no voltage present, remove the jumper wire and service the faulty wiring circuit or alternator.

5. Connect the positive voltmeter lead to the positive battery terminal and connect the wiring connector to the regulator. Repeat the Load Test.

FUSE LINK CONTINUITY

1. Make sure the battery is okay (See Section 1).

2. Turn on the headlights or any accessory. If the headlights or accessory do not operate, the fuse link is probably burned out.

3. On some vehicles there are several fuse links. Proceed as in Step 2 to test other fuse links.

4. To test the fuse link that protects the alternator, check for voltage at the BAT terminal of the alternator and A terminal of the regulator, using a voltmeter. If there is no voltage, the fuse link is probably burned out.

FIELD CIRCUIT DRAIN

In all of the Field Circuit Drain test steps, connect the negative voltmeter lead to the alternator rear housing.

1. With the ignition switch in the **OFF** position, connect the positive voltmeter lead to the regulator F terminal screw. The voltmeter should read battery voltage if the system is operating normally. If less than battery voltage is indicated, go to Step 2.

2. Disconnect the wiring connector from the regulator and connect the positive voltmeter lead to the wiring connector I terminal. There should be no voltage indicated. If voltage is indicated, service the I lead from the ignition switch to identify and eliminate the voltage source.

3. If there was no voltage indicated in Step 2, connect the positive voltmeter lead to the wiring connector S terminal. No voltage should be indicated. If no voltage is indicated, replace the regulator.

4. If there was voltage indicated in Step 3, disconnect the wiring connector from the alternator rectifier connector. Connect the positive voltmeter lead to the regulator wiring connector S terminal. If voltage is indicated, service the S lead to the alternator connector to eliminate the voltage source. If no voltage is indicated, the alternator rectifier assembly is faulty.

1992–94 Vehicles with Integral Regulator/Internal Fan Alternator

BASE VOLTAGE TEST

♦ **See Figure 3**

1. Connect the negative and positive leads of a voltmeter to the negative and positive battery cable clamps.

2. Make sure the ignition switch is in the **OFF** position and all electrical loads (lights, radio, etc.) are OFF.

3. Record the battery voltage shown on the voltmeter; this is the base voltage.

➡ **Turn the headlights ON for 10–15 seconds to remove any surface charge from the battery, then wait until the voltage stabilizes, before performing the base voltage test.**

NO-LOAD TEST

1. Connect a suitable tachometer to the engine.
2. Start the engine and bring the engine speed to 1500 rpm. With no other electrical loads (doors closed, foot off the brake pedal), the reading on the voltmeter should increase, but no more than 3 volts above the base voltage.

➡**The voltage reading should be taken when the voltage stops rising. This may take a few minutes.**

3. If the voltage increases as in Step 2, perform the Load Test.
4. If the voltage continues to rise, perform the Over Voltage Tests.
5. If the voltage does not rise to the proper level, perform the Under Voltage Tests.

LOAD TEST

1. With the engine running, turn the blower speed switch to the high speed position and turn the headlights on to high beam.
2. Raise the engine speed to approximately 2000 rpm. The voltmeter reading should be a minimum of 0.5 volts above the base voltage. If not, perform the Under Voltage Tests.

➡**If the voltmeter readings in the No-Load Test and Load Test are as specified, the charging system is operating properly. Go to the following tests if one or more of the voltage readings differs, and also check for battery drain.**

OVER VOLTAGE TESTS

♦ **See Figure 16**

If the voltmeter reading was more than 3 volts above base voltage in the No-Load Test, proceed as follows:

1. Turn the ignition switch to the **RUN** position, but do not start the engine.
2. Connect the negative voltmeter lead to ground. Connect the positive voltmeter lead first to the alternator output connection at the starter solenoid (1992) or load distribution point (1993–94) and then to the regulator A screw head.
3. If there is greater than 0.5 volts difference between the 2 locations, service the A wiring circuit to eliminate the high resistance condition indicated by excessive voltage drop.
4. If the over voltage condition still exists, check for loose regulator and alternator grounding screws. Tighten loose regulator grounding screws to 16–24 inch lbs. (1.7–2.8 Nm).
5. If the over voltage condition still exists, connect the negative voltmeter lead to ground. Turn the ignition switch to the **OFF** position and connect the positive voltmeter lead first to the regulator A screw head and then to the regulator F screw head. If there are different voltage readings at the 2 screw heads, a malfunctioning regulator grounded brush lead or a grounded rotor coil is indicated; replace the regulator/brush set or the entire alternator.
6. If the same voltage reading, battery voltage, is obtained at both screw heads in Step 5, then there is no short to ground through the alternator field/brushes. Replace the regulator.

UNDER VOLTAGE TESTS

♦ **See Figures 16, 17 and 18**

If the voltmeter reading was not more than 0.5 volts above base voltage, proceed as follows:

1. Disconnect the wiring connector from the regulator and connect an ohmmeter between the regulator A and F terminal screws. The ohmmeter should read more than 2.4 ohms. If the ohmmeter reads less than 2.4 ohms, check the alternator for shorted rotor to field coil or for shorted brushes. Replace the brush holder or the entire alternator assembly. Perform the Load Test after replacement.

✳✳ WARNING

Do not replace the regulator if a shorted rotor coil or field circuit has been diagnosed, or regulator damage could result. Replace the alternator assembly.

2. If the ohmmeter reading is greater than 2.4 ohms, connect the regulator wiring connector and connect the negative voltmeter lead to ground. Connect the positive voltmeter lead to the regulator A terminal screw; battery voltage should be indicated. If there is no voltage, service the A wiring circuit and then perform the Load Test.
3. If battery voltage is indicated in Step 2, connect the negative voltmeter lead to ground. Turn the ignition switch to the **OFF** position, then connect the positive voltmeter lead to the regulator F terminal screw. Battery voltage should be indicated on the voltmeter. If there is no voltage, replace the alternator and then perform the Load Test.
4. If battery voltage is indicated in Step 3, connect the negative voltmeter lead to ground. Turn the ignition switch to the **RUN** position, but leave the engine OFF. Connect the positive voltmeter lead to the regulator F terminal screw; the voltmeter reading should be 2 volts or less. If more than 2 volts is indicated, perform the I circuit tests and service the I circuit, if needed. If the I circuit tests normal, replace the regulator, if needed, then perform the Load Test.
5. If 2 volts or less is indicated in Step 4, perform the Load Test, but connect the positive voltmeter lead to the alternator output stud. If the voltage increases more than 0.5 volts above base voltage, service the alternator-to-starter relay (1992) or alternator-to-load distribution point (1993–94) wiring. Repeat the Load Test, measuring the voltage at the battery cable clamps after servicing.
6. If the voltage does not increase more than 0.5 volts above base voltage in Step 5, perform the Load Test and measure the voltage drop from the battery to the A terminal of the regulator (regulator connected). If the voltage drop exceeds 0.5 volts, service the wiring from the A terminal to the starter relay (1992) or load distribution point (1993–94).
7. If the voltage drop does not exceed 0.5 volts, connect a jumper wire from the alternator rear housing to the regulator F terminal. Repeat the Load Test with the positive voltmeter lead connected to the alternator output stud. If the voltage increases more than 0.5 volts, replace the regulator. If voltage does not increase more than 0.5 volts, replace the alternator.

ALTERNATOR S CIRCUIT TEST

♦ **See Figure 19**

1. Disconnect the wiring connector from the regulator. Connect a jumper wire from the regulator A terminal to the wiring connector A lead. Connect a jumper wire from the regulator F screw to the alternator rear housing.
2. With the engine idling and the negative voltmeter lead connected to ground, connect the positive voltmeter lead first to the S terminal and then to the A terminal of the regulator wiring connector. The S circuit voltage should be approximately ½ the A circuit voltage. If the voltage readings are normal, remove the jumper wire, replace the regulator and connect the wiring connector. Repeat the Load Test.

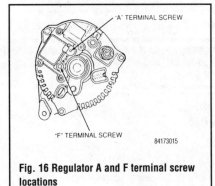

Fig. 16 Regulator A and F terminal screw locations

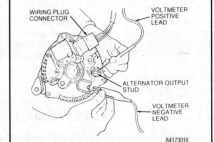

Fig. 17 Voltmeter connections for Under Voltage Tests, Step 5

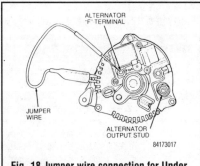

Fig. 18 Jumper wire connection for Under Voltage Tests, Step 7

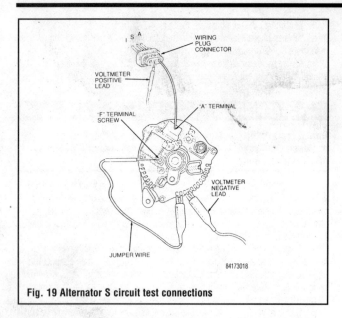

Fig. 19 Alternator S circuit test connections

3. If there is no voltage present, remove the jumper wire and service the damaged or worn wiring circuit or alternator.

4. Connect the positive voltmeter lead to the positive battery terminal. Connect the wiring connector to the regulator and repeat the Load Test.

FUSE LINK CONTINUITY

1. Make sure the battery is okay (See Section 1).

2. Turn on the headlights or any accessory. If the headlights or accessory do not operate, the fuse link is probably burned out.

3. On some vehicles there are several fuse links. Proceed as in Step 2 to test other fuse links.

4. To test the fuse link that protects the alternator, check for voltage at the BAT terminal of the alternator and A terminal of the regulator, using a voltmeter. If there is no voltage, the fuse link is probably burned out.

FIELD CIRCUIT DRAIN

In all of the Field Circuit Drain test steps, connect the negative voltmeter lead to the alternator rear housing.

1. With the ignition switch in the **OFF** position, connect the positive voltmeter lead to the regulator F terminal screw. The voltmeter should read battery voltage if the system is operating normally. If less than battery voltage is indicated, go to Step 2.

2. Disconnect the wiring connector from the regulator and connect the positive voltmeter lead to the wiring connector I terminal. There should be no voltage indicated. If voltage is indicated, service the I lead from the ignition switch to identify and eliminate the voltage source.

3. If there was no voltage indicated in Step 2, connect the positive voltmeter lead to the wiring connector S terminal. No voltage should be indicated. If no voltage is indicated, replace the regulator.

4. If there was voltage indicated in Step 3, disconnect the 1-pin S terminal connector. Again, connect the positive voltmeter lead to the regulator wiring connector S terminal. If voltage is indicated, service the S lead wiring to eliminate the voltage source. If no short is found, replace the alternator.

REMOVAL & INSTALLATION

♦ See Figure 20

1. Disconnect the negative battery cable.

2. Tag and disconnect the wiring connectors from the rear of the alternator. To disconnect push-on type terminals, depress the lock tab and pull straight off.

3. On 5.0L and 5.8L engines, loosen the alternator pivot bolt and remove the adjusting bolt. Disengage the drive belt from the alternator pulley.

4. On 4.6L engines, rotate the automatic tensioner away from the drive belt and disengage the drive belt from the alternator pulley. Remove the alternator brace.

5. On 5.0L and 5.8L engines, remove the alternator pivot bolt and the alternator. On 4.6L engines, remove the alternator mounting bolts and remove the alternator.

6. Installation is the reverse of the removal procedure. On 4.6L engines,

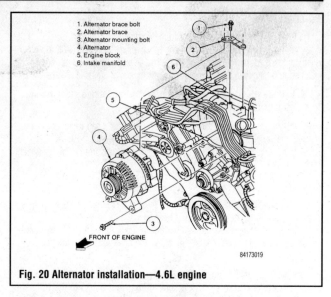

Fig. 20 Alternator installation—4.6L engine

tighten the alternator mounting bolts to 15–22 ft. lbs. (20–30 Nm) and the alternator brace bolts to 70–106 inch lbs. (8–12 Nm). On 5.0L and 5.8L engines, adjust the drive belt tension (refer to Section 1).

Regulator

REMOVAL & INSTALLATION

External Regulator

1. Disconnect the negative battery cable.

2. Disconnect the regulator from the wiring harness.

3. Remove the regulator retaining screws and the regulator.

4. Installation is the reverse of the removal procedure.

Integral Regulator

EXTERNAL FAN ALTERNATOR

♦ See Figures 21, 22 and 23

1. Disconnect the negative battery cable.

2. Remove the alternator, if necessary.

3. Remove the four T20 TORX® head screws holding the regulator to the alternator rear housing. Remove the regulator, with the brush holder attached.

4. Hold the regulator in 1 hand and break off the tab covering the A screw head with a small prybar.

5. Remove the two T20 TORX® head screws retaining the regulator to the brush holder. Separate the regulator from the brush holder.

To install:

6. Wipe the regulator base plate with a clean cloth. Position the regulator against the brush holder and install the retaining screws. Tighten to 20–30 inch lbs. (2.3–3.4 Nm).

7. Cover the head of the A terminal screw head with electrical tape.

8. Place the brush springs in the brush holder. Locate the brushes in the holder and hold in place with a thin, flat piece of steel or similar tool. Loop the brush leads toward the brush end of the brush holder.

9. Wipe the regulator mounting surface of the alternator rear housing with a clean cloth. Position the regulator and brush holder assembly in the alternator rear housing and pull the retaining tool.

10. Install the regulator retaining screws and tighten to 25–35 inch lbs. (2.8–4.0 Nm).

INTERNAL FAN ALTERNATOR

♦ See Figures 24 and 25

1. Disconnect the negative battery cable.

2. Remove the four T20 TORX® head screws holding the regulator to the alternator rear housing. Remove the regulator, with the brush holder attached.

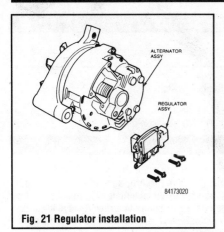

Fig. 21 Regulator installation

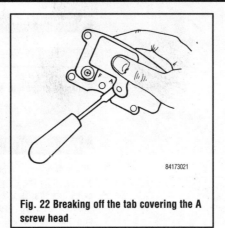

Fig. 22 Breaking off the tab covering the A screw head

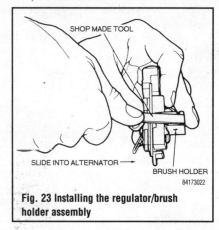

Fig. 23 Installing the regulator/brush holder assembly

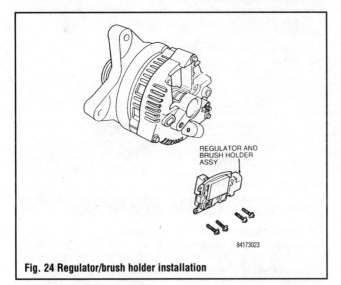

Fig. 24 Regulator/brush holder installation

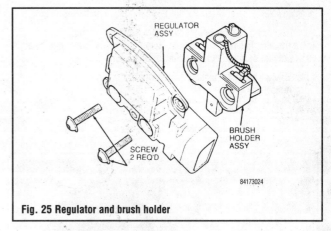

Fig. 25 Regulator and brush holder

3. Hold the regulator in 1 hand and pry off the cap covering the A screw head with a small prybar.

4. Remove the two T20 TORX® head screws retaining the regulator to the brush holder. Separate the regulator from the brush holder.

To install:

5. Install the brush holder on the regulator with the attaching screws. Tighten the screws to 25–35 inch lbs. (2.8–4.0 Nm).

6. Install the cap on the head of the A terminal screw.

7. Depress the brushes into the holder and hold the brushes in position by inserting a standard size paper clip, or equivalent tool, through both the location hole in the regulator and through the holes in the brushes.

8. Install the regulator/brush holder assembly and remove the paper clip. Install the attaching screws and tighten to 20–30 inch lbs. (2.3–3.4 Nm).

Starter

TESTING

Place the transmission in **N** or **P**. Disconnect the vacuum line to the Thermactor bypass valve, if equipped, before performing any cranking tests. After tests, run the engine for 3 minutes before connecting the vacuum line.

Starter Cranks Slowly

1. Connect jumper cables as shown in the Jump Starting procedure in Section 1. If, with the aid of the booster battery, the starter now cranks normally, check the condition of the battery. Recharge or replace the battery, as necessary. Clean the cables and battery posts and make sure connections are tight.

2. If Step 1 does not correct the problem, clean and tighten the connections at the starter relay and battery ground on the engine. You should not be able to

rotate the eyelet terminals easily, by hand. Also make sure the positive cable is not shorted to ground.

3. If the starter still cranks slowly, it must be replaced.

Starter Relay Operates But Starter Doesn't Crank

1. Connect jumper cables as shown in the Jump Starting procedure in Section 1. If, with the aid of the booster battery, the starter now cranks normally, check the condition of the battery. Recharge or replace the battery, as necessary. Clean the cables and battery posts and make sure connections are tight.

2. If Step 1 does not correct the problem, clean and tighten the connections at the starter and relay. Make sure the wire strands are secure in the eyelets.

3. On 1989 vehicles, if the starter still doesn't crank, it must be replaced.

4. On 1990–94 vehicles with starter mounted solenoid: Connect a jumper cable across terminals B and M of the starter solenoid. If the starter does not operate, replace the starter. If the starter does operate, replace the solenoid.

✳✳ CAUTION

Making the jumper connections could cause a spark. Battery jumper cables or equivalent, should be used due to the high current in the starting system.

Starter Doesn't Crank—Relay Chatters or Doesn't Click

1. Connect jumper cables as shown in the Jump Starting procedure in Section 1. If, with the aid of the booster battery, the starter now cranks normally, check the condition of the battery. Recharge or replace the battery, as necessary. Clean the cables and battery posts and make sure connections are tight.

2. If Step 1 does not correct the problem, remove the push-on connector from the relay (red with blue stripe wire). Make sure the connection is clean and secure and the relay bracket is grounded.

3. If the connections are good, check the relay operation with a jumper wire. Remove the push-on connector from the relay and, using a jumper wire, jump from the now exposed terminal on the starter relay to the main terminal (battery side or battery positive post). If this corrects the problem, check the ignition

switch, neutral safety switch and the wiring in the starting circuit for open or loose connections.

4. If a jumper wire across the relay does not correct the problem, replace the relay.

Start Spins But Doesn't Crank Engine

1. Remove the starter.
2. Check the armature shaft for corrosion and clean or replace, as necessary.
3. If there is no corrosion, replace the starter drive.

REMOVAL & INSTALLATION

▶ **See Figure 26**

1. Disconnect the negative battery cable.
2. Raise the vehicle and support it safely.
3. Disconnect the starter cable from the starter. If equipped with starter mounted solenoid, disconnect the push-on connector from the solenoid.

➡**To disconnect the hard-shell connector from the solenoid S terminal, grasp the plastic shell and pull off; do not pull on the wire. Pull straight off to prevent damage to the connector and S terminal.**

4. Remove the starter bolts and the starter.
To install:
5. Position the starter to the engine and tighten the mounting bolts to 15–20 ft. lbs. (20–27 Nm).
6. Reconnect the electrical leads. Connect the negative battery cable.

84173025

Fig. 26 View of a typical starter motor mounting

SOLENOID OR RELAY REPLACEMENT

Solenoid

STARTER MOUNTED SOLENOID

1. Disconnect the negative battery cable.
2. Remove the starter.
3. Remove the positive brush connector from the solenoid M terminal.
4. Remove the solenoid retaining screws and remove the solenoid.
5. Attach the solenoid plunger rod to the slot in the lever and tighten the solenoid retaining screws to 45–54 inch lbs. (5.1–6.1 Nm).
6. Attach the positive brush connector to the solenoid M terminal and tighten the retaining nut to 80–120 inch lbs. (9.0–13.5 Nm).
7. Install the starter and connect the negative battery terminal.

Relay

1. Disconnect the negative battery cable.
2. Label and disconnect the wires from the relay.
3. Remove the relay retaining bolts and remove the relay.
4. Installation is the reverse of the removal procedure.

Sending Units and Sensors

REMOVAL & INSTALLATION

Coolant Temperature Sender/Switch

1. Disconnect the negative battery cable.
2. Drain the cooling system into a suitable container.

✳✳ CAUTION

When draining the coolant, keep in mind that cats and dogs are attracted by the ethylene glycol antifreeze, and are quite likely to drink any that is left in an uncovered container or in puddles on the ground. This will prove fatal in sufficient quantity. Always drain the coolant into a sealable container. Coolant should be reused unless it is contaminated or several years old.

3. Disconnect the electrical connector at the temperature sender/switch.
4. Remove the temperature sender/switch.
To install:
5. Apply pipe sealant or teflon tape to the threads of the new sender/switch.
6. Install the temperature sender/switch and connect the electrical connector.
7. Connect the negative battery cable. Fill the cooling system.
8. Run the engine and check for leaks.

Oil Pressure Sender/Switch

▶ **See Figures 27 and 28**

✳✳ WARNING

The pressure switch used with the oil pressure warning light is not interchangeable with the sending unit used with the oil pressure gauge. If the incorrect part is installed the oil pressure indicating system will be inoperative and the sending unit or gauge will be damaged.

1. Disconnect the negative battery cable.
2. Disconnect the electrical connector and remove the oil pressure sender/switch.
To install:
3. Apply pipe sealant to the threads of the new sender/switch.
4. Install the oil pressure sender/switch and tighten to 9–11 ft. lbs. (12–16 Nm).
5. Connect the electrical connector to the sender/switch and connect the negative battery cable.
6. Run the engine and check for leaks and proper operation.

Low Oil Level Sensor

▶ **See Figure 29**

1. Disconnect the negative battery cable.
2. Raise and safely support the vehicle.
3. Drain at least 2 quarts of oil from the engine into a suitable container.
4. Disconnect the electrical connector from the sensor.
5. Remove the sensor using a 1 in. socket or wrench.
To install:
6. Install the sensor and tighten to 15–25 ft. lbs. (20–34 Nm).
7. Connect the electrical connector.
8. Tighten the oil pan drain plug to 8–12 ft. lbs. (11–16 Nm) on 4.6L engines or 15–25 ft. lbs. (20–34 Nm) on 5.0L and 5.8L engines.
9. Lower the vehicle.
10. Add oil to the proper level.
11. Connect the negative battery cable, start the engine and check for leaks.

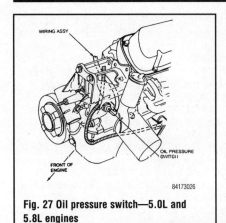

Fig. 27 Oil pressure switch—5.0L and 5.8L engines

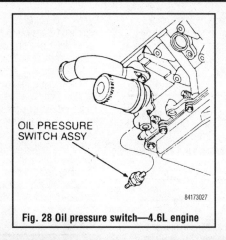

Fig. 28 Oil pressure switch—4.6L engine

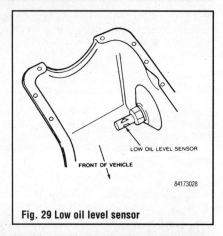

Fig. 29 Low oil level sensor

ENGINE MECHANICAL

Description

▶ See Figures 30 and 31

All engines have 8 cylinders configured in a 90° V design with 4 cylinders on each bank, in a cast iron cylinder block. The crankshaft is supported in 5 main bearing saddles. The pistons are aluminum and drive the crankshaft by way of connecting rods.

The cylinder heads on the 5.0L and 5.8L engines are cast iron and contain 1 each intake and exhaust valve per cylinder. The valves are actuated by rocker arms which are driven by the camshaft by way of pushrods and hydraulic lifters. The camshaft and hydraulic lifters are housed in the engine block and the camshaft is driven off the crankshaft by a chain and 2 sprockets.

The cylinder heads on the 4.6L engine are aluminum and contain 1 each intake and exhaust valve per cylinder. The valves are actuated by roller followers

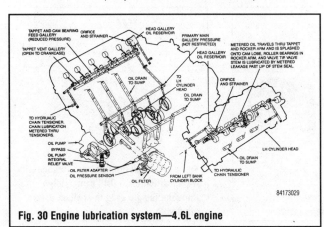

Fig. 30 Engine lubrication system—4.6L engine

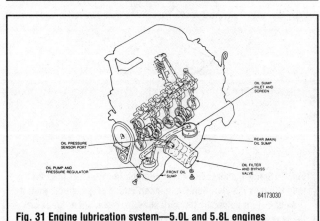

Fig. 31 Engine lubrication system—5.0L and 5.8L engines

which are driven directly off the camshaft. A single camshaft is mounted on each cylinder head. Both camshafts are driven off the crankshaft by a chain and sprockets.

Engine Overhaul Tips

Most engine overhaul procedures are fairly standard. In addition to specific parts replacement procedures and complete specifications for your individual engine, this section also is a guide to accepted rebuilding procedures. Examples of standard rebuilding practice are shown and should be used along with specific details concerning your particular engine.

Competent and accurate machine shop services will ensure maximum performance, reliability and engine life. In most instances it is more profitable for the do-it-yourself mechanic to remove, clean and inspect the component, buy the necessary parts and deliver these to a shop for actual machine work.

On the other hand, much of the rebuilding work (crankshaft, block, bearings, piston, rods, and other components) is still within the scope of the do-it-yourself mechanic.

TOOLS

The tools required for an engine overhaul or parts replacement will depend on the depth of your involvement. With a few exceptions, they will be the tools found in a mechanic's tool kit (see Section 1). More in-depth work will require any or all of the following:

- dial indicator (reading in thousandths) mounted on a universal base.
- micrometers and telescope gauges.
- jaw and screw-type pullers.
- scraper.
- valve spring compressor.
- ring groove cleaner.
- piston ring expander and compressor.
- ridge reamer.
- cylinder hone or glaze breaker.
- Plastigage®.
- engine stand.

The use of most of these tools is illustrated in this section. Many can be rented for a one-time use from a local parts jobber or tool supply house specializing in automotive work.

Occasionally, the use of special tools is called for. See the information on Special Tools and the Safety Notice in the front of this book before substituting another tool.

INSPECTION TECHNIQUES

Procedures and specifications are given in this section for inspecting, cleaning and assessing the wear limits of most major components. Other procedures such as Magnaflux® and Zyglo® can be used to locate material flaws and stress cracks. Magnaflux® is a magnetic process applicable only to ferrous materials. The Zyglo® process coats the material with a fluorescent dye penetrant and can be used on any material. Checks for suspected surface cracks can be more readily made using spot check dye. The dye is sprayed onto the suspected area, wiped off and area sprayed with a developer. Cracks will show up brightly.

OVERHAUL TIPS

Aluminum has become extremely popular for use in engines, due to its low weight. Observe the following precautions when handling aluminum parts:

Never hot tank aluminum parts (the caustic hot-tank solution will eat the aluminum).

Remove all aluminum parts (identification tag, etc) from engine parts prior to hot-tanking.

Always coat threads lightly with engine oil or anti-seize compounds before installation, to prevent seizure.

Never over-torque bolts or spark plugs, especially in aluminum threads. Stripped threads in any component can be repaired using any of several commercial repair kits (Heli-Coil®, Microdot®, Keenserts®, etc.)

When assembling the engine, any parts that will be in frictional contact must be prelubed to provide lubrication at initial start-up.

When semi-permanent (locked, but removable) installation of bolts or nuts is desired, threads should be cleaned and coated with Loctite® or other similar, commercial non-hardening sealant.

REPAIRING DAMAGED THREADS

▶ **See Figures 32, 33, 34, 35 and 36**

Several methods of repairing damaged threads are available. Heli-Coil® (shown here), Keenserts® and Microdot® are among the most widely used. All involve basically the same principle—drilling out stripped threads, tapping the hole and installing a prewound insert—making welding, plugging and oversize fasteners unnecessary.

Two types of thread repair inserts are usually supplied: a standard type for most Inch Coarse, Inch Fine, Metric Coarse and Metric Fine thread sizes and a spark plug type to fit most spark plug port sizes. Consult the individual manufacturer's catalog to determine exact applications. Typical thread repair kits will contain a selection of prewound threaded inserts, a tap (corresponding to the outside diameter threads of the insert) and an installation tool. Spark plug inserts usually differ because they require a tap equipped with pilot threads and combined reamer/tap section. Most manufacturers also supply blister-packed thread repair inserts separately in addition to a master kit containing a variety of taps and inserts plus installation tools.

Before effecting a repair to a threaded hole, remove any snapped, broken or damaged bolts or studs. Penetrating oil can be used to free frozen threads; the offending item can be removed with locking pliers or with a screw or stud extractor. After the hole is clear, the thread can be repaired, as shown in the figures.

CHECKING ENGINE COMPRESSION

▶ **See Figure 37**

A noticeable lack of engine power, excessive oil consumption and/or poor fuel mileage measured over an extended period are all indicators of internal engine wear. Worn piston rings, scored or worn cylinder bores, blown head gaskets, sticking or burnt valves and worn valve seats are all possible culprits here. A check of each cylinder's compression will help you locate the problems.

As mentioned earlier, a screw-in type compression gauge is more accurate than the type you simply hold against the spark plug hole, although it takes slightly longer to use. It's worth it to obtain a more accurate reading. Check engine compression as follows:

1. Make sure the engine oil level is correct and the battery is properly charged. Warm up the engine to normal operating temperature.

2. Turn the ignition switch **OFF**. Remove all spark plugs.

3. Screw the compression gauge into the No. 1 cylinder spark plug hole until the fitting is snug.

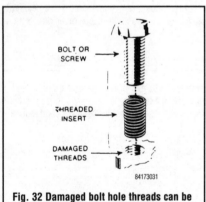

Fig. 32 Damaged bolt hole threads can be replaced with thread repair inserts

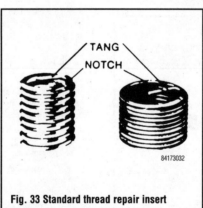

Fig. 33 Standard thread repair insert (left), and spark plug thread insert

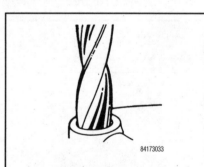

Fig. 34 Drill out the damaged threads with the specified drill. Drill completely through the hole or to the bottom of a blind hole

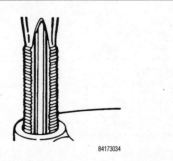

Fig. 35 With the tap supplied, tap the hole to receive the thread insert. Keep the tap well oiled and back it out frequently to avoid clogging the threads

Fig. 36 Screw the threaded insert onto the installer tool until the tang engages the slot. Screw the insert into the tapped hole until it is ¼ or ½ turn below the top surface. After installation, break off the tang with a hammer and punch

➡ **Be careful not to crossthread the plug hole. On aluminum cylinder heads use extra care, as the threads in these heads are easily ruined.**

4. Install an auxiliary starter switch in the starter circuit.

5. Ask an assistant to depress the accelerator pedal fully. Then, while you read the compression gauge, crank the engine at least 5 compression strokes using the auxiliary starter switch (ignition switch in **OFF** position). Note the approximate number of compression strokes required to obtain the highest reading.

6. Repeat the compression test on each cylinder, cranking the engine approximately the same number of compression strokes.

7. Compare your lowest and highest compression readings with those in the figure. Compression pressures are considered within specification if the lowest reading cylinder is within 75% of the highest.

8. If a cylinder is unusually low, pour a tablespoon of clean 20W-50 engine oil into the cylinder through the spark plug hole and repeat the compression test. If the compression comes up after adding the oil, it appears that the cylinder's piston rings or bore are damaged or worn. If the pressure remains low, the valves may not be seating properly (a valve job is needed), or the head gasket may be blown near that cylinder. If compression in any two adjacent cylinders is low, and if the addition of oil doesn't help the compression, there is leakage past the head gasket. Oil and coolant water in the combustion chamber can result from this problem. There may be evidence of water droplets on the engine dipstick when a head gasket has blown.

Maximum PSI	Minimum PSI	Maximum PSI	Minimum PSI	Maximum PSI	Minimum PSI	Maximum PSI	Minimum PSI
134	101	164	123	194	145	224	168
136	102	166	124	196	147	226	169
138	104	168	126	198	148	228	171
140	105	170	127	200	150	230	172
142	107	172	129	202	151	232	174
144	108	174	131	204	153	234	175
146	110	176	132	206	154	236	177
148	111	178	133	208	156	238	178
150	113	180	135	210	157	240	180
152	114	182	136	212	158	242	181
154	115	184	138	214	160	244	183
156	117	186	140	216	162	246	184
158	118	188	141	218	163	248	186
160	120	190	142	220	165	250	187
162	121	192	144	222	166		

84173036

Fig. 37 Compression pressure limits

GENERAL ENGINE SPECIFICATIONS

Year	Engine ID/VIN	Engine Displacement Liters (cc)	Fuel System Type	Net Horsepower @ rpm	Net Torque @ rpm (ft. lbs.)	Bore × Stroke (in.)	Compression Ratio	Oil Pressure @ rpm
1989	F	5.0 (4943)	SEFI	①	②	4.00 × 3.00	8.9:1	40–60 @ 2000 ③
	G	5.8 (5767)	VV	180 @ 3600	285 @ 2400	4.00 × 3.50	8.3:1	40–60 @ 2000 ③
1990	F	5.0 (4943)	SEFI	①	②	4.00 × 3.00	8.9:1	40–60 @ 2000 ③
	G	5.8 (5767)	VV	180 @ 3600	285 @ 2400	4.00 × 3.50	8.3:1	40–60 @ 2000 ③
1991	F	5.0 (4943)	SEFI	①	②	4.00 × 3.00	8.9:1	40–60 @ 2000 ③
	G	5.8 (5767)	VV	180 @ 3600	285 @ 2400	4.00 × 3.50	8.3:1	40–60 @ 2000 ③
1992	W	4.6 (4593)	SEFI	④	⑤	3.55 × 3.54	9.0:1	20–45 @ 1500 ③
1993-94	W	4.6 (4593)	SEFI	④	⑤	3.55 × 3.54	9.0:1	20–45 @ 1500 ③

SEFI—Sequential Electronic Fuel Injection
VV—Variable Venturi carburetor
① Single exhaust: 150 @ 3200
　Dual exhaust: 160 @ 3400
② Single exhaust: 270 @ 2000
　Dual exhaust: 280 @ 2200
③ Engine at normal operating temperature
④ Single exhaust: 190 @ 4200
　Dual exhaust: 210 @ 4600
⑤ Single exhaust: 260 @ 3200
　Dual exhaust: 270 @ 3400

84173R08

VALVE SPECIFICATIONS

All measurements given in inches.

Year	Engine ID/VIN	Engine Displacement Liters (cc)	Seat Angle (deg.)	Face Angle (deg.)	Spring Test Pressure (lbs. @ in.)	Spring Installed Height (in.)	Stem-to-Guide Clearance (in.) Intake	Exhaust	Stem Diameter (in.) Intake	Exhaust
1989	F	5.0 (4943)	45	44	①	②	0.0010–0.0027	0.0015–0.0032	0.3416–0.3423	0.3411–0.3418
	G	5.8 (5767)	45	44	195–215 @ 1.05	②	0.0010–0.0027	0.0015–0.0032	0.3416–0.3423	0.3411–0.3418
1990	F	5.0 (4943)	45	44	①	②	0.0010–0.0027	0.0015–0.0032	0.3416–0.3423	0.3411–0.3418
	G	5.8 (5767)	45	44	195–215 @ 1.05	②	0.0010–0.0027	0.0015–0.0032	0.3416–0.3423	0.3411–0.3418
1991	F	5.0 (4943)	45	44	①	②	0.0010–0.0027	0.0015–0.0032	0.3416–0.3423	0.3411–0.3418
	G	5.8 (5767)	45	44	195–215 @ 1.05	②	0.0010–0.0027	0.0015–0.0032	0.3416–0.3423	0.3411–0.3418
1992	W	4.6 (4593)	45	45.5	132 @ 1.10	1.57	0.0008–0.0027	0.0018–0.0037	0.2746–0.2754	0.2736–0.2744
1993 -94	W	4.6 (4593)	45	45.5	132 @ 1.10	1.57	0.0008–0.0027	0.0018–0.0037	0.2746–0.2754	0.2736–0.2744

① Intake: 194–214 @ 1.36
  Exhaust: 190–210 @ 1.20
② Intake: 1.75–1.80
  Exhaust: 1.58–1.64

84173R11

CAMSHAFT SPECIFICATIONS

All measurements given in inches.

Year	Engine ID/VIN	Engine Displacement Liters (cc)	Journal Diameter 1	2	3	4	5	Elevation In.	Ex.	Bearing Clearance	Camshaft End Play
1989	F	5.0 (4943)	2.0805–2.0815	2.0655–2.0665	2.0505–2.0515	2.0355–2.0365	2.0205–2.0215	0.2325–0.2375	0.2424–0.2474	0.001–0.006	0.005–0.009
	G	5.8 (5767)	2.0805–2.0815	2.0655–2.0665	2.0505–2.0515	2.0355–2.0365	2.0205–2.0215	0.273–0.278	0.278–0.283	0.001–0.006	0.001–0.009
1990	F	5.0 (4943)	2.0805–2.0815	2.0655–2.0665	2.0505–2.0515	2.0355–2.0365	2.0205–2.0215	0.2325–0.2375	0.2424–0.2474	0.001–0.006	0.005–0.009
	G	5.8 (5767)	2.0805–2.0815	2.0655–2.0665	2.0505–2.0515	2.0355–2.0365	2.0205–2.0215	0.273–0.278	0.278–0.283	0.001–0.006	0.001–0.009
1991	F	5.0 (4943)	2.0805–2.0815	2.0655–2.0665	2.0505–2.0515	2.0355–2.0365	2.0205–2.0215	0.2325–0.2375	0.2424–0.2474	0.001–0.006	0.005–0.009
	G	5.8 (5767)	2.0805–2.0815	2.0655–2.0665	2.0505–2.0515	2.0355–2.0365	2.0205–2.0215	0.273–0.278	0.278–0.283	0.001–0.006	0.001–0.009
1992	W	4.6 (4593)	1.0605–1.0615	1.0605–1.0615	1.0605–1.0615	1.0605–1.0615	1.0605–1.0615	0.259	0.259	0.0010–0.0047	0.001–0.007
1993 -94	W	4.6 (4593)	1.0605–1.0615	1.0605–1.0615	1.0605–1.0615	1.0605–1.0615	1.0605–1.0615	0.259	0.259	0.0010–0.0047	0.001–0.007

84173R09

PISTON AND RING SPECIFICATIONS

All measurements are given in inches.

Year	Engine ID/VIN	Engine Displacement Liters (cc)	Piston Clearance	Ring Gap Top Compression	Bottom Compression	Oil Control	Ring Side Clearance Top Compression	Bottom Compression	Oil Control
1989	F	5.0 (4943)	0.0014–0.0022	0.010–0.020	0.010–0.020	0.015–0.055	0.002–0.004	0.002–0.004	Snug
	G	5.8 (5767)	0.0018–0.0026	0.010–0.020	0.010–0.020	0.015–0.055	0.002–0.004	0.002–0.004	Snug
1990	F	5.0 (4943)	0.0014–0.0022	0.010–0.020	0.010–0.020	0.015–0.055	0.002–0.004	0.002–0.004	Snug
	G	5.8 (5767)	0.0018–0.0026	0.010–0.020	0.010–0.020	0.015–0.055	0.002–0.004	0.002–0.004	Snug
1991	F	5.0 (4943)	0.0014–0.0022	0.010–0.020	0.010–0.020	0.015–0.055	0.002–0.004	0.002–0.004	Snug
	G	5.8 (5767)	0.0018–0.0026	0.010–0.020	0.010–0.020	0.015–0.055	0.002–0.004	0.002–0.004	Snug
1992	W	4.6 (4593)	0.0008–0.0018	0.009–0.019	0.009–0.019	0.010–0.030	0.0016–0.0035	0.0012–0.0031	Snug
1993 -94	W	4.6 (4593)	0.0008–0.0018	0.009–0.019	0.009–0.019	0.010–0.030	0.0016–0.0035	0.0012–0.0031	Snug

84173R12

CRANKSHAFT AND CONNECTING ROD SPECIFICATIONS

All measurements are given in inches.

Year	Engine ID/VIN	Engine Displacement Liters (cc)	Crankshaft Main Brg. Journal Dia.	Main Brg. Oil Clearance	Shaft End-play	Thrust on No.	Connecting Rod Journal Diameter	Oil Clearance	Side Clearance
1989	F	5.0 (4943)	2.2482–2.2490	0.0004–0.0021	0.004–0.012	3	2.1228–2.1236	0.0008–0.0024	0.010–0.023
	G	5.8 (5767)	2.9994–3.0002	0.0008–0.0026	0.004–0.012	3	2.3103–2.3111	0.0007–0.0025	0.010–0.023
1990	F	5.0 (4943)	2.2482–2.2490	0.0004–0.0021	0.004–0.012	3	2.1228–2.1236	0.0008–0.0024	0.010–0.023
	G	5.8 (5767)	2.9994–3.0002	0.0008–0.0026	0.004–0.012	3	2.3103–2.3111	0.0007–0.0025	0.010–0.023
1991	F	5.0 (4943)	2.2482–2.2490	0.0004–0.0024	0.004–0.012	3	2.1228–2.1236	0.0007–0.0026	0.010–0.023
	G	5.8 (5767)	2.9994–3.0002	0.0008–0.0025	0.004–0.012	3	2.3103–2.3111	0.0007–0.0025	0.010–0.023
1992	W	4.6 (4593)	2.6578–2.6698	0.0011–0.0025	0.005–0.010	5	2.0866	0.0011–0.0027	0.006–0.019
1993 -94	W	4.6 (4593)	2.6578–2.6698	0.0011–0.0025	0.005–0.011	5	2.0873–2.0890	0.0011–0.0027	0.006–0.019

84173R10

TORQUE SPECIFICATIONS

All readings in ft. lbs.

Year	Engine ID/VIN	Engine Displacement Liters (cc)	Cylinder Head Bolts	Main Bearing Bolts	Rod Bearing Bolts	Crankshaft Damper Bolts	Flywheel Bolts	Manifold Intake	Manifold Exhaust	Spark Plugs	Lug Nut
1989	F	5.0 (4943)	①	60–70	19–24	70–90	75–85	23–25②	18–24	5–10	85–105
	G	5.8 (5767)	③	90–105	40–45	70–90	75–85	23–25②	18–24	10–15	85–105
1990	F	5.0 (4943)	①	60–70	19–24	70–90	75–85	23–25②	18–24	5–10	85–105
	G	5.8 (5767)	③	90–105	40–45	70–90	75–85	23–25②	18–24	10–15	85–105
1991	F	5.0 (4943)	①	60–70	19–24	70–90	75–85	23–25②	18–24	5–10	85–105
	G	5.8 (5767)	③	95–105	40–45	70–90	75–85	23–25②	18–24	10–15	85–105
1992	W	4.6 (4593)	④	⑤	⑥	114–121	54–64	15–22②	15–22	7	85–105
1993-94	W	4.6 (4593)	④	⑤	⑥	114–121	54–64	15–22②	15–22	7	85–105

① Tighten in 2 steps:
  Step 1: 55–65
  Step 2: 65–72
② Retorque with engine hot
③ Tighten in 3 steps:
  Step 1: 85
  Step 2: 95
  Step 3: 105–112
④ Tighten in 3 steps:
  Step 1: 25–30 ft. lbs.
  Step 2: Turn each bolt 85–95 degrees, in
    sequence
  Step 3: Turn each bolt 85–95 degrees, in
    sequence
⑤ Tighten in 2 steps:
  Step 1: 22–25 ft. lbs.
  Step 2: Turn each bolt 85–95 degrees.
⑥ Tighten in 2 steps:
  Step 1: 12 ft. lbs.
  Step 2: Turn each bolt 85–95 degrees

84173R13

Engine

REMOVAL & INSTALLATION

➡Label all wiring, vacuum hoses, fuel lines, etc. before disconnecting them; thereby making installation much easier.

4.6L Engine

▶ See Figures 38, 39, 40 and 41

1. Disconnect the negative, then the positive battery cable. Drain the crankcase and the cooling system into suitable containers.

❊❊❊ CAUTION

When draining the coolant, keep in mind that cats and dogs are attracted by the ethylene glycol antifreeze, and are quite likely to drink any that is left in an uncovered container or in puddles on the ground. This will prove fatal in sufficient quantity. Always drain the coolant into a sealable container. Coolant should be reused unless it is contaminated or several years old.

2. Relieve the fuel system pressure and disconnect the fuel lines; refer to Section 5. Discharge the air conditioning system; refer to Section 1.
3. Mark the position of the hood on the hinges and remove the hood.
4. Remove the cooling fan, shroud and radiator.
5. Remove the wiper module and support bracket. Remove the air inlet tube.
6. Remove the 42-pin connector from the retaining bracket on the brake vacuum booster. Disconnect the 42-pin connector and transmission harness connector and position aside.

7. Disconnect the accelerator and cruise control cables. Disconnect the throttle valve cable.
8. Disconnect the electrical connector and vacuum hose from the purge solenoid. Disconnect the power supply from the power distribution box and starter relay.
9. Disconnect the vacuum supply hose from the throttle body adapter vacuum port. Disconnect the heater hoses.
10. Disconnect the alternator harness from the fender apron and junction block. Disconnect the air conditioning hoses from the compressor; refer to Section 6.
11. Disconnect the Electronic Variable Orifice (EVO) sensor connector from the power steering pump and disconnect the body ground strap from the dash panel.
12. Raise and safely support the vehicle.
13. Disconnect the exhaust system from the exhaust manifolds and support with wire hung from the crossmember.
14. Remove the retaining nut from the transmission line bracket and remove the 3 bolts and stud retaining the engine to the transmission knee braces.
15. Remove the starter. Remove the 4 bolts retaining the power steering pump to the engine block and position aside.
16. Remove the plug from the engine block to access the torque converter retaining nuts. Rotate the crankshaft until each of the 4 nuts is accessible and remove the nuts.
17. Remove the 6 transmission-to-engine retaining bolts. Remove the engine mount through bolts, 2 on the left mount and 1 on the right mount.
18. Lower the vehicle. Support the transmission with a floor jack and remove the bolt retaining the right engine mount to the lower engine bracket.
19. Install an engine lifting bracket to the left cylinder head on the front and the right cylinder head on the rear. Connect suitable engine lifting equipment to the lifting brackets.
20. Raise the engine slightly and carefully separate the engine from the transmission.

21. Carefully lift the engine out of the engine compartment and position on a workstand. Remove the engine lifting equipment.

To install:

22. Install the engine lifting brackets as in Step 19. Connect the engine lifting equipment to the brackets and remove the engine from the workstand.

23. Carefully lower the engine into the engine compartment. Start the converter pilot into the flexplate and align the paint marks on the flexplate and torque converter. Make sure the studs on the torque converter align with the holes in the flexplate.

24. Fully engage the engine to the transmission and lower onto the mounts. Remove the engine lifting equipment and brackets. Install the bolt retaining the right engine mount to the frame.

25. Raise and safely support the vehicle. Install the 6 engine-to-transmission bolts and tighten to 30–44 ft. lbs. (40–60 Nm).

26. Install the engine mount through bolts and tighten to 15–22 ft. lbs. (20–30 Nm). Install the 4 torque converter retaining nuts and tighten to 22–25 ft. lbs. (20–30 Nm). Install the plug into the access hole in the engine block.

27. Position the power steering pump on the engine block and install the 4 retaining nuts. Tighten to 15–22 ft. lbs. (20–30 Nm). Install the starter.

28. Position the engine to transmission braces and install the 3 bolts and 1 stud. Tighten the bolts and stud to 18–31 ft. lbs. (25–43 Nm).

29. Position the transmission line bracket to the knee brace stud and install the retaining nut. Tighten to 15–22 ft. lbs. (20–30 Nm).

30. Cut the wire and position the exhaust system to the manifolds. Install the 4 nuts and tighten to 20–30 ft. lbs. (27–41 Nm).

➡**Make sure the exhaust system clears the No. 3 crossmember. Adjust as necessary.**

31. Lower the vehicle and connect the EVO sensor.

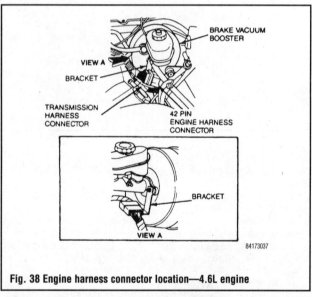

Fig. 38 Engine harness connector location—4.6L engine

32. Connect the air conditioner lines to the compressor; refer to Section 6. Connect the alternator harness from the fender apron and junction block.

33. Connect the heater hoses and connect the vacuum supply hose to the throttle body adapter vacuum port.

34. Connect the power supply to the power distribution box and starter relay. Connect the electrical connector and vacuum hose to the purge solenoid.

35. Connect and if necessary, adjust the throttle valve cable; refer to Section 7. Connect the accelerator and cruise control cables.

36. Connect the 42-pin engine harness connector and transmission harness connector. Install the 42-pin connector to the retaining bracket on the brake vacuum booster.

37. Install the wiper module and support bracket. Connect the fuel lines.

38. Install the radiator, cooling fan and shroud. Install the air inlet tube.

39. Fill the crankcase with the proper type and quantity of engine oil. Fill the cooling system.

40. Install the hood, aligning the marks that were made during removal. Connect the battery cables.

41. Start the engine and bring to operating temperature. Check for leaks. Check all fluid levels. Evacuate and charge the air conditioning system.

42. Road test the vehicle.

5.0L and 5.8L Engines

1. Disconnect the negative, then the positive battery cable. Drain the crankcase and the cooling system into suitable containers.

> ✳✳ **CAUTION**
>
> **When draining the coolant, keep in mind that cats and dogs are attracted by the ethylene glycol antifreeze, and are quite likely to drink any that is left in an uncovered container or in puddles on the ground. This will prove fatal in sufficient quantity. Always drain the coolant into a sealable container. Coolant should be reused unless it is contaminated or several years old.**

2. Relieve the fuel system pressure; refer to Section 5. Discharge the air conditioning system; refer to Section 1.

3. Mark the position of the hood on the hinges and remove the hood. Disconnect the battery ground cables from the cylinder block.

4. Remove the air intake duct and the air cleaner, if engine mounted.

5. Disconnect the upper radiator hose from the thermostat housing and the lower hose from the water pump. Disconnect the oil cooler lines from the radiator.

6. Remove the bolts attaching the radiator fan shroud to the radiator. Remove the radiator. Remove the fan, belt pulley and shroud.

7. Remove the alternator bolts and position the alternator aside.

8. Disconnect the oil pressure sending unit wire from the sending unit. Disconnect the fuel lines; refer to Section 5.

9. Disconnect the accelerator cable from the carburetor or throttle body. Disconnect the throttle valve rod. Disconnect the cruise control cable, if equipped.

10. Disconnect the throttle valve vacuum line from the intake manifold, if equipped. Disconnect the transmission filler tube bracket from the cylinder block.

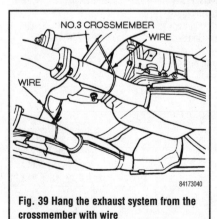

Fig. 39 Hang the exhaust system from the crossmember with wire

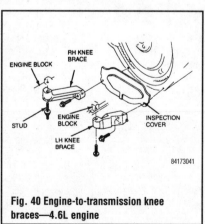

Fig. 40 Engine-to-transmission knee braces—4.6L engine

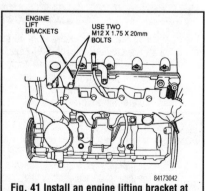

Fig. 41 Install an engine lifting bracket at the front of the left cylinder head—4.6L engine

11. Disconnect the air conditioning lines and electrical connectors at the compressor and remove the compressor; refer to Section 6. Plug the lines and the compressor fittings to prevent the entrance of dirt and moisture.

12. Disconnect the power steering pump bracket from the cylinder head. Remove the drive belt. Position the power steering pump aside in a position that will prevent the fluid from leaking.

13. Disconnect the power brake vacuum line from the intake manifold.

14. On 5.0L engines, disconnect the heater hoses from the heater tubes. On 5.8L engines, disconnect the heater hoses from the water pump and intake manifold. Disconnect the electrical connector from the coolant temperature sending unit.

15. Remove the transmission-to-engine upper bolts.

16. On 5.8L engines, disconnect the primary wiring connector from the ignition coil. Disconnect the wiring to the solenoid on the left rocker cover. Remove the wire harness from the left rocker arm cover and position the wires aside. Disconnect the ground strap from the block.

17. On 5.0L engines, disconnect the wiring harness at the two 10-pin connectors.

18. Raise and safely support the vehicle. Disconnect the starter cable from the starter and remove the starter.

19. Disconnect the muffler inlet pipes from the exhaust manifolds. Disconnect the engine mounts from the chassis. Disconnect the downstream thermactor tubing and check valve from the right exhaust manifold stud, if equipped.

20. Disconnect the transmission cooler lines from the retainer and remove the transmission inspection cover. Disconnect the flywheel from the converter and secure the converter assembly in the transmission. Remove the remaining transmission-to-engine bolts.

21. Lower the vehicle and then support the transmission. Attach suitable engine lifting equipment and hoist the engine.

22. Raise the engine slightly and carefully pull it from the transmission. Carefully lift the engine out of the engine compartment. Avoid bending or damaging the rear cover plate or other components. Install the engine on a workstand.

To install:

23. Attach the engine lifting equipment and remove the engine from the workstand.

24. Lower the engine carefully into the engine compartment. Make sure the exhaust manifolds are properly aligned with the muffler inlet pipes.

25. Start the converter pilot into the crankshaft. Align the paint mark on the flywheel to the paint mark on the torque converter.

26. Install the transmission upper bolts, making sure the dowels in the cylinder block engage the transmission.

27. Install the engine mount-to-chassis attaching fasteners and remove the engine lifting equipment.

28. Raise and safely support the vehicle. Connect both muffler inlet pipes to the exhaust manifolds. Install the starter and connect the starter cable.

29. Remove the retainer holding the torque converter in the transmission. Attach the converter to the flywheel. Install the converter housing inspection cover and install the remaining transmission attaching bolts.

30. Remove the support from the transmission and lower the vehicle.

31. On 5.8L engines, connect the wiring harness to the left rocker arm cover and connect the coil wiring connector. On 5.0L engines, connect the wiring harness at the two 10-pin connectors.

32. Connect the coolant temperature sending unit wire and connect the heater hoses. Connect the wiring to the metal heater tubes and the engine coolant temperature, air charge temperature and oxygen sensors.

33. Connect the transmission filler tube bracket. Connect the manual shift rod and the retracting spring. Connect the throttle valve vacuum line, if equipped.

34. Connect the accelerator cable and throttle valve cable. Connect the cruise control cable, if equipped.

35. Connect the fuel lines and the oil pressure sending unit wire.

36. Install the pulley, water pump belt and fan/clutch assembly.

37. Position the alternator bracket and install the alternator bolts. Connect the alternator and ground cables. Adjust the drive belt tension.

38. Install the air conditioning compressor. Unplug and connect the refrigerant lines and connect the electrical connector to the compressor.

39. Install the power steering drive belt and power steering pump bracket. Connect the power brake vacuum line.

40. Place the shroud over the fan and install the radiator. Connect the radiator hoses and the transmission oil cooler lines. Position the shroud and install the bolts.

41. Connect the heater hoses to the heater tubes. Fill the cooling system.

Fill the crankcase with the proper type and quantity of engine oil. Adjust the transmission throttle linkage; refer to Section 7.

42. Connect the negative battery cable. Start the engine and bring to normal operating temperature. Check for leaks. Check all fluid levels.

43. Install the air intake duct assembly. Install the hood, aligning the marks that were made during removal.

44. Evacuate and charge the air conditioning system. Road test the vehicle.

Rocker Arm/Valve Cover

REMOVAL & INSTALLATION

4.6L Engine

▶ See Figure 42

1. Disconnect the negative battery cable.
2. Remove the right valve cover as follows:
   a. Disconnect the positive battery cable at the battery and at the power distribution box. Remove the retaining bolt from the positive battery cable bracket located on the side of the right cylinder head.
   b. Disconnect the crankshaft position sensor, air conditioning compressor clutch and canister purge solenoid connectors. Position the harness out of the way.
   c. Disconnect the vent hose from the purge solenoid and position the positive battery cable out of the way.
   d. Disconnect the spark plug wires from the spark plugs. Remove the spark plug wire brackets from the camshaft cover studs and position the wires out of the way.
   e. Remove the PCV valve from the valve cover grommet and position out of the way.
   f. Remove the bolts and stud bolts (note their positions for reassembly) and remove the valve cover.
3. Remove the left valve cover as follows:
   a. Remove the air inlet tube. Relieve the fuel system pressure and disconnect the fuel lines; refer to Section 5.
   b. Raise and safely support the vehicle.
   c. Disconnect the Electronic Variable Orifice (EVO) sensor and oil pressure sending unit and position the harness out of the way. Lower the vehicle.
   d. Remove the 42-pin engine harness connector from the retaining bracket on the brake vacuum booster. Disconnect and position out of the way.
   e. Remove the windshield wiper module.
   f. Disconnect the spark plug wires from the spark plugs. Remove the spark plug wire brackets from the studs and position the wires out of the way.
   g. Remove the bolts and stud bolts (noting their position for reassembly) and remove the valve cover.

To install:

4. Clean the sealing surfaces of the valve covers and cylinder heads. Apply silicone sealer to the places where the front engine cover meets the cylinder head.

5. Attach new gaskets to the valve covers, using suitable sealant. Install the covers with the bolts and stud bolts and tighten to 6.0–8.8 ft. lbs. (8–12 Nm).

6. When installing the right valve cover, proceed as follows:
   a. Install the PCV into the valve cover grommet.
   b. Install the spark plug wire brackets on the studs and connect the wires to the spark plugs.
   c. Position the harness and connect the canister purge solenoid, air conditioning compressor clutch and crankshaft position sensor.
   d. Position the positive battery cable harness on the right cylinder head. Install the bolt retaining the cable bracket to the cylinder head.
   e. Connect the positive battery cable at the power distribution box and the battery.

7. When installing the left valve cover, proceed as follows:
   a. Install the spark plug wire brackets on the studs and connect the wires to the spark plugs.
   b. Install the windshield wiper module.
   c. Connect the 42-pin connector and transmission harness connector. Install the connector on the retaining bracket.
   d. Raise and safely support the vehicle. Position and connect the EVO sensor and oil pressure sending unit harness.
   e. Lower the vehicle. Connect the fuel lines.

8. Connect the negative battery cable. Start the engine and check for leaks.

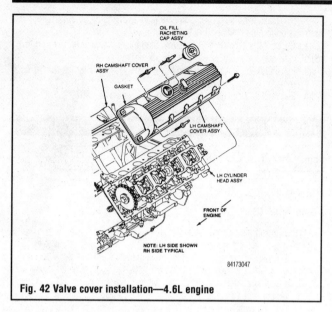

Fig. 42 Valve cover installation—4.6L engine

5.0L Engine

1. Disconnect the negative battery cable.
2. Before removing the right rocker arm cover, disconnect the PCV closure tube from the oil fill stand pipe at the rocker cover.
3. Remove the thermactor bypass valve and air supply hoses as necessary to provide clearance.
4. Disconnect the spark plug wires from the spark plugs. Remove the wires and bracket assembly from the rocker arm cover attaching stud and position the wires out of the way.
5. Remove the upper intake manifold as follows:
   a. Tag and disconnect the electrical connectors at the air bypass valve, throttle position sensor and EGR position sensor.
   b. Disconnect the throttle and transmission linkage at the throttle body. Remove the cable bracket from the intake manifold and position the bracket and cables aside.
   c. Tag and disconnect the vacuum lines from the vacuum tree, EGR valve, fuel pressure regulator and evaporative canister.
   d. Disconnect the PCV hose from the fitting on the rear of the upper manifold and disconnect the PCV vent closure tube at the throttle body.
   e. Remove the 2 EGR coolant lines from the EGR spacer.
   f. Remove the upper intake manifold cover plate.
   g. Remove the 6 retaining bolts and remove the upper intake manifold.
6. Remove the attaching bolts and remove the rocker arm covers.

To install:

7. Clean all gasket mating surfaces of the rocker arm covers and cylinder heads.
8. Attach new rocker arm cover gaskets to the rocker arm covers, using suitable sealant. Install the rocker arm covers and tighten the bolts to 10–13 ft. lbs. (14–18 Nm), wait 2 minutes and tighten again to the same specification.
9. Install the crankcase ventilation tube in the right cover.
10. Install the upper intake manifold in the reverse order of removal. Use a new gasket and tighten the retaining bolts to 12–18 ft. lbs. (16–24 Nm).
11. Install the spark plug wires and bracket assembly on the rocker cover attaching stud. Connect the spark plug wires.
12. Install the air cleaner and intake duct assembly. Install the thermactor bypass valve and air supply hoses, if required.
13. Connect the negative battery cable, start the engine and check for leaks.

5.8L Engine

1. Disconnect the negative battery cable.
2. Before removing the right rocker arm cover, remove the air cleaner assembly. Disconnect the automatic choke heat chamber air inlet hose from the inlet tube near the right rocker arm cover, if equipped.
3. Remove the crankcase ventilation fresh air tube from the rocker arm cover.
4. Remove the thermactor bypass valve and air supply hoses as necessary to provide clearance.

5. Disconnect the spark plug wires from the spark plugs. Remove the wires and bracket assembly from the rocker arm cover attaching stud and position the wires out of the way.
6. On the left side rocker arm cover, remove the wire harness from the retaining clips. Disconnect the wires at the solenoid mounted on the left rocker cover.
7. Remove the rocker arm cover attaching bolts and remove the rocker arm cover.

To install:

8. Clean all gasket mating surfaces of the rocker arm covers and cylinder heads.
9. Attach new rocker arm cover gaskets to the rocker arm covers, using suitable sealant. Install the rocker arm covers and tighten the bolts to 3–5 ft. lbs. (4–7 Nm) on 1989–90 vehicles or 10–13 ft. lbs. (14–18 Nm) on 1991 vehicles. Wait 2 minutes and tighten again to the same specification.
10. Install the crankcase ventilation hoses on the rocker arm covers.
11. Install the spark plug wires and bracket assembly on the rocker arm cover attaching stud. Connect the spark plug wires.
12. Install the air cleaner, the thermactor bypass valve and air supply hoses.
13. Connect the negative battery cable, start the engine and check for leaks.

Rocker Arms/Roller Followers

REMOVAL & INSTALLATION

4.6L Engine

♦ See Figure 43

1. Disconnect the negative battery cable.
2. Remove the valve cover(s).
3. Position the piston of the cylinder being serviced at the bottom of its stroke and position the camshaft lobe on the base circle.
4. Install valve spring spacer tool T91P–6565–AH or equivalent, between the spring coils to prevent valve seal damage.

✳✳ WARNING

If the valve spring spacer tool is not used, the retainer will hit the valve stem seal and damage the seal.

5. Install valve spring compressor tool T91P–6565–A or equivalent, under the camshaft and on top of the valve spring retainer.
6. Compress the valve spring and remove the roller follower. Remove the valve spring compressor and spacer.
7. Repeat Steps 3–6 for each roller follower to be removed. Inspect the roller follower(s) for wear and/or damage and replace, as necessary.

To install:

8. Apply engine oil or assembly lubricant to the valve stem tip and roller follower contact surfaces.

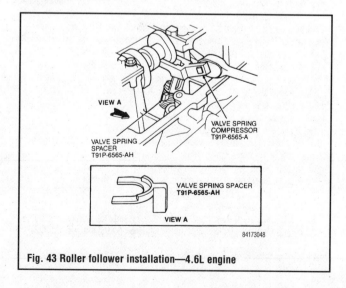

Fig. 43 Roller follower installation—4.6L engine

9. Install valve spring spacer tool T91P–6565–AH or equivalent, between the spring coils. Compress the valve spring using valve spring compressor tool T91P–6565–A or equivalent, and install the roller follower.

➡The piston must be at the bottom of its stroke and the camshaft at the base circle.

10. Remove the valve spring compressor and spacer.
11. Repeat Steps 8–10 for each roller follower to be installed.
12. Install the valve cover(s). Connect the negative battery cable.

5.0L and 5.8L Engines

♦ See Figure 44

1. Disconnect the negative battery cable.
2. Remove the rocker arm cover(s).
3. Remove the rocker arm fulcrum bolt, fulcrum seat and rocker arm. Keep all rocker arm assemblies together. Identify each assembly so it may be reinstalled in its original position.
4. Inspect the rocker arm and fulcrum seat contact surfaces for wear and/or damage. Also check the rocker arm for wear on the valve stem tip contact surface and the pushrod socket. Replace complete rocker arm assemblies, as necessary.
5. Inspect the pushrod end and the valve stem tip. Replace pushrods, as necessary. If the valve stem tip is worn, the cylinder head must be removed to replace or machine the valve.

To install:

6. Apply engine oil or assembly lubricant to the valve stem tip and pushrod end. Also apply lubricant to the rocker arm and fulcrum seat contact surfaces.
7. Rotate the crankshaft until the lifter is on the camshaft base circle (all the way down) and install the rocker, fulcrum seat and fulcrum bolt. Tighten the bolts to 18–25 ft. lbs. (24–34 Nm).
8. Install the rocker arm cover(s).
9. Connect the negative battery cable.

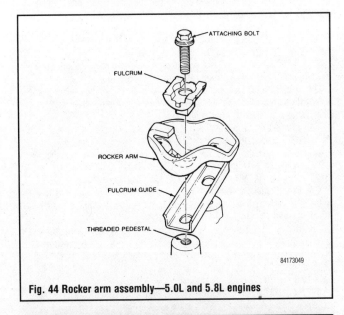

Fig. 44 Rocker arm assembly—5.0L and 5.8L engines

Thermostat

REMOVAL & INSTALLATION

4.6L Engine

♦ See Figure 45

1. Drain the cooling system to a level below the thermostat.

✳✳ CAUTION

When draining the coolant, keep in mind that cats and dogs are attracted by the ethylene glycol antifreeze, and are quite likely to

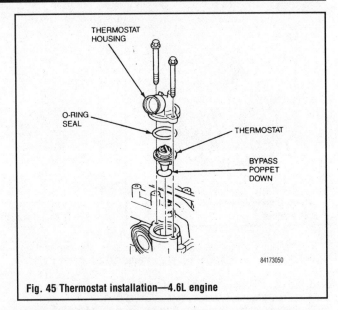

Fig. 45 Thermostat installation—4.6L engine

drink any that is left in an uncovered container or in puddles on the ground. This will prove fatal in sufficient quantity. Always drain the coolant into a sealable container. Coolant should be reused unless it is contaminated or several years old.

2. Disconnect the upper radiator hose at the thermostat housing.
3. Remove the 2 thermostat housing retaining bolts and remove the thermostat housing.
4. Remove the thermostat and O-ring seal. Inspect the O-ring for damage and replace, as necessary.

To install:

5. Make sure all mating surfaces are clean.
6. Install the thermostat, O-ring and thermostat housing. Make sure the thermostat is positioned as shown in the figure.
7. Install and alternately tighten the thermostat housing retaining bolts to 15–22 ft. lbs. (20–30 Nm). Connect the upper radiator hose.
8. Fill the cooling system as described in Section 1. Check for leaks.

5.0L and 5.8L Engines

♦ See Figures 46 and 47

1. Drain the cooling system to a level below the thermostat.

✳✳ CAUTION

When draining the coolant, keep in mind that cats and dogs are attracted by the ethylene glycol antifreeze, and are quite likely to drink any that is left in an uncovered container or in puddles on the ground. This will prove fatal in sufficient quantity. Always drain the coolant into a sealable container. Coolant should be reused unless it is contaminated or several years old.

2. Disconnect the upper radiator hose and the bypass hose at the thermostat housing.
3. To gain access to the thermostat housing, either mark the location of the distributor, loosen the hold-down clamp and rotate the distributor, or remove the distributor cap and rotor.
4. Remove the thermostat housing retaining bolts and the housing and gasket. Remove the thermostat from the housing.

To install:

5. Clean the gasket mating surfaces. Position a new gasket on the intake manifold.
6. Install the thermostat in the housing, rotating slightly to lock the thermostat in place on the flats cast into the housing. Install the housing on the manifold and tighten the bolts to 12–18 ft. lbs. (16–24 Nm).

➡If the thermostat has a bleeder valve, the thermostat should be positioned with the bleeder valve at the 12 o'clock position as viewed from the front of the engine.

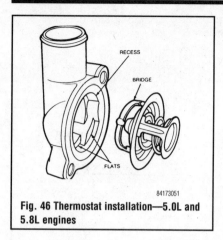

Fig. 46 Thermostat installation—5.0L and 5.8L engines

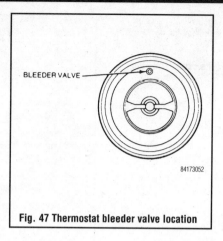

Fig. 47 Thermostat bleeder valve location

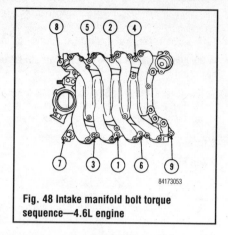

Fig. 48 Intake manifold bolt torque sequence—4.6L engine

7. Install the distributor cap and rotor, or reposition the distributor for correct ignition timing, as necessary. Tighten the hold-down bolt to 18–26 ft. lbs. (24–35 Nm).

8. Connect the bypass hose and the upper radiator hose to the thermostat housing. Fill the cooling system as described in Section 1.

9. Check for leaks.

Intake Manifold

REMOVAL & INSTALLATION

4.6L Engine

▶ See Figure 48

1. Disconnect the negative battery cable.

2. Drain the cooling system. Relieve the fuel system pressure and disconnect the fuel lines; refer to Section 5.

✳✳ CAUTION

When draining the coolant, keep in mind that cats and dogs are attracted by the ethylene glycol antifreeze, and are quite likely to drink any that is left in an uncovered container or in puddles on the ground. This will prove fatal in sufficient quantity. Always drain the coolant into a sealable container. Coolant should be reused unless it is contaminated or several years old.

3. Remove the wiper module and the air inlet tube. Release the belt tensioner and remove the accessory drive belt.

4. Tag and disconnect the spark plug wires from the spark plugs. Disconnect the spark plug wire brackets from the valve cover studs.

5. Disconnect both ignition coils and CID sensor. Tag and disconnect all spark plug wires from both ignition coils. Remove the 2 bolts retaining the spark plug wire tray to the coil brackets and remove the spark plug wire assembly.

6. Disconnect the alternator wiring harness from the junction block at the fender apron and alternator. Remove the bolts retaining the alternator brace to the intake manifold and the alternator to the engine block and remove the alternator.

7. Raise and safely support the vehicle. Disconnect the oil sending unit and EVO harness sensor and position the wiring harness out of the way.

8. Disconnect the EGR tube from the right exhaust manifold and lower the vehicle.

9. Remove the 42-pin engine harness connector from the retaining bracket on the vacuum brake booster and disconnect the connector.

10. Disconnect the air conditioning compressor, crankshaft position sensor and canister purge solenoid.

11. Remove the PCV valve from the valve cover and disconnect the canister purge vent hose from the PCV valve.

12. Disconnect the accelerator and cruise control cables from the throttle body using a small prybar. Remove the accelerator cable bracket from the intake manifold and position out of the way.

13. Disconnect the throttle valve cable from the throttle body and the vacuum hose from the throttle body adapter port.

14. Disconnect both oxygen sensors and the heater supply hose.

15. Remove the 2 bolts retaining the thermostat housing to the intake manifold and position the upper hose and thermostat housing out of the way.

➡**The 2 thermostat housing bolts also retain the intake manifold.**

16. Remove the bolts retaining the intake manifold to the cylinder heads and remove the intake manifold. Remove and discard the gaskets.

To install:

17. Clean all gasket mating surfaces. Position new intake manifold gaskets on the cylinder heads. Make sure the alignment tabs on the gaskets are aligned with the holes in the cylinder heads.

18. Install the intake manifold and the retaining bolts. Tighten the bolts, in sequence, to 15–22 ft. lbs. (20–30 Nm).

19. Inspect and if necessary, replace the O-ring seal on the thermostat housing. Position the housing and upper hose and install the 2 bolts. Tighten to 15–22 ft. lbs. (20–30 Nm).

20. Connect the heater supply hose and connect both oxygen sensors.

21. Connect the vacuum hose to the throttle body adapter vacuum port. Connect and, if necessary, adjust the throttle valve cable.

22. Install the accelerator cable bracket on the intake manifold and connect the accelerator and cruise control cables to the throttle body.

23. Install the PCV valve in the valve cover and connect the canister purge solenoid vent hose. Connect the air conditioning compressor, crankshaft position sensor and canister purge solenoid.

24. Connect the 42-pin engine harness connector. Install the connector on the retaining bracket on the vacuum brake booster.

25. Raise and safely support the vehicle. Connect the EGR tube to the right exhaust manifold and tighten the line nut to 26–33 ft. lbs. (35–45 Nm).

26. Connect the EVO sensor and oil sending unit. Lower the vehicle.

27. Position the alternator and install the retaining bolts. Tighten to 15–22 ft. lbs. (20–30 Nm). Install the 2 bolts retaining the alternator brace to the intake manifold and tighten to 6.0–8.8 ft. lbs. (8–12 Nm).

28. Connect the alternator wiring harness to the alternator, right-hand fender apron and junction block.

29. Position the spark plug wire assembly on the engine and install the 2 bolts retaining the spark plug wire tray to the coil brackets. Tighten the bolts to 6.0–8.8 ft. lbs. (8–12 Nm).

30. Connect the spark plug wires to the ignition coils in their proper positions. Connect the spark plug wires to the spark plugs.

31. Connect the spark plug wire brackets on the valve cover studs. Connect both ignition coils and CID sensor.

32. Install the accessory drive belt and the air inlet tube. Install the wiper module and connect the fuel lines.

33. Fill the cooling system. Connect the negative battery cable, start the engine and bring to normal operating temperature. Check for leaks.

34. Shut the engine OFF and retighten the intake manifold bolts, in sequence, to 15–22 ft. lbs. (20–30 Nm).

5.0L Engine

▶ See Figures 49, 50, 51 and 52

1. Disconnect the negative battery cable.

2. Drain the cooling system. Relieve the fuel system pressure; refer to Section 5.

When draining the coolant, keep in mind that cats and dogs are attracted by the ethylene glycol antifreeze, and are quite likely to drink any that is left in an uncovered container or in puddles on the ground. This will prove fatal in sufficient quantity. Always drain the coolant into a sealable container. Coolant should be reused unless it is contaminated or several years old.

3. Disconnect the accelerator cable and cruise control linkage, if equipped, from the throttle body. Disconnect the throttle valve cable, if equipped. Label and disconnect the vacuum lines at the intake manifold fitting.

4. Label and disconnect the spark plug wires from the spark plugs. Remove the wires and bracket assembly from the rocker arm cover attaching stud. Remove the distributor cap and wires assembly.

5. Disconnect the fuel lines (see Section 5) and the distributor wiring connector. Mark the position of the rotor on the distributor housing and the position of the distributor housing in the block. Remove the hold-down bolt and remove the distributor.

6. Disconnect the upper radiator hose at the thermostat housing and the water temperature sending unit wire at the sending unit. Disconnect the heater hose from the intake manifold and disconnect the 2 throttle body cooler hoses.

7. Disconnect the water pump bypass hose from the thermostat housing. Label and disconnect the connectors from the engine coolant temperature, air charge temperature, throttle position and EGR sensors and the idle speed control solenoid. Disconnect the injector wire connections and the fuel charging assembly wiring.

8. Remove the PCV valve from the grommet at the rear of the lower intake manifold. Disconnect the fuel evaporative purge hose from the plastic connector at the front of the upper intake manifold.

9. Remove the upper intake manifold cover plate and upper intake bolts. Remove the upper intake manifold.

10. Remove the heater tube assembly from the lower intake manifold studs. Remove the alternator and air conditioner braces from the intake studs. Disconnect the heater hose from the lower intake manifold.

11. Remove the lower intake manifold retaining bolts and remove the lower intake manifold.

➡If it is necessary to pry the intake manifold away from the cylinder heads, be careful to avoid damaging the gasket sealing surfaces.

To install:

12. Clean all gasket mating surfaces. Apply a ⅛ in. bead of silicone sealer to the points where the cylinder block rails meet the cylinder heads.

13. Position new seals on the cylinder block and new gaskets on the cylinder heads with the gaskets interlocked with the seal tabs. Make sure the holes in the gaskets are aligned with the holes in the cylinder heads.

14. Apply a ³⁄₁₆ in. bead of sealer to the outer end of each intake manifold seal for the full width of the seal.

15. Using guide pins to ease installation, carefully lower the intake manifold into position on the cylinder block and cylinder heads.

➡After the intake manifold is in place, run a finger around the seal area to make sure the seals are in place. If the seals are not in place, remove the intake manifold and position the seals.

16. Make sure the holes in the manifold gaskets and the manifold are in alignment. Remove the guide pins. Install the intake manifold attaching bolts and tighten, in sequence, to 23–25 ft. lbs. (31–34 Nm).

17. If required, install the heater tube assembly to the lower intake manifold studs.

18. Install the water pump bypass hose and upper radiator hose on the thermostat housing. Install the hoses to the heater tubes and intake manifold. Connect the fuel lines.

19. Install the distributor, aligning the housing and rotor with the marks that were made during removal. Install the distributor cap. Position the spark plug wires in the harness brackets on the rocker arm cover attaching stud and connect the wires to the spark plugs.

20. Install a new gasket and the upper intake manifold. Tighten the bolts to 12–18 ft. lbs. (16–24 Nm). Install the cover plate and connect the crankcase vent tube.

21. Connect the accelerator, throttle valve cable and cruise control cable, if equipped, to the throttle body. Connect the electrical connectors and vacuum lines to their proper locations.

22. Connect the coolant hoses to the EGR spacer. Fill the cooling system.

23. Connect the negative battery cable, start the engine and check for leaks. Check the ignition timing.

24. Operate the engine at fast idle. When engine temperatures have stabilized, tighten the intake manifold bolts to 23–25 ft. lbs. (31–34 Nm).

25. Connect the air intake duct and the crankcase vent hose.

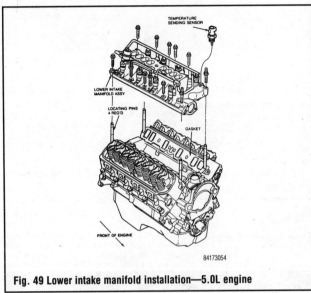

Fig. 49 Lower intake manifold installation—5.0L engine

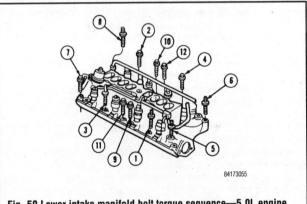

Fig. 50 Lower intake manifold bolt torque sequence—5.0L engine

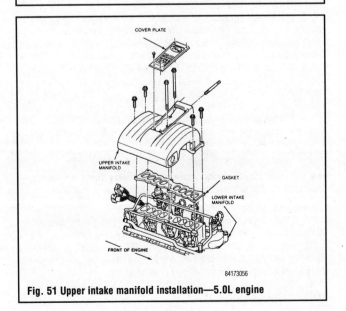

Fig. 51 Upper intake manifold installation—5.0L engine

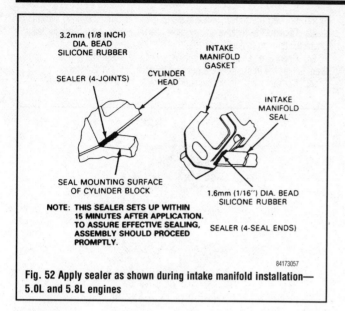

Fig. 52 Apply sealer as shown during intake manifold installation—5.0L and 5.8L engines

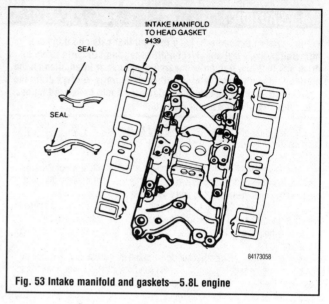

Fig. 53 Intake manifold and gaskets—5.8L engine

5.8L Engine

♦ See Figures 53 and 54

1. Disconnect the negative battery cable and drain the cooling system.

❊❊ CAUTION

When draining the coolant, keep in mind that cats and dogs are attracted by the ethylene glycol antifreeze, and are quite likely to drink any that is left in an uncovered container or in puddles on the ground. This will prove fatal in sufficient quantity. Always drain the coolant into a sealable container. Coolant should be reused unless it is contaminated or several years old.

2. Remove the air cleaner, crankcase ventilation hose and intake duct assembly. If equipped, disconnect the automatic choke heat tube.

3. Disconnect the accelerator cable and cruise control linkage, if equipped, from the carburetor. Disconnect the throttle valve rod, if equipped, and remove the accelerator cable bracket.

4. Tag and disconnect the vacuum lines at the intake manifold and the wires from the coil.

5. Tag and disconnect the spark plug wires from the spark plugs. Remove the wires and bracket assembly from the rocker arm cover attaching stud. Remove the distributor cap and spark plug wires assembly.

6. Remove the carburetor fuel inlet line.

7. Disconnect the vacuum hoses and the wiring connector from the distributor. Mark the position of the rotor on the distributor housing and the position of the distributor housing in the block. Remove the hold-down bolt and remove the distributor.

8. Disconnect the upper radiator hose at the thermostat housing and the water temperature sending unit wire at the sending unit. Disconnect the heater hose from the intake manifold. Disconnect the EGR cooler T-fitting from the heater return hose, if equipped.

9. Disconnect the water pump bypass hose at the thermostat housing. Disconnect the crankcase vent hose at the rocker arm cover. Disconnect the fuel evaporative purge tube, if equipped.

10. Remove the intake manifold and carburetor as an assembly.

➡If it is necessary to pry the intake manifold away from the cylinder heads, be careful to avoid damaging the gasket sealing surfaces.

To install:

11. Clean all gasket mating surfaces. Apply a ⅛ in. bead of silicone sealer to the points where the cylinder block rails meet the cylinder heads.

12. Position new seals on the cylinder block and new gaskets on the cylinder heads with the gaskets interlocked with the seal tabs. Make sure the holes in the gaskets are aligned with the holes in the cylinder heads.

13. Apply a ³⁄₁₆ in. bead of sealer to the outer end of each intake manifold seal for the full width of the seal.

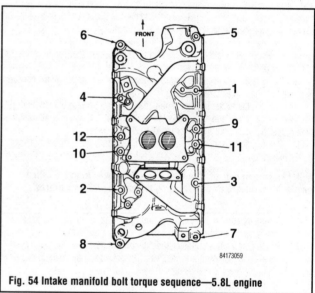

Fig. 54 Intake manifold bolt torque sequence—5.8L engine

14. Using guide pins to ease installation, carefully lower the intake manifold into position on the cylinder block and cylinder heads.

➡After the intake manifold is in place, run a finger around the seal area to make sure the seals are in place. If the seals are not in place, remove the intake manifold and position the seals.

15. Make sure the holes in the manifold gaskets and the manifold are in alignment. Remove the guide pins. Install the intake manifold attaching bolts and tighten, in sequence, to 23–25 ft. lbs. (31–34 Nm).

16. Install the water pump bypass hose on the thermostat housing. Connect the upper radiator hose and the heater hose. Install the carburetor fuel line.

17. Install the distributor, aligning the distributor housing and rotor with the marks that were made during removal. Install the distributor cap. Position the spark plug wires in the harness brackets on the rocker arm cover attaching stud and connect the wires to the spark plugs.

18. Connect the crankcase vent tube. Connect the coil wire and primary wiring connector.

19. Connect the accelerator cable and cable bracket. Connect the throttle valve rod and the cruise control linkage, if equipped.

20. Connect all electrical connections and vacuum lines disconnected during removal. Fill the cooling system.

21. Connect the negative battery cable, start the engine and check for leaks. Adjust the ignition timing and connect the vacuum hoses to the distributor.

22. Operate the engine at fast idle. When engine temperatures have stabilized, tighten the intake manifold bolts to 23–25 ft. lbs. (31–34 Nm).

23. Connect the air cleaner and intake duct assembly and the crankcase vent hose.

Exhaust Manifold

REMOVAL & INSTALLATION

4.6L Engine

▶ See Figure 55

1. Disconnect the battery cables, negative cable first. Remove the air inlet tube.

2. Drain the cooling system and remove the cooling fan and shroud. Relieve the fuel system pressure and disconnect the fuel lines; refer to Section 5.

❋❋ CAUTION

When draining the coolant, keep in mind that cats and dogs are attracted by the ethylene glycol antifreeze, and are quite likely to drink any that is left in an uncovered container or in puddles on the ground. This will prove fatal in sufficient quantity. Always drain the coolant into a sealable container. Coolant should be reused unless it is contaminated or several years old.

3. Remove the upper radiator hose. Remove the wiper module and support bracket.

4. Discharge the air conditioning system; refer to Section 1. Disconnect and plug the compressor outlet hose at the compressor and remove the bolt retaining the hose assembly to the right coil bracket. Cap the compressor opening.

5. Remove the 42-pin engine harness connector from the retaining bracket on the brake vacuum booster. Disconnect the connector.

6. Disconnect the throttle valve cable from the throttle body. Disconnect the heater outlet hose.

7. Remove the nut retaining the ground strap to the right cylinder head. Remove the upper stud and lower bolt retaining the heater outlet hose to the right cylinder head and position out of the way.

8. Remove the blower motor resistor and remove the bolt retaining the right engine mount to the lower engine bracket. Disconnect both oxygen sensors.

9. Raise and safely support the vehicle. Remove the engine mount through bolts.

10. Remove the EGR tube line nut from the right exhaust manifold.

11. Disconnect the exhaust pipes from the manifolds. Lower the exhaust system and hang it from the crossmember with wire.

12. To remove the left exhaust manifold, remove the engine mount from the engine block and remove the 8 bolts retaining the exhaust manifold.

13. Position a jack and a block of wood under the oil pan, rearward of the oil drain hole. Raise the engine approximately 4 in. (100mm).

14. Remove the 8 bolts retaining the right exhaust manifold and remove the manifold.

To install:

15. If the exhaust manifolds are being replaced, transfer the oxygen sensors and tighten to 27–33 ft. lbs. (37–45 Nm). On the right manifold, transfer the EGR tube connector and tighten to 33–48 ft. lbs. (45–65 Nm).

16. Clean the mating surfaces of the exhaust manifolds and cylinder heads.

17. Position the exhaust manifolds to the cylinder heads and install the retaining bolts. Tighten, in sequence, to 15–22 ft. lbs. (20–30 Nm).

18. Position and connect the EGR valve and tube assembly to the exhaust manifold. Tighten the line nut to 26–33 ft. lbs. (35–45 Nm).

19. Install the left engine mount and tighten the bolts to 15–22 ft. lbs. (20–30 Nm). Lower the engine onto the mounts and remove the jack. Install the engine mount through bolts and tighten to 15–22 ft. lbs. (20–30 Nm).

20. Cut the wire and position the exhaust system. Tighten the nuts to 20–30 ft. lbs. (27–41 Nm).

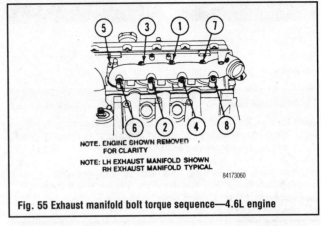

Fig. 55 Exhaust manifold bolt torque sequence—4.6L engine

➡ **Make sure the exhaust system clears the No. 3 crossmember. Adjust as necessary.**

21. Lower the vehicle. Connect both oxygen sensors and install the bolt retaining the right engine mount to the frame. Tighten to 15–22 ft. lbs. (20–30 Nm).

22. Install the blower motor resistor. Position the heater outlet hoses. Install the upper stud and lower bolt and tighten to 15–22 ft. lbs. (20–30 Nm). Install the ground strap onto the stud and tighten the nut to 15–22 ft. lbs. (20–30 Nm).

23. Connect the heater outlet hose. Connect and if necessary, adjust the throttle valve cable.

24. Connect the 42-pin connector and transmission harness connector. Install the connector to the retaining bracket on the brake vacuum booster.

25. Connect the air conditioning compressor outlet hose to the compressor and install the bolt retaining the hose assembly to the right coil bracket.

26. Install the upper radiator hose and connect the fuel lines. Install the wiper module and retaining bracket.

27. Install the cooling fan and shroud. Fill the cooling system.

28. Install the air inlet tube. Connect the battery cables, start the engine and check for leaks.

29. Evacuate and charge the air conditioning system.

5.0L and 5.8L Engines

1. Disconnect the negative battery cable.

2. Remove the thermactor hardware from the right exhaust manifold. Remove the air cleaner and inlet duct, if necessary.

3. Tag and disconnect the spark plug wires. Remove the spark plugs.

4. Disconnect the engine oil dipstick tube from the exhaust manifold stud.

5. Raise and safely support the vehicle. Disconnect the exhaust pipes from the exhaust manifolds.

6. Remove the engine oil dipstick tube by carefully tapping upward on the tube. Disconnect the oxygen sensor connector.

7. Lower the vehicle.

8. Remove the attaching bolts and washers and remove the exhaust manifolds.

To install:

9. Clean the manifold, cylinder head and exhaust pipe mating surfaces.

10. Position the manifolds on the cylinder heads and install the mounting bolts and washers. Working from the center to the ends, tighten the bolts to 18–24 ft. lbs. (24–32 Nm).

11. Install the engine oil dipstick tube. Connect the oxygen sensor connector.

12. Install the spark plugs and connect the spark plug wires.

13. Install the thermactor hardware to the right exhaust manifold. Install the air cleaner and inlet duct, if removed.

14. Raise and safely support the vehicle. Position the exhaust pipes to the manifolds. Alternately tighten the exhaust pipe flange nuts to 20–30 ft. lbs. (27–41 Nm).

15. Lower the vehicle, start the engine and check for exhaust leaks.

Radiator

REMOVAL & INSTALLATION

▶ See Figures 56, 57 and 58

> ❈❈ **CAUTION**
>
> Never remove the radiator cap while the engine is running or personal injury from scalding hot coolant or steam may result. If possible, wait until the engine has cooled to remove the radiator cap. If this is not possible, wrap a thick cloth around the radiator cap and turn it slowly to the first stop. Step back while the pressure is released from the cooling system. When it is certain all the pressure has been released, press down on the cap, still with the cloth, and turn and remove it.

1. Disconnect the negative battery cable.
2. Remove the radiator cap. Place a drain pan under the radiator, open the draincock and drain the coolant.

> ❈❈ **CAUTION**
>
> When draining the coolant, keep in mind that cats and dogs are attracted by the ethylene glycol antifreeze, and are quite likely to

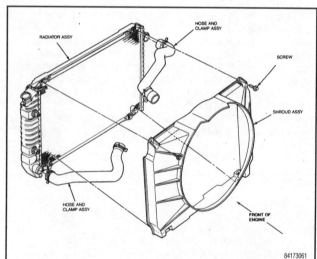

Fig. 56 Radiator and related components—1990–91 vehicles (except California)

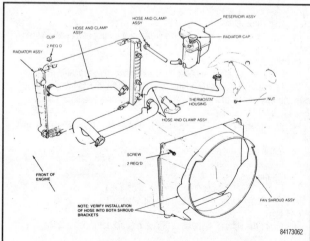

Fig. 57 Radiator and related components—1992–94 vehicles

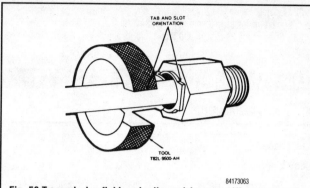

Fig. 58 Transmission fluid cooler line quick connect/disconnect tool, for 1989–90 vehicles

drink any that is left in an uncovered container or in puddles on the ground. This will prove fatal in sufficient quantity. Always drain the coolant into a sealable container. Coolant should be reused unless it is contaminated or several years old.

3. Disconnect the upper, lower and coolant reservoir hoses at the radiator.
4. Disconnect the fluid cooler lines at the radiator. On 1989–90 vehicles, tool T82L–9500–AH or equivalent, is required to disconnect the fluid cooler lines. On 1991–94 vehicles, use a backup wrench to hold the radiator fitting while loosening the fluid cooler lines.
5. Remove the 2 upper fan shroud retaining bolts at the radiator support, lift the fan shroud sufficiently to disengage the lower retaining clips and lay the shroud back over the fan.
6. Remove the radiator upper support retaining bolts and remove the supports. Lift the radiator from the vehicle.

To install:

7. If a new radiator is to be installed, transfer the petcock from the old radiator to the new one. Remove the fluid cooler line fittings from the old radiator and install them on the new one, using an oil resistant sealer.
8. Position the radiator assembly into the vehicle. Install the upper supports and the retaining bolts. Connect the fluid cooler lines.
9. Place the fan shroud into the clips on the lower radiator support and install the 2 upper shroud retaining bolts. Position the shroud to maintain approximately 1 in. (25mm) clearance between the fan blades and the shroud.
10. Connect the radiator hoses. Close the radiator petcock. Fill the cooling system as explained in Section 1.
11. Start the engine and bring to operating temperature. Check for coolant and transmission fluid leaks.
12. Check the coolant and transmission fluid levels.

Engine Fan

REMOVAL & INSTALLATION

4.6L Engine

▶ See Figure 59

1. Loosen the fan clutch mounting shaft from the water pump hub.
2. Loosen the fan shroud from its radiator mounting and remove the lower hose from the shroud.
3. Lift the fan and clutch assembly and the fan shroud from the vehicle.
4. If necessary, remove the fan-to-fan clutch retaining bolts and separate the fan from the fan clutch.

> ❈❈ **CAUTION**
>
> Closely examine the fan for cracks or separation, to avoid the possibility of personal injury or vehicle damage.

To install:

5. Assemble the fan and fan clutch. Tighten the retaining bolts to 15–20 ft. lbs. (20–27 Nm).

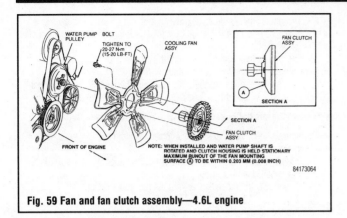

Fig. 59 Fan and fan clutch assembly—4.6L engine

6. Install the fan and clutch assembly and the fan shroud. Mount the fan clutch shaft to the water pump hub and tighten to 37–46 ft. lbs. (50–62 Nm).

7. Slip the shroud into the lower mounting clips and install the shroud retaining screws.

5.0L and 5.8L Engines

1. Loosen the fan clutch-to-water pump hub retaining bolts.
2. If necessary, remove the drive belt from the water pump pulley.
3. Remove the fan shroud upper retaining screws. Lift the shroud to disengage it from the lower retaining clips.
4. Remove the fan clutch-to-water pump hub bolts and remove the fan and clutch assembly and the fan shroud.
5. If necessary, remove the fan-to-fan clutch retaining bolts and separate the fan from the fan clutch.

�֍ CAUTION

Closely examine the fan for cracks or separation, to avoid the possibility of personal injury or vehicle damage.

To install:

6. Assemble the fan and fan clutch. Tighten the retaining bolts evenly and alternately to 12–18 ft. lbs. (16–24 Nm).
7. Install the fan and clutch assembly and the fan shroud.
8. Install the fan clutch-to-water pump hub bolts.
9. Slip the shroud into the lower mounting clips and install the shroud retaining screws.
10. If removed, install the water pump drive pulley and adjust the belt tension; refer to Section 1.
11. Tighten the fan clutch-to-water pump hub bolts evenly and alternately to 15–22 ft. lbs. (20–27 Nm). Recheck the belt tension.

Water Pump

REMOVAL & INSTALLATION

4.6L Engine

▶ See Figure 60

1. Disconnect the negative battery cable.
2. Drain the cooling system, remove the cooling fan and the shroud.

✖✖ CAUTION

When draining the coolant, keep in mind that cats and dogs are attracted by the ethylene glycol antifreeze, and are quite likely to drink any that is left in an uncovered container or in puddles on the ground. This will prove fatal in sufficient quantity. Always drain the coolant into a sealable container. Coolant should be reused unless it is contaminated or several years old.

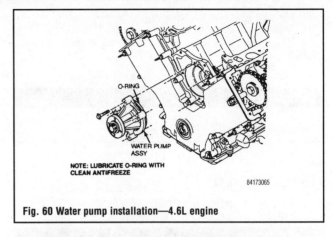

Fig. 60 Water pump installation—4.6L engine

3. Release the belt tensioner and remove the accessory drive belt.
4. Remove the 4 bolts retaining the water pump pulley to the water pump and remove the pulley.
5. Remove the 4 bolts retaining the water pump to the engine assembly and remove the water pump.

To install:

6. Clean the sealing surfaces of the water pump and engine block.
7. Lubricate a new O-ring seal with clean antifreeze and install on the water pump.
8. Install the water pump and tighten the retaining bolts to 15–22 ft. lbs. (20–30 Nm).
9. Install the water pump pulley and tighten the retaining bolts to 15–22 ft. lbs. (20–30 Nm).
10. Install the accessory drive belt; refer to Section 1.
11. Install the cooling fan and shroud. Connect the negative battery cable and fill the cooling system as explained in Section 1.
12. Run the engine and check for leaks.

5.0L and 5.8L Engines

1. Disconnect the negative battery cable.
2. Drain the cooling system. Remove the air inlet tube.

✖✖ CAUTION

When draining the coolant, keep in mind that cats and dogs are attracted by the ethylene glycol antifreeze, and are quite likely to drink any that is left in an uncovered container or in puddles on the ground. This will prove fatal in sufficient quantity. Always drain the coolant into a sealable container. Coolant should be reused unless it is contaminated or several years old.

3. Remove the fan shroud attaching bolts and position the shroud over the fan. Remove the fan and clutch assembly from the water pump shaft and remove the shroud.
4. Remove the air conditioner drive belt and idler pulley bracket. Remove the alternator and power steering drive belts. Remove the power steering pump and position aside, leaving the hoses attached. Remove all accessory brackets that attach to the water pump.
5. Remove the water pump pulley. Disconnect the lower radiator hose, heater hose and water pump bypass hose at the water pump.
6. Remove the water pump attaching bolts and remove the water pump. Discard the gasket.

To install:

7. Clean all old gasket material from the timing cover and water pump.
8. Apply a suitable waterproof sealing compound to both sides of a new gasket and install the gasket on the timing cover.
9. Install the water pump and tighten the mounting bolts to 12–18 ft. lbs. (16–24 Nm).
10. Connect the hoses and accessory brackets to the water pump. Install the pulley on the water pump shaft.
11. Install the power steering pump and air conditioner idler pulley bracket. Install the accessory drive belts.

12. Install the fan and fan clutch assembly and the fan shroud.
13. Adjust the accessory drive belt tension; refer to Section 1.
14. Connect the negative battery cable and fill the cooling system, as explained in Section 1.
15. Run the engine and check for leaks.

Cylinder Head

REMOVAL & INSTALLATION

4.6L Engine

♦ **See Figures 61 thru 67**

1. Disconnect the negative battery cable.
2. Drain the cooling system and remove the cooling fan and shroud.

✳✳ CAUTION

When draining the coolant, keep in mind that cats and dogs are attracted by the ethylene glycol antifreeze, and are quite likely to drink any that is left in an uncovered container or in puddles on the ground. This will prove fatal in sufficient quantity. Always drain the coolant into a sealable container. Coolant should be reused unless it is contaminated or several years old.

3. Relieve the fuel system pressure and disconnect the fuel lines; refer to Section 5.
4. Remove the air inlet tube and the wiper module. Release the belt tensioner and remove the accessory drive belt.
5. Tag and disconnect the spark plug wires from the spark plugs. Disconnect the spark plug wire brackets from the valve cover studs and remove the 2 bolts retaining the spark plug wire tray to the coil brackets.
6. Remove the bolt retaining the air conditioner high pressure line to the right coil bracket. Disconnect both ignition coils and CID sensor.
7. Remove the nuts retaining the coil brackets to the front cover. Slide the ignition coil brackets and spark plug wire assembly off the mounting studs and remove from the vehicle.
8. Remove the water pump pulley. Disconnect the alternator wiring harness from the junction block, fender apron and alternator. Disconnect the bolts retaining the alternator to the intake manifold and engine block and remove the alternator.
9. Disconnect the positive battery cable at the power distribution box. Remove the retaining bolt from the positive battery cable bracket located on the side of the right cylinder head.
10. Disconnect the vent hose from the canister purge solenoid and position the positive battery cable out of the way. Disconnect the canister purge solenoid vent hose from the PCV valve and remove the PCV valve from the valve cover.
11. Remove the 42-pin engine harness connector from the retaining bracket on the brake vacuum booster, disconnect and position out of the way.
12. Disconnect the crankshaft position sensor, air conditioning compressor clutch and canister purge solenoid connectors.
13. Raise and safely support the vehicle.
14. Remove the bolts retaining the power steering pump to the engine block and front cover. The front lower bolt on the power steering pump will not come all the way out. Wire the power steering pump out of the way.
15. Remove the 4 bolts retaining the oil pan to the front cover. Remove the crankshaft damper retaining bolt and remove the damper, using a suitable puller.
16. Disconnect the Electronic Variable Orifice (EVO) sensor and oil sending unit. Position the EVO sensor and oil pressure sending unit harness out of the way.
17. Disconnect the EGR tube from the right exhaust manifold. Disconnect the exhaust pipes from the exhaust manifolds. Lower the exhaust pipes and hang with wire from the crossmember.
18. Remove the bolt retaining the starter wiring harness to the rear of the right cylinder head. Lower the vehicle.
19. Remove the bolts and stud bolts retaining the valve covers to the cylinder heads and remove the covers.

20. Disconnect the accelerator, cruise control and throttle valve cables. Remove the accelerator cable bracket from the intake manifold and position out of the way.
21. Disconnect the vacuum hose from the throttle body elbow vacuum port, both oxygen sensors and the heater supply hose.
22. Remove the 2 bolts retaining the thermostat housing to the intake manifold and position the upper hose and thermostat housing out of the way.

➡**The two thermostat housing bolts also retain the intake manifold.**

23. Remove the 9 bolts retaining the intake manifold to the cylinder heads and remove the intake manifold and gaskets.
24. Remove the 7 stud bolts and 4 bolts retaining the front cover to the engine and remove the front cover.
25. Remove the timing chains; refer to the procedure in this Section.
26. Remove the 10 bolts retaining the left cylinder head to the engine block and remove the head.

➡**The lower rear bolt cannot be removed due to interference with the brake vacuum booster. Use a rubber band to hold the bolt away from the engine block.**

27. Remove the ground strap, 1 stud and 1 bolt retaining the heater return line to the right cylinder head.
28. Remove the 10 bolts retaining the right cylinder head to the engine block and remove the head.

➡**The lower rear bolt cannot be removed due to interference with the evaporator housing. Use a rubber band to hold the bolt away from the engine block.**

29. Clean all gasket mating surfaces. Check the cylinder head and engine block for flatness. Check the cylinder head for scratches near the coolant passage and combustion chamber that could provide leak paths.
To install:
30. Rotate the crankshaft counterclockwise 45 degrees. The crankshaft keyway should be at the 9 o'clock position viewed from the front of the engine. This ensures that all pistons are below the top of the engine block deck face.
31. Rotate the camshaft to a stable position where the valves do not extend below the head face.
32. Position new head gaskets on the engine block. Install the lower rear bolts on both cylinder heads and retain with rubber bands as explained during the removal procedure.

➡**New cylinder head bolts must be used whenever the cylinder head is removed and reinstalled. The cylinder head bolts are a torque-to-yield design and cannot be reused.**

33. Position the cylinder heads on the engine block dowels, being careful not to score the surface of the head face. Apply clean oil to the head bolts, remove the rubber band from the lower rear bolt and install all bolts hand-tight.
34. Tighten the head bolts as follows:
   a. Tighten the bolts, in sequence, to 25–30 ft. lbs. (35–45 Nm).
   b. Rotate each bolt, in sequence, 85–95 degrees.
   c. Rotate each bolt, in sequence, an additional 85–95 degrees.
35. Position the heater return hose and install the 2 bolts. Rotate the camshafts using the flats matched at the center of the camshaft until both are in time. Install cam positioning tools T91P–6256–A or equivalent, on the flats of the camshafts to keep them from rotating.
36. Rotate the crankshaft clockwise 45 degrees to position the crankshaft at TDC on No. 1 cylinder.

➡**The crankshaft must only be rotated in the clockwise direction and only as far as TDC.**

37. Install the timing chains according to the procedure in this Section.
38. Install a new front cover seal and gasket. Apply silicone sealer to the lower corners of the cover where it meets the junction of the oil pan and cylinder block and to the points where the cover contacts the junction of the cylinder block and cylinder head.
39. Install the front cover and the stud bolts and bolts. Tighten to 15–22 ft. lbs. (20–30 Nm).

40. Position new intake manifold gaskets on the cylinder heads. Make sure the alignment tabs on the gaskets are aligned with the holes in the cylinder heads.

➡**Before installing the intake manifold, inspect it for nicks and cuts that could provide leak paths.**

41. Position the intake manifold on the cylinder heads and install the retaining bolts. Tighten the bolts, in sequence, to 15–22 ft. lbs. (20–30 Nm).

42. Install the thermostat and O-ring, then position the thermostat housing and upper hose and install the 2 bolts. Tighten to 15–22 ft. lbs. (20–30 Nm).

43. Connect the heater supply hose and both oxygen sensors. Connect the vacuum hose to the throttle body adapter vacuum port.

44. Connect and, if necessary, adjust the throttle valve cable. Install the accelerator cable bracket on the intake manifold and connect the accelerator and cruise control cables to the throttle body.

45. Apply silicone sealer to both places where the front cover meets the cylinder head. Install new gaskets on the valve covers.

46. Install the valve covers on the cylinder heads. Install the bolts and stud bolts and tighten to 6.0–8.8 ft. lbs. (8–12 Nm).

47. Raise and safely support the vehicle. Position the starter wiring harness to the right cylinder head and install the retaining bolt.

48. Cut the wire and position the exhaust pipes to the exhaust manifolds. Tighten the 4 nuts to 20–30 ft. lbs. (27–41 Nm).

➡**Make sure the exhaust system clears the No. 3 crossmember. Adjust as necessary.**

49. Connect the EGR tube to the right exhaust manifold and tighten the line nut to 26–33 ft. lbs. (35–45 Nm). Connect the EVO sensor and oil sending unit.

50. Apply a small amount of silicone sealer in the rear of the keyway on the damper. Position the damper on the crankshaft, making sure the crankshaft key and keyway are aligned.

51. Using damper installer T74P–6316–B or equivalent, install the crankshaft damper. Install the damper bolt and washer and tighten to 114–121 ft. lbs. (155–165 Nm).

52. Install the 4 bolts retaining the oil pan to the front cover and tighten to 15–22 ft. lbs. (20–30 Nm).

53. Position the power steering pump on the engine and install the 4 retaining bolts. Tighten to 15–22 ft. lbs. (20–30 Nm). Lower the vehicle.

54. Connect the air conditioning compressor, crankshaft position sensor and canister purge solenoid.

55. Connect the 42-pin engine harness connector and transmission harness connector. Install the 42-pin connector on the retaining bracket on the vacuum brake booster.

56. Install the PCV valve in the right valve cover and connect the canister purge solenoid vent hose.

57. Position the positive battery cable harness on the right cylinder head and install the bolt retaining the cable bracket to the cylinder head. Connect the positive battery cable at the power distribution box and battery.

58. Position the alternator and install the 2 retaining bolts. Tighten to 15–22 ft. lbs. (20–30 Nm). Install the 2 bolts retaining the alternator brace to the intake manifold and tighten to 6–8 ft. lbs. (8–12 Nm).

59. Install the water pump pulley and tighten the bolts to 15–22 ft. lbs. (20–30 Nm).

60. Position the ignition coil brackets and spark plug wire assembly onto the mounting studs. Install the 7 nuts retaining the coil brackets to the front cover and tighten to 15–22 ft. lbs. (20–30 Nm).

61. Install the 2 bolts retaining the spark plug wire tray to the coil bracket and tighten to 6.0–8.8 ft. lbs. (8–12 Nm). Connect both ignition coils and CID sensor.

62. Position the air conditioner high pressure line on the right coil bracket and install the bolt. Connect the spark plug wires to the spark plugs and install the bracket onto the valve cover studs.

63. Install the accessory drive belt and the wiper module. Connect the fuel lines and install the cooling fan and shroud. Fill the cooling system.

64. Install the air inlet tube and connect the negative battery cable. Start the engine and bring to normal operating temperature. Check for leaks. Check all fluid levels.

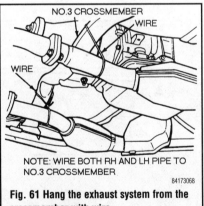

Fig. 61 Hang the exhaust system from the crossmember with wire

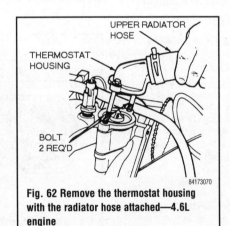

Fig. 62 Remove the thermostat housing with the radiator hose attached—4.6L engine

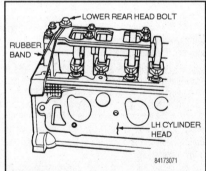

Fig. 63 Hold the lower rear bolt on the left cylinder head with a rubber band—4.6L engine

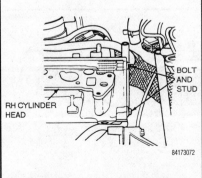

Fig. 64 Heater return line retaining bolt and stud location—4.6L engine

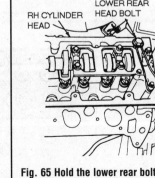

Fig. 65 Hold the lower rear bolt on the right cylinder head with a rubber band—4.6L engine

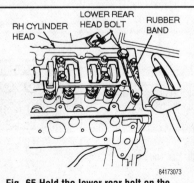

Fig. 66 Position the crankshaft as shown before installing the cylinder heads—4.6L engine

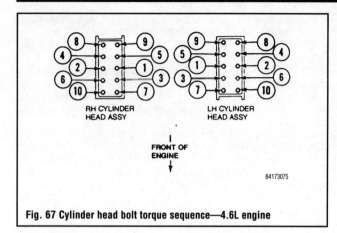

Fig. 67 Cylinder head bolt torque sequence—4.6L engine

5.0L and 5.8L Engines

▶ See Figures 68 and 69

1. Disconnect the negative battery cable.
2. Relieve the fuel system pressure; refer to Section 5. Drain the cooling system.

⁂ CAUTION

When draining the coolant, keep in mind that cats and dogs are attracted by the ethylene glycol antifreeze, and are quite likely to drink any that is left in an uncovered container or in puddles on the ground. This will prove fatal in sufficient quantity. Always drain the coolant into a sealable container. Coolant should be reused unless it is contaminated or several years old.

3. On 5.0L engine, remove the upper and lower intake manifold and throttle body assembly. On 5.8L engine, remove the intake manifold and carburetor assembly.
4. If the air conditioning compressor is in the way of a cylinder head that is to be removed, proceed as follows:
   a. Discharge the air conditioning system; refer to Section 1.
   b. Disconnect and plug the refrigerant lines at the compressor. Cap the openings on the compressor.
   c. Disconnect the electrical connector to the compressor.
   d. Remove the compressor and the necessary mounting brackets.
5. If the left cylinder head is to be removed, disconnect the power steering pump bracket from the cylinder head and remove the drive belt from the pump pulley. Position the pump out of the way in a position that will prevent the oil from draining out.
6. Disconnect the oil level dipstick tube bracket from the exhaust manifold stud, if necessary.
7. If the right cylinder head is to be removed, on some vehicles it is necessary to disconnect the alternator mounting bracket from the cylinder head.
8. Remove the thermactor crossover tube from the rear of the cylinder heads. If equipped, remove the fuel line from the clip at the front of the right cylinder head.
9. Raise and safely support the vehicle. Disconnect the exhaust manifolds from the muffler inlet pipes. Lower the vehicle.
10. Loosen the rocker arm fulcrum bolts so the rocker arms can be rotated to the side. Remove the pushrods in sequence so they may be installed in their original positions.
11. Remove the cylinder head attaching bolts and the cylinder heads. If necessary, remove the exhaust manifolds to gain access to the lower bolts. Remove and discard the head gaskets.
12. Clean all gasket mating surfaces. Check the flatness of the cylinder head using a straightedge and a feeler gauge. The cylinder head must not be warped any more than 0.003 in. in any 6.0 in. span; 0.006 in. overall. Machine as necessary.

To install:

13. Position the new cylinder head gasket over the dowels on the block. Position the cylinder heads on the block and install the attaching bolts.
14. On 5.0L engine, tighten the bolts, in sequence, in 2 steps, first to 55–65 ft. lbs. (75–88 Nm), then to 65–72 ft. lbs. (88–97 Nm). On 5.8L engine, tighten the bolts, in sequence, in 3 steps, first to 85 ft. lbs. (116 Nm), then to 95 ft. lbs. (129 Nm), and finally to 105–112 ft. lbs. (142–152 Nm).

➡**When the cylinder head bolts have been tightened following this procedure, it is not necessary to retighten the bolts after extended operation.**

15. If removed, install the exhaust manifolds. Tighten the retaining bolts to 18–24 ft. lbs. (24–32 Nm).
16. Clean the pushrods, making sure the oil passages are clean. Check the ends of the pushrods for wear. Visually check the pushrods for straightness or check for runout using a dial indicator. Replace pushrods, as necessary.
17. Apply a suitable grease to the ends of the pushrods and install them in their original positions. Position the rocker arms over the pushrods and the valves.
18. Before tightening each fulcrum bolt, bring the lifter for the fulcrum bolt to be tightened onto the base circle of the camshaft by rotating the engine. When the lifter is on the base circle of the camshaft, tighten the fulcrum bolt to 18–25 ft. lbs. (24–34 Nm).

➡**If all the original valve train parts are reinstalled, a valve clearance check is not necessary. If any valve train components are replaced, a valve clearance check must be performed.**

19. Install new rocker arm cover gaskets on the rocker arm covers and install the covers on the cylinder heads.
20. Raise and safely support the vehicle. Connect the exhaust manifolds to the muffler inlet pipes. Lower the vehicle.
21. If necessary, install the air conditioning compressor and brackets. Connect the refrigerant lines and electrical connector to the compressor.
22. If necessary, install the alternator bracket.
23. If the left cylinder head was removed, install the power steering pump.
24. Install the drive belts. Install the thermactor tube at the rear of the cylinder heads.
25. Install the intake manifold. Fill and bleed the cooling system.
26. Connect the negative battery cable, start the engine and bring to normal operating temperature. Check for leaks. Check all fluid levels.
27. If necessary, evacuate and charge the air conditioning system.

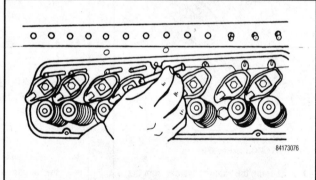

Fig. 68 Keep the pushrods in order so they can be reinstalled in their original locations

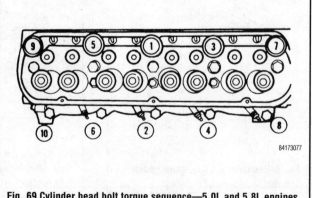

Fig. 69 Cylinder head bolt torque sequence—5.0L and 5.8L engines

CLEANING AND INSPECTION

▶ **See Figure 70**

➡️On the 4.6L engine, the roller followers, hydraulic lash adjusters and camshaft should be removed before proceeding further; refer to the procedures in this Section.

✳✳ WARNING

Be careful when scraping and cleaning the 4.6L engine cylinder heads, as aluminum is easily damaged.

1. With the valves installed to protect the valve seats, remove deposits from the combustion chambers and valve heads with a scraper and drill-mounted wire brush. Be careful not to damage the cylinder head gasket surface. If the head is to be disassembled, proceed to Step 3. If the head is not to be disassembled, proceed to Step 2.
2. Remove all dirt, oil and old gasket material from the cylinder head with solvent. Clean the bolt holes and the oil passage. Be careful not to get solvent on the valve seals as the solvent may damage them. Dry the cylinder head with compressed air, if available. Check the head for cracks or other damage, and check the gasket surface for burrs, nicks and flatness. If you are in doubt about the head's serviceability, consult a reputable automotive machine shop.
3. Remove the valves, springs and retainers. If the valve seats are to be refaced, clean the carbon from the valve seat areas using a drill-mounted wire brush. Clean the valve guide bores with a valve guide cleaning tool. Remove all dirt, oil and old gasket material from the cylinder head with solvent. Clean the bolt holes and the oil passages.
4. Remove all deposits from the valves with a wire brush or buffing wheel.
5. Check the head for cracks in the valve seat area and ports, and check the gasket surface for burrs, nicks and flatness.
6. Refer to the valve, valve spring, valve seat and valve guide servicing procedures in this Section. If you are in doubt about the head's serviceability, consult a reputable automotive machine shop.

➡️If the cylinder head was removed due to an overheating condition and a crack is suspected, do not assume that the head is not cracked because a crack is not visually found. A crack can be so small that it cannot be seen by eye, but can pass coolant when the engine is at operating temperature. Consult an automotive machine shop that has pressure testing equipment to make sure the head is not cracked.

RESURFACING

▶ **See Figure 71**

Whenever the cylinder head is removed, check the flatness of the cylinder head gasket surface as follows:
1. Make sure all dirt and old gasket material has been cleaned from the cylinder head. Any foreign material left on the head gasket surface can cause a false measurement.
2. Place a straightedge on the gasket surface. Check the flatness of the cylinder head with the straightedge positioned across the center of the head,

positioned corner to opposite corner, and positioned on either side of the combustion chamber. Use the appropriate thickness feeler gauge to determine warpage.
3. On the 5.0L and 5.8L engines, if warpage exceeds 0.003 in. in any 6 inch span—0.006 in. overall, the cylinder head must be resurfaced. If resurfacing is necessary, do not plane or grind off more than 0.010 in. (0.254mm) from the original gasket surface.
4. On the 4.6L engine, if any warpage is found, the cylinder head must be replaced.

Valves

REMOVAL & INSTALLATION

▶ **See Figures 72, 73 and 74**

1. Remove the cylinder head.
2. On the 4.6L engine, remove the roller followers, hydraulic lash adjusters and camshaft.
3. Block the head on its side, or install a pair of head-holding brackets made especially for valve removal.
4. Using a socket slightly larger than the valve stem and keepers, place the socket over the valve spring retainer and gently hit the socket with a plastic hammer to break loose any varnish buildup.
5. Remove the valve keepers, retainer, (sleeve on 5.0L and 5.8L engine intake valve) and valve spring using a valve spring compressor (the locking C-clamp type is the easiest to use).
6. Place the parts from each valve in a separate container, numbered and identified for the valve and cylinder.
7. Remove and discard the valve stem oil seal, a new seal will be used at assembly time.
8. Remove the valves from the cylinder head and place, in order, through holes punched in a stiff piece of cardboard.
9. Use an electric drill and rotary wire brush to clean the intake and exhaust valve ports, combustion chamber and valve seats. In some cases, the carbon build-up will have to be chipped away. Use a blunt pointed drift for carbon chipping, being careful around valve seat areas.

✳✳ WARNING

Be careful when cleaning and removing carbon from the 4.6L engine cylinder head, as aluminum is easily damaged.

10. Use a valve guide cleaning brush and safe solvent to clean the valve guides. Remove all dirt, oil and old gasket material from the cylinder head with solvent. Clean the bolt holes and the oil passages.
11. Clean the valves with a revolving wire brush. Heavy carbon deposits may be removed with a blunt drift.

➡️When using a wire brush to remove carbon from the cylinder head or valves, make sure the deposits are actually removed and not just burnished.

Fig. 70 Cleaning the combustion chamber with drill-mounted wire brush—5.0L engine shown

84173078

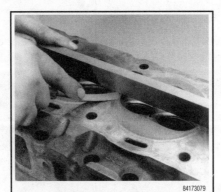

84173079

Fig. 71 Checking cylinder head flatness using a straightedge

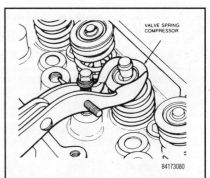

84173080

Fig. 72 Compressing the valve spring with a valve spring compressor—5.0L and 5.8L engine shown

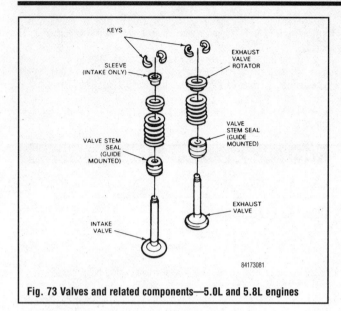

Fig. 73 Valves and related components—5.0L and 5.8L engines

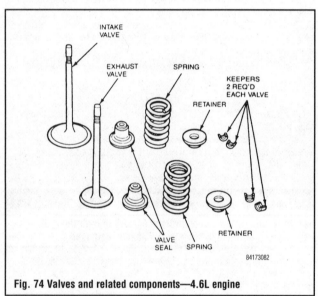

Fig. 74 Valves and related components—4.6L engine

12. Wash and clean all valves, valve springs, keepers, retainers etc., in safe solvent. Remember to keep parts from each valve separate.

13. Check the cylinder head for cracks. Cracks usually start around the exhaust valve seat because it is the hottest part of the combustion chamber. If a crack is suspected but cannot be detected visually, have the area checked by pressure testing, with a dye penetrant or other method by an automotive machine shop.

14. Inspect the valves, guides, springs and seats and machine or replace parts, as necessary.

To install:

15. Dip each valve in clean engine oil and install in its original location.

16. On the 5.0L and 5.8L engines, install new valve seals, using a ⅝ in. deep-well socket and a light mallet to seat the seal on the cylinder head and valve stem.

17. On the 4.6L engine, install new valve seals using seal replacer tool T91P–6751–A and driver handle T80T–4000–W, or equivalents.

18. Install any required shims, the valve spring and the retainer over the valve stem. Compress the spring with the valve spring compressor and install the keepers.

19. After all the valves and springs have been assembled, take a mallet and lightly strike each valve stem tip squarely to seat the keepers.

20. On the 4.6L engine, install the camshaft, hydraulic lash adjusters and roller followers

INSPECTION

▶ **See Figures 75, 76, 77, 78 and 79**

1. Remove the valves from the cylinder head. Clean the valves, valve guides, valve seats and related components, as explained earlier.

2. Visually check the valves for obvious wear or damage. A burnt valve will have discoloration, severe galling or pitting and even cracks on one area of the valve face. Minor pits, grooves, etc. on the valve face can be removed by refacing. Check the valve stem for bends and for obvious wear that is indicated by a step between the part of the stem that travels in the valve guide and the part of the stem near the keeper grooves.

3. Check the valve stem-to-guide clearance. If a dial indicator is not on hand, a visual inspection can give you a fairly good idea if the guide, valve stem or both are worn. Insert the valve into the guide until the valve head is slightly away from the valve seat. Wiggle the valve sideways. A small amount of wobble is normal, excessive wobble means a worn guide and/or valve stem. If a dial indicator is on hand, mount the indicator so that gauge stem is 90° to the valve stem as close to the top of the valve guide as possible. Move the valve from the seat, and measure the valve guide-to-stem clearance by rocking the stem back and forth to actuate the dial indicator. Measure the valve stem using a micrometer and compare to specifications, to determine whether stem or guide, is causing excessive clearance.

4. The valve guide, if worn, must be repaired before the valve seats can be refaced. Refer to the valve guide service procedure in this Section.

5. If the valve guide is okay, measure the valve seat concentricity using a runout gauge. Follow the manufacturers instructions. If runout is excessive, machine or replace the valve seat; refer to the procedure in this Section.

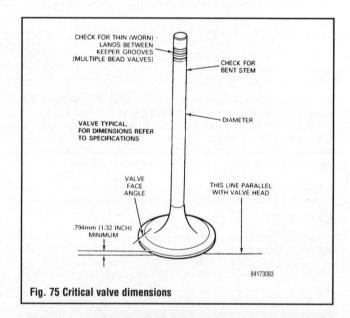

Fig. 75 Critical valve dimensions

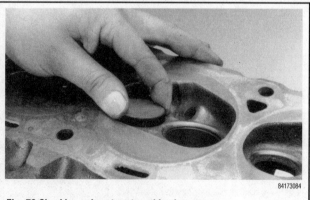

Fig. 76 Checking valve stem-to-guide clearance

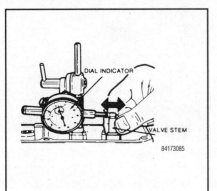

Fig. 77 Checking valve stem-to-guide clearance using a dial indicator

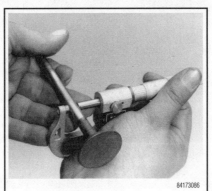

Fig. 78 Measuring the valve stem using a micrometer

Fig. 79 Checking valve seat concentricity

6. Valves and seats must always be machined together. Never use a refaced valve on a valve seat that has not been machined; never use a valve that has not been refaced on a machined valve seat.

REFACING

1. Determine if the valve is usable as explained in the Inspection procedure.

2. Refer to specifications for the correct valve face machining angle. Make sure the valve refacer grinding wheels are properly dressed.

3. Reface the valve face only enough to remove the pits and grooves or correct any runout. If the edge of the valve head is less than 1/32 in. (0.8mm) thick after grinding, replace the valve, as the valve will run too hot in the engine.

4. Remove all grooves or score marks from the end of the valve stem, and chamfer it, as necessary. Do not remove more than 0.010 in. (0.254mm) from the end of the valve stem.

5. When the engine is reassembled, it will be necessary to check the clearance between the rocker arm or roller follower pad and the valve stem tip. Refer to Section 2.

Valve Stem Seals

REPLACEMENT

Cylinder Head Removed

▶ **See Figures 80 and 81**

1. Remove the cylinder head.

2. On the 4.6L engine, remove the roller followers, hydraulic lash adjusters and camshaft.

3. Block the head on its side, or install a pair of head-holding brackets made especially for valve removal.

4. Using a socket slightly larger than the valve stem and keepers, place the socket over the valve spring retainer and gently hit the socket with a plastic hammer to break loose any varnish buildup.

5. Remove the valve keepers, retainer, (sleeve on 5.0L and 5.8L engine intake valve) and valve spring using a valve spring compressor (the locking C-clamp type is the easiest to use).

6. Place the parts from each valve in a separate container, numbered and identified for the valve and cylinder.

7. Remove and discard the valve stem oil seal.

8. On the 5.0L and 5.8L engines, install new valve seals, using a 5/8 in. deep-well socket and a light mallet to seat the seal on the cylinder head and valve stem.

9. On the 4.6L engine, install new valve seals using seal replacer tool T91P–6751–A and driver handle T80T–4000–W, or equivalents.

10. Install any required shims, the valve spring and the retainer over the valve stem. Compress the spring with the valve spring compressor and install the keepers.

11. After all the valves and springs have been assembled, take a mallet and lightly strike each valve stem tip squarely to seat the keepers.

12. On the 4.6L engine, install the camshaft, hydraulic lash adjusters and roller followers

Cylinder Head Installed

4.6L ENGINE

▶ **See Figures 82, 83 and 84**

1. Disconnect the negative battery cable.

2. Remove the valve cover(s) and roller followers as explained in this Section.

3. Remove the spark plug from the cylinder where the seals are to be replaced.

4. Rotate the crankshaft until the piston is at Top Dead Center (TDC) with both valves closed.

5. Install a suitable adapter in the spark plug hole and connect an air supply line to the adapter. Turn on the air supply.

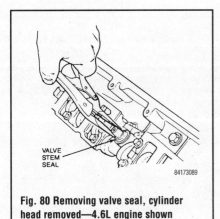

Fig. 80 Removing valve seal, cylinder head removed—4.6L engine shown

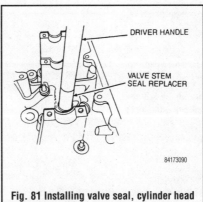

Fig. 81 Installing valve seal, cylinder head removed—4.6L engine

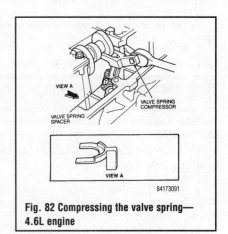

Fig. 82 Compressing the valve spring—4.6L engine

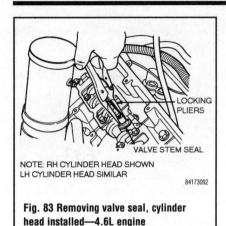

NOTE: RH CYLINDER HEAD SHOWN
LH CYLINDER HEAD SIMILAR

84173092

Fig. 83 Removing valve seal, cylinder head installed—4.6L engine

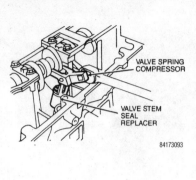

84173093

Fig. 84 Installing valve seal, cylinder head installed—4.6L engine

84173094

Fig. 85 Compressing the valve spring—5.0L and 5.8L engines

➥If the air pressure does not hold the valves closed during the following steps, there is probably valve and/or valve seat damage; remove the cylinder head.

6. Install valve spring spacer tool T91P–6565–AH or equivalent, between the spring coils.
7. Compress the valve spring using valve spring compressor tool T91–6565–A or equivalent.
8. Remove the keepers, retainer and valve spring. Remove and discard the valve stem seal.

➥If air pressure has forced the piston to the bottom of the cylinder, any loss of air pressure will let the valve(s) fall into the cylinder. Wrap a rubber band, tape or string around the end of the valve stem to prevent this.

9. Make sure the piston is at TDC. Remove the air pressure from the spark plug adapter and inspect the valve stem for damage. Rotate the valve and check the valve stem tip for eccentric movement. Move the valve up and down in the guide through its normal travel and check for binding. If the valve is damaged, the cylinder head must be removed.
10. If the valve is okay, apply clean engine oil to the valve stem and hold the valve closed. Apply the air pressure to the cylinder.
11. Install a new valve seal using seal replacer tool T91–6571–A or equivalent.
12. Position the valve spring and retainer over the valve stem. Install valve spring spacer tool T91P–6565–AH or equivalent, between the spring coils.
13. Compress the valve spring using valve spring compressor tool T91P–6565–A or equivalent, and install the keepers.
14. Remove the valve spring compressor and spacer. Turn off the air supply and remove the adapter from the spark plug hole.
15. Install the spark plug. Install the roller follower(s) and valve cover(s), as explained in this Section.
16. Connect the negative battery cable, start the engine and check for leaks.

5.0L AND 5.8L ENGINES

♦ See Figure 85

1. Disconnect the negative battery cable.
2. Remove the rocker arm cover.
3. Remove the spark plug from the cylinder where the seals are to be replaced.
4. Rotate the crankshaft until the piston is at Top Dead Center (TDC) with both valves closed.
5. Install a suitable adapter in the spark plug hole and connect an air supply line to the adapter. Turn on the air supply.

➥If the air pressure does not hold the valves closed during the following steps, there is probably valve and/or valve seat damage; remove the cylinder head.

6. Remove the rocker arm fulcrum bolts, fulcrum, rocker arm, fulcrum guide and pushrod. Note their positions so they can be reinstalled in their original locations.
7. Install the fulcrum bolt and position valve spring compressor tool T70P–6049–A or equivalent. Compress the valve spring and remove the keepers, sleeve (intake valve only), retainer and spring.
8. Remove and discard the valve stem seal.

➥If air pressure has forced the piston to the bottom of the cylinder, any loss of air pressure will let the valve(s) fall into the cylinder. Wrap a rubber band, tape or string around the end of the valve stem to prevent this.

9. Make sure the piston is at TDC. Remove the air pressure from the spark plug adapter and inspect the valve stem for damage. Rotate the valve and check the valve stem tip for eccentric movement. Move the valve up and down in the guide through its normal travel and check for binding. If the valve is damaged, the cylinder head must be removed.
10. If the valve is okay, apply clean engine oil to the valve stem and hold the valve closed. Apply the air pressure to the cylinder.
11. Install a new valve seal using a ⅝ in. deep well socket and light hammer or mallet to seat the seal on the valve stem or use valve seal installer kit (guide mounted) T87L–6571–BH or equivalent.
12. Position the spring and retainer (and sleeve, if equipped) over the valve stem and compress the valve spring. Install the keepers and release the compressor. Remove the compressor and fulcrum bolt.
13. Turn off the air pressure and remove the air line and adapter.
14. Apply multi-purpose grease or equivalent lubricant to the pushrod ends and install the pushrods. Apply multi-purpose grease or equivalent lubricant to the valve stem tips.
15. Apply multi-purpose grease or equivalent lubricant to the rocker arm pushrod socket, fulcrum seat and valve stem pad.
16. Install the rocker arms, fulcrum seats and fulcrum bolts. Rotate the crankshaft until the lifter is on the base circle of the camshaft, then tighten the fulcrum bolt to 18–25 ft. lbs. (24–34 Nm).
17. Install the spark plug and the rocker arm cover.
18. Connect the negative battery cable, start the engine and check for leaks.

Valve Springs

REMOVAL & INSTALLATION

♦ See Figure 86

1. Remove the cylinder head.
2. On the 4.6L engine, remove the roller followers, hydraulic lash adjusters and camshaft.
3. Block the head on its side, or install a pair of head-holding brackets made especially for valve removal.
4. Using a socket slightly larger than the valve stem and keepers, place the socket over the valve spring retainer and gently hit the socket with a plastic hammer to break loose any varnish buildup.
5. Position a suitable valve spring compressor on the valve head and valve spring retainer. Compress the spring and remove the valve keepers.
6. Release the spring compressor and remove the retainer, sleeve on 5.0L and 5.8L engine intake valve, and valve spring. Remove any shims that may have been under the valve spring.
7. Place the parts from each valve in a separate container, numbered and identified for the valve and cylinder.

8. Inspect the valve springs for damage or wear and replace as necessary. Check the spring pressure and spring squareness.

To install:

9. Install the valve spring retainer (and sleeve on 5.0L and 5.8L engine intake valve) on the valve without the spring and retain it with the keepers. Pull the valve firmly against the seat.

10. Using a suitable measuring tool (calipers, or a telescope gauge with a micrometer work well), measure the distance between the cylinder head and the retainer and compare this distance with the installed height specification. Shims are available to make up the difference and are usually necessary after a valve job.

11. Install the required shim(s) on the valve spring seat.

12. Install the spring and retainer (and sleeve on 5.0L and 5.8L engine intake valve) over the valve stem.

13. Compress the spring using the spring compressor and install the keepers. Release the spring compressor.

14. After all the valves and springs have been assembled, take a mallet and lightly strike each valve stem tip squarely to seat the keepers.

15. On the 4.6L engine, install the camshaft, hydraulic lash adjusters and roller followers.

INSPECTION

▶ **See Figures 87 and 88**

1. Check the springs for cracks or other damage.

2. Check each spring for squareness using a steel square and a flat surface. Stand the spring and square on end on the flat surface. Slide the spring up to the square, revolve the spring slowly and observe the space between the top coil of the spring and the square. If the space exceeds specification, replace the spring.

3. Check each spring for the proper pressure at the specified spring lengths, using a valve spring tester. Replace any springs that are not within specifications.

Valve Seats

REFACING

▶ **See Figures 89 and 90**

1. Inspect the valve guides to make sure they are usable, as described under valve inspection.

2. Make sure the refacer grinding wheels are properly dressed to ensure a good finish.

3. Grind the valve seats to a 45° angle, only removing enough metal to clean up the pits and grooves and correct valve seat runout.

4. After the seat has been refaced, measure the seat width using a suitable measuring tool and compare to specification.

5. If the seat is too wide, grinding wheels of 60° and 30° can be used to remove stock from the bottom and the top of the seat, respectively, and narrow the seat.

6. Once the correct seat width has been obtained, find out where the seat contacts the valve. The finished seat should contact the approximate center of the valve face.

7. Coat the seat with Prussian Blue and set the valve in place. Rotate the valve with light pressure, then remove it and check the seat contact.

8. If the blue is transferred to the center of the valve face, contact is satisfactory. If the blue is transferred to the top edge of the valve face, lower the valve seat. If the blue is transferred to the bottom edge of the valve face, raise the valve seat.

REMOVAL & INSTALLATION

If the valve seat is so worn that refacing cannot bring the seat dimensions within specification, it must be replaced.

Valve seat replacement should be left to an automotive machine shop, due to the high degree of precision and special equipment required. Seat replacement

Fig. 86 Measuring valve spring installed height

Fig. 87 Checking the valve spring for squareness

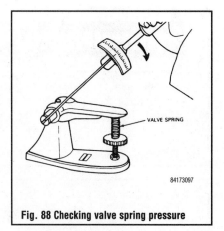

Fig. 88 Checking valve spring pressure

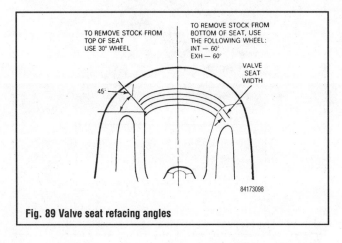

Fig. 89 Valve seat refacing angles

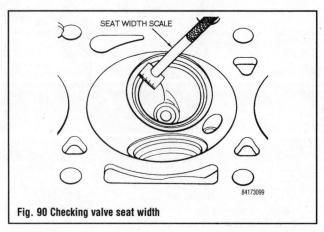

Fig. 90 Checking valve seat width

procedures differ between the 4.6L and 5.0L/5.8L engines due to their respective aluminum and cast iron construction. The following procedures can be construed as what is generally acceptable for aluminum and cast iron cylinder heads; the actual method employed should be the decision of the machinist.

The 4.6L engine uses replaceable seat inserts. These inserts can be removed by cutting them out to within a few thousandths of their outside diameter and then collapsing the remainder, or by heating the head to a high temperature and then driving the seat out. The valve seats are integral with the cylinder head on the 5.0L and 5.8L engines. To install a replacement seat, the old seat must be completely cut out with a special cutter tool mounted on a cylinder head machine.

To install a new seat on the 4.6L engine, the cylinder head is usually heated to a high temperature, then the seat, which is at room temperature or slightly chilled, is pressed into the head. The head is then allowed to cool and as it does, it contracts and grips the seat. On the 5.0L and 5.8L engines, the new seat is usually driven in with both the head and seat at room temperature. The calculated press-fit interference retains the seat in the head.

After a new seat is installed, it must be refaced.

Valve Guides

▶ **See Figures 91 and 92**

If the valve guides are determined to be worn during the valve inspection procedure, there are 3 possible repair alternatives: knurling, reaming oversize or replacement.

If guide wear is minimal, the correct inside diameter can be restored by knurling. Knurling involves using a special tool to raise a spiral ridge on the inside of the guide while it is installed in the head. This effectively reduces the inside diameter of the guide. A reamer is then usually passed through the guide to make the inside diameter smooth and uniform, and to restore the guide to its

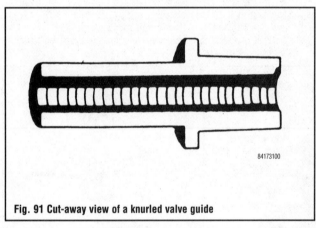

Fig. 91 Cut-away view of a knurled valve guide

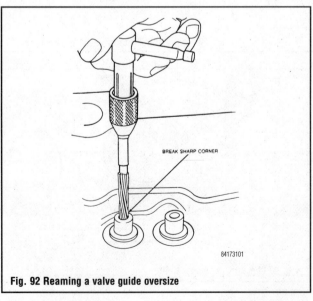

Fig. 92 Reaming a valve guide oversize

original inside diameter. Knurling is only an alternative if there is minimum guide wear.

The valve guide can also be reamed oversize, necessitating the use of a valve with a corresponding oversize valve stem, to restore the proper valve stem-to-guide clearance. Valves are generally available with 0.015 in. and 0.030 in. oversize stems. Check oversize availability before you choose this alternative.

Due to the high degree of precision and special equipment required, valve guide replacement should be left to an automotive machine shop.

➡**The valve seats must be refaced after guide knurling, reaming or replacement.**

Valve Lifters/Lash Adjusters

REMOVAL & INSTALLATION

4.6L Engine

▶ **See Figure 93**

1. Disconnect the negative battery cable.
2. Remove the valve cover(s); refer to the procedure in this Section.
3. Position the piston of the cylinder being serviced at the bottom of its stroke and position the camshaft lobe on the base circle.
4. Install valve spring spacer tool T91P-6565-AH or equivalent, between the spring coils to prevent valve seal damage.

➡**If the valve spring spacer tool is not used, the retainer will hit the valve stem seal and damage the seal.**

5. Install valve spring compressor tool T91P-6565-A or equivalent, under the camshaft and on top of the valve spring retainer.
6. Compress the valve spring and remove the roller follower. Remove the valve spring compressor and spacer.
7. Remove the hydraulic lash adjuster.
   To install:
8. Check the hydraulic lash adjusters. They must have no more than 1.5mm of plunger travel prior to installation.
9. Apply engine oil to the valve stem and tip, roller follower contact surfaces and lash adjuster bore. Install the lash adjusters.
10. Install valve spring spacer tool T91P-6565-AH or equivalent, between the spring coils. Compress the valve spring using valve spring compressor tool T91P-6565-A or equivalent, and install the roller follower.

➡**The piston must be at the bottom of its stroke and the camshaft at the base circle.**

11. Remove the valve spring compressor and spacer.
12. Install the valve cover(s).
13. Connect the negative battery cable. Start the engine and check for leaks.

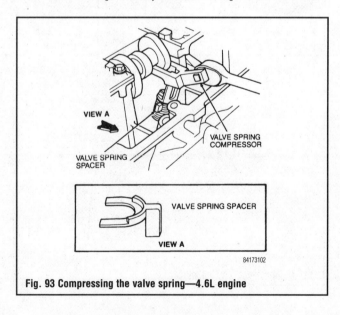

Fig. 93 Compressing the valve spring—4.6L engine

5.0L and 5.8L Engines

▶ **See Figures 94 and 95**

1. Disconnect the negative battery cable. Remove the intake manifold and related parts.

2. Remove the crankcase ventilation hoses, PCV valve and elbows from the valve rocker arm covers.

3. Remove the valve rocker arm covers. Loosen the valve rocker arm fulcrum bolts and rotate the rocker arms to the side.

4. Remove the valve pushrods and identify them so they can be installed in their original position.

5. On 5.0L engine equipped with roller lifters, remove the lifter guide retainer bolts. Remove the retainer and lifter guide plates. Identify the guide plates so they may be reinstalled in their original positions.

6. Using a magnet, remove the lifters and place them in a rack so they can be installed in their original bores.

➡**If the lifters are stuck in the bores due to excessive varnish or gum deposits, it may be necessary to use a claw-type tool to aid removal. When using a remover tool, rotate the lifter back and forth to loosen it from gum or varnish that may have formed on the lifter.**

7. Inspect the lifter(s) for pitting, scoring or excessive wear and replace as necessary. If the camshaft contact surface of the lifter is worn, it is recommended that all the lifters and the camshaft be replaced.

To install:

8. Lubricate the lifters and install them in their original bores. If new lifters are being installed, check them for free fit in their respective bores.

9. On 5.0L engine equipped with roller lifters, install the lifter guide plates in their original positions, then install the guide plate retainer.

10. Install the pushrods in their original positions. Apply grease to the ends prior to installation.

11. Lubricate the rocker arms and fulcrum seats with heavy engine oil. Position the rocker arms over the pushrods and install the fulcrum bolts.

12. Before tightening each fulcrum bolt, rotate the crankshaft until the lifter is on the base circle of the cam. Tighten the fulcrum bolt to 18–25 ft. lbs. (24–34 Nm). Check the valve clearance.

13. Install the rocker arm covers and the intake manifold. Connect the negative battery cable, start the engine and check for leaks.

OVERHAUL

The internal parts of each hydraulic lifter are matched sets. The parts must not be intermixed. Keep all assemblies intact until they are to be cleaned.

4.6L Engine

If the hydraulic lash adjuster plunger has more than 1.5mm of travel prior to installation, the entire lash adjuster must be replaced.

5.0L and 5.8L Engines

▶ **See Figures 96 and 97**

1. Use needle nose pliers to release the lock ring from the groove. It may be necessary to depress the plunger to release the lock ring.

2. Remove the pushrod cup, metering valve disc, plunger and spring.

3. Remove the plunger assembly, check valve and check valve retainer, and plunger spring. Carefully remove the plunger spring, check valve retainer and check valve disc from the plunger.

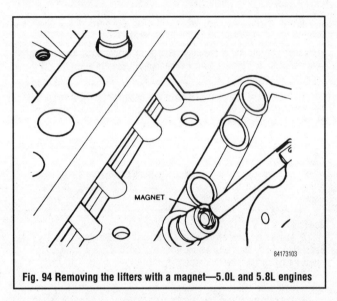

Fig. 94 Removing the lifters with a magnet—5.0L and 5.8L engines

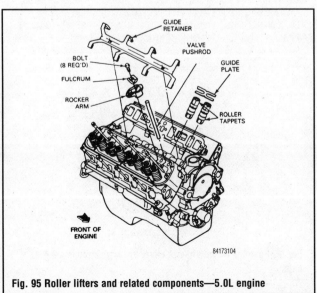

Fig. 95 Roller lifters and related components—5.0L engine

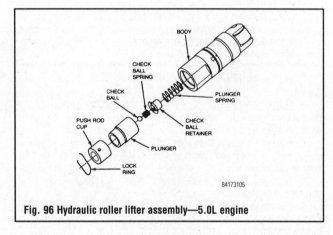

Fig. 96 Hydraulic roller lifter assembly—5.0L engine

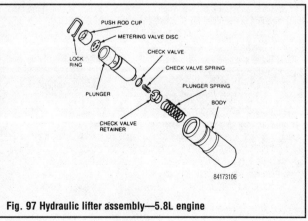

Fig. 97 Hydraulic lifter assembly—5.8L engine

To assemble:

4. Place the plunger upside down on a clean work bench.

5. Place the check valve (disc or ball check) in position over the oil hole on the bottom of the plunger. Set the check valve spring on top of the check valve (disc or ball check).

6. Position the check valve retainer over the check valve and spring and push the retainer down into place on the plunger.

7. Place the plunger spring, and then the plunger (open end up) into the lifter body.

8. Position the metering valve disc in the plunger, and then place the pushrod cup in the plunger.

9. Depress the plunger, and position the closed end of the lock ring in the groove of the lifter body. With the plunger still depressed, position the open ends of the lock ring in the groove. Release the plunger, then depress it again to fully seat the lock ring.

10. Submerge the lifter upright in a container of clean engine oil. Use a suitable tool to push the plunger up and down, bleeding the air from the lifter. The lifter is bled when no more air bubbles appear.

Oil Pan

REMOVAL & INSTALLATION

4.6L Engine

▶ **See Figures 98, 99 and 100**

1. Disconnect the battery cables, negative cable first, and remove the air inlet tube.

2. Relieve the fuel system pressure and disconnect the fuel lines; refer to Section 5. Drain the cooling system and remove the cooling fan and shroud.

✳✳ CAUTION

When draining the coolant, keep in mind that cats and dogs are attracted by the ethylene glycol antifreeze, and are quite likely to drink any that is left in an uncovered container or in puddles on the ground. This will prove fatal in sufficient quantity. Always drain the coolant into a sealable container. Coolant should be reused unless it is contaminated or several years old.

3. Remove the upper radiator hose. Remove the wiper module and support bracket.

4. Discharge the air conditioning system. Disconnect and plug the compressor outlet hose at the compressor and remove the bolt retaining the hose assembly to the right coil bracket. Cap the compressor outlet.

5. Remove the 42-pin engine harness connector from the retaining bracket on the brake vacuum booster and disconnect the connector and transmission harness connector.

6. Disconnect the throttle valve cable from the throttle body and disconnect the heater outlet hose.

7. Remove the nut retaining the ground strap to the right cylinder head. Remove the upper stud and loosen the lower bolt retaining the heater outlet hose to the right cylinder head and position out of the way.

8. Remove the blower motor resistor. Remove the bolt retaining the right engine mount to the lower engine bracket.

9. Disconnect the vacuum hoses from the EGR valve and tube. Remove the 2 bolts retaining the EGR valve to the intake manifold.

10. Raise and safely support the vehicle. Drain the crankcase and remove the engine mount through bolts.

11. Remove the EGR tube line nut from the right exhaust manifold and remove the EGR valve and tube assembly.

12. Disconnect the exhaust from the exhaust manifolds. Lower the exhaust system and support it with wire from the crossmember.

13. Position a jack and a block of wood under the oil pan, rearward of the oil drain hole. Raise the engine approximately 4 in. and insert 2 wood blocks approximately 2½ in. thick under each engine mount. Lower the engine onto the wood blocks and remove the jack.

14. Remove the 16 bolts retaining the oil pan to the engine block and remove the oil pan.

➡**It may be necessary to loosen, but not remove, the 2 nuts on the rear transmission mount and with a jack, raise the transmission extension housing slightly to remove the pan.**

15. If necessary, remove the 2 bolts retaining the oil pickup tube to the oil pump and remove the bolt retaining the pickup tube to the main bearing stud spacer. Remove the pickup tube.

To install:

16. Clean the oil pan and inspect for damage. Clean the sealing surfaces of the front cover and engine block. Clean and inspect the oil pickup tube and replace the O-ring.

17. If removed, position the oil pickup tube on the oil pump and hand start the 2 bolts. Install the bolt retaining the pickup tube to the main bearing stud spacer hand tight.

18. Tighten the pickup tube-to-oil pump bolts to 6.0–8.8 ft. lbs. (8–12 Nm), then tighten the pickup tube-to-main bearing stud spacer bolt to 15–22 ft. lbs. (20–30 Nm).

19. Position a new gasket on the oil pan. Apply silicone sealer to where the front cover meets the cylinder block and rear seal retainer meets the cylinder block. Position the oil pan on the engine and install the bolts. Tighten the bolts, in sequence, to 15–22 ft. lbs. (20–30 Nm).

20. Position the jack and wood block under the oil pan, rearward of the oil drain hole, and raise the engine enough to remove the wood blocks. Lower the engine and remove the jack.

21. Install the engine mount through bolts and tighten to 15–22 ft. lbs. (20–30 Nm).

22. Position the EGR valve and tube assembly in the vehicle and connect to the exhaust manifold. Tighten the line nut to 26–33 ft. lbs. (35–45 Nm).

➡**Loosen the line nut at the EGR valve prior to installing the assembly into the vehicle. This will allow enough movement to align the EGR valve retaining bolts.**

23. Cut the wire and position the exhaust system to the manifolds. Install the 4 nuts and tighten to 20–30 ft. lbs. (27–41 Nm). Make sure the exhaust system clears the crossmember. Adjust as necessary.

24. Install a new oil filter and lower the vehicle.

25. Install the bolt retaining the right engine mount to the lower engine bracket. Tighten to 15–22 ft. lbs. (20–30 Nm).

26. Install a new gasket on the EGR valve and position on the intake manifold. Install the 2 bolts retaining the EGR valve to the intake manifold and tighten to 15–22 ft. lbs. (20–30 Nm). Tighten the EGR tube line nut at the EGR valve to 26–33 ft. lbs. (35–45 Nm). Connect the vacuum hoses to the EGR valve and tube.

27. Install the blower motor resistor. Position the heater outlet hose, install the upper stud and tighten the upper and lower bolts to 15–22 ft. lbs. (20–30 Nm). Install the ground strap on the stud and tighten to 15–22 ft. lbs. (20–30 Nm).

28. Connect the heater outlet hose and the throttle valve cable. If necessary, adjust the throttle valve cable.

29. Connect the 42-pin connector and transmission harness connector. Install the harness connector on the brake vacuum booster.

30. Connect the air conditioning compressor outlet hose to the compressor and install the bolt retaining the hose to the right coil bracket.

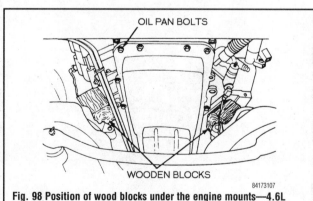

OIL PAN BOLTS

WOODEN BLOCKS

84173107

Fig. 98 Position of wood blocks under the engine mounts—4.6L engine

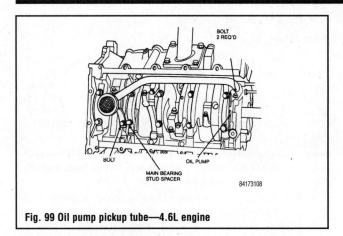

Fig. 99 Oil pump pickup tube—4.6L engine

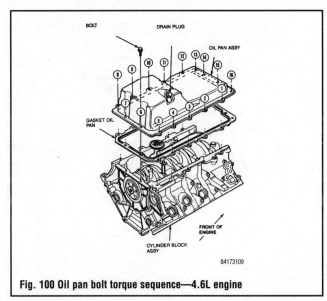

Fig. 100 Oil pan bolt torque sequence—4.6L engine

31. Install the upper radiator hose and connect the fuel lines. Install the wiper module and retaining bracket.

32. Install the cooling fan and shroud and fill the cooling system. Fill the crankcase with the proper type and quantity of engine oil.

33. Connect the negative battery cable and install the air inlet tube. Start the engine and check for leaks.

34. Evacuate and recharge the air conditioning system.

5.0L and 5.8L Engines

▶ **See Figure 101**

1. Disconnect the negative battery cable. Relieve the fuel system pressure; refer to Section 5.

2. On 5.8L engine, remove the air cleaner assembly and air ducts.

3. Disconnect the accelerator and throttle valve cables at the throttle body or carburetor. On 5.8L engine, remove the accelerator mounting bracket retaining bolts and remove the bracket.

4. Remove the fan shroud attaching bolts, positioning the fan shroud back over the fan. Remove the dipstick and tube assembly.

5. Disconnect the wiper motor electrical connector and remove the wiper motor. Disconnect the windshield washer hose and remove the wiper motor mounting cover.

6. Remove the thermactor air dump tube retaining clamp on 5.0L engine. Remove the thermactor crossover tube at the rear of the vehicle.

7. Raise and safely support the vehicle. Drain the crankcase. Remove the filler tube from the oil pan and drain the transmission.

8. Disconnect the starter cable and remove the starter. Disconnect the fuel line.

9. Disconnect the exhaust system from the manifolds. Remove the oxygen sensors from the exhaust manifolds.

10. Remove the thermactor secondary air tube to torque converter housing clamps. Remove the converter inspection cover.

11. Disconnect the exhaust pipes to the catalytic converter outlet. Remove the catalytic converter secondary air tube and the inlet pipes to the exhaust manifold.

12. Loosen the rear engine mount attaching nuts and remove the engine mount through bolts. Remove the shift crossover bolts at the transmission.

13. Remove the brake line retainer from the front crossmember and disconnect the transmission kickdown rod.

14. Position a jack and wood block under the engine and raise the engine as high as it will go. Place wood blocks between the engine mounts and the chassis brackets, lower the engine and remove the jack.

15. Remove the oil pan retaining bolts and lower the oil pan. Remove the 2 bolts retaining the oil pump pickup tube and screen to the oil pump and the nut from the main bearing cap stud. Allow the pickup tube to drop into the oil pan.

16. Rotate the crankshaft, as required, for clearance and remove the oil pan from the vehicle.

To install:

17. Clean the oil pan and the gasket mating surfaces. Clean the oil pump pickup tube and screen assembly.

18. Install a new oil filter. Position a new oil pan gasket on the cylinder block. Place the oil pickup tube and screen in the oil pan and position the oil pan on the crossmember.

19. Install the pickup tube and screen with a new gasket. Install the bolts and tighten to 12–18 ft. lbs. (16–24 Nm). Position the oil pan and install the retaining bolts. Tighten to 7–10 ft. lbs. (9–14 Nm).

20. Position the jack and wood block under the engine and raise the engine enough to remove the wood blocks. Lower the engine and remove the jack. Install the engine mount through bolts and tighten to 33–46 ft. lbs. (45–62 Nm).

21. Connect the fuel lines. Install the converter inspection cover. Tighten the rear mount attaching nuts to 35–50 ft. lbs. (48–68 Nm).

22. Install the shift crossover. Position the catalytic converters, secondary air tube and inlet pipes to the exhaust manifold and install the retaining nuts.

23. Install the catalytic converter outlet attaching bolts and install the secondary air tube on the converter housing. Install the starter and connect the starter cable.

24. Install the oxygen sensors and lower the vehicle. Install the dipstick and tube. Install the thermactor air dump valve to exhaust manifold clamp.

25. Connect the windshield wiper hose and install the wiper motor mounting plate. Install the wiper motor.

26. Install the accelerator cable mounting bracket with the attaching screws on 5.8L engine. Connect the accelerator and throttle valve cables to the throttle body or carburetor.

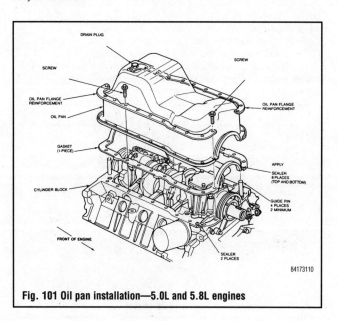

Fig. 101 Oil pan installation—5.0L and 5.8L engines

27. Position the shroud and install the retaining bolts. Install the thermactor tube to the rear of the engine. Install the air cleaner assembly and air ducts.

28. Fill the crankcase with the proper type and quantity of engine oil. Fill the transmission with the proper type and quantity of transmission fluid.

29. Connect the negative battery cable. Start the engine and check for leaks.

Oil Pump

REMOVAL

4.6L Engine

1. Disconnect the negative battery cable.
2. Remove the valve covers, timing chain cover, and oil pan. Refer to the procedures in this Section.
3. Remove the timing chains according to the procedure in this Section.
4. Remove the 4 bolts retaining the oil pump to the cylinder block and remove the pump.
5. Remove the 2 bolts retaining the oil pickup tube to the oil pump and remove the bolt retaining the oil pickup tube to the main bearing stud spacer. Remove the pickup tube.

5.0L and 5.8L Engines

1. Disconnect the negative battery cable. Remove the oil pan; see the procedure in this Section.
2. Remove the oil pump inlet tube and screen assembly.
3. Remove the oil pump attaching bolts and gasket. Remove the oil pump intermediate shaft.

INSTALLATION

4.6L Engine

▶ See Figure 102

1. Clean the oil pickup tube and replace the O-ring.
2. Position the tube on the oil pump and hand-start the 2 bolts. Install the bolt retaining the pickup tube to the main bearing stud spacer hand tight.
3. Tighten the pickup tube-to-oil pump bolts to 6.0–8.8 ft. lbs. (8–12 Nm). Tighten the pickup tube to main bearing stud spacer bolt to 15–22 ft. lbs. (20–30 Nm).
4. Rotate the inner rotor of the oil pump to align with the flats on the crankshaft and install the oil pump flush with the cylinder block. Install the 4 retaining bolts and tighten to 6.0–8.8 ft. lbs. (8–12 Nm).
5. Install a new oil filter. Install the timing chains.
6. Install the oil pan, front cover and camshaft covers.
7. Fill the crankcase with the proper type and quantity of engine oil. Connect the negative battery cable, start the engine and check for leaks.

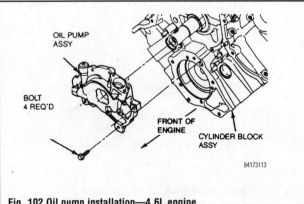

Fig. 102 Oil pump installation—4.6L engine

5.0L and 5.8L Engines

▶ See Figure 103

1. Prime the oil pump by filling either the inlet or outlet ports with engine oil and rotating the pump shaft to distribute the oil within the pump body.
2. Position the intermediate driveshaft into the distributor socket. With the shaft firmly seated in the distributor socket, the stop on the shaft should touch the roof of the crankcase. Remove the shaft and position the stop, as necessary.
3. Position a new gasket on the pump body, insert the intermediate shaft into the oil pump and install the pump and shaft as an assembly.

➥Do not attempt to force the pump into position if it will not seat readily. The driveshaft hex may be misaligned with the distributor shaft. To align, rotate the intermediate shaft into a new position.

4. Tighten the oil pump attaching bolts to 22–32 ft. lbs. (30–43 Nm).
5. Clean and install the oil pump inlet tube and screen assembly.
6. Install the oil pan and the remaining components in the reverse order of removal. Start the engine and check for leaks.

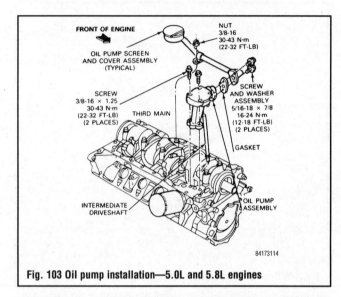

Fig. 103 Oil pump installation—5.0L and 5.8L engines

Crankshaft Damper

REMOVAL & INSTALLATION

4.6L Engine

▶ See Figures 104, 105 and 106

1. Disconnect the negative battery cable.
2. Release the belt tensioner and remove the accessory drive belt.
3. Raise and safely support the vehicle.
4. Remove the crankshaft damper retaining bolt and washer. Remove the damper using a suitable puller.
   To install:
5. Apply clean engine oil to the sealing surface of the damper. Apply a small amount of silicone sealer to the rear of the damper keyway. Using a damper installer, install the crankshaft damper. Be sure the key on the crankshaft aligns with the keyway in the damper.

❋❋ WARNING

Do not drive the damper onto the crankshaft with a hammer; damage to the crankshaft and/or thrust bearings may result. Always use a crankshaft damper installation tool.

6. Install the crankshaft damper retaining bolt and washer and tighten to 114–121 ft. lbs. (155–165 Nm).
7. Lower the vehicle and install the accessory drive belt.
8. Connect the negative battery cable, start the engine and check for leaks.

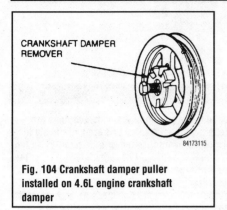

Fig. 104 Crankshaft damper puller installed on 4.6L engine crankshaft damper

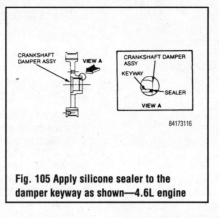

Fig. 105 Apply silicone sealer to the damper keyway as shown—4.6L engine

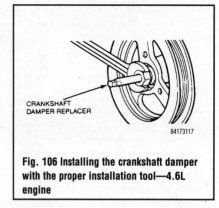

Fig. 106 Installing the crankshaft damper with the proper installation tool—4.6L engine

5.0L and 5.8L Engines

♦ See Figures 107 and 108

1. Disconnect the negative battery cable.
2. Remove the fan shroud and position it back over the fan. Remove the fan/clutch assembly and shroud.
3. Remove the accessory drive belts.
4. Remove the crankshaft pulley from the damper and remove the damper retaining bolt. Remove the damper using a suitable puller.

To install:

5. Apply clean engine oil to the sealing surface of the damper. Apply a small amount of silicone sealer to the damper keyway. Line up the crankshaft damper keyway with the crankshaft key and install the damper using a damper installation tool.

❄❄ WARNING

Do not drive the damper onto the crankshaft with a hammer; damage to the crankshaft and/or thrust bearings may result. Always use a crankshaft damper installation tool.

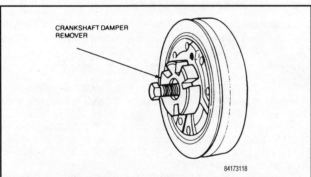

Fig. 107 Crankshaft damper puller installed on 5.0L/5.8L engine crankshaft damper

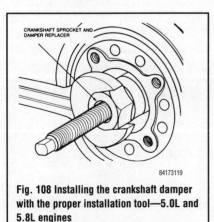

Fig. 108 Installing the crankshaft damper with the proper installation tool—5.0L and 5.8L engines

6. Install the damper retaining bolt and tighten to 70–90 ft. lbs. (95–122 Nm).
7. Install the remaining components in the reverse order of their removal.

Timing Chain Cover Seal

REMOVAL & INSTALLATION

♦ See Figures 109 and 110

1. Remove the crankshaft damper as described in this Section.
2. Use a suitable seal removal tool to remove the seal from the cover. Be careful not to damage the crankshaft or the seal bore in the timing chain cover.

To install:

3. Lubricate the seal bore in the front cover and the seal lip with clean engine oil.
4. Install the new seal using a suitable seal installation tool. Make sure the seal is installed evenly and straight.
5. Install the crankshaft damper. Be sure to lubricate the sealing surface of the damper with clean engine oil prior to installation.
6. Start the engine and check for leaks.

Timing Chain Cover

REMOVAL & INSTALLATION

4.6L Engine

♦ See Figure 111

1. Disconnect the negative battery cable.
2. Remove the cooling fan and shroud. Loosen the water pump pulley bolts, remove the accessory drive belt and remove the water pump pulley.
3. Raise and safely support the vehicle.

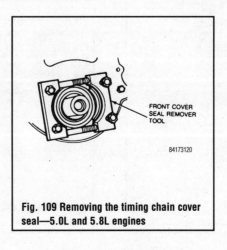

Fig. 109 Removing the timing chain cover seal—5.0L and 5.8L engines

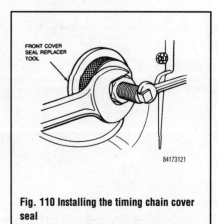

Fig. 110 Installing the timing chain cover seal

4. Remove the bolts retaining the power steering pump to the engine block and cylinder front cover. The lower front bolt on the power steering pump will not come all the way out. Wire the power steering pump out of the way.

5. Remove the 4 bolts retaining the oil pan to the front cover. Remove the crankshaft damper retaining bolt and washer. Remove the damper using a puller.

6. Lower the vehicle. Remove the bolt retaining the air conditioner high pressure line to the right coil bracket.

7. Remove the front bolts and loosen the remaining bolts on the valve covers. Using plastic wedges or similar tools, prop up both valve covers. Disconnect both ignition coils and Camshaft Identification (CID) sensor.

8. Remove the nuts retaining the right coil bracket to the front cover. Position the power steering hose out of the way.

9. Remove the nuts retaining the left coil bracket to the front cover. Slide both coil brackets and spark plug wires off the mounting studs and lay the assembly on top of the engine.

10. Disconnect the crankshaft position sensor. Remove the 7 stud bolts and 4 bolts retaining the front cover to the engine and remove the front cover.

To install:

11. Inspect and replace the front cover seal as necessary and clean the sealing surfaces of the cylinder block. Apply silicone sealer to the oil pan where it meets the cylinder block and to the points where the cylinder head meets the cylinder block.

12. Install the front cover and the attaching studs and bolts. Tighten to 15–22 ft. lbs. (20–30 Nm). Connect the crankshaft position sensor.

13. Position the coil brackets and spark plug wires as an assembly onto the mounting studs. Position the power steering hose and install the nuts retaining the coil brackets to the front cover. Tighten the nuts to 15–22 ft. lbs. (20–30 Nm). Connect both ignition coils and CID sensor.

14. Remove the plastic wedges holding up the valve covers. Apply silicone sealer where the front cover meets the cylinder head and make sure the valve cover gaskets are properly positioned. Install the front retaining bolts into the valve cover and tighten the bolts to 6.0–8.8 ft. lbs. (8–12 Nm).

15. Position the air conditioner high pressure line on the right coil bracket and install the bolt. Raise and safely support the vehicle.

16. Apply a small amount of silicone sealer in the rear of the keyway in the damper. Position the damper on the crankshaft and install, using a suitable installation tool. Install the damper bolt and washer and tighten to 114–121 ft. lbs. (155–165 Nm).

17. Install the 4 bolts retaining the oil pan to the front cover. Tighten to 15–22 ft. lbs. (20–30 Nm).

18. Position the power steering pump on the engine and install the 4 retaining bolts. Tighten to 15–22 ft. lbs. (20–30 Nm). Lower the vehicle.

19. Install the water pump pulley with the 4 bolts. Tighten to 15–22 ft. lbs. (20–30 Nm). Install the accessory drive belt and the cooling fan and shroud.

20. Connect the negative battery cable, start the engine and check for leaks.

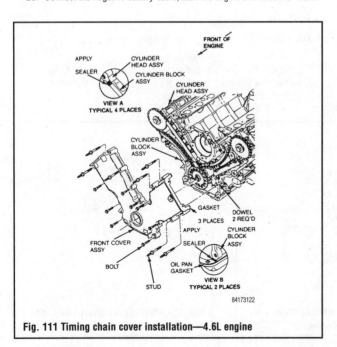

Fig. 111 Timing chain cover installation—4.6L engine

5.0L and 5.8L Engines

▶ **See Figure 112**

1. Disconnect the negative battery cable.
2. Drain the cooling system. Remove the air inlet tube.

✳✳ CAUTION

When draining the coolant, keep in mind that cats and dogs are attracted by the ethylene glycol antifreeze, and are quite likely to drink any that is left in an uncovered container or in puddles on the ground. This will prove fatal in sufficient quantity. Always drain the coolant into a sealable container. Coolant should be reused unless it is contaminated or several years old.

3. Remove the fan shroud attaching bolts and position the shroud over the fan. Remove the fan and clutch assembly from the water pump shaft and remove the shroud.

4. Remove the air conditioner drive belt and idler pulley bracket. Remove the alternator and power steering drive belts. Remove the power steering pump and position aside, leaving the hoses attached. Remove all accessory brackets that attach to the water pump.

5. Remove the water pump pulley. Disconnect the lower radiator hose, heater hose and water pump bypass hose at the water pump.

6. Remove the crankshaft pulley from the crankshaft vibration damper. Remove the damper attaching bolt and washer and remove the damper using a puller.

7. On 5.8L engines, disconnect the fuel pump outlet line from the fuel pump. Remove the fuel pump attaching bolts and lay the pump to 1 side with the flexible fuel line still attached.

8. Remove the fuel line from the clip on the front cover, if equipped.

9. Remove the oil pan-to-front cover attaching bolts. Use a thin blade knife to cut the oil pan gasket flush with the cylinder block face prior to separating the cover from the cylinder block.

10. Remove the cylinder front cover and water pump as an assembly.

➡ **Cover the front oil pan opening while the cover assembly is off to prevent foreign material from entering the pan.**

To install:

11. If a new front cover is to be installed, remove the water pump from the old front cover and install it on the new front cover.

12. Clean all gasket mating surfaces. Pry the old oil seal from the front cover and install a new one, using a seal installer.

13. Coat the gasket surface of the oil pan with sealer, cut and position the required sections of a new gasket on the oil pan and apply silicone sealer at the corners. Apply sealer to a new front cover gasket and install on the block.

14. Position the front cover on the cylinder block. Use care to avoid seal damage or gasket mislocation. It may be necessary to force the cover downward to slightly compress the pan gasket. Use front cover aligner tool T61P–6019–B or equivalent to assist the operation.

15. Coat the threads of the front cover attaching screws with pipe sealant and install. While pushing in on the alignment tool, tighten the oil pan to cover attaching screws to 9–11 ft. lbs. (12–15 Nm).

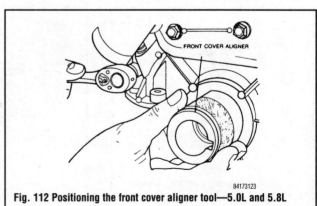

Fig. 112 Positioning the front cover aligner tool—5.0L and 5.8L engines

16. Tighten the front cover to cylinder block attaching bolts to 15–18 ft. lbs. (20–24 Nm). Remove the alignment tool.

17. Apply multi-purpose grease to the sealing surface of the vibration damper. Apply silicone sealer to the keyway of the vibration damper.

18. Line up the vibration damper keyway with the crankshaft key and install the damper using a suitable installation tool. Tighten the retaining bolt to 70–90 ft. lbs. (95–122 Nm). Install the crankshaft pulley.

19. On 5.8L engines, install the fuel pump with a new gasket. Connect the fuel pump outlet line.

20. Install the remaining components in the reverse order of their removal.

21. Fill the crankcase with the proper type and quantity of engine oil. Fill the cooling system.

22. Connect the negative battery cable, start the engine and check for leaks.

Timing Chain and Sprockets

REMOVAL & INSTALLATION

4.6L Engine

♦ See Figures 113 thru 121

➡This is not a free wheeling engine. If it has "jumped time," there will be damage to the valves and/or pistons and will require the removal of the cylinder heads.

☆☆ WARNING

The camshafts and/or crankshaft must never be rotated when the cylinder heads are installed and the timing chain is removed. Failure to heed this warning will result in valve and/or piston damage.

1. Disconnect the negative battery cable.
2. Remove the valve covers and the timing chain front cover.
3. Remove the crankshaft position sensor tooth wheel.
4. Rotate the engine to set the No. 1 piston at TDC on the compression stroke.
5. Install cam positioning tools T92P–6256–A or equivalent, on the flats of the camshaft. This will prevent accidental rotation of the camshafts.
6. Remove the 2 bolts retaining the right tensioner to the cylinder head and remove the tensioner. Remove the right tensioner arm.
7. Remove the 2 bolts retaining the right chain guide to the cylinder head and remove the chain guide. Remove the right chain and right crankshaft sprocket. If necessary, remove the right camshaft sprocket retaining bolt, washer, sprocket and spacer.

➡Cam positioning tools T92P–6256–A or equivalent, must be installed on the camshaft to prevent the camshaft from rotating.

8. Remove the 2 bolts retaining the left tensioner to the cylinder head and remove the tensioner. Remove the left tensioner arm.
9. Remove the 2 bolts retaining the left chain guide to the cylinder head and remove the chain guide. Remove the left chain and left crankshaft sprocket.

If necessary, remove the left camshaft sprocket retaining bolt, washer, sprocket and spacer.

➡Cam positioning tools T92P–6256–A or equivalent, must be installed on the camshaft to prevent the camshaft from rotating.

10. Inspect the friction material on the tensioner arms and chain guides. If worn or damaged, remove and clean the oil pan and replace the oil pickup tube.

☆☆ WARNING

Do not rotate the crankshaft and/or camshafts.

To install:

11. Make sure cam positioning tools T92P–6256–A or equivalent, are installed on the camshafts to prevent them from rotating.
12. If removed, position the camshaft spacers and sprockets on the camshafts and install the washers and retaining bolts. Do not tighten at this time.
13. Install the left crankshaft sprocket with the tapered part of the sprocket facing away from the engine block.

➡The crankshaft sprockets are identical. They may only be installed 1 way, with the tapered part of the sprocket facing each other.

14. Install the left timing chain on the camshaft and crankshaft sprockets. Make sure the copper links of the chain line up with the timing marks of the sprockets.

➡If the copper links of the timing chain are not visible, pull the chain taught until the opposite sides of the chain contact one another and lay it on a flat surface. Mark the links at each end of the chain and use them in place of the copper links.

15. Install the right crankshaft sprocket with the tapered part of the sprocket facing the left crankshaft sprocket.
16. Install the right timing chain on the camshaft and crankshaft sprockets. Make sure the copper links of the chain line up with the timing marks of the sprockets.
17. It is necessary to bleed the timing chain tensioners before installation. Proceed as follows:

  a. Position the timing chain tensioner in a soft-jawed vice.

  b. Using a small pick or similar tool, hold the ratchet lock mechanism away from the ratchet stem and slowly compress the tensioner plunger by rotating the vise handle.

☆☆ WARNING

The tensioner must be compressed slowly or damage to the internal seals will result.

  c. Once the tensioner plunger bottoms in the tensioner bore, continue to hold the ratchet lock mechanism and push down on the ratchet stem until flush with the tensioner face.

  d. While holding the ratchet stem flush to the tensioner face, release the ratchet lock mechanism and install a paper clip or similar tool in the tensioner body to lock the tensioner in the collapsed position.

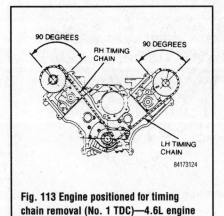

Fig. 113 Engine positioned for timing chain removal (No. 1 TDC)—4.6L engine

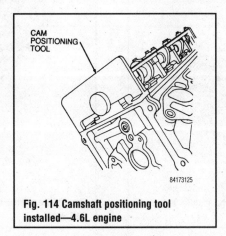

Fig. 114 Camshaft positioning tool installed—4.6L engine

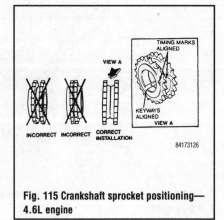

Fig. 115 Crankshaft sprocket positioning—4.6L engine

e. The paper clip must not be removed until the timing chain, tensioner, tensioner arm and timing chain guide are completely installed on the engine.

18. Install the right and left timing chain tensioners and secure with 2 bolts on each. Tighten the bolts to 15–22 ft. lbs. (20–30 Nm).

19. On 1993–94 vehicles, install crankshaft positioning tool T93P–6265–A or equivalent, over the crankshaft and front cover alignment dowel, to position the crankshaft.

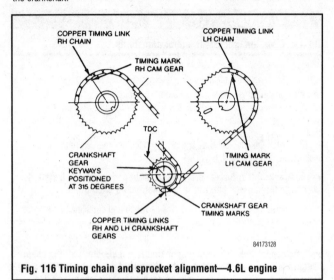

Fig. 116 Timing chain and sprocket alignment—4.6L engine

20. Lubricate the tensioner arm contact surfaces with engine oil and install the right and left tensioner arms on their dowels.

21. Install the right and left timing chain guides and secure with 2 bolts on each. Tighten the bolts to 6.0–8.8 ft. lbs. (8–12 Nm).

22. Position a suitable C-clamp around the tensioner arm and chain guide, to remove all slack from the chain.

23. Remove the paper clips from the timing chain tensioners and make sure all timing marks are aligned.

24. Using camshaft positioning tool T92P–6265–A or equivalent, to align the camshaft, tighten the camshaft sprocket-to-camshaft bolt to 81–95 ft. lbs. (110–130 Nm).

25. On 1993–94 vehicles, position a suitable dial indicator in the No. 1 cylinder spark plug hole. Check that the camshaft is at maximum lift for the intake valve when the piston is at 114° after TDC. If it is not, loosen the camshaft sprocket bolt and repeat Steps 18–22.

26. Remove the camshaft and crankshaft positioning tools.

27. Installation of the remaining components is the reverse of removal.

28. Connect the negative battery cable, start the engine and check for leaks and proper operation.

5.0L and 5.8L Engines

▶ See Figure 122

1. Disconnect the negative battery cable and drain the cooling system.

❄❄ **CAUTION**

When draining the coolant, keep in mind that cats and dogs are attracted by the ethylene glycol antifreeze, and are quite likely to

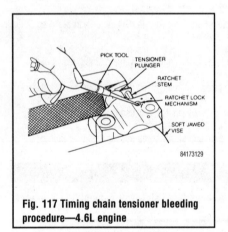

Fig. 117 Timing chain tensioner bleeding procedure—4.6L engine

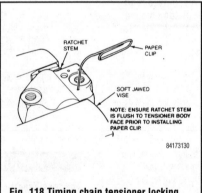

Fig. 118 Timing chain tensioner locking procedure—4.6L engine

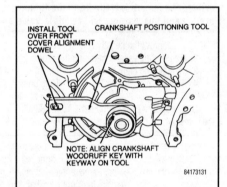

Fig. 119 Crankshaft positioning tool installation—4.6L engine

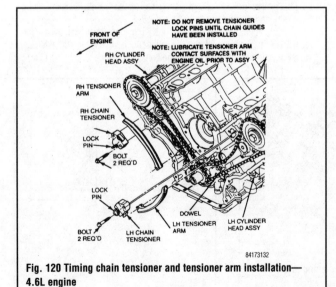

Fig. 120 Timing chain tensioner and tensioner arm installation—4.6L engine

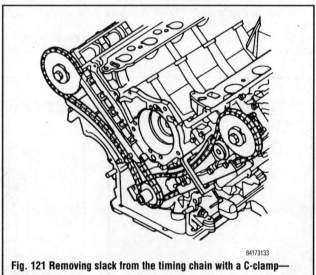

Fig. 121 Removing slack from the timing chain with a C-clamp—4.6L engine

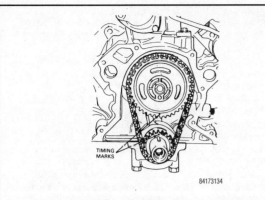

Fig. 122 Timing sprocket alignment—5.0L and 5.8L engines

drink any that is left in an uncovered container or in puddles on the ground. This will prove fatal in sufficient quantity. Always drain the coolant into a sealable container. Coolant should be reused unless it is contaminated or several years old.

2. Remove the timing chain front cover.
3. Rotate the crankshaft until the timing marks on the sprockets are aligned.
4. Remove the camshaft retaining bolt, washer and eccentric. Slide both sprockets and the timing chain forward and remove them as an assembly.
To install:
5. Position the sprockets and timing chain on the camshaft and crankshaft simultaneously. Make sure the timing marks on the sprockets are aligned.
6. Install the washer, eccentric and camshaft sprocket retaining bolt. Tighten the bolt to 40–45 ft. lbs. (54–61 Nm).
7. Install the timing chain front cover and remaining components.
8. Fill the cooling system. Connect the negative battery cable, start the engine and check for leaks.
9. Check and adjust the ignition timing and idle speed, as necessary.

Camshaft

REMOVAL & INSTALLATION

4.6L Engine

▸ **See Figures 123 thru 128**

1. Disconnect the negative battery cable and drain the cooling system. Relieve the fuel system pressure as described in Section 5.

❋❋ CAUTION

When draining the coolant, keep in mind that cats and dogs are attracted by the ethylene glycol antifreeze, and are quite likely to drink any that is left in an uncovered container or in puddles on the

ground. This will prove fatal in sufficient quantity. Always drain the coolant into a sealable container. Coolant should be reused unless it is contaminated or several years old.

2. Remove the right and left valve covers.
3. Remove the timing chain front cover. Remove the timing chains.
4. Rotate the crankshaft counterclockwise 45 degrees from TDC to make sure all pistons are below the top of the engine block deck face.

❋❋ WARNING

The crankshaft must be in this position prior to rotating the camshafts or damage to the pistons and/or valve train will result.

5. Install valve spring compressor tool T91P–6565–A or equivalent, under the camshaft and on top of the valve spring retainer.

➡**Valve spring spacer tool T91P–6565–AH or equivalent, must be installed between the spring coils and the camshaft must be at the base circle before compressing the valve spring.**

6. Compress the valve spring far enough to remove the roller follower. Repeat Steps 5 and 6 until all roller followers are removed.
7. Remove the bolts retaining the camshaft cap cluster assemblies to the cylinder heads. Tap upward on the camshaft caps at points near the upper bearing halves and gradually lift the camshaft clusters from the cylinder heads.
8. Remove the camshafts straight upward to avoid bearing damage.
To install:
9. Apply heavy engine oil to the camshaft journals and lobes. Position the camshafts on the cylinder heads.

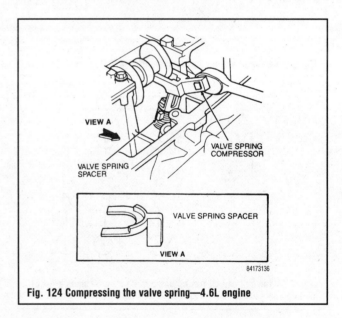

Fig. 124 Compressing the valve spring—4.6L engine

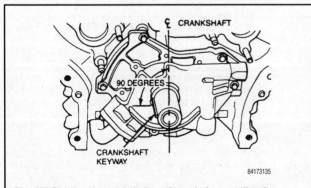

Fig. 123 Position the crankshaft as shown before rotating the camshafts—4.6L engine

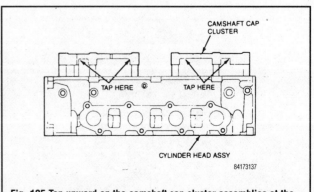

Fig. 125 Tap upward on the camshaft cap cluster assemblies at the points shown—4.6L engine

10. Install and seat the camshaft cap cluster assemblies. Hand start the bolts.

11. Tighten the camshaft cluster retaining bolts in sequence to 6.0–8.8 ft. lbs. (8–12 Nm).

➡ **Each camshaft cap cluster assembly is tightened individually.**

12. Loosen the camshaft cap cluster retaining bolts approximately 2 turns or until the heads of the bolts are free. Retighten all bolts, in sequence, to 6.0–8.8 ft. lbs. (8–12 Nm).

➡ **The camshafts should turn freely with a slight drag.**

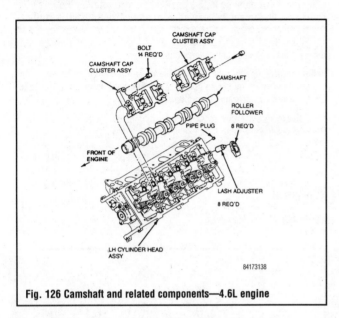

Fig. 126 Camshaft and related components—4.6L engine

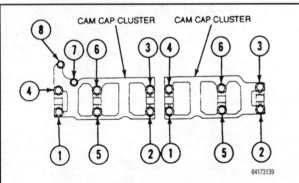

Fig. 127 Camshaft cap cluster retaining bolt torque sequence—4.6L engine

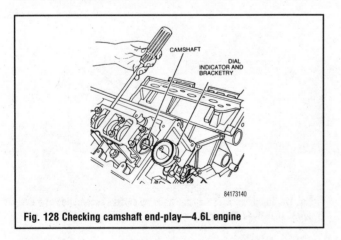

Fig. 128 Checking camshaft end-play—4.6L engine

13. Check camshaft end-play as follows:
    a. Install a suitable dial indicator on the front of the engine. Position it so the indicator foot is resting on the camshaft sprocket bolt or the front of the camshaft.
    b. Push the camshaft toward the rear of the engine and zero the dial indicator.
    c. Pull the camshaft forward and release it. Compare the dial indicator reading with specification.
    d. If end-play is too tight, check for binding or foreign material in the camshaft thrust bearing. If end-play is excessive, check for worn camshaft thrust plate and replace the cylinder head, as required.
    e. Remove the dial indicator.

14. If necessary, install cam positioning tools T92P–6256–A or equivalent, on the flats of the camshafts and install the spacers and camshaft sprockets. Install the bolts and washers and tighten to 81–95 ft. lbs. (110–130 Nm).

15. Install valve spring compressor T91P–6565–A or equivalent, under the camshaft and on top of the valve spring retainer.

➡ **Valve spring spacer tool T91P–6565–AH or equivalent, must be installed between the spring coils and the camshaft must be at the base circle before compressing the valve spring.**

16. Compress the valve spring far enough to install the roller followers.

17. Repeat Steps 15 and 16 until all roller followers are installed.

18. Rotate the crankshaft clockwise 45 degrees to position the crankshaft at TDC.

➡ **The crankshaft must only be rotated in the clockwise direction and only as far as TDC.**

19. Install the timing chains and install the timing chain front cover. Install the valve covers.

20. Install the remaining components in the reverse order of removal.

21. Connect the negative battery cable. Start the engine and check for leaks.

5.0L and 5.8L Engines

▶ **See Figures 129 and 130**

1. Disconnect the negative battery cable and drain the cooling system.

✳✳ CAUTION

When draining the coolant, keep in mind that cats and dogs are attracted by the ethylene glycol antifreeze, and are quite likely to drink any that is left in an uncovered container or in puddles on the ground. This will prove fatal in sufficient quantity. Always drain the coolant into a sealable container. Coolant should be reused unless it is contaminated or several years old.

2. Relieve the fuel system pressure as described in Section 5. Discharge the air conditioning system.

3. Remove the radiator and air conditioner condenser.

4. Remove the grille.

5. Remove the intake manifold and the lifters.

6. Remove the timing chain front cover, the timing chain and camshaft sprocket.

7. Check the camshaft end-play as follows:
    a. Position a dial indicator on the front of the engine, with the indicator foot resting on the end of the camshaft.
    b. Push the camshaft toward the rear of the engine and set the indicator pointer to 0.
    c. Pull the camshaft forward and release it. Check the dial indicator reading.
    d. If end-play exceeds specification, replace the thrust plate.
    e. Recheck the end-play with the new thrust plate installed. If end-play is still excessive, check the camshaft and rear camshaft bore plug.

8. Remove the thrust plate. Remove the camshaft, being careful not to damage the bearing surfaces.

To install:

9. Lubricate the cam lobes and journals with heavy engine oil. Install the camshaft, being careful not to damage the bearing surfaces while sliding into position.

10. Install the thrust plate. Tighten the bolts to 9–12 ft. lbs. (12–16 Nm).

11. Install the timing chain and sprockets. Install the engine front cover.

12. Install the lifters and the intake manifolds.

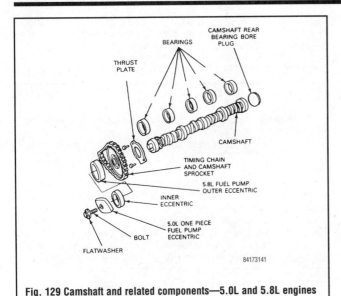

Fig. 129 Camshaft and related components—5.0L and 5.8L engines

Fig. 130 Checking camshaft end-play—5.0L and 5.8L engines

13. Install the grille and the air conditioner condenser.
14. Install the radiator. Fill the cooling system.
15. Connect the negative battery cable. Start the engine and check for leaks.
16. Evacuate and recharge the air conditioning system.

INSPECTION

♦ **See Figure 131**

1. Clean the camshaft in solvent and allow to dry.
2. Inspect the camshaft for obvious signs of wear: scores, nicks or pits on the journals or lobes. Light scuffs or nicks can be removed with an oil stone.

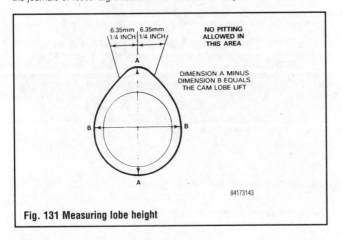

Fig. 131 Measuring lobe height

➥Lobe pitting except in the area shown in the figure will not hurt the operation of the camshaft; do not replace the camshaft because of pitting unless the pitting has occurred in the lobe lift area.

3. Using a micrometer, measure the diameter of the journals and compare to specifications. Replace the camshaft if any journals are not within specification.
4. Measure the camshaft lobes at the major (A–A) and minor (B–B) diameters, using a micrometer. The difference in readings is the lobe height. Compare your measurements with the lobe height specifications. Replace the camshaft if any lobe heights are not within specification.

Pistons and Connecting Rods

REMOVAL

♦ **See Figures 132, 133, 134 and 135**

➥Although the pistons and connecting rods can be removed from the engine (after the cylinder heads and oil pan are removed) while the engine is still in the car; it is far easier to work on the engine when removed from the car, and advisable for assembly cleanliness.

1. Remove the engine from the vehicle and mount it on a suitable workstand.
2. Remove the cylinder head(s) and the oil pan.
3. The position of each piston, connecting rod and connecting rod cap should be noted before any are removed, so they can be reinstalled in the same location.
4. Check the tops of the pistons and the sides of the connecting rods for identifying marks. In some engines, the top of the piston will be numbered to correspond with the cylinder number. The connecting rod and connecting rod cap should have numbers stamped on them where they meet that also correspond with their cylinder number. Refer to the firing order diagrams in Section 2 to see how the cylinders are numbered. If you cannot see any identifying numbers, use a number punch set and stamp in the numbers yourself.
5. Rotate the crankshaft until the piston to be removed is at the bottom of the cylinder. Check for a ridge at the top of the cylinder bore before removing the piston and connecting rod assembly, referring to the Ridge Removal and Honing procedure.
6. On the 4.6L engine, loosen the rod bolts and remove the rod cap and lower bearing insert.

➥On the 4.6L engine, the connecting rod bolts have been torqued to yield at least twice and must be replaced. The bolts are retained in the bolt hole with a light press fit; support the rod cap and drive the bolts from the holes using a hammer and punch.

7. On 5.0L and 5.8L engines, loosen the connecting rod nuts until the nuts are flush with the ends of the rod bolts. Using a hammer and a brass drift or piece of wood, lightly tap on the nuts/bolts until the connecting rod cap is loos-

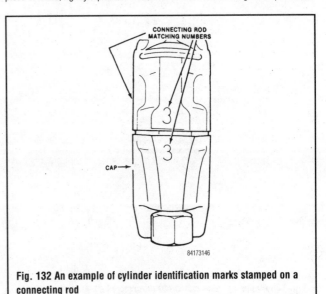

Fig. 132 An example of cylinder identification marks stamped on a connecting rod

ened from the connecting rod. Remove the nuts, rod cap and lower bearing insert.

8. If rod bearing clearance is to be checked at this time, refer to the procedure under Rod Bearing Replacement in this Section.

9. On the 5.0L and 5.8L engines, slip a piece of snug fitting rubber hose over each rod bolt, to prevent the bolt threads from damaging the crankshaft during removal.

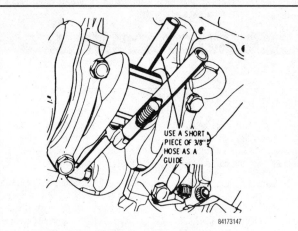

Fig. 133 Slip pieces of rubber hose over the 5.0L and 5.8L engine connecting rod bolts to protect the crankshaft during the removal procedure

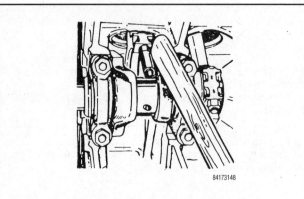

Fig. 134 Removing the piston and connecting rod assembly

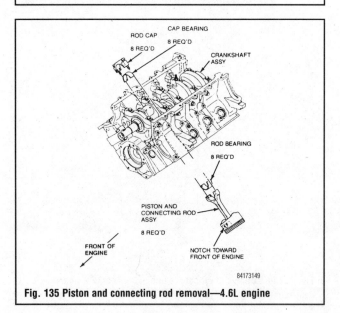

Fig. 135 Piston and connecting rod removal—4.6L engine

10. Using a hammer handle or piece of wood or plastic, tap the rod and piston upward in the bore until the piston rings clear the cylinder block. Remove the piston and connecting rod assembly from the top of the cylinder bore.

CLEANING AND INSPECTION

◗ See Figures 136 thru 143

1. Remove the piston rings using a piston ring expander. Refer to the Piston Ring Replacement procedure.

2. Clean the ring grooves with a ring groove cleaner, being careful not to cut into the piston metal. Heavy carbon deposits can be cleaned from the top of the piston with a scraper or wire brush, however, do not use a wire wheel on the ring grooves or lands. Clean the oil drain holes in the ring grooves. Clean all remaining dirt, carbon and varnish from the piston with a suitable solvent and a brush; do not use a caustic solution.

3. After cleaning, inspect the piston for scuffing, scoring, cracks, pitting or excessive ring groove wear. Replace any piston that is obviously worn.

4. If the piston appears okay, measure the piston diameter using a micrometer. Measure the piston diameter in the thrust direction, 90° to the piston pin axis. On the 4.6L engine, measure 1.65 in. (42mm) from the piston dome. On 5.0L and 5.8L engines, measure in line with the centerline of the piston pin.

5. Measure the cylinder bore diameter using a bore gauge, or with a telescope gauge and micrometer. The measurement should be made in the piston thrust direction at the top, middle and bottom of the bore.

➡ Piston diameter and cylinder bore measurements should be made with the parts at room temperature, 70°F (21°C).

6. Subtract the piston diameter measurement made in Step 4 from the cylinder bore measurement made in Step 5. This is the piston-to-bore clearance. If the clearance is within specification, light finish honing is all that is necessary. If the clearance is excessive, the cylinder must be bored and the piston replaced. Consult an automotive machine shop. If the pistons are replaced, the piston rings must also be replaced.

7. If the piston-to-bore clearance is okay, check the ring groove clearance. Insert the ring that will be used in the ring groove and check the clearance with a feeler gauge. Compare your measurement with specification. Replace the piston if the ring groove clearance is not within specification.

8. Check the connecting rod for damage or obvious wear. Check for signs of fractures and check the bearing bore for out-of-round and taper.

9. A shiny surface on the pin boss side of the piston usually indicates that the connecting rod is bent or the wrist pin hole is not in proper relation to the piston skirt and ring grooves.

10. Abnormal connecting rod bearing wear can be caused by either a bent connecting rod, an improperly machined journal, or a tapered connecting rod bore.

11. Twisted connecting rods will not create an easily identifiable wear pattern, but badly twisted rods will disturb the action of the entire piston, rings,

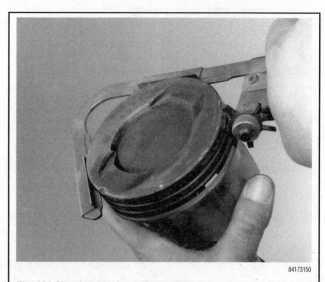

Fig. 136 Cleaning the piston ring grooves

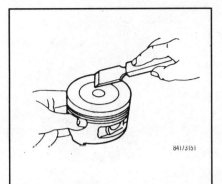

Fig. 137 Cleaning the top of the piston with a scraper

Fig. 138 Cleaning the top of the piston with a wire brush

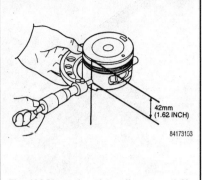

Fig. 139 Measuring piston diameter—4.6L engine

Fig. 140 Measuring piston diameter—5.0L engine

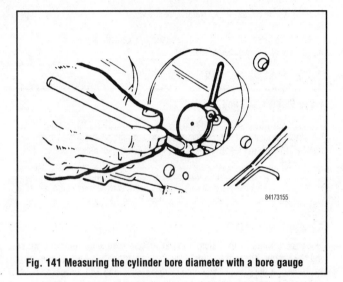

Fig. 141 Measuring the cylinder bore diameter with a bore gauge

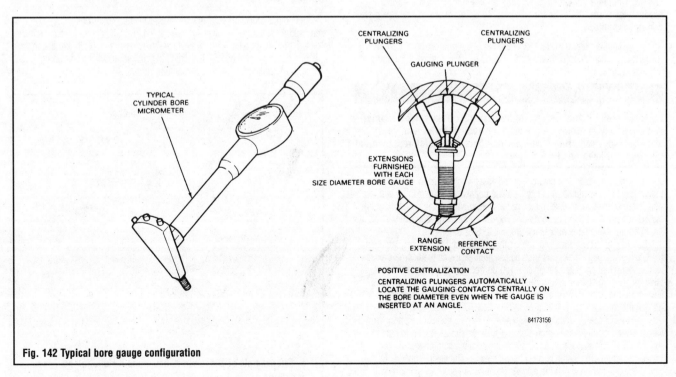

Fig. 142 Typical bore gauge configuration

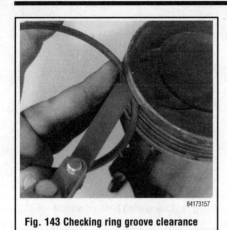

Fig. 143 Checking ring groove clearance

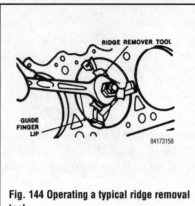

Fig. 144 Operating a typical ridge removal tool

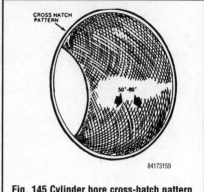

Fig. 145 Cylinder bore cross-hatch pattern after honing

and connecting rod assembly and may be the cause of excessive oil consumption.

12. If a connecting rod problem is suspected, consult an automotive machine shop to have the rod checked.

RIDGE REMOVAL AND HONING

♦ **See Figures 144 and 145**

1. Before the piston is removed from the cylinder, check for a ridge at the top of the cylinder bore. This ridge occurs because the piston ring does not travel all the way to the top of the bore, thereby leaving an unused portion of cylinder bore.

2. Clean away any carbon buildup at the top of the cylinder with sand paper, in order to see the extent of the ridge more clearly. If the ridge is slight, it will be safe to remove the pistons without damaging the rings or piston ring lands. If the ridge is severe, and easily catches your fingernail, it will have to be removed using a ridge reamer.

➡ **A severe ridge is an indication of excessive bore wear. Before removing the piston, check the cylinder bore diameter with a bore gauge, as explained in the piston and connecting rod cleaning and inspection procedure. Compare your measurement with specification. If the bore is excessively worn, the cylinder will have to bored oversize and the piston and rings replaced.**

3. Install the ridge removal tool in the top of the cylinder bore. Carefully follow the manufacturers instructions for operation. Only remove the amount of material necessary to remove the ridge.

❊❊ WARNING

Be very careful if you are unfamiliar with operating a ridge reamer. It is very easy to remove more cylinder bore material than you want, possibly requiring a cylinder overbore and piston replacement that may not have been necessary.

4. After the piston and connecting rod assembly have been removed, check the clearances as explained in the piston and connecting rod cleaning and inspection procedure, to determine whether boring and honing or just light honing are required. If boring is necessary, consult an automotive machine shop. If light honing is all that is necessary, proceed to Step 5.

5. Honing is best done with the crankshaft removed, to prevent damage to the crankshaft and to make post-honing cleaning easier, as the honing process will scatter metal particles. However, if you do not want to remove the crankshaft, position the connecting rod journal for the cylinder being honed as far away from the bottom of the cylinder bore as possible, and wrap a shop cloth around the journal.

6. Honing can be done either with a flexible glaze breaker type hone or with a rigid hone that has honing stones and guide shoes. The flexible hone removes the least amount of metal, and is especially recommended if your piston-to-cylinder bore clearance is on the loose side. The flexible hone is useful to provide a finish on which the new piston rings will seat. A rigid hone will remove more material than the flexible hone and requires more operator skill.

7. Regardless of which type of hone you use, carefully follow the manufacturers instructions for operation.

8. The hone should be moved up and down the bore at sufficient speed to obtain a uniform finish. A rigid hone will provide a more definite cross-hatch finish; operate the rigid hone at a speed to obtain a 45–65° included angle in the cross-hatch. The finish marks should be clean but not sharp, free from embedded particles and torn or folded metal.

9. Periodically during the honing procedure, thoroughly clean the cylinder bore and check the piston-to-bore clearance with the piston for that cylinder.

10. After honing is completed, thoroughly wash the cylinder bores and the rest of the engine with hot water and detergent. Scrub the bores well with a stiff bristle brush and rinse thoroughly with hot water. Thorough cleaning is essential, for if any abrasive material is left in the cylinder bore, it will rapidly wear the new rings and the cylinder bore. If any abrasive material is left in the rest of the engine, it will be picked up by the oil and carried throughout the engine, damaging bearings and other parts.

11. After the bores are cleaned, wipe them down with a clean cloth coated with light engine oil, to keep them from rusting.

PISTON PIN REPLACEMENT

♦ **See Figure 146**

All engines utilize pressed-in wrist pins, which can only be removed/installed with a press and special fixtures. Attempting to remove/install the wrist pins with other than these special fixtures can result in damage to the piston and/or connecting rod. If a wrist pin problem is suspected (too tight, too loose, etc.) consult an automotive machine shop.

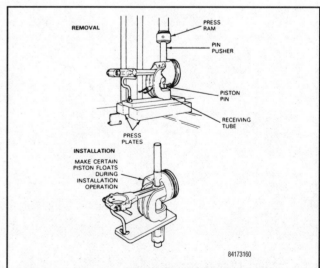

Fig. 146 Example of piston pin removal and installation using special fixtures

PISTON RING REPLACEMENT

♦ **See Figures 147, 148 and 149**

1. Remove the piston rings from the piston using a piston ring expander.
2. Clean the piston ring grooves, check the piston-to-cylinder bore clearance and check the ring groove clearance as explained in the piston and connecting rod cleaning and inspection procedure.
3. After the cylinder bores have been finish honed and cleaned, check the piston ring end gap. Compress the piston rings to be used in the cylinder, one at a time, into that cylinder. Using an inverted piston, push the ring down into the cylinder bore area where normal ring wear is not encountered.
4. Measure the ring end gap with a feeler gauge and compare to specification. A gap that is too tight is more harmful than one that is too loose (If ring end gap is excessively loose, the cylinder bore is probably worn beyond specification).
5. If the ring end gap is too tight, carefully remove the ring and file the ends squarely with a fine file to obtain the proper clearance.
6. Install the rings on the piston, lowest ring first. The lowest (oil) ring is installed by hand; the top 2 (compression) rings must be installed using a piston ring expander. There is a high risk of breaking or distorting the compression rings if they are installed by hand.
7. Install the oil ring expander in the bottom ring groove. Make sure the ends butt together and do not overlap. The ends must be on a solid portion of the piston, not over a drain hole.
8. Start the end of an oil ring rail ring into the oil ring groove above the spacer. On the 5.0L and 5.8L engines, the end gap must be approximately 1 in. (25.4mm) away from the expander ends. On the 4.6L engine, the end gap must be 90° from the expander ends. Finish installing the rail ring by spiraling it the remainder of the way on. Repeat the rail installation with the other rail ring. Its gap must be approximately the same as the other rail ring, except on the other side of the expander ends.

➡**If the instructions on the ring packaging differ from this information regarding oil ring gap positioning, follow the ring manufacturers instructions.**

9. Install the lower compression ring in the piston ring expander with the proper side up. The piston ring packaging should contain instructions as to the directions the ring sides should face. Spread the ring with the expander and install it on the piston.
10. Repeat Step 9 to install the top compression ring. Space the compression ring gaps according to the instructions on the ring packaging. The piston ring end gaps must not be aligned.

ROD BEARING REPLACEMENT

♦ **See Figures 150 and 151**

1. Inspect the rod bearings for scoring, chipping or other wear. See the figure for typical bearing wear patterns.
2. Inspect the crankshaft rod bearing journal for wear. Measure the journal diameter in several locations around the journal and compare to specification. If the crankshaft journal is scored or has deep ridges, or its diameter is below specification, the crankshaft must be removed from the engine and reground. Consult an automotive machine shop.
3. If the crankshaft journal appears usable, clean it and the rod bearing shells until they are completely free of oil. Blow any oil from the oil hole in the crankshaft.

➡**The journal surfaces and bearing shells must be completely free of oil to get an accurate reading with Plastigage®.**

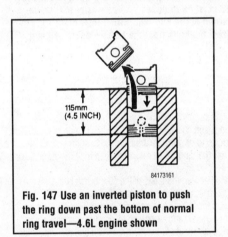

Fig. 147 Use an inverted piston to push the ring down past the bottom of normal ring travel—4.6L engine shown

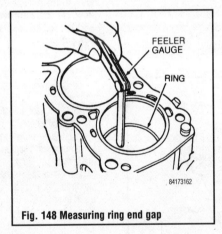

Fig. 148 Measuring ring end gap

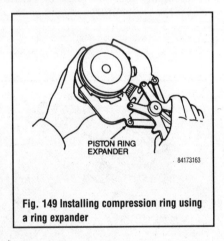

Fig. 149 Installing compression ring using a ring expander

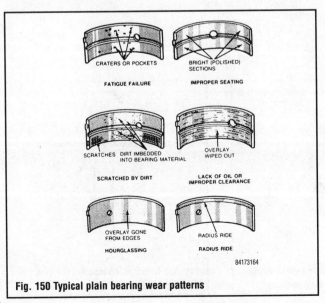

Fig. 150 Typical plain bearing wear patterns

4. Place a strip of Plastigage® lengthwise along the bottom center of the lower bearing shell, then install the cap with the shell and torque the connecting rod nuts or bolts to specification. Do not turn the crankshaft with the Plastigage® installed in the bearing.
5. Remove the bearing cap with the shell. The flattened Plastigage® will either be sticking to the bearing shell or the crankshaft journal.
6. Using the printed scale on the Plastigage® package, measure the flattened Plastigage® at its widest point. The number on the scale that most closely corresponds to the width of the Plastigage® indicates the bearing clearance in thousandths of an inch or hundreths of a millimeter.
7. Compare your findings with the bearing clearance specification. If the bearing clearance is excessive, the bearing must be replaced or the crankshaft must be ground and the bearing replaced.

➡**If the crankshaft is still at standard size (has not been ground undersize), bearing shell sets of 0.001, (0.0254mm) 0.002 (0.050mm) and 0.003 in. (0.0762mm) over standard size are usually available to correct excessive bearing clearance.**

8. After clearance measuring is completed, be sure to remove the Plastigage® from the crankshaft and/or bearing shell.
9. For final bearing shell installation, make sure the connecting rod and rod cap bearing saddles are clean and free of nicks or burrs. Install the bearing

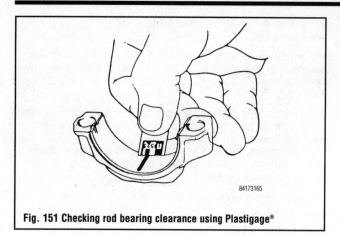

Fig. 151 Checking rod bearing clearance using Plastigage®

shells in the connecting rod, making sure the bearing shell tangs are seated in the notches.

➡**Be careful when handling any plain bearings. Your hands and the working area should be clean. Dirt is easily embedded in the bearing surface and the bearings are easily scratched or damaged.**

INSTALLATION

▶ **See Figures 152, 153, 154 and 155**

1. Make sure the cylinder bore and crankshaft journal are clean.
2. Position the crankshaft journal at its furthest position away from the bottom of the cylinder bore.
3. Coat the cylinder bore with light engine oil.
4. Make sure the rod bearing shells are correctly installed. On 5.0L and

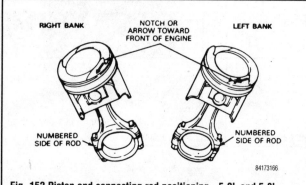

Fig. 152 Piston and connecting rod positioning—5.0L and 5.8L engines

5.8L engines, install the rubber hoses over the connecting rod bolts to protect the crankshaft during installation.

5. Make sure the piston rings are properly installed and the ring end gaps are correctly positioned. Install a piston ring compressor over the piston and rings and compress the piston rings into their grooves. Follow the ring compressor manufacturers instructions.

6. Place the piston and connecting rod assembly into the cylinder bore. Make sure the assembly is the correct one for that bore and that the piston and connecting rod are facing in the proper direction. Most pistons have an arrow or notch on the top of the piston, or the letter **F** appears somewhere on the piston to indicate "front", meaning this side should face the front of the engine.

7. Make sure the ring compressor is seated squarely on the block deck surface. If the compressor is not seated squarely, a ring could pop out from beneath the compressor and hang up on the deck surface, as the piston is tapped into the bore, possibly breaking the ring.

8. Make sure that the connecting rod is not hung up on the crankshaft counterweights and is in position to come straight on to the crankshaft.

9. Tap the piston slowly into the bore, making sure the compressor remains squarely against the block deck. When the piston is completely in the bore, remove the ring compressor.

10. Coat the crankshaft journal and the bearing shells with engine assembly lube or clean engine oil. Pull the connecting rod onto the crankshaft journal. After the rod is seated, remove the rubber hoses from the rod bolts on 5.0L and 5.8L engines.

11. On 4.6L engine, lightly oil the connecting rod bolt threads and install the rod bearing cap. Torque the connecting rod bolts in 2 steps, first to 12 ft. lbs. (15 Nm), then give each bolt an 85–95 degree turn.

➡**On the 4.6L engine, the connecting rod bolts have been torqued to yield at least twice and must be replaced with new prior to installation. The bolts are retained in the bolt hole with a light press fit; support the rod cap and drive the bolts from the holes using a hammer and punch.**

12. On the 5.0L and 5.8L engines, install the rod bearing cap. Lightly oil the connecting rod bolt threads and install the rod nuts. Torque the nuts to 19–24 ft. lbs. (26–32 Nm) on 5.0L engine and 40–45 ft. lbs. (54–61 Nm) on 5.8L engine.

13. After each piston and connecting rod assembly is installed, turn the crankshaft over several times and check for binding. If there is a problem and the crankshaft will not turn, or turns with great difficulty, it will be easier to find the problem (rod cap on backwards, broken ring, etc.) than if all the assemblies are installed.

14. Check the clearance between the sides of the connecting rods and the crankshaft using a feeler gauge. Spread the rods slightly with a screwdriver to insert the gauge. If the clearance is below the minimum specification, the connecting rod will have to be removed and machined to provide adequate clearance. If the clearance is excessive, substitute an unworn rod and recheck. If the clearance is still excessive, the crankshaft must be welded and reground, or replaced.

15. Install the oil pan and cylinder head(s).
16. Install the engine in the vehicle.

Fig. 153 The notch should face the front of the engine

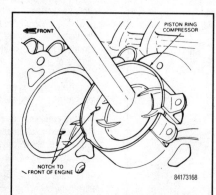

Fig. 154 Installing the piston using a ring compressor—5.0L/5.8L engine shown

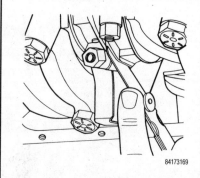

Fig. 155 Checking connecting rod side clearance

Rear Main Seal

REMOVAL & INSTALLATION

4.6L Engine

♦ **See Figures 156 and 157**

1. Disconnect the negative battery cable.
2. Remove the transmission; refer to Section 7.
3. Remove the flexplate from the crankshaft.
4. Remove the rear main seal retainer from the cylinder block.
5. Securely support the seal retainer and remove the seal, using a sharp pick.

To install:

6. Clean and inspect the retainer and retainer-to-cylinder block mating surfaces.
7. Apply a 0.060 in. (1.5mm) continuous bead of a suitable gasket maker to the cylinder block.
8. Install the seal retainer and tighten the bolts, in sequence, to 6.0–8.8 ft. lbs. (8–12 Nm).
9. Install the new rear main seal using rear main seal installer T82L–6701–A and adapter T91P–6701–A or equivalents.
10. Install the flexplate and tighten the bolts, in a crisscross pattern, to 54–64 ft. lbs. (73–87 Nm).
11. Install the transmission and lower the vehicle.
12. Connect the negative battery cable, start the engine and check for leaks.

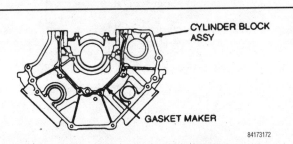

Fig. 156 Apply gasket maker to the cylinder block as shown—4.6L engine

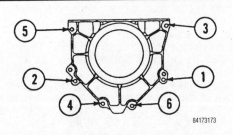

Fig. 157 Rear main seal retainer bolt torque sequence—4.6L engine

5.0L and 5.8L Engines

♦ **See Figure 158**

1. Disconnect the negative battery cable.
2. Remove the transmission; refer to Section 7.
3. Remove the flexplate from the crankshaft.
4. Punch 2 holes in the crankshaft rear oil seal on opposite sides of the crankshaft, just above the bearing cap to cylinder block split line. Install a sheet metal screw in each of the holes or use a small slide hammer and pry the crankshaft rear main oil seal from the block.

➡ **Use extreme caution not to scratch the crankshaft oil seal surface.**

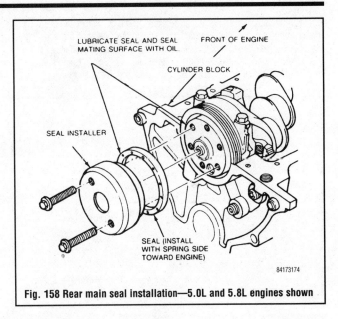

Fig. 158 Rear main seal installation—5.0L and 5.8L engines shown

To install:

5. Clean the oil seal recess in the cylinder block and main bearing cap.
6. Coat the seal and all of the seal mounting surfaces with oil. Position the seal on rear main seal installer T82L–6701–A or equivalent, and position the tool and seal to the rear of the engine.
7. Alternate bolt tightening to seat the seal properly. The rear face of the seal must be within 0.005 in. (0.127mm) of the rear face of the block.
8. Install the flexplate. Apply pipe sealant to the flexplate bolt threads, then tighten them, in a crisscross pattern, to 75–85 ft. lbs. (102–115 Nm).
9. Install the transmission and lower the vehicle.
10. Connect the negative battery cable, start the engine and check for leaks.

Crankshaft and Main Bearings

REMOVAL & INSTALLATION

4.6L Engine

♦ **See Figures 159, 160, 161, 162 and 163**

1. Remove the engine from the vehicle and position on a workstand.
2. Remove the crankshaft damper, flexplate, valve covers, timing chain cover, and timing chain and sprockets.
3. Remove the intake manifold, exhaust manifolds, cylinder heads and water pump.
4. Remove the oil pan, oil pump, oil pump pickup tube and rear main seal housing.
5. Remove the piston and connecting rod assemblies as explained earlier in this Section.
6. Make sure the main bearing caps are numbered so they can be reinstalled in their original positions.
7. Loosen the main bearing cap bolts, jack screws and side bolts and remove the main bearing caps. If main bearing clearance is to be checked at this time, refer to the procedure under Bearing Replacement.

➡ **The main bearing bolts are a torque-to-yield design and cannot be reused. They must be replaced with new prior to crankshaft installation.**

8. Carefully lift the crankshaft from the cylinder block.
9. Inspect the crankshaft and bearings and repair and/or replace, as necessary. If the bearings are removed and are to be reused, they must be identified so they can be reinstalled in their original locations.

To install:

10. Make sure the main cap and cylinder block main bearing saddles are clean and free of burrs and nicks, that would prevent the bearings from fully seating. Install the bearings shells.

11. After cleaning, inspecting and measuring the crankshaft and checking the main bearing clearance, install the crankshaft. Apply engine assembly lube or clean engine oil to the upper bearing shells prior to crankshaft installation.

12. Apply engine assembly lube or clean engine oil to the lower bearing shells, then install the main bearing caps in their original positions.

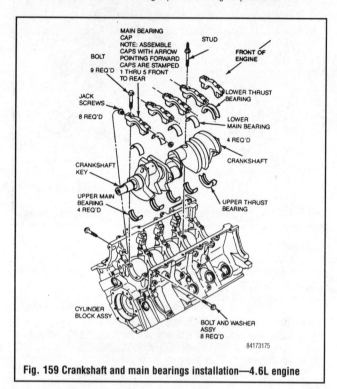

Fig. 159 Crankshaft and main bearings installation—4.6L engine

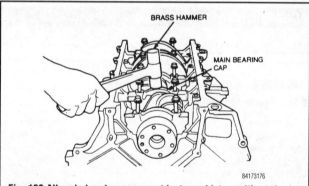

Fig. 160 All main bearing caps must be tapped into position prior to tightening—4.6L engine

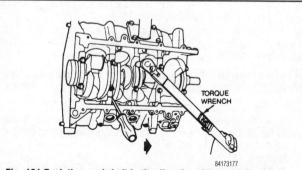

Fig. 161 Push the crankshaft in the direction shown to fully seat the thrust bearing. Leave the prybar in position until all main bearing bolts are tightened—4.6L engine

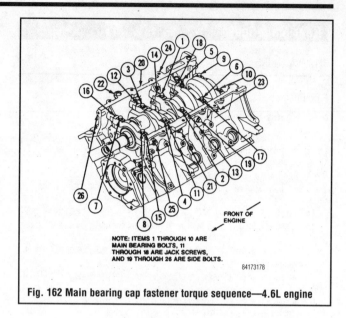

Fig. 162 Main bearing cap fastener torque sequence—4.6L engine

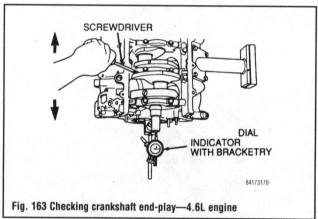

Fig. 163 Checking crankshaft end-play—4.6L engine

➡The jack screws must be bottomed on the main cap prior to installation.

13. Tap all of the main caps with a brass hammer, to make sure they are seated properly. Incorrect torque may result if this Step is not performed.

14. Push the crankshaft forward using a small prybar, to seat the thrust bearing.

15. Tighten the new main bearing bolts in 2 steps. First tighten, in sequence, to 22–25 ft. lbs. (30–35 Nm), then turn each bolt, in sequence, 85–95 degrees.

16. Tighten the jack screws in 2 steps. First tighten, in sequence, to 44 inch lbs. (5 Nm), then tighten, in sequence, to 80–97 inch lbs. (9–11 Nm).

17. Tighten the side bolts in 2 steps. First tighten, in sequence, to 7 ft. lbs. (10 Nm), then tighten, in sequence, to 14–17 ft. lbs. (19–23 Nm).

18. Position a dial indicator on the front of the engine with the indicator foot resting on the tip of the crankshaft. Use a small prybar against the No. 2 main bearing cap to move the crankshaft back and forth. Check the end-play reading against specification. If end-play is excessive, it can be corrected using a thicker thrust bearing or by removing the crankshaft and welding and regrinding the thrust journal.

19. Install the remaining components in the reverse order of their removal.

20. Install the engine in the vehicle.

5.0L and 5.8L Engines

♦ See Figures 164, 165 and 166

1. Remove the engine from the vehicle and position on a workstand.
2. Remove the rocker arm covers, rocker arms and pushrods.
3. Remove the intake and exhaust manifolds and the cylinder heads.
4. Remove the crankshaft damper, timing chain cover, oil pan, oil pump and rear main seal.

5. Remove the timing chain and sprockets, lifters and camshaft.

6. Remove the piston and connecting rod assemblies as described earlier.

7. Identify the location of the main bearing caps so they can be reinstalled in their original positions.

8. Loosen the main bearing cap bolts and remove the main bearing caps. If main bearing clearance is to be checked at this time, refer to the procedure under Bearing Replacement.

9. Carefully lift the crankshaft from the cylinder block.

10. Inspect the crankshaft and bearings and repair and/or replace, as necessary. If the bearings are removed and are to be reused, they must be identified so they can be reinstalled in their original locations.

To install:

11. Make sure the main cap and cylinder block main bearing saddles are clean and free of burrs and nicks, that would prevent the bearings from fully seating. Install the bearings shells.

12. After cleaning, inspecting and measuring the crankshaft and checking the main bearing clearance, install the crankshaft. Apply engine assembly lube or clean engine oil to the upper bearing shells prior to crankshaft installation.

13. Lightly oil the main bearing cap bolt threads. Apply engine assembly lube or clean engine oil to the lower bearing shells, then install the main bearing caps, except the thrust bearing cap (No. 3), in their original positions. Tighten the bolts to 60–70 ft. lbs. (81–95 Nm) on the 5.0L engine or 95–105 ft. lbs. (128–142 Nm) on the 5.8L engine.

➡ **Prior to installation, apply a ³/₁₆ in. bead of sealant in each corner of the rear main bearing cap saddle, the full length of the saddle.**

14. Install the thrust bearing cap, but leave the bolts finger tight.

15. Pry the crankshaft forward against the thrust surface of the upper half of the bearing.

16. Hold the crankshaft forward and pry the thrust bearing cap to the rear. This will align the thrust surfaces of both halves of the bearing.

17. While retaining the forward pressure on the crankshaft, tighten the thrust bearing cap bolts to the specification listed in Step 13.

18. Install a suitable dial indicator on the front of the cylinder block and position the indicator foot on the tip of the crankshaft.

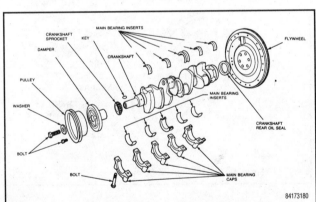

Fig. 164 Crankshaft, main bearings and related components—5.0L and 5.8L engines

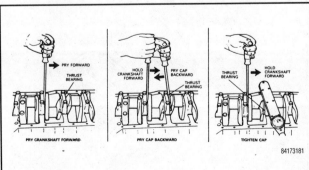

Fig. 165 Crankshaft thrust bearing alignment—5.0L and 5.8L engines

Fig. 166 Checking crankshaft end-play—5.0L and 5.8L engines

19. Use a small prybar against a main bearing cap, to push the crankshaft to the rear of the cylinder block. Zero the dial indicator.

20. Push the crankshaft forward and note the indicator reading. Check the end-play reading against specification. If end-play is excessive, it can be corrected using a thicker thrust bearing or by removing the crankshaft and welding and regrinding the thrust journal.

21. Install the remaining components in the reverse order of their removal.

22. Install the engine in the vehicle.

CLEANING AND INSPECTION

▶ **See Figures 167 and 168**

1. Clean the crankshaft with solvent and a brush. Clean the oil passages with a suitable brush, then blow them out with compressed air.

2. Inspect the crankshaft for obvious damage or wear. Check the main and connecting rod journals for cracks, scratches, grooves or scores. Inspect the crankshaft oil seal surface for nicks, sharp edges or burrs that could damage the oil seal or cause premature seal wear.

3. If the crankshaft passes a visual inspection, measure the main and connecting rod journals for wear, out-of-roundness or taper, using a micrometer. Measure in at least 4 places around each journal and compare your findings with the journal diameter specifications.

4. Check journal runout using a dial indicator. Support the crankshaft in V-blocks as shown in the figure and check the runout as shown. Compare to specifications.

5. If the crankshaft fails any inspection for wear or damage, it must be reground or replaced.

BEARING REPLACEMENT

▶ **See Figures 169 and 170**

1. Inspect the bearings for scoring, chipping or other wear. See the figure for typical bearing wear patterns.

2. Inspect the crankshaft journals as detailed in the Cleaning and Inspection procedure.

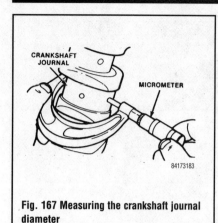

Fig. 167 Measuring the crankshaft journal diameter

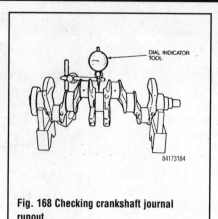

Fig. 168 Checking crankshaft journal runout

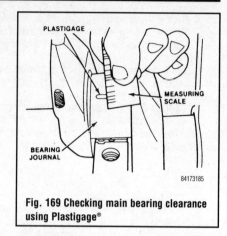

Fig. 169 Checking main bearing clearance using Plastigage®

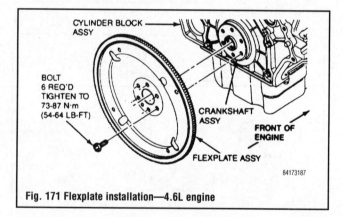

Fig. 170 Typical plain bearing wear patterns

3. If the crankshaft journals appear usable, clean them and the bearing shells until they are completely free of oil. Blow any oil from the oil hole in the crankshaft.

➡The journal surfaces and bearing shells must be completely free of oil to get an accurate reading with Plastigage®.

4. Place a strip of Plastigage® lengthwise along the bottom center of the lower bearing shell, then install the cap with the shell and torque the main cap fasteners to specification. Do not turn the crankshaft with the Plastigage® installed in the bearing.

5. Remove the bearing cap with the shell. The flattened Plastigage® will either be sticking to the bearing shell or the crankshaft journal.

6. Using the printed scale on the Plastigage® package, measure the flattened Plastigage® at its widest point. The number on the scale that most closely corresponds to the width of the Plastigage® indicates the bearing clearance in thousandths of an inch or hundredths of a millimeter.

7. Compare your findings with the bearing clearance specification. If the bearing clearance is excessive, the bearing must be replaced or the crankshaft must be ground and the bearing replaced.

➡If the crankshaft is still at standard size (has not been ground under-size), bearing shell sets of 0.001 in. , (0.0254mm) 0.002 in. (0.050mm) and 0.003 in. (0.0762mm) over standard size are usually available to correct excessive bearing clearance.

8. After clearance measuring is completed, be sure to remove the Plasti-gage® from the crankshaft and/or bearing shell.

9. For final bearing shell installation, make sure the main cap bearing saddles are clean and free of nicks or burrs. Install the bearing shells in the bearing saddles, making sure the bearing shell tangs are seated in the notches.

➡Be careful when handling any plain bearings. Your hands and the working area should be clean. Dirt is easily embedded in the bearing surface and the bearings are easily scratched or damaged.

10. After all of the main bearing cap fasteners have been tightened, check crankshaft end-play as detailed in the removal and installation procedure.

Flexplate

REMOVAL & INSTALLATION

◆ **See Figures 171 and 172**

1. Disconnect the negative battery cable.
2. Remove the transmission; refer to Section 7.

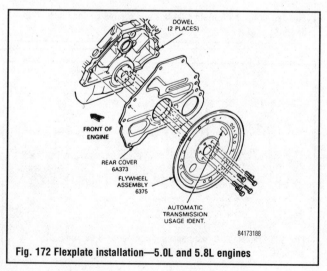

Fig. 171 Flexplate installation—4.6L engine

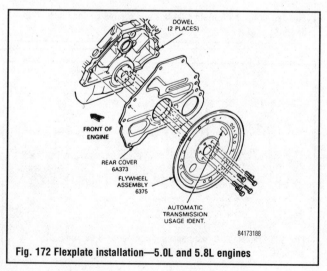

Fig. 172 Flexplate installation—5.0L and 5.8L engines

3. Remove the retaining bolts and remove the flexplate from the crankshaft.

4. Inspect the flexplate for cracks or other damage. Check the ring gear for worn, chipped or cracked teeth. If the teeth are damaged, the entire flexplate must be replaced.

To install:

5. Make sure the crankshaft flange and flexplate mating surfaces are clean.

6. Position the flexplate on the crankshaft and install the retaining bolts.

➡ **On 5.0L and 5.8L engines, apply suitable pipe sealant to the flexplate bolt threads prior to installation.**

7. On 4.6L engine, tighten the flexplate retaining bolts, in a crisscross pattern, to 54–64 ft. lbs. (73–87 Nm).

8. On 5.0L and 5.8L engines, tighten the flexplate retaining bolts, in a crisscross pattern, to 75–85 ft. lbs. (102–115 Nm).

9. Install the transmission and lower the vehicle. Connect the negative battery cable.

EXHAUST SYSTEM

◆ **See Figures 173 and 174**

Safety Precautions

Exhaust system work can be the most dangerous type of work you can do on your car. Always observe the following precautions:

• Support the car extra securely. Not only will you often be working directly under it, but you'll frequently be using a lot of force, say, heavy hammer blows, to dislodge rusted parts. This can cause a car that's improperly supported to shift and possibly fall.

• Wear goggles. Exhaust system parts are always rusty. Metal chips can be dislodged, even when you're only turning rusted bolts. Attempting to pry pipes apart with a chisel makes the chips fly even more frequently.

• If you're using a cutting torch, keep it a great distance from either the fuel tank or lines. Stop what you're doing and feel the temperature of the fuel bearing pipes on the tank frequently. Even slight heat can expand and/or vaporize fuel, resulting in accumulated vapor, or even a liquid leak, near your torch.

• Watch where your hammer blows fall and make sure you hit squarely. You could easily tap a brake or fuel line when you hit an exhaust system part with a glancing blow. Inspect all lines and hoses in the area where you've been working.

❊❊ CAUTION

Be very careful when working on or near the catalytic converter! External temperatures can reach 1,500°F (816°C) and more, causing severe burns. Removal or installation should be performed only on a cold exhaust system.

Special Tools

A number of special exhaust system tools can be rented from auto supply houses or local stores that rent special equipment. A common one is a tail pipe expander, designed to enable you to join pipes of identical diameter.

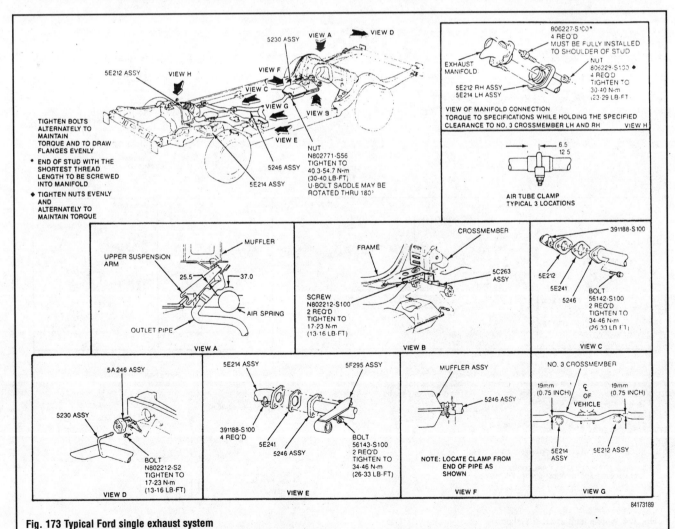

Fig. 173 Typical Ford single exhaust system

It may also be quite helpful to use solvents designed to loosen rusted bolts or flanges. Soaking rusted parts the night before you do the job can speed the work of freeing rusted parts considerably. Remember that these solvents are often flammable. Apply only to parts after they are cool!

INSPECTION

Once or twice a year, check the muffler(s) and pipes for signs of corrosion and damage. Check the hangers for wear, cracks or hardening. Check the heat shields for corrosion or damage. Replace components as necessary.

All vehicles are equipped with a catalytic converter, which is attached to the front exhaust pipe. The exhaust system is bolted together. Replacement parts are usually the same as the original system, with the exception of some mufflers.

Use only the proper size sockets or wrenches when unbolting system components. Do not tighten completely until all components are attached, aligned, and suspended. Check the system for leaks after the installation is completed.

Catalytic Converter

REMOVAL & INSTALLATION

1. Disconnect the negative battery cable. Raise and safely support the vehicle.
2. Disconnect the air injection tube from the converter, if equipped.
3. Remove the retaining bolts at each converter to the Y pipe/H pipe flange.
4. Remove the converter-to-exhaust manifold nuts.
5. Slide the pipe rearward until the catalytic converter(s) can be removed. It

may be necessary to obtain sufficient clearance to separate the converter at the manifold connection(s).

6. Discard the gasket(s) and any damaged parts.
7. Remove the heat shield(s) from the converter(s), if equipped. On vehicles with 5.0L engine, the shields are welded on.

To install:

8. Clean all gasket material from the Y pipe/H pipe flanges and the converter(s), if a replacement converter is not being installed.
9. Install the heat shield(s), if removed.
10. Position the catalytic converter(s) on the exhaust manifold and loosely install the nuts.
11. Install new gaskets between the inlet Y pipe/H pipe converter flat flanges. Position the inlet pipe flange to the converter outlet flange connections and insert new retaining bolts.
12. Alternately tighten the converter to the inlet pipe flange connection(s) to 26–33 ft. lbs. (34–46 Nm).

➡ **To provide uniform clamping, alternate tightening of the joint fasteners is required. This prevents joint distortion, a major cause of leaks and misadjustment.**

13. Align the system to the proper clearance specifications; refer to the figures.
14. Alternately tighten the manifold nuts to 16–24 ft. lbs. (22–33 Nm) on 1989 vehicles, 20–30 ft. lbs. (27–41 Nm) on 1990–91 vehicles or 26–33 ft. lbs. (34–46 Nm) on 1992–94 vehicles.
15. Connect the air injection tube to the converter, if equipped.
16. Connect the negative battery cable, start the engine and check for exhaust leaks.
17. Lower the vehicle.

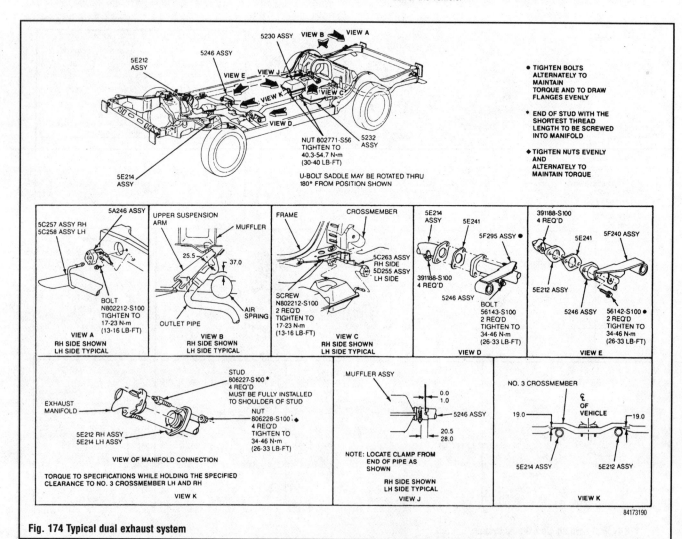

Fig. 174 Typical dual exhaust system

Muffler Inlet Y Pipe/H Pipe

REMOVAL & INSTALLATION

1. Disconnect the negative battery cable. Raise and safely support the vehicle.

2. Remove the U-bolts at the muffler inlets.

3. Remove the bolts retaining the Y pipe/H pipe inlet flanges to the converters.

4. Lower the Y pipe/H pipe until the inlet flanges clear the converter. It may be necessary to remove the support bracket-to-pipe retaining screws, to gain sufficient clearance.

5. When the Y pipe/H pipe is lowered sufficiently, separate the Y pipe/H pipe from the muffler slip joints and discard the gaskets.

6. With the muffler bracket screws removed, it may be necessary to support the muffler in position with wire.

To install:

7. Clean all gasket material from the converter outlet flanges and Y pipe/H pipe flanges.

8. Loosen the right and left converter-to-manifold retaining nuts enough to allow converter movement without binding.

9. Slide new U-bolt clamps over the outlet ends of the inlet Y pipe/H pipe. Insert the inlet pipe into the muffler slip joints and loosely secure the U-bolt clamps. The inlet pipe tab must fully engage the muffler alignment slot.

10. Install new gaskets and position the Y pipe/H pipe to the converters. Install new retaining bolts but do not tighten at this time.

11. Install the muffler support bracket retaining screws, if removed.

12. Align the system to specification; refer to the figures.

13. With the system held to alignment specification:

   a. Make sure the inlet pipe tab is fully engaged into the muffler alignment slot. Alternately tighten the U-bolt nuts to 30 ft. lbs. (40 Nm).

   b. Tighten the muffler support bracket screws to 13–16 ft. lbs. (17–23 Nm), if required. Tighten the Y pipe/H pipe-to-converter flange bolts to 26–33 ft. lbs. (34–46 Nm).

   c. Alternately tighten the right and left manifold nuts to 16–24 ft. lbs. (22–33 Nm) on 1989 vehicles, 20–30 ft. lbs. (27–41 Nm) on 1990–91 vehicles or 26–33 ft. lbs. (34–46 Nm) on 1992–94 vehicles.

14. Remove the alignment restraints and support wire.

15. Connect the negative battery cable, start the engine and check for exhaust leaks and proper alignment.

16. Lower the vehicle.

Muffler

REMOVAL & INSTALLATION

1. Disconnect the negative battery cable. Raise and safely support the vehicle so the rear axle hangs to the full extent of its travel.

➡ **This provides the necessary clearance to remove the muffler.**

2. Remove the U-bolt at the Y pipe/H pipe-to-muffler inlet connection.

3. On 1989 vehicles, remove the screws attaching the support bracket to the tailpipe. On 1990–94 vehicles, remove the rubber insulators from the muffler hangers.

4. Remove the support bracket-to-muffler retaining screws.

5. Separate the muffler from the Y pipe/H pipe and remove the muffler.

To install:

6. Slide a new U-bolt clamp over the outlet end of the inlet pipe. Install the muffler heat shield, if equipped.

7. Position the muffler on the Y pipe/H pipe and loosely install the clamp. Make sure the tab is fully inserted into the locating slot and muffler.

8. Position the tailpipe. On 1989 vehicles, install the support bracket screws and tighten to 12–18 ft. lbs. (16–24 Nm). On 1990–94 vehicles, install the rubber insulators. Replace any worn or deteriorated insulators.

9. Install the support bracket-to-muffler retaining screws and tighten to 13–16 ft. lbs. (17–23 Nm).

10. Align the exhaust system to conform to the clearance specifications in the figures.

➡ **If the specified alignment specifications cannot be obtained, loosen the right and left exhaust manifold flange nuts. After the proper clearance is obtained, retighten the nuts to 16–24 ft. lbs. (22–33 Nm) on 1989 vehicles, 20–30 ft. lbs. (27–41 Nm) on 1990–91 vehicles or 26–33 ft. lbs. (34–46 Nm) on 1992–94 vehicles.**

11. Position and alternately tighten the U-bolt clamp nuts to 30 ft. lbs. (40 Nm). Make sure the tab and slot are properly engaged.

12. Connect the negative battery cable, start the engine and check for exhaust leaks.

13. Lower the vehicle.

ENGINE REBUILDING SPECIFICATIONS CHART

Component	U.S.	Metric
Camshaft		
Lobe lift		
4.6L engine		
Intake	0.259 in.	6.589mm
Exhaust	0.259 in.	6.588mm
5.0L engine		
Intake	0.2325-0.2375 in.	5.914-6.041mm
Exhaust	0.2424-0.2474 in.	6.166-6.2931mm
5.8L engine		
Intake	0.273-0.278 in.	6.944-7.071mm
Exhaust	0.278-0.283 in.	7.071-7.199mm
Journal diameter		
4.6L engine	1.0605-1.0615 in.	26.936-26.962mm
5.0L and 5.8L engines		
No. 1	2.0805-2.0815 in.	52.927-52.947mm
No. 2	2.0655-2.0665 in.	52.540-52.566mm
No. 3	2.0505-2.0515 in.	52.159-52.184mm
No. 4	2.0355-2.0365 in.	51.777-51.802mm
No. 5	2.0205-2.0215 in.	51.395-51.421mm
Journal-to-bearing clearance		
4.6L engine	0.001-0.0047 in.	0.025-0.121mm
5.0L engine	0.001-0.006 in.	0.025-0.152mm
5.8L engine	0.001-0.006 in.	0.025-0.152mm
Endplay		
4.6L engine	0.001-0.007 in.	0.025-0.190mm
5.0L engine	0.0005-0.009 in.	0.0127-0.229mm
5.8L engine		
1989-90	0.001-0.009 in.	0.025-0.229mm
1991	0.0005-0.009 in.	0.0127-0.229mm
Cylinder block		
Cylinder bore		
Diameter		
4.6L engine	3.5512-3.5527 in.	90.200-90.239mm
5.0L engine	4.000-4.0048 in.	101.748-101.870mm
5.8L engine	4.000-4.0048 in.	101.748-101.870mm
Out-of-round service limit		
4.6L engine	0.00078 in.	0.020mm
5.0L engine	0.005 in.	0.127mm
5.8L engine	0.005 in.	0.127mm
Taper service limit		
4.6L engine	0.00024 in.	0.006mm
5.0L engine	0.010 in.	0.254mm
5.8L engine	0.010 in.	0.254mm
Hydraulic lifter bore diameter		
5.0L engine	0.8752-0.8767 in.	22.262mm
5.8L engine	0.8752-0.8767 in.	22.262mm
Hydraulic lifter diameter		
5.0L engine	0.8740-0.8745 in.	22.232mm
5.8L engine	0.8740-0.8745 in.	22.232mm
Hydraulic lifter-to-bore clearance		
5.0L engine	0.0007-0.0027 in.	0.0178-0.06867mm
5.8L engine	0.0007-0.0027 in.	0.0178-0.06867mm
Main bearing bore diameter		
4.6L engine	2.8505-2.8512 in.	72.402-72.422mm
5.0L engine	2.4412-2.4420 in.	62.096-62.117mm
5.8L engine	3.1922-3.1930 in.	81.199-81.220mm

8417321 7

ENGINE REBUILDING SPECIFICATIONS CHART

Component	U.S.	Metric
Cylinder head		
Valve stem diameter		
4.6L engine		
Intake	0.2746-0.2754 in.	6.995-6.975mm
Exhaust	0.2736-0.2744 in.	6.949-6.970mm
5.0L engine		
Intake	0.3416-0.3423 in.	8.689-8.707mm
Exhaust	0.3411-0.3418 in.	8.676-8.694mm
5.8L engine		
Intake	0.3416-0.3423 in.	8.689-8.707mm
Exhaust	0.3411-0.3418 in.	8.676-8.694mm
Valve stem-to-guide clearance		
4.6L engine		
Intake	0.0008-0.0027 in.	0.020-0.069mm
Exhaust	0.0018-0.0037 in.	0.046-0.095mm
5.0L engine		
Intake	0.0010-0.0027 in.	0.025-0.069mm
Exhaust	0.0015-0.0032 in.	0.038-0.081mm
5.8L engine		
Intake	0.0010-0.0027 in.	0.025-0.069mm
Exhaust	0.0015-0.0032 in.	0.038-0.081mm
Valve face angle		
4.6L engine	45.5°	45.5°
5.0L engine	44°	44°
5.8L engine	44°	44°
Valve seat angle		
4.6L engine	45°	45°
5.0L engine	45°	45°
5.8L engine	45°	45°
Valve seat width		
4.6L engine	0.075-0.083 in.	1.9-2.1mm
5.0L engine	0.060-0.080 in.	1.5-2.0mm
5.8L engine	0.060-0.080 in.	1.5-2.0mm
Valve spring pressure		
4.6L engine	132 lbs. @ 1.10 in.	587N @ 28.02mm
5.0L engine		
Intake	194-214 lbs. @ 1.36 in.	862-951N @ 34.59mm
Exhaust	190-210 lbs. @ 1.20 in.	845-934N @ 30.52mm
5.8L engine	195-215 lbs. @ 1.05 in.	867-956N @ 26.71mm
Valve spring free length		
4.6L engine	1.95 in.	49.55mm
5.0L engine	2.04 in.	51.89mm
5.8L engine	1.88 in.	47.82mm
Valve spring installed height		
4.6L engine		
Intake	2.05 in.	52.14mm
Exhaust	1.87 in.	47.57mm
5.0L engine	1.57 in.	40.00mm
5.8L engine		
Intake	1.75-1.80 in.	44.51-45.78mm
Exhaust	1.58-1.64 in.	40.19-41.72mm
Intake	1.75-1.80 in.	44.51-45.78mm
Exhaust	1.58-1.64 in.	40.19-41.72mm
Valve spring out-of-square limit		
4.6L engine	2°	2°
5.0L engine	0.078 in.	1.98mm
5.8L engine	0.078 in.	1.98mm

8417321 8

ENGINE REBUILDING SPECIFICATIONS CHART

Component	U.S.	Metric
Cylinder head		
Collapsed lash adjuster gap		
4.6L engine		
Desired	0.0177–0.0335 in.	0.45–0.85mm
Collapsed lifter gap		
5.0L engine		
Allowable	0.071–0.171 in.	1.81–4.35mm
Desired	0.096–0.146 in.	2.44–3.71mm
5.8L engine		
Allowable	0.092–0.192 in.	2.34–4.88mm
Desired	0.096–0.146 in.	2.44–3.71mm
Piston and connecting rod		
Piston diameter		
4.6L engine		
Coded red	3.5499–3.5509 in.	90.167–90.180mm
Coded blue	3.5503–3.5509 in.	90.180–90.193mm
Coded yellow	3.5509–3.5514 in.	90.193–90.206mm
5.0L engine		
Coded red	3.9989–3.9995 in.	101.720–101.735mm
Coded blue	4.0001–4.0007 in.	101.750–101.766mm
Coded yellow	4.0013–4.0019 in.	101.781–101.796mm
5.8L engine		
Coded red	3.9978–3.9984 in.	101.692–101.707mm
Coded blue	3.9990–3.9996 in.	101.722–101.738mm
Coded yellow	4.0014–4.0020 in.	101.784–101.799mm
Piston-to-bore clearance		
4.6L engine	0.0008–0.0018 in.	0.0203–0.0457mm
5.0L engine	0.0014–0.0022 in.	0.0356–0.0560mm
5.8L engine	0.0018–0.0026 in.	0.0458–0.0661mm
Piston pin bore diameter		
4.6L engine	0.8662–0.8663 in.	22.0015–22.004mm
5.0L engine	0.9124–0.9127 in.	23.2087–23.2163mm
5.8L engine	0.9124–0.9127 in.	23.2087–23.2163mm
Piston pin diameter		
4.6L engine	0.8659–0.8661 in.	21.994–21.999mm
5.0L engine	0.9119–0.9124 in.	23.196–23.2087mm
5.8L engine	0.9119–0.9124 in.	23.196–23.2087mm
Piston pin-to-piston clearance		
4.6L engine	0.0002–0.0004 in.	0.005–0.010mm
5.0L engine	0.0002–0.0004 in.	0.005–0.010mm
5.8L engine	0.0003–0.0005 in.	0.008–0.013mm
Ring groove width		
4.6L engine		
Top compression ring	0.0602–0.0610 in.	1.530–1.550mm
Bottom compression ring	0.0598–0.0602 in.	1.520–1.530mm
Oil ring	0.2754–0.2844 in.	6.996–7.224mm
5.0L engine		
Top compression ring	0.060–0.061 in.	1.526–1.550mm
Bottom compression ring	0.060–0.061 in.	1.526–1.550mm
Oil ring	0.1587–0.1597 in.	4.037–4.062mm
5.8L engine		
Top compression ring	0.080–0.081 in.	2.035–2.060mm
Bottom compression ring	0.080–0.081 in.	2.035–2.060mm
Oil ring	0.188–0.189 in.	4.782–4.807mm

84173219

ENGINE REBUILDING SPECIFICATIONS CHART

Component	U.S.	Metric
Piston and connecting rod		
Ring groove clearance		
4.6L engine		
Top compression ring	0.0016–0.0035 in.	0.040–0.090mm
Bottom compression ring	0.0012–0.0031 in.	0.030–0.080mm
Oil ring	Snug fit	Snug fit
5.0L engine		
Top compression ring	0.002–0.004 in.	0.051–0.102mm
Bottom compression ring	0.002–0.004 in.	0.051–0.102mm
Oil ring	Snug fit	Snug fit
5.8L engine		
Top compression ring	0.002–0.004 in.	0.051–0.102mm
Bottom compression ring	0.002–0.004 in.	0.051–0.102mm
Oil ring	Snug fit	Snug fit
Ring end gap		
4.6L engine		
Top compression ring	0.009–0.019 in.	0.23–0.49mm
Bottom compression ring	0.009–0.019 in.	0.23–0.49mm
Oil ring	0.010–0.030 in.	0.25–0.77mm
5.0L engine		
Top compression ring	0.010–0.020 in.	0.25–0.51mm
Bottom compression ring	0.010–0.020 in.	0.25–0.51mm
Oil ring	0.015–0.055 in.	0.38–1.40mm
5.8L engine		
Top compression ring	0.010–0.020 in.	0.25–0.51mm
Bottom compression ring	0.010–0.020 in.	0.25–0.51mm
Oil ring	0.015–0.055 in.	0.38–1.40mm
Connecting rod pin bore diameter		
4.6L engine	0.8645–0.8653 in.	21.959–21.979mm
5.0L engine	0.9096–0.9112 in.	23.137–23.178mm
5.8L engine	0.9096–0.9112 in.	23.137–23.178mm
Connecting rod bearing bore diameter		
4.6L engine	2.2388–2.2396 in.	56.866–56.886mm
5.0L engine	2.2390–2.2398 in.	56.953–56.974mm
5.8L engine	2.4265–2.4273 in.	61.723–61.743mm
Connecting rod center-to-center length		
4.6L engine	5.9330 in.	150.7mm
5.0L engine	5.0885–5.0915 in.	129.44–129.51mm
5.8L engine	5.945–5.9575 in.	151.22–151.54mm
Connecting rod side clearance		
4.6L engine	0.006–0.019 in.	0.15–0.50mm
5.0L engine	0.010–0.023 in.	0.25–0.58mm
5.8L engine	0.010–0.023 in.	0.25–0.58mm
Crankshaft		
Main journal diameter		
4.6L engine	2.6578–2.6598 in.	67.508–67.559mm
5.0L engine	2.2482–2.2490 in.	57.187–57.208mm
5.8L engine	2.9994–3.0002 in.	76.296–76.316mm
Main bearing oil clearance		
4.6L engine	0.0011–0.0025 in.	0.027–0.065mm
5.0L engine		
Allowable	0.0001–0.0024 in.	0.0025–0.0610mm
Desired	0.0004–0.0015 in.	0.0102–0.0381mm
5.8L engine		
Allowable	0.0008–0.0026 in.	0.0203–0.0661mm
Desired	0.0008–0.0015 in.	0.0203–0.0381mm
Connecting rod journal diameter		
4.6L engine	2.0873–2.0890 in.	53.019–53.083mm
5.0L engine	2.1228–2.1236 in.	53.997–54.018mm
5.8L engine	2.3103–2.3111 in.	58.767–58.787mm

84173220

ENGINE REBUILDING SPECIFICATIONS CHART

Component	U.S.	Metric
Crankshaft		
Connecting rod bearing oil clearance		
4.6L engine	0.0011-0.0027 in.	0.027-0.069mm
5.0L engine		
Allowable	0.0008-0.0026 in.	0.0203-0.0661mm
Desired	0.0008-0.0015 in.	0.0203-0.0381mm
5.8L engine		
Allowable	0.0007-0.0025 in.	0.0178-0.0636mm
Desired	0.0008-0.0015 in.	0.0203-0.0381mm
Crankshaft journal runout limit		
5.0L engine	0.002 in.	0.0509mm
5.8L engine	0.002 in.	0.0509mm
Crankshaft endplay		
4.6L engine	0.005-0.011 in.	0.130-0.301mm
5.0L engine	0.004-0.012 in.	0.102-0.305mm
5.8L engine	0.004-0.012 in.	0.102-0.305mm
Oil pump		
5.0L engine		
Relief valve spring tension	10.6-12.2 lbs. @ 1.70 in.	47.1-54.2N @ 43.3mm
Driveshaft-to-housing clearance	0.0015-0.0030 in.	0.0381-0.0763mm
Relief valve-to-bore clearance	0.0015-0.0030 in.	0.0381-0.0763mm
Rotor assembly end clearance	0.004 in. Max.	0.102mm Max.
Outer race-to-housing clearance	0.001-0.013 in.	0.025-0.331mm
5.8L engine		
Relief valve spring tension	18.2-20.2 lbs. @ 2.49 in.	80.9-89.8N @ 63.3mm
Driveshaft-to-housing clearance	0.0015-0.0030 in.	0.0381-0.0763mm
Relief valve-to-bore clearance	0.0015-0.0030 in.	0.0381-0.0763mm
Rotor assembly end clearance	0.004 in. Max.	0.102mm Max.
Outer race-to-housing clearance	0.001-0.013 in.	0.025-0.331mm

84173221

TORQUE SPECIFICATIONS

Component	U.S.	Metric
Camshaft cap bolts		
4.6L engine		
Step 1:	6.0-8.8 ft. lbs.	8-12 Nm
Step 2:	loosen bolts 2-3 turns	loosen bolts 2-3 turns
Step 3:	6.0-8.8 ft. lbs.	8-12 Nm
Camshaft sprocket bolt		
4.6L engine	81-95 ft. lbs.	110-130 Nm
5.0L engine	40-45 ft. lbs.	54-61 Nm
5.8L engine	40-45 ft. lbs.	54-61 Nm
Camshaft thrust plate		
5.0L engine	9-12 ft. lbs.	12-16 Nm
5.8L engine	9-12 ft. lbs.	12-16 Nm
Carburetor-to-intake manifold		
5.8L engine	12-15 ft. lbs.	16-20 Nm
Connecting rod bearing cap nuts/bolts		
4.6L engine*		
Step 1:	12 ft. lbs.	15 Nm
Step 2:	+ 85-95 degrees turn	+ 85-95 degrees turn
5.0L engine	19-24 ft. lbs.	25-33 Nm
5.8L engine	40-45 ft. lbs.	54-61 Nm
* NOTE: Use new bolts		
Crankshaft damper bolt		
4.6L engine	114-121 ft. lbs.	155-165 Nm
5.0L engine	70-90 ft. lbs.	95-122 Nm
5.8L engine	70-90 ft. lbs.	95-122 Nm
Cylinder head bolt		
4.6L engine*		
Step 1:	25-30 ft. lbs.	35-45 Nm
Step 2:	+ 85-95 degrees turn	+ 85-95 degrees turn
Step 3:	+ 85-95 degrees turn	+ 85-95 degrees turn
5.0L engine		
Step 1:	55-65 ft. lbs.	75-88 Nm
Step 2:	65-72 ft. lbs.	88-98 Nm
5.8L engine		
Step 1:	85 ft. lbs.	116 Nm
Step 2:	95 ft. lbs.	129 Nm
Step 3:	105-112 ft. lbs.	143-152 Nm
* NOTE: Use new bolts and oil the threads		
EGR valve		
4.6L engine	15-22 ft. lbs.	20-30 Nm
5.0L, 5.8L engine	15-22 ft. lbs.	20-30 Nm
EGR valve-to-spacer plate		
5.0L engine	12-18 ft. lbs.	16-24 Nm
5.8L engine	12-18 ft. lbs.	16-24 Nm
EGR supply tube		
4.6L engine	33-48 ft. lbs.	45-65 Nm
Engine-to-transmission	40 ft. lbs.	55 Nm

84173214

TORQUE SPECIFICATIONS

Component	U.S.	Metric
Engine/transmission mounts		
4.6L engine		
Front		
Mount-to-engine block	45–60 ft. lbs.	60–81 Nm
Mount through bolts	15–22 ft. lbs.	20–30 Nm
Rear		
Mount-to-transmission	50–70 ft. lbs.	68–95 Nm
Mount-to-crossmember	35–50 ft. lbs.	48–68 Nm
5.0L and 5.8L engines		
Front		
Mount-to-frame	26–38 ft. lbs.	35–52 Nm
Mount through bolts	45–65 ft. lbs.	61–88 Nm
Rear		
Mount-to-transmission	50–70 ft. lbs.	68–95 Nm
Mount-to-crossmember	35–50 ft. lbs.	48–68 Nm
Exhaust flange-to-manifold nuts		
1989	16–24 ft. lbs.	22–33 Nm
1990–91	20–30 ft. lbs.	27–41 Nm
1992–94	26–33 ft. lbs.	34–46 Nm
Exhaust manifold		
4.6L engine	15–22 ft. lbs.	20–30 Nm
5.0L engine	18–24 ft. lbs.	25–33 Nm
5.8L engine	18–24 ft. lbs.	25–33 Nm
Flywheel/flexplate-to-crankshaft bolts		
4.6L engine	54–64 ft. lbs.	75–87 Nm
5.0L engine	75–85 ft. lbs.	102–116 Nm
5.8L engine	75–85 ft. lbs.	102–116 Nm
Flywheel-to-converter bolts	20–34 ft. lbs.	27–46 Nm
Fuel pump-to-block		
5.8L engine	19–27 ft. lbs.	26–37 Nm
Fuel rail-to-intake manifold bolts	70–105 ft. lbs.	8–12 Nm
Intake manifold		
4.6L engine		
Step 1:	15–22 ft. lbs.	20–30 Nm
Step 2:	retorque when hot	retorque when hot
5.0L and 5.8L engines		
Step 1:	23–25 ft. lbs.	31–34 Nm
Step 2:	retorque when hot	retorque when hot
Intake plenum-to-lower manifold		
5.0L engine	12–18 ft. lbs.	16–24 Nm
Main bearing cap bolts		
4.6L engine*		
Step 1:	22–25 ft. lbs.	30–35 Nm
Step 2:	+ 85–95 degrees turn	+ 85–95 degrees turn
5.0L engine	60–70 ft. lbs.	81–95 Nm
5.8L engine	95–105 ft. lbs.	129–143 Nm
* NOTE: Use new bolts		
Main bearing cap jack screws/side bolts		
4.6L engine		
Screws		
Step 1:	44 inch lbs.	5 Nm
Step 2:	80–97 inch lbs.	9–11 Nm
Side bolts		
Step 1:	88 inch lbs.	10 Nm
Step 2:	14–17 ft. lbs.	19–23 Nm

84173R15

TORQUE SPECIFICATIONS

Component	U.S.	Metric
Oil pan-to-block		
4.6L engine	15–22 ft. lbs.	20–30 Nm
5.0L and 5.8L engines	10 ft. lbs.	14 Nm
Oil pan drain plug		
4.6L engine	8–12 ft. lbs.	11–16 Nm
5.0L and 5.8L engines	15–25 ft. lbs.	20–34 Nm
Oil pump attaching bolts		
4.6L engine	6.0–8.8 ft. lbs.	8–12 Nm
5.0L engine	22–32 ft. lbs.	30–43 Nm
5.8L engine	22–32 ft. lbs.	30–43 Nm
Rocker arm bolt		
5.0L engine	18–25 ft. lbs.	24–34 Nm
5.8L engine	18–25 ft. lbs.	24–34 Nm
Rocker arm (valve) cover		
4.6L engine	6.0–8.8 ft. lbs.	8–12 Nm
5.0L engine	10–13 ft. lbs.	14–18 Nm
5.8L engine		
1989–90	3–5 ft. lbs.	4–7 Nm
1991	10–13 ft. lbs.	14–18 Nm
Spark plug		
4.6L engine	7 ft. lbs.	10 Nm
5.0L engine	5–10 ft. lbs.	7–14 Nm
5.8L engine	10–15 ft. lbs.	14–20 Nm
Starter-to-block bolts	15–20 ft. lbs.	20–27 Nm
Thermostat housing		
4.6L engine	15–22 ft. lbs.	20–30 Nm
5.0L and 5.8L engine	12–18 ft. lbs.	16–24 Nm
Throttle body nuts/bolts		
4.6L engine	6.0–8.5 ft. lbs.	8.0–11.5 Nm
5.0L engine	12–18 ft. lbs.	16–24 Nm
Timing chain tensioner bolt		
4.6L engine	15–22 ft. lbs.	20–30 Nm
Timing cover		
4.6L engine	15–22 ft. lbs.	20–30 Nm
5.0L engine	15–18 ft. lbs.	20–24 Nm
5.8L engine	15–18 ft. lbs.	20–24 Nm
Water pump		
4.6L engine	15–22 ft. lbs.	20–30 Nm
5.0L engine	12–18 ft. lbs.	16–24 Nm
5.8L engine	12–18 ft. lbs.	16–24 Nm

84173216

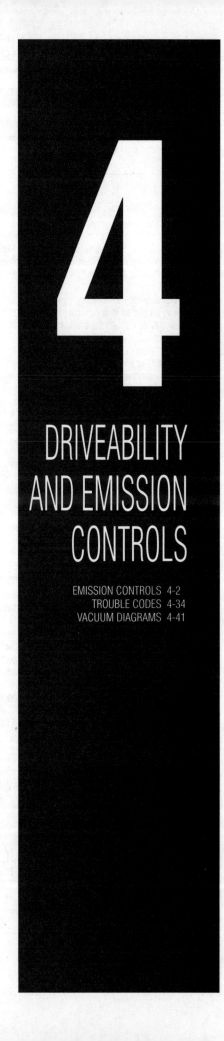

4

DRIVEABILITY AND EMISSION CONTROLS

EMISSION CONTROLS

Crankcase Ventilation System

OPERATION

▶ **See Figure 1**

Your car is equipped with a closed Positive Crankcase Ventilation (PCV) system. The PCV system vents crankcase gases into the engine air intake where they are burned with the air/fuel mixture. The PCV system keeps pollutants from being released into the atmosphere, and also helps to keep the engine oil clean, by ridding the crankcase of moisture and corrosive fumes. The PCV system consists of the PCV valve, a closed oil fill cap and the various connecting hoses.

The PCV system recycles crankcase gases as follows: When the engine is running, clean filtered air is drawn into the crankcase through the intake air filter. As the air passes through the crankcase, it picks up the combustion gases and carries them out of the crankcase, up through the PCV valve and into the intake manifold. After they enter the intake manifold, they are drawn into the combustion chamber and burned.

The most critical component of the PCV system is the PCV valve. The PCV valve regulates the amount of ventilating air and blow-by gas to the intake manifold and also prevents backfire from traveling into the crankcase, avoiding the explosion of crankcase gases. At low engine speeds, the PCV valve is partially closed, limiting the flow of gases into the intake manifold. As engine speed increases, the valve opens to admit greater quantities of gases into the intake manifold.

If the PCV valve becomes blocked or plugged, crankcase gases will not be able to escape by the normal route. Since these gases are under pressure, they will seek an alternate route, which is usually an oil seal or gasket. As the gases escape, an oil leak will be created.

Besides causing oil leaks, a clogged PCV valve will also allow gases to remain in the crankcase for an extended period, promoting the formation of sludge in the engine.

SERVICE

1. Visually inspect the PCV valve hose and the fresh air supply hose and their attaching nipples or grommets for splits, cuts, damage, clogging, or restrictions. Repair or replace, as necessary.

2. If the hoses pass inspection, remove the PCV valve from its mounting grommet. Shake the PCV valve and listen or feel for the rattle of the valve plunger within the valve body. If the valve plunger does not rattle, the PCV valve must be cleaned or replaced. If the valve plunger rattles, the PCV valve is okay; reinstall it.

3. Start the engine and bring it to normal operating temperature. Remove the fresh air supply hose from the air cleaner or air outlet tube. Place a stiff piece of paper over the hose end and wait 1 minute. If vacuum holds the paper in place, the system is okay.

4. On the 4.6L engine, the PCV system is connected with the evaporative emission system. If the paper is not held in place, disconnect the evaporative hose, cap the connector and retest as in Step 3. If vacuum now holds the paper in place, the problem is in the evaporative emission system. If not, go to Step 5.

5. If the paper is not held by vacuum, check the fresh air and PCV hoses for leaks or loose connections. Also check for a loose fitting oil fill cap or loose dipstick. Correct as required until vacuum can be felt at the end of the supply hose.

➡ **If air pressure and oil or sludge is present at the end of the fresh air supply hose, the engine has excessive blow-by and cylinder bore or piston ring wear.**

REMOVAL & INSTALLATION

PCV Valve

▶ **See Figures 2, 3 and 4**

1. Remove the PCV valve from the grommet or elbow.
2. Disconnect the hose(s) from the PCV valve and remove it from the vehicle.
3. Installation is the reverse of the removal procedure.

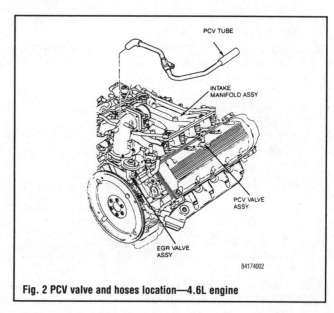

Fig. 2 PCV valve and hoses location—4.6L engine

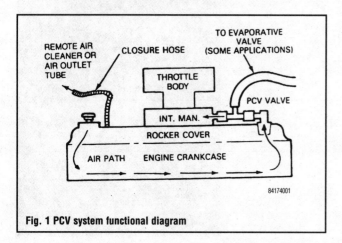

Fig. 1 PCV system functional diagram

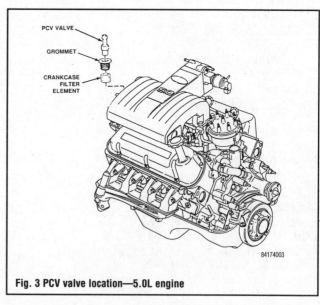

Fig. 3 PCV valve location—5.0L engine

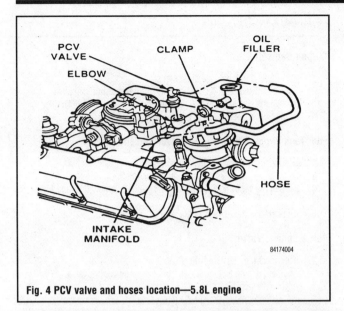

Fig. 4 PCV valve and hoses location—5.8L engine

Evaporative Emission Controls

OPERATION

▶ **See Figures 5 and 6**

The fuel evaporative emission control system prevents the escape of fuel vapors to the atmosphere.

Fuel vapors trapped in the sealed fuel tank are vented through the orifices vapor valve assembly in the top of the tank. The vapors leave the valve assembly through a single vapor line and continue to the carbon canister for storage until they are purged to the engine for burning.

On vehicles with 5.8L engine, fuel vapors from the carburetor fuel bowl are vented to the carbon canister for storage. The flow of vapors is controlled by the fuel bowl solenoid vent valve and/or fuel bowl thermal vent valve.

Purging the carbon canister removes the fuel vapor stored in the carbon canister. The fuel vapor flow from the canister to the engine is controlled by a purge solenoid or vacuum controlled purge valve. Purging occurs when the engine is at operating temperature and, in most systems, off idle.

The evaporative emission control system consists of the carbon canister, fuel tank vapor orifice and roll over valve assembly, purge control valve and/or purge solenoid valve and the pressure/vacuum relief valve. In addition, carbureted vehicles also employ a fuel bowl solenoid vent valve and/or fuel bowl thermal vent valve.

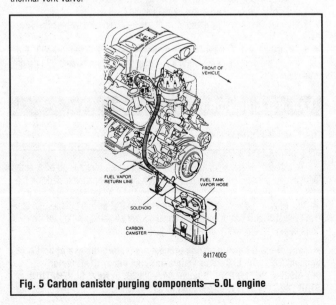

Fig. 5 Carbon canister purging components—5.0L engine

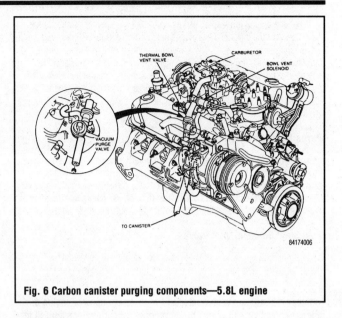

Fig. 6 Carbon canister purging components—5.8L engine

Carbon Canister

▶ **See Figure 7**

The fuel vapors from the fuel tank (and carburetor, if equipped) are stored in the carbon canister until the vehicle is operated, at which time, the vapors will purge from the canister into the engine for consumption. The carbon canister contains activated carbon, which absorbs the fuel vapor. The canister is located in the engine compartment or along the frame rail.

Fuel Tank Vapor Orifice and Rollover Valve Assembly

Fuel vapor in the fuel tank is vented to the carbon canister through the vapor valve assembly. The valve is mounted in a rubber grommet at a central location in the upper surface of the fuel tank. A vapor space between the fuel level and the tank upper surface is combined with a small orifice and float shut-off valve in the vapor valve assembly to prevent liquid fuel from passing to the carbon canister. The vapor space also allows for thermal expansion of the fuel.

Purge Control Valve

The purge control valve is in-line with the carbon canister and controls the flow of fuel vapors out of the canister.

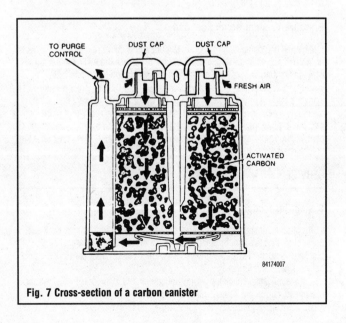

Fig. 7 Cross-section of a carbon canister

When the engine is stopped, vapors from the fuel tank and carburetor fuel bowl flow into the canister. On systems using spark port or EGR port vacuum to actuate the purge control valve, the vacuum signal is strong enough during normal cruise to open the valve and vapors are drawn from the canister to the engine vacuum connection. At the same time, vapors from the fuel tank are routed directly into the engine. On some systems where purging does not affect idle quality, the purge control valve is connected to engine manifold vacuum and opens any time there is enough manifold vacuum.

Purge Solenoid Valve

The purge solenoid valve is in-line with the carbon canister and controls the flow of fuel vapors out of the canister. It is normally closed. When the engine is shut off, the vapors from the fuel tank flow into the canister. After the engine is started, the solenoid is engaged and opens, purging the vapors into the engine. With the valve open, vapors from the fuel tank are routed directly into the engine.

Fuel Bowl Solenoid Vent Valve

The fuel bowl solenoid vent valve is located in the fuel bowl vent line on carbureted engines. The valve is open when the ignition switch is in the **OFF** position and closes when the engine is running.

➡️**If lean fuel mixture is suspected as the cause of improper engine operation, check either the solenoid vent valve or the carburetor's built-in fuel bowl vent valve to make sure they are closed when the engine is running. If the valve is open, purge vacuum will affect the fuel bowl balanced air pressure, and the carburetor will have a leaner air/fuel mixture.**

Fuel Bowl Thermal Vent Valve

The thermal vent valve is located in the carburetor-to-carbon canister vent line. The valve's function is to prevent fuel tank vapors from being vented through the carburetor fuel bowl when the engine is cold.

The valve is closed when the engine compartment is cold, blocking fuel vapors from entering the now-open carburetor fuel bowl vent, and instead routing them to the carbon canister. When the engine runs and the engine compartment warms up, the thermal vent valve opens. When the engine is turned off, the fuel bowl (or solenoid) vent valve opens, allowing fuel vapor to flow through the open thermal vent valve and into the carbon canister. The thermal vent valve closes as it cools, and the cycle repeats.

Auxiliary Fuel Bowl Vent Tube

On some carbureted vehicles, an auxiliary fuel bowl vent tube is connected to the fuel bowl vent tube to vent the fuel bowl when the internal fuel bowl vent or the solenoid vent valve is closed and the thermal vent valve is also closed. An air filter is installed on the air cleaner end of the tube to prevent the entrance of contaminants into the carburetor fuel bowl.

Pressure/Vacuum Relief Fuel Cap

The fuel cap contains an integral pressure and vacuum relief valve. The vacuum valve acts to allow air into the fuel tank to replace the fuel as it is used, while preventing vapors from escaping the tank through the atmosphere. The vacuum relief valve opens after a vacuum of −0.5 psi. The pressure valve acts as a backup pressure relief valve in the event the normal venting system is overcome by excessive generation of internal pressure or restriction of the normal venting system. The pressure relief range is 1.6–2.1 psi. Fill cap damage or contamination that stops the pressure vacuum valve from working may result in deformation of the fuel tank.

SERVICE

System Inspection

1. Visually inspect the vapor and vacuum lines and connections for looseness, pinching, leakage, or other damage. If fuel line, vacuum line, or orifice blockage is suspected as the obvious cause of a malfunction, correct the cause before proceeding further.
2. If applicable, check the wiring and connectors to the purge solenoid for looseness, corrosion, damage or other problems.
3. If all checks are okay, go to the diagnostic charts

REMOVAL & INSTALLATION

Carbon Canister

1. Disconnect the negative battery cable.
2. Label and disconnect the vapor hoses from the carbon canister.
3. Remove the canister attaching screws and remove the canister.
4. Installation is the reverse of the removal procedure.

Fuel Tank Vapor Orifice and Roll over Valve Assembly

1. Disconnect the negative battery cable.
2. Remove the fuel tank as described in Section 5.
3. Remove the vapor orifice and roll over valve assembly from the fuel tank.
4. Installation is the reverse of the removal procedure.

Purge Control Valve

1. Disconnect the negative battery cable.
2. Label and disconnect the hoses from the purge control valve.
3. Remove the purge control valve.
4. Installation is the reverse of the removal procedure.

Purge Solenoid Valve

1. Disconnect the negative battery cable.
2. Label and disconnect the hoses from the purge solenoid valve.
3. Disconnect the electrical connector from the valve.
4. Remove the purge solenoid valve.
5. Installation is the reverse of the removal procedure.

Fuel Bowl Solenoid Vent Valve

1. Disconnect the negative battery cable.
2. Label and disconnect the hoses from the fuel bowl solenoid vent valve.
3. Disconnect the electrical connector from the valve.
4. Remove the fuel bowl solenoid vent valve.
5. Installation is the reverse of the removal procedure.

Fuel Bowl Thermal Vent Valve

1. Disconnect the negative battery cable.
2. Label and disconnect the hoses from the fuel bowl thermal vent valve.
3. Remove the fuel bowl thermal vent valve.
4. Installation is the reverse of the removal procedure.

Pressure/Vacuum Relief Fuel Cap

1. Unscrew the fuel filler cap. The cap has a pre-vent feature that allows the tank to vent for the first ¾ turn before unthreading.
2. Remove the screw retaining the fuel cap tether and remove the fuel cap.
3. Installation is the reverse of the removal procedure. When installing the cap, continue to turn clockwise until the ratchet mechanism gives off 3 or more loud clicks.

Exhaust Emission Control System

GENERAL INFORMATION

The exhaust emission control system begins at the air intake and ends at the tailpipe. The exhaust emission control system includes the thermostatic air inlet system, exhaust gas recirculation system, thermactor air injection system and exhaust catalyst, as well as the electronic controls that govern the fuel and ignition system. These components combined control engine operation for maximum engine efficiency and minimal exhaust emissions.

➡️**Many of the following testing procedures require the use of breakout box tool T83L–50–EEC–IV or equivalent, and either STAR tester 007–00004, SUPER STAR II tester 007–00028, or NEW GENERATION STAR (NGS) scan tool 007–00500 or equivalents.**

DIAGNOSTIC TEST NUMBER	SOURCE COMPONENT	DIAGNOSTIC ACTION
EE1	Thermostatic Bowl Vent Valve	• At a temperature of 120°F or more, the Vacuum Vent Valve (E3EE-9G332-AA) should flow air between carburetor port and canister port when no vacuum is applied to vacuum signal nipple. It should not flow air with a vacuum applied at the vacuum signal nipple At a temperature of 90°F or less, the valve should not flow air or be very restrictive to airflow. *Vacuum/Thermostatic Bowl Vent Valve*

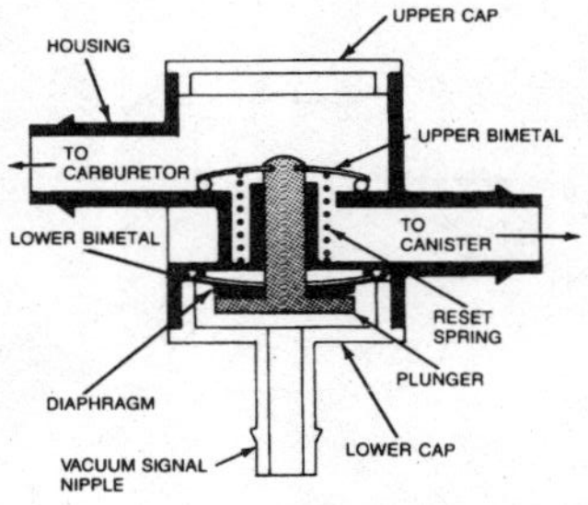

8417418

Fig. 9 Evaporative emission system diagnosis, carbureted engines

CONDITION	POSSIBLE SOURCE *	ACTION
• Cranks Normally But Slow to Start	1. Thermostatic Bowl Vent Valve or Carburetor Fuel Bowl Thermal Vent Valve malfunction.	• Go to Diagnostic Test EE1 and/or EE5.
• Rough Idle	1. Thermostatic or Vacuum Bowl Vent Valve open or leaking. 2. Canister Purge Regulator Valve open. 3. Carburetor Fuel Bowl Solenoid Vent Valve open. 4. Canister Purge Valve open or leaking.	• Go to Diagnostic Test EE1 and/or EE2. • Go to Diagnostic Test EE3. • Go to Diagnostic Test EE4. • Go to Diagnostic Test EE3.
• Surge at Steady Speed	1. Liquid fuel in Carbon Canister.	• Replace carbon canister. Check fuel tank vent system and carburetor for malfunction.
• Gas Smell	1. Thermostatic Bowl Vent Valve or Carburetor Fuel Bowl Thermal Vent Valve malfunction. 2. Blockage of Carburetor Bowl Vent line. 3. Canister Purge Regulator Valve or Canister Purge Valve malfunction. 4. Carburetor Fuel Bowl Solenoid Vent Valve malfunction. 5. Liquid fuel in Carbon Canister. 6. Fuel Tank Vent System blocked. 7. Hole or cut in Carburetor Bowl Vent Line or Fuel Tank Vent Line.	• Go to Diagnostic Test EE1 and/or EE5. • Check line for blockage and route with downhill slope to canister. • Go to Diagnostic Test EE6 and/or EE3. • Go to Diagnostic Test EE4. • Replace Canister. Check fuel tank vent system and carburetor for malfunction. • Check fuel tank vent system. • Visually inspect and replace damaged line.

* System component fault in order of occurrence.

8417418

Fig. 8 Evaporative emission system diagnosis, carbureted engines

DIAGNOSTIC TEST NUMBER	SOURCE COMPONENT	DIAGNOSTIC ACTION
EE3	Canister Purge Valve	**Important: Never apply vacuum to Port(s) C. Doing so may dislodge internal diaphram and valve will be permanently damaged.** • Application of vacuum to Port A (only) should indicate no flow. If flow occurs, replace valve. • Application of vacuum Port B (only) should indicate no flow, valve should be closed (all valves except E5VE-9B963-AA, E4VE-9B963-AA, E77E-9B963-AA, which should indicate slight flow). If valve flows (except E5VE-AA, E4VE-AA, E77E-AA), replace valve. • After applying and maintaining 54 kPa (16 in-Hg) vacuum to port A, apply vacuum to Port B. Air should pass. **NOTE: Valves E5VE-AA, E4VE-AA, E77E-AA should indicate higher flow than that indicated in above test.**

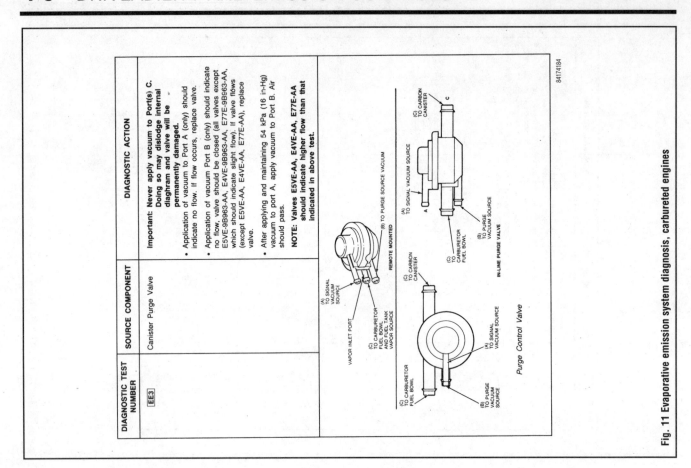

Fig. 11 Evaporative emission system diagnosis, carbureted engines

DIAGNOSTIC TEST NUMBER	SOURCE COMPONENT	DIAGNOSTIC ACTION
EE2	Vacuum Bowl Vent Valve	• The Vacuum Bowl Vent Valve (E3TE-9G332-AA) should flow air between carburetor port and canister port when no vacuum is applied to vacuum signal nipple and should not flow air with a vacuum applied at the vacuum signal nipple

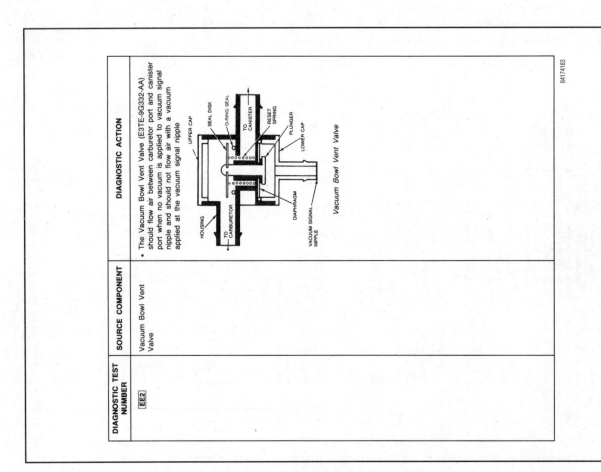

Fig. 10 Evaporative emission system diagnosis, carbureted engines

DIAGNOSTIC TEST NUMBER	SOURCE COMPONENT	DIAGNOSTIC ACTION
EE5	Carburetor Fuel Bowl Thermal Vent Valve	• Fill a container with water. While using a thermometer to measure the appropriate temperature of the water, submerse the Fuel Bowl Thermal Vent Valve (9E589) in the water for one to two minutes and try to pull air through the valve using a vacuum pump. At 90°F and below, the vent valve is fully closed and at 120°F and above, the vent valve is fully open. At temperatures between 90°F and 120°F, the valve may be open or closed

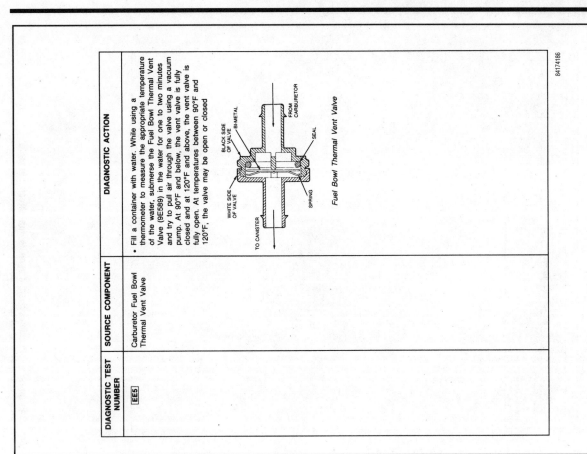

84174186

Fig. 13 Evaporative emission system diagnosis, carbureted engines

DIAGNOSTIC TEST NUMBER	SOURCE COMPONENT	DIAGNOSTIC ACTION
EE4	Carburetor Fuel Solenoid Vent Valve	• Apply 9 to 14 volts DC to the Fuel Bowl Vent Solenoid Valve (9B982). The valve should close, not allowing air to pass. If valve does not close or leaks when voltage and 1 in-Hg vacuum is applied to carburetor port, replace the valve

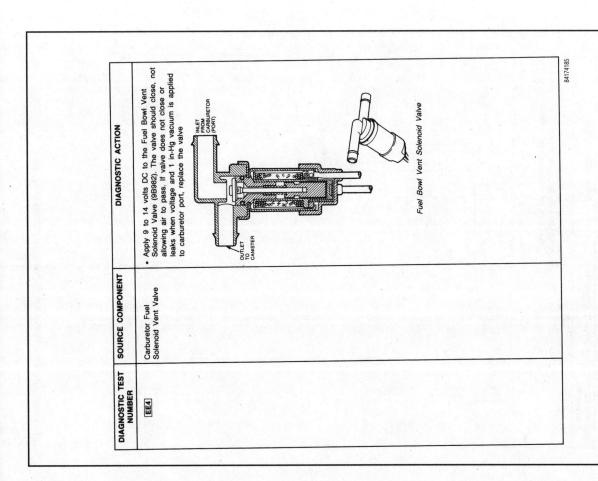

84174185

Fig. 12 Evaporative emission system diagnosis, carbureted engines

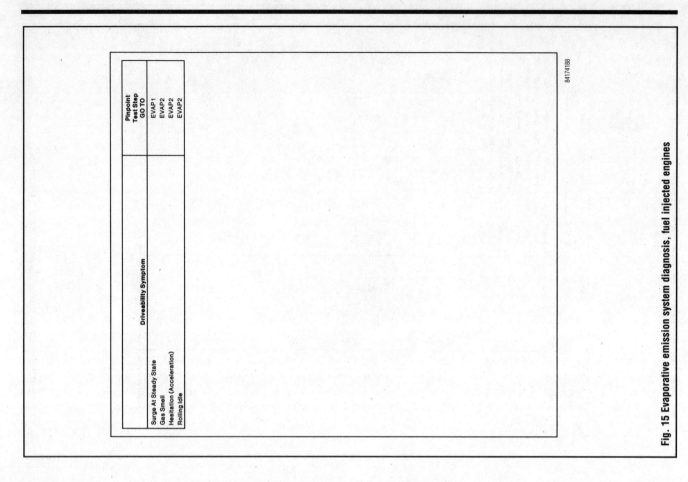

Driveability Symptom	Pinpoint Test Step GO TO
Surge At Steady State	EVAP1
Gas Smell	EVAP2
Hesitation (Acceleration)	EVAP2
Rolling Idle	EVAP2

84174188

Fig. 15 Evaporative emission system diagnosis, fuel injected engines

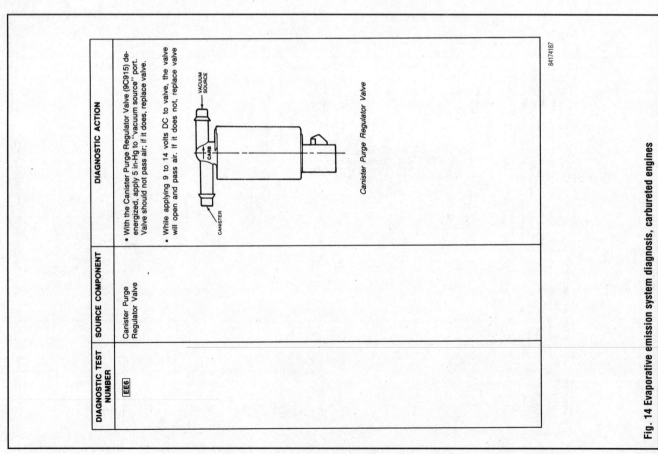

DIAGNOSTIC TEST NUMBER	SOURCE COMPONENT	DIAGNOSTIC ACTION
EE6	Canister Purge Regulator Valve	• With the Canister Purge Regulator Valve (9C915) de-energized, apply 5 in-Hg to "vacuum source" port. Valve should not pass air; if it does, replace valve. • While applying 9 to 14 volts DC to valve, the valve will open and pass air. If it does not, replace valve

Canister Purge Regulator Valve

84174187

Fig. 14 Evaporative emission system diagnosis, carbureted engines

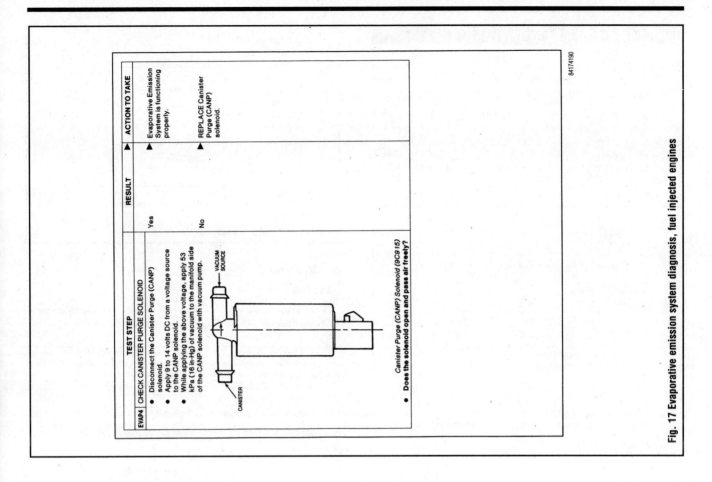

TEST STEP	RESULT		ACTION TO TAKE
EVAP4 CHECK CANISTER PURGE SOLENOID • Disconnect the Canister Purge (CANP) solenoid. • Apply 9 to 14 volts DC from a voltage source to the CANP solenoid. • While applying the above voltage, apply 53 kPa (16 in-Hg) of vacuum to the manifold side of the CANP solenoid with vacuum pump.	Yes	▲	Evaporative Emission System is functioning properly.
	No	▲	REPLACE Canister Purge (CANP) solenoid.
Canister Purge (CANP) Solenoid (9C915) • Does the solenoid open and pass air freely?			

84174190

Fig. 17 Evaporative emission system diagnosis, fuel injected engines

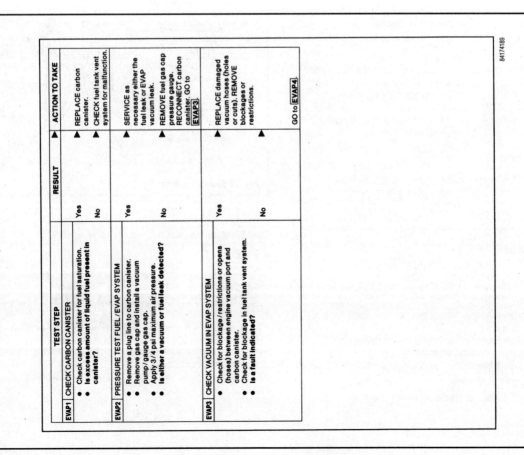

TEST STEP	RESULT		ACTION TO TAKE
EVAP1 CHECK CARBON CANISTER • Check carbon canister for fuel saturation. • **Is excess amount of liquid fuel present in canister?**	Yes	▲	REPLACE carbon canister.
	No	▲	CHECK fuel tank vent system for malfunction.
EVAP2 PRESSURE TEST FUEL / EVAP SYSTEM • Remove a plug line to carbon canister. • Remove gas cap and install a vacuum pump / gauge gas cap. • Apply 3 / 4 psi maximum air pressure. • **Is either a vacuum or fuel leak detected?**	Yes	▲	SERVICE as necessary either the fuel leak or EVAP vacuum leak.
	No	▲	REMOVE fuel gas cap and pressure gauge. RECONNECT carbon canister. GO to **EVAP3**.
EVAP3 CHECK VACUUM IN EVAP SYSTEM • Check for blockage / restrictions or opens (hoses) between engine vacuum port and carbon canister. • Check for blockage in fuel tank vent system. • **Is a fault indicated?**	Yes	▲	REPLACE damaged vacuum hoses (holes or cuts). REMOVE blockages or restrictions.
	No		GO to **EVAP4**.

84174189

Fig. 16 Evaporative emission system diagnosis, fuel injected engines

Thermostatic Air Inlet System

OPERATION

▶ **See Figure 18**

The thermostatic air inlet system is used on the 5.8L engine. The thermostatic air inlet system regulates the air inlet temperature by drawing air in from a cool air source as well as heated air from a heat shroud which is mounted on the exhaust manifold. The system consists of the following components: duct and valve assembly, heat shroud, bimetal sensor, cold weather modulator and the necessary vacuum lines and air ducts.

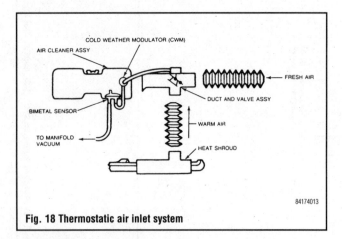

Fig. 18 Thermostatic air inlet system

Duct and Valve Assembly

The duct and valve assembly which regulates the air flow from the cool and heated air sources is attached to the air cleaner. The flow is regulated by means of a door that is operated by a vacuum motor. The operation of the motor is controlled by the bimetal sensor and cold weather modulator.

Bimetal Sensor

The core of the bimetal sensor is made of 2 different types of metals bonded together, each having different temperature expansion rates. At a given increase in temperature, the shape of the sensor core changes, bleeding off vacuum available at the vacuum motor. This permits the vacuum motor to open the duct door to allow fresh air in while shutting off full heat. The bimetal sensor is calibrated according to the needs of each particular application.

Cold Weather Modulator

The cold weather modulator modifies the vacuum signal to the duct and valve assembly vacuum motor, based on temperature calibration.

SERVICE

Duct and Valve Assembly

▶ **See Figure 19**

1. If the duct door is in the closed to fresh air position, remove the hose from the air cleaner vacuum motor.
2. The door should go to the open to fresh air position. If it sticks or binds, service or replace, as required.
3. If the door is in the open to fresh air position, check the door by applying 8 in. Hg or greater of vacuum to the vacuum motor.
4. The door should move freely to the closed to fresh air position. If it binds or sticks, service or replace, as required.

➡**Make sure the vacuum motor is functional before changing the duct and valve assembly.**

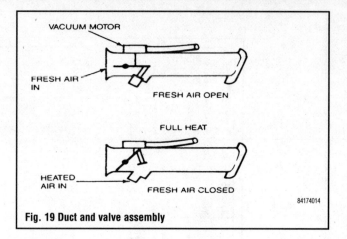

Fig. 19 Duct and valve assembly

Bimetal Sensor

▶ **See Figure 20**

1. Bring the temperature of the bimetal sensor below 75°F (24°C) and apply 16 in. Hg of vacuum with a vacuum pump at the vacuum source port of the sensor.
2. The duct door should stay closed. If not, replace the bimetal sensor.
3. The sensor will bleed off vacuum to allow the duct door to open and let in fresh air at or above the following temperatures:
   a. Brown—75°F (24°C)
   b. Pink, black or red—90°F (32.2°C)
   c. Blue, yellow or green—105°F (40.6°C)

➡**Do not cool the bimetal sensor while the engine is running.**

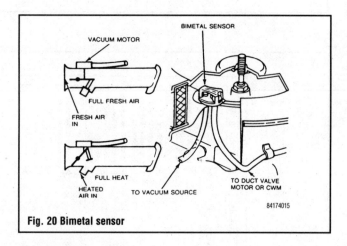

Fig. 20 Bimetal sensor

Cold Weather Modulator

▶ **See Figure 21**

1. Hold the cold weather modulator in the closed palm of your hand for about 15 minutes.
2. Check the chart in the figure for leaks using a vacuum pump at 16 in. Hg applied vacuum.
3. Place the modulator in a container of ice water for 30–40 minutes.
4. Check the chart in the figure for holding vacuum using a vacuum pump at 16 in. Hg applied vacuum.
5. Replace the cold weather modulator if it does not perform as specified.

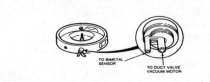

COLOR	TYPE	HOLDS	LEAKS
Black	N/O	Below −6.7°C (20°F)	Above 1.7°C (35°F)
Blue	N/O	Below 4.4°C (40°F)	Above 12.8°C (55°F)
Green	N/O	Below 10°C (50°F)	Above 24.4°C (76°F)
Yellow	N/C	Above 18.3°C (65°F)	Below 10°C (50°F)

84174016

Fig. 21 Cold weather modulator

REMOVAL & INSTALLATION

Vacuum Motor

1. Disconnect the vacuum hose from the vacuum motor.
2. Separate the vacuum motor from the vacuum operated door and remove the vacuum motor.
3. Installation is the reverse of the removal procedure.

Bimetal Sensor

1. Remove the air cleaner housing lid to gain access to the sensor.
2. Label and disconnect the vacuum hoses from the sensor. It may be necessary to move the air cleaner housing to accomplish this.
3. Remove the sensor from the air cleaner housing.
4. Installation is the reverse of the removal procedure.

Cold Weather Modulator

1. Remove the air cleaner housing lid to gain access to the modulator.
2. Label and disconnect the vacuum hoses from the modulator.
3. Remove the modulator from the air cleaner housing.
4. Installation is the reverse of the removal procedure.

Mass Air Flow Sensor

OPERATION

▶ See Figure 22

The Mass Air Flow (MAF) sensor is used on all 4.6L engines and on 1990–91 5.0L engines installed in sedans sold in California. The MAF sensor directly measures the mass of the air flowing into the engine. The sensor output

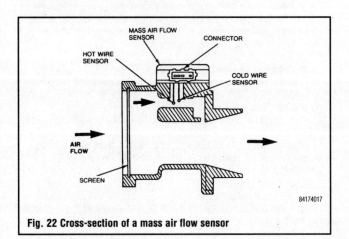

Fig. 22 Cross-section of a mass air flow sensor

is an analog signal ranging from about 0.5–5.0 volts. The signal is used by the Powertrain Control Module (PCM) to calculate the injector pulse width. The sensing element is a thin platinum wire wound on a ceramic bobbin and coated with glass. This "hot wire" is maintained at 200°C above the ambient temperature as measured by a constant "cold wire". The MAF sensor is located in the outlet side of the air cleaner lid assembly.

SERVICE

▶ See Figures 23 and 24

The wire color to test pin 50 is dark blue/orange on 1990 vehicles and light blue/red on all others. The wire color to test pin 9 is tan/light blue. The wire color to test pin 40/60 is black/light green on 1990–91 vehicles, black on 1992 vehicles and black/white on 1993–94 vehicles. The wire color to test pin 37/57 is red.

1. Service Code 26 or 159 indicates the MAF sensor is out of Self-Test range and that the MAF signal was greater than 0.7 volts during the Key On, Engine Off (KOEO) Self-Test. Key On, Engine Running (KOER) Code 26 or 159 indicates that the MAF signal was not between 0.2–1.5 volts during the KOER Self-Test. Possible causes are as follows:
   - Damaged Idle Air Control (IAC) solenoid.
   - Damaged MAF sensor.
   - MAF sensor partially connected.
   - Damaged PCM.
   - Air leaks before or after the MAF sensor.

If Code 12, 13, 411 and/or 412 is present, refer to Idle Air Control (IAC) solenoid testing. If not, go to Step 2.

2. Check VPWR circuit voltage as follows:
   a. Turn the ignition key **OFF**.
   b. Disconnect the MAF sensor.
   c. Turn the ignition key **ON**, but do not start the engine.

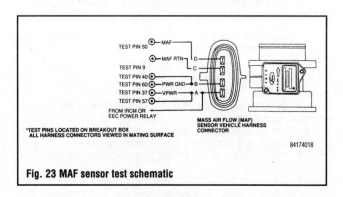

84174018

Fig. 23 MAF sensor test schematic

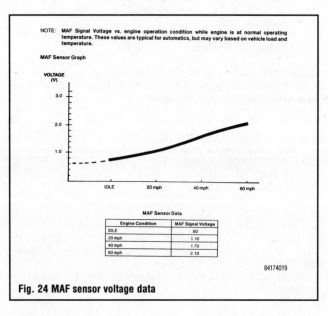

84174019

Fig. 24 MAF sensor voltage data

d. Measure the voltage between the VPWR circuit at the MAF sensor vehicle harness connector and negative battery terminal.

e. If the voltage reading is greater than 10.5 volts, go to Step 3. If it is not, service the open in the VPWR circuit and rerun the Quick Test.

3. Check the MAF sensor ground as follows:

a. Turn the ignition key **ON**, but do not start the engine.

b. Disconnect the MAF sensor.

c. Measure the voltage between the VPWR circuit and the PWR GND circuit at the MAF sensor vehicle harness connector.

d. If the voltage reading is greater than 10.5 volts, go to Step 7. If it is not, service the open in the PWR GND circuit, reconnect the MAF sensor and rerun the Quick Test.

4. Continuous Memory Code 66 or 157 indicates the MAF sensor signal went below 0.4 volts sometime during the last 80 warm-up cycles. Possible causes are:

- Poor continuity in the MAF sensor harness or connectors.
- Intermittent open or short in the MAF sensor or harness.
- Damaged MAF sensor.
- IAC system (possible closed throttle position indication).

5. Start the engine and let it idle for 5–10 minutes.

6. RUN the KOEO Self-Test.

7. If Continuous Memory Code 66 or 157 is present, go to Step 7. If it is not, go to Step 5.

8. Monitor the MAF circuit under simulated road shock as follows:

a. Turn the ignition key **OFF**.

b. Disconnect the PCM and inspect for damaged or pushed out pins, corrosion, loose wires, etc. Service as necessary.

c. Install breakout box tool T83L–50–EEC–IV or equivalent, and reconnect the PCM.

d. Connect a volt-ohmmeter between test pin 50 and test pin 9 at the breakout box.

e. Start the engine.

f. Lightly tap on the MAF sensor and wiggle the harness connector to simulate road shock.

➡**MAF voltage is normally above 0.4 volts. A sudden change down from this minimum limit indicates a fault.**

g. If a fault is indicated, disconnect and inspect the MAF sensor connector. If it is okay, replace the MAF sensor, clear Continuous Memory and rerun the Quick Test.

h. If a fault is not indicated, leave the volt-ohmmeter and PCM connected; go to Step 6.

9. Check the vehicle harness for intermittent opens or shorts as follows:

a. Turn the ignition key **ON**, but do not start the engine.

b. Connect a volt-ohmmeter between test pin 50 and test pin 9 at the breakout box.

c. Grasp the vehicle harness closest to the MAF sensor connector. Shake and bend a small section of the vehicle harness while working your way to the dash panel. Also wiggle, shake and bend the vehicle harness from the dash panel to the PCM.

d. If a fault is indicated, isolate the fault and service as necessary. Clear the Continuous Memory and rerun the Quick Test.

e. If a fault is not indicated, reconnect all components, the fault is not able to be duplicated or identified at this time.

10. Engine Running Code 72 or 129 indicates insufficient change during the Dynamic Response Test. Possible causes are:

- Open MAF circuit.
- Open VPWR circuit to MAF sensor.
- Open PWR GND circuit to MAF sensor.
- Open MAF RTN circuit to MAF sensor.
- MAF circuit shorted to ground.
- Damaged PCM.
- Damaged MAF sensor.
- Air leak before or after MAF sensor.
- MAF sensor disconnected.
- IAC system (possible closed throttle position indication).

11. Check for broken and/or loose air outlet tube clamps at the throttle body and air cleaner ends, cracks and/or holes in the air outlet tube, and worn gaskets between the MAF sensor and air cleaner.

12. If a fault is indicated, service as necessary. Reconnect all components and rerun the Quick Test.

13. If a fault is not indicated, go to Step 8.

14. Check the continuity of the MAF and VPWR circuits as follows:

a. Turn the ignition key **OFF**.

b. Disconnect the MAF sensor.

c. Disconnect the PCM and inspect for damaged or pushed out pins, corrosion, loose wires, etc. Service as necessary.

d. Install breakout box tool T83L–50–EEC–IV or equivalent, and leave the PCM disconnected.

e. Measure the resistance between the VPWR circuit at the MAF sensor vehicle harness connector and test pins 37 and 57 at the breakout box.

f. Measure the resistance between the MAF circuit at the MAF sensor vehicle harness connector and test pin 50 at the breakout box.

g. If each resistance is less than 5 ohms, go to Step 9. If not, service the open circuit, remove the breakout box, reconnect all components and rerun the Quick Test.

15. Check the MAF circuit for shorts to ground and the MAF RTN circuit as follows:

a. Turn the ignition key **OFF**.

b. Disconnect the MAF sensor.

c. Install breakout box tool T83L–50–EEC–IV or equivalent, and leave the PCM disconnected.

d. Measure the resistance between test pin 50 and test pins 9, 40 and 60 at the breakout box.

e. If each resistance is greater than 10,000 ohms, go to Step 10. If not, service the short circuit(s), remove the breakout box, reconnect all components and rerun the Quick Test.

16. Check the PWR GND circuit continuity as follows:

a. Turn the ignition key **OFF**.

b. Disconnect the MAF sensor.

c. Install breakout box tool T83L–50–EEC–IV or equivalent, and leave the PCM disconnected.

d. Measure the resistance between the PWR GND circuit at the MAF sensor vehicle harness connector and the negative battery terminal.

e. If resistance is less than 10 ohms, go to Step 11. If not, service the open circuit, remove the breakout box, reconnect all components and rerun the Quick Test.

17. Check MAF RTN circuit continuity as follows:

a. Turn the ignition key **OFF**.

b. Disconnect the MAF sensor.

c. Install breakout box tool T83L–50–EEC–IV or equivalent, and leave the PCM disconnected.

d. Measure the resistance between the MAF RTN circuit at the MAF sensor vehicle harness connector and test pin 9 at the breakout box.

e. If the resistance is less than 5 ohms, go to Step 12. If not, service the open circuit, remove the breakout box, reconnect all components and rerun the Quick Test.

18. Check MAF circuit for short to ground as follows:

a. Turn the ignition key **OFF**.

b. Disconnect the MAF sensor.

c. Install breakout box tool T83L–50–EEC–IV or equivalent, and connect the PCM to the breakout box.

d. Measure the resistance between test pin 50 and test pins 9, 40 and 60 at the breakout box.

e. If each resistance is greater than 10,000 ohms, go to Step 13. If not, replace the PCM, remove the breakout box, reconnect the MAF sensor and rerun the Quick Test.

19. Check MAF circuit output as follows:

a. Turn the ignition key **OFF**.

b. Reconnect the MAF sensor.

c. Install breakout box tool T83L–50–EEC–IV or equivalent, and connect the PCM.

d. Start the engine.

e. Measure the voltage between test pin 50 and the negative battery terminal.

f. If the voltage is 0.36–1.50 volts, go to Step 14. If not, replace the MAF sensor, remove the breakout box, reconnect the PCM and rerun the Quick Test.

20. Check MAF circuit output as follows:

a. Turn the ignition key **OFF**.

b. Reconnect the MAF sensor.

c. Install breakout box tool T83L–50–EEC–IV or equivalent, and connect the PCM.

d. Start the engine.

e. Measure the voltage between test pin 50 and test pin 9 at the breakout box.

f. If the voltage is 0.36–1.50 volts, replace the PCM, remove the breakout box and rerun the Quick Test. If not, replace the MAF sensor, remove the breakout box, reconnect the PCM and rerun the Quick Test.

21. Service Code 56 or 158 indicates the MAF sensor signal went above 4.5 volts during normal engine operation (continuous) or during the Self-Test.

➡ **Service Code 56 or 158 could be generated by foreign material blocking the MAF sensor screen causing an air flow restriction. If contaminants are found on the screen, check the air filter installation in the air cleaner housing and proper sealing of the air cleaner and tube before proceeding further.**

22. Turn the ignition key **OFF**.

23. Disconnect the MAF sensor.

24. Start the engine and let it idle for 1 minute.

25. Turn the ignition key **OFF**.

26. Run the KOEO Self-Test.

27. If Service Code 66 or 157 is present, replace the MAF sensor and rerun the Quick Test. If it is not, go to Step 16.

28. Check the MAF circuit for short to VPWR as follows:

a. Turn the ignition key **OFF**.

b. Disconnect the MAF sensor.

c. Disconnect the PCM and inspect for pushed out pins, corrosion, loose wires, etc. Service as necessary.

d. Measure the resistance between the MAF circuit and the VPWR circuit at the MAF sensor vehicle harness connector.

e. If resistance is greater than 10,000 ohms, replace the PCM, remove the breakout box, reconnect the MAF sensor and rerun the Quick Test. If not, service the short circuit, remove the breakout box, reconnect all components and rerun the Quick Test.

REMOVAL & INSTALLATION

1. Disconnect the negative battery cable.
2. Remove the air intake tube.
3. Disconnect the MAF sensor electrical connector.
4. Remove the sensor attaching screws and remove the sensor.

➡ **Inspect the MAF sensor-to-air cleaner lid gasket for any signs of deterioration. Replace the gasket, as necessary. If scraping is necessary, be careful not to damage the air cleaner lid or the MAF sensor gasket surfaces.**

5. Installation is the reverse of the removal procedure.

Manifold Absolute Pressure Sensor

OPERATION

▶ **See Figure 25**

The Manifold Absolute Pressure (MAP) sensor is used on the 5.0L engine, except on 1990–91 sedans sold in California. The MAP sensor operates as a pressure sensing disc. It does not generate a voltage, instead its output is a frequency change. The sensor changes frequency according to intake manifold vacuum; as vacuum increases sensor frequency increases. This gives the Powertrain Control Module (PCM) information on engine load. The PCM uses the MAP sensor signal to help determine spark advance, EGR flow and air/fuel ratio.

SERVICE

▶ **See Figures 26, 27 and 28**

The wire color to test pin 45 is dark blue/light green on 1989 vehicles and light green/black on 1990–91 vehicles. The wire color to test pin 46 is black/white. The wire color to test pin 26 is orange/white on 1989–90 vehicles and brown/white on 1991 vehicles.

1. Service Code 22 indicates that the MAP sensor is out of Self-Test range. The correct MAP sensor tester measurement range is 1.4–1.6 volts. Possible causes are as follows:

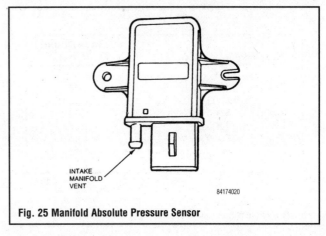

Fig. 25 Manifold Absolute Pressure Sensor

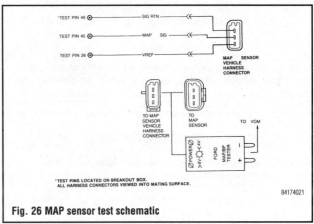

Fig. 26 MAP sensor test schematic

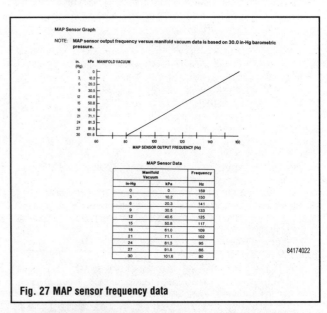

Fig. 27 MAP sensor frequency data

- MAP SIG circuit open between sensor harness connector and PCM.
- MAP SIG circuit shorted to VREF, SIG RTN or GND.
- Damaged MAP sensor.
- Vacuum trapped at MAP sensor.
- High atmospheric pressure.
- Damaged PCM.
- VREF circuit open at MAP sensor.
- SIG RTN circuit open at MAP sensor.

2. Check for power to the MAP sensor as follows:

a. Turn the ignition **OFF**.

Approximate Altitude (Ft.)	Voltage Output (±.04 Volts)
0	1.59
1000	1.56
2000	1.53
3000	1.50
4000	1.47
5000	1.44
6000	1.41
7000	1.39

84174023

Fig. 28 MAP sensor altitude/voltage output relationship

b. Disconnect the MAP sensor from the vehicle harness.

c. Connect the MAP sensor tester between the vehicle harness connector and the MAP sensor.

d. Insert the MAP sensor tester plugs into a voltmeter.

➡**The green light on the tester indicates that the VREF circuit is okay, 4–6 volts. A red light or no light, indicates the VREF is either too low or too high.**

e. Turn the ignition ON. If the green light is ON, go to Step 4. If the green light is not ON, go to Step 3.

3. Check for power at the sensor harness connector as follows:

a. Turn the ignition **ON**.

b. Connect the MAP sensor tester and the voltmeter as in Step 2.

c. Disconnect the MAP sensor.

d. If the green light comes ON, replace the MAP sensor and rerun the Quick Test. If not, check the wiring harness.

4. Check the MAP sensor output as follows:

a. Measure several known good MAP sensors on available vehicles. The measured voltage will be typical for the location on the day of testing.

b. Turn the ignition **ON**.

c. Connect the MAP sensor tester and voltmeter as in Step 2.

d. Measure the MAP sensor voltage. If the voltage is in range for the altitude shown in the figure, remove the MAP sensor tester and go to Step 5. If not, remove the tester and go to Step 6.

5. Check the MAP SIG circuit continuity as follows:

a. Turn the ignition **OFF** and disconnect the MAP sensor.

b. Disconnect the PCM connector. Check for damaged or pushed out pins, corrosion, loose wires, etc. and service, as necessary.

c. Install breakout box tool T83L–50–EEC–IV or equivalent, and leave the PCM disconnected.

d. Measure the resistance between the MAP SIG circuit at the MAP sensor harness connector and test pin 45 at the breakout box.

e. If the resistance is less than 5 ohms, replace the PCM, remove the breakout box and reconnect the MAP sensor; rerun the Quick Test. If not, service the open circuit, remove the breakout box, reconnect all components and rerun the Quick Test.

6. Check the MAP SIG circuit for shorts to VREF, SIG RTN and ground, as follows:

a. Turn the ignition **OFF** and disconnect the MAP sensor.

b. Disconnect the PCM connector. Check for damaged or pushed out pins, corrosion, loose wires, etc. and service, as necessary.

c. Install breakout box tool T83L–50–EEC–IV or equivalent and leave the PCM disconnected.

d. Measure the resistance between test pin 45 and test pins 26, 46, 40 and 60 at the breakout box.

e. If each resistance is greater than 10,000 ohms, replace the MAP sensor, remove the breakout box, reconnect the PCM and rerun the Quick Test. If not, service the short circuit, remove the breakout box, reconnect all components and rerun the Quick Test.

7. Check MAP sensor operation as follows:

a. Turn the ignition **OFF**.

b. Disconnect the vacuum hose from the MAP sensor and connect a vacuum pump in its place.

c. Apply 18 in. Hg of vacuum to the MAP sensor.

d. If the MAP sensor holds vacuum, go to Step 8. If the MAP sensor does not hold vacuum, it must be replaced; rerun the Quick Test.

8. If a Code 22 is obtained during the Engine Running Self-Test, attempt to eliminate the code as follows:

a. Turn the ignition **OFF**. Plug the MAP sensor vacuum supply hose.

b. Start the engine and run it at 1500 rpm.

c. Slowly apply 15 in. Hg of vacuum to the MAP sensor.

d. While maintaining 1500 rpm, perform the Engine Running Self-Test. If Code 22 is still present, replace the MAP sensor and rerun the Quick Test. If not, inspect the vacuum supply hose to the MAP sensor and service, as necessary. If okay, service other Engine Running Codes.

9. A Code 72 indicates that the MAP sensor output did not change enough during the Dynamic Response Test. Possible causes are as follows:

• System failed to detect partial wide-open throttle.

• MAP sensor vacuum supply hose is blocked or kinked.

• Damaged MAP sensor.

➡**The Dynamic Response Test is used on some applications to verify operation of the TP and MAP sensors during the brief Wide-Open Throttle (WOT) performed during the Engine Running Self-Test. The signal to perform the brief WOT is a single pulse or Code 10 on the STAR tester.**

10. Rerun the Engine Running Self-Test and make sure the WOT is performed during the Dynamic Response portion of the test. If Code 72 is still present, go to Step 11.

11. A Code 81 indicates that MAP sensor vacuum has not changed greater than 2 in. Hg during normal vehicle operation. This could be caused by a blocked or kinked or improperly routed MAP sensor vacuum supply hose or a MAP sensor leak. Check the vacuum hoses; if they are okay, go to Step 12. If not, service, as necessary and rerun the Quick Test.

12. Check MAP sensor operation as follows:

a. Turn the ignition **OFF**.

b. Disconnect the vacuum hose from the MAP sensor and connect a vacuum pump in its place.

c. Apply 18 in. Hg of vacuum to the MAP sensor.

d. If the MAP sensor holds vacuum, go to Step 13. If the MAP sensor does not hold vacuum, it must be replaced; rerun the Quick Test.

13. Check that vacuum to the MAP sensor decreases during Dynamic Response as follows:

a. Turn the ignition **OFF**.

b. Tee a vacuum gauge into the intake manifold vacuum supply hose at the MAP sensor.

c. Perform the Engine Running Self-Test while observing the vacuum.

d. If the vacuum decreased by more than 10 in. Hg vacuum during the Dynamic Response test, replace the MAP sensor and rerun the Quick Test. If not, check for probable causes affecting engine vacuum.

14. Continuous Memory Code 22 indicates the MAP sensor was out of self-test range. The code was set during normal driving conditions. The correct range of measurement is typically 1.4–1.6 volts. Possible causes for Continuous Memory Code 22 are as follows:

• Damaged MAP sensor.

• Damaged wiring harness.

• Damaged wiring harness connectors and/or terminals.

• Unusually high/low barometric pressures.

15. Using the Key On, Engine Off Continuous Monitor Mode, observe the volt-ohmmeter or STAR LED for indication of a fault while doing the following:

a. Connect a vacuum pump to the MAP sensor.

b. Slowly apply 25 in. Hg of vacuum to the MAP sensor.

c. Slowly bleed vacuum off the MAP sensor.

d. Lightly tap on the MAP sensor to simulate road shock.

e. Wiggle the MAP sensor connector.

f. If a fault is indicated, disconnect and check the connectors. If the connectors and terminals are good, replace the MAP sensor.

g. If a fault is not indicated, go to Step 16.

16. While still in the Key On, Engine Off Continuous Monitor Mode, observe the volt-ohmmeter or STAR LED for a fault while grasping the wiring harness closest to the MAP sensor connector. Wiggle, shake or bend a small section of the harness while working toward the dash panel and from the dash panel to the PCM. If a fault is indicated, service as necessary.

REMOVAL & INSTALLATION

1. Disconnect the negative battery cable.
2. Disconnect the electrical connector and the vacuum line from the sensor.
3. Remove the sensor mounting bolts and remove the sensor.
4. Installation is the reverse of the removal procedure.

Temperature Sensors

OPERATION

The Air Charge Temperature (ACT) and Engine Coolant Temperature (ECT) sensors change resistance according to temperature change. ACT and ECT sensor resistance decreases as the surrounding temperature increases, providing a signal to the Powertrain Control Module (PCM) that indicates either the temperature of the incoming air charge or engine coolant temperature. If the ACT or ECT sensor malfunctions, the lack of accurate temperature information could cause the PCM to provide output information resulting in an incorrect air/fuel ratio. This could cause poor vehicle performance and/or emission test failure.

SERVICE

♦ See Figures 29 and 30

The wire color to test pin 25 is light green/purple on 1989–92 vehicles and grey on 1993–94 vehicles. The wire color to test pin 46 is black/white on 1989–90 vehicles and grey/red on 1991–94 vehicles. The wire color to test pin 7 is light green/yellow on 1989–90 vehicles and light green/red on 1992–94 vehicles.

1. A Code 21 or 116 for the ECT or Code 24 or 114 for the ACT indicates that the corresponding sensor is out of Self-Test range. The correct range of measure is 0.3–3.7 volts. Possible causes are:
  • Low coolant level (ECT).
  • Ambient temperature below 50°F (10°C) (ACT).
  • Faulty harness connector.
  • Faulty sensor.
2. Start the engine and run it at 2000 rpm for 2 minutes. If the engine will not start, go to Step 5. If the engine stalls, check the Idle Air Control (IAC) system.
3. Make sure the upper radiator hose is hot and pressurized, then rerun the Quick Test. If Codes 21, 24, 114 or 116 are present, go to Step 4. If they are not, service other codes as necessary.

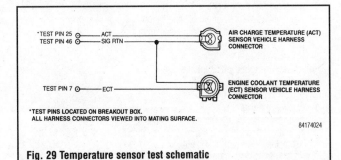

*TEST PINS LOCATED ON BREAKOUT BOX.
ALL HARNESS CONNECTORS VIEWED INTO MATING SURFACE.

84174024

Fig. 29 Temperature sensor test schematic

Temperature		Engine Coolant / Air Charge Temperature Sensor Values	
°F	°C	Voltage (volts)	Resistance (K ohms)
248	120	.27	1.18
230	110	.35	1.55
212	100	.46	2.07
194	90	.60	2.80
176	80	.78	3.84
158	70	1.02	5.37
140	60	1.33	7.70
122	50	1.70	10.97
104	40	2.13	16.15
86	30	2.60	24.27
68	20	3.07	27.30
50	10	3.51	58.75

84174025

Fig. 30 Temperature sensor data

4. Check the VREF circuit voltage at the Throttle Position (TP) sensor as follows:
  a. Turn the ignition key **OFF**.
  b. Disconnect the TP sensor.
  c. Turn the ignition key **ON**, but do not start the engine.
  d. Using a volt-ohmmeter, measure the voltage between the VREF circuit and the SIG RTN circuit at the TP sensor vehicle harness connector.
  e. If the voltage is between 4–6 volts, reconnect the TP sensor and go to Step 5. If not, check the vehicle battery power circuit.
5. Check the resistance of the temperature sensor with the engine off as follows:
  a. Turn the ignition key **OFF**.
  b. Disconnect the suspect temperature sensor.
  c. Measure the resistance between the sensor signal circuit and the SIG RTN circuit at the temperature sensor.
  d. If the resistance is within specification, check the ignition system if the suspect sensor is an ECT and the vehicle will not start, otherwise go to Step 6. If the resistance is not within specification, replace the sensor and reconnect the vehicle harness. Rerun the Quick Test.
6. Check the resistance of the temperature sensor with the engine running as follows:

→**The engine may have cooled down. Always warm the engine before taking ECT sensor resistance measurements. Check for an open thermostat.**

  a. Turn the ignition key **OFF**.
  b. Disconnect the suspect temperature sensor.
  c. Run the engine for 2 minutes at 2000 rpm.
  d. Using a volt-ohmmeter, measure the resistance between the sensor signal circuit and the SIG RTN circuit at the temperature sensor.
  e. If the resistance is within specification, replace the PCM and reconnect the vehicle harness. Rerun the Quick Test. If the resistance is not within specification, replace the sensor, reconnect the vehicle harness and rerun the Quick Test.
7. A Code 51 or 118 for the ECT or Code 54 or 113 for the ACT indicates that the corresponding sensor signal is greater than the Self-Test maximum. The maximum for ECT and ACT sensors is 4.6 volts. Possible causes are:
  • Open in the wiring harness.
  • Faulty connection.
  • Faulty sensor.
  • Faulty PCM.
8. Attempt to induce opposite Code 61 or 117, or 64 or 112, as follows:
  a. Turn the ignition key **OFF**.
  b. Disconnect the suspect temperature sensor.
  c. Connect a jumper wire between the sensor signal circuit and SIG RTN circuit at the temperature sensor vehicle harness connector.
  d. Run the Key On Engine Off Self-Test.
  e. If Code, 61, 64, 112 or 117 is present, replace the sensor, remove the jumper wire and reconnect the vehicle harness. Rerun the Quick Test. If not, remove the jumper wire and go to Step 9.
9. Check the continuity of the sensor signal and SIG RTN circuits as follows:
  a. Turn the ignition key **OFF**.
  b. Disconnect the suspect temperature sensor.
  c. Disconnect the PCM connector and inspect for damaged or pushed out pins, corrosion, loose wires, etc. Repair, as necessary.
  d. Install breakout box tool T83L–50–EEC–IV or equivalent, and leave the PCM disconnected.
  e. Measure the resistance between the sensor signal circuit at the temperature sensor vehicle harness connector and test pin 7 (ECT) or 25 (ACT) at the breakout box.
  f. Measure the resistance between the SIG RTN circuit at the temperature sensor vehicle harness connector and test pin 46 at the breakout box.
  g. If each resistance is less than 5 ohms, replace the PCM, remove the breakout box, reconnect all components and rerun the Quick Test. If each resistance is not less than 5 ohms, service the open circuits, remove the breakout box, reconnect all components and rerun the Quick Test.
10. A Code 61 or 117 for the ECT or Code 64 or 112 for the ACT indicates that the corresponding sensor's signal is less than the Self-Test minimum. The ACT and ECT sensor minimum is 0.2 volts. Possible causes are:
  • Grounded circuit in harness.

- Faulty sensor.
- Faulty PCM.
- Faulty connection.

11. Attempt to induce opposite Code 51 or 118 or Code 54 or 113 as follows:

a. Turn the ignition key **OFF**.

b. Disconnect the vehicle harness from the suspect sensor. Inspect for damaged, corroded, pushed out pins or loose wires, etc. Repair as necessary.

c. Run the Key On Engine Off Self-Test.

d. If Code 51, 54, 113 or 118 is present, replace the sensor, reconnect the harness and rerun the Quick Test. If not, go to Step 12.

12. Check the VREF circuit voltage at the TP sensor as follows:

a. Turn the ignition key **OFF**.

b. Disconnect the suspect temperature sensor.

c. Disconnect the TP sensor.

d. Turn the ignition key **ON**, but do not start the engine.

e. Measure the voltage between the VREF circuit and the SIG RTN circuit at the TP sensor vehicle sensor connector.

f. If the voltage is between 4–6 volts, reconnect the TP sensor and go to Step 13. If not, check the vehicle battery power circuit.

13. Check the temperature sensor signal circuit for short to ground as follows:

a. Turn the ignition key **OFF**.

b. Disconnect the suspect temperature sensor.

c. Disconnect the PCM connector and inspect for damaged or pushed out pins, corrosion, loose wires, etc. Repair, as necessary.

d. Install breakout box tool T83L–50–EEC–IV or equivalent, and leave the PCM disconnected.

e. Measure the resistance between test pin 7 (ECT) or 25 (ACT) and test pins 40, 46 and 60 at the breakout box.

f. If each resistance is greater than 10,000 ohms, replace the PCM, remove the breakout box, reconnect all components and rerun the Quick Test. If each resistance is not greater than 10,000 ohms, service the short circuit, remove the breakout box, reconnect all components and rerun the Quick Test.

14. Continuous Memory Codes 51 or 118 (ECT) and 54 or 113 (ACT) indicate that the sensor signal was greater than the Self-Test maximum of 4.6 volts. Continuous Memory Codes 61 or 117 (ECT) and 64 or 112 (ACT) indicate that the sensor signal was less than the Self-Test minimum of 0.2 volts. The code was generated under normal driving conditions. Possible causes are:

- Faulty sensor.
- Open circuit in harness.
- Grounded circuit in harness.
- Faulty PCM.

15. Check the sensor as follows:

a. Enter the Key On Engine Off continuous monitor mode.

b. Observe the volt-ohmmeter or STAR LED for indication of a fault while tapping on the sensor to simulate road shock.

c. Observe the volt-ohmmeter or STAR LED for indication of a fault while wiggling the sensor connector.

d. If a fault is indicated, disconnect and inspect the connectors. If they are okay, replace the sensor and clear the Continuous Memory. Rerun the Quick Test. If a fault is not indicated, go to Step 16.

16. While still in the Key On Engine Off continuous monitor mode, observe the volt-ohmmeter or STAR LED for fault indication while wiggling, shaking or bending small sections of the EEC-IV system vehicle harness from the sensor to the PCM. If a fault is indicated, repair as necessary, clear Continuous Memory and rerun the Quick Test. If a fault is not indicated, go to Step 17.

17. Check the PCM and vehicle harness connectors for damage, loose or pushed out pins, loose or poorly crimped wires. Service as necessary.

18. A Continuous Memory Code 338 or 339 indicates a cooling system problem. Check the thermostat, water pump, radiator cap and radiator. Check for low coolant level and check for coolant leaks.

REMOVAL & INSTALLATION

1. Disconnect the negative battery cable.
2. Disconnect the electrical connector from the sensor.
3. If replacing the engine coolant temperature sensor, drain the cooling system, as necessary.
4. Remove the sensor.
5. Installation is the reverse of the removal procedure.

Idle Air Control Solenoid

OPERATION

♦ **See Figure 31**

The Idle Air Control (IAC) solenoid is used on all fuel injected engines. It is used to control engine idle speed and dashpot functions. The IAC solenoid is mounted on the throttle body and allows air to bypass the throttle plate. The amount of air allowed to bypass is determined by the Powertrain Control Module (PCM) and controlled by a duty cycle.

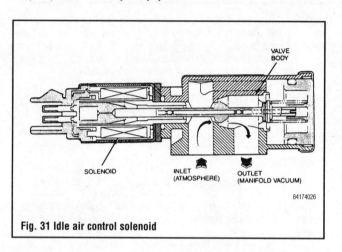

Fig. 31 Idle air control solenoid

SERVICE

♦ **See Figure 32**

The wire color to test pin 21 is white/light blue. The wire color to test pin 37 and 57 is red.

1. Service Code 12 or 412 indicates that during the Engine Running Self-Test, engine rpm could not be controlled within the Self-Test upper limit band. Possible causes are:

- Open or shorted circuit.
- Throttle linkage binding.
- Improper idle airflow set.
- Throttle body/IAC solenoid contamination.
- Items external to Idle Air Control system that could affect engine rpm.
- Damaged IAC solenoid.
- Damaged PCM.

2. Check for rpm drop as follows:

a. Turn the ignition key **OFF**.

b. Connect a tachometer to the engine.

c. Start the engine.

d. Disconnect the IAC harness connector.

e. If the rpm drops or the engine stalls, go to Step 3. If not, go to Step 4.

3. Check for EGR codes. If Codes 31 or 327, 32 or 326, 328, 33 or 332, 34 or 336, 334, 232 or 213 are present, reconnect the IAC solenoid and service the appropriate system to eliminate the code(s). If not, go to Step 4.

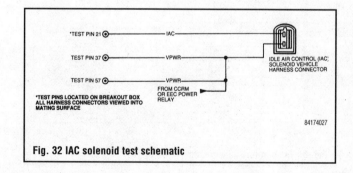

Fig. 32 IAC solenoid test schematic

4. Check for other EEC codes. If Codes 22 or 126, 41 or 172, 42 or 173, 91 or 136, or 92 or 137 are present, reconnect the IAC solenoid and service the appropriate system to eliminate the code(s). If not, go to Step 5.

5. Measure IAC solenoid resistance as follows:
   a. Turn the ignition key **OFF**.
   b. Disconnect the IAC solenoid.
   c. Measure the IAC solenoid resistance.

➥**Due to the diode in the solenoid, place the ohmmeter positive lead on the VPWR pin and the negative lead on the IAC pin.**

   d. If the resistance is 6–13 ohms, go to Step 6. If not, replace the IAC solenoid and rerun the Quick Test.

6. Check for internal short to the IAC solenoid case as follows:
   a. Turn the ignition key **OFF**.
   b. Disconnect the IAC solenoid.
   c. Measure the resistance from either IAC solenoid pin to the IAC housing.
   d. If the resistance is greater than 10,000 ohms, go to Step 7. If not, replace the IAC solenoid and rerun the Quick Test.

7. Check the VPWR circuit voltage as follows:
   a. Turn the ignition key **ON**, but do not start the engine.
   b. Disconnect the IAC solenoid.
   c. Measure the voltage between the VPWR circuit at the IAC solenoid vehicle harness connector and battery ground.
   d. If the voltage is greater than 10.5 volts, go to Step 8. If not, service the open circuit and rerun the Quick Test.

8. Check IAC circuit continuity as follows:
   a. Turn the ignition key **OFF** and disconnect the IAC solenoid.
   b. Disconnect the PCM and inspect both 60 pin connectors for damaged or pushed out pins, corrosion, loose wires, etc. and service, as necessary.
   c. Install breakout box tool T83L–50–EEC–IV or equivalent, and leave the PCM disconnected.
   d. Measure the resistance between test pin 21 at the breakout box and the IAC circuit at the IAC solenoid vehicle harness connector.
   e. If the resistance is less than 5 ohms, go to Step 9. If not, service the open circuit, remove the breakout box and reconnect all components; rerun the Quick Test.

9. Check the IAC circuit for short to ground as follows:
   a. Turn the ignition key **OFF** and disconnect the IAC solenoid.
   b. Install breakout box tool T83L–50–EEC–IV or equivalent, and leave the PCM disconnected.
   c. Measure the resistance between test pin 21 and test pins 40, 46 and 60 at the breakout box.
   d. If each resistance is greater than 10,000 ohms, go to Step 10. If not, service the short circuit, remove the breakout box and reconnect all components; rerun the Quick Test.

10. Check the IAC circuit for short to power as follows:
   a. Turn the ignition key **OFF** and disconnect the IAC solenoid.
   b. Install breakout box tool T83L–50–EEC–IV or equivalent, and leave the PCM disconnected.
   c. Turn the ignition key **ON**.
   d. Measure the voltage between test pin 21 at the breakout box and chassis ground.
   e. If the voltage is less than 1 volt, go to Step 11. If not, service the short circuit, remove the breakout box and reconnect all components. Rerun the Quick Test. If code or symptom is still present, replace the PCM.

11. Check for IAC signal from the PCM as follows:
   a. Turn the ignition key **OFF**.
   b. Install breakout box tool T83L–50–EEC–IV or equivalent, and reconnect the PCM to the breakout box.
   c. Reconnect the IAC solenoid.
   d. Connect a volt-ohmmeter between test pin 21 and test pin 40 at the breakout box.
   e. Start the engine and slowly increase engine speed to 3000 rpm.
   f. If the voltage reading is 3–11.5 volts, go to Step 12. If not, remove the IAC solenoid and make sure it is not stuck open. If it is okay, replace the PCM and remove the breakout box; rerun the Quick Test.

12. Check engine idle speed. If engine idle speed appears normal, remove the IAC solenoid and inspect it for contamination. If there is contamination, replace the IAC solenoid and rerun the Quick Test.

13. If engine idle speed does not appear normal, reset the idle airflow to specification. If unable to set idle to specification, go to Step 14.

14. Check for problems affecting proper engine speed, such as binding throttle and/or cruise control linkage, contaminated throttle body, engine vacuum hoses and leaks around the IAC solenoid. If all checks out okay, remove the IAC solenoid and inspect it for contamination. If there is contamination, replace the IAC solenoid and rerun the Quick Test. If any of the problems exist, service as necessary, remove the breakout box and reconnect the PCM; rerun the Quick Test.

15. Code 13 or 411 indicates that during the Engine Running Self-Test, engine rpm could not be controlled within the Self-Test lower limit band. Possible causes are:
   • Improper idle airflow set.
   • Vacuum leaks.
   • Throttle linkage binding.
   • Throttle plates open.
   • Improper ignition timing (distributor ignition only).
   • Throttle body/IAC solenoid contamination.
   • IAC circuit short to ground.
   • Damaged IAC solenoid.

16. If engine idle speed appears normal, remove the IAC solenoid and inspect it for contamination. If there is contamination, replace the IAC solenoid and rerun the Quick Test.

17. If engine idle speed does not appear normal, reset the idle airflow to specification. If unable to set to specification, go to Step 18.

18. Check for conditions affecting idle as follows:
   a. Check engine vacuum hoses for leaks.
   b. Check throttle and/or cruise control linkage for binding.
   c. Check that throttle plates are closed.
   d. Check for induction system leaks. Check the IAC solenoid-to-throttle body gasket, EGR flange gasket, loose IAC/EGR/PCV, etc.
   e. Check the throttle body for contamination.
   f. Make sure the base timing is set to specification (distributor ignition only).
   g. Make sure the purge solenoid is not stuck open.
   h. If all of the above checks are okay, go to Step 19. If not, service as necessary and rerun the Quick Test.

19. Check for internal short to IAC solenoid case as follows:
   a. Turn the ignition key **OFF** and disconnect the IAC solenoid.
   b. Measure the resistance from either IAC solenoid pin to the IAC solenoid housing.
   c. If the resistance is greater than 10,000 ohms, go to Step 20. If not, replace the IAC solenoid and rerun the Quick Test.

20. Check the IAC circuit for short to ground as follows:
   a. Turn the ignition key **OFF** and disconnect the IAC solenoid.
   b. Disconnect the PCM connector and inspect for damaged or pushed out pins, corrosion, loose wires, etc. and service as necessary.
   c. Install breakout box tool T83L–50–EEC–IV or equivalent, and leave the PCM disconnected.
   d. Measure the resistance between test pin 21 and test pins 40, 46 and 60 at the breakout box.
   e. If all resistances are greater than 10,000 ohms, go to Step 21. If not, service the short circuit, remove the breakout box and reconnect all components; rerun the Quick Test.

21. Check PCM output as follows:
   a. Turn the ignition key **OFF**.
   b. Install breakout box tool T83L–50–EEC–IV or equivalent, and reconnect the PCM to the breakout box.
   c. Reconnect the IAC solenoid.
   d. Connect a volt-ohmmeter between test pin 21 and test pin 40 at the breakout box.
   e. Start the engine and slowly increase engine speed to 3000 rpm.
   f. If the voltage reading is 3–11.5 volts, remove the IAC solenoid and inspect for contamination. If contamination is present, replace IAC solenoid.
   g. If voltage reading is not 3–11.5 volts, replace PCM and remove breakout box. Rerun Quick Test.

REMOVAL & INSTALLATION

▶ **See Figure 33**

1. Disconnect the negative battery cable.
2. Disconnect the IAC solenoid connector.

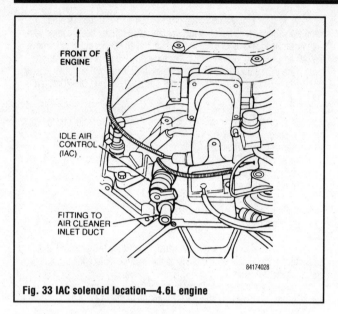

Fig. 33 IAC solenoid location—4.6L engine

3. Remove the 2 retaining bolts and remove the IAC solenoid and gasket from the throttle body.

4. Installation is the reverse of the removal procedure. Use a new gasket and tighten the retaining bolts to 71–97 inch lbs. (8–11 Nm).

➡**If scraping is necessary to remove old gasket material, be careful not to damage the IAC solenoid or the throttle body gasket surfaces or drop material into the throttle body.**

Throttle Position Sensor

OPERATION

The Throttle Position (TP) sensor is used on all fuel injected engines. The TP sensor is a rotary potentiometer that is attached to the throttle shaft blade. As the TP sensor is rotated by the throttle shaft blade, the Powertrain Control Module (PCM) determines 4 operating modes from the TP signal: closed throttle, part throttle, wide open throttle and throttle angle rate.

The PCM uses the TP signal to control spark advance, EGR flow, air/fuel mixture, A/C clutch wide open throttle cutout and thermactor air flow.

SERVICE

♦ **See Figures 34 and 35**

The wire color to test pin 46 is black/white on 1989–90 vehicles and grey/red on 1991–94 vehicles. The wire color to test pin 47 is dark green/light green on 1989–90 vehicles and grey/white on 1991–94 vehicles. The wire color to test pin 26 is orange/white on 1989–90 vehicles and brown/white on 1991–94 vehicles.

1. An Engine Running Code 23 or 121 indicates that the TP sensor's rotational setting may be out of Self-Test range. Possible causes are:
- Binding throttle linkage.
- TP sensor may not be seated properly.
- Damaged TP sensor.
- Damaged PCM.

2. Check for a Code 31 or 327 in the Key On Engine Running Self-Test. If Code 31 or 327 is present along with Code 23 or 121, service must be performed to eliminate Code 31 or 327. If Code 31 or 327 is not present with Code 23 or 121, go to Step 3.

3. Visually inspect the throttle body and throttle linkage for binding or sticking. Make sure the throttle linkage is at mechanical closed throttle. Check for binding throttle or cruise control linkage, vacuum line/wiring harness interference, etc. If the throttle moves freely and returns to the closed throttle position, go to Step 4. If not, service as necessary and rerun the Quick Test.

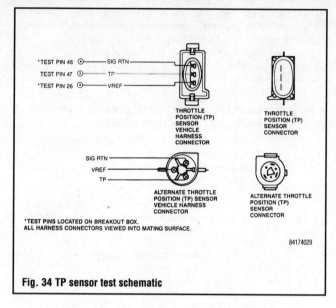

Fig. 34 TP sensor test schematic

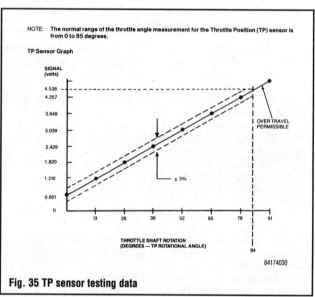

Fig. 35 TP sensor testing data

4. A Code 53 or 123 indicates that the TP sensor signal is greater than the Self-Test maximum value. Possible causes are:
- TP sensor may not be seated properly (tightened down).
- Damaged TP sensor.
- Short to power in harness.
- Damaged PCM.

5. Attempt to generate Code 63 or 122 as follows:
   a. Turn the ignition key **OFF**.
   b. Disconnect the TP sensor and inspect for pushed out pins, corrosion and loose wires. Service as necessary.
   c. Rerun the Key On Engine Off Self-Test. If Code 63 or 122 is present (ignore all other codes), go to Step 6. If not, go to Step 7.

6. Check VREF circuit voltage as follows:
   a. Turn the ignition key **OFF**.
   b. Disconnect the TP sensor.
   c. Turn the ignition key **ON**, but leave the engine off.
   d. Measure the voltage between the VREF circuit and the SIG RTN circuit at the TP sensor vehicle harness connector.
   e. If the voltage reading is 4–6 volts, replace the TP sensor and rerun the Quick Test.
   f. If the voltage reading is not 4–6 volts, reconnect all components and check reference voltage.

7. Check the TP circuit for shorts to power as follows:

a. Turn the ignition key **OFF** and disconnect the TP sensor.

b. Disconnect the PCM connector and inspect for damaged or pushed out pins, corrosion, loose wires, etc. and service as necessary.

c. Install breakout box tool T83L–50–EEC–IV or equivalent, and leave the PCM disconnected.

d. Measure the resistance between test pin 47 and test pins 26 and 57 at the breakout box.

e. If each resistance is greater than 10,000 ohms, replace the PCM, remove the breakout box, reconnect the TP sensor and rerun the Quick Test. If each resistance is not greater than 10,000 ohms, service the short circuit, remove the breakout box, reconnect all components and rerun the Quick Test.

8. Code 63 or 122 indicates that the TP sensor signal is less than the Self-Test minimum value. Possible causes are:
- TP sensor not seated properly (tightened down).
- Damaged TP sensor.
- Open harness.
- Grounded harness.
- Damaged PCM.

9. Attempt to generate Code 23 or 121, or Code 53 or 123 as follows:

a. Turn the ignition key **OFF**.

b. Disconnect the TP sensor and check for pushed out pins, corrosion, loose wires, etc. and service as necessary.

c. Connect a jumper wire between the VREF circuit and the TP circuit at the TP sensor vehicle harness connector.

d. Perform the Key On Engine Off Self-Test.

e. If no codes are generated, immediately remove the jumper wire and go to Step 12.

f. If Code 23 or 121 or Code 53 or 123 is present (ignore all other codes), replace the TP sensor and remove the jumper wire; rerun the Quick Test. If the specified codes are not present, remove the jumper wire and go to Step 10.

10. Check VREF circuit voltage as follows:

a. Turn the ignition key **OFF** and disconnect the TP sensor.

b. Turn the ignition key **ON** but do not start the engine.

c. Measure the voltage between the VREF circuit and the SIG RTN circuit at the TP sensor vehicle harness connector.

d. If the voltage reading is 4–6 volts, go to Step 11. If not, reconnect all components and check reference voltage.

11. Check TP circuit continuity as follows:

a. Turn the ignition key **OFF** and disconnect the TP sensor.

b. Disconnect the PCM connector and inspect for damaged or pushed out pins, corrosion, loose wires, etc. and service as necessary.

c. Install breakout box tool T83L–50–EEC–IV or equivalent, and leave the PCM disconnected.

d. Measure the resistance between the TP circuit at the TP sensor vehicle harness connector and test pin 47 at the breakout box.

e. If the resistance is less than 5 ohms, go to Step 12. If not, service the open circuit, remove the breakout box, reconnect all components and rerun the Quick Test.

12. Check the TP circuit for shorts to ground as follows:

a. Turn the ignition key **OFF** and disconnect the TP sensor.

b. Disconnect the PCM connector and inspect for damaged or pushed out pins, corrosion, loose wires, etc. and service as necessary.

c. Install breakout box tool T83L–50–EEC–IV or equivalent, and leave the PCM disconnected.

d. Measure the resistance between test pin 47 and test pins 40, 46 and 60 at the breakout box.

e. If each resistance is greater than 10,000 ohms, replace the PCM, remove the breakout box, reconnect all components and rerun the Quick Test. If each resistance is not greater than 10,000 ohms, service the short circuit, remove the breakout box, reconnect all components and rerun the Quick Test.

13. An Engine Running Code 73 or 167 indicates that the TP sensor did not exceed 25 percent of its rotation during the Dynamic Response test.

➡The Dynamic Response Test is used on some applications to verify operation of the TP, MAF and MAP sensors during the brief Wide-Open Throttle (WOT) performed during the Engine Running Self-Test. The signal to perform the brief WOT is a single pulse or 10 Code on the STAR tester.

14. Run the Key On Engine Running Self-Test and make sure a complete WOT is performed during the Dynamic Response portion of the test. If Code 73

or 167 is still present, go to Step 15. If not, service other Engine Running codes as necessary, otherwise testing is completed.

15. Check TP sensor movement during the Dynamic Response test as follows:

a. Turn the ignition key **OFF**.

b. Disconnect the PCM connector and inspect for damaged or pushed out pins, corrosion, loose wires, etc. and service as necessary.

c. Install breakout box tool T83L–50–EEC–IV or equivalent, and connect the PCM to the breakout box.

d. Connect a voltmeter to test pin 47 and test pin 46 at the breakout box.

e. Rerun the Engine Running Self-Test with a proper WOT Dynamic Response portion of the test.

f. If the voltage increases to greater than 3.5 volts during the Dynamic Response test, replace the PCM and remove the breakout box; rerun the Quick Test. If the voltage does not increase to greater than 3.5 volts, make sure the TP sensor is properly installed on the throttle body; if it is, replace the TP sensor and rerun the Quick Test.

16. Check the TP circuit under simulated road shock as follows:

a. Enter the Key On Engine Off Continuous Monitor mode.

b. Connect a volt-ohmmeter or STAR LED to the STO.

c. Observe the volt-ohmmeter or STAR LED for an indication of a fault while: moving the throttle slowly to the WOT position, releasing the throttle slowly to the closed position and lightly tapping on the TP sensor, and wiggling the TP harness connector.

d. If the volt-ohmmeter or STAR LED indicates a fault, go to Step 17. If not, go to Step 18.

17. Measure the TP signal voltage while exercising the TP sensor as follows:

a. Turn the ignition key **OFF**.

b. Disconnect the PCM connector and inspect for damaged or pushed out pins, corrosion, loose wires, etc. and service as necessary.

c. Install breakout box tool T83L–50–EEC–IV or equivalent, and connect the PCM to the breakout box.

d. Leave the volt-ohmmeter or STAR LED connected to the STO as in Step 16.

e. Connect a voltmeter from test pin 47 to test pin 46 at the breakout box.

f. Turn the ignition key **ON**, but do not start the engine.

g. While observing the voltmeter, repeat Step 16.

h. If the fault occurs below 4.25 volts, disconnect and inspect the connectors. If the connector and terminals are good, replace the TP sensor and clear Continuous Memory. Rerun the Quick Test.

i. If the fault does not occur below 4.25 volts, TP sensor overtravel may have caused Continuous Memory Code 53 or 123. Check the vehicle wiring harness and go to Step 18.

18. While still in the Key On Engine Off Continuous Monitor mode, observe the volt-ohmmeter or STAR LED for a fault indication while wiggling, shaking, or bending a small section of the EEC harness while working towards the dash panel to the PCM. If a fault is indicated, service as necessary, clear Continuous Memory and rerun the Quick Test. If a fault is not indicated, go to Step 19.

19. Check the PCM and vehicle harness connectors for damage, loose or pushed out pins, loose or poorly crimped wires. Service as necessary.

REMOVAL & INSTALLATION

♦ **See Figures 36 and 37**

1. Disconnect the negative battery cable.
2. Disconnect the TP sensor connector.
3. Scribe a reference mark across the edge of the sensor and the throttle body so the sensor can be reinstalled in the same position.
4. Remove the TP sensor retaining screws and remove the sensor.

To install:

5. The TP sensor bushing, if present, must be reused. Install the bushing with the larger diameter facing outward.
6. Install the TP sensor on the throttle shaft and rotate the TP sensor 10–20 degrees counterclockwise to align the screw holes.
7. Install the 2 TP sensor retaining screws and tighten to 11–16 inch lbs. (1.2–1.8 Nm).
8. Cycle the throttle lever to WOT; it should return without interference.
9. Connect the TP sensor connector and connect the negative battery cable.

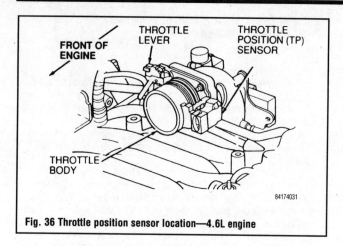

Fig. 36 Throttle position sensor location—4.6L engine

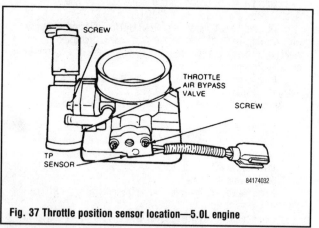

Fig. 37 Throttle position sensor location—5.0L engine

Exhaust Gas Oxygen Sensor

OPERATION

The Heated Exhaust Gas Oxygen (HEGO) sensor is used on all fuel injected vehicles. The HEGO sensor detects the presence of oxygen in the exhaust and produces a variable voltage between 0 and 1.1 volts, according to the amount of oxygen detected. A high concentration of oxygen (lean air/fuel ratio) produces a low voltage signal, less than 0.4 volts. A low concentration of oxygen (rich air/fuel ratio) produces a high voltage signal, greater than 0.6 volts.

The Powertrain Control Module (PCM) uses the HEGO sensor signal to achieve a near stoichiometric air/fuel ratio of 14.7:1 during closed loop engine operation.

SERVICE

▶ **See Figures 38 and 39**

In the figure, the wire color to test pin 44 is grey/light blue, the wire color to test pin 46 is grey/red, and the wire color to test pin 43 is red/black.

1. If the HEGO is always lean, slow to switch or lack of switching; fuel at adaptive limit, possible causes are:
- Moisture inside the HEGO sensor/harness connector resulting in a short to ground.
- HEGO sensor being coated with contaminants.
- HEGO circuit open.
- HEGO circuit shorted to ground.
2. Check HEGO integrity as follows:
   a. Turn the ignition **OFF**.
   b. Inspect the HEGO harness for chaffing, burns or other indications of damage and service, as necessary.
   c. Inspect the HEGO sensor and connector for indication of submerging in water, oil, coolant, etc. Service as necessary.

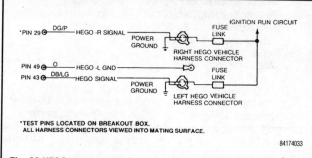

Fig. 38 HEGO sensor test schematic—all 1989–90 vehicles and 1991 non MAF sensor equipped vehicles

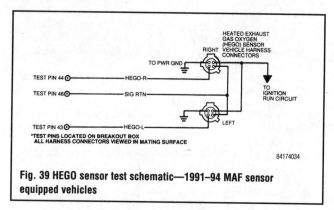

Fig. 39 HEGO sensor test schematic—1991–94 MAF sensor equipped vehicles

   d. Start the engine and run it at 2000 rpm for 2 minutes.
   e. Turn the ignition **OFF**.
   f. Run the Engine Running Self Test.
   g. If any fault codes are present and the engine is equipped with a MAP sensor, go to Step 3. If any fault codes are present and the engine is equipped with a MAF sensor, go to Step 4. If no fault codes are present, go to Step 9.
3. Check the HEGO sensor on engines equipped with MAP sensors as follows:

➡**Vacuum/air leaks could cause Code 41, 91, 136, 172 or 176. Check for: leaking vacuum actuator, engine sealing, EGR system, PCV system or lead contaminated HEGO sensor.**

   a. Turn the ignition **OFF**.
   b. Make sure the MAP sensor output voltage is in range for the vehicle's altitude.
   c. Disconnect the appropriate HEGO sensor from the vehicle harness. If equipped with a 4-wire HEGO, connect a volt-ohmmeter to HEGO SIGNAL and HEGO GND or SIG RTN at the HEGO sensor connector. If equipped with a 3-wire HEGO, connect the volt-ohmmeter to HEGO SIGNAL at the sensor and negative battery post.
   d. Disconnect and plug the line at the MAP sensor. Place the volt-ohmmeter on the 20 volt scale.
   e. Start the engine and apply 10–14 in. Hg of vacuum to the MAP sensor using a vacuum pump.
   f. Run the engine for 2 minutes at approximately 2000 rpm.
   g. If the volt-ohmmeter indicates greater than 0.5 volts within 2 minutes, go to Step 5. If it does not, replace the HEGO sensor, reconnect the MAP sensor vacuum line and rerun the Quick Test.
4. Check the HEGO sensor on engines equipped with MAF sensors as follows:

➡**Vacuum/air leaks could cause Code 41, 91, 136, 172 or 176. Check for: leaking vacuum actuator, engine sealing, EGR system, PCV system, unmetered air leak between MAF sensor and throttle body or lead contaminated HEGO sensor.**

   a. Turn the ignition **OFF**.
   b. Disconnect the appropriate HEGO sensor from the vehicle harness. If equipped with a 4-wire HEGO, connect a volt-ohmmeter to HEGO SIGNAL

and HEGO GND at the HEGO sensor connector. If equipped with a 3-wire HEGO, connect the volt-ohmmeter to HEGO SIGNAL at the sensor and negative battery post.

    c. Place the volt-ohmmeter on the 20 volt scale.

    d. Run the engine for 2 minutes at approximately 2000 rpm.

    e. Rerun the Engine Running Self-Test and monitor the HEGO sensor voltage.

    f. If the volt-ohmmeter indicates greater than 0.5 volts at the end of the Self-Test, go to Step 5. If it does not, replace the HEGO sensor and rerun the Quick Test.

5. Check continuity of HEGO SIGNAL and HEGO GND as follows:

    a. Turn the ignition **OFF**.

    b. Install breakout box tool T83L–50–EEC–IV or equivalent, and leave the PCM disconnected.

    c. Disconnect the suspect HEGO sensor from the vehicle harness. Inspect both ends of the connector for damaged or pushed out pins, moisture, corrosion, loose wires, etc. Repair as necessary.

    d. Measure the resistance between HEGO SIGNAL test pin at the breakout box and HEGO SIGNAL at the vehicle harness connector. If equipped with a 3-wire HEGO, measure the resistance between HEGO GND test pin at the breakout box and negative battery post.

    e. If equipped with a 4-wire HEGO, measure the resistance between HEGO GND test pin at the breakout box and HEGO GND at the vehicle harness connector. Where applicable, measure the resistance between HEGO GND and SIG RTN at the breakout box.

    f. If each resistance is less than 5 ohms, go to Step 6. If each resistance is not less than 5 ohms, service the open circuit, remove the breakout box, reconnect the PCM, HEGO sensor and any other components that have been disconnected. Drive the vehicle 5 miles at 55 mph, then rerun the Quick Test.

6. Check the HEGO circuit for short to ground as follows:

    a. Turn the ignition **OFF**.

    b. Install breakout box tool T83L–50–EEC–IV or equivalent, and leave the PCM disconnected.

    c. Disconnect the HEGO sensor.

    d. Measure the resistance between the HEGO SIGNAL test pin at the breakout box and test pins 40, 46 or 49 where applicable at the breakout box.

    e. If each resistance is greater than 10,000 ohms, go to Step 7. If not, service the short circuit, remove the breakout box, reconnect the PCM, HEGO sensor and any other components that have been disconnected. Drive the vehicle 5 miles at 55 mph, then rerun the Quick Test.

7. Check the HEGO sensor for short to ground as follows:

    a. Turn the ignition **OFF**.

    b. Install breakout box tool T83L–50–EEC–IV or equivalent, and leave the PCM disconnected.

    c. Disconnect the HEGO sensor.

    d. Measure the resistance between PWR GND and HEGO SIGNAL at the HEGO sensor connector.

    e. If equipped with a 4-wire HEGO, also measure the resistance between HEGO GND and/or SIG RTN at the HEGO sensor connector.

    f. If the resistance is greater than 10,000 ohms, for Codes 144 or 41, 139 or 91, 171, 174, 175 or 178, go to Step 19. If the resistance is greater than 10,000 ohms and the vehicle is equipped with a MAP sensor, go to Step 8.

    g. If the resistance is greater than 10,000 ohms and the vehicle is equipped with a MAF sensor, remove the breakout box and reconnect the HEGO sensor. Replace the PCM, drive the vehicle 5 miles at 55 mph, then rerun the Quick Test.

    h. If the resistance is not greater than 10,000 ohms, replace the HEGO sensor, remove the breakout box and reconnect the PCM. Drive the vehicle 5 miles at 55 mph, then rerun the Quick Test.

8. Attempt to eliminate Code 41 or 172, 91 or 136, or 176 on engines equipped with a MAP sensor as follows:

    a. Turn the ignition **OFF**.

    b. Install breakout box tool T83L–50–EEC–IV or equivalent.

    c. Disconnect and plug the MAP sensor vacuum line.

    d. Connect the PCM to the breakout box.

    e. Reconnect the HEGO sensor.

    f. Start the engine and apply 10–14 in. Hg of vacuum to the MAP sensor with a vacuum pump.

    g. Run the engine for 2 minutes at approximately 2000 rpm, then allow the engine to return to idle.

    h. Rerun the Engine Running Self-Test.

➡ **If directed here for Continuous Memory Codes the vehicle has to be driven 5 miles at 55 mph.**

    i. If Code 41 or 172, 91 or 136, or 176 is still present, ignoring all other codes, remove the breakout box and reconnect the MAP sensor vacuum line. If the engine runs rough, check the IAC solenoid. On all other vehicles, replace the PCM, drive the vehicle 5 miles at 55 mph and rerun the Quick Test.

    j. If Code 41 or 172, 91 or 136, or 176 are not present, ignoring all other codes, remove the breakout box, reconnect the PCM and MAP sensor vacuum line. The HEGO sensor input is okay and the fuel delivery is okay. The problem is in an area common to all cylinders: air/vacuum leak, fuel contamination, EGR, Thermactor, MAP frequency, ignition system, etc. Repair as necessary.

9. Check the resistance of the heater element on the HEGO sensor as follows:

    a. Turn the ignition **OFF**.

    b. Disconnect the suspect HEGO sensor from the vehicle harness.

    c. Inspect both ends of the connector for damaged or pushed out pins, moisture, corrosion, loose wires, etc. Repair as necessary.

    d. Measure the resistance between the KEY PWR circuit and PWR GND circuit at the HEGO sensor connector.

    e. The hot to warm resistance specification is 5–30 ohms. The room temperature resistance specification is 2–5 ohms.

    f. If the resistance is within specification, go to Step 10. If the resistance is not within specification, replace the HEGO sensor and rerun the Quick Test.

10. Check for power at the HEGO harness connector as follows:

    a. Turn the ignition **ON** but do not start the engine.

    b. Disconnect the HEGO sensor.

    c. Measure the voltage between KEY POWER circuit and PWR GND circuit at the HEGO vehicle harness connector.

    d. If the voltage is greater than 10.5 volts, reconnect the HEGO sensor. The HEGO sensor system and fuel delivery is okay. The HEGO sensor may have cooled prior to the Engine Running Self-Test. If the symptom persists, the problem is in an area common to all cylinders: air/vacuum leak, fuel contamination, EGR, Thermactor, MAP frequency, ignition system, etc. Repair as necessary.

    e. If the voltage is not greater than 10.5 volts, go to Step 11.

11. Check the continuity of the POWER GND circuit as follows:

    a. Turn the ignition **OFF**.

    b. Disconnect the HEGO sensor.

    c. Measure the resistance between PWR GND circuit at the HEGO vehicle harness connector and negative battery post.

    d. If the resistance is less than 5 ohms, service the open in the KEY PWR circuit. Reconnect the HEGO sensor and rerun the Quick Test.

    e. If the resistance is not less than 5 ohms, service the open in the PWR GND circuit. Reconnect the HEGO sensor and rerun the Quick Test.

12. Check the HEGO SIGNAL for short to power. HEGO always rich could be caused by moisture inside the HEGO harness connector resulting in a short to power, or the HEGO circuit shorted to power. Proceed as follows:

➡ **With dual HEGO sensors, Code 42 or 173 refers to right HEGO sensor; Code 92 or 137, 177 refers to left HEGO sensor.**

    a. Turn the ignition **OFF**.

    b. Disconnect the suspect HEGO sensor from the vehicle harness.

    c. Inspect both ends of the connector for damaged or pushed out pins, moisture, corrosion, loose wires, etc. Repair as necessary.

    d. Turn the ignition **ON** but do not start the engine.

    e. Measure the voltage between HEGO SIG and PWR GND at the HEGO vehicle harness connector.

    f. If the voltage is less than 0.5 volts, go to Step 14. If the voltage is not less than 0.5 volts, go to Step 13.

13. Check for a short to power as follows:

    a. Turn the ignition **OFF**.

    b. Inspect the HEGO GND and HEGO signal harness for chaffing, burns or other indications of a short to power. Repair as necessary.

    c. Disconnect the PCM and inspect for damaged or pushed out pins, corrosion, loose wires, etc. Repair as necessary.

    d. Install breakout box tool T83L–50–EEC–IV or equivalent, and leave the PCM disconnected.

    e. Disconnect the suspect HEGO sensor.

    f. Measure the resistance between HEGO SIG and KEY PWR at the breakout box.

g. If the resistance is greater than 10,000 ohms, replace the PCM, remove the breakout box and reconnect the HEGO sensor. Drive the vehicle 5 miles at 55 mph, then rerun the Quick Test.

h. If the resistance is not greater than 10,000 ohms, repair the short to power, remove the breakout box and reconnect the PCM. Drive the vehicle 5 miles at 55 mph, then rerun the Quick Test.

14. Check the HEGO sensor for a short to the ignition run circuit as follows:
   a. Turn the ignition **OFF**.
   b. Disconnect the HEGO sensor.
   c. Measure the resistance between the KEY PWR circuit and HEGO SIG circuit at the HEGO sensor connector.
   d. If the resistance is greater than 10,000 ohms, for Codes 42 or 173, 92 or 137, or 177, go to Step 15.
   e. If the resistance is greater than 10,000 ohms, for Codes 171, 174, 175, 178 and equipped with a MAP sensor, go to Step 16.
   f. If the resistance is greater than 10,000 ohms, for Codes 171, 174, 175, 178 and equipped with a MAF sensor, go to Step 18.
   g. If the resistance is not greater than 10,000 ohms, replace the HEGO sensor. Drive the vehicle 5 miles at 55 mph, then rerun the Quick Test.

15. Attempt to generate Code 41 or 172, 91 or 136, or 176 as follows:
   a. Turn the ignition **OFF**.
   b. Disconnect the HEGO sensor.
   c. Connect a jumper wire between the HEGO SIG circuit at the HEGO vehicle harness connector to the negative battery post.
   d. Rerun the Engine Running Self-Test.
   e. If Code 41 or 172, 91, 136 or 176 is present, remove the jumper wire. If equipped with a MAP sensor, go to Step 16. If equipped with a MAF sensor, go to Step 18.
   f. If Code 41 or 172, 91, 136 or 176 is not present, remove the jumper wire and reconnect the HEGO sensor. Disconnect the PCM connector and inspect for damaged or pushed out pins, corrosion, loose wires, etc. Repair as necessary. If okay, replace the PCM. Drive the vehicle 5 miles at 55 mph, then rerun the Quick Test.

16. Check the MAP sensor for a vacuum leak as follows:

➡**Due to the MAP sensor's large influence on fuel control, there is a possibility that the MAP sensor could be at fault without a Code 22 or 126. The next 2 steps will verify proper vacuum to the MAP sensor and its ability to hold vacuum.**

   a. Turn the ignition **OFF**.
   b. Disconnect the vacuum line from the MAP sensor.
   c. Inspect the hose for blockage, damage from wear or aging. Repair as necessary.
   d. Plug the vacuum hose at the MAP side.
   e. Connect a vacuum pump to the MAP sensor and apply 18 in. Hg of vacuum to the MAP sensor.
   f. If the MAP sensor holds vacuum, release the vacuum and go to Step 17. If the MAP sensor does not hold vacuum, replace it. Reconnect the HEGO sensor and drive the vehicle 5 miles at 55 mph, then rerun the Quick Test.

17. Check for loss of vacuum to the MAP sensor as follows:
   a. Tee a vacuum gauge into the manifold vacuum line at the MAP sensor.
   b. Start the engine and let the engine speed stabilize. Note the vacuum level.
   c. Turn the ignition **OFF**.
   d. Remove the vacuum gauge and Tee and reconnect the vacuum line to the MAP sensor.
   e. Tee in the vacuum gauge at a different source of intake manifold vacuum and restart the engine. Note the vacuum level.
   f. If the vacuum level differs greater than 1 in. Hg, inspect the engine vacuum integrity and repair as necessary. Remove the vacuum gauge and Tee. Reconnect the HEGO sensor and drive the vehicle 5 miles at 55 mph, then rerun the Quick Test.
   g. If the vacuum level does not differ greater than 1 in. Hg, go to Step 18.

18. Check the HEGO sensor as follows:
   a. Turn the ignition **OFF**.
   b. Disconnect the HEGO sensor.
   c. If equipped with a 4-wire HEGO sensor, connect a volt-ohmmeter to HEGO SIGNAL and HEGO GND or SIG RTN at the HEGO sensor connector.
   d. If equipped with a 3-wire HEGO sensor, connect the volt-ohmmeter to HEGO SIGNAL at the HEGO sensor connector and to the negative battery post.
   e. Place the volt-ohmmeter on the 20 volt scale.

f. Create a vacuum leak to cause the HEGO sensor to go lean. On engines equipped with MAF sensors, disconnect any vacuum hose from the manifold vacuum tree. For all other applications, disconnect the PCV valve hose from the PCV valve.
   g. Start the engine and run at approximately 2000 rpm.
   h. If the volt-ohmmeter indicates less than 0.4 volts within 30 seconds, go to Step 19.
   i. If the volt-ohmmeter does not indicate less than 0.4 volts within 30 seconds, replace the HEGO sensor. Reconnect the vacuum hoses and drive the vehicle 5 miles at 55 mph. Rerun the Quick Test.

19. Check the Continuous Monitor Mode as follows:
   a. Turn the ignition **OFF**.
   b. Make sure the engine is at operating temperature.
   c. Start the engine and run at 2000 rpm for 2 minutes.
   d. With the engine at idle, enter the Engine Running Continuous Monitor Mode.
   e. Observe the volt-ohmmeter or STAR LED for indication of a fault.
   f. Wiggle, shake or bend a small section of the EEC harness while working from the HEGO sensor to the PCM.
   g. Wiggle, shake or bend a small section of the EEC harness while working from the HEGO GND to the PCM.
   h. If a fault is indicated, isolate the fault and repair as necessary. Remove the breakout box and clear Continuous Memory. Rerun the Quick Test.
   i. If a fault is not indicated, remain in the Engine Running Continuous Monitor Mode and go to Step 20.

20. Perform a Continuous Monitor test drive check as follows:
   a. Remain in the Engine Running Continuous Monitor Mode.
   b. Test drive the vehicle at 55 mph with a minimum road load for 5 miles.
   c. Continue to drive on a rough road at 55 mph for 5 miles.
   d. If possible, drive the vehicle through a pool of water on the road to shower the HEGO sensor and/or connector.
   e. If a fault is indicated, isolate the fault and repair as necessary. Remove the breakout box and clear Continuous Memory. Rerun the Quick Test.
   f. If a fault is not indicated, exit the Engine Running Continuous Monitor Mode. Go to Step 21.

21. Check HEGO switching as follows:
   a. Turn the ignition **OFF**.
   b. Inspect the EEC wire harness for proper routing and insulation; burnt, chaffed, intermittently shorted or open. Repair as necessary.
   c. Disconnect the PCM connector and inspect for damaged or pushed out pins, corrosion, loose wires, etc. Repair as necessary.
   d. Install breakout box tool T83L–50–EEC–IV or equivalent, and connect the PCM to the breakout box.
   e. Connect an analog voltmeter to the suspect **HEGO** sensor test pin and HEGO GND at the breakout box.
   f. Test drive the vehicle at 55 mph with minimum road load for 5 miles.
   g. Observe the voltmeter for HEGO switching from 0.3–0.9 volts within 3 seconds.
   h. If the HEGO voltage did not switch, replace the HEGO sensor and remove the breakout box. Reconnect the PCM and rerun the Quick Test.

REMOVAL & INSTALLATION

1. Disconnect the negative battery cable.
2. Raise and safely support the vehicle, as necessary.
3. Disconnect the HEGO sensor electrical connector.
4. Remove the HEGO sensor from the exhaust manifold.
5. Installation is the reverse of the removal procedure.

Fuel Injector

OPERATION

▶ **See Figure 40**

The fuel injector nozzle is an electromechanical device which meters and atomizes the fuel delivered to the engine. The injector valve body consists of a solenoid actuated pintle and needle valve assembly that sits on a fixed size orifice. An electrical signal from the Powertrain Control Module (PCM) activates the solenoid causing the pintle to move inward off its seat and allows fuel to

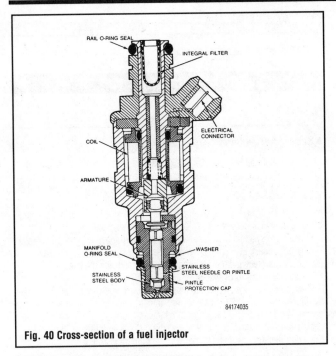

Fig. 40 Cross-section of a fuel injector

flow through the orifice. The fuel supply pressure is constant; therefore, fuel flow to the engine is controlled by how long the solenoid is energized. Atomization is obtained by contouring the pintle at the point where the fuel separates.

The fuel injectors are mounted in the lower intake manifold on 4.6L and 5.0L engines, and are positioned so their tips direct fuel just ahead of the intake valves.

SERVICE

◆ **See Figures 41, 42 and 43**

1. Check fuel pressure as follows:
   a. Turn the ignition key **OFF**.
   b. Relieve the fuel pressure as described in Section 5, then connect fuel pressure gauge T80L–9974–B or equivalent, to the pressure relief valve on the fuel supply manifold.
   c. Make sure that manifold vacuum is connected to the fuel pressure regulator.
   d. If the engine will start, run the engine and check the fuel pressure. It should be 30–45 psi.
   e. If the engine will not start, cycle the ignition key **ON** and **OFF** several times and check the fuel pressure. It should be 35–40 psi.
   f. If the fuel pressure is within specification, proceed with testing. If it is not, check the fuel delivery system (fuel pump, fuel pump relay, pressure regulator, etc.).
2. Check the system's ability to hold fuel pressure as follows:
   a. Pressurize the fuel system, as in Step 1.
   b. Visually check for fuel leaking at the injector O-ring, fuel pressure regulator, and the fuel lines to the fuel charging assembly. Service as necessary.
   c. Turn the ignition key **ON**, but do not start the engine.
   d. Using a mechanics stethoscope, listen for leaking fuel injectors.
   e. If fuel pressure remains at specification for 60 seconds and the vehicle does not start, go to Step 3.
   f. If fuel pressure remains at specification for 60 seconds, for service codes or other symptoms, go to Step 4.
   g. If the fuel pressure does not remain at specification, check the fuel delivery system.
3. Check fuel delivery as follows:
   a. Turn the ignition key **OFF**.
   b. Relieve the fuel system pressure as described in Section 5, then connect fuel pressure gauge T80L–9974–B or equivalent, to the pressure relief valve on the fuel supply manifold.
   c. Pressurize the fuel system, as in Step 1.
   d. Disconnect the fuel pump inertia switch, located on the left side of the trunk on sedans or behind the left service panel on wagons.

e. Crank the engine for 5 seconds.
   f. If pressure drops greater than 5 psi by the end of the 5 second crank cycle, the EEC system is not the cause of the No Start condition; check other systems.
   g. If pressure does not drop greater than 5 psi by the end of the 5 second crank cycle, remove the pressure gauge, reconnect the inertia switch, and go to Step 5.
4. Check cylinder balance as follows:
   a. Run the Engine Running Self-Test.
   b. After the last repeated code, wait 5–10 seconds.
   c. "Goose" the throttle lightly but not wide-open throttle. The Cylinder Balance Test will now be performed.

➡ **The Cylinder Balance Test switches each injector OFF and ON 1 at a time. Codes correspond to the cylinder, as shown in the figure. The Cylinder Balance Test is designed to aid in the detection of a weak or non-contributing cylinder.**

   d. If a cylinder balance fault code is present, go to Step 6. If not, the injectors are okay.
5. Check the resistance of the injector(s) and harness as follows:
   a. Turn the ignition **OFF**.

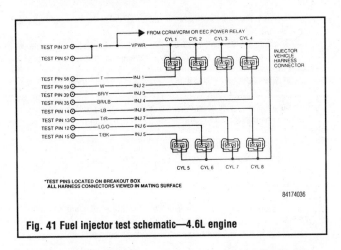

Fig. 41 Fuel injector test schematic—4.6L engine

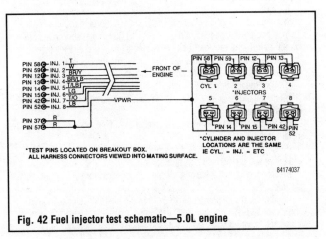

Fig. 42 Fuel injector test schematic—5.0L engine

SERVICE CODE	90	10	20	30	40	50	60	70	80	77/538
CYLINDER/INJECTOR NUMBER	PASS	1	2	3	4	5	6	7	8	RERUN TEST

Fig. 43 Cylinder balance table

b. Disconnect the PCM. Inspect for damaged or pushed out pins, corrosion, loose wires, etc. and service, as necessary.

➡**This erases Continuous Memory**

c. Install breakout box T83L–50–EEC–IV or equivalent, and leave the PCM disconnected.

d. Measure the resistance between the suspect injector circuit test pin and test pin 37 at the breakout box and record the resistance.

e. If the vehicle will not start, pick any injector and measure the resistance between that injector circuit's test pin and test pin 37 at the breakout box; record the resistance.

f. The resistance should be 13.5–19 ohms on 1989 vehicles, 13–16 ohms on 1990–92 vehicles, or 11–18 ohms on 1993–94 vehicles. If the resistance is within specification, go to Step 10. If the resistance is not within specification and the vehicle will not start, service the open in the VPWR circuit; all others go to Step 7.

6. Check the continuity of the fuel injector harness as follows:

a. Turn the ignition **OFF**.

b. Install breakout box T83L–50–EEC–IV or equivalent, and leave the PCM disconnected.

c. Disconnect the injector vehicle harness connector at the suspect injector.

d. Measure the resistance between test pin 37/57 at the breakout box and the VPWR pin at the injector vehicle harness connector.

e. Measure the resistance between the injector test pin(s) at the breakout box and the same injector circuit signal pin at each injector vehicle harness connector.

f. If each resistance is less than 5 ohms, go to Step 8. If not, service the open circuit, remove the breakout box and reconnect the PCM and injectors. Drive the vehicle 5 miles at 55 miles per hour and rerun the Quick Test.

7. Check the injector harness circuit for short to power or ground as follows:

a. Turn the ignition **OFF**.

b. Install breakout box T83L–50–EEC–IV or equivalent, and leave the PCM disconnected.

c. Disconnect the injector vehicle harness connector at the suspect injector.

d. Measure the resistance between the injector test pin(s) and test pin 37/57, 40, 46 and 60 at the breakout box.

e. Measure the resistance between the injector test pin(s) at the breakout box and chassis ground.

f. If each resistance is greater than 10,000 ohms, replace the injector according to the Cylinder Balance Test fault code. Rerun the Quick Test.

g. If each resistance is not greater than 10,000 ohms, service the short circuit, remove the breakout box and reconnect the PCM and injectors. Drive the vehicle 5 miles at 55 miles per hour and rerun the Quick Test.

8. Isolate the faulty injector circuit as follows:

a. Turn the ignition **OFF**.

b. Install breakout box T83L–50–EEC–IV or equivalent, and leave the PCM disconnected.

c. Disconnect all the injectors on the suspect bank. Place the volt-ohmmeter on the 200 ohm scale.

d. Connect one injector and measure the resistance between test pin 37 and either test pin 58 or 59, as appropriate.

e. Disconnect that injector and repeat the process for each of the remaining injectors.

f. The resistance should be 13.5–19 ohms on 1989 vehicles, 13–16 ohms on 1990–92 vehicles, or 11–18 ohms on 1993–94 vehicles. If each resistance is within specification, go to Step 10. If not, replace the injector, reconnect the PCM and the injectors. Drive the vehicle 5 miles at 55 miles per hour and rerun the Quick Test.

9. Check the injector driver signal as follows:

a. Turn the ignition **OFF**.

b. Install breakout box T83L–50–EEC–IV or equivalent, and connect the PCM to the breakout box.

c. Connect a 12 volt test light between test pin 37 and the suspect injector's test pin at the breakout box.

d. Crank or start the engine.

e. A properly operating system will show a dim glow on the test light. If there is no light or a bright light, replace the PCM and remove the breakout box. Drive the vehicle 5 miles at 55 miles per hour and rerun the Quick Test.

REMOVAL & INSTALLATION

For fuel injector removal and installation procedures, refer to Section 5.

Exhaust Gas Recirculation System

OPERATION

♦ **See Figures 44 thru 51**

The Exhaust Gas Recirculation (EGR) system reintroduces exhaust gas into the combustion cycle, thereby lowering combustion temperatures and reducing the formation of Nitrous Oxide. The amount of exhaust gas reintroduced and the timing of the cycle varies by calibration and is controlled by factors such as engine speed, engine vacuum, exhaust system back pressure, coolant temperature and throttle angle. All EGR valves are vacuum actuated.

There are 3 systems used: The 4.6L engine is equipped with the Differential Pressure Feedback EGR (DPFE) system, the 5.0L engine uses the Electronic EGR (EEGR) system and the 5.8L engine is equipped with the Integral Back Pressure Transducer EGR system.

The DPFE is a subsonic closed loop EGR system that controls EGR flow rate by directly monitoring the pressure drop across a remotely located sharp-edged orifice. The DPFE sensor then converts the pressure signal into a proportional analog voltage which is sent to the Powertrain Control Module (PCM). The PCM digitizes the signal and computes the optimum EGR flow. The output signal from the PCM is varied by valve modulation using vacuum output of the EGR Vacuum Regulator (EVR). In the DPFE system, the EGR valve serves as a pressure regulator rather than a flow metering device.

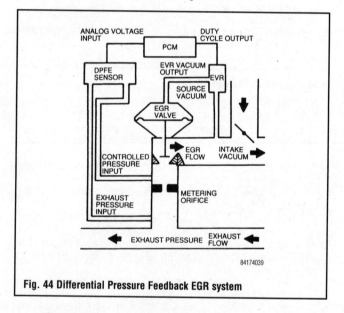

Fig. 44 Differential Pressure Feedback EGR system

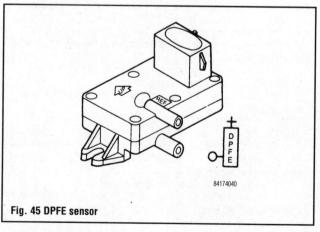

Fig. 45 DPFE sensor

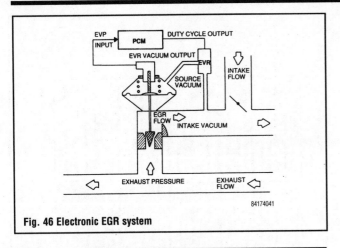

Fig. 46 Electronic EGR system

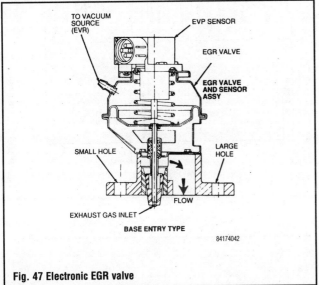

Fig. 47 Electronic EGR valve

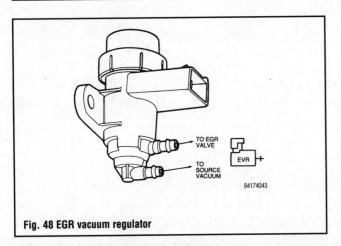

Fig. 48 EGR vacuum regulator

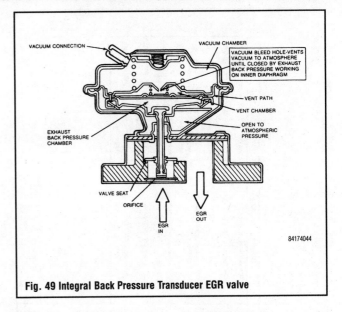

Fig. 49 Integral Back Pressure Transducer EGR valve

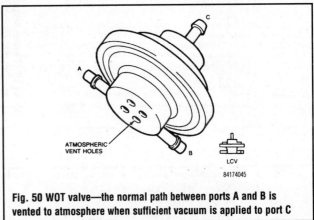

Fig. 50 WOT valve—the normal path between ports A and B is vented to atmosphere when sufficient vacuum is applied to port C

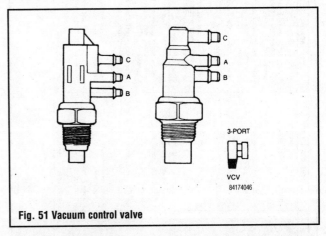

Fig. 51 Vacuum control valve

In the EEGR system, EGR flow is controlled according to computer demands by means of an EGR Valve Position (EVP) sensor attached to the valve. The valve is operated by a vacuum signal from the electronic vacuum regulator which actuates the valve diaphragm. As supply vacuum overcomes the spring load, the diaphragm is actuated. This lifts the pintle off its seat allowing exhaust gas to recirculate. The amount of flow is proportional to the pintle position. The EVP sensor mounted on the valve sends an electrical signal of its position to the PCM.

The Integral Back Pressure Transducer EGR valve combines inputs of back pressure and EGR port vacuum into one unit. Both inputs are required for the valve to operate, it will not operate on vacuum alone. The Integral Back Pressure Transducer EGR system also includes the EGR Load Control (WOT) valve and the Vacuum Control Valve (VCV). The WOT valve dumps EGR vacuum at or near wide open throttle and the VCV controls vacuum to the EGR valve during engine warm-up.

SYMPTOM	POSSIBLE SOURCE	ACTION
• Rough Idle Cold	• EGR valve malfunction.	• Run EEC-IV Quick Test.
	• EGR flange gasket leaking.	• Replace flange gasket and tighten valve attaching nuts or bolts to specification.
	• EGR valve attaching nuts or bolts loose or missing.	• Replace flange gasket and tighten valve attaching nuts or bolts to specification.
	• EGR or VCV malfunction.	• Perform EGR or VCV diagnosis.
	• Load control (WOT) valve malfunction.	• Perform load control (WOT) valve diagnosis.
	• Vacuum leak at EVP sensor.	• Replace O-ring seal and tighten EVP sensor attaching nuts to specification.
	• EGR valve contamination.	• Clean EGR valve.
• Rough Idle Hot	• EGR valve malfunction.	• Run EEC-IV Quick Test.
	• EGR flange gasket leaking.	• Replace flange gasket and tighten valve attaching nuts or bolts to specification.
	• EGR valve attaching nuts or bolts loose or missing.	• Replace flange gasket and tighten valve attaching nuts or bolts to specification.
	• Load control (WOT) valve malfunction.	• Perform load control (WOT) valve diagnosis.
	• Vacuum leak at EVP sensor.	• Replace O-ring seal and tighten EVP sensor attaching nuts to specification.
	• EGR valve contamination.	• Clean EGR valve.

84174191

Fig. 52 EGR System diagnosis

SYMPTOM	POSSIBLE SOURCE	ACTION
• Rough Running, Surge, Hesitation, Poor Part Throttle Performance — Cold	• EGR valve malfunction.	• Perform EGR valve diagnosis.
	• EGR flange gasket leaking.	• Replace flange gasket and tighten valve attaching nuts or bolts to specification.
	• EGR valve attaching nuts or bolts loose or missing.	• Replace flange gasket and tighten valve attaching nuts or bolts to specification.
	• EGR solenoid malfunction.	• Run EEC-IV Quick Test.
	• EGR or VCV malfunction.	• Perform EGR or VCV diagnosis.
	• Load control (WOT) valve malfunction.	• Perform load control (WOT) valve diagnosis.
	• Vacuum leak at EVP sensor.	• Replace O-ring seal and tighten EVP sensor attaching nuts to specification.
	• EGR valve contamination.	• Clean EGR valve.
• Rough Running, Surge, Hesitation, Poor Part Throttle Performance — Hot	• EGR valve malfunction.	• Perform EGR valve diagnosis.
	• EGR flange gasket leaking.	• Replace flange gasket and tighten valve attaching nuts or bolts to specification.
	• EGR valve attaching nuts or bolts loose or missing.	• Replace flange gasket and tighten valve attaching nuts or bolts to specification.
	• EGR or VCV malfunction.	• Perform EGR or VCV diagnosis.
	• EGR valve contamination.	• Clean EGR valve and if necessary, replace EGR valve.
	• Load control (WOT) valve malfunction.	• Perform load control (WOT) valve diagnosis.
	• Vacuum leak at EVP sensor.	• Replace O-ring seal and tighten EVP sensor attaching nuts to specification.
	• Insufficient exhaust back pressure to activate valve.	• Check exhaust system for leaks.

84174192

Fig. 53 EGR System diagnosis

SYMPTOM	POSSIBLE SOURCE	ACTION
• Engine Stalls On Deceleration — Hot and Cold	• EGR valve malfunction.	• Perform EGR valve diagnosis.
	• EGR flange gasket leaking.	• Replace flange gasket and tighten valve attaching nuts or bolts to specification.
	• EGR valve attaching nuts or bolts loose or missing.	• Replace flange gasket and tighten valve attaching nuts or bolts to specification.
	• EGR solenoid malfunction.	• Run EEC-IV Quick Test.
	• EGR or VCV malfunction.	• Perform EGR or VCV diagnosis.
	• EGR valve contamination.	• Clean EGR valve and if necessary, replace EGR valve.
	• Load control (WOT) valve malfunction.	• Perform load control (WOT) valve diagnosis.

84174193

Fig. 54 EGR System diagnosis

SYMPTOM	POSSIBLE SOURCE	ACTION
• Engine Spark Knock or Ping	• EGR malfunction.	• Perform EGR valve diagnosis.
	• EGR flange gasket leaking.	• Replace flange gasket and tighten valve attaching nuts or bolts to specification.
	• EGR valve attaching nuts or bolts loose or missing.	• Replace flange gasket and tighten valve attaching nuts or bolts to specification.
		• Run EEC-IV Quick Test.
	• EGR solenoid malfunction.	• Perform EGR or VCV diagnosis.
	• EGR or VCV malfunction.	• Clean passages in EGR spacer and EGR valve.
	• Blocked or restricted passages in valve or spacer.	• Replace O-ring seal and tighten EVP sensor attaching nuts to specification.
	• Vacuum leak at EVP sensor.	• Check exhaust system for leaks.
	• Insufficient exhaust back pressure to actuate valve.	
• Engine Stalls At Idle — Cold	• EGR valve malfunction.	• Perform EGR valve diagnosis.
	• EGR flange gasket leaking.	• Replace flange gasket and tighten valve attaching nuts or bolts to specification.
	• EGR valve attaching nuts or bolts loose or missing.	• Replace flange gasket and tighten valve attaching nuts or bolts to specification.
	• EGR solenoid malfunction.	• Run EEC-IV Quick Test.
	• EGR or PVS malfunction.	• Perform EGR or PVS diagnosis.
	• EGR valve contamination.	• Clean EGR valve.
	• Load control (WOT) valve malfunction.	• Perform load control (WOT) valve diagnosis.

84174194

Fig. 55 EGR System diagnosis

Fig. 58 Back pressure transducer system functional test

TEST STEP	RESULT	▲	ACTION TO TAKE
IBP1 CHECK SYSTEM INTEGRITY **WARNING** **DO NOT USE EGR CLEANER ON THIS VALVE.** • Check vacuum hoses and connections for looseness, pinching, leakage, splitting, blockage and proper routing. • Inspect EGR valve for loose attaching bolts or damaged flange gasket. • Does system appear to be in good condition and vacuum hoses properly routed?	Yes No	▲ ▲	GO to IBP2. SERVICE EGR system as required. RE-EVALUATE symptom.
IBP2 CHECK EGR VALVE FUNCTION • Install a tachometer • Plug the tailpipe(s) to increase the exhaust system back pressure, leaving a half-inch diameter opening to allow exhaust gases to escape. • Remove and plug the vacuum supply hose from the EGR valve nipple. • Start engine, idle with transmission in NEUTRAL, and observe idle speed • Tee into a manifold vacuum source and apply direct manifold vacuum to the EGR valve vacuum nipple. NOTE: Vacuum applied to the EGR valve may bleed down if not applied continuously. • Does idle speed drop more than 100 rpm with vacuum continuously applied and return to normal (± 25 rpm) after the vacuum is removed?	Yes No	▲ ▲	The EGR system is OK. UNPLUG and RECONNECT the EGR valve vacuum supply hose. REMOVE tailpipe plug(s). REPLACE the EGR valve. RE-EVALUATE symptom.

Fig. 59 Differential feedback EGR system functional diagnosis

TEST STEP	RESULT	▲	ACTION TO TAKE
PEV1 CHECK SYSTEM INTEGRITY • Check vacuum hoses and connections for looseness, pinching, leakage, splitting, blockage and proper routing. • Inspect EGR valve for loose attaching bolts or damaged flange gasket. • Does system appear to be in good condition and vacuum hoses properly routed?	Yes No	▲ ▲	GO to PEV2. SERVICE EGR system as required. RE-EVALUATE symptom.
PEV2 CHECK EGR VACUUM AT IDLE • Run engine until normal operating temperature is reached. • With engine running at idle, disconnect EGR vacuum supply at the EGR valve and check for a vacuum signal. NOTE: The EVR solenoid has a constant internal leak. You may notice a small vacuum signal. This signal should be less than 1.0 in-Hg at idle. • Is EGR vacuum signal less than 1.0 in-Hg at idle?	Yes No	▲ ▲	GO to PEV3. RECONNECT EGR vacuum hose. INSPECT EVR solenoid for leakage. RUN EEC-IV Quick Test.

Fig. 56 EGR System diagnosis

SYMPTOM	POSSIBLE SOURCE	ACTION
• Engine Stalls At Idle — Hot	• EGR valve malfunction.	• Perform EGR valve diagnosis.
	• EGR flange gasket leaking.	• Replace flange gasket and tighten valve attaching nuts or bolts to specification.
	• EGR valve attaching nuts or bolts loose or missing.	• Replace flange gasket and tighten valve attaching nuts or bolts to specification.
	• EGR valve contamination.	• Clean EGR valve and if necessary, replace EGR valve.
	• Load control (WOT) valve malfunction.	• Perform load control (WOT) valve diagnosis.
	• Vacuum leak at EVP sensor.	• Replace O-ring seal and tighten EVP sensor attaching nuts to specification.
	• EGR solenoid malfunction.	• Run EEC-IV Quick Test
• Low Power at Wide-Open Throttle	• EGR valve malfunction.	• Perform EGR valve diagnosis.
	• EGR flange gasket leaking.	• Replace flange gasket and tighten valve attaching nuts or bolts to specification.
	• EGR valve attaching nuts or bolts loose or missing.	• Replace flange gasket and tighten valve attaching nuts or bolts to specification.
	• Load control (WOT) valve malfunction.	• Perform load control (WOT) valve diagnosis.
	• EGR solenoid malfunction.	• Run EEC-IV Quick Test

Fig. 57 EGR System diagnosis

SYMPTOM	POSSIBLE SOURCE	ACTION
• Engine Starts But Will Not Run — Engine Hard To Start Or Will Not Start	• EGR valve malfunction.	• Perform EGR valve diagnosis.
	• EGR flange gasket leaking.	• Replace flange gasket and tighten valve attaching nuts or bolts to specification.
	• EGR valve attaching nuts or bolts loose or missing.	• Replace flange gasket and tighten valve attaching nuts or bolts to specification.
	• EGR solenoid malfunction.	• Run EEC-IV Quick Test
	• EGR or VCV malfunction.	• Perform EGR or VCV diagnosis.
	• EGR valve contamination.	• Clean EGR valve.
	• Vacuum leak at EVP sensor.	• Replace O-ring seal and tighten EVP sensor attaching nuts to specification.
• Poor Fuel Economy	• EGR valve malfunction.	• Perform EGR valve diagnosis.
	• EGR flange gasket leaking.	• Replace flange gasket and tighten valve attaching nuts or bolts to specification.
	• EGR valve attaching nuts or bolts loose or missing.	• Replace flange gasket and tighten valve attaching nuts or bolts to specification.
	• EGR solenoid malfunction.	• Run EEC-IV Quick Test
	• EGR or PVS malfunction.	• Perform EGR or PVS diagnosis.
	• Blocked or restricted EGR passages in valve or spacer.	• Clean passages in EGR spacer and replace EGR valve.
	• Load control (WOT) valve malfunction.	• Perform load control (WOT) valve diagnosis.
	• Vacuum leak at EVP sensor.	• Replace O-ring seal and tighten EVP sensor attaching nuts to specification.
	• Insufficient exhaust back pressure to activate valve.	• Check exhaust system for leaks.

TEST STEP	RESULT ▶	ACTION TO TAKE
PEV3 CHECK EGR VALVE FUNCTION		
• Install a tachometer	Yes ▶	The EGR system is OK. UNPLUG and RECONNECT the EGR valve vacuum supply hose. RECONNECT the idle air bypass valve connector.
• Disconnect the Idle Air Bypass Valve electrical connector (EFI engines only).		
• Remove and plug the vacuum supply hose from the EGR valve nipple.		
• Start engine, idle with transmission in NEUTRAL, and observe idle speed. If necessary, adjust idle speed	NO ▶	INSPECT the EGR valve for blockage or contamination. CLEAN the valve using
• Slowly apply 5-10 inches of vacuum to the EGR valve nipple using a hand vacuum pump		EGR valve cleaner. INSPECT valve for vacuum leakage. REPLACE if necessary.
• **Does idle speed drop more than 100 rpm with vacuum applied and return to normal (± 25 rpm) after the vacuum is removed?**		

84174199

Fig. 60 Differential feedback EGR system functional diagnosis

TEST STEP	RESULT ▶	ACTION TO TAKE
EEGR1 CHECK SYSTEM INTEGRITY		
• Check vacuum hoses and connections for looseness, pinching, leakage, splitting, blockage, and proper routing.	Yes ▶	GO to EEGR2 .
• Inspect EGR valve for loose attaching bolts or damaged flange gasket.	NO ▶	SERVICE EGR system as required. RE-EVALUATE symptom.
• **Does system appear to be in good condition and vacuum hoses properly routed?**		
EEGR2 CHECK EGR VACUUM AT IDLE		
• Run engine until normal operating temperature is reached.	Yes ▶	GO to EEGR3 .
• With engine running at idle, disconnect EGR vacuum supply at the EGR valve and check for a vacuum signal.	No ▶	RECONNECT EGR vacuum hose. INSPECT EVR solenoid for leakage. RUN EEC-IV Quick Test
NOTE: The EVR solenoid has a constant internal leak. You may notice a small vacuum signal. This signal should be less than 1.0 in-Hg at idle.		
• **Is EGR vacuum signal less than 1.0 in-Hg at idle?**		

84174200

Fig. 61 Electronic EGR system functional test

TEST STEP	RESULT	▶	ACTION TO TAKE
EEGR3 **CHECK EGR VALVE FUNCTION**			
• Install a tachometer • Disconnect the Idle Air Bypass Valve electrical connector (EFI engines only). • Remove and plug the vacuum supply hose from the EGR valve nipple. • Start engine, idle with transmission in NEUTRAL, and observe idle speed. If necessary, adjust idle speed • Slowly apply 5-10 inches of vacuum to the EGR valve nipple using a hand vacuum pump • **Does idle speed drop more than 100 rpm with vacuum applied and return to normal (± 25 rpm) after the vacuum is removed?**	Yes No	▶ ▶	The EGR system is OK. UNPLUG and RECONNECT the EGR valve vacuum supply hose. RECONNECT the idle air bypass valve connector. INSPECT the EGR valve for blockage or contamination. CLEAN the valve using EGR valve cleaner. INSPECT valve for vacuum leakage. REPLACE if necessary.

84174201

Fig. 62 Electronic EGR system functional test

REMOVAL & INSTALLATION

EGR Valve

1. Disconnect the negative battery cable.
2. Disconnect the vacuum line from the EGR valve. If equipped, disconnect the connector from the EVP sensor.
3. Remove the mounting bolts and remove the EGR valve.
4. If equipped, remove the EVP sensor from the EGR valve.
5. Installation is the reverse of the removal procedure. Be sure to remove all old gasket material before installation. Use a new gasket during installation.

DPFE EGR Transducer

1. Disconnect the negative battery cable.
2. Disconnect the electrical connector from the transducer. Label and disconnect the vacuum lines.
3. Remove the transducer.
4. Installation is the reverse of the removal procedure.

EGR Vacuum Regulator

1. Disconnect the negative battery cable.
2. Disconnect the electrical connector from the regulator. Label and disconnect the vacuum lines.
3. Remove the regulator mounting bolts and remove the regulator.
4. Installation is the reverse of the removal procedure.

EVP Sensor

1. Disconnect the negative battery cable.
2. Disconnect the electrical connector from the sensor.
3. Remove the sensor mounting nuts and remove the sensor from the EGR valve.
4. Installation is the reverse of the removal procedure.

WOT Valve

1. Disconnect the negative battery cable.
2. Label and disconnect the vacuum lines from the valve.
3. Remove the valve from the vehicle.
4. Installation is the reverse of the removal procedure.

Vacuum Control Valve

1. Disconnect the negative battery cable.
2. Drain the cooling system, as necessary.

❋❋ CAUTION

When draining the coolant, keep in mind that cats and dogs are attracted by the ethylene glycol antifreeze, and are quite likely to drink any that is left in an uncovered container or in puddles on the ground. This will prove fatal in sufficient quantity. Always drain the coolant into a sealable container. Coolant should be reused unless it is contaminated or several years old.

3. Label and disconnect the vacuum lines from the valve.
4. Remove the valve.
5. Installation is the reverse of the removal procedure. Fill the cooling system as explained in Section 1.

Thermactor Air Injection System

OPERATION

♦ See Figures 63 and 64

The thermactor air injection system reduces the hydrocarbon and carbon monoxide content of the exhaust gases by continuing the combustion of unburned gases after they leave the combustion chamber. This is done by injecting fresh air

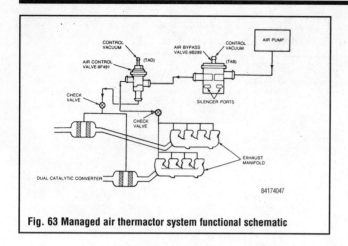

Fig. 63 Managed air thermactor system functional schematic

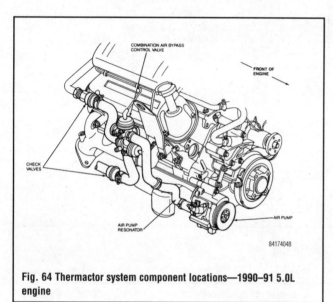

Fig. 64 Thermactor system component locations—1990–91 5.0L engine

into the hot exhaust stream leaving the exhaust ports or into the catalyst. At this point, the fresh air mixes with hot exhaust gases to promote further oxidation of both the hydrocarbons and carbon monoxide, thereby reducing their concentration and converting some of them into harmless carbon dioxide and water.

All vehicles with 5.0L and 5.8L engines are equipped with a managed air thermactor system. This system is utilized in electronic control systems to divert thermactor air either upstream to the exhaust manifold check valve or downstream to the rear section check valve and dual bed catalyst. The system will also dump thermactor air to atmosphere during some operating modes.

The thermactor air injection system consists of the air supply pump, air bypass valve, check valves, air supply control valve, combination air bypass/air control valve, solenoid vacuum valve, thermactor idle vacuum valve and vacuum control valve. Componentry will vary according to year and application.

Air Supply Pump

♦ See Figure 65

The air supply pump is a belt-driven, positive displacement, vane-type pump that provides air for the thermactor system. It is available in 19 and 22 cu. in. sizes, either of which may be driven with different pulley ratios for different applications. The pump receives air from a remote silencer filter on the rear side of the engine air cleaner attached to the pump's air inlet nipple or through an impeller-type centrifugal filter fan.

Air Bypass Valve

The air bypass valve supplies air to the exhaust system with medium and high applied vacuum signals when the engine is at normal operating tempera-

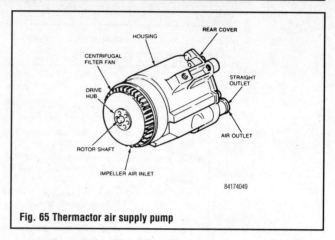

Fig. 65 Thermactor air supply pump

ture. With low or no vacuum applied, the pumped air is dumped through the silencer ports of the valve or through the dump port.

Air Check Valve

♦ See Figure 66

The air check valve is a 1-way valve that allows thermactor air to pass into the exhaust system while preventing exhaust gases from passing in the opposite direction.

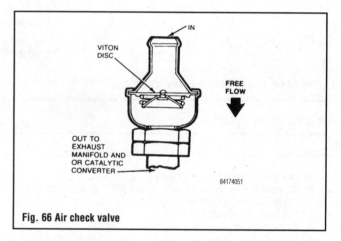

Fig. 66 Air check valve

Air Supply Control Valve

The air supply control valve directs air pump output to the exhaust manifold or downstream to the catalyst system depending upon the engine control strategy. It may also be used to dump air to the air cleaner or dump silencer.

Combination Air Bypass/Air Control Valve

The combination air control/bypass valve combines the secondary air bypass and air control functions. The valve is located in the air supply line between the air pump and the upstream/downstream air supply check valves.

The air bypass portion controls the flow of thermactor air to the exhaust system or allows thermactor air to be bypassed to atmosphere. When air is not being bypassed, the air control portion of the valve switches the air injection point to either an upstream or downstream location.

Solenoid Vacuum Valve

The normally closed solenoid valve assembly consists of 2 vacuum ports with an atmospheric vent. The valve assembly can be with or without control bleed. The outlet port of the valve is opened to atmospheric vent and closed to the inlet port when de-energized. When energized, the outlet port is opened to the inlet port and closed to atmospheric vent. The control bleed is provided to prevent contamination entering the solenoid valve assembly from the intake manifold.

Thermactor Idle Vacuum Valve

The Thermactor Idle Vacuum (TIV) valve vents the vacuum signal to atmosphere when the preset manifold vacuum or pressure is exceeded. It is used to divert thermactor airflow during cold starts to control exhaust backfire.

Vacuum Control Valve

The Vacuum Control Valve (VCV) controls vacuum to other emission devices during engine warm-up. The 2-port VCV opens when engine coolant reaches a pre-determined calibration temperature. The 4-port VCV functions in the same manner, as it is nothing more than two 2-port VCVs in one housing. The 3 port VCV switches the vacuum source to the center port from the top or bottom ports. Electrical switches can be either open or closed until the VCV is fully cycled. The VCV responds to a sensing bulb immersed in engine coolant by utilizing a wax pellet principle.

Vacuum Check Valve

The vacuum check valve blocks airflow in one direction, allowing free airflow in the other direction. The check valve side of the valve will hold the highest vacuum seen on the vacuum side.

SERVICE

▶ See Figure 67, 68, 69

Air Supply Pump

1. Check belt tension and adjust if needed.

✳ WARNING

Do not pry on the pump to adjust the belt. The aluminum housing is likely to collapse.

2. Disconnect the air supply hose from the bypass control valve.
3. The pump is operating properly if airflow is felt at the pump outlet and the flow increases as engine speed increases.

SYMPTOM	POSSIBLE SOURCE	ACTION
• Backfire (Exhaust)	• Air bypass valve malfunction	• Perform bypass valve diagnosis
	• Air control valve malfunction	• Perform air control valve diagnosis
	• Combination air bypass/control valve malfunction	• Perform combination valve diagnosis
	• Thermactor solenoid valve malfunction	• Perform solenoid diagnosis
	• Thermactor idle vacuum valve malfunction	• Perform TIV diagnosis
	• Exhaust manifolds or pipes loose	• Inspect and tighten nuts or bolts to specification.
• Surge at Steady Speed	• Air control valve malfunction	• Perform air control valve diagnosis
	• Combination air bypass/control valve malfunction	• Perform combination valve diagnosis
	• Thermactor solenoid malfunction	• Perform solenoid diagnosis
• Engine Noise - (Hiss)	• Thermactor hose leaks or disconnects	• Visual inspection of hoses and connections
• Engine Noise - (Rap, Roar)	• Thermactor hose or valves leak exhaust	• Visual inspection of hoses and valves. Perform air check valve diagnosis
• Poor Fuel Economy	• Air control valve malfunction	• Perform air control valve diagnosis
	• Combination air bypass/control valve malfunction	• Perform combination valve diagnosis
	• Thermactor solenoid valve malfunction	• Perform solenoid diagnosis
	• Disconnected vacuum or electrical connections for thermactor components	• Visual inspection
• Exhaust Smoke - (White)	• Disconnected vacuum or electrical connections for thermactor components	• Visual inspection
	• Air bypass valve malfunction	• Perform bypass valve diagnosis
	• Air control valve malfunction	• Perform air control valve diagnosis
	• Combination air bypass/control valve malfunction	• Perform combination valve diagnosis
	• Thermactor solenoid valve malfunction	• Perform solenoid diagnosis
• State Emission Test Failure	• Disconnected vacuum or electrical connections for thermactor components	• Visual inspection
	• Air bypass valve malfunction	• Perform bypass valve diagnosis
	• Air control valve malfunction	• Perform air control valve diagnosis
	• Combination air bypass/control valve malfunction	• Perform combination valve diagnosis
	• Thermactor solenoid valve malfunction	• Perform solenoid diagnosis
• Rolling Idle	• Thermactor solenoid valve malfunction	• Perform solenoid diagnosis
	• Disconnected vacuum or electrical connections for thermactor components	• Visual inspection
	• Air bypass valve malfunction	• Perform bypass valve diagnosis
	• Air control valve malfunction	• Perform air control valve diagnosis
	• Combination air bypass/control valve malfunction	• Perform combination valve diagnosis

84174202

Fig. 67 Thermactor air injection system functional diagnosis

THERMACTOR SYSTEM NOISE TEST

⚠ CAUTION

Do not use a pry bar to move the air pump for belt adjustment.

NOTE: The thermactor system is not completely noiseless. Under normal conditions, noise rises in pitch as engine speed increases. To determine if noise is the fault of the air injection system, disconnect the belt drive (only after verifying that belt tension is correct), and operate the engine. If the noise disappears, proceed with the following diagnosis.

Diagnosis

SYMPTOM	POSSIBLE SOURCE	ACTION
• Excessive Belt Noise	• Loose belt.	• Tighten to specification using Tool T75L-9480-A or equivalent to hold belt tension and Belt Tension Gauge T63L-8620-A or equivalent. CAUTION: Do not use a pry bar to move air pump.
	• Seized pump.	• Replace pump.
	• Loose pulley.	• Replace pulley and/or pump if damaged. Tighten bolts to 13.6-17.0 N·m (120-150 lb-in).
	• Loose or broken mounting brackets or bolts.	• Replace parts as required and tighten bolts to specification.
• Excessive Mechanical Noise, Chirps, Squeaks, Clicks or Ticks	• Overtightened mounting bolt.	• Tighten to 34 N·m (25 lb-ft).
	• Overtightened drive belt.	• Same as loose belt.
	• Excessive flash on the air pump adjusting arm boss.	• Remove flash from the boss.
	• Distorted adjusting arm.	• Replace adjusting arm.
	• Pump or pulley mounting fasteners loose.	• Tighten fasteners to specifications.

84174203

Fig. 68 Thermactor air injection system functional diagnosis

SYMPTOM	POSSIBLE SOURCE	ACTION
• Excessive Thermactor System Noise (Putt-Putt, Whirling or Hissing)	• Leak in hose.	• Locate source of leak using soap solution and replace hoses as necessary.
	• Loose, pinched or kinked hose.	• Reassemble, straighten or replace hose and clamps as required.
	• Hose touching other engine parts.	• Adjust hose to prevent contact with other engine parts.
	• Bypass valve inoperative.	• Test the valve.
	• Check valve inoperative.	• Test the valve.
	• Restricted or bent pump outlet fitting.	• Inspect fitting and remove any flash blocking the air passage way. Replace bent fittings.
	• Air dumping through bypass valve (at idle only).	• On many vehicles, the thermactor system has been designed to dump air at idle to prevent overheating the catalyst. This condition is normal. Determine that the noise persists at higher speeds before proceeding.
	• Air dump through bypass valve (decel and cruise).	• On many vehicles, the thermactor air is dumped in the air cleaner or in remote silencer. Make sure hoses are connected and not cracked.
	• Air pump resonator leaking or blocked.	• Check resonator for hole or restricted inlet/outlet tubes.
• Excessive Pump Noise - (Chirps, Squeaks and Ticks)	• Worn or damaged pump.	• Check the thermactor system for wear or damage and make necessary corrections.
• Engine noise - (Rap or Roar)	• Hose disconnected.	• Audible and visual inspection to assure all hoses are connected.
• State Emissions Test Failure	• Restricted hose.	• Inspect hoses for crimped and/or kinked hoses.
	• Plugged pulse air silencer.	• Remove inlet hose and inspect silencer inlet for dirt and foreign material. Clean or replace silencer as appropriate.
	• Pulse air valve malfunction, leaking or restricted.	• Perform pulse air check valve diagnosis.
	• Pulse air control valve malfunction.	• Perform pulse air control valve diagnosis.

84174204

Fig. 69 Thermactor air injection system functional diagnosis

4. If the pump is not operating as described in Step 3 and the system is equipped with a silencer/filter, check the silencer/filter for possible obstruction before replacing the pump.

Air Bypass Valve

1. Turn the ignition key **OFF**.
2. Remove the control vacuum line from the bypass valve.
3. Start the engine and bring to normal operating temperature.
4. Check for vacuum at the vacuum line. If there is no vacuum, check the solenoid vacuum valve assembly. If vacuum is present, inspect the air bypass valve.

5. Turn the engine **OFF** and disconnect the air hose at the bypass valve outlet.

6. Inspect the outlet for damage from the hot exhaust gas.

7. If the valve is damaged, replace it. If the valve is not damaged, check the bypass valve diaphragm.

8. Connect a vacuum pump to the bypass valve and apply 10 in. Hg of vacuum.

9. If the valve holds vacuum, leave the vacuum applied and go to Step 10. If the valve does not hold vacuum, it must be replaced.

10. Start the engine and increase the engine speed to 1500 rpm.

11. Check for air flow at the valve outlet, either audibly or by feel. If there is air flow, go to Step 12. If there is no air flow, replace the air bypass valve.

12. Release the vacuum applied by the vacuum pump and check that the air flow switches from the valve outlet to the dump port or silencer ports, either audibly or by feel.

13. If the air flow does not switch, replace the air bypass valve. If the air flow switches, the air bypass valve is okay, check the air supply control valve, or check the air check valve.

Air Check Valve

1. Turn the ignition **OFF**.

2. Visually inspect the thermactor system hoses, tubes, control valve(s) and check valve(s) for leaks or external signs of damage, from the back flow of hot exhaust gases.

3. If the hoses and valves are okay, go to Step 4. If they are not, service or replace the damaged parts, including the check valve.

4. Remove the hose from the check valve inlet and visually check the inside of the hose for damage from hot exhaust gas.

5. If the hose is clean and undamaged, go to Step 6. If not, replace the hose and check valve.

6. Start the engine and listen for escaping exhaust gas from the check valve. Feel for the gas only if the engine temperature is at an acceptable level.

7. If any exhaust gas is escaping, replace the check valve.

Air Supply Control Valve

♦ See Figure 70

1. Turn the ignition **OFF**.

2. Remove the hoses from the air control valve outlets and inspect the outlets for damage from hot exhaust gases.

3. If the air supply control valve is damaged, it must be replaced, then check the air check valve. If the air supply control valve is not damaged, go to Step 4.

4. Remove the vacuum line from the air supply control valve. Start the engine and bring to normal operating temperature, then shut the engine **OFF**.

5. Restart the engine and immediately check for vacuum at the hose. If vacuum was present at the start, go to Step 6. If vacuum was not present at the start, check the solenoid vacuum valve.

6. Start the engine and let it run. Check for the vacuum to change from high to low.

7. If the vacuum dropped to 0 within a few minutes after the engine started, go to Step 8. If not, check the solenoid vacuum valve.

8. Connect a vacuum pump to the air supply control valve and apply 10 in. Hg of vacuum.

9. If the valve holds vacuum, go to Step 10. If it does not hold vacuum, replace the air supply control valve.

10. Start the engine and bring to normal operating temperature. Make sure air is being supplied to the air supply control valve.

11. If air is present, go to Step 12. If air is not present, check air pump operation.

12. Leave the engine running and apply 10 in. Hg of vacuum to the air supply control valve. Increase engine speed to 1500 rpm.

13. If air flow comes out of outlet A, go to Step 14. If not, replace the air supply control valve.

14. Leave the engine running. Vent the vacuum pump until there is 0 vacuum.

15. If the air flow switches from outlet A to outlet B, the air supply control valve is okay. If the air flow does not switch, replace the air supply control valve.

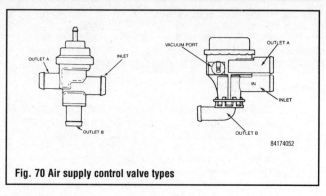

Fig. 70 Air supply control valve types

Combination Air Bypass/Air Control Valve

♦ See Figure 71

1. Turn the ignition **OFF**.

2. Remove the hoses from the combination air control valve outlets A and B and inspect the outlets for damage from hot exhaust gases.

3. If the valve appears damaged, replace it, then check the air check valve. If the valve is not damaged, go to Step 4.

4. Leave the hoses disconnected from the valve. Disconnect and plug the vacuum line to port D.

5. Start the engine and run at 1500 rpm. If air flow is present at the valve, go to Step 6. If it is not, check the air pump. If the air pump is okay, replace the combination air control valve.

6. Leave the engine running. Disconnect both vacuum lines from ports D and S.

7. Measure the manifold vacuum at both ports. If the proper vacuum is present, go to Step 8. If not, check the solenoid vacuum valve.

8. Turn the ignition **OFF**. Reconnect the vacuum line to port D but leave the vacuum line to port S disconnected and plugged.

9. Start the engine and run it at 1500 rpm. If air flow is present at outlet B but not at outlet A, go to Step 10. If not, replace the combination air control valve and reconnect all hoses.

10. Turn the ignition **OFF** and leave the vacuum line to port S disconnected and unplugged.

11. Apply 8–10 in. Hg of vacuum to port S on the combination valve. Start the engine and run at 1500 rpm. If air flow is present at outlet A, the combination valve is okay. If not, replace the combination air control valve.

➡**If the combination valve is a bleed type, this will affect the amount of air flow.**

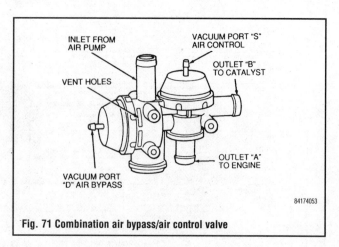

Fig. 71 Combination air bypass/air control valve

Solenoid Vacuum Valve

♦ See Figure 72

1. The ports should flow air when the solenoid is energized.

2. Check the resistance at the solenoid terminals with an ohmmeter. The resistance should be 51–108 ohms.

3. If the resistance is not as specified, replace the solenoid.

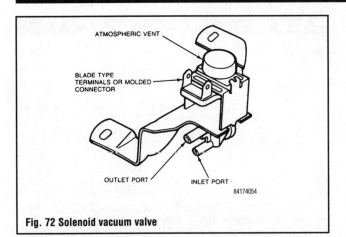

Fig. 72 Solenoid vacuum valve

➡The valve can be expected to have a very small leakage rate when energized or de-energized. This leakage is not measurable in the field and is not detrimental to valve function.

TIV Valve

♦ See Figure 73

➡The following tests apply to valves with the words ASH or RED on the decal.

1. Start the engine and let it idle. Apply the parking brake, block the drive wheels and place the transmission in **N**.
2. Apply vacuum to the small nipple and place your fingers over the TIV valve atmospheric vent holes. If no vacuum is sensed, the TIV valve is damaged and must be replaced.
3. With the engine still idling in **N**, use a suitable vacuum source to apply 1.5–3.0 in. Hg vacuum to the ASH TIV valve large nipple, or 3.5–4.5 in. Hg vacuum to the RED TIV valve large nipple. If vacuum is still sensed when placing your fingers over the vent holes, the TIV valve is damaged and must be replaced.

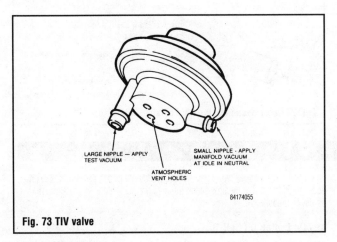

Fig. 73 TIV valve

Vacuum Control Valve

♦ See Figure 74

1. When the engine is cold, passage A to B should be closed and passage A to C should be open.
2. When the engine is at normal operating temperature, the valve should be open between A and B and closed between A and C.

➡On 4-port valves, check A$BSB1to B$BSB1and A$BSB2to B$BSB2separately.

3. If the valve does not operate as specified in Steps 2 and 3, it must be replaced.

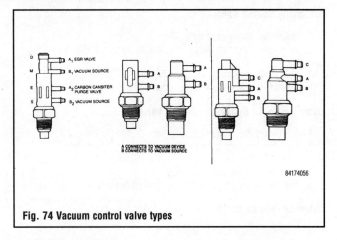

Fig. 74 Vacuum control valve types

Vacuum Check Valve

♦ See Figure 75

1. Apply 16 in. Hg vacuum to the "check" side of the valve and trap.
2. If vacuum remains above 15 in. Hg for 10 seconds, the valve is okay. If not, the valve must be replaced.

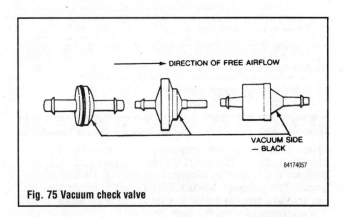

Fig. 75 Vacuum check valve

REMOVAL & INSTALLATION

Air Supply Pump

1. Disconnect the negative battery cable.
2. Remove the drive belt from the air pump pulley.
3. Label and disconnect the air hose(s) from the air pump.
4. Remove the mounting bolts and, if necessary, the mounting brackets.
5. Remove the air pump from the vehicle.
6. Installation is the reverse of the removal procedure. Adjust the drive belt tension as explained in Section 1.

Air Bypass Valve

1. Disconnect the negative battery cable.
2. Label and disconnect the air inlet and outlet hoses and the vacuum hose from the bypass valve.
3. Remove the bypass valve from the vehicle.
4. Installation is the reverse of the removal procedure.

Air Check Valve

1. Disconnect the negative battery cable.
2. Disconnect the input hose from the check valve.
3. Remove the check valve from the connecting tube.
4. Installation is the reverse of the removal procedure.

Air Supply Control Valve

1. Disconnect the negative battery cable.
2. Label and disconnect the air hoses and the vacuum line from the air control valve.
3. Remove the air control valve from the vehicle.
4. Installation is the reverse of the removal procedure.

Combination Air Bypass/Air Control Valve

1. Disconnect the negative battery cable.
2. Label and disconnect the air hoses and vacuum lines from the valve.
3. Remove the valve from the vehicle.
4. Installation is the reverse of the removal procedure.

Solenoid Vacuum Valve

1. Disconnect the negative battery cable.
2. Disconnect the electrical connector from the solenoid valve. Label and disconnect the vacuum lines.
3. Remove the mounting bolts and remove the solenoid valve.
4. Installation is the reverse of the removal procedure.

TIV Valve

1. Disconnect the negative battery cable.
2. Label and disconnect the vacuum lines from the valve.
3. Remove the valve from the vehicle.
4. Installation is the reverse of the removal procedure.

Vacuum Control Valve

1. Disconnect the negative battery cable.
2. Drain the cooling system, as necessary.

✳✳ CAUTION

When draining the coolant, keep in mind that cats and dogs are attracted by the ethylene glycol antifreeze, and are quite likely to drink any that is left in an uncovered container or in puddles on the ground. This will prove fatal in sufficient quantity. Always drain the coolant into a sealable container. Coolant should be reused unless it is contaminated or several years old.

3. Label and disconnect the vacuum lines from the valve.
4. Remove the valve.
5. Installation is the reverse of the removal procedure. Fill the cooling system as explained in Section 1.

Exhaust Catalyst System

OPERATION

▶ **See Figure 76**

Engine exhaust consists mainly of Nitrogen (N_2), however, it also contains Carbon Monoxide (CO), Carbon Dioxide (CO_2), Water Vapor (H_2O), Oxygen (O_2), Nitrogen Oxides (NOx) and Hydrogen, as well as various, unburned Hydrocarbons (HC). Three of these exhaust components, CO, NOx and HC, are major air pollutants, so their emission to the atmosphere has to be controlled.

The catalytic converter, mounted in the engine exhaust stream, plays a major role in the emission control system. The converter works as a gas reactor and it's catalytic function is to speed up the heat producing chemical reaction between the exhaust gas components in order to reduce the air pollutants in the engine exhaust. The catalyst material, contained inside the converter, is made of a ceramic substrate that is coated with a high surface area alumina and impregnated with catalytically active, precious metals.

All vehicles use a 3-way catalyst in conjunction with a conventional oxidation catalyst. The conventional oxidation catalyst, containing Platinum (Pt) and Palladium (Pd), is effective for catalyzing the oxidation reactions of HC and CO. The 3-way catalyst, containing Platinum (Pt) and Rhodium (RH) or Palladium (Pd) and Rhodium (RH), is not only effective for catalyzing the oxidation reactions of HC and CO, but it also catalyzes the reduction of NOx.

The catalytic converter assembly consists of a structured shell containing a ceramic, honeycomb construction. In order to maintain the converter's exhaust oxygen content at a high level to obtain the maximum oxidation for producing the heated chemical reaction, the oxidation catalyst sometimes requires the use of a secondary air source. This is provided by the thermactor air injection system.

REMOVAL & INSTALLATION

For catalytic converter removal and installation procedures, see Section 3.

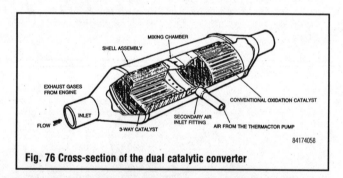

Fig. 76 Cross-section of the dual catalytic converter

TROUBLE CODES

Self-Diagnostic System

GENERAL INFORMATION

All fuel injected vehicles have self-diagnostic capabilities. The Powertrain Control Module (PCM) monitors all input and output functions within the system. If a malfunction is detected, the information will be stored in the PCM memory in the form of a 2 or 3 digit code. These codes can be accessed using the Quick Test procedure.

The Quick Test procedure is divided into 2 sections, the Key On Engine Off (KOEO) and Key On Engine Running (KOER) Self-Tests. Codes can be obtained from each test using a scan tool, such as the Ford STAR, SUPER STAR II or NEW GENERATION STAR (NGS) testers, an analog voltmeter or the dashboard Malfunction Indicator Light (MIL).

If using the scan tool, codes will be output and displayed as numbers, such as the number 116. If codes are being read through the dashboard MIL, the codes will be displayed as groups of flashes separated by pauses. Code 116 would be shown as a flash, a pause, a flash, another pause, followed by 6

flashes. A longer pause will occur between codes. If codes are being read on an analog voltmeter, the needle sweeps indicate the code digits in the same manner as the MIL flashes.

Key On Engine Off Self-Test

▶ **See Figure 77**

1. Connect the scan tool to the self-test connectors. Make sure the test button is unlatched or up.
2. Set the STAR, SUPER STAR II or NEW GENERATION STAR (NGS) tester switch to the EEC-IV position.
3. Start the engine and run it until normal operating temperature is reached.
4. Turn the engine **OFF** for 10 seconds.
5. Turn on the power to the tester. Activate the test button to the test position.
6. Turn the ignition switch **ON** but do not start the engine.
7. The KOEO codes will be transmitted. Six to nine seconds after the last KOEO code, a single separator pulse will be transmitted. Six to nine seconds after this pulse, the codes from the Continuous Memory will be transmitted.

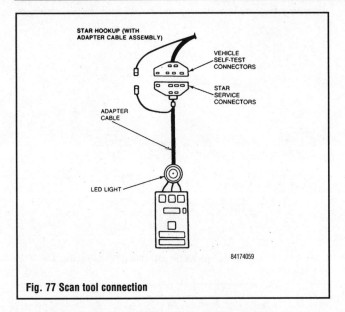

Fig. 77 Scan tool connection

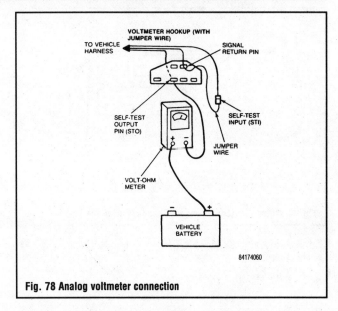

Fig. 78 Analog voltmeter connection

8. Record all codes displayed. Do not depress the throttle during the test.

➡ **The original Ford STAR tester cannot be used to read 3-digit codes. If the STAR tester is used, the display will be blank.**

Key On Engine Running Self-Test

1. Make sure the self-test button is released or de-activated on the STAR, SUPER STAR II or NEW GENERATION STAR (NGS) tester.

2. Start the engine and run it at 2000 rpm for 2 minutes to warm the oxygen sensor.

3. Turn the ignition switch **OFF** for 10 seconds.

4. Depress the test button to the test position, then restart the engine.

5. An engine identification code will be transmitted only on vehicles with 2-digit codes. This is a single digit number representing ½ the number of cylinders in a gasoline engine. On the STAR tester this number may appear with a zero, i.e., 40 = 4. The code is used to confirm that the correct processor is installed and that the Self-Test has begun.

6. If equipped with a Brake On/Off (BOO) switch, the brake pedal must be depressed and released after the ID code is transmitted.

7. If equipped with a power steering pressure switch, the steering wheel must be turned at least ½ turn within 2 seconds after the engine ID code is transmitted.

8. Certain vehicles will display a Dynamic Response code 6–20 seconds after the engine ID code. This will appear as 1 pulse on a meter or as a 10 on the STAR tester. When this code appears, briefly take the engine to WOT. This allows the system to test the TP sensor, MAF and MAP sensors. For 3-digit code applications, the Dynamic Response indicator will light on the SUPER STAR II tester but no Dynamic Response code will be displayed.

9. All relevant codes will be displayed and should be recorded. These codes refer only to faults present during this test cycle. Codes stored in Continuous Memory are not displayed in this test mode.

10. Do not depress the throttle during testing unless a dynamic response code is displayed.

Reading Codes With Analog Voltmeter

♦ **See Figures 78 and 79**

In the absence of a scan tool, an analog voltmeter may be used to obtain codes. Set the meter range to read DC 0–15 volts. Connect the positive lead of the meter to the positive battery terminal and connect the negative lead of the meter to the self-test output pin of the diagnostic connector.

Follow the directions for performing the KOEO and KOER tests. To activate the tests, use a jumper wire to connect the signal return pin on the diagnostic connector to the self-test input connector. The self-test input line is the separate wire and connector near the diagnostic connector.

Codes will be transmitted as groups of needle sweeps. The Continuous Memory codes are separated from the KOEO codes by 6 seconds, a single sweep and another 6 second delay.

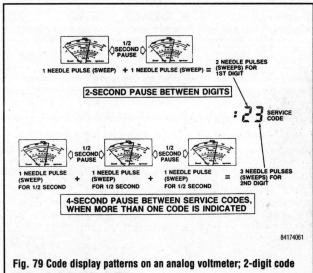

Fig. 79 Code display patterns on an analog voltmeter; 2-digit code shown, 3-digit code similar

Reading Codes With MIL

♦ **See Figures 80, 81 and 82**

The MIL on the dashboard may also be used to obtain codes. Follow the directions for performing the KOEO and KOER tests. To activate the tests, use a jumper wire to connect the signal return pin on the diagnostic connector to the self-test input connector. The self-test input line is the separate wire and connector with or near the diagnostic connector.

Codes are transmitted as flashes with a pause between the digits. A Code 332 would be sent as 3 flashes, a pause, 3 flashes and another pause, followed by 2 flashes. A slightly longer pause divides codes from each other. Be ready to count and record the codes; the only way to repeat a code is to re-cycle the system. The Continuous Memory codes are separated from the KOEO codes by 6 seconds, single flash and another 6 second delay.

Clearing Codes

CONTINUOUS MEMORY CODES

These codes are retained in memory for 80 warm-up cycles. To clear the codes for the purpose of testing or confirming repair, perform the KOEO test. When codes begin to be displayed, de-activate the test by either disconnecting the jumper wire or releasing the test button on the scan tool. Stopping the test during code transmission will erase the Continuous Memory. Do not disconnect

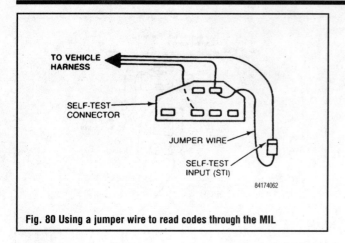

Fig. 80 Using a jumper wire to read codes through the MIL

the negative battery cable to clear these codes as the Keep Alive Memory (KAM) will be cleared.

KEEP ALIVE MEMORY (KAM)

The KAM contains the adaptive factors used by the PCM to compensate for component tolerances and wear. It should not be routinely cleared during diagnosis. If an emissions related part is replaced during repair, the KAM must be cleared. Failure the clear the KAM may cause driveability problems since the correction factor for the old component will be applied to the new component.

To clear the KAM, disconnect the negative battery cable for at least 5 min-

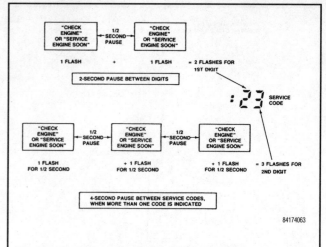

Fig. 81 Code display pattern on the MIL; 2-digit code shown, 3-digit code similar

utes. After the memory is cleared and the battery reconnected, the vehicle must be driven at least 10 miles so the PCM can relearn the needed correction factors. The distance to be driven depends on the engine and vehicle, but all drives should include steady-throttle cruise on open roads. Certain driveability problems may be noted during the drive because the adaptive factors are not yet functioning.

SERVICE CODE		SERVICE CODE DEFINITION
11	orc	System PASS
12	r	Unable to control rpm to Self-Test upper limit band
13	r	Unable to control rpm to Self-Test lower limit band
14	c	PIP circuit failure
15	o	ROM test failure
15	c	Power interruption to Keep Alive Memory (KAM)
16	r	RPM too low to perform fuel test
18	r	SPOUT circuit open
18	c	Loss of tach input to Processor/SPOUT circuit grounded
19	o	Failure of EEC power supply
21	or	ECT sensor input is out of Self-Test range
22	orc	MAP sensor input is out of Self-Test range
23	or	TP sensor input is out of Self-Test range
24	or	ACT sensor input is out of Self-Test range
29	c	Insufficient input from the Vehicle Speed Sensor (VSS)
31	orc	EVP circuit is below minimum voltage
32	orc	EVP voltage is below closed limit (SONIC)
33	rc	EGR valve is not opening (SONIC)
34	orc	EVP voltage is above closed limit (SONIC)
35	orc	EVP circuit is above maximum voltage
41	r	HEGO sensor circuit indicates system lean (right HEGO)
41	c	No HEGO switching detected (right HEGO)
42	r	HEGO sensor circuit indicates system rich (right HEGO)
44	r	Thermactor air system inoperative (cyl. 1-4)
45	r	Thermactor air upstream during Self-Test
46	r	Thermactor air not bypassed during Self-Test
51	oc	ECT sensor input is greater than Self-Test maximum
53	oc	TP sensor input is greater than Self-Test maximum
54	oc	ACT sensor input is greater than Self-Test maximum
61	oc	ECT sensor input is less than Self-Test minimum
63	oc	TP sensor input is less than Self-Test minimum
64	oc	ACT sensor input is less than Self-Test minimum
67	o	Neutral Drive Switch (NDS) circuit open
74	r	Brake On/Off (BOO) circuit open — not actuated during test
75	r	Brake On/Off (BOO) circuit closed - always high
79	o	A/C on during Self-Test
81	o	Air Management 2 (AM2) circuit failure
82	o	Air Management 1 (AM1) circuit failure
84	o	EGR Vacuum Regulator (EVR) circuit failure
85	o	Canister Purge (CANP) circuit failure
87	oc	Fuel pump primary circuit failure
91	r	HEGO sensor circuit indicates system lean (left HEGO)
91	c	No HEGO switching detected (left HEGO)
92	r	HEGO sensor circuit indicates system rich (left HEGO)
94	r	Thermactor air system inoperative (cyl. 5-8)
98	r	Hard fault is present
NO CODES		Unable to initiate Self-Test or unable to output Self-Test codes
CODES NOT LISTED		Service codes displayed are not applicable to the vehicle being tested

KEY: o = Key On Engine Off (KOEO) r = Engine Running (ER) c = Continuous Memory

Fig. 82 Diagnostic service codes; 1989 5.0L engine

SERVICE CODE		SERVICE CODE DEFINITION
11	orc	System PASS
12	r	Cannot control rpm during Self-Test high rpm check
13	r	Cannot control rpm during Self-Test low rpm check
14	c	PIP circuit failure
15	o	EEC processor Read Only Memory (ROM) test failed
15	c	EEC processor Keep Alive Memory (KAM) test failed
16	r	Rpm too low to perform EGO test
18	r	SPOUT circuit open
18	c	IDM circuit failure/SPOUT circuit grounded
19	o	Failure in EEC processor internal voltage
21	or	ECT out of Self-Test range
22	or	MAP/BP out of Self-Test range
23	or	TP out of Self-Test range
24	or	ACT out of Self-Test range
26	or	MAF out of Self-Test range
29	orc	Insufficient input from the Vehicle Speed Sensor (VSS)
31	orc	EVP circuit below minimum voltage
32	orc	EVP voltage below closed limit (SONIC)
33	rc	EGR valve opening not detected (SONIC)
34	oc	EVP voltage above closed limit (SONIC)
35	orc	EVP circuit above maximum voltage
41	r	HEGO sensor circuit indicates system lean (right HEGO)
41	c	No HEGO switch detected (right HEGO)
42	r	HEGO sensor circuit indicates system rich (right HEGO)
44	r	Thermactor air system inoperative (right side)
45	r	Thermactor air upstream during Self-Test
46	r	Thermactor air not bypassed during Self-Test
51	oc	ECT indicated -40°F/circuit open
53	oc	TP circuit above maximum voltage
54	oc	ACT indicated -40°F/circuit open
56	oc	MAF circuit above maximum voltage (MA only)
61	oc	ECT indicated 254°F/circuit grounded
63	oc	TP circuit below minimum voltage
64	oc	ACT indicated 254°F/circuit grounded
66	c	MAF circuit below minimum voltage (MA only)
67	o	Neutral Drive Switch (NDS) circuit open
74	r	Brake On/Off (BOO) circuit open/not actuated during Self-Test
75	r	Brake On/Off (BOO) circuit closed/ECA input open
77	r	Brief WOT not sensed during Self-Test/Operator error
79	o	A/C on/Defrost on during Self-Test
81	o	Air Management 2 (AM2) circuit failure
82	o	Air Management 1 (AM1) circuit failure
84	o	EGR Vacuum Regulator (EVR) circuit failure
85	o	Canister Purge (CANP) circuit failure
87	oc	Fuel pump primary circuit failure
91	r	HEGO sensor circuit indicates system lean (left HEGO)
91	c	No HEGO switching detected (left HEGO)
92	r	HEGO sensor circuit indicates system rich (left HEGO)
94	r	Thermactor air system inoperative (left side)
95	oc	Fuel pump secondary circuit failure
96	oc	Fuel pump secondary circuit failure
98	r	Hard fault is present - FMEM mode
NO CODES	▲	Unable to initiate Self-Test or unable to output Self-Test codes
CODES NOT LISTED	▲	Service codes displayed are not applicable to the vehicle being tested

KEY: o = Key On Engine Off (KOEO) r = Engine Running (ER) c = Continuous Memory

Fig. 84 Diagnostic service codes; 1991 5.0L engine

SERVICE CODE		SERVICE CODE DEFINITION
11	orc	System PASS
12	r	Cannot control rpm during Self-Test high rpm check
13	r	Cannot control rpm during Self-Test low rpm check
14	c	PIP circuit failure
15	o	ECA Read Only Memory (ROM) test failed
15	c	ECA Keep Alive Memory (KAM) test failed
16	r	Rpm too low to perform EGO test
18	r	SPOUT circuit open
18	c	IDM circuit failure/SPOUT circuit grounded
19	o	Failure in ECA internal voltage
21	or	ECT out of Self-Test range
22	or	MAP/BP out of Self-Test range
23	or	TP out of Self-Test range
24	or	ACT out of Self-Test range
26	or	MAF out of Self-Test range (MA only)
29	orc	Insufficient input from the Vehicle Speed Sensor (VSS)
31	orc	EVP circuit below minimum voltage
32	orc	EVP voltage below closed limit (SONIC)
33	rc	EGR valve opening not detected (SONIC)
34	oc	EVP voltage above closed limit (SONIC)
35	orc	EVP circuit above maximum voltage
41	r	HEGO sensor circuit indicates system lean (right HEGO)
41	c	No HEGO switch detected (right HEGO)
42	r	HEGO sensor circuit indicates system rich (right HEGO)
44	r	Thermactor air system inoperative (right side)
45	r	Thermactor air upstream during Self-Test
46	r	Thermactor air not bypassed during Self-Test
51	oc	ECT indicated -40°F/circuit open
53	oc	TP circuit above maximum voltage
54	oc	ACT indicated -40°F/circuit open
56	oc	MAF circuit above maximum voltage (MA only)
61	oc	ECT indicated 254°F/circuit grounded
63	oc	TP circuit below minimum voltage
64	oc	ACT indicated 254°F/circuit grounded
66	c	MAF circuit below minimum voltage (MA only)
67	o	Neutral Drive Switch (NDS) circuit open
74	r	Brake ON/OFF (BOO) circuit open/not actuated during Self-Test
75	r	Brake ON/OFF (BOO) circuit closed/ECA input open
77	r	Brief WOT not sensed during Self-Test/Operator error
79	o	A/C on/Defrost on during Self-Test
81	o	Air Management 2 (AM2) circuit failure
82	o	Air Management 1 (AM1) circuit failure
84	o	EGR Vacuum Regulator (EVR) circuit failure
85	o	Canister Purge (CANP) circuit failure
87	oc	Fuel pump primary circuit failure
91	r	HEGO sensor circuit indicates system lean (left HEGO)
91	c	No HEGO switching detected (left HEGO)
92	r	HEGO sensor circuit indicates system rich (left HEGO)
94	r	Thermactor air system inoperative (left side)
95	oc	Fuel pump secondary circuit failure
96	oc	Fuel pump secondary circuit failure
98	r	Hard fault is present - FMEM mode
NO CODES	▲	Unable to initiate Self-Test or unable to output Self-Test codes
CODES NOT LISTED	▲	Service codes displayed are not applicable to the vehicle being tested

KEY: o = Key On Engine Off (KOEO) r = Engine Running (ER) c = Continuous Memory

Fig. 83 Diagnostic service codes; 1990 5.0L engine

Fig. 85 Diagnostic service codes; 1992 4.6L engine

SERVICE CODE	SERVICE CODE DEFINITION
111 orc	System PASS
112 or	ACT indicated 123°C (254°F) / circuit grounded
113 or	ACT indicated -40°C (-40°F) / circuit open
114 or	ACT out of Self-Test range
116 or	ECT out of Self-Test range
117 oc	ECT indicated 123°C (254°F) / circuit grounded
118 oc	ECT indicated -40°C (-40°F) / circuit open
121 orc	TP out of Self-Test range
122 oc	TP circuit below minimum voltage
123 oc	TP circuit above maximum voltage
124 c	TP circuit output higher than expected
125 c	TP circuit output lower than expected
129 r	Insufficient MAF change during Dynamic Response Test
136 r	HEGO sensor indicates system lean (left side)
137 r	HEGO sensor indicates system rich (left side)
139 c	No HEGO switching detected (left side)
144 c	No HEGO switching detected (right side)
157 rc	MAF circuit below minimum voltage
158 orc	MAF circuit above maximum voltage
159 or	MAF out of Self-Test range
167 r	Insufficient TP change during Dynamic Response Test
171 c	No HEGO switching detected / adaptive fuel at limit (right side)
172 rc	HEGO sensor indicates system lean (right side)
173 rc	HEGO sensor indicates system rich (right side)
174 c	HEGO switching time is slow (right side)
175 c	No HEGO switching detected / adaptive fuel at limit (left side)
176 c	HEGO sensor indicates system lean (left side)
177 c	HEGO sensor indicates system rich (left side)
178 c	HEGO switching time is slow (left side)
179 c	Adaptive fuel lean limit is reached (right side)
181 c	Adaptive fuel rich limit is reached (right side)
182 c	Adaptive fuel lean limit is reached at idle (right side)
183 c	Adaptive fuel rich limit is reached at idle (right side)
184 c	MAF circuit output higher than expected
185 c	MAF circuit output lower than expected
186 c	Injector pulsewidth higher than expected
187 c	Injector pulsewidth lower than expected
188 c	Adaptive fuel lean limit is reached (left side)
189 c	Adaptive fuel rich limit is reached (left side)
191 c	Adaptive fuel lean limit is reached at idle (left side)
192 c	Adaptive fuel rich limit is reached at idle (left side)
211 c	PIP circuit failure
212 c	IDM circuit failure / SPOUT circuit grounded
213 r	SPOUT circuit open
327 orc	DPFE circuit output below minimum voltage
326 rc	DPFE circuit voltage lower than expected
332 rc	EGR valve opening not detected
335 o	DPFE sensor voltage higher or lower than expected

Fig. 86 Diagnostic service codes; 1992 4.6L engine, continued

SERVICE CODE	SERVICE CODE DEFINITION
337 orc	DPFE circuit above maximum voltage
341 o	Octane Adjust circuit open
519 o	Power Steering Pressure Switch (PSPS) circuit open
521 r	Power Steering Pressure Switch (PSPS) circuit did not change states
536 rc	Brake On / Off (BOO) circuit failure
411 r	Cannot control rpm during Self-Test low rpm check
412 r	Cannot control rpm during Self-Test high rpm check
452 c	Insufficient input from the Vehicle Speed Sensor (VSS)
511 o	EEC processor Read Only Memory (ROM) test failed
512 c	EEC processor Keep Alive Memory (KAM) test failed
513 o	Failure in EEC processor internal voltage
522 o	Indicates vehicle in gear
538 r	Operator error (Dynamic response / Cylinder Balance Test)
539 o	A/C on / Defrost on during Self-Test
542 oc	Fuel pump secondary circuit failure
543 oc	Fuel pump secondary circuit failure
556 oc	Fuel pump primary circuit failure
558 o	EGR Vacuum Regulator (EVR) circuit failure
565 o	Canister Purge Solenoid (CANP) circuit failure
617 c	1-2 Shift error
618 c	2-3 Shift error
619 c	3-4 Shift error
621 oc	Shift Solenoid 1 (SS1) circuit failure
622 oc	Shift Solenoid 2 (SS2) circuit failure
624 o	Electronic Pressure Control (EPC) circuit failure
625 o	Electronic Pressure Control (EPC) driver open in ECA
628 c	Excessive Converter Clutch slippage
634 oc	Manual Lever Position (MLP) sensor out of range
636 o	Transmission Oil Temperature (TOT) out of Self-Test range
637 oc	TOT indicated -40°C (140°F) / circuit open
638 oc	TOT indicated 143°C (290°F) / circuit grounded
639 rc	Ouput Shaft Speed Sneisor (OSS) circuit failure
652 c	Modulated / Converter Clutch Control (M/CCC) circuit failure
998 r	Hard fault is present - FMEM mode
NO CODES	Unable to initiate Self-Test or unable to output Self-Test codes
CODES NOT LISTED	Service codes displayed are not applicable to the vehicle being tested

KEY: o = Key On Engine Off (KOEO), r = Engine Running (ER), c = Continuous Memory

DIAGNOSTIC TROUBLE CODES	DEFINITIONS
111	System Pass
112	Intake Air Temp (IAT) sensor circuit below minimum voltage / 254°F indicated
113	Intake Air Temp (IAT) sensor circuit above maximum voltage / -40°F indicated
114	Intake Air Temp (IAT) higher or lower than expected
116	Engine Coolant Temp (ECT) higher or lower than expected
117	Engine Coolant Temp (ECT) sensor circuit below minimum voltage / 254°F indicated
118	Engine Coolant Temp (ECT) sensor circuit above maximum voltage / -40°F indicated
121	Closed throttle voltage higher or lower than expected
121	Indicates throttle position voltage inconsistent with the MAF sensor
122	Throttle Position (TP) sensor circuit below minimum voltage
123	Throttle Position (TP) sensor circuit above maximum voltage
124	Throttle Position (TP) sensor voltage higher than expected
125	Throttle Position (TP) sensor voltage lower than expected
126	MAP/BARO sensor higher or lower than expected
128	MAP sensor vacuum hose damaged/disconnected
129	Insufficient MAP / Mass Air Flow (MAF) change during dynamic response test KOER
136	Lack of Heated Oxygen Sensor (HO2S-2) switch during KOER, indicates lean (Bank #2)
137	Lack of Heated Oxygen Sensor (HO2S-2) switch during KOER, indicates rich (Bank #2)
138	Cold Start Injector (CSI) flow insufficient KOER
139	No Heated Oxygen Sensor (HO2S-2) switches detected (Bank #2)
144	No Heated Oxygen Sensor (HO2S-1) switches detected (Bank #1)
157	Mass Air Flow (MAF) sensor circuit below minimum voltage
158	Mass Air Flow (MAF) sensor circuit above minimum voltage
159	Mass Air Flow (MAF) higher or lower than expected
167	Insufficient throttle position change during dynamic response test KOER
171	Fuel system at adaptive limits, Heated Oxygen Sensor (HO2S-1) unable to switch (Bank #1)
172	Lack of Heated Oxygen Sensor (HO2S-1) switches, indicates lean (Bank #1)
173	Lack of Heated Oxygen Sensor (HO2S-1) switches, indicates rich (Bank #1)
175	Fuel system at adaptive limits, Heated Oxygen Sensor (HO2S-2) unable to switch (Bank #2)
176	Lack of Heated Oxygen Sensor (HO2S-2) switches, indicates lean (Bank #2)
177	Lack of Heated Oxygen Sensor (HO2S-2) switches, indicates rich (Bank #2)
179	Fuel system at lean adaptive limit at part throttle, system rich (Bank #1)
181	Fuel system at rich adaptive limit at part throttle, system lean (Bank #1)
184	Mass Air Flow (MAF) higher than expected
185	Mass Air Flow (MAF) lower than expected
186	Injector pulsewidth higher than expected (with BARO sensor)
186	Injector pulsewidth higher than expected (without BARO sensor)
187	Injector pulsewidth lower than expected (with BARO sensor)
187	Injector pulsewidth lower than expected (without BARO sensor)
188	Fuel system at lean adaptive limit at part throttle, system rich (Bank #1)
189	Fuel system at rich adaptive limit at part throttle, system lean (Bank #2)
193	Flexible Fuel (FF) sensor circuit failure

Fig. 87 Diagnostic service codes; 1993–94 4.6L engine

DIAGNOSTIC TROUBLE CODES	DEFINITIONS
211	Profile Ignition Pickup (PIP) circuit failure
212	Loss of Ignition Diagnostic Monitor (IDM) input to PCM / SPOUT circuit grounded
213	SPOUT circuit open
214	Cylinder Identification (CID) circuit failure
215	PCM detected coil 1 primary circuit failure (EI)
216	PCM detected coil 2 primary circuit failure (EI)
217	PCM detected coil 3 primary circuit failure (EI)
218	Loss of Ignition Diagnostic Monitor (IDM) signal-left side (dual plug EI)
219	Spark timing defaulted to 10 degrees-SPOUT circuit open (EI)
221	Spark timing error (EI)
222	Loss of Ignition Diagnostic Monitor (IDM) signal-right side (dual plug EI)
223	Loss of Dual Plug Inhibit (DPI) control (dual plug EI)
224	PCM detected coil 1, 2, 3 or 4 primary circuit failure (dua plug EI)
225	Knock not sensed during dynamic response test KOER
226	Ignition Diagnostic Module (IDM) signal not received (EI)
232	PCM detected coil 1, 2, 3 or 4 primary circuit failure (EI)
238	PCM detected coil 4 primary circuit failure (EI)
241	ICM to PCM IDM pulsewidth transmission error (EI)
244	CID circuit fault present when cylinder balance test requested
311	AIR system inoperative during KOER (Bank #1 w/dual HO2S)
312	AIR misdirected during KOER
313	AIR not bypassed during KOER
314	AIR system inoperative during KOER (Bank #2 w/dual HO2S)
326	EGR (PFE/DPFE) circuit voltage lower than expected
327	EGR (EVP/PFE/DPFE) circuit below minimum voltage
328	EGR (EVP) closed valve voltage lower than expected
332	Insufficient EGR flow detected (EVP/PFE/DPFE)
334	EGR (EVP) closed valve voltage higher than expected
335	EGR (PFE/DPFE) sensor voltage higher or lower than expected during KOEO
336	Exhaust pressure high / EGR (PFE/DPFE) circuit voltage higher than expected
337	EGR (EVP/PFE/DPFE) circuit above maximum voltage
338	Engine Coolant Temperature (ECT) lower than expected (thermostat test)
339	Engine Coolant Temperature (ECT) higher than expected (thermostat test)
341	Octane adjust service pin open
411	Cannot control RPM during KOER low RPM check
412	Cannot control RPM during KOER high RPM check
415	Idle Air Control (IAC) system at maximum adaptive lower limit
416	Idle Air Control (IAC) system at upper adaptive learning limit
452	Insufficient input from Vehicle Speed Sensor (VSS) to PCM
453	Servo leaking up (KOER IVSC test)
454	Servo leaking down (KOER IVSC test)
455	Insufficient RPM increase (KOER IVSC test)
456	Insufficient RPM decrease (KOER IVSC test)
457	Speed control command switch(s) circuit not functioning (KOEO IVSC test)

Fig. 88 Diagnostic service codes; 1993–94 4.6L engine, continued

DIAGNOSTIC TROUBLE CODES	DEFINITIONS
585	Power to A/C clutch over current (VCRM module)
586	A/C clutch circuit open (VCRM module)
587	Variable Control Relay Module (VCRM) communication failure
617	1-2 shift error
618	2-3 shift error
619	3-4 shift error
621	Shift Solenoid 1 (SS1) circuit failure KOEO
622	Shift Solenoid 2 (SS2) circuit failure KOEO
624	Electronic Pressure Control (EPC) circuit failure
625	Electronic Pressure Control (EPC) driver open in PCM
626	Coast Clutch Solenoid (CCS) circuit failure KOEO
627	Torque Converter Clutch (TCC) solenoid circuit failure
628	Excessive converter clutch slippage
629	Torque Converter Clutch (TCC) solenoid circuit failure
631	Transmission Control Indicator Lamp (TCIL) circuit failure KOEO
632	Transmission Control Switch (TCS) circuit did not change states during KOER
633	4x4L switch closed during KOEO
634	Manual Lever Position (MLP) voltage higher or lower than expected
636	Transmission Oil Temp (TOT) higher or lower than expected
637	Transmission Oil Temp (TOT) sensor circuit above maximum voltage / -40°F (-40°C) indicated / circuit open
638	Transmission Oil Temp (TOT) sensor circuit below minimum voltage / 290°F (143°C) indicated / circuit shorted
639	Insufficient input from Transmission Speed Sensor (TSS)
641	Shift Solenoid 3 (SS3) circuit failure
643	Torque Converter Clutch (TCC) circuit failure
645	Incorrect gear ratio obtained for first gear
646	Incorrect gear ratio obtained for second gear
647	Incorrect gear ratio obtained for third gear
648	Incorrect gear ratio obtained for fourth gear
649	Electronic Pressure Control (EPC) higher or lower than expected
651	Electronic Pressure Control (EPC) circuit failure
652	Torque Converter Clutch (TCC) solenoid circuit failure
654	Manual Lever Position (MLP) sensor not indicating PARK during KOEO
656	Torque Converter Clutch continuous slip error
657	Transmission over temperature condition occurred
998	Hard fault present ****FMEM MODE****

Fig. 90 Diagnostic service codes; 1993–94 4.6L engine, continued

DIAGNOSTIC TROUBLE CODES	DEFINITIONS
458	Speed control command switch(es) stuck / circuit grounded (KOEO IVSC test)
459	Speed control ground circuit open (KOEO IVSC test)
511	PCM Read Only Memory (ROM) test failure KOEO
512	PCM Keep Alive Memory (KAM) test failure
513	PCM internal voltage failure (KOEO)
519	Power Steering Pressure (PSP) switch circuit open KOEO
521	Power Steering Pressure (PSP) switch circuit did not change states KOEO
522	Vehicle not in PARK or NEUTRAL during KOEO / PNP switch circuit open
524	Low speed fuel pump circuit open—battery to PCM
525	Indicates vehicle in gear / A/C on
527	Park / Neutral Position (PNP) switch circuit open—A/C on KOEO
528	Clutch Pedal Position (CPP) switch circuit failure
529	Data Communication Link (DCL) or PCM circuit failure
532	Cluster Control Assembly (CCA) circuit failure
533	Data Communication Link (DCL) or Electronic Instrument Cluster (EIC) circuit failure
536	Brake On / Off (BOO) circuit failure / not actuated during KOER
538	Insufficient RPM change during KOER dynamic response test
538	Invalid cylinder balance test due to throttle movement during test (SFI only)
538	Invalid cylinder balance test due to CID circuit failure
539	A/C on / Defrost on during Self-Test
542	Fuel pump secondary circuit failure
543	Fuel pump secondary circuit failure
551	Idle Air Control (IAC) circuit failure KOEO
552	Secondary Air Injection Bypass (AIRB) circuit failure KOEO
553	Secondary Air Injection Diverter (AIRD) circuit failure KOEO
554	Fuel Pressure Regulator Control (FPRC) circuit failure
556	Fuel pump relay primary circuit failure
557	Low speed fuel pump primary circuit failure
558	EGR Vacuum Regulator (EVR) circuit failure KOEO
559	Air Conditioning On (ACON) relay circuit failure KOEO
563	High Fan Control (HFC) circuit failure KOEO
564	Fan Control (FC) circuit failure KOEO
565	Canister Purge (CANP) circuit failure KOEO
566	3-4 shift solenoid circuit failure KOEO (A4LD)
567	Speed Control Vent (SCVNT) circuit failure (KOEO IVSC test)
568	Speed Control Vacuum (SCVAC) circuit failure (KOEO IVSC test)
569	Auxiliary Canister Purge (CANP2) circuit failure KOEO
578	A/C pressure sensor circuit shorted (VCRM module)
579	Insufficient A/C pressure change (VCRM module)
581	Power to Fan circuit over current (VCRM module)
582	Fan circuit open (VCRM module)
583	Power to Fuel pump over current (VCRM module)
584	Power ground circuit open (Pin 1) (VCRM module)

Fig. 89 Diagnostic service codes; 1993–94 4.6L engine, continued

VACUUM DIAGRAMS

Following are vacuum diagrams for most of the engine and emissions package combinations covered by this manual. Because vacuum circuits will vary based on various engine and vehicle options, always refer first to the vehicle emission control information label, if present. Should the label be missing, or should the vehicle be equipped with a different engine from the vehicle's original equipment, refer to the diagrams below for the same or similar configuration.

If you wish to obtain a replacement emissions label, most manufacturers make the labels available for purchase. The labels can usually be ordered from a local dealer.

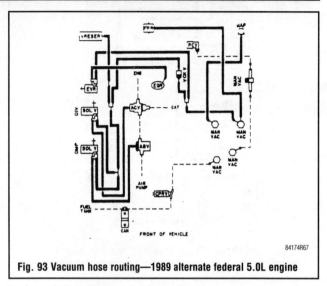

Fig. 93 Vacuum hose routing—1989 alternate federal 5.0L engine

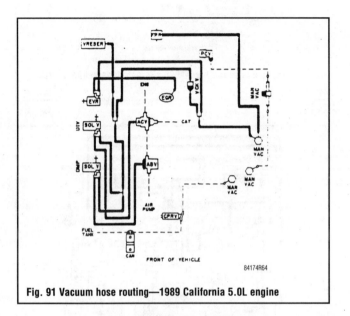

Fig. 91 Vacuum hose routing—1989 California 5.0L engine

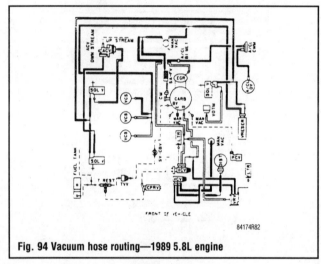

Fig. 94 Vacuum hose routing—1989 5.8L engine

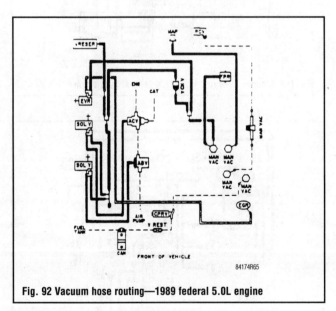

Fig. 92 Vacuum hose routing—1989 federal 5.0L engine

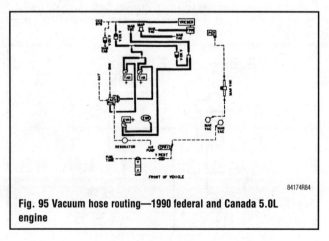

Fig. 95 Vacuum hose routing—1990 federal and Canada 5.0L engine

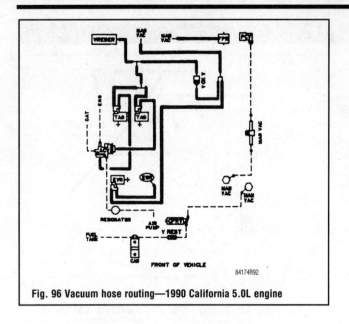

Fig. 96 Vacuum hose routing—1990 California 5.0L engine

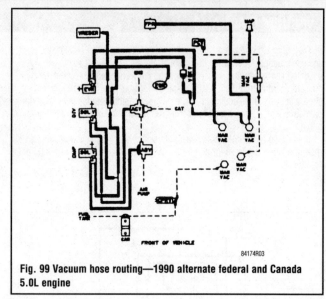

Fig. 99 Vacuum hose routing—1990 alternate federal and Canada 5.0L engine

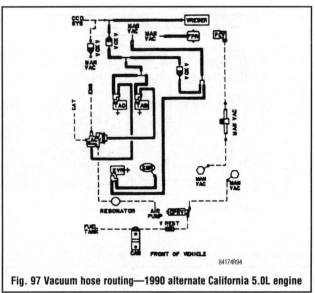

Fig. 97 Vacuum hose routing—1990 alternate California 5.0L engine

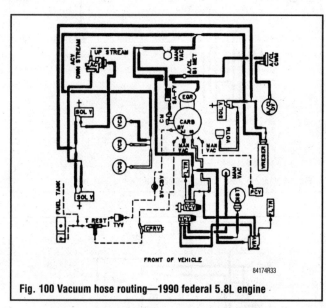

Fig. 100 Vacuum hose routing—1990 federal 5.8L engine

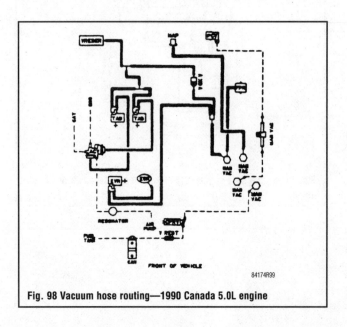

Fig. 98 Vacuum hose routing—1990 Canada 5.0L engine

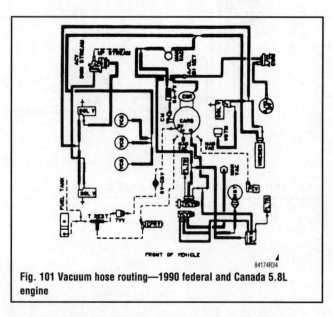

Fig. 101 Vacuum hose routing—1990 federal and Canada 5.8L engine

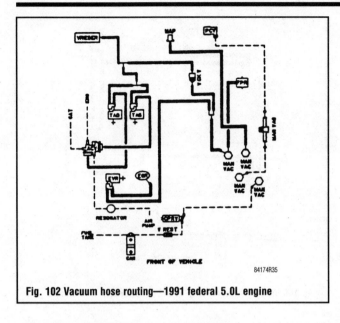

Fig. 102 Vacuum hose routing—1991 federal 5.0L engine

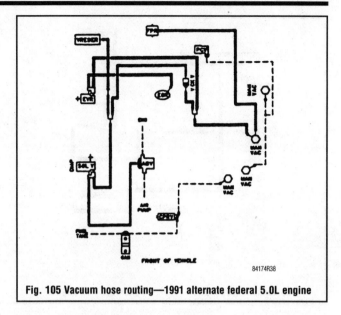

Fig. 105 Vacuum hose routing—1991 alternate federal 5.0L engine

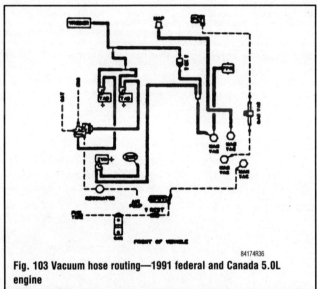

Fig. 103 Vacuum hose routing—1991 federal and Canada 5.0L engine

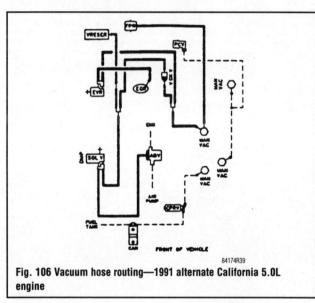

Fig. 106 Vacuum hose routing—1991 alternate California 5.0L engine

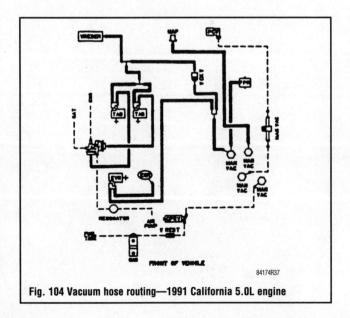

Fig. 104 Vacuum hose routing—1991 California 5.0L engine

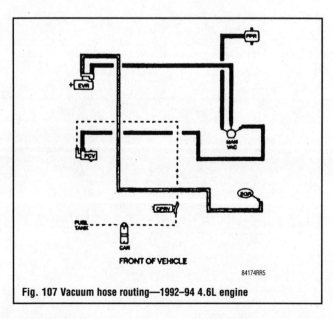

Fig. 107 Vacuum hose routing—1992–94 4.6L engine

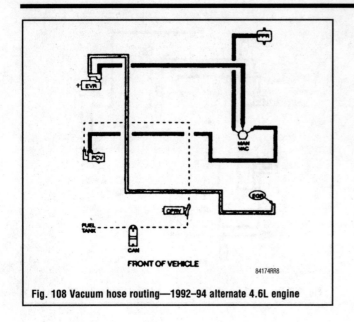

Fig. 108 Vacuum hose routing—1992-94 alternate 4.6L engine

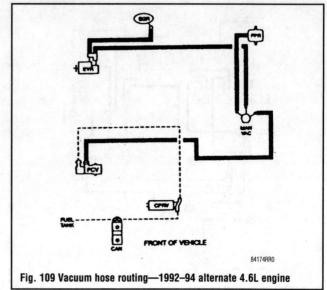

Fig. 109 Vacuum hose routing—1992-94 alternate 4.6L engine

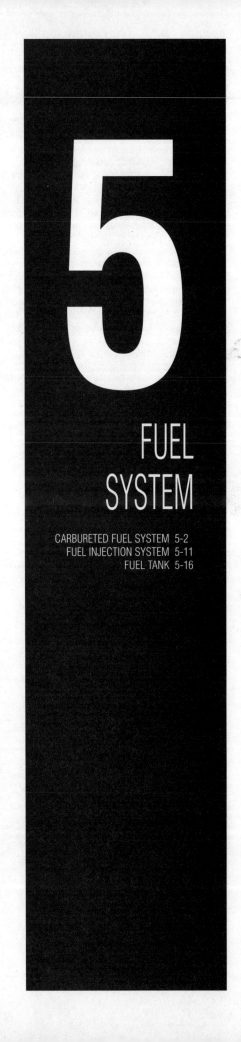

5

FUEL
SYSTEM

CARBURETED FUEL SYSTEM

Description

All vehicles with the 5.8L engine are equipped with a Motorcraft 7200 Variable Venturi (VV) carburetor. Fuel is supplied to the carburetor by a mechanical fuel pump mounted on the engine. The fuel pump is driven by an eccentric attached to the front of the camshaft.

The 7200 VV carburetor is unique in that it is able to vary the venturi area according to engine speed and load, which is quite different from standard carburetors which have a fixed venturi area. The venturi area is varied by dual venturi valves that are controlled by engine vacuum and throttle position. The position of the venturi valves change, depending on engine demands, to determine the area for airflow to the two throats of the carburetor.

The venturi valves are connected to two tapered main metering rods that ride in the main metering jets. When the venturi valve position varies, the metering rods vary the fuel flow by changing the flow area of the main metering jets. During engine operation, air speed through the carburetor is fairly constant, causing more even air/fuel mixtures throughout the engine operating range.

In a traditional fixed venturi carburetor, airflow speed varies according to throttle opening and engine speed, making a supplementary idle system and power enrichment system necessary in order to work with the changing flow speed. In the variable venturi carburetor, these supplementary systems are not necessary.

The variable venturi carburetor varies the air/fuel ratio in response to signals from a control module. The air bleed feedback system used on the variable venturi carburetor uses a stepper motor, activated by a signal from the control module, to regulate bleed air admitted into the main fuel metering system. The stepper motor modulates the pintle movement in the metering orifice, varying the air bleed into the main system. The air/fuel mixture becomes leaner as the amount of air becomes greater.

Mechanical Fuel Pump

REMOVAL & INSTALLATION

♦ **See Figure 1**

1. Loosen the threaded fuel line connection(s) with a tubing wrench, then tighten snugly. Do not remove the lines yet.
2. Loosen the fuel pump mounting bolts 1–2 turns. If the fuel pump does not come loose from its mounting, the gasket is probably stuck; apply force with your hands to loosen the pump.
3. Rotate the crankshaft with the starter until the fuel pump eccentric is near its low position, reducing the tension on the fuel pump rocker arm. It will now be easier to remove and install the fuel pump.
4. Disconnect the negative battery cable.
5. Disconnect the fuel pump inlet, outlet and fuel vapor return line, if equipped.

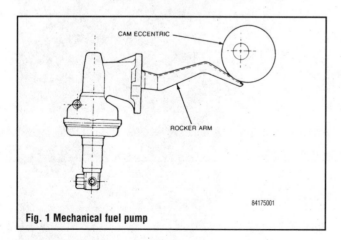

CAM ECCENTRIC

ROCKER ARM

84175001

Fig. 1 Mechanical fuel pump

✳✳ CAUTION

The outlet line is pressurized. Wrap a rag around the line, release pressure slowly and contain spillage. Observe no smoking/no open flame precautions. Have a class B-C (dry powder) fire extinguisher within arm's reach at all times.

6. Remove the fuel pump mounting bolts and remove the fuel pump. Discard the old gasket.

To install:

7. Clean all old gasket material from the pump mounting surface on the engine and from the fuel pump, if it is to be reused.
8. Apply a coat of oil resistant sealer to a new gasket.
9. Install the mounting bolts into the fuel pump and install the gasket on the bolts. Position the pump on the engine. Turn the mounting bolts alternately and evenly and tighten to 19–27 ft. lbs. (26–37 Nm).
10. Connect the fuel pump outlet line. If it is a threaded connection, start the fitting by hand to avoid cross-threading. Tighten the fitting to 15–18 ft. lbs. (20–24 Nm).
11. Connect the inlet line and fuel vapor return line, if equipped. Tighten the hose clamp(s).

➥**Prior to installation, check the rubber fuel lines and make sure they are not cracked, hardened or frayed. If replacement is necessary, use only rubber hose made for fuel line use.**

12. Connect the negative battery cable, start the engine and check for leaks.
13. Stop the engine and check all fuel line connections for leaks. Check the fuel pump mounting pad for oil leaks.

TESTING

Capacity Test

1. Remove the air cleaner assembly.
2. Using a backup wrench on the carburetor inlet nut, slowly disconnect the fuel line from the carburetor.

✳✳ CAUTION

The fuel line is pressurized. Wrap a rag around the line, release pressure slowly and contain spillage. Observe no smoking/no open flame precautions. Have a class B-C (dry powder) fire extinguisher within arm's reach at all times.

3. Attach a piece of rubber hose to the end of the fuel line and direct the other end of the hose into a suitable container.
4. Crank the engine 10 revolutions. If little or no fuel flows from the fuel line during the tenth revolution, check the following:
    a. Make sure there is fuel in the fuel tank and the fuel tank outlet is not plugged or restricted.
    b. If there is an in-line filter between the fuel pump and carburetor, make sure it is not plugged.
    c. Check all fuel lines for kinks, cracks and leaks.
    d. Check the fuel pump diaphragm crimp area and breather hole(s) for fuel or oil leaks.
5. If there is an adequate fuel supply and there are no restrictions or leaks, replace the fuel pump.
6. If the fuel flow is adequate, perform the pressure test.

Pressure Test

1. Connect a suitable pressure gauge to the carburetor end of the fuel line.
2. Start the engine and read the pressure after 10 seconds. The engine should be able to run for over 30 seconds on the fuel in the carburetor bowl.
3. The fuel pump pressure should be 6–8 psi. If pump pressure is too low or too high, install a new fuel pump.
4. Connect the fuel line to the carburetor, using a backup wrench on the carburetor inlet fitting.
5. Install the air cleaner assembly.

Carburetor

ADJUSTMENTS

Choke

COLD ENRICHMENT ROD (CER) ADJUSTMENT

♦ See Figures 2 and 3

➡The CER mechanism affects carburetor air/fuel mixtures throughout engine operation, cold and warm. Several adjustments are required. Although each adjustment affects a particular phase of operation, and a maladjustment can lead to a particular performance symptom, the adjustment procedure must be performed completely and in the following sequence.

If adjustment cannot be accomplished due to epoxy in the adjustment nut, a new service assembly must be installed.

1. Remove the carburetor from the engine.
2. Install a suitable dial indicator on the carburetor, as shown in the Fig. 3.

➡The CER adjustment specifications are listed on a tag attached to the carburetor above the choke cap, as shown in Fig. 2.

3. Remove the choke diaphragm cover and spring.
4. Remove the choke cap.
5. Compress the idle speed positioner where applicable and insert a 5/16–1/2 in. spacer between the positioner stem and the throttle lever contact paddle. Retain in this position with a rubber band. This will locate the fast idle pick-up lever away from the cam and allow the cam to rotate freely.
6. Install Stator Cap T77L–9848–A or equivalent as a weight to rotate the bimetal lever counterclockwise and seat the CER.
7. Position the dial indicator with the tip centered on the top surface of the CER. Zero the dial indicator, then raise the weight slightly and release to check for accurate zero.

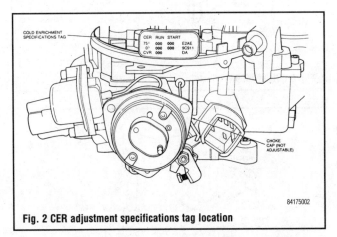

Fig. 2 CER adjustment specifications tag location

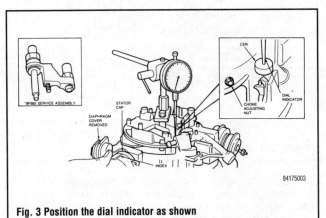

Fig. 3 Position the dial indicator as shown

➡This adjustment will be the reference for other adjustments. Make sure the dial indicator reading is accurate.

CONTROL VACUUM REGULATOR (CVR)SWIVEL ASSEMBLY REPLACEMENT

♦ See Figures 4 and 5

The CVR/CER nuts have cylindrical projections above the threads which are filled with epoxy after final adjustment. To adjust, the existing parts must be removed and a new assembly installed.

1. Remove the E-clip and hinge pin.
2. Turn the CER adjusting nut counterclockwise until the nut disengages from the rod.
3. Remove the CVR and replace with a new assembly.
4. The unbroken rod must be in place first before further assembly. Install the assembly and tighten the CER adjusting nut to lower and locate into position. Connect the lever to the swivel.
5. Install the hinge pin and E-clip.

➡The rod has an undercut designed to break. If breakage does occur, a new rod assembly must be installed. The upper body must be loosened to position the rod through the opening. Replace the upper body gasket as necessary.

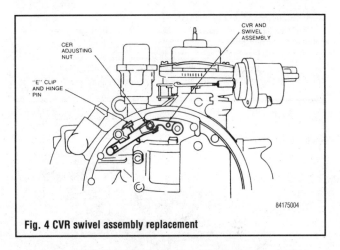

Fig. 4 CVR swivel assembly replacement

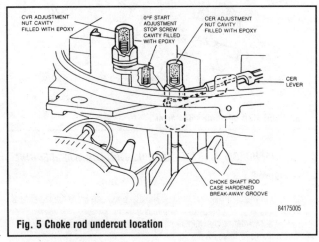

Fig. 5 Choke rod undercut location

CER RUN POSITION ADJUSTMENT

♦ See Figure 6

1. Install the stator cap and rotate clockwise to index. The dial should indicate the tag specification for Run at 75°F (24°C) plus or minus 0.010 in.
2. Adjust by turning the choke adjusting nut clockwise to increase or counterclockwise to decrease the height.

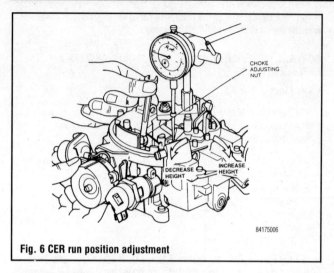

Fig. 6 CER run position adjustment

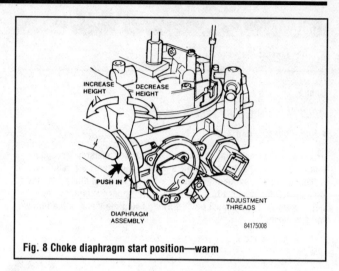

Fig. 8 Choke diaphragm start position—warm

CER START (CRANK) POSITION ADJUSTMENT

♦ See Figure 7

1. Remove the stator cap.
2. Rotate the choke bimetal lever clockwise until the CER travel stop screw bottoms on the choke seal retainer (full travel). The dial should indicate the tag specification for Start at 0°F (18°C) plus or minus 0.005 in.
3. Adjust by turning the CER travel stop screw with a 5/64 in. hex wrench. clockwise to decrease or counterclockwise to increase height.

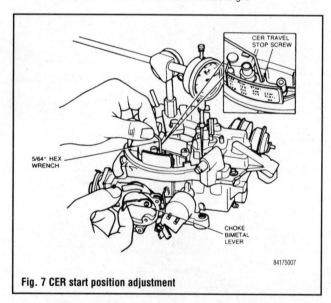

Fig. 7 CER start position adjustment

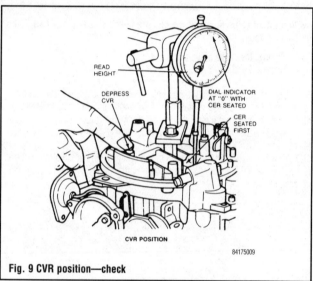

Fig. 9 CVR position—check

CHOKE DIAPHRAGM START (CRANK)POSITION FOR WARM ENGINE

♦ See Figure 8

1. Push in the diaphragm assembly. The dial should indicate the tag specification for Start at 75°F (24°C) plus or minus 0.020 in.
2. Adjust by rotating the diaphragm assembly clockwise to decrease or counterclockwise to increase height.

CONTROL VACUUM ROD (CVR) POSITION

♦ See Figures 9 and 10

1. Seat the CER again using the stator cap weight and check for zero dial indicator reading. Reset the zero position of the indicator, if required. Remove the stator cap weight.
2. Depress the CVR until seated. The dial should indicate the tag specification for CVR plus or minus 0.10 in.

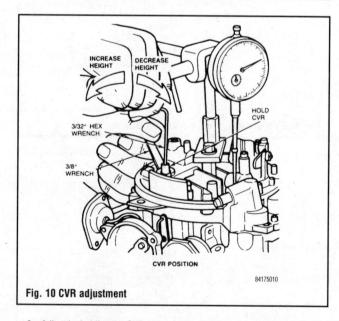

Fig. 10 CVR adjustment

3. Adjust by holding the CVR with a ⅜ in. wrench and turning the adjustment with a ³⁄₃₂ in. hex wrench, clockwise to decrease or counterclockwise to increase height.
4. Reinstall the original choke diaphragm cover with the original spring.

CHOKE DIAPHRAGM RUN POSITION FOR COLD ENGINE

▶ See Figure 11

1. Apply vacuum to the choke diaphragm cover, or depress the choke diaphragm rod to the seated position.
2. Rotate the choke bimetal lever clockwise until the choke shaft lever pin contacts the fast idle intermediate lever. The dial should indicate the tag specification for Run at 0°F plus or minus 0.005 in.
3. If an adjustment is required, remove the choke diaphragm cover and install a new cover with the original spring. This is necessary because of the tamper-resistant material on the adjustment screw.
4. Adjust by rotating the screw in the diaphragm housing with a 5/64 in. hex wrench, clockwise to increase or counterclockwise to decrease height.
5. Apply sealing liquid on the adjustment screw to secure the adjustment.
6. Install lead ball plug in the adjusting screw hole.

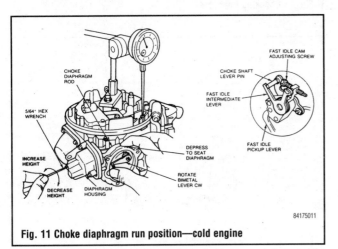

Fig. 11 Choke diaphragm run position—cold engine

FAST IDLE CAM SETTING

▶ See Figure 12

1. Position the fast idle pick-up lever on the second step of the fast idle cam against the shoulder of the high step.
2. Install the stator cap and rotate clockwise until the fast idle pick-up lever contacts the fast idle cam adjusting screw. The dial should indicate specification 0.360 in. plus or minus 0.005 in.
3. Adjust by rotating the fast idle cam adjusting screw.
4. Remove the stator cap.
5. Assemble the choke cap, gasket and retainer with breakaway screws.
6. Remove the dial indicator and rubber band.
7. Install the carburetor and adjust the idle speeds.

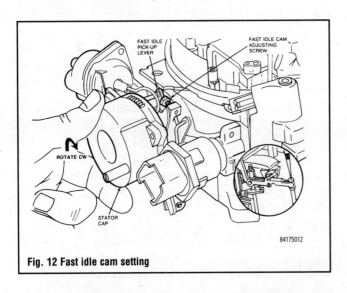

Fig. 12 Fast idle cam setting

Venturi Valve Wide Open Throttle(WOT) Opening

▶ See Figures 13, 14, 15, 16 and 17

1. Remove the carburetor from the engine.
2. Remove the expansion plug covering the venturi valve limiter adjustment screw (center punch until loose).
3. Remove the (WOT) stop adjustment screw and spring, using a 5/32 in. Allen wrench.
4. Hold the throttle plates wipe open, lightly push the venturi valve toward "close position" and check the gap between the valve and venturi opening wall. Set the closing gap specification at 0.39–0.41 in. (9.91–10.41mm).
5. Using a 5/64 in. Allen wrench, turn the venturi valve limiter adjustment screw (on the venturi valve arm) to set the closing gap to specification.

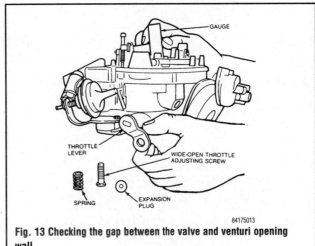

Fig. 13 Checking the gap between the valve and venturi opening wall

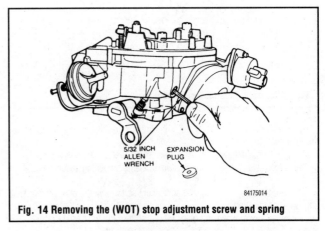

Fig. 14 Removing the (WOT) stop adjustment screw and spring

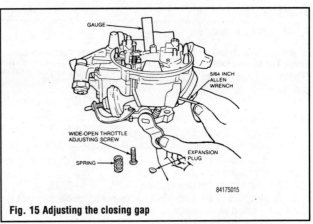

Fig. 15 Adjusting the closing gap

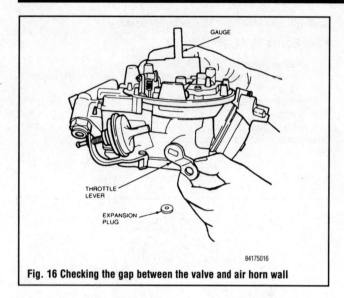

Fig. 16 Checking the gap between the valve and air horn wall

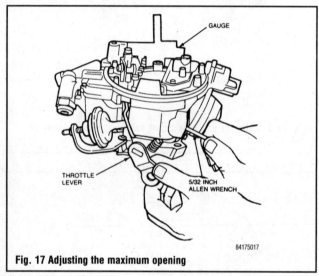

Fig. 17 Adjusting the maximum opening

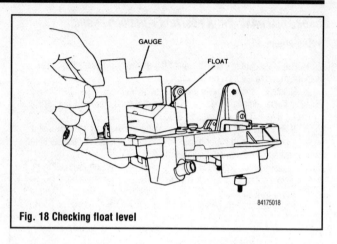

Fig. 18 Checking float level

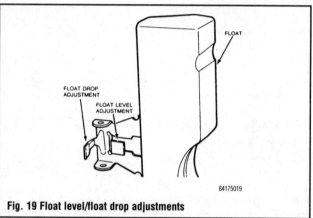

Fig. 19 Float level/float drop adjustments

6. Install the throttle (WOT) stop adjustment screw and spring, using a ⁵⁄₃₂ in. Allen wrench.

7. Lightly push the venturi valve "wide open to stop" and check the gap between the valve and air horn wall. This "maximum opening specification" is 0.99–1.01 in. (25.15–25.65mm).

8. Turn the throttle (WOT) stop adjustment screw until the maximum opening is to specification.

9. Install a new expansion plug and install the carburetor on the engine.

Float Level

▶ **See Figures 18 and 19**

➡The variable venturi carburetor is very insensitive to float level settings. The factory setting does not change with time and usage. Adjusting the float level setting will not correct any typical start/drive problems.

1. Remove the carburetor.
2. Remove the upper body assembly and the upper body gasket.
3. If necessary, fabricate a gauge to the specified dimension.
4. With the upper body inverted, place the float level gauge on the cast surface of the upper body and measure the vertical distance from the cast surface of the upper body and the bottom of the float.
5. The float level specification is 1.010–1.070 in. (25.66–27.17mm).
6. To adjust, bend the float operating lever away from the fuel inlet needle to decrease the setting and toward the needle to increase the setting.
7. Check and/or adjust the float drop.

Float Drop

▶ **See Figures 19 and 20**

1. If necessary, fabricate a gauge to 1.430–1.490 in. (36.33–37.84mm).
2. With the carburetor upper body assembly held in an upright position, place the gauge against the cast surface of the upper body and measure the vertical distance between the cast surface of the upper body and the bottom of the float.
3. The float drop specification is 1.430–1.490 in. (36.33–37.84mm).
4. To adjust, bend the stop tab on the float lever away from the hinge pin to increase the setting and toward the hinge pin to decrease the setting.
5. Install a new upper body gasket and install the upper body assembly.

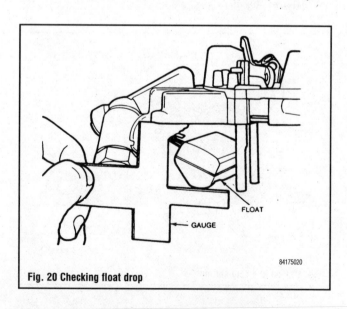

Fig. 20 Checking float drop

REMOVAL & INSTALLATION

➡In many instances, flooding, stumble on acceleration, and other performance complaints are caused by the presence of dirt, water or other foreign material in the carburetor. To aid in complaint diagnosis, the carburetor should be carefully removed from the engine without removing the fuel from the bowl. The contents of the bowl can then be examined for contamination as the carburetor is disassembled.

1. Disconnect the negative battery cable. Remove the air cleaner.
2. Remove the throttle cable and transmission kickdown levers from the throttle lever. Tag and disconnect all vacuum lines, emission hoses, and electrical connections.
3. Using a backup wrench on the carburetor inlet nut, slowly disconnect the fuel line from the carburetor.

✳✳ CAUTION

The fuel line is pressurized. Wrap a rag around the line, release pressure slowly and contain spillage. Observe no smoking/no open flame precautions. Have a class B-C (dry powder) fire extinguisher within arm's reach at all times.

4. Remove the carburetor mounting nuts; then remove the carburetor. Remove the carburetor mounting gasket spacer, if equipped, and lower gasket from the intake manifold.

To install:

5. Clean the gasket mounting surfaces of the spacer and carburetor. Place the spacer between 2 new gaskets and place the spacer and gaskets on the intake manifold. Position the carburetor on the spacer and gasket.
6. Install the spark and EGR vacuum lines and fuel fitting before bolting the carburetor in place. Install the carburetor mounting nuts and hand tighten them. Then, alternately tighten each nut in a crisscross pattern to 12–15 ft. lbs. (16–20 Nm).

7. Connect the throttle cable and all emission and vacuum lines. Observe the color coded vacuum line connections on the carburetor.
8. Run the engine and adjust the idle speeds. Check for fuel leaks. Adjust the throttle valve lever.

OVERHAUL

➡To ensure proper assembly, use a separate container for the component parts of each subassembly.

Disassembly

UPPER BODY

▶ **See Figures 21, 22, 23, 24 and 25**

1. Remove the fuel inlet fitting, fuel filter, gasket and spring.
2. Remove the E-ring on the accelerator pump rod and the choke control rod and disengage the rods.
3. Remove the air cleaner stud.
4. Remove the 7 screws attaching the upper body to the main body and remove the upper body. Place the upper body, inverted, on a clean work surface.

➡For assembly purposes, note the position of the screws: 5 long—silver; 2 short—black.

5. Remove the float hinge pin and the float. Remove the float bowl gasket.
6. Remove the fuel inlet valve, seat and gasket.
7. Remove the accelerator pump link retaining screw and nut. Remove the accelerator link and swivel assembly. Remove the overtravel spring and washer.
8. Remove the accelerator pump rod and the dust seal.
9. Remove the E-ring on the choke hinge pin and slide the pin out of the casting.
10. Turn counterclockwise to remove the Cold Enrichment Rod (CER) adjusting nut.

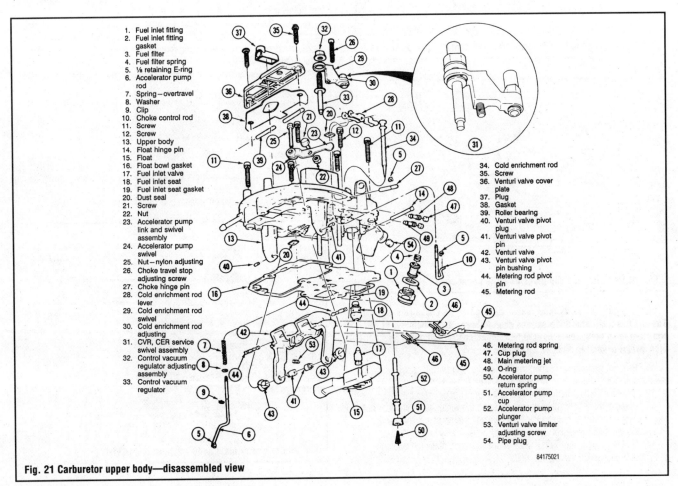

1. Fuel inlet fitting
2. Fuel inlet fitting gasket
3. Fuel filter
4. Fuel filter spring
5. ⅛ retaining E-ring
6. Accelerator pump rod
7. Spring—overtravel
8. Washer
9. Clip
10. Choke control rod
11. Screw
12. Screw
13. Upper body
14. Float hinge pin
15. Float
16. Float bowl gasket
17. Fuel inlet valve
18. Fuel inlet seat
19. Fuel inlet seat gasket
20. Dust seal
21. Screw
22. Nut
23. Accelerator pump link and swivel assembly
24. Accelerator pump swivel
25. Nut—nylon adjusting
26. Choke travel stop adjusting screw
27. Choke hinge pin
28. Cold enrichment rod lever
29. Cold enrichment rod swivel
30. Cold enrichment rod adjusting
31. CVR, CER service swivel assembly
32. Control vacuum regulator adjusting assembly
33. Control vacuum regulator

34. Cold enrichment rod
35. Screw
36. Venturi valve cover plate
37. Plug
38. Gasket
39. Roller bearing
40. Venturi valve pivot plug
41. Venturi valve pivot pin
42. Venturi valve
43. Venturi valve pivot pin bushing
44. Metering rod pivot pin
45. Metering rod

46. Metering rod spring
47. Cup plug
48. Main metering jet
49. O-ring
50. Accelerator pump return spring
51. Accelerator pump cup
52. Accelerator pump plunger
53. Venturi valve limiter adjusting screw
54. Pipe plug

Fig. 21 Carburetor upper body—disassembled view

84175021

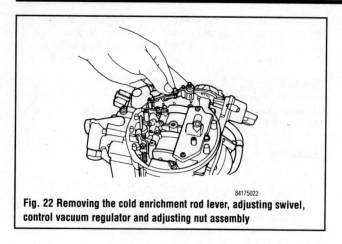

Fig. 22 Removing the cold enrichment rod lever, adjusting swivel, control vacuum regulator and adjusting nut assembly

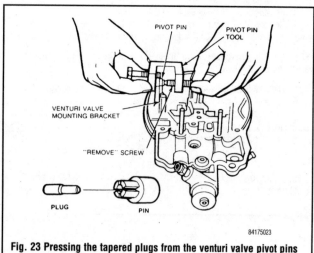

Fig. 23 Pressing the tapered plugs from the venturi valve pivot pins

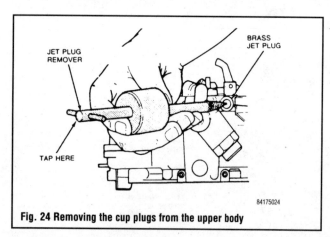

Fig. 24 Removing the cup plugs from the upper body

➡**Epoxy on the nut cavity may cause breakage of the choke control rod. The rod has a circular undercut designed to break at 10 inch lbs. (1.13 Nm) torque. If breakage occurs, a new choke control rod and a new service swivel assembly must be installed.**

11. Remove the cold enrichment rod lever, adjusting swivel, control vacuum regulator and adjusting nut as an assembly. Disassemble as required.

12. Slide the cold enrichment rod out of the upper body casting.

13. Remove the 2 Torx® head screws securing the venturi valve cover. Invert the carburetor assembly, holding the venturi valve cover in place, and remove the venturi valve cover, gasket and bearings as an assembly.

14. Using pivot pin tool T77L–9928–A or equivalent, press the tapered plugs out of the venturi valve pivot pins.

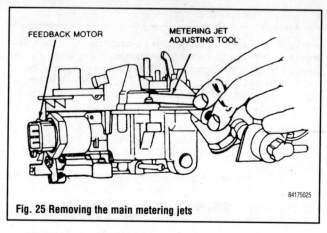

Fig. 25 Removing the main metering jets

15. Push the venturi pivot pins out and slide the venturi valve to the rear until it is free of the casting. Remove the venturi valve pivot pin bushings.

16. Remove the metering rod pins (on the outboard sides of the venturi valve), the metering rods and the springs. Be sure to identify the rods, "throttle" or "choke" side for assembly reference.

➡**Always block the venturi valve wide open when removing brass jet plug or working on the jets.**

17. Using jet plug remover T77L–9533–B or equivalent, remove the cup plugs recessed in the upper body casting.

➡**Because the main metering jet setting is an important factor in the overall carburetor calibration, the following Steps must be carefully followed.**

18. Use metering jet adjusting tool T77L–9533–A or equivalent, to turn each main metering jet clockwise, counting the number of turns, until they bottom lightly in the casting. Record the number of turns.

19. Turn the jet assembly counterclockwise to remove. Remove the O-ring and identify the jets, "throttle" or "choke" side, for proper assembly.

20. Remove the accelerator pump plunger and assemble and disassemble, as required.

21. Remove the venturi valve limiter adjusting screw from the throttle side of the venturi valve.

22. Remove the ⅛ in. pipe plug in the fuel inlet boss, if required for cleaning.

MAIN BODY

♦ **See Figure 26**

1. Remove the venturi valve diaphragm cover retaining screws, cover, spring guide and spring. Tap lightly to loosen the cover; do not pry.

2. Carefully loosen the diaphragm and slide it out of the main body

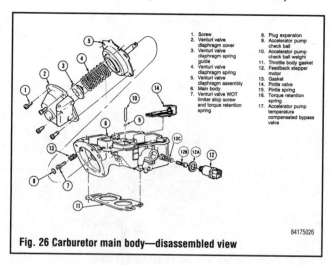

1. Screw
2. Venturi valve diaphragm cover
3. Venturi valve diaphragm spring guide
4. Venturi valve diaphragm spring
5. Venturi valve diaphragm assembly
6. Main body
7. Venturi valve WOT limiter stop screw and torque retention spring
8. Plug expansion
9. Accelerator pump check ball
10. Accelerator pump check ball weight
11. Throttle body gasket
12. Feedback stepper motor
13. Gasket
14. Pintle valve
15. Pintle spring
16. Torque retention spring
17. Accelerator pump temperature compensated bypass valve

Fig. 26 Carburetor main body—disassembled view

3. Place the carburetor inverted on a clean surface. Position your hand to catch the accelerator pump check ball and weight as the carburetor is turned over.

4. Remove the 5 screws attaching the throttle body and remove the throttle body and gasket.

5. Using a 1⅝ in. socket, remove the feedback stepper motor, gasket, pintle valve and pintle spring.

THROTTLE BODY

▶ **See Figures 27 and 28**

1. Remove the throttle control device, solenoid, dashpot and bracket.

2. Remove the thermostatic choke cap retaining screws as follows:

   a. Center punch the choke cap retaining screw heads and, using a ¼ in. drill, drill the screw heads deep enough to remove the retainer from the choke cap.

   b. Carefully remove the choke cap.

   c. Remove the remaining portion of the choke cap screws with small locking pliers.

3. Remove the choke thermostatic lever screw and lever.

4. Slide the choke shaft and lever assembly out of the casing and remove the fast idle cam and E-clip. Remove the fast idle cam adjusting screw. Remove the choke diaphragm rod E-clip attaching the rod to the fast idle intermediate lever. Disengage the deloading rod, if equipped.

5. Remove the fast idle intermediate lever.

6. Remove the choke control diaphragm cover screws, cover and return spring.

7. Remove the choke control diaphragm and rod. Disassemble, if necessary.

8. The choke housing bushing is pressed into the casting and staked in place. If replacement is required, it will have to be carefully pressed out. Support the casting while pressing, to prevent damage.

➡ **Before pressing, file or grind off the staked areas.**

9. Remove the (TSP off) idle speed adjusting screw.

10. Remove the throttle shaft retaining nut and spring, if equipped, the fast idle adjusting lever, the nylon bushing, the fast idle lever and the fast idle adjusting screw. Remove the deloading lever, if equipped. Remove the large E-clip.

11. If it is necessary to remove the throttle plates, lightly scribe along the shaft and mark the plates T or C for throttle or choke side to ensure proper assembly.

➡ **The throttle plate screws are staked at assembly. The staked ends should be filed before removal and the old screws discarded once removed.**

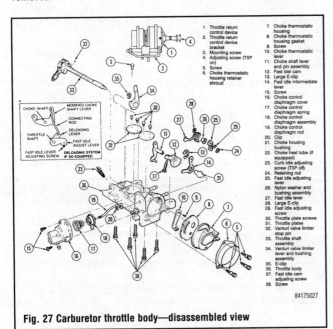

Fig. 27 Carburetor throttle body—disassembled view

1. Throttle return control device
2. Throttle return control device bracket
3. Mounting screw
4. Adjusting screw (TSP on)
5. Screw
6. Choke thermostatic housing retainer shroud
7. Choke thermostatic housing
8. Choke thermostatic housing gasket
9. Screw
10. Choke thermostatic lever
11. Choke shaft lever and pin assembly
12. Fast idel cam
13. Large E-clip
14. Fast idle intermediate lever
15. Screw
16. Choke control diaphragm cover
17. Choke control diaphragm spring
18. Choke control diaphragm assembly
19. Choke control diaphragm rod
20. Clip
21. Choke housing bushing
22. Choke heat tube (if equipped)
23. Curb idle adjusting screw (TSP off)
24. Retaining nut
25. Fast idle adjusting lever
26. Nylon washer and bushing assembly
27. Fast idle lever
28. Large E-clip
29. Fast idle adjusting screw
30. Throttle plate screws
31. Throttle plates
32. Venturi valve limiter stop pin
33. Throttle shaft assembly
34. Venturi valve limiter lever and bushing assembly
35. E-clip
36. Throttle body
37. Fast idle cam adjusting screw
38. Screw

84175027

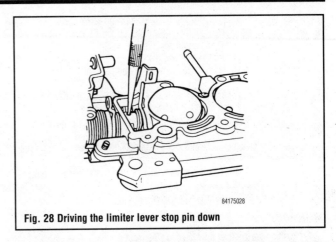

Fig. 28 Driving the limiter lever stop pin down

84175028

12. In order to remove the throttle shaft, it is necessary to drive the limiter lever stop pin down until it is flush with the shaft. Remove the E-clip next to the venturi valve limiter lever.

13. Slide the throttle shaft out of the casting.

14. Remove the venturi valve limiter lever and bushing assembly.

Assembly

Obtain a quality carburetor overhaul service kit that contains the necessary replacement parts and gaskets. All applicable gaskets and parts included in the kit should be installed during assembly. Discard the old parts and gaskets.

Wash all carburetor parts, except those containing diaphragms, electrical components and other non-metallic parts, in clean commercial carburetor cleaning solvent. Rinse the parts in kerosene to remove all traces of the cleaning solvent, then dry them with compressed air. Wipe all parts clean that cannot be immersed in solvent with a clean, soft, lint-free cloth. Make sure all dirt, gum, carbon and other foreign matter are removed from all parts.

Force compressed air through all carburetor passages. Do not use a wire brush to clean any parts, or a drill or wire to clean out any openings or passages in the carburetor. A drill or wire may enlarge the hole or passage, changing the carburetor calibration.

Check the Cold Enrichment Rod (CER) and Control Vacuum Rod (CVR) for grooves, wear and excessive looseness or binding. Inspect the choke linkage for ease of operation and free it, if necessary. Make sure all carbon and foreign material has been removed from the automatic choke housing. Check the operation of the choke pulldown diaphragm to ensure it has free movement. Replace worn parts as necessary.

Check the throttle shafts in the bores for excessive looseness or binding and check the throttle plates for burrs that could prevent proper closure. Inspect the main body, throttle body, venturi valve assembly, underbody assemblies, choke housing and thermostatic spring housing, enrichment valve cover and accelerator pump cover for cracks. Replace worn parts as necessary. If a float leaks, replace it. Replace the float if the arm needle contact surface is grooved. If the float is usable, polish the needle contact surface of the arm with crocus cloth. Replace the float shaft if it is worn. Replace all screws and nuts that have stripped threads. Replace all distorted or broken springs.

Inspect all gasket mating surfaces for nicks and burrs. Service or replace any parts that have a damaged gasket surface. Make sure all traces of old gasket material have been removed from the gasket mating surfaces.

THROTTLE BODY

1. Carefully support the throttle shaft and drive out the venturi valve limiter stop pin, if equipped. Discard the pin.

2. Place the venturi valve limiter assembly in the throttle body and slide the throttle shaft into place. Install the E-clip.

3. Place the throttle plates in position, aligning the scribe marks made during disassembly, and turn the screws in until they are snug, but not tight. With the throttle closed, tap the plates lightly to ensure proper centering. Tighten the screws to 10–15 inch lbs. (1.1–1.7 Nm), then carefully stake them.

4. Drive the new venturi valve limiter stop pin into the shaft, leaving approximately ⅛ in. (3.18mm) exposed. Install the retaining screws and E-clip.

5. Install the E-clip, fast idle lever, nylon bushing, fast idle adjusting lever,

the throttle shaft retaining nut, and the fast idle adjusting screw. Install the deloading lever, if equipped.

6. Install the (TSP off) idle speed adjusting screw.

7. If the choke housing bushing was removed, it must be carefully pressed into the housing and staked in place. Carefully support the casting while pressing and staking.

8. Install the fast idle intermediate lever, large E-clip, and the fast idle cam and adjusting screw. Install the deloading lever, if equipped.

9. Slide the choke control diaphragm rod into position and engage the rod and E-clip.

10. Slide the choke shaft lever and pin assembly into the casting and install the choke thermostatic lever and screw.

11. Install the choke control diaphragm, spring, cover and screws. Tighten the screws to 13–19 inch lbs. (1.5–2.1 Nm).

12. Install the throttle return control device and bracket.

MAIN BODY

1. Position the throttle body gasket on the main body and assemble the main body to the throttle body. Tighten the retaining screws to 24–35 inch lbs. (2.7–4.0 Nm).

2. Drop the accelerator pump check ball and weight into the pump discharge channel.

3. Do not install the venturi valve limiter stop screw, torque retention spring and plug at this time. They should be installed after complete assembly. Refer to the Venturi Valve WOT Opening adjustment.

4. Slide the venturi valve diaphragm into the main body.

5. Install the venturi valve diaphragm spring, spring guide and cover. Loosely install the retaining screws. Depress the diaphragm stem with your finger to prevent pinching the diaphragm between the cover and casting. Diagonally tighten the screws to 15–22 inch lbs. (1.7–2.5 Nm), then release the diaphragm stem.

6. Install the feedback motor, gasket, pintle valve and pintle spring. Tighten the motor to 8–10 ft. lbs. (11–14 Nm).

UPPER BODY

▶ **See Figures 29 and 30**

1. Install the ⅛ in. pipe plug in the fuel inlet boss and tighten to 5–7 ft. lbs. (7–9 Nm).

2. Install the venturi valve limiter screw in the venturi valve.

3. Lubricate the O-ring seals with a mild solution of soapy water and install on the metering jets.

➡**Do not use silicone lubricant on the O-ring seals.**

4. Using metering jet adjusting tool T77L–9533–A or equivalent, turn each main metering jet clockwise until it is seated lightly in the casting. Then turn each jet counterclockwise the number of turns recorded during disassembly.

5. Using jet plug installer T77L–9533–C or equivalent, install the jet plugs. Tap lightly until the tool bottoms on the face of the casting.

6. Install the metering rods, metering rod springs and the metering rod pivot pins on the venturi valve.

7. Install the venturi valve, carefully guiding the metering rods into the main metering jets. Press down on the metering rods. If the springs are properly assembled they will spring back.

8. Install the venturi valve pivot pin bushings and the pivot pins.

9. Carefully press the tapered plugs into the venturi valve pivot pins with pivot pin tool T77L–9928–A or equivalent.

10. Install the venturi valve cover plate roller bearings, a new gasket and the attaching screws. Tighten the screws to 24–35 inch lbs. (2.7–4.0 Nm).

11. Install the accelerator pump operating rod and the dust seal. Attach the E-clip and washer. Slide the accelerator pump overtravel spring on to the rod.

12. Insert the accelerator pump lever and swivel assembly into the cold enrichment lever. Install the accelerator pump link screw and nut. Install the accelerator pump adjusting nut.

13. Install a new fuel inlet valve seat gasket, the seat and the valve. Install a new float bowl gasket.

14. Install the float and the float hinge pin. Check and adjust the float level according to the procedure in this Section.

15. Assemble the accelerator pump return spring, cup and plunger. Place the pump piston assembly in position in the hole in the upper body.

16. Install a new service swivel assembly as follows:

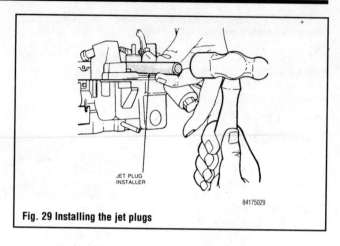

Fig. 29 Installing the jet plugs

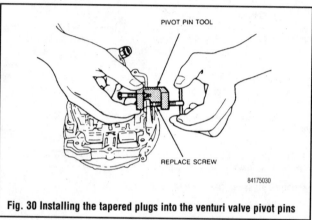

Fig. 30 Installing the tapered plugs into the venturi valve pivot pins

a. Assemble the lever to the swivel.

b. Position the assembly and tighten the CER nut 4–5 turns on the choke control rod.

c. Seat the assembly.

17. Install the choke control rod. For final adjustment after complete assembly, refer to the Choke adjustment procedure in this Section.

18. Assemble the upper body to the main body. Hold the accelerator pump piston assembly with your finger and guide it into the pump cavity in the main body.

19. Install the choke control rod dust seal and tap gently to straighten the retainer. If the choke control rod broke during disassembly, prior to installing the upper body, a new rod must be positioned through the opening. Tighten the upper body retaining screws to 24–35 inch lbs. (2.7–4.0 Nm).

➡**Make sure the venturi valve diaphragm stem engages the venturi valve.**

20. Install the fuel filter spring, a new filter, a new inlet fitting gasket and the inlet fitting. Tighten the fitting to 7–10 ft. lbs. (10.2–14.1 Nm).

21. After setting the choke rod adjustment, install the air cleaner stud and tighten to 6–9 ft. lbs. (8–12 Nm).

22. Slide the cold enrichment rod into the upper body. Install the choke hinge pin and the E-ring.

23. Engage the accelerator pump operating rod, the choke control rod and install the E-ring retainers.

24. Check and adjust the fast idle cam.

25. After setting the choke adjustment, position the gasket and install the choke cap, retaining shroud and new breakaway screws.

➡**Make sure the bimetal spring tab is engaged in the slotted choke shaft lever.**

26. Set the choke cap to specification, then tighten the screws until the Torx® heads break off.

27. Install the venturi valve limiter stop screw and tighten the retention spring (omitted when assembling the main body). Follow the venturi valve limiter adjusting procedure. Install the plug after the adjustment is made.

28. Install the carburetor and adjust the idle speeds.

FUEL INJECTION SYSTEM

Description

▶ **See Figures 31 and 32**

All vehicles with the 4.6L and 5.0L engines are equipped with a Sequential Electronic Fuel Injection (SEFI) system. In this system, fuel is metered into each intake port in sequence with the engine firing order, according to engine demand, through fuel injectors mounted on a tuned intake manifold.

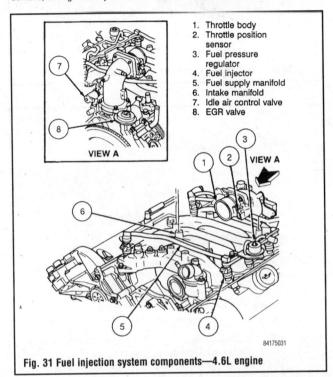

1. Throttle body
2. Throttle position sensor
3. Fuel pressure regulator
4. Fuel injector
5. Fuel supply manifold
6. Intake manifold
7. Idle air control valve
8. EGR valve

Fig. 31 Fuel injection system components—4.6L engine

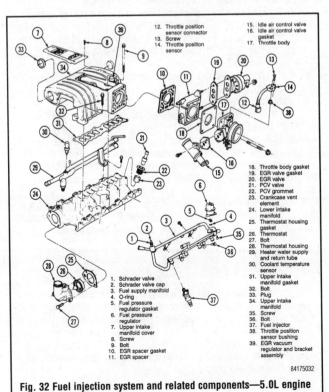

12. Throttle position sensor connector
13. Screw
14. Throttle position sensor
15. Idle air control valve
16. Idle air control valve gasket
17. Throttle body
18. Throttle body gasket
19. EGR valve gasket
20. EGR valve
21. PCV valve
22. PCV grommet
23. Crankcase vent element
24. Lower intake manifold
25. Thermostat housing gasket
26. Thermostat
27. Bolt
28. Thermostat housing
29. Heater water supply and return tube
30. Coolant temperature sensor
31. Upper intake manifold gasket
32. Bolt
33. Plug
34. Upper intake manifold
35. Screw
36. Bolt
37. Fuel injector
38. Throttle position sensor bushing
39. EGR vacuum regulator and bracket assembly

1. Schrader valve
2. Schrader valve cap
3. Fuel supply manifold
4. O-ring
5. Fuel pressure regulator gasket
6. Fuel pressure regulator
7. Upper intake manifold cover
8. Bolt
9. Bolt
10. EGR spacer gasket
11. EGR spacer

Fig. 32 Fuel injection system and related components—5.0L engine

The SEFI system consists of two subsystems, the fuel delivery system and the electronic control system. The fuel delivery system supplies fuel to the fuel injectors at a specified pressure. The electronic control system regulates the flow of fuel from the injectors into the engine.

The fuel delivery system consists of an electric fuel pump, fuel filters, fuel supply manifold (fuel rail), fuel pressure regulator and fuel injectors. The electric fuel pump, mounted in the fuel tank, draws fuel through a filter screen attached to the fuel pump/sending unit assembly. Fuel is pumped through a frame mounted fuel filter, to the engine compartment, and into the fuel supply manifold. The fuel supply manifold supplies fuel directly to the injectors. A constant fuel pressure to the injectors is maintained by the fuel pressure regulator. The fuel pressure regulator is mounted on the fuel supply manifold, downstream from the fuel injectors. The excess fuel supplied by the fuel pump but not required by the engine, passes through the regulator and returns to the fuel tank through the fuel return line. The fuel injectors spray a metered quantity of fuel into the intake air stream when they are energized. The quantity of fuel is determined by the electronic control system.

Air entering the engine is monitored by speed, pressure and temperature sensors. The outputs of these sensors are processed by the Powertrain Control Module (PCM). The PCM computes the required fuel flow rate and determines the needed injector pulse width (injector "on" time) and sends a signal to the injector to meter the exact quantity of fuel. Each fuel injector is energized once every other crankshaft revolution, in sequence with the ignition firing order.

➡**For description and testing of electronic control system components, see Section 4.**

Relieving Fuel System Pressure

❊❊ CAUTION

Fuel supply lines on fuel injected vehicles will remain pressurized for some time after the engine is shut off. Fuel pressure must be relieved before servicing the fuel system.

1. Disconnect the negative battery cable.
2. Remove the fuel tank cap to relieve the pressure in the fuel tank.
3. Remove the cap from the Schrader valve located on the fuel supply manifold.
4. Attach fuel pressure gauge T80L–9974–A or equivalent, to the Schrader valve and drain the fuel through the drain tube into a suitable container.
5. After the fuel system pressure is relieved, remove the fuel pressure gauge and install the cap on the Schrader valve.

Fuel Line Couplings

REMOVAL & INSTALLATION

There are 3 methods in use to connect the fuel lines and fuel system components, the hairpin clip push connect fitting, the duck bill clip or steel push connect fitting, and the spring lock coupling. Each requires a different procedure to disconnect and connect.

Hairpin Clip Push Connect Fitting

▶ **See Figure 33**

1. Inspect the visible internal portion of the fitting for dirt accumulation. If more than a light coating of dust is present, clean the fitting before disassembly.
2. Some adhesion between the seals in the fitting and the tubing will occur with time. To separate, twist the fitting on the tube, then push and pull the fitting until it moves freely on the tube.
3. Remove the hairpin clip from the fitting by first bending and breaking the shipping tab. Next, spread the 2 clip legs by hand about ⅛ in. each to disengage the body and push the legs into the fitting. Lightly pull the triangular end of the clip and work it clear of the tube and fitting.

➡**Do not use hand tools to complete this operation.**

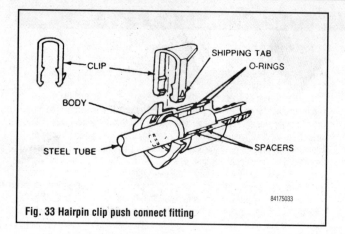

Fig. 33 Hairpin clip push connect fitting

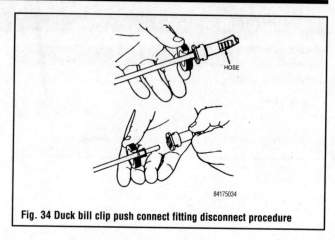

Fig. 34 Duck bill clip push connect fitting disconnect procedure

4. Grasp the fitting and pull in an axial direction to remove the fitting from the tube. Be careful on 90 degree elbow connectors, as excessive side loading could break the connector body.

5. After disassembly, inspect and clean the tube end sealing surfaces. The tube end should be free of scratches and corrosion that could provide leak paths. Inspect the inside of the fitting for any internal parts such as O-rings and spacers that may have been dislodged from the fitting. Replace any damaged connector.

To connect:

6. Install a new connector if damage was found. Insert a new clip into any 2 adjacent openings with the triangular portion pointing away from the fitting opening. Install the clip until the legs of the clip are locked on the outside of the body. Piloting with an index finger is necessary.

7. Before installing the fitting on the tube, wipe the tube end with a clean cloth. Inspect the inside of the fitting to make sure it is free of dirt and/or obstructions.

8. Apply a light coating of engine oil to the tube end. Align the fitting and tube axially and push the fitting onto the tube end. When the fitting is engaged, a definite click will be heard. Pull on the fitting to make sure it is fully engaged.

Duck Bill Clip or Steel Push Connect Fitting

▶ **See Figures 34 and 35**

This fitting consists of a body, spacers, O-rings and a retaining clip. The retaining clip is referred to as a "duck bill" retaining clip on 1989–90 vehicles.

1. Inspect the visible internal portion of the fitting for dirt accumulation. If more than a light coating of dust is present, clean the fitting before disassembly.

2. Some adhesion between the seals in the fitting and the tubing will occur with time. To separate, twist the fitting on the tube, then push and pull the fitting until it moves freely on the tube.

3. On 1989–90 vehicles, align the slot on push connect disassembly tool T82L–9500–AH or equivalent, with either tab on the clip, 90 degrees from the slots on the side of the fitting and insert the tool. This disengages the duck bill retainer from the tube. Holding the tool and the tube with 1 hand, pull the fitting away from the tube.

4. On 1991–94 vehicles, snap disassembly tool T90T–9550–B (⁵⁄₁₆ in.) or T90T–9550–C (³⁄₈ in.) or equivalent, with either tab on the fuel line to be disconnected. Push the tool into the connector to release the internal locking fingers. Separate the fuel line from the connector and remove the tool.

➡**Use hands only. Only moderate effort is required if the tube has been properly disengaged.**

5. After disassembly, inspect and clean the tube end sealing surfaces. The tube end should be free of scratches and corrosion that could provide leak paths. Inspect the inside of the fitting for any internal parts such as O-rings and spacers that may have been dislodged from the fitting. Replace any damaged connector.

6. Some fuel tubes have a secondary bead which aligns with the outer surface of the clip. These beads can make tool insertion difficult. If there is extreme difficulty, on 1989–90 vehicles use the following disassembly method:

    a. Using pliers with a jaw width of 0.2 in. (5mm) or less, align the jaws with the openings in the side of the fitting case and compress the portion of the retaining clip that engages the fitting case. This disengages the retaining

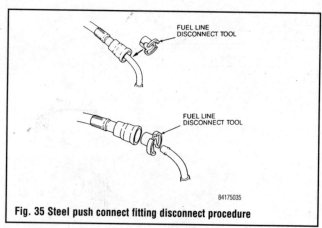

Fig. 35 Steel push connect fitting disconnect procedure

clip from the case. Often 1 side of the clip will disengage before the other. The clip must be disengaged from both openings.

    b. Pull the fitting off the tube by hand only. Only moderate effort is required if the retaining clip has been properly disengaged.

    c. After disassembly, inspect and clean the tube end sealing surfaces. The tube end should be free of scratches and corrosion that could provide leak paths. Inspect the inside of the fitting for any internal parts such as O-rings and spacers that may have been dislodged from the fitting. Replace any damaged connector.

    d. The retaining clip will remain on the tube. Disengage the clip from the tube bead and remove.

To connect:

7. Install a new connector if damage was found. On 1989–90 vehicles, install the new replacement clip into the body by inserting 1 of the retaining clip serrated edges on the duck bill portion into 1 side of the window openings. Push on the other side until the clip snaps into place.

8. Before installing the fitting on the tube, wipe the tube end with a clean cloth. Inspect the inside of the fitting to make sure it is free of dirt and/or obstructions.

9. Apply a light coating of engine oil to the tube end. Align the fitting and tube axially and push the fitting onto the tube end. When the fitting is engaged, a definite click will be heard. Pull on the fitting to make sure it is fully engaged.

Spring Lock Coupling

▶ **See Figures 36 and 37**

The spring lock coupling is a fuel line coupling held together by a garter spring inside a circular cage. When the coupling is connected together, the flared end of the female fitting slips behind the garter spring inside the cage of the male fitting. The garter spring and cage then prevent the flared end of the female fitting from pulling out of the cage. As an additional locking feature, a horseshoe shaped retaining clip is incorporated that improves the retaining reliability of the spring lock coupling.

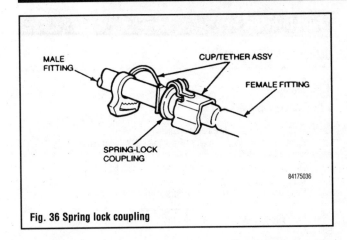

Fig. 36 Spring lock coupling

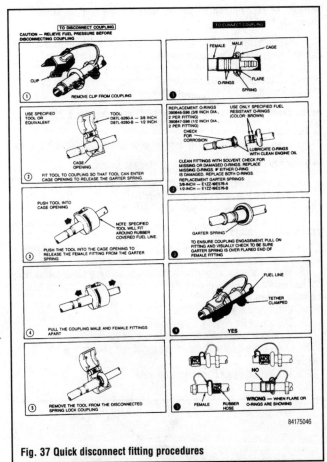

Fig. 37 Quick disconnect fitting procedures

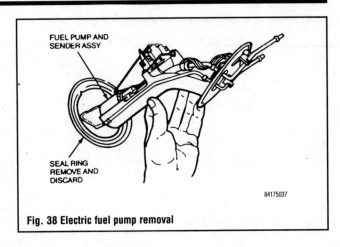

Fig. 38 Electric fuel pump removal

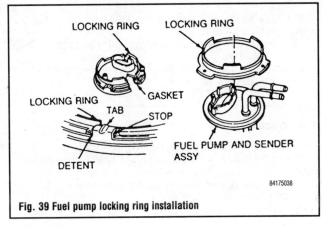

Fig. 39 Fuel pump locking ring installation

Electric Fuel Pump

REMOVAL & INSTALLATION

▶ **See Figures 38 and 39**

1. Disconnect the negative battery cable. Relieve the fuel system pressure as explained in this Section.
2. Remove the fuel tank and place it on a bench.
3. Remove any dirt that has accumulated around the fuel pump retaining flange so it will not enter the tank during pump removal and installation.
4. Turn the fuel pump locking ring counterclockwise and remove the locking ring.
5. Remove the fuel pump/sending unit assembly. Remove and discard the seal ring.

To install:

6. Clean the fuel pump mounting flange, fuel tank mounting surface and seal ring groove.
7. Apply a light coating of grease on a new seal ring to hold it in place during assembly and install in the seal ring groove.
8. Install the fuel pump/sending unit assembly carefully to ensure the filter is not damaged. Make sure the locating keys are in the keyways and the seal ring remains in the groove.
9. Hold the pump assembly in place and install the locking ring finger-tight. Make sure all the locking tabs are under the tank lock ring tabs.
10. Rotate the locking ring clockwise until the ring is against the stops.
11. Install the fuel tank in the vehicle. Add a minimum of 10 gallons of fuel to the tank and check for leaks.
12. Install a suitable fuel pressure gauge to the Schrader valve on the fuel supply manifold.
13. Turn the ignition switch from **OFF** to **ON** for 3 seconds. Repeat this procedure 5–10 times until the pressure gauge shows at least 35 psi. Check for fuel leaks.
14. Remove the pressure gauge, start the engine and check for leaks.

Throttle Body

REMOVAL & INSTALLATION

4.6L Engine

▶ **See Figure 40**

1. Disconnect the negative battery cable.
2. Disconnect the throttle position sensor and throttle linkage at the throttle lever.
3. Remove the 4 throttle body mounting bolts.
4. Carefully separate the throttle body from the intake manifold adapter.
5. Remove and discard the gasket between the throttle body adapter.

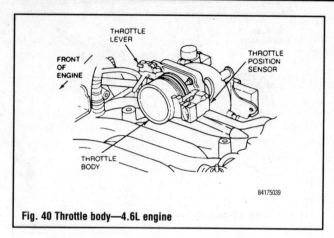

Fig. 40 Throttle body—4.6L engine

To install:

6. Clean all gasket mating surfaces, being careful not to damage them or allow material to drop into the manifold.

7. Install the throttle body, a new gasket and the 4 mounting bolts. Tighten the bolts to 6–8.5 ft. lbs. (8–11.5 Nm).

8. Connect the throttle position sensor and the throttle linkage. Connect the negative battery cable.

5.0L Engine

▶ **See Figure 41**

1. Disconnect the negative battery cable.

2. Disconnect the throttle position sensor and idle air control valve connectors.

3. Remove the PCV vent closure hose at the throttle body.

4. Remove the 4 throttle body mounting nuts.

5. Carefully separate the throttle body from the EGR spacer and intake manifold.

6. Remove and discard the gasket between the throttle body and EGR spacer.

To install:

7. Clean all gasket mating surfaces, being careful not to damage them or allow material to drop into the manifold.

8. Install the throttle body with a new gasket on the 4 studs of the EGR spacer. Install the nuts and tighten to 12–18 ft. lbs. (16–24 Nm).

9. Connect the PCV vent closure hose. Connect the throttle position sensor and idle air control valve connectors.

10. Connect the negative battery cable.

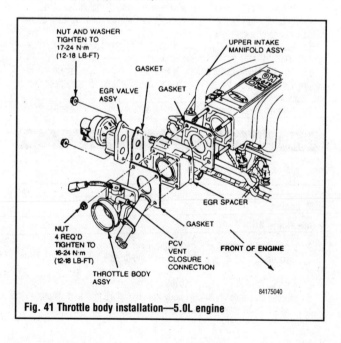

Fig. 41 Throttle body installation—5.0L engine

Fuel Injectors

REMOVAL & INSTALLATION

4.6L Engine

▶ **See Figures 42, 43 and 44**

1. Disconnect the negative battery cable.

2. Remove the fuel tank cap and relieve the fuel system pressure, as explained in this Section.

3. Disconnect the vacuum line at the pressure regulator.

4. Disconnect the fuel lines from the fuel rail.

5. Disconnect the electrical connectors from the injectors.

6. Remove the fuel rail assembly retaining bolts.

7. Carefully disengage the fuel rail from the fuel injectors and remove the fuel rail.

➡ **It may be easier to remove the injectors with the fuel rail as an assembly.**

8. Grasping the injector body, pull while gently rocking the injector from side-to-side to remove the injector from the fuel rail or intake manifold.

9. Inspect the pintle protection cap and washer for signs of deterioration. Replace the complete injector, as required. If the cap is missing, look for it in the intake manifold.

➡ **The pintle protection cap is not available as a separate part.**

To install:

10. Lubricate new O-rings with light grade oil and install 2 on each injector.

➡ **Never use silicone grease as it will clog the injectors.**

11. Install the injectors using a light, twisting, pushing motion.

12. Install the fuel rail, pushing it down to ensure all injector O-rings are fully seated in the fuel rail cups and intake manifold.

13. Install the retaining bolts while holding the fuel rail down and tighten to 71–106 inch lbs. (8–12 Nm).

14. Connect the fuel lines to the fuel rail and the vacuum line to the pressure regulator.

15. With the injector wiring disconnected, connect the negative battery cable and turn the ignition switch to the **RUN** position to allow the fuel pump to pressurize the system.

16. Check for fuel leaks.

17. Disconnect the negative battery cable.

18. Connect the electrical connectors to the fuel injectors.

19. Connect the negative battery cable and start the engine. Let it idle for 2 minutes.

20. Turn the engine **OFF** and check for leaks.

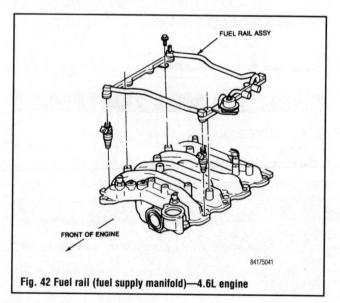

Fig. 42 Fuel rail (fuel supply manifold)—4.6L engine

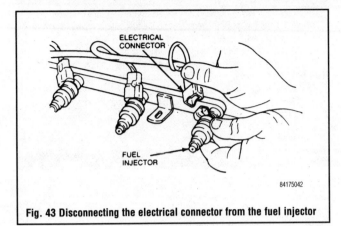

Fig. 43 Disconnecting the electrical connector from the fuel injector

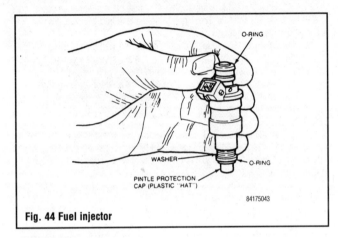

Fig. 44 Fuel injector

5.0L Engine

♦ See Figures 43, 44 and 45

1. Disconnect the negative battery cable.
2. Remove the fuel tank cap and relieve the fuel system pressure, as explained in this Section.
3. Partially drain the cooling system into a suitable container.

✶✶✶ CAUTION

When draining the coolant, keep in mind that cats and dogs are attracted by the ethylene glycol antifreeze, and are quite likely to drink any that is left in an uncovered container or in puddles on the ground. This will prove fatal in sufficient quantity. Always drain the coolant into a sealable container. Coolant should be reused unless it is contaminated or several years old.

4. Label and disconnect the electrical connectors at the idle air control valve, throttle position sensor and EGR sensor.
5. Disconnect the throttle linkage at the throttle ball and transmission linkage from the throttle body. Remove the 2 bolts securing the bracket to the intake manifold and position the bracket with the cables aside.
6. Label and disconnect the upper intake manifold vacuum fitting connections by disconnecting all vacuum lines to the vacuum tree, EGR valve, fuel pressure regulator and evaporative canister.
7. Disconnect the PCV hose from the fitting on the rear of the upper manifold and disconnect the PCV vent closure tube at the throttle body.
8. Remove the 2 EGR coolant lines from the fittings on the EGR spacer.
9. Remove the 6 upper intake manifold retaining bolts.
10. Remove the upper intake and throttle body as an assembly from the lower intake manifold.
11. Disconnect the fuel lines from the fuel rail.
12. Remove the 4 fuel rail assembly retaining bolts.
13. Disconnect the electrical connectors from the injectors.
14. Carefully disengage the fuel rail from the fuel injectors.

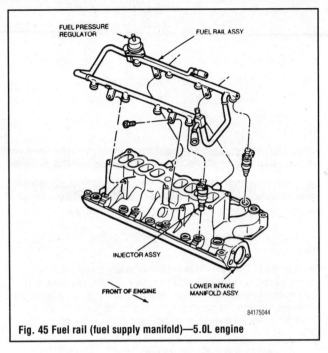

Fig. 45 Fuel rail (fuel supply manifold)—5.0L engine

➡**It may be easier to remove the injectors with the fuel rail as an assembly.**

15. Grasping the injector body, pull up while gently rocking the injector from side-to-side to remove the injector from the fuel rail or intake manifold.
16. Inspect the pintle protection cap and washer for signs of deterioration. Replace the complete injector, as required. If the cap is missing, look for it in the intake manifold.

➡**The pintle protection cap is not available as a separate part.**

To install:
17. Lubricate new O-rings with light grade oil and install 2 on each injector.

➡**Never use silicone grease as it will clog the injectors.**

18. Install the injectors using a light, twisting, pushing motion.
19. Install the fuel rail, pushing it down to ensure all the injector O-rings are fully seated in the fuel rail cups and intake manifold.
20. Install the retaining bolts while holding the fuel rail down and tighten to 71–106 inch lbs. (8–12 Nm).
21. Connect the fuel lines to the fuel rail.
22. With the injector wiring disconnected, connect the negative battery cable and turn the ignition switch to the **RUN** position to allow the fuel pump to pressurize the system.
23. Check for fuel leaks.
24. Disconnect the negative battery cable.
25. Connect the electrical connectors to the injectors.
26. Install the upper intake manifold and throttle body assembly by reversing the removal procedure. Use a new gasket and tighten the retaining bolts to 12–18 ft. lbs. (16–24 Nm).
27. Refill the cooling system and connect the negative battery cable.
28. Start the engine and let it idle for 2 minutes. Turn the engine **OFF** and check for leaks.

Fuel Pressure Regulator

REMOVAL & INSTALLATION

1. Disconnect the negative battery cable.
2. Remove the fuel tank cap and relieve the fuel system pressure, as explained in this Section.
3. Disconnect the vacuum line at the pressure regulator.
4. Remove and discard the 3 Allen head screws retaining the regulator housing.

5. Remove the pressure regulator, gasket and O-ring.

6. If scraping is necessary to remove old gasket material, be careful not to damage the pressure regulator or fuel supply manifold gasket surfaces.

To install:

7. Lubricate a new fuel pressure regulator O-ring with clean engine oil.

➡ **Never use silicone grease as it will clog the injectors.**

8. Make sure the pressure regulator and fuel supply manifold gasket mating surfaces are clean.

9. Install the new O-ring and new gasket on the pressure regulator.

10. Install the fuel pressure regulator on the fuel supply manifold. Install new Allen screws and tighten to 27–40 inch lbs. (3–4.5 Nm).

11. Connect the vacuum line to the pressure regulator.

12. Connect the negative battery cable and turn the ignition switch to the **RUN** position to allow the fuel pump to pressurize the system.

13. Check for fuel leaks.

14. Start the engine and let it idle for 2 minutes. Turn the engine **OFF** and check for leaks.

FUEL TANK

REMOVAL & INSTALLATION

1. Disconnect the negative battery cable and relieve the fuel system pressure.

2. Siphon or pump as much fuel as possible out through the fuel filler pipe.

➡ **Fuel injected vehicles have reservoirs inside the fuel tank to maintain fuel near the fuel pickup during cornering and under low fuel operating conditions. These reservoirs could block siphon tubes or hoses from reaching the bottom of the fuel tank. Repeated attempts using different hose orientations can overcome this obstacle.**

3. Raise and safely support the vehicle.

4. If equipped with a metal retainer that fastens the filler pipe to the fuel tank, remove the screw attaching the retainer to the fuel tank flange.

5. Disconnect the fuel lines and the electrical connector to the fuel tank sending unit. On some vehicles, these are inaccessible on top of the tank. In these cases they must be disconnected with the tank partially removed.

6. Place a safety support under the fuel tank and remove the bolts or nuts from the fuel tank straps. Allow the straps to swing out of the way.

7. Partially remove the tank and disconnect the fuel lines and electrical connector from the sending unit, if not disconnected previously.

8. Remove the tank from the vehicle.

To install:

9. Raise the fuel tank into position in the vehicle. Connect the fuel lines and sending unit electrical connector if it is necessary to connect them before the tank is in the final installed position.

10. Lubricate the fuel filler pipe with water base tire mounting lubricant and install the tank onto the filler pipe, then bring the tank into final position. Be careful not to deform the tank.

11. Bring the fuel tank straps around the tank and start the retaining nut or bolt. Align the tank with the straps. If equipped, make sure the fuel tank shields are installed with the straps and are positioned correctly on the tank.

12. Check the hoses and wiring mounted on the tank top to make sure they are correctly routed and will not be pinched between the tank and body.

13. Tighten the fuel tank strap retaining nuts or bolts to 20–30 ft. lbs. (28–40 Nm).

14. If not already connected, connect the fuel hoses and lines which were disconnected. Make sure the fuel supply, fuel return, if present, and vapor vent connections are made correctly. If not already connected, connect the sending unit electrical connector.

15. Lower the vehicle. Replace the fuel that was drained from the tank. Check all connections for leaks.

SENDING UNIT REPLACEMENT

Refer to the Electric Fuel Pump removal & installation procedure.

TORQUE SPECIFICATIONS

Component	U.S.	Metric
Carburetor		
Air cleaner stud	6–9 ft. lbs.	8–12 Nm
Choke control diaphragm screws	13–19 inch lbs.	1.5–2.1 Nm
Feedback motor	8–10 ft. lbs.	11–14 Nm
Fuel filter inlet fitting	7–10 ft. lbs.	10.2–14.1 Nm
Fuel inlet boss pipe plug	5–7 ft. lbs.	7–9 Nm
Main body-to-throttle body screws	24–35 inch lbs.	2.7–4.0 Nm
Mounting nuts	12–15 ft. lbs.	16–20 Nm
Throttle plate screws	10–15 inch lbs.	1.1–1.7 Nm
Upper body retaining screws	24–35 inch lbs.	2.7–4.0 Nm
Venturi valve cover plate screws	24–35 inch. lbs.	2.7–4.0 Nm
Venturi valve diaphragm screws	15–22 inch lbs.	1.7–2.5 Nm
Fuel pressure regulator screws	27–40 inch lbs.	3–4.5 Nm
Fuel pump mounting bolts		
5.8L engine	19–27 ft. lbs.	26–37 Nm
Fuel pump outlet line fitting		
5.8L engine	15–18 ft. lbs.	20–24 Nm
Fuel supply manifold retaining bolts	71–106 inch lbs.	8–12 Nm
Fuel tank strap nuts/bolts	20–30 ft. lbs.	28–40 Nm
Throttle body bolts		
4.6L engine	6–8.5 ft. lbs.	8–11.5 Nm
Throttle body nuts		
5.0L engine	12–18 ft. lbs.	16–24 Nm
Upper intake manifold retaining bolts		
5.0L engine	12–18 ft. lbs.	16–24 Nm

84175045

6

CHASSIS ELECTRICAL

UNDERSTANDING AND TROUBLESHOOTING ELECTRICAL SYSTEMS

Basic Electrical Theory

♦ **See Figure 1**

For any 12 volt, negative ground, electrical system to operate, the electricity must travel in a complete circuit. This simply means that current (power) from the positive (+) terminal of the battery must eventually return to the negative (–) terminal of the battery. Along the way, this current will travel through wires, fuses, switches and components. If, for any reason, the flow of current through the circuit is interrupted, the component fed by that circuit will cease to function properly.

Perhaps the easiest way to visualize a circuit is to think of connecting a light bulb (with two wires attached to it) to the battery—one wire attached to the negative (–) terminal of the battery and the other wire to the positive (+) terminal. With the two wires touching the battery terminals, the circuit would be complete and the light bulb would illuminate. Electricity would follow a path from the battery to the bulb and back to the battery. It's easy to see that with longer wires on our light bulb, it could be mounted anywhere. Further, one wire could be fitted with a switch so that the light could be turned on and off.

The normal automotive circuit differs from this simple example in two ways. First, instead of having a return wire from the bulb to the battery, the current travels through the frame of the vehicle. Since the negative (–) battery cable is attached to the frame (made of electrically conductive metal), the frame of the vehicle can serve as a ground wire to complete the circuit. Secondly, most automotive circuits contain multiple components which receive power from a single circuit. This lessens the amount of wire needed to power components on the vehicle.

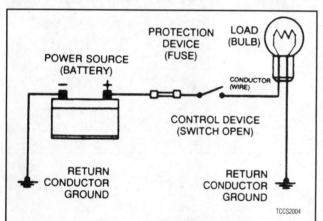

Fig. 1 This example illustrates a simple circuit. When the switch is closed, power from the positive (+) battery terminal flows through the fuse and the switch, and then to the light bulb. The light illuminates and the circuit is completed through the ground wire back to the negative (–) battery terminal. In reality, the two ground points shown in the illustration are attached to the metal frame of the vehicle, which completes the circuit back to the battery

HOW DOES ELECTRICITY WORK: THE WATER ANALOGY

Electricity is the flow of electrons—the subatomic particles that constitute the outer shell of an atom. Electrons spin in an orbit around the center core of an atom. The center core is comprised of protons (positive charge) and neutrons (neutral charge). Electrons have a negative charge and balance out the positive charge of the protons. When an outside force causes the number of electrons to unbalance the charge of the protons, the electrons will split off the atom and look for another atom to balance out. If this imbalance is kept up, electrons will continue to move and an electrical flow will exist.

Many people have been taught electrical theory using an analogy with water. In a comparison with water flowing through a pipe, the electrons would be the water and the wire is the pipe.

The flow of electricity can be measured much like the flow of water through a pipe. The unit of measurement used is amperes, frequently abbreviated as amps

(a). You can compare amperage to the volume of water flowing through a pipe. When connected to a circuit, an ammeter will measure the actual amount of current flowing through the circuit. When relatively few electrons flow through a circuit, the amperage is low. When many electrons flow, the amperage is high.

Water pressure is measured in units such as pounds per square inch (psi); The electrical pressure is measured in units called volts (v). When a voltmeter is connected to a circuit, it is measuring the electrical pressure.

The actual flow of electricity depends not only on voltage and amperage, but also on the resistance of the circuit. The higher the resistance, the higher the force necessary to push the current through the circuit. The standard unit for measuring resistance is an ohm. Resistance in a circuit varies depending on the amount and type of components used in the circuit. The main factors which determine resistance are:

• Material—some materials have more resistance than others. Those with high resistance are said to be insulators. Rubber materials (or rubber-like plastics) are some of the most common insulators used in vehicles as they have a very high resistance to electricity. Very low resistance materials are said to be conductors. Copper wire is among the best conductors. Silver is actually a superior conductor to copper and is used in some relay contacts, but its high cost prohibits its use as common wiring. Most automotive wiring is made of copper.

• Size—the larger the wire size being used, the less resistance the wire will have. This is why components which use large amounts of electricity usually have large wires supplying current to them.

• Length—for a given thickness of wire, the longer the wire, the greater the resistance. The shorter the wire, the less the resistance. When determining the proper wire for a circuit, both size and length must be considered to design a circuit that can handle the current needs of the component.

• Temperature—with many materials, the higher the temperature, the greater the resistance (positive temperature coefficient). Some materials exhibit the opposite trait of lower resistance with higher temperatures (negative temperature coefficient). These principles are used in many of the sensors on the engine.

OHM'S LAW

There is a direct relationship between current, voltage and resistance. The relationship between current, voltage and resistance can be summed up by a statement known as Ohm's law.

Voltage (E) is equal to amperage (I) times resistance (R): $E = I \times R$
Other forms of the formula are $R = E/I$ and $I = E/R$

In each of these formulas, E is the voltage in volts, I is the current in amps and R is the resistance in ohms. The basic point to remember is that as the resistance of a circuit goes up, the amount of current that flows in the circuit will go down, if voltage remains the same.

The amount of work that the electricity can perform is expressed as power. The unit of power is the watt (w). The relationship between power, voltage and current is expressed as:

Power (w) is equal to amperage (I) times voltage (E): $W = I \times E$

This is only true for direct current (DC) circuits; The alternating current formula is a tad different, but since the electrical circuits in most vehicles are DC type, we need not get into AC circuit theory.

Electrical Components

POWER SOURCE

Power is supplied to the vehicle by two devices: The battery and the alternator. The battery supplies electrical power during starting or during periods when the current demand of the vehicle's electrical system exceeds the output capacity of the alternator. The alternator supplies electrical current when the engine is running. Just not does the alternator supply the current needs of the vehicle, but it recharges the battery.

The Battery

In most modern vehicles, the battery is a lead/acid electrochemical device consisting of six 2 volt subsections (cells) connected in series, so that the unit is capable of producing approximately 12 volts of electrical pressure. Each sub-section consists of a series of positive and negative plates held a short distance apart in a solution of sulfuric acid and water.

The two types of plates are of dissimilar metals. This sets up a chemical reaction, and it is this reaction which produces current flow from the battery when its positive and negative terminals are connected to an electrical load. The power removed from the battery is replaced by the alternator, restoring the battery to its original chemical state.

The Alternator

On some vehicles there isn't an alternator, but a generator. The difference is that an alternator supplies alternating current which is then changed to direct current for use on the vehicle, while a generator produces direct current. Alternators tend to be more efficient and that is why they are used.

Alternators and generators are devices that consist of coils of wires wound together making big electromagnets. One group of coils spins within another set and the interaction of the magnetic fields causes a current to flow. This current is then drawn off the coils and fed into the vehicles electrical system.

GROUND

Two types of grounds are used in automotive electric circuits. Direct ground components are grounded to the frame through their mounting points. All other components use some sort of ground wire which is attached to the frame or chassis of the vehicle. The electrical current runs through the chassis of the vehicle and returns to the battery through the ground (–) cable; if you look, you'll see that the battery ground cable connects between the battery and the frame or chassis of the vehicle.

➡ **It should be noted that a good percentage of electrical problems can be traced to bad grounds.**

PROTECTIVE DEVICES

♦ See Figure 2

It is possible for large surges of current to pass through the electrical system of your vehicle. If this surge of current were to reach the load in the circuit, the surge could burn it out or severely damage it. It can also overload the wiring, causing the harness to get hot and melt the insulation. To prevent this, fuses, circuit breakers and/or fusible links are connected into the supply wires of the electrical system. These items are nothing more than a built-in weak spot in the system. When an abnormal amount of current flows through the system, these protective devices work as follows to protect the circuit:

• Fuse—when an excessive electrical current passes through a fuse, the fuse "blows" (the conductor melts) and opens the circuit, preventing the passage of current.

• Circuit Breaker—a circuit breaker is basically a self-repairing fuse. It will open the circuit in the same fashion as a fuse, but when the surge subsides, the circuit breaker can be reset and does not need replacement.

• Fusible Link—a fusible link (fuse link or main link) is a short length of special, high temperature insulated wire that acts as a fuse. When an excessive electrical current passes through a fusible link, the thin gauge wire inside the link melts, creating an intentional open to protect the circuit. To repair the circuit, the link must be replaced. Some newer type fusible links are housed in plug-in modules, which are simply replaced like a fuse, while older type fusible links must be cut and spliced if they melt. Since this link is very early in the electrical path, it's the first place to look if nothing on the vehicle works, yet the battery seems to be charged and is properly connected.

❋❋ CAUTION

Always replace fuses, circuit breakers and fusible links with identically rated components. Under no circumstances should a component of higher or lower amperage rating be substituted.

SWITCHES & RELAYS

♦ See Figures 3 and 4

Switches are used in electrical circuits to control the passage of current. The most common use is to open and close circuits between the battery and the various electric devices in the system. Switches are rated according to the amount of amperage they can handle. If a sufficient amperage rated switch is not used in a circuit, the switch could overload and cause damage.

Some electrical components which require a large amount of current to operate use a special switch called a relay. Since these circuits carry a large amount of current, the thickness of the wire in the circuit is also greater. If this large wire were connected from the load to the control switch, the switch would have to carry the high amperage load and the fairing or dash would be twice as large to accommodate the increased size of the wiring harness. To prevent these problems, a relay is used.

Relays are composed of a coil and a set of contacts. When the coil has a current passed though it, a magnetic field is formed and this field causes the contacts to move together, completing the circuit. Most relays are normally open, preventing current from passing through the circuit, but they can take any electrical form depending on the job they are intended to do. Relays can be considered "remote control switches." They allow a smaller current to operate devices

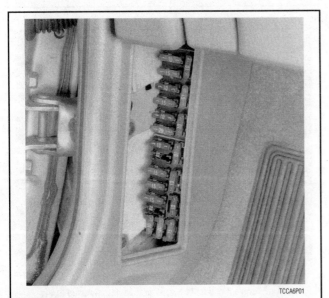

TCCA6P01

Fig. 2 Most vehicles use one or more fuse panels. This one is located on the driver's side kick panel

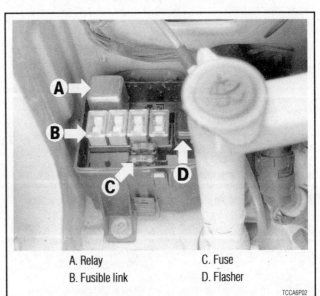

A. Relay C. Fuse
B. Fusible link D. Flasher

TCCA6P02

Fig. 3 The underhood fuse and relay panel usually contains fuses, relays, flashers and fusible links

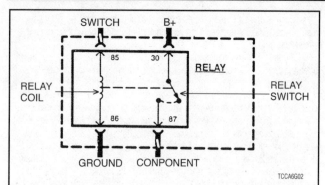

Fig. 4 Relays are composed of a coil and a switch. These two components are linked together so that when one operates, the other operates at the same time. The large wires in the circuit are connected from the battery to one side of the relay switch (B+) and from the opposite side of the relay switch to the load (component). Smaller wires are connected from the relay coil to the control switch for the circuit and from the opposite side of the relay coil to ground

that require higher amperages. When a small current operates the coil, a larger current is allowed to pass by the contacts. Some common circuits which may use relays are the horn, headlights, starter, electric fuel pump and other high draw circuits.

LOAD

Every electrical circuit must include a "load" (something to use the electricity coming from the source). Without this load, the battery would attempt to deliver its entire power supply from one pole to another. This is called a "short circuit." All this electricity would take a short cut to ground and cause a great amount of damage to other components in the circuit by developing a tremendous amount of heat. This condition could develop sufficient heat to melt the insulation on all the surrounding wires and reduce a multiple wire cable to a lump of plastic and copper.

WIRING & HARNESSES

The average vehicle contains meters and meters of wiring, with hundreds of individual connections. To protect the many wires from damage and to keep them from becoming a confusing tangle, they are organized into bundles, enclosed in plastic or taped together and called wiring harnesses. Different harnesses serve different parts of the vehicle. Individual wires are color coded to help trace them through a harness where sections are hidden from view.

Automotive wiring or circuit conductors can be either single strand wire, multi-strand wire or printed circuitry. Single strand wire has a solid metal core and is usually used inside such components as alternators, motors, relays and other devices. Multi-strand wire has a core made of many small strands of wire twisted together into a single conductor. Most of the wiring in an automotive electrical system is made up of multi-strand wire, either as a single conductor or grouped together in a harness. All wiring is color coded on the insulator, either as a solid color or as a colored wire with an identification stripe. A printed circuit is a thin film of copper or other conductor that is printed on an insulator backing. Occasionally, a printed circuit is sandwiched between two sheets of plastic for more protection and flexibility. A complete printed circuit, consisting of conductors, insulating material and connectors for lamps or other components is called a printed circuit board. Printed circuitry is used in place of individual wires or harnesses in places where space is limited, such as behind instrument panels.

Since automotive electrical systems are very sensitive to changes in resistance, the selection of properly sized wires is critical when systems are repaired. A loose or corroded connection or a replacement wire that is too small for the circuit will add extra resistance and an additional voltage drop to the circuit.

The wire gauge number is an expression of the cross-section area of the conductor. Vehicles from countries that use the metric system will typically describe the wire size as its cross-sectional area in square millimeters. In this method, the larger the wire, the greater the number. Another common system for

expressing wire size is the American Wire Gauge (AWG) system. As gauge number increases, area decreases and the wire becomes smaller. An 18 gauge wire is smaller than a 4 gauge wire. A wire with a higher gauge number will carry less current than a wire with a lower gauge number. Gauge wire size refers to the size of the strands of the conductor, not the size of the complete wire with insulator. It is possible, therefore, to have two wires of the same gauge with different diameters because one may have thicker insulation than the other.

It is essential to understand how a circuit works before trying to figure out why it doesn't. An electrical schematic shows the electrical current paths when a circuit is operating properly. Schematics break the entire electrical system down into individual circuits. In a schematic, usually no attempt is made to represent wiring and components as they physically appear on the vehicle; switches and other components are shown as simply as possible. Face views of harness connectors show the cavity or terminal locations in all multi-pin connectors to help locate test points.

CONNECTORS

♦ **See Figures 5 and 6**

Three types of connectors are commonly used in automotive applications—weatherproof, molded and hard shell.

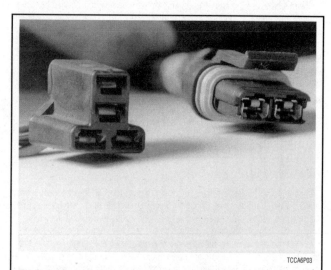

Fig. 5 Hard shell (left) and weatherproof (right) connectors have replaceable terminals

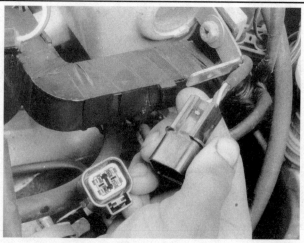

Fig. 6 Weatherproof connectors are most commonly used in the engine compartment or where the connector is exposed to the elements

• Weatherproof—these connectors are most commonly used where the connector is exposed to the elements. Terminals are protected against moisture and dirt by sealing rings which provide a weathertight seal. All repairs require the use of a special terminal and the tool required to service it. Unlike standard blade type terminals, these weatherproof terminals cannot be straightened once they are bent. Make certain that the connectors are properly seated and all of the sealing rings are in place when connecting leads.

• Molded—these connectors require complete replacement of the connector if found to be defective. This means splicing a new connector assembly into the harness. All splices should be soldered to insure proper contact. Use care when probing the connections or replacing terminals in them, as it is possible to create a short circuit between opposite terminals. If this happens to the wrong terminal pair, it is possible to damage certain components. Always use jumper wires between connectors for circuit checking and NEVER probe through weatherproof seals.

• Hard Shell—unlike molded connectors, the terminal contacts in hardshell connectors can be replaced. Replacement usually involves the use of a special terminal removal tool that depresses the locking tangs (barbs) on the connector terminal and allows the connector to be removed from the rear of the shell. The connector shell should be replaced if it shows any evidence of burning, melting, cracks, or breaks. Replace individual terminals that are burnt, corroded, distorted or loose.

Test Equipment

Pinpointing the exact cause of trouble in an electrical circuit is most times accomplished by the use of special test equipment. The following describes different types of commonly used test equipment and briefly explains how to use them in diagnosis. In addition to the information covered below, the tool manufacturer's instructions booklet (provided with the tester) should be read and clearly understood before attempting any test procedures.

JUMPER WIRES

✳ CAUTION

Never use jumper wires made from a thinner gauge wire than the circuit being tested. If the jumper wire is of too small a gauge, it may overheat and possibly melt. Never use jumpers to bypass high resistance loads in a circuit. Bypassing resistances, in effect, creates a short circuit. This may, in turn, cause damage and fire. Jumper wires should only be used to bypass lengths of wire or to simulate switches.

Jumper wires are simple, yet extremely valuable, pieces of test equipment. They are basically test wires which are used to bypass sections of a circuit. Although jumper wires can be purchased, they are usually fabricated from lengths of standard automotive wire and whatever type of connector (alligator clip, spade connector or pin connector) that is required for the particular application being tested. In cramped, hard-to-reach areas, it is advisable to have insulated boots over the jumper wire terminals in order to prevent accidental grounding. It is also advisable to include a standard automotive fuse in any jumper wire. This is commonly referred to as a "fused jumper". By inserting an in-line fuse holder between a set of test leads, a fused jumper wire can be used for bypassing open circuits. Use a 5 amp fuse to provide protection against voltage spikes.

Jumper wires are used primarily to locate open electrical circuits, on either the ground (–) side of the circuit or on the power (+) side. If an electrical component fails to operate, connect the jumper wire between the component and a good ground. If the component operates only with the jumper installed, the ground circuit is open. If the ground circuit is good, but the component does not operate, the circuit between the power feed and component may be open. By moving the jumper wire successively back from the component toward the power source, you can isolate the area of the circuit where the open is located. When the component stops functioning, or the power is cut off, the open is in the segment of wire between the jumper and the point previously tested.

You can sometimes connect the jumper wire directly from the battery to the "hot" terminal of the component, but first make sure the component uses 12 volts in operation. Some electrical components, such as fuel injectors or sensors, are designed to operate on about 4 to 5 volts, and running 12 volts directly to these components will cause damage.

TEST LIGHTS

▶ **See Figure 7**

The test light is used to check circuits and components while electrical current is flowing through them. It is used for voltage and ground tests. To use a 12 volt test light, connect the ground clip to a good ground and probe wherever necessary with the pick. The test light will illuminate when voltage is detected. This does not necessarily mean that 12 volts (or any particular amount of voltage) is present; it only means that some voltage is present. It is advisable before using the test light to touch its ground clip and probe across the battery posts or terminals to make sure the light is operating properly.

✳ WARNING

Do not use a test light to probe electronic ignition, spark plug or coil wires. Never use a pick-type test light to probe wiring on computer controlled systems unless specifically instructed to do so. Any wire insulation that is pierced by the test light probe should be taped and sealed with silicone after testing.

Like the jumper wire, the 12 volt test light is used to isolate opens in circuits. But, whereas the jumper wire is used to bypass the open to operate the load, the 12 volt test light is used to locate the presence of voltage in a circuit. If the test light illuminates, there is power up to that point in the circuit; if the test light does not illuminate, there is an open circuit (no power). Move the test light in successive steps back toward the power source until the light in the handle illuminates. The open is between the probe and a point which was previously probed.

The self-powered test light is similar in design to the 12 volt test light, but contains a 1.5 volt penlight battery in the handle. It is most often used in place of a multimeter to check for open or short circuits when power is isolated from the circuit (continuity test).

The battery in a self-powered test light does not provide much current. A weak battery may not provide enough power to illuminate the test light even when a complete circuit is made (especially if there is high resistance in the circuit). Always make sure that the test battery is strong. To check the battery, briefly touch the ground clip to the probe; if the light glows brightly, the battery is strong enough for testing.

➡**A self-powered test light should not be used on any computer controlled system or component. The small amount of electricity transmitted by the test light is enough to damage many electronic automotive components.**

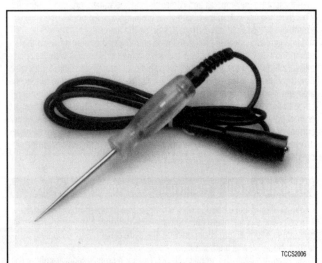

TCCS2006

Fig. 7 A 12 volt test light is used to detect the presence of voltage in a circuit

MULTIMETERS

Multimeters are an extremely useful tool for troubleshooting electrical problems. They can be purchased in either analog or digital form and have a price range to suit any budget. A multimeter is a voltmeter, ammeter and ohmmeter (along with other features) combined into one instrument. It is often used when testing solid state circuits because of its high input impedance (usually 10 megaohms or more). A brief description of the multimeter main test functions follows:

• Voltmeter—the voltmeter is used to measure voltage at any point in a circuit, or to measure the voltage drop across any part of a circuit. Voltmeters usually have various scales and a selector switch to allow the reading of different voltage ranges. The voltmeter has a positive and a negative lead. To avoid damage to the meter, always connect the negative lead to the negative (–) side of the circuit (to ground or nearest the ground side of the circuit) and connect the positive lead to the positive (+) side of the circuit (to the power source or the nearest power source). Note that the negative voltmeter lead will always be black and that the positive voltmeter will always be some color other than black (usually red).

• Ohmmeter—the ohmmeter is designed to read resistance (measured in ohms) in a circuit or component. Most ohmmeters will have a selector switch which permits the measurement of different ranges of resistance (usually the selector switch allows the multiplication of the meter reading by 10, 100, 1,000 and 10,000). Some ohmmeters are "auto-ranging" which means the meter itself will determine which scale to use. Since the meters are powered by an internal battery, the ohmmeter can be used like a self-powered test light. When the ohmmeter is connected, current from the ohmmeter flows through the circuit or component being tested. Since the ohmmeter's internal resistance and voltage are known values, the amount of current flow through the meter depends on the resistance of the circuit or component being tested. The ohmmeter can also be used to perform a continuity test for suspected open circuits. In using the meter for making continuity checks, do not be concerned with the actual resistance readings. Zero resistance, or any ohm reading, indicates continuity in the circuit. Infinite resistance indicates an opening in the circuit. A high resistance reading where there should be none indicates a problem in the circuit. Checks for short circuits are made in the same manner as checks for open circuits, except that the circuit must be isolated from both power and normal ground. Infinite resistance indicates no continuity, while zero resistance indicates a dead short.

WARNING

Never use an ohmmeter to check the resistance of a component or wire while there is voltage applied to the circuit.

• Ammeter—an ammeter measures the amount of current flowing through a circuit in units called amperes or amps. At normal operating voltage, most circuits have a characteristic amount of amperes, called "current draw" which can be measured using an ammeter. By referring to a specified current draw rating, then measuring the amperes and comparing the two values, one can determine what is happening within the circuit to aid in diagnosis. An open circuit, for example, will not allow any current to flow, so the ammeter reading will be zero. A damaged component or circuit will have an increased current draw, so the reading will be high. The ammeter is always connected in series with the circuit being tested. All of the current that normally flows through the circuit must also flow through the ammeter; if there is any other path for the current to follow, the ammeter reading will not be accurate. The ammeter itself has very little resistance to current flow and, therefore, will not affect the circuit, but it will measure current draw only when the circuit is closed and electricity is flowing. Excessive current draw can blow fuses and drain the battery, while a reduced current draw can cause motors to run slowly, lights to dim and other components to not operate properly.

Troubleshooting Electrical Systems

When diagnosing a specific problem, organized troubleshooting is a must. The complexity of a modern automotive vehicle demands that you approach any problem in a logical, organized manner. There are certain troubleshooting techniques, however, which are standard:

• Establish when the problem occurs. Does the problem appear only under certain conditions? Were there any noises, odors or other unusual symptoms? Isolate the problem area. To do this, make some simple tests and observations, then eliminate the systems that are working properly. Check for obvious problems, such as broken wires and loose or dirty connections. Always check the obvious before assuming something complicated is the cause.

• Test for problems systematically to determine the cause once the problem area is isolated. Are all the components functioning properly? Is there power going to electrical switches and motors? Performing careful, systematic checks

will often turn up most causes on the first inspection, without wasting time checking components that have little or no relationship to the problem.

• Test all repairs after the work is done to make sure that the problem is fixed. Some causes can be traced to more than one component, so a careful verification of repair work is important in order to pick up additional malfunctions that may cause a problem to reappear or a different problem to arise. A blown fuse, for example, is a simple problem that may require more than another fuse to repair. If you don't look for a problem that caused a fuse to blow, a shorted wire (for example) may go undetected.

Experience has shown that most problems tend to be the result of a fairly simple and obvious cause, such as loose or corroded connectors, bad grounds or damaged wire insulation which causes a short. This makes careful visual inspection of components during testing essential to quick and accurate troubleshooting.

Testing

OPEN CIRCUITS

▶ **See Figure 8**

This test already assumes the existence of an open in the circuit and it is used to help locate the open portion.

1. Isolate the circuit from power and ground.
2. Connect the self-powered test light or ohmmeter ground clip to the ground side of the circuit and probe sections of the circuit sequentially.
3. If the light is out or there is infinite resistance, the open is between the probe and the circuit ground.
4. If the light is on or the meter shows continuity, the open is between the probe and the end of the circuit toward the power source.

SHORT CIRCUITS

➡**Never use a self-powered test light to perform checks for opens or shorts when power is applied to the circuit under test. The test light can be damaged by outside power.**

1. Isolate the circuit from power and ground.
2. Connect the self-powered test light or ohmmeter ground clip to a good ground and probe any easy-to-reach point in the circuit.
3. If the light comes on or there is continuity, there is a short somewhere in the circuit.
4. To isolate the short, probe a test point at either end of the isolated circuit (the light should be on or the meter should indicate continuity).
5. Leave the test light probe engaged and sequentially open connectors or switches, remove parts, etc. until the light goes out or continuity is broken.
6. When the light goes out, the short is between the last two circuit components which were opened.

VOLTAGE

This test determines voltage available from the battery and should be the first step in any electrical troubleshooting procedure after visual inspection. Many electrical problems, especially on computer controlled systems, can be caused by a low state of charge in the battery. Excessive corrosion at the battery cable terminals can cause poor contact that will prevent proper charging and full battery current flow.

1. Set the voltmeter selector switch to the 20V position.
2. Connect the multimeter negative lead to the battery's negative (–) post or terminal and the positive lead to the battery's positive (+) post or terminal.
3. Turn the ignition switch **ON** to provide a load.
4. A well charged battery should register over 12 volts. If the meter reads below 11.5 volts, the battery power may be insufficient to operate the electrical system properly.

VOLTAGE DROP

▶ **See Figure 9**

When current flows through a load, the voltage beyond the load drops. This voltage drop is due to the resistance created by the load and also by small

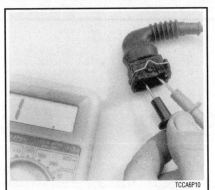

Fig. 8 The infinite reading on this multimeter indicates that the circuit is open

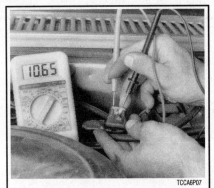

Fig. 9 This voltage drop test revealed high resistance (low voltage) in the circuit

Fig. 10 Checking the resistance of a coolant temperature sensor with an ohmmeter. Reading is 1.04 kilohms

resistances created by corrosion at the connectors and damaged insulation on the wires. The maximum allowable voltage drop under load is critical, especially if there is more than one load in the circuit, since all voltage drops are cumulative.

1. Set the voltmeter selector switch to the 20 volt position.
2. Connect the multimeter negative lead to a good ground.
3. Operate the circuit and check the voltage prior to the first component (load).
4. There should be little or no voltage drop in the circuit prior to the first component. If a voltage drop exists, the wire or connectors in the circuit are suspect.
5. While operating the first component in the circuit, probe the ground side of the component with the positive meter lead and observe the voltage readings. A small voltage drop should be noticed. This voltage drop is caused by the resistance of the component.
6. Repeat the test for each component (load) down the circuit.
7. If a large voltage drop is noticed, the preceding component, wire or connector is suspect.

RESISTANCE

♦ See Figures 10 and 11

�֍ WARNING

Never use an ohmmeter with power applied to the circuit. The ohmmeter is designed to operate on its own power supply. The normal 12 volt electrical system voltage could damage the meter!

1. Isolate the circuit from the vehicle's power source.
2. Ensure that the ignition key is **OFF** when disconnecting any components or the battery.
3. Where necessary, also isolate at least one side of the circuit to be checked, in order to avoid reading parallel resistances. Parallel circuit resistances will always give a lower reading than the actual resistance of either of the branches.
4. Connect the meter leads to both sides of the circuit (wire or component) and read the actual measured ohms on the meter scale. Make sure the selector switch is set to the proper ohm scale for the circuit being tested, to avoid misreading the ohmmeter test value.

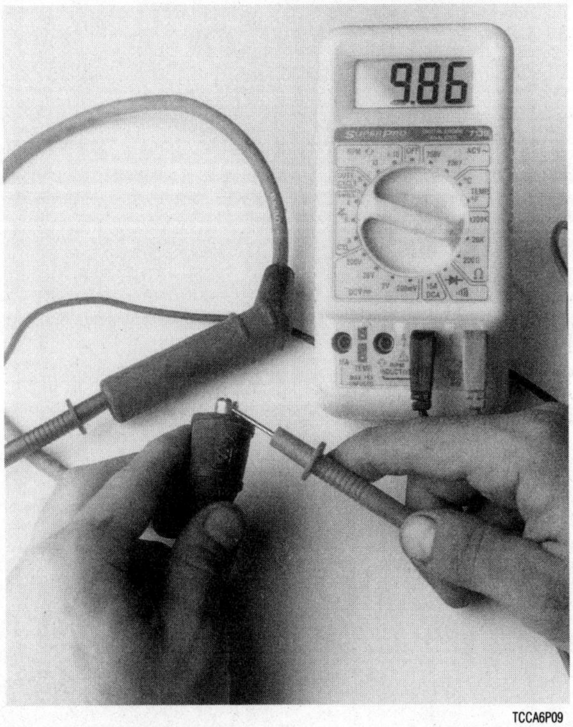

Wire and Connector Repair

Almost anyone can replace damaged wires, as long as the proper tools and parts are available. Wire and terminals are available to fit almost any need. Even

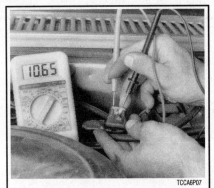

Fig. 11 Spark plug wires can be checked for excessive resistance using an ohmmeter

the specialized weatherproof, molded and hard shell connectors are now available from aftermarket suppliers.

Be sure the ends of all the wires are fitted with the proper terminal hardware and connectors. Wrapping a wire around a stud is never a permanent solution and will only cause trouble later. Replace wires one at a time to avoid confusion. Always route wires exactly the same as the factory.

➡ **If connector repair is necessary, only attempt it if you have the proper tools. Weatherproof and hard shell connectors require special tools to release the pins inside the connector. Attempting to repair these connectors with conventional hand tools will damage them.**

SUPPLEMENTAL RESTRAINT SYSTEM (AIR BAG)

General Information

The Supplemental Air Bag Restraint System (SRS) provides increased protection for the driver and front seat passenger, (if equipped with passenger air bag) in an accident. The word "supplemental" is key, as the SRS is designed to

be used in addition to the seat belts. In the event of an accident, the air bag(s) will be the most effective if the vehicle occupant(s) is held in position by the seat belts.

A driver's side air bag first became standard equipment on 1990 vehicles. In 1992, a passenger's side air bag became optional.

SYSTEM COMPONENTS

▶ See Figure 12

The SRS consists of two subsystems: the driver and, if equipped, passenger air bags, and the electrical system, which includes the impact sensors and electronic diagnostic monitor.

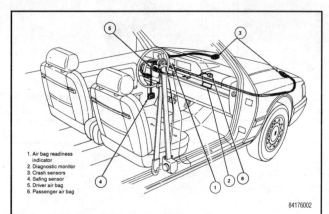

1. Air bag readiness indicator
2. Diagnostic monitor
3. Crash sensors
4. Safing sensor
5. Driver air bag
6. Passenger air bag

84176002

Fig. 12 Typical air bag system component locations—1992–94 vehicles shown

Air Bag Module

▶ See Figures 13 and 14

The air bag module consists of: the inflator, bag assembly, a mounting plate or housing, and a trim cover.

➡**The air bag module components cannot be serviced. The air bag module is only serviced as a complete assembly.**

INFLATOR

Inside the inflator is an igniter. When the impact sensors detect a crash and sensor contacts close, battery power flows to the igniter, which then converts the electrical energy to thermal (heat) energy, igniting the sodium azide/copper oxide gas inside the air bag. The combustion process produces nitrogen gas, which inflates the air bag.

AIR BAG

The driver air bag is constructed of neoprene coated nylon. The passenger air bag is made of ripstop nylon. Fill volume of the driver air bag is 2.3 cubic feet while fill volume of the passenger air bag is approximately 8 cubic feet.

Diagnostic Monitor

The diagnostic monitor continually monitors all air bag system components and wiring connections for possible faults. If a fault is detected, a code

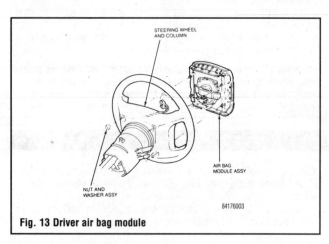

84176003

Fig. 13 Driver air bag module

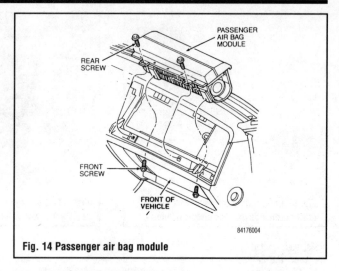

84176004

Fig. 14 Passenger air bag module

will be displayed on the air bag warning light, located on the instrument cluster.

The diagnostic monitor illuminates the air bag light for approximately 6 seconds when the ignition switch is turned **ON**, then turns it off. This indicates that the air bag light is operational. If the air bag light does not illuminate, or if it stays on or flashes at any time, a fault has been detected by the diagnostic monitor.

➡**If a system fault exists and the air bag light is malfunctioning, an audible tone will be heard indicating the need for service.**

Performing system diagnostics is the main purpose of the diagnostic monitor. The diagnostic monitor does not deploy the air bags in the event of a crash.

SERVICE PRECAUTIONS

- Always wear safety glasses when servicing an air bag vehicle, and when handling an air bag.
- Never attempt to service the steering wheel or steering column on an air bag equipped vehicle without first properly disarming the air bag system. The air bag system should be properly disarmed whenever ANY service procedure in this manual indicates that you should do so.
- When carrying a live air bag module, always make sure the bag and trim cover are pointed away from your body. In the unlikely event of an accidental deployment, the bag will then deploy with minimal chance of injury.
- When placing a live air bag on a bench or other surface, always face the bag and trim cover up, away from the surface. This will reduce the motion of the air bag if is accidentally deployed.
- If you should come in contact with a deployed air bag, be advised that the air bag surface may contain deposits of sodium hydroxide, which is a product of the gas generant combustion and is irritating to the skin. Always wear gloves and safety glasses when handling a deployed air bag, and wash your hands with mild soap and water afterwards.

DISARMING THE SYSTEM

1990–91

▶ See Figures 15 and 16

1. Disconnect the negative battery cable.
2. Disconnect the electrical connector from the backup power supply.

➡**The backup power supply allows air bag deployment if the battery or battery cables are damaged in an accident before the crash sensors close. The power supply is a capacitor that will leak down in approximately 15 minutes after the battery is disconnected or in 1 minute if the battery positive cable is grounded. It is located in the instrument panel and is combined with the diagnostic monitor. The backup power supply must be disconnected before any air bag related service is performed.**

3. Remove the 4 nut and washer assemblies retaining the driver air bag module to the steering wheel.

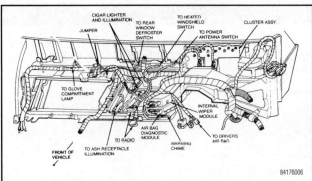

Fig. 15 Rear view of instrumental panel showing diagnostic monitor location—1990–91 vehicles

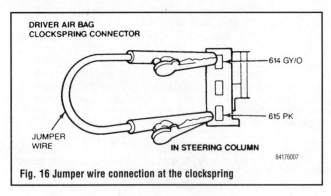

Fig. 16 Jumper wire connection at the clockspring

4. Disconnect the driver air bag module connector and attach a jumper wire to the air bag terminals on the clockspring.

5. Connect the backup power supply and negative battery cable.

1992–94

♦ See Figure 17

❊❊ WARNING

The air bag system is considered disarmed once all power is cut from the module and the backup power supply is depleted. BUT, as long as the modules are left installed, there remains a possibility that someone could accidentally provide power to the circuit and deploy the bags. However unlikely this may seem, your best bet to assure safety would be to completely remove the inflator modules from the vehicle. Also, MAKE SURE that no-one is near the modules when power is initially re-supplied, after they are installed again.

1. Disconnect the negative, then the positive battery cables. Wait 1 minute for the backup power supply in the diagnostic monitor to deplete its stored energy.

2. Remove the 4 nut and washer assemblies retaining the driver air bag module to the steering wheel.

3. Disconnect the driver air bag connector. Ford recommends connecting the air bag simulator tool 105–00010 or equivalent in order to prevent the possibility of setting trouble codes if power is supplied to the system during service. Since you will likely not have access to this tool, you should take steps to avoid supplying power to the module including, leaving the negative battery cable disconnected, removing the air bag fuse(s), and/or disconnecting the wiring harness from the module.

4. Remove the air bag module from the steering wheel and place it on a bench with the trim cover facing up.

❊❊ CAUTION

When carrying a live air bag, make sure the bag and trim cover are pointed away from the body. In the unlikely event of an accidental deployment, the bag will then deploy with minimal chance of injury.

When placing a live air bag on a bench or other surface, always face the bag and trim cover up, away from the surface. This will reduce the motion of the module if it is accidently deployed.

5. If equipped with a passenger air bag, proceed as follows:
   a. Remove the right-hand instrument panel lower moulding.
   b. On Crown Victoria, remove the right-hand instrument cluster finish panel retaining screws and remove the panel. On Grand Marquis, remove the right-hand register applique retaining screws and remove the applique.
   c. On Grand Marquis, remove the cluster finish panel retaining screws and remove the panel.
   d. Open the glove compartment, press the sides inward and lower the glove compartment to the floor.
   e. Remove the air bag module retaining bolts. Disconnect the electrical connector and remove the module.
   f. Connect air bag simulator tool 105–00010 or equivalent, to the vehicle harness connector.

6. Connect the positive, then the negative battery cables.

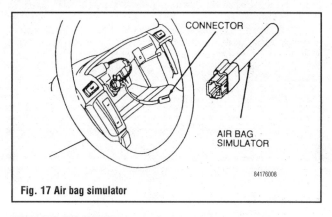

Fig. 17 Air bag simulator

ENABLING THE SYSTEM

1990–91

1. Disconnect the negative battery cable and the backup power supply.

2. Remove the jumper wire from the air bag terminals on the clockspring assembly and reconnect the air bag connector.

3. Position the driver air bag on the steering wheel with the 4 nut and washer assemblies. Tighten the nuts to 24–32 inch lbs. (2.7–3.7 Nm).

4. Connect the backup power supply and negative battery cable. Verify the air bag light.

1992–94

1. Disconnect the negative, then the positive battery cables. Wait 1 minute for the backup power supply in the diagnostic monitor to deplete its stored energy.

2. Remove the air bag simulator from the vehicle harness connector at the top of the steering column. Reconnect the driver air bag connector.

3. Position the driver air bag on the steering wheel with the 4 nut and washer assemblies. Tighten the nuts to 24–32 inch lbs. (2.7–3.7 Nm).

4. If equipped with a passenger air bag, remove the air bag simulator from the vehicle harness connector and reconnect the passenger air bag. Proceed as follows:
   a. Position the air bag module in the instrument panel.
   b. Install the 2 rear screws and tighten to 24–32 inch lbs. (2.7–3.7 Nm). Install the 2 front screws and tighten to 68–92 inch lbs. (7.6–10.4 Nm).
   c. Return the glove compartment to its proper position.
   d. Install the instrument cluster finish panel and tighten the screws to 17–27 inch lbs. (2.0–2.9 Nm).
   e. On Grand Marquis, install the right-hand register applique and tighten the screws to 17–27 inch lbs. (2.0–2.9 Nm).
   f. Install the instrument panel lower moulding.

5. Connect the positive, then the negative battery cables and verify the air bag light.

HEATER AND AIR CONDITIONER

Blower Motor

REMOVAL & INSTALLATION

▶ **See Figure 18**

1. Disconnect the negative battery cable.
2. Disconnect the blower motor lead connector from the wiring harness connector.
3. Remove the blower motor cooling tube from the blower motor.
4. Remove the 4 retaining screws.
5. Turn the blower motor and wheel assembly slightly to the right so the bottom edge of the mounting plate follows the contour of the wheel well splash panel. While still in the blower housing, lift the motor and wheel assembly up and maneuver it out of the blower housing.
6. If necessary, remove the pushnut from the motor shaft and slide the wheel from the shaft.
7. Installation is the reverse of removal. If the wheel was removed from the motor shaft, make sure it is reinstalled so the outside of the wheel is 3.62–3.70 in. (92–94mm) from the blower motor mounting plate.
8. Connect the negative battery cable and check for proper blower motor operation.

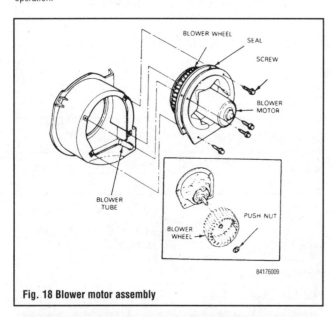

Fig. 18 Blower motor assembly

Heater Core

REMOVAL & INSTALLATION

▶ **See Figures 19, 20, 21 and 22**

1. Disconnect the negative battery cable.
2. Drain the cooling system and disconnect the heater hoses from the heater core tubes. Plug the hoses and the heater core tubes to prevent coolant leakage.

✱✱ CAUTION

When draining the coolant, keep in mind that cats and dogs are attracted by the ethylene glycol antifreeze, and are quite likely to drink any that is left in an uncovered container or in puddles on the ground. This will prove fatal in sufficient quantity. Always drain the coolant into a sealable container. Coolant should be reused unless it is contaminated or several years old.

3. Remove the 3 nuts located below the windshield wiper motor attaching the left end of the plenum to the dash panel. Remove the 1 nut retaining the upper left corner of the evaporator case to the dash panel.
4. Disconnect the vacuum supply hose(s) from the vacuum source. Push the grommet and vacuum supply hose(s) into the passenger compartment.
5. Remove the right and left lower instrument panel insulators.
6. On 1989 vehicles, remove the 3 glove compartment hinge screws, disconnect the check arms and remove the glove compartment. Loosen the right door sill plate and remove the right side cowl trim panel. Remove the bolt attaching the lower right end of the instrument panel to the side cowl. Remove the instrument panel pad as follows:
   a. Remove the 2 screws attaching the pad to the instrument panel at each defroster opening. Be careful not to drop the screws into the defroster openings.
   b. Remove the one screw attaching each outboard end of the pad to the instrument panel.
   c. On Crown Victoria, remove one pad attaching screw near the upper right corner of the glove compartment door.
   d. Remove the 5 screws attaching the lower edge of the pad to the instrument panel. Pull the instrument panel pad rearward and remove it from the vehicle.
7. On 1990–94 vehicles, remove all instrument panel mounting screws and pull the instrument panel back as far as it will go without disconnecting any wiring harnesses. Make sure the nuts attaching the instrument panel braces to the dash panel are removed. Loosen the right door sill plate and remove the right side cowl trim panel.
8. If equipped with manual air conditioning, disengage the temperature control cable housing from the bracket on top of the plenum. Disconnect the cable from the temperature blend door crank arm.
9. If equipped with Automatic Temperature Control (ATC), proceed as follows:
   a. On 1989 vehicles, disconnect the temperature control cable from the ATC sensor. Disconnect the vacuum harness line connector from the ATC sensor harness and disconnect the electrical connector from the ATC servo connector.
   b. On 1990–94 vehicles, remove the cross body brace and disconnect the wiring harness from the temperature blend door actuator. Disconnect the ATC sensor tube from the evaporator case connector.
10. Disconnect the vacuum jumper harness at the multiple vacuum connector near the floor air distribution duct. Disconnect the white vacuum hose from the outside-recirculating door vacuum motor.
11. Remove the 2 hush panels.
12. Remove 1 plastic push fastener retaining the floor air distribution duct to the left end of the plenum. Remove the left screw and loosen the right screw on the rear face of the plenum and remove the floor air distribution duct.
13. Remove the 2 nuts from the 2 studs along the lower flange of the plenum.
14. Carefully move the plenum rearward to allow the heater core tubes and the stud at the top of the plenum to clear the holes in the dash panel. Remove the plenum from the vehicle by rotating the top of the plenum forward, down and out from under the instrument panel. Carefully pull the lower edge of the instrument panel rearward, as necessary, while rolling the plenum from behind the instrument panel.
15. On 1989 vehicles with ATC, remove the ATC servo from the plenum.
16. Remove the 4 retaining screws from the heater core cover and remove the cover from the plenum assembly. Pull the heater core and seal assembly from the plenum assembly.

To install:
17. Carefully install the heater core and seal assembly into the plenum assembly. Visually check to ensure that the core seal is properly positioned. Position the heater core cover and install the 4 retaining screws.
18. On 1989 vehicles with ATC, install the ATC servo on the plenum.
19. Route the vacuum supply hose through the dash panel and seat the grommet in the opening.
20. Position the plenum under the instrument panel with the register duct opening up and the heater core tubes down. Rotate the plenum up behind the instrument panel and position the plenum to the dash panel. Insert the heater core tubes and mounting studs through their respective holes in the dash panel and the evaporator case.
21. Install the 3 nuts on the studs along the lower flange and one on the upper flange of the plenum. Install the 3 nuts below the windshield wiper motor to attach the left end of the plenum to the dash panel and the one nut to retain the upper left corner of the evaporator case to the dash panel.

22. Position the floor air distribution duct on the plenum. Install the 2 screws and plastic push fastener. If removed, position the panel door vacuum motor to the mounting bracket and install the 2 attaching screws.

23. Connect the white vacuum hose to the outside-recirculating door vacuum motor. Connect the vacuum jumper harness to the plenum harness at the multiple vacuum connector near the floor air distribution duct. Install the floor duct.

24. If equipped with manual air conditioning, connect the temperature control cable housing to the bracket on top of the plenum and connect the temperature control cable to the temperature blend door crank arm. Adjust the temperature cable.

25. If equipped with ATC, proceed as follows:

    a. On 1989 vehicles, connect the temperature control cable to the ATC sensor and adjust the cable. Route and connect the vacuum harness connector to the ATC sensor and connect the electrical connector to the ATC servo connector. Do not block the sensor aspirator exhaust port with the excess vacuum harness. Install the ATC sensor tube between the sensor and the evaporator connector.

    b. On 1990–94 vehicles, connect the ATC sensor tube to the evaporator case connector. Install the cross body brace and connect the wiring harness to the blend door actuator.

26. Install the bolt to attach the lower right end of the instrument panel to the side cowl. Install the right side cowl trim panel and tighten the right door sill plate attaching screws.

27. On 1989 vehicles, install the instrument panel pad and the glove compartment door. On 1990–94 vehicles, push the instrument panel back into position and install all instrument panel mounting screws. Install the right and left lower instrument panel insulators.

28. Connect the vacuum supply hose(s) to the vacuum source.

29. Install the right and left lower instrument panel insulators and install the 2 hush panels.

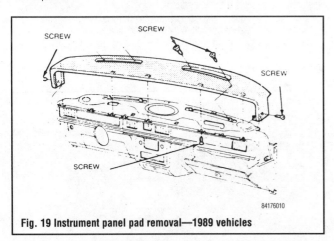

Fig. 19 Instrument panel pad removal—1989 vehicles

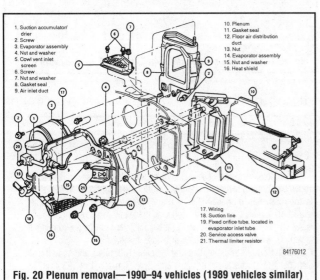

1. Suction accumulator/drier
2. Screw
3. Evaporator assembly
4. Nut and washer
5. Cowl vent inlet screen
6. Screw
7. Nut and washer
8. Gasket seal
9. Air inlet duct
10. Plenum
11. Gasket seal
12. Floor air distribution duct
13. Nut
14. Evaporator assembly
15. Nut and washer
16. Heat shield
17. Wiring
18. Suction line
19. Fixed orifice tube, located in evaporator inlet tube
20. Service access valve
21. Thermal limiter resistor

Fig. 20 Plenum removal—1990–94 vehicles (1989 vehicles similar)

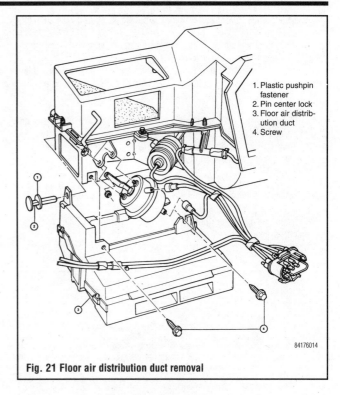

1. Plastic pushpin fastener
2. Pin center lock
3. Floor air distribution duct
4. Screw

Fig. 21 Floor air distribution duct removal

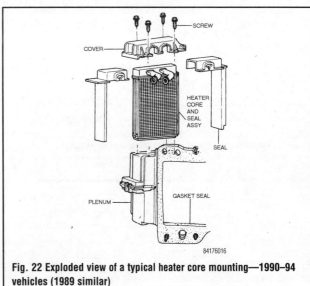

Fig. 22 Exploded view of a typical heater core mounting—1990–94 vehicles (1989 similar)

30. Unplug the heater core tubes and the heater hoses and connect the heater hoses to the heater core tubes. Fill the cooling system.

31. Connect the negative battery cable and check the system for proper operation.

Control Cables

REMOVAL & INSTALLATION

Vehicles with Manual Air Conditioning

▶ **See Figures 23 and 24**

1. Disconnect the negative battery cable.

2. Press the glove compartment door stops inward and allow the door to hang by the hinge.

3. Remove the control panel from the instrument panel, as explained in this Section.

4. Disconnect the cable housing from the control assembly and disengage the cable from the temperature control lever.

5. Working through the glove compartment opening, disconnect the cable from the plenum temperature blend door crank arm and cable mounting bracket.

6. Note the cable routing and remove the cable from the vehicle.

To install:

7. Make sure the self-adjusting clip is at least 1 in. (25.4mm) from the end loop of the control cable.

8. Route the cable behind the instrument panel and connect the control cable to the mounting bracket on the plenum.

9. Install the self-adjusting clip on the temperature blend door crank arm.

10. Connect the other end of the cable to the temperature lever arm on the control assembly. Snap the cable housing into place at the control assembly.

11. Install the control panel in the instrument panel.

12. Return the glove compartment door to the normal position and connect the negative battery cable.

13. Check the system for proper operation.

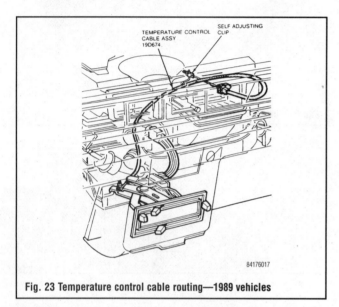

Fig. 23 Temperature control cable routing—1989 vehicles

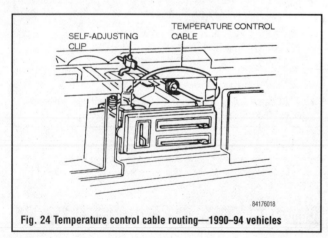

Fig. 24 Temperature control cable routing—1990–94 vehicles

1989 Vehicles with Automatic Temperature Control (ATC)

♦ See Figure 25

1. Disconnect the negative battery cable.

2. Remove the instrument panel pad as follows:

a. Remove the 2 screws attaching the pad to the instrument panel at each defroster opening. Be careful not to drop the screws into the defroster openings.

b. Remove the one screw attaching each outboard end of the pad to the instrument panel.

c. On Crown Victoria, remove one pad attaching screw near the upper right corner of the glove compartment door.

d. Remove the 5 screws attaching the lower edge of the pad to the instrument panel. Pull the instrument panel pad rearward and remove it from the vehicle.

3. Remove the one screw attaching the cable to the ATC sensor and remove the cable from the sensor.

4. If equipped with a mechanically controlled radio, pull the knobs from the radio control shafts.

5. Open the ash tray and remove the 2 screws attaching the center finish panel to the instrument panel at the ash tray opening.

6. Pull the lower edge of the center finish panel away from the instrument panel and disengage the upper tabs of the finish panel from the instrument panel.

7. Remove the 4 screws attaching the control panel to the instrument panel and pull the control out from the opening.

8. Remove the pushnut retaining the cable end loop on the temperature lever arm. Disconnect the cable housing from the control panel.

9. Note the cable routing and remove the cable from the vehicle.

To install:

10. Route the cable behind the instrument panel and connect the cable to the sensor. Loosely assemble; do not tighten the attaching screw at this time.

11. Connect the other end of the cable to the temperature lever arm of the control panel. Snap the cable housing into place at the control panel.

12. Install a new pushnut to retain the cable end loop on the temperature lever arm.

13. Install the control panel and secure with the 4 screws. Install the center finish panel and secure with the 2 screws.

14. Install the knobs on the radio control shafts, if equipped.

15. Adjust the cable according to the procedure in this Section.

16. Install the instrument panel pad in the reverse order of removal.

17. Connect the negative battery cable and check the system for proper operation.

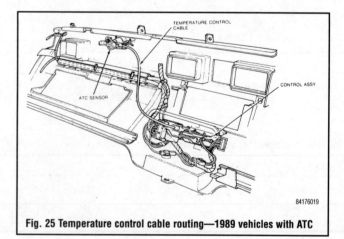

Fig. 25 Temperature control cable routing—1989 vehicles with ATC

ADJUSTMENT

Vehicles with Manual Air Conditioning

♦ See Figure 26

The temperature control cable is self-adjusting with a firm movement of the temperature control lever to the extreme right of the slot (WARM) in the face of the control panel. To prevent kinking of the control cable wire during cable installation, a preset adjustment should be made before attempting to perform the self-adjustment procedure. The preset adjustment can be performed either in the vehicle, with the cable installed or before installation.

1. Grip the self-adjusting clip and the cable with pliers and slide the clip down the control wire (away from the end) approximately 1 in. (25.4mm).

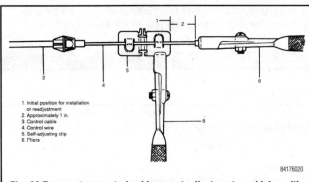

Fig. 26 Temperature control cable preset adjustment—vehicles with manual air conditioning

2. With the temperature selector lever in the maximum COOL position, snap the temperature cable housing into the mounting bracket. Attach the self-adjusting clip to the temperature door crank arm.

3. Firmly move the temperature selector lever to the extreme right of the slot (WARM) to position the self-adjusting clip.

4. Check for proper control operation.

1989 Vehicles with Automatic Temperature Control (ATC)

1. Remove the instrument panel pad as follows:

a. Remove the 2 screws attaching the pad to the instrument panel at each defroster opening. Be careful not to drop the screws into the defroster openings.

b. Remove the one screw attaching each outboard end of the pad to the instrument panel.

c. On Crown Victoria, remove one pad attaching screw near the upper right corner of the glove compartment door.

d. Remove the 5 screws attaching the lower edge of the pad to the instrument panel. Pull the instrument panel pad rearward and remove it from the vehicle.

2. Move the temperature selector lever to the 75°F position.

3. The control arm of the ATC sensor should be aligned with the arrow on the sensor body.

4. If it is not, loosen the cable housing-to-sensor attaching screw and align the sensor control arm with the arrow while maintaining the 75°F position of the temperature selector control lever.

5. Tighten the cable housing-to-sensor attaching screw. Make sure the temperature control stays at 75°F and the sensor arm stays locked.

Control Panel

REMOVAL & INSTALLATION

1989 Vehicles

▶ **See Figure 27**

1. Disconnect the negative battery cable.

2. If equipped with a mechanically controlled radio, pull the knobs from the radio control shafts.

3. Open the ash tray and remove the 2 screws attaching the center finish panel to the instrument panel at the ash tray opening.

4. Pull the lower edge of the center finish panel away from the instrument panel and disengage the upper tabs of the finish panel from the instrument panel.

5. Remove the 4 screws attaching the control panel to the instrument panel, then pull the control panel from the instrument panel opening. Disconnect the wire connectors.

6. Disconnect the vacuum harness and temperature control cable from the control panel.

To install:

7. Connect the temperature cable to the control panel and use a new push-nut to retain the cable end loop to the control arm.

8. Connect the wire connectors and the vacuum harness to the control panel.

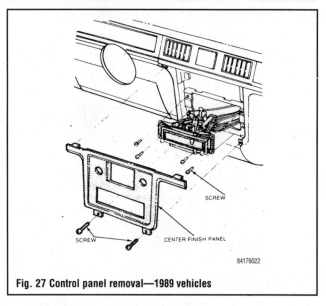

Fig. 27 Control panel removal—1989 vehicles

➡**Push on the vacuum harness retaining nut. Do not attempt to screw it onto the post.**

9. Install the control panel and secure with the 4 screws. Install the center finish panel and secure with the 2 screws.

10. Install the knobs on the radio control shafts, if equipped.

11. Connect the negative battery cable and check the system for proper operation.

1990–94 Vehicles

▶ **See Figure 28**

1. Disconnect the negative battery cable.

2. Remove the left and right instrument panel mouldings.

3. Remove the cluster finish panel screws made visible in Step 2 as well as the 6 screws along the top surface of the cluster finish panel.

4. Pull off the knob from the headlight auto dim switch.

5. Remove the headlight switch shaft as follows:

a. Locate the headlight switch assembly body under the instrument panel.

b. Push the spring loaded shaft release button located on the side of the switch body and simultaneously pull out the headlight switch shaft.

6. Remove 2 screws on the left side, one screw on the right side and the 3 screws from the bottom and remove the steering column close out bolster panel.

7. Remove the 2 screws retaining the steering column close out bolster panel bracket and remove the bracket.

8. Lower the steering column as follows:

a. Place the gearshift lever in **1**.

b. Remove the transmission range indicator cable from the steering column arm and remove the bolt from the steering column transmission range indicator bracket. Remove the transmission range indicator cable assembly.

c. Remove the 4 nuts retaining the steering column and let the steering column rest on the front seat.

9. Disconnect the electrical connectors from the accessory pushbutton switches and remove the cluster finish panel.

10. Remove the top 2 screws from the center finish panel. Gently rock the top of the center finish panel back while unsnapping the bottom tabs from the instrument panel. Disconnect the electrical connector from the clock and remove the center finish panel.

11. Remove the 4 retaining screws and pull the control panel out of the instrument panel.

12. Disconnect the electrical connectors, temperature control cable (manual air conditioning), and vacuum connector from the control panel.

To install:

13. Connect the temperature cable, if equipped, electrical connectors and vacuum connector to the control panel.

14. Install the control panel and secure with the 4 screws.

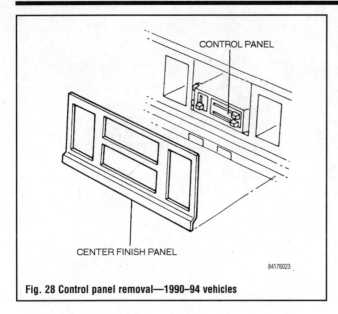

CONTROL PANEL

CENTER FINISH PANEL

84176023

Fig. 28 Control panel removal—1990–94 vehicles

15. Connect the clock electrical connector. Snap in the bottom of the center finish panel and secure the top of the panel with the 2 screws.

16. Connect the electrical connectors and install the cluster finish panel.

17. Raise the steering column and install the 4 nuts to the steering column bracket. Tighten the nuts to 9–14 ft. lbs. (13–19 Nm).

18. Install the bolt to the steering column transmission range indicator bracket and connect the transmission range indicator cable to the steering column arm.

19. Install the steering column close out bolster panel bracket and secure with the 2 screws. Install the steering column close out bolster panel.

20. Install the cluster finish panel screws.

21. Install the headlight switch knob/shaft assembly, which is a snap lock fit. Install the headlight auto dim knob.

22. Snap the left and right instrument panel mouldings in place.

23. Connect the negative battery cable and check the system for proper operation.

Blower Switch

REMOVAL & INSTALLATION

1. Disconnect the negative battery cable.
2. Remove the control panel according to the procedure in this Section.
3. Pull the blower switch knob from the blower switch lever.
4. Remove the one screw, from the underside of the control panel, retaining the switch to the control panel.
5. Disconnect the electrical connector and remove the switch.
6. Installation is the reverse of the removal procedure.

Air Conditioning Components

REMOVAL & INSTALLATION

Repair or service of air conditioning components is not covered by this manual, because of the risk of personal injury or death, and because of the legal ramifications of servicing these components without the proper EPA certification and experience. Cost, personal injury or death, environmental damage, and legal considerations (such as the fact that it is a federal crime to vent refrigerant into the atmosphere), dictate that the A/C components on your vehicle should be serviced only by a Motor Vehicle Air Conditioning (MVAC) trained, and EPA certified automotive technician.

➡**If your vehicle's A/C system uses R-12 refrigerant and is in need of recharging, the A/C system can be converted over to R-134a refrigerant (less environmentally harmful and expensive). Refer to Section 1 for**

additional information on R-12 to R-134a conversions, and for additional considerations dealing with your vehicle's A/C system.

Vacuum Motors

REMOVAL & INSTALLATION

Panel Door Vacuum Motor

♦ See Figures 29 and 30

1. Disconnect the negative battery cable.
2. Drain the cooling system and disconnect the heater hoses from the heater core tubes. Plug the hoses and the heater core tubes to prevent coolant leakage.

❄ CAUTION

When draining the coolant, keep in mind that cats and dogs are attracted by the ethylene glycol antifreeze, and are quite likely to drink any that is left in an uncovered container or in puddles on the ground. This will prove fatal in sufficient quantity. Always drain the coolant into a sealable container. Coolant should be reused unless it is contaminated or several years old.

3. Remove the 3 nuts located below the windshield wiper motor attaching the left end of the plenum to the dash panel. Remove the 1 nut retaining the upper left corner of the evaporator case to the dash panel.

4. Disconnect the vacuum supply hose(s) from the vacuum source. Push the grommet and vacuum supply hose(s) into the passenger compartment.

5. Remove the right and left lower instrument panel insulators.

6. On 1989 vehicles, remove the 3 glove compartment hinge screws, disconnect the check arms and remove the glove compartment. Loosen the right door sill plate and remove the right side cowl trim panel. Remove the bolt attaching the lower right end of the instrument panel to the side cowl. Remove the instrument panel pad as follows:

   a. Remove the 2 screws attaching the pad to the instrument panel at each defroster opening. Be careful not to drop the screws into the defroster openings.

   b. Remove the one screw attaching each outboard end of the pad to the instrument panel.

   c. On Crown Victoria, remove one pad attaching screw near the upper right corner of the glove compartment door.

   d. Remove the 5 screws attaching the lower edge of the pad to the instrument panel. Pull the instrument panel pad rearward and remove it from the vehicle.

7. On 1990–94 vehicles, remove all instrument panel mounting screws and pull the instrument panel back as far as it will go without disconnecting any wiring harnesses. Make sure the nuts attaching the instrument panel braces to the dash panel are removed. Loosen the right door sill plate and remove the right side cowl trim panel.

8. If equipped with manual air conditioning, disengage the temperature control cable housing from the bracket on top of the plenum. Disconnect the cable from the temperature blend door crank arm.

9. If equipped with Automatic Temperature Control (ATC), proceed as follows:

   a. On 1989 vehicles, disconnect the temperature control cable from the ATC sensor. Disconnect the vacuum harness line connector from the ATC sensor harness and disconnect the electrical connector from the ATC servo connector.

   b. On 1990–94 vehicles, remove the cross body brace and disconnect the wiring harness from the temperature blend door actuator. Disconnect the ATC sensor tube from the evaporator case connector.

10. Disconnect the vacuum jumper harness at the multiple vacuum connector near the floor air distribution duct. Disconnect the white vacuum hose from the outside-recirculating door vacuum motor.

11. Remove the 2 hush panels.

12. Remove 1 plastic push fastener retaining the floor air distribution duct to the left end of the plenum. Remove the left screw and loosen the right screw on the rear face of the plenum and remove the floor air distribution duct.

13. Remove the 2 nuts from the 2 studs along the lower flange of the plenum.

14. Carefully move the plenum rearward to allow the heater core tubes and the stud at the top of the plenum to clear the holes in the dash panel. Remove the plenum from the vehicle by rotating the top of the plenum forward, down and out from under the instrument panel. Carefully pull the lower edge of the instrument panel rearward, as necessary, while rolling the plenum from behind the instrument panel.

15. Reach through the defroster nozzle opening and remove the sleeve nut attaching the vacuum motor arm to the door.

16. Remove the 2 screws attaching the vacuum motor to the mounting bracket. Disengage the vacuum motor from the plenum and disconnect the vacuum hose from the vacuum motor.

To install:

17. Position the vacuum motor to the mounting bracket and the door bracket. Install the 2 screws to attach the motor to the mounting bracket.

18. Connect the vacuum motor arm to the panel door with a new sleeve nut and connect the vacuum hose to the vacuum motor.

19. Route the vacuum supply hose through the dash panel and seat the grommet in the opening.

20. Position the plenum under the instrument panel with the register duct opening up and the heater core tubes down. Rotate the plenum up behind the instrument panel and position the plenum to the dash panel. Insert the heater core tubes and mounting studs through their respective holes in the dash panel and the evaporator case.

21. Install the 3 nuts on the studs along the lower flange and one on the upper flange of the plenum. Install the 3 nuts below the windshield wiper motor to attach the left end of the plenum to the dash panel and the one nut to retain the upper left corner of the evaporator case to the dash panel.

22. Position the floor air distribution duct on the plenum. Install the 2 screws and plastic push fastener. If removed, position the panel door vacuum motor to the mounting bracket and install the 2 attaching screws.

23. Connect the white vacuum hose to the outside-recirculating door vacuum motor. Connect the vacuum jumper harness to the plenum harness at the multiple vacuum connector near the floor air distribution duct. Install the floor duct.

24. If equipped with manual air conditioning, connect the temperature control cable housing to the bracket on top of the plenum and connect the temperature control cable to the temperature blend door crank arm. Adjust the temperature cable.

25. If equipped with ATC, proceed as follows:

   a. On 1989 vehicles, connect the temperature control cable to the ATC sensor and adjust the cable. Route and connect the vacuum harness connector to the ATC sensor and connect the electrical connector to the ATC servo connector. Do not block the sensor aspirator exhaust port with the excess vacuum harness. Install the ATC sensor tube between the sensor and the evaporator connector.

   b. On 1990–94 vehicles, connect the ATC sensor tube to the evaporator case connector. Install the cross body brace and connect the wiring harness to the blend door actuator.

26. Install the bolt to attach the lower right end of the instrument panel to the side cowl. Install the right side cowl trim panel and tighten the right door sill plate attaching screws.

27. On 1989 vehicles, install the instrument panel pad and the glove compartment door. On 1990–94 vehicles, push the instrument panel back into position and install all instrument panel mounting screws. Install the right and left lower instrument panel insulators.

28. Connect the vacuum supply hose(s) to the vacuum source.

29. Install the right and left lower instrument panel insulators and install the 2 hush panels.

30. Unplug the heater core tubes and the heater hoses and connect the heater hoses to the heater core tubes. Fill the cooling system.

31. Connect the negative battery cable and check the system for proper operation.

Floor-Defrost Door Vacuum Motor

◆ See Figures 21 and 31

1. Remove the 2 screws retaining the passenger (rear) side of the floor air distribution duct to the plenum. It may be necessary to remove the 2 nuts retaining the vacuum motor to the mounting bracket to gain access to the right duct screw.

2. Remove the one plastic push pin fastener retaining the floor air distribution duct to the left end of the plenum and remove the floor air distribution duct.

3. Remove the pushnut retaining the vacuum motor arm to the floor-defrost door crank arm.

4. If not previously removed, remove the 2 nuts retaining the vacuum motor to the motor bracket.

5. Disengage the motor from the mounting bracket and the motor arm from the door crank arm.

6. Disconnect the vacuum hoses from the motor and remove the motor from the plenum.

To install:

7. Connect the yellow vacuum hose to the vacuum motor end nipple and the red vacuum hose to the vacuum motor side nipple. Position the motor to the floor-defrost door crank arm and the motor mounting bracket.

8. Install the 2 nuts to retain the vacuum motor to the mounting bracket and install a new pushnut to retain the motor arm on the door crank arm.

9. Position the floor air distribution duct to the plenum air duct opening. Install the plastic push pin fastener to the left end of the plenum and duct.

10. Install the 2 screws that attach the passenger (rear) side of the floor air distribution duct to the plenum.

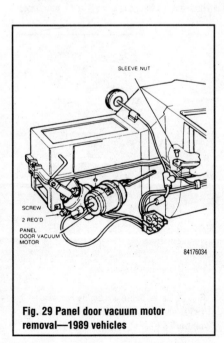

Fig. 29 Panel door vacuum motor removal—1989 vehicles

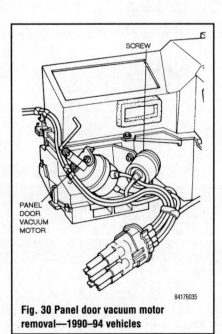

Fig. 30 Panel door vacuum motor removal—1990–94 vehicles

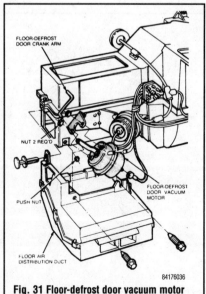

Fig. 31 Floor-defrost door vacuum motor removal—1989 vehicles

11. If not previously installed, install the 2 nuts retaining the vacuum motor to the mounting bracket.

12. Check the system for proper operation.

Outside-Recirculating Door Vacuum Motor

♦ See Figures 32 and 33

1. Remove the spring nut retaining the outside-recirculating air door vacuum motor arm to the door crank arm.

2. Disengage the vacuum motor arm and washer from the crank arm.

3. Disengage the assist spring and the second washer from the crank arm.

4. Disconnect the white vacuum hose connector from the vacuum motor.

5. Remove the 2 nuts retaining the vacuum motor and the assist spring bracket to the air inlet duct mounting bracket. Remove the vacuum motor and the assist spring mounting bracket.

To install:

6. Install the vacuum motor and the assist spring bracket to the air inlet duct mounting bracket and secure with the retaining nuts.

7. Install one of the washers on the crank arm and install the loop end of the assist spring.

8. Install the second washer and the vacuum motor arm on the crank arm. Secure the 2 washers, the assist spring and the vacuum motor arm on the crank arm with a new spring nut.

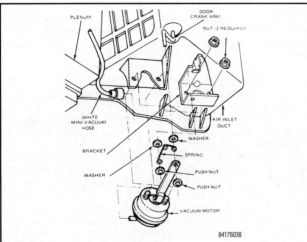

Fig. 32 Outside-recirculating air door vacuum motor removal—1989 vehicles

9. Connect the white vacuum hose connector onto the vacuum motor.

10. Check the system for proper operation.

Thermal Blower Lock Out Switch

REMOVAL & INSTALLATION

Vehicles with Automatic Temperature Control

♦ See Figure 34

1. Disconnect the negative battery cable and drain the cooling system.

✳✳ CAUTION

When draining the coolant, keep in mind that cats and dogs are attracted by the ethylene glycol antifreeze, and are quite likely to drink any that is left in an uncovered container or in puddles on the ground. This will prove fatal in sufficient quantity. Always drain the coolant into a sealable container. Coolant should be reused unless it is contaminated or several years old.

2. Disconnect the electrical and vacuum connections at the switch.

3. Loosen the hose clamps at the switch remove the switch from the hose.

To install:

4. Slide new hose clamps over the ends of the hoses.

5. Apply soapy water to the ends of the hoses.

6. Insert the switch in the hose ends and tighten the clamps to 16–21 inch lbs. (1.8–2.5 Nm).

7. Connect the electrical and vacuum connectors to the switch.

8. Connect the negative battery cable and fill the cooling system.

9. Check the system for proper operation.

Servo Motor

REMOVAL & INSTALLATION

1989 Vehicles with Automatic Temperature Control

♦ See Figure 35

1. Disconnect the negative battery cable.

2. Disconnect the glove compartment door stop (one screw) and let the door hang by the hinges.

3. Disconnect the vacuum hose and electrical connector from the servo motor.

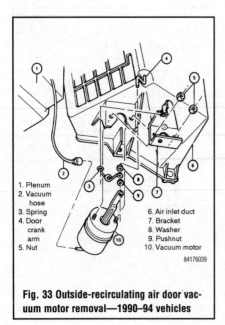

1. Plenum
2. Vacuum hose
3. Spring
4. Door crank arm
5. Nut
6. Air inlet duct
7. Bracket
8. Washer
9. Pushnut
10. Vacuum motor

Fig. 33 Outside-recirculating air door vacuum motor removal—1990–94 vehicles

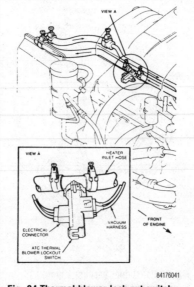

Fig. 34 Thermal blower lock out switch

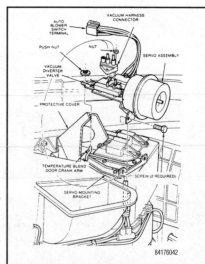

Fig. 35 Servo motor assembly removal—1989 vehicles with automatic temperature control

4. Remove the 2 screws from the servo motor mounting bracket and position the servo for access to the vacuum diverter valve.

5. Remove the retaining pushnut and vacuum connector clip, then unplug the multiple vacuum connector from the vacuum diverter valve.

6. Remove the pushnut that retains the servo motor overtravel spring and arm link to the blend door crank arm. Remove the servo assembly.

To install:

7. Connect the servo motor overtravel spring and arm link to the blend door crank arm. Install a new pushnut.

8. Connect the multiple vacuum connector to the vacuum diverter valve and secure it with a vacuum connector and a new retaining pushnut.

9. Position the servo motor and install the 2 mounting screws.

10. Connect the vacuum hose to the servo motor and connect the electrical connector to the harness.

11. Replace the glove compartment door stop screw and connect the negative battery cable.

12. Check the system for proper operation.

Variable Blower Speed Controller

REMOVAL & INSTALLATION

1990–94 Vehicles with Automatic Temperature Control

▶ See Figure 36

1. Disconnect the negative battery cable.
2. Disconnect the electrical connector from the blower speed controller.
3. Remove the 2 screws attaching the controller to the evaporator case and remove the blower speed controller.
4. Installation is the reverse of the removal procedure. Check the blower for proper operation.

Fig. 36 Variable blower speed controller—1990–94 vehicles with automatic temperature control

Temperature Blend Door Actuator

REMOVAL & INSTALLATION

1990–94 Vehicles with Automatic Temperature Control

▶ See Figure 37

1. Disconnect the negative battery cable.
2. Remove the instrument panel; refer to Section 10.
3. Disconnect the electrical harness to the temperature controller on the control assembly, from the blend door actuator.
4. Remove the 4 screws and remove the blend door actuator from the plenum.

To install:

5. Position the blend door actuator on the plenum. Make sure the actuator cam is properly engaged with the temperature blend door crank arm.
6. Secure the blend door actuator to the plenum with the 4 screws.
7. Connect the temperature controller electrical harness to the blend door actuator.
8. Install the instrument panel and connect the negative battery cable.

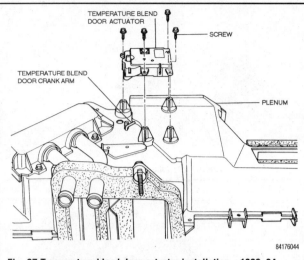

Fig. 37 Temperature blend door actuator installation—1990–94 vehicles with automatic temperature control

Sensor

REMOVAL & INSTALLATION

Vehicles with Automatic Temperature Control

1989 VEHICLES

▶ See Figure 38

1. Disconnect the negative battery cable.
2. Remove the instrument panel pad as follows:

   a. Remove the 2 screws attaching the pad to the instrument panel at each defroster opening. Be careful not to drop the screws into the defroster openings.

   b. Remove the one screw attaching each outboard end of the pad to the instrument panel.

   c. On Crown Victoria, remove one pad attaching screw near the upper right corner of the glove compartment door.

   d. Remove the 5 screws attaching the lower edge of the pad to the instrument panel. Pull the instrument panel pad rearward and remove it from the vehicle.

3. Remove the 2 mounting screws from the sensor.
4. Remove the control cable housing-to-sensor attachment screw.
5. Disconnect the cable end loop from the lever arm and remove the cable from the sensor.

➡**Secure the control cable with tape or wire to prevent it from falling from sight behind the instrument panel.**

6. Disconnect the sensor vacuum harness from the servo vacuum harness.
7. Remove the ambient air hose from the end of the sensor by rotating the sensor in a clockwise direction.
8. Remove the sensor from the vehicle.

To install:

9. Connect the ambient air hose to the sensor by turning it counterclockwise.
10. Route and connect the vacuum harness connector to the jumper line connector. Make sure the locking tab is snapped onto the jumper line connector.
11. Position the sensor to the screw mounting bosses and install the mounting screws.

➡**Use a mirror to help align the sensor screw holes to the mounting bosses. If necessary, position a trouble light on the windshield for additional light. A small amount of body caulk in the end of the ratchet socket will help prevent the screws from falling from the socket.**

12. Remove the tape or wire securing the cable and connect the control cable to the lever arm. Loosely install the attaching screw. Adjust the cable according to the procedure in this Section.

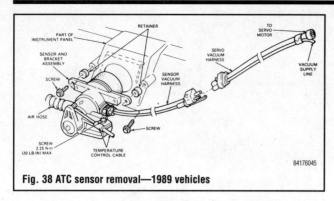

Fig. 38 ATC sensor removal—1989 vehicles

13. Do not block the sensor aspirator exhaust port with the excess vacuum harness.

14. Install the instrument panel pad and connect the negative battery cable. Check the system for proper operation.

1990–94 VEHICLES

▶ See Figures 39 and 40

1. Disconnect the negative battery cable.
2. Remove the left and right instrument panel mouldings.
3. Remove the cluster finish panel screws made visible in Step 2 as well as the 6 screws along the top surface of the cluster finish panel.
4. Pull off the knob from the headlight auto dim switch.
5. Remove the headlight switch shaft as follows:
   a. Locate the headlight switch assembly body under the instrument panel.
   b. Push the spring loaded shaft release button located on the side of the switch body and simultaneously pull out the headlight switch shaft.
6. Remove 2 screws on the left side, one screw on the right side and the 3 screws from the bottom and remove the steering column close out bolster panel.
7. Remove the 2 screws retaining the steering column close out bolster panel bracket and remove the bracket.
8. Lower the steering column as follows:
   a. Place the gearshift lever in **1**.
   b. Remove the transmission range indicator cable from the steering column arm and remove the bolt from the steering column transmission range indicator bracket. Remove the transmission range indicator cable assembly.
   c. Remove the 4 nuts retaining the steering column and let the steering column rest on the front seat.
9. Disconnect the electrical connectors from the accessory pushbutton switches and remove the cluster finish panel.
10. Remove the top 2 screws from the center finish panel. Gently rock the top of the center finish panel back while unsnapping the bottom tabs from the instrument panel. Disconnect the electrical connector from the clock and remove the center finish panel.
11. Grasp the sensor, remove the 2 screws and rotate the sensor down and out of the instrument panel.
12. Disconnect the electrical connector and the air hose from the sensor.
To install:
13. Connect the electrical lead and the air hose to the sensor.

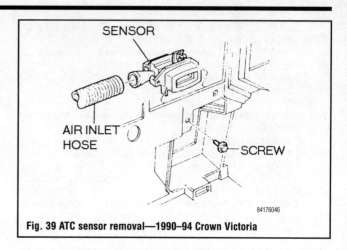

Fig. 39 ATC sensor removal—1990–94 Crown Victoria

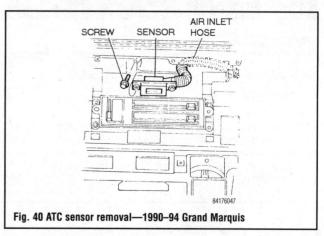

Fig. 40 ATC sensor removal—1990–94 Grand Marquis

14. Position the sensor on the instrument panel and install the 2 retaining screws.
15. Connect the clock electrical connector. Snap in the bottom of the center finish panel and secure the top of the panel with the 2 screws.
16. Connect the electrical connectors and install the cluster finish panel.
17. Raise the steering column and install the 4 nuts to the steering column bracket. Tighten the nuts to 9–14 ft. lbs. (13–19 Nm).
18. Install the bolt to the steering column transmission range indicator bracket and connect the transmission range indicator cable to the steering column arm.
19. Install the steering column close out bolster panel bracket and secure with the 2 screws. Install the steering column close out bolster panel.
20. Install the cluster finish panel screws.
21. Install the headlight switch knob/shaft assembly, which is a snap lock fit. Install the headlight auto dim knob.
22. Snap the left and right instrument panel mouldings in place.
23. Connect the negative battery cable and check the system for proper operation.

CRUISE CONTROL

Control Switches

REMOVAL & INSTALLATION

1989 Vehicles

▶ See Figure 41

1. Disconnect the negative battery cable.
2. Remove the steering wheel center horn pad by inserting a punch through the holes in the back of the steering wheel.

3. Remove and discard the steering wheel attaching bolt.
4. Remove the steering wheel from the upper shaft using a suitable steering wheel puller.
5. Remove the 6 steering wheel-to-back cover screws. Separate the control switch connector carefully from the terminal on the cover.
6. Remove the back cover and disconnect the control switch connector from the back cover.
7. Remove the cruise control switch assembly.
To install:
8. Position the control switch into the steering wheel.
9. Carefully attach the control switch connector to the terminal on the back cover. Support the slip rings at the connector while sliding on the connector.

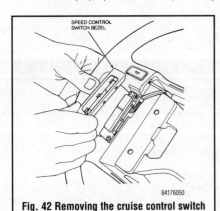

Fig. 41 Cruise control switch removal and installation—1989 vehicles

10. Position the back cover to the steering wheel. Make sure the control switch wire harness is positioned properly in the lower spoke. Press back the cover until it snaps into place. Install the cover retaining screws.

11. Install the steering wheel on the end of the steering shaft. Make sure the index mark on the wheel aligns with the mark on the steering shaft and the front wheels are in the straight-ahead position.

12. Install a new steering wheel bolt and tighten to 23–33 ft. lbs. (31–45 Nm).

13. Install the steering wheel center horn pad.

14. Connect the negative battery cable.

1990–94 Vehicles

▶ See Figures 42, 43, 44 and 45

1. Safely disarm the system and remove the air bag module from the vehicle. Refer to the proper procedure before proceeding.

2. Pry off the cruise control switch bezel and remove the bezel from the steering wheel.

3. Remove the 4 Phillips head screws from the cruise control switch assemblies

4. Remove the wire organizer from the steering wheel.

5. Disconnect the cruise control and horn switch connectors. Remove the cruise control switches and wiring assembly.

To install:

6. Install the cruise control switches on the steering wheel and secure with the Phillips head screws.

7. Connect all harness connectors and route the wiring in the steering wheel cavity. Install the wire organizer.

➥**Make sure the wires are positioned so that no interference is encountered when installing the air bag module.**

8. Position the cruise control switch bezel and snap into place.

9. Position the air bag module on the steering wheel and connect the clockspring contact.

10. Secure the air bag module to the steering wheel with the 4 nut and washer assemblies. Tighten to 35–53 inch lbs. (4–6 Nm) on 1990 vehicles or 24–32 inch lbs. (2.7–3.7 Nm) on 1991–94 vehicles.

11. Enable the air bag system according to the procedure in this Section.

Speed Sensor

REMOVAL & INSTALLATION

▶ See Figures 46 and 47

1. Disconnect the negative battery cable.

2. Raise and safely support the vehicle.

3. Remove the bolt retaining the speed sensor mounting clip to the transmission.

4. Remove the sensor and driven gear from the transmission.

5. Disconnect the electrical connector, and if equipped, speedometer cable from the speed sensor.

6. If equipped with a speedometer cable, disconnect it by pulling it out of the speed sensor.

➥**Do not attempt to remove the spring retainer clip with the speedometer cable in the sensor.**

7. Remove the driven gear retainer and remove the driven gear from the sensor.

To install:

8. Position the driven gear to the sensor and install the gear retainer.

9. Connect the electrical connector.

10. If equipped with a speedometer cable, make sure the internal O-ring is properly seated in the sensor housing, then snap the speedometer cable into the sensor housing.

11. Insert the sensor into the transmission housing and install the retaining bolt.

12. Lower the vehicle and connect the negative battery cable.

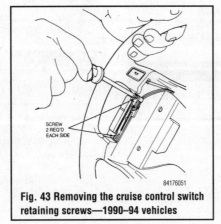

Fig. 42 Removing the cruise control switch bezel—1990–94 vehicles

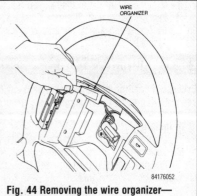

Fig. 43 Removing the cruise control switch retaining screws—1990–94 vehicles

Fig. 44 Removing the wire organizer—1990–94 vehicles

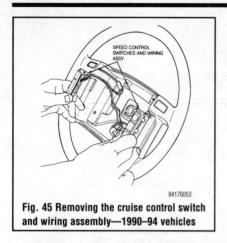

Fig. 45 Removing the cruise control switch and wiring assembly—1990–94 vehicles

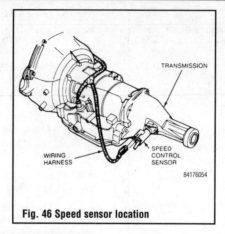

Fig. 46 Speed sensor location

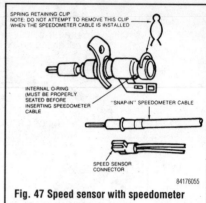

Fig. 47 Speed sensor with speedometer cable, if equipped

Actuator Cable

REMOVAL & INSTALLATION

1989–91 Vehicles

To replace the actuator assembly, remove the servo assembly, attach the new actuator cable assembly to the servo and install the total assembly.

1992 Vehicles

1. Remove the screw attaching the resonator to the throttle cable bracket. Remove the 2 hoses from the resonator and loosen the clamp at the throttle body. Pull the resonator from the throttle body and position out of the way.
2. Remove the screw attaching the actuator cable to the throttle cable bracket. Disconnect the actuator cable from the throttle cable.
3. Remove the 2 nuts retaining the servo to its mounting bracket. Carefully remove the servo and cable assembly from the bracket.
4. Remove the 2 nuts retaining the cable housing to the servo. Pull the housing from the servo and remove the cable ball end from the servo clip.
5. Remove the cable from the retaining clips and pull out from under the fuel lines.
6. Installation is the reverse of the removal procedure. Tighten the cable housing nuts to 36–53 inch lbs. (4–6 Nm) and the servo mounting nuts to 45–61 inch lbs. (5–7 Nm). Adjust the actuator cable.

1993–94 Vehicles

1. Remove the screw attaching the resonator to the throttle cable bracket. Remove the 2 hoses from the resonator and loosen the clamp at the throttle body. Pull the resonator from the throttle body and position out of the way.
2. Remove the screw attaching the actuator cable to the throttle cable bracket. Disconnect the actuator cable from the accelerator cable.
3. Remove the actuator cable cap from the cruise control servo by depressing the cap locking arm and rotating the cap counterclockwise.
4. Remove the cable slug from the cruise control servo pulley by prying up the plastic locking arm slightly with a small prybar, and at the same time push the slug out of the pulley slot.

✳✳ WARNING

Excessive bending of the arm will cause it to break. Do not use servos with damaged or missing locking arms.

To install:

5. Make sure the rubber seal is fully seated onto the actuator cable cap.
6. Lock the cable ball slug into the cruise control servo pulley slot.
7. Pull on the throttle attachment end of the cable to draw the cable cap on to the cruise control servo pulley.

8. Align the cable cap tabs with the slots in the cruise control servo housing. Insert the cap into the cruise control servo and rotate clockwise until the locking arm engages.
9. Route the cable behind the brake booster and along the valve cover underneath the fuel lines. Position the cable into the retaining clips.
10. Snap the actuator cable onto the accelerator cable and install the screw at the bracket. Tighten to 27–35 inch lbs. (3–4 Nm).
11. Check the cable adjustment following the procedure in this Section.
12. Connect the resonator and hose.

➡**Incorrect wrapping of the cable core wire around the cruise control servo pulley may result in a high idle condition. Make sure the throttle lever is at idle position after cable installation and adjustment.**

ADJUSTMENT

1989–92 Vehicles

1. Remove the cable retaining clip.
2. Make sure the throttle is in the fully closed position.
3. Pull on the actuator cable end tube to take up any slack. Maintain a light tension on the cable.
4. Insert the cable retaining clip and snap into place.
5. Check that the throttle linkage operates freely and smoothly.

➡**The cable should be adjusted as tight as possible without opening the throttle or increasing the engine speed.**

1993–94 Vehicles

1. Remove the retaining clip from the actuator cable adjuster at the throttle.
2. Make sure the throttle is in the fully closed position.
3. Pull on the actuator cable to take up slack, then back off at least one notch so there is approximately 0.118 in. (3mm) of slack in the cable.

➡**The cable must not be pulled tight, otherwise the cruise control may not operate properly.**

4. Insert the cable retaining clip and snap into place.
5. Check that the throttle linkage operates freely and smoothly.

Vacuum Dump Valve

REMOVAL & INSTALLATION

▶ **See Figure 48**

1. Remove the vacuum hose from the valve and remove the bracket mounting screw.
2. Remove the valve and bracket assembly.
3. Remove the valve from the bracket
4. Installation is the reverse of the removal procedure. Adjust the valve.

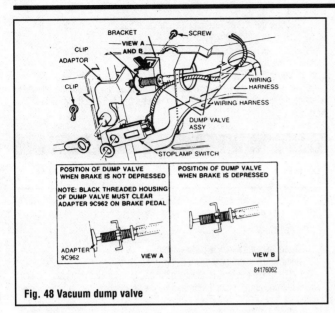

Fig. 48 Vacuum dump valve

ADJUSTMENT

▶ See Figure 48

The vacuum dump valve is movable in its mounting bracket. It should be adjusted so it is closed, no vacuum leaks, when the brake pedal is in its normal release position. Adjust the dump valve as follows:

1. Hold the brake pedal down and push the dump valve forward through its adjustment collar.
2. Install a 0.05 in. (1.27mm) shim on the surface of the adapter and pull the brake pedal fully rearward.
3. Release the brake pedal and remove the shim. The adapter should be in contact with the white or yellow dump valve plunger and not with the black dump valve housing.
4. Use a hand vacuum pump to check the vacuum dump valve for sealing off vacuum.

➡**The black dump valve housing in contact with the adapter can cause the stoplights to activate with temperature change.**

ENTERTAINMENT SYSTEMS

Radio/Tape Player/CD Player

REMOVAL & INSTALLATION

1989 Vehicles

▶ See Figure 50

1. Disconnect the negative battery cable.
2. Remove the screws attaching the bezel to the instrument panel. Remove the radio attaching screws.

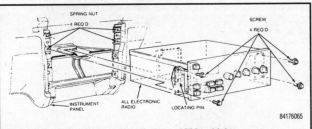

Fig. 50 Radio/tape player installation—1989 vehicles

Deactivator Switch

REMOVAL & INSTALLATION

1993–94 Vehicles

▶ See Figure 49

1. Disconnect the negative battery cable.
2. Disconnect the electrical connector from the switch.
3. Unscrew the switch and remove it from the rear brake proportioning valve (if equipped with anti-lock brakes) or the junction block below the brake booster (without anti-lock brakes).
   To install:
4. Screw the switch into the proportioning valve or junction block. Tighten to 12–14 ft. lbs. (15–20 Nm).
5. Connect the electrical connector to the switch and connect the negative battery cable.
6. Bleed the brake system, as explained in Section 9.

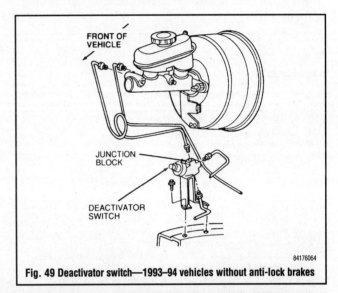

Fig. 49 Deactivator switch—1993–94 vehicles without anti-lock brakes

3. Pull the radio to disengage it from the lower rear support bracket. Disconnect the power antenna and speaker leads and remove the radio.
4. Remove the lower rear support retaining nut and remove the support.
5. Installation is the reverse of the removal procedure.

1990–94 Vehicles

▶ See Figure 51

1. Disconnect the negative battery cable.
2. Install radio removal tools T87P–19061–A or equivalent into the radio face plate. Push the tools in approximately 1 in. (25.4mm) to release the retaining clips.

➡**Do not use excessive force when installing the radio removal tools, as this will damage the retaining clips, making radio removal difficult.**

3. Apply a slight spreading force on the tools and pull the radio from the dash.
4. Disconnect the power, antenna and speaker leads and remove the radio.
   To install:
5. Connect the power, antenna and speaker leads.
6. Slide the radio into the dash making sure that the rear bracket is engaged on the lower support rail.
7. Push the radio inward until the retaining clips are fully engaged.
8. Connect the negative battery cable. Check for proper operation.

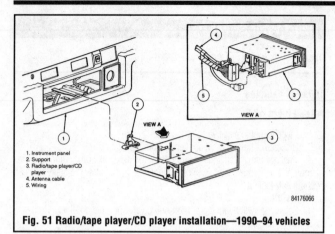

Fig. 51 Radio/tape player/CD player installation—1990–94 vehicles

1. Instrument panel
2. Support
3. Radio/tape player/CD player
4. Antenna cable
5. Wiring

Amplifier

REMOVAL & INSTALLATION

Sedan

♦ **See Figure 52**

1. Disconnect the negative battery cable.
2. Lift and remove the rear seat cushion.
3. Remove the 2 safety belt retaining bolts.
4. Carefully remove the sound insulation material.
5. Remove the retaining screws.
6. Remove the spare tire.
7. Disconnect the hardshell connectors and remove the amplifier.
8. Installation is the reverse of the removal procedure.

Station Wagon

1. Disconnect the negative battery cable.
2. Remove the spare tire cover and the spare tire.
3. Remove the 4 amplifier retaining screws from the mounting bracket.
4. Remove the 2 amplifier retaining screws.
5. Disconnect the hardshell connectors and remove the amplifier.
6. Installation is the reverse of the removal procedure.

Compact Disc Changer

REMOVAL & INSTALLATION

1. Disconnect the negative battery cable.
2. Remove the luggage compartment trim cover.

3. Remove the screws retaining the compact disc changer bracket to the body.
4. Disconnect the connectors and remove the compact disc changer and bracket assembly.
5. Remove the screws retaining the compact disc changer to the bracket.
6. Installation is the reverse of the removal procedure. Tighten the screws retaining the compact disc changer to the bracket to 24–32 inch lbs. (2.7–3.7 Nm).

Speakers

REMOVAL & INSTALLATION

Front

1989 VEHICLES

1. Disconnect the negative battery cable.
2. Remove the instrument panel pad as follows:
   a. Remove the 2 screws attaching the pad to the instrument panel at each defroster opening. Be careful not to drop the screws into the defroster openings.
   b. Remove the one screw attaching each outboard end of the pad to the instrument panel.
   c. On Crown Victoria, remove one pad attaching screw near the upper right corner of the glove compartment door.
   d. Remove the 5 screws attaching the lower edge of the pad to the instrument panel. Pull the instrument panel pad rearward and remove it from the vehicle.
3. Remove the 3 retaining screws for each of the front speakers.
4. Raise the speakers and disconnect the leads at the connectors.
5. Installation is the reverse of the removal procedure.

Door Mounted

1989 AND 1992–94 VEHICLES

♦ **See Figure 53**

1. Disconnect the negative battery cable.
2. Remove the door panel as explained in Section 10.
3. Remove the retaining screws and pull the speaker from the opening.
4. Disconnect the speaker lead at the connector and remove the speaker.
5. Installation is the reverse of the removal procedure.

1990–91 VEHICLES

♦ **See Figure 54**

1. Disconnect the negative battery cable.
2. Remove the door speaker grille.
3. Remove the 3 retaining screws for the door speakers.
4. Remove the speaker and disconnect the lead.

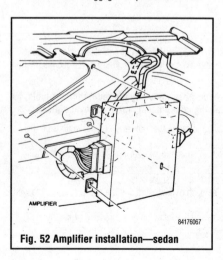

Fig. 52 Amplifier installation—sedan

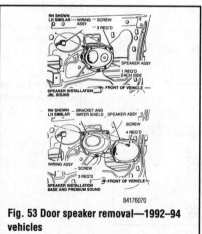

Fig. 53 Door speaker removal—1992–94 vehicles

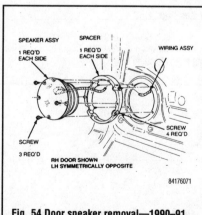

Fig. 54 Door speaker removal—1990–91 vehicles

Rear

1989–91 SEDAN

♦ **See Figure 55**

1. Disconnect the negative battery cable.
2. Remove the spare tire and jack assembly from the luggage compartment, if necessary.
3. Working inside the luggage compartment, disconnect the speaker lead from the wire harness.
4. Disengage the strap from the retaining clips and remove the speaker.
5. Installation is the reverse of the removal procedure.

1992–94 SEDAN

♦ **See Figure 56**

1. Disconnect the negative battery cable.
2. Remove the package tray trim.

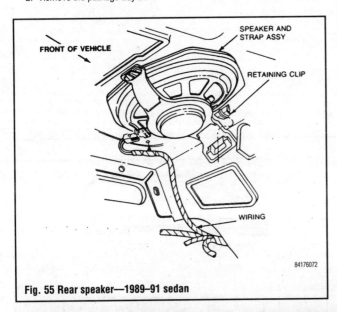

Fig. 55 Rear speaker—1989–91 sedan

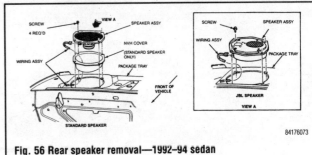

Fig. 56 Rear speaker removal—1992–94 sedan

3. Remove the 4 speaker retaining screws.
4. Disconnect the connector and lift out the speaker.
5. If equipped with standard speakers, remove the NVH cover if necessary.
6. Installation is the reverse of the removal procedure.

STATION WAGON

1. Disconnect the negative battery cable.
2. Remove the speaker and grille assembly retaining screws from the quarter trim panel.
3. Lift the speaker and grille assembly from the trim panel and disconnect the speaker connector lead.
4. Remove the retaining nuts and remove the speaker from the grille.
5. Installation is the reverse of the removal procedure.

Subwoofer

1. Disconnect the negative battery cable.
2. Remove the spare tire.
3. Remove the 4 nut and washer assemblies from the bottom of the subwoofer. Remove the subwoofer by lowering straight down.
4. Disconnect the power connector and amplifier input connector located on the forward face of the subwoofer enclosure.
5. The subwoofer and amplifier assembly is now free of the vehicle.
6. To remove the subwoofer amplifier from the enclosure, disconnect the power and input connectors.
7. Remove the 4 retaining screws from the amplifier and remove the amplifier from the subwoofer enclosure.
8. Installation is the reverse of the removal procedure.

WINDSHIELD WIPERS AND WASHERS

Windshield Wiper Blade and Arm

REMOVAL & INSTALLATION

1989–91 Vehicles

♦ **See Figures 57 and 58**

Raise the blade end of the arm off of the windshield and move the slide latch away from the pivot shaft. This will unlock the wiper arm from the pivot shaft and hold the blade end of the arm off of the glass at the same time. The wiper arm can now be pulled off of the pivot shaft without the aid of any tools.

➡**To prevent glass and/or paint damage, do not pry the arm from the pivot with metal or sharp tools.**

Turn on the wiper switch and allow the motor to move the pivot shafts 3–4 cycles, then turn off the wiper switch. This will place the pivot shafts in the PARK position. Make sure the switch is not rotated into the INTERVAL position, before installing the blade and arm assembly.

Position the auxiliary arm over the pivot pin, hold it down and push the main arm head over the pivot shaft. Install the blade and arm assemblies to dimension X, as shown in the figure. Dimension X is the distance between the centerline of the blade element and the arm stop. At the lower settings the arm will be beyond the stop. This is normal. In operation, the arms will assume slightly different positions.

1992–94 Vehicles

♦ **See Figures 58, 59 and 60**

Raise the blade end of the arm off of the windshield and move the slide latch away from the pivot shaft. This will unlock the wiper arm from the pivot shaft and hold the blade end of the arm off of the glass at the same time. The wiper arm can now be pulled off of the pivot shaft without the aid of any tools.

➡**To prevent glass and/or paint damage, do not pry the arm from the pivot with metal or sharp tools.**

To install the blade and arm assembly, line up the key on the wiper arm with the keyway in the pivot shaft. Push the arm onto the pivot shaft.

Hold the main arm head onto the pivot shaft while raising the blade end of the wiper arm and push the slide latch into the lock under the pivot shaft. Then lower the blade to the windshield. If the blade does not touch the windshield, the slide latch is not completely in place.

After blade and arm installation, operate the wiper switch to cycle the linkage and bring the blade and arm back to the parked position. Check dimension X in the figure. Dimension X in Section A should be 0.2–1.3 in. and dimension X in Section B should be 0.08–1.02 in.

If adjustment is necessary, remove the blade and arm assemblies and use a small prybar to remove the plastic key from the arm. Turn on the wiper switch and allow the motor to move the pivot shafts 3–4 cycles, then turn off the wiper switch. Reinstall the blade and arm assemblies to dimension X. Install the arm

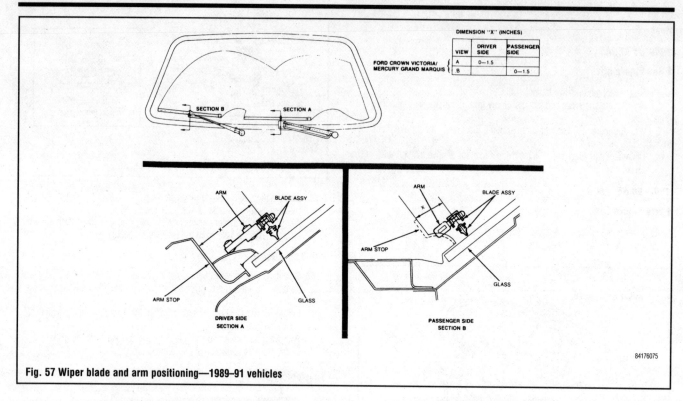

	DIMENSION "X" (INCHES)	
VIEW	DRIVER SIDE	PASSENGER SIDE
A	0—1.5	
B		0—1.5

FORD CROWN VICTORIA/
MERCURY GRAND MARQUIS

84176075

Fig. 57 Wiper blade and arm positioning—1989–91 vehicles

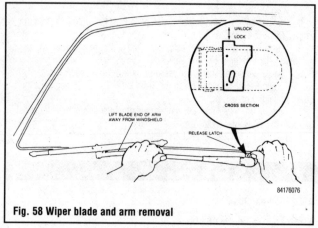

84176076

Fig. 58 Wiper blade and arm removal

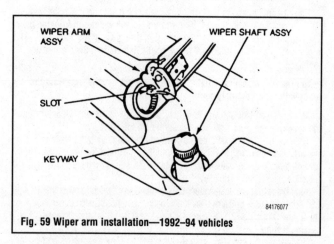

84176077

Fig. 59 Wiper arm installation—1992–94 vehicles

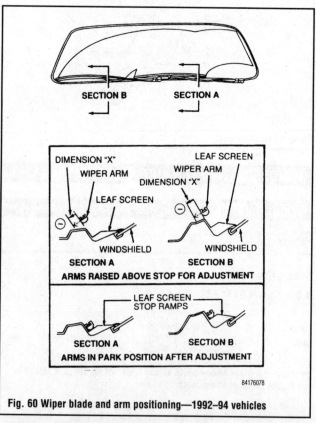

84176078

Fig. 60 Wiper blade and arm positioning—1992–94 vehicles

on the pivot shaft, then apply downward pressure on the arm head. Allow the latch to slide under the the pivot shaft and slide latch using finger pressure only.

Windshield Wiper Motor

REMOVAL & INSTALLATION

➥**The internal permanent magnets used in the wiper motor are a ceramic (glass-like) material. Be careful when handling the motor to** avoid damaging the magnets. The motor must not be struck or tapped with a hammer or other object.

1989–91 Vehicles

▶ **See Figures 61 and 62**

1. Disconnect the negative battery cable.
2. Disconnect the 2 push-on wire connectors from the motor.
3. Remove the hood seal. Remove the right wiper arm and blade assembly from the pivot shaft.
4. Remove the windshield wiper linkage cover by removing the 2 attaching screws and hose clip.
5. Remove the linkage retaining clip from the operating arm on the motor by lifting the locking tab up and pulling the clip away from the pin.
6. Remove the 3 bolts that retain the motor to the dash panel extension and remove the motor.
7. Installation is the reverse of the removal procedure.

1992–94 Vehicles

▶ **See Figure 61**

1. Disconnect the negative battery cable.
2. Remove the rear hood seal. Remove the wiper arm assemblies.
3. Remove the cowl vent screws and disconnect the washer hoses from the washer jets.
4. Remove the wiper assembly attaching screws, lift the assembly out and disconnect the washer hose.
5. Disconnect the electrical connectors from the wiper motor.
6. Unsnap and remove the linkage cover.
7. Remove the linkage retaining clip from the motor operating arm by lifting the locking tab and pulling the clip away from the pin.
8. Remove the motor retaining screws and remove the motor from the vehicle.
9. Installation is the reverse of removal.

Wiper Linkage

REMOVAL & INSTALLATION

1989–91 Vehicles

➡ **The pivot shafts and wiper linkage assemblies are connected together with non-removable plastic ball joints. The right and left pivot shafts and linkage assemblies are serviced as one unit.**

1. Disconnect the negative battery cable.
2. Remove the blade and arm assemblies and the rear hood seal.
3. Remove the windshield wiper motor and linkage cover, for access to the linkage.
4. Remove the linkage retaining clip from the operating arm on the motor by lifting the locking tab up and pulling the clip away from the pin.

5. Remove the 6 bolts retaining the left and right pivot shafts to the cowl and remove the complete linkage assembly.
6. Installation is the reverse of the removal procedure. When installing the pivot shaft retaining bolts, tighten to 62–88 inch lbs. (7–10 Nm). When installing the linkage connecting clip on the wiper motor crank pin, force the clip locking flange into the locked position.

1992–94 Vehicles

The pivot shafts and linkage are not serviceable; they can only be replaced as a complete assembly. For pivot shaft removal and installation, refer to the wiper motor removal and installation procedure in this Section.

Windshield Washer Motor

REMOVAL & INSTALLATION

1989–91 Vehicles

▶ **See Figures 63 and 64**

➡ **1991 California vehicles with 5.0L engine are equipped with a motor similar to that installed in 1992–94 vehicles, therefore the procedure for 1992–94 vehicles should be followed.**

1. Disconnect the negative battery cable.
2. Remove the fluid reservoir from the vehicle and drain the fluid into a container.
3. Using a small prybar, pry out the retaining ring.
4. Using pliers to grip one wall around the electrical terminals, pull out the motor, seal and impeller assembly.

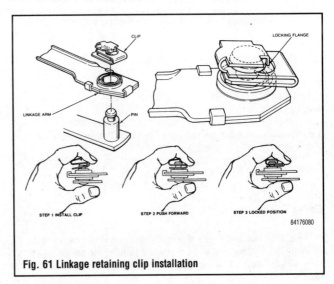

Fig. 61 Linkage retaining clip installation

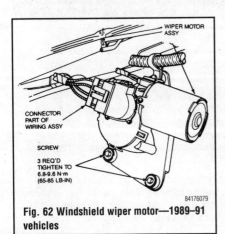

Fig. 62 Windshield wiper motor—1989–91 vehicles

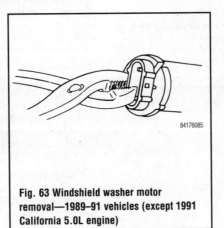

Fig. 63 Windshield washer motor removal—1989–91 vehicles (except 1991 California 5.0L engine)

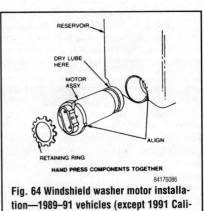

Fig. 64 Windshield washer motor installation—1989–91 vehicles (except 1991 California 5.0L engine)

To install:

5. Make sure the reservoir pump chamber is free of foreign material prior to installing the motor in the reservoir.

6. Lubricate the outside diameter of the seal with a dry lubricant such as powdered graphite. This will prevent the seal from sticking to the wall of the reservoir motor cavity and make assembly easier.

7. Align the small projection on the motor end cap with the slot in the reservoir and assemble so the seal seats against the bottom of the motor cavity.

8. Using a 1-inch 12-point socket, hand press the retaining ring securely against the motor end plate.

9. Connect the electrical connector and hose. Install the fluid reservoir in the vehicle.

10. Fill the reservoir and connect the negative battery cable. Operate the washer system and check for leaks and hose kinks.

➡ **Do not operate the pump until fluid is added to the reservoir.**

1992–94 Vehicles

1. Disconnect the negative battery cable.
2. Remove the fluid reservoir.
3. Using a small prybar, pry out the pump, being careful not to damage the plastic housing.
4. Remove the one-piece seal/filter and inspect for damage or debris.

To install:

5. Insert the seal.
6. Lubricate the inside diameter of the seal with a soapy solution and insert the pump into the cavity until it is firmly seated in the seal.
7. Connect the electrical connectors and hoses and install the fluid reservoir.
8. Fill the reservoir slowly (otherwise air will be trapped in the reservoir causing it to overflow). Connect the negative battery cable.
9. Operate the washer system and check for leaks.

➡ **Do not operate the pump until fluid is added to the reservoir.**

INSTRUMENTS AND SWITCHES

Instrument Cluster

REMOVAL & INSTALLATION

Conventional Cluster

1. Disconnect the negative battery cable.
2. On 1989 vehicles, disconnect the speedometer cable. On 1989 Crown Victoria and Grand Marquis, remove the headlight switch knob and shaft assembly.
3. Remove the instrument cluster trim cover attaching screws and remove the trim cover.
4. Except 1992–94 Grand Marquis, remove the lower steering column cover retaining screws and remove the lower cover. On 1992–94 Grand Marquis, remove the knee bolster retaining screws and remove the knee bolster.
5. On all except 1992–94 Grand Marquis, remove the lower half of the steering column shroud.
6. Remove the screw holding the transmission range indicator column bracket to the steering column. Detach the cable loop from the pin and cane shift lever. Remove the column bracket from the column.
7. Remove the 4 cluster retaining screws. Disconnect the cluster feed plugs from the receptacle and remove the cluster assembly.
8. Installation is the reverse of the removal procedure.

Electronic Cluster

➡ **The electronics within the electronic instrument cluster are not serviceable. In the event of an electronic failure, the entire instrument cluster must be replaced or returned to the manufacturer for repair.**

1. Disconnect the negative battery cable and set the parking brake.
2. Unsnap the center moulding on the left and right sides of the instrument panel. Remove the steering column cover and column shroud.
3. Remove the knobs from the auto dim and auto lamp switches, if equipped. Remove the 13 screws retaining the instrument panel and pull the panel out.
4. Move the shift lever to the **1** position, if required, for easier access.
5. Disconnect the electrical connectors from the warning lamp module, switch module and center panel switches, if equipped.
6. Remove the instrument cluster carefully so as not to scratch the cluster lens. Disconnect the electrical connector from the front of the cluster.
7. Disconnect the transmission range indicator assembly from the cluster by carefully bending the bottom tab down and pulling the indicator assembly forward.
8. Pull the cluster out and disconnect the electrical connectors on the rear of the cluster. Remove the instrument cluster.
9. Installation is the reverse of the removal procedure.

Speedometer

REMOVAL & INSTALLATION

Conventional Cluster

1989 VEHICLES

1. Disconnect the negative battery cable.
2. Remove the instrument cluster assembly.
3. Remove the screws attaching the lens and mask assembly to the cluster backplate. Remove the lens and mask assembly.
4. Remove the insulator from the rear of the speedometer at the back of the instrument cluster.
5. Remove the terminal nuts from the housing studs on the back of the speedometer.
6. Remove the screws attaching the speedometer to the cluster backplate and remove the speedometer assembly.
7. Installation is the reverse of the removal procedure.

1990–94 VEHICLES

1. Disconnect the negative battery cable.
2. Remove the instrument cluster assembly.
3. Keeping the cluster face up, remove the lens and mask retaining screws.
4. Remove the lens and mask assembly. Use caution handling the mask to prevent scratches.
5. Remove the transmission indicator assembly. Lift the temperature gauge and fuel gauge from the cluster. Set them face up to avoid damage.
6. Lift the speedometer assembly out of the cluster.
7. Installation is the reverse of the removal procedure.

Speedometer Cable

REMOVAL & INSTALLATION

1989 Vehicles

1. Disconnect the negative battery cable.
2. Disconnect the speedometer cable from the speedometer head and push the cable and grommet through the opening in the floorpan or dash panel.
3. Raise and safely support the vehicle.
4. Disconnect the cable from all retaining clips and disconnect the cable from the transmission.

➡ **If equipped with cruise control, remove the speedometer cable by pulling it out of the transmission mounted speed sensor. Do not attempt to remove the spring retainer clip with the speedometer cable in the sensor. To install the speedometer cable, snap it into the sensor.**

To install:

5. Remove the driven gear and connect the new cable to the driven gear and the transmission.

6. Engage the new cable in the retaining clips and route it through the opening in the floorpan or dash panel. Push the grommet in place.

7. Lower the vehicle.

8. Apply a ³⁄₁₆ in. (4.6mm) diameter ball of silicone grease in the drive hole of the speedometer head. Connect the cable to the speedometer head.

9. Connect the negative battery cable.

Gauges

REMOVAL & INSTALLATION

1. Disconnect the negative battery cable.
2. Remove the instrument cluster.
3. Remove the screws retaining the cluster backplate and remove the mask and lens.
4. On 1989 Crown Victoria, remove the speedometer, if necessary.
5. Pull the gauge out of the backplate clips (if used).
6. Remove the gauge from the cluster.
7. Installation is the reverse of the removal procedure.

Headlight Switch

REMOVAL & INSTALLATION

1989 Vehicles

▶ **See Figure 65**

1. Disconnect the negative battery cable.
2. Pull the headlight switch shaft out to the headlight **ON** position.
3. From under the instrument panel, depress the headlight switch knob and shaft retainer button on the headlight switch. Hold the button in and pull the knob and shaft assembly straight out.
4. Remove the autolamp control bezel and remove the locknut.
5. From under the instrument panel, move the switch toward the front of the vehicle while tilting it downward.

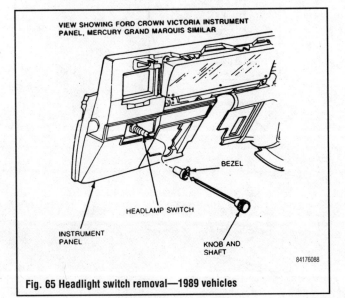

Fig. 65 Headlight switch removal—1989 vehicles

6. Disconnect the wiring from the switch and remove the switch from the vehicle.

7. Installation is the reverse of removal.

1990–94 Vehicles

▶ **See Figure 66**

1. Disconnect the negative battery cable.
2. Remove the right and left mouldings from the instrument panel by pulling up and snapping out of the retainers.
3. Remove the screws retaining the finish panel to the instrument panel.
4. Remove the headlight switch knob from the shaft and remove the finish panel.
5. Remove the 2 headlight bracket retaining screws and pull the bracket and switch from from the instrument panel.
6. Remove the nut retaining the switch to the bracket.
7. Disconnect the electrical connector and remove the switch.
8. Installation is the reverse of removal.

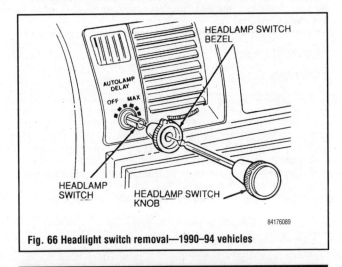

Fig. 66 Headlight switch removal—1990–94 vehicles

Back-up Light Switch

REMOVAL & INSTALLATION

1. Disconnect the negative battery cable.
2. Disconnect the back-up light switch wires at the plug connector.
3. If equipped, disconnect the 2 parking brake release vacuum hoses.
4. Remove the 2 screws retaining the back-up light switch to the steering column and lift the switch from the column.
5. Check the column to be sure the metal switch actuator is secured to the shift tube and that it is seated as far forward against the shift tube bearing as is possible. Check for a broken or damaged actuator.

To install:

6. Before installing a new switch to the column, make sure the drive position gauge is inserted in the drive pinning hole. If the pin is missing, align the 2 holes at the drive pinning hole on top of the switch and install a No. 43 drill bit or 0.092–0.093 in. gauge pin.

7. While holding the selector lever against the stop in the drive detent position, place the switch on the column and install the 2 retaining screws.

8. Remove the drill bit or gauge pin.

9. Connect the switch wires to the plug connector. If equipped, connect the 2 parking brake release vacuum hoses.

10. Connect the negative battery cable. Check the back-up lights for proper operation.

LIGHTING

Headlights

All 1989–91 vehicles are equipped with sealed-beam halogen headlights. All 1992–94 vehicles are equipped with aerodynamically styled headlight bodies using replaceable halogen bulbs.

REMOVAL & INSTALLATION

Headlight Bulb

✳✳ CAUTION

The halogen headlight bulb contains gas under pressure. The bulb may shatter if the glass envelope is scratched or the bulb is dropped. Handle the bulb carefully. Grasp the bulb only by its plastic base. Avoid touching the glass envelope. Keep the bulb out of the reach of children.

1989–91 VEHICLES

◆ **See Figure 67**

1. Remove the headlight door mounting screws and remove the headlight door.
2. Remove the 4 retainer ring screws and remove the retainer ring from the headlight.
3. Pull the headlight bulb forward and disconnect the wiring connector.
To install:
4. Connect the wiring connector to the headlight bulb and place the bulb in position, locating the bulb glass tabs in the positioning slots.
5. Attach the bulb retainer ring to the assembly with the retainer ring screws.
6. Install the headlight door and secure with the screws.
7. Check the headlight bulb aim and adjust as necessary.

1992–94 VEHICLES

◆ **See Figures 68, 69, 70, 71 and 72**

1. Make sure the headlight switch is in the OFF position.
2. Lift the hood and remove the trim panel located above the headlight bulb.
3. Rotate the bulb counterclockwise (when viewed from the rear) about an ⅛–¼ turn.
4. Carefully remove the bulb from the socket in the reflector by gently pulling straight out of the socket. Do not rotate the bulb during removal.
5. Disconnect the electrical connector from the bulb.
To install:
6. Connect the electrical connector to the bulb.
7. Insert the glass envelope of the bulb into the socket while aligning the locking tabs.
8. Rotate the bulb ¼ turn.
9. Turn the headlights on and check for proper operation.

➡**A properly aimed headlight normally does not need to be re-aimed after bulb installation. A burned out bulb should not be removed from the headlight reflector until just before a replacement bulb is to be installed. Removal of a bulb for an extended period of time may allow contaminants to enter the headlight body and affect the performance of the headlight. The headlight bulb should be energized only while it is contained within the headlight body.**

Headlight Body

1992–94 VEHICLES

◆ **See Figure 73**

1. Make sure the headlight switch is in the OFF position.
2. Disconnect the electrical connectors from the headlight bulbs by grasping the wires firmly and carefully snapping the connectors downward.
3. Remove the 3 retainers attaching the headlight body to the grille opening panel. Use snap-ring pliers to spread the retainers, then pull straight upwards to disengage.

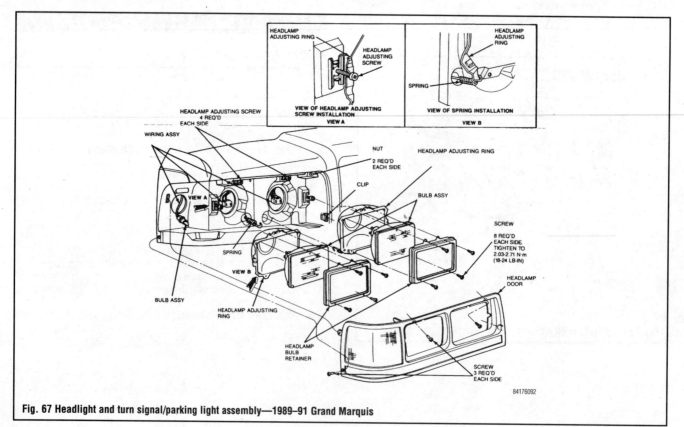

Fig. 67 Headlight and turn signal/parking light assembly—1989–91 Grand Marquis

Fig. 68 Removing the trim panel—Crown Victoria shown

Fig. 69 Headlight bulb in installed position

Fig. 70 Rotate the bulb ⅛–¼ turn counterclockwise

Fig. 71 When removing the headlight bulb, handle it by the base only

Fig. 72 Disconnect the electrical connector from the bulb

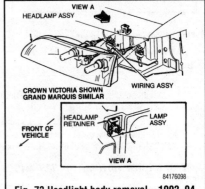

Fig. 73 Headlight body removal—1992–94 vehicles

4. Remove the headlight body from the vehicle.
5. Installation is the reverse of the removal procedure. Check headlight aim.

AIMING

On 1989–91 vehicles, the headlights can be aimed using the adjusting screws located above and to the side of the headlight bulbs. A rough adjustment can be made while shining the headlights on a wall or on the rear of another vehicle, but headlight adjustment should really be made using proper headlight aiming equipment.

On 1992–94 vehicles, the aerodynamically styled headlights necessitate the use of headlight aiming kit 107–00003 or equivalent. The adjustable aimer adapters provided in the kit must be used to aim the headlights. Adjustment aimer adapter positions are moulded into the bottom edge of the headlight lens. Set and lock the adjustable adapters, attach each adapter to its mechanical aimer and aim the headlights according to the instructions in the kit.

Headlight aim adjustment should be made with the fuel tank approximately half full, the vehicle unloaded and the trunk empty, except for the spare tire and jacking equipment. Make sure all tires are inflated to the proper pressure.

Signal and Marker Lights

REMOVAL & INSTALLATION

Front Turn Signal and Parking Lights

1989–91 VEHICLES

▶ See Figure 67

1. Remove the screws retaining the headlight door to the grille opening panel.
2. Pull the headlight door and turn signal/parking light assembly away from the grille opening panel.
3. Remove the turn signal/parking light bulb and socket assembly from the headlight door by rotating the socket ⅓ turn counterclockwise.

4. Remove the bulb from the socket.
5. Installation is the reverse of the removal procedure.

➡On Crown Victoria, if only bulb replacement is necessary, the bulb socket can be accessed by reaching up behind the bumper reinforcement and grille opening panel.

1992–94 CROWN VICTORIA

▶ See Figure 74

1. Remove the headlight body as described in this Section.
2. Remove the nut and screw retaining the turn signal/parking light assembly to the fender.
3. Pull the light assembly away from the fender, rotate the socket and remove it from the light.
4. Remove the bulb from the socket.
5. Installation is the reverse of the removal procedure.

1992–94 GRAND MARQUIS

▶ See Figure 75

1. Remove the 2 screws retaining the turn signal/parking light assembly to the bumper cover.
2. Pull the light assembly away from the cover, rotate the socket and remove it from the light.
3. Remove the bulb from the socket.
4. Installation is the reverse of the removal procedure.

Side Marker/Cornering Lights

1989–91 VEHICLES—FRONT

▶ See Figure 76

1. If only bulb replacement is necessary, reach up behind the fender, rotate the bulb socket ⅓ turn and remove the bulb and socket assembly. Remove the bulb from the socket.

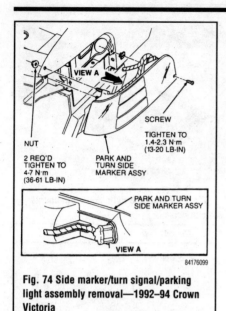

Fig. 74 Side marker/turn signal/parking light assembly removal—1992–94 Crown Victoria

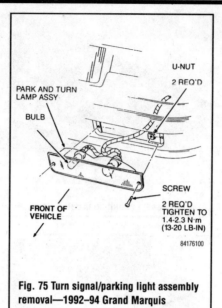

Fig. 75 Turn signal/parking light assembly removal—1992–94 Grand Marquis

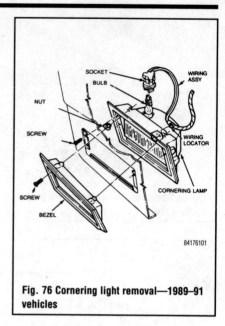

Fig. 76 Cornering light removal—1989–91 vehicles

2. If the light body is to be removed, first remove the bezel retaining screws and the bezel.

3. Remove the exposed housing retaining screws and remove the housing from behind the fender. Disconnect the harness locator.

4. Installation is the reverse of the removal procedure.

1989–91 CROWN VICTORIA STATION WAGON/COUNTRY SQUIRE—REAR

1. Remove the 4 screws retaining the side marker light to the quarter panel.

2. Pull the light body away from the opening.

3. Remove the socket from the light body.

4. Remove the bulb from the socket.

5. Installation is the reverse of the removal procedure.

1992–94 CROWN VICTORIA

For side marker light removal and installation, refer to the turn signal/parking light removal and installation procedure in this Section.

1992–94 GRAND MARQUIS

▶ **See Figure 77**

1. Remove the headlight body as described in this Section.

2. Remove the nut and screw retaining the side marker/cornering light assembly to the fender.

3. Pull the light assembly away from the fender, rotate the socket and remove it from the light.

4. Remove the bulb from the socket.

5. Installation is the reverse of the removal procedure.

Rear Turn Signal, Brake and Parking Lights

1989–91 SEDAN

▶ **See Figures 78 and 79**

1. Remove the luggage compartment rear trim panel.

2. Turn the light sockets counterclockwise to the stop and remove the bulb and socket assemblies from the light assembly. Remove the bulb from the socket.

3. If the light assembly is to be removed, remove the nuts and remove the light assembly from the vehicle.

4. Installation is the reverse of the removal procedure.

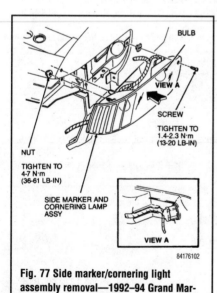

Fig. 77 Side marker/cornering light assembly removal—1992–94 Grand Marquis

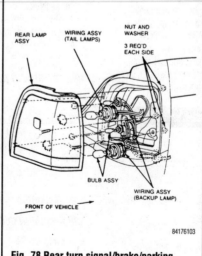

Fig. 78 Rear turn signal/brake/parking light assembly removal—1989–91 Crown Victoria sedan

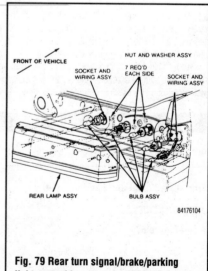

Fig. 79 Rear turn signal/brake/parking light assembly removal—1989–91 Grand Marquis sedan

1992–94 SEDAN

♦ See Figures 80 thru 85

1. Remove the screw(s) and wing nut retainers at the rear of the luggage compartment and push the trim away from the back of the light.
2. Remove the wing nuts retaining the light assembly to the lower back panel and pull the light body assembly from the vehicle.
3. Turn the bulb socket(s) counterclockwise to the stop and remove the socket(s) from the light assembly. Remove the bulb(s) from the socket(s).
4. Installation is the reverse of the removal procedure.

STATION WAGON

♦ See Figures 86 and 87

1. On Crown Victoria/Country Squire, remove the screws retaining the light assembly to the quarter panel. Pull the light from the quarter panel opening, remove the light socket and remove the bulb from the socket.

2. On Grand Marquis/Colony Park, remove the quarter trim panel to gain access to the attaching nuts. Remove the nuts and the bulb sockets, then remove the light assembly from the quarter panel opening. Remove the bulb from the socket.
3. Installation is the reverse of the removal procedure.

High-Mount Brake Light

1989–92 SEDAN

♦ See Figures 88 and 89

1. If equipped, remove the retainer screw covers from each side of the light assembly. Remove the screws from the retainer.
2. Pull the light assembly up and forward to detach from the retainer brackets.

➡ Be careful not to move the plastic attachment brackets.

3. On the bottom of the light body, pull the wire locator from the light body.

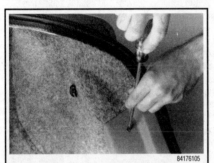

Fig. 80 Remove the screw retaining the rear luggage compartment trim—1992 Crown Victoria shown

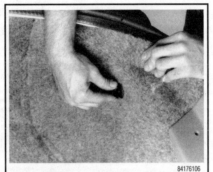

Fig. 81 Remove the wing nut retaining the rear luggage compartment trim

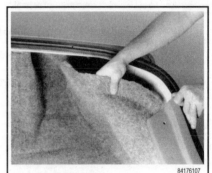

Fig. 82 Push the trim away from the back of the light

Fig. 83 Remove the wing nuts retaining the light assembly to the lower back panel

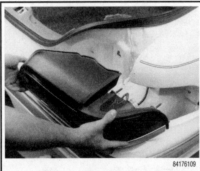

Fig. 84 Pull the light assembly away from the vehicle

Fig. 85 Remove the bulb and socket assembly from the light assembly

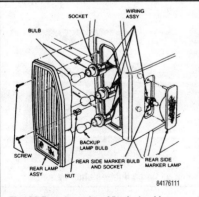

Fig. 86 Rear turn signal/brake/parking light assembly removal—Crown Victoria/Country Squire wagon

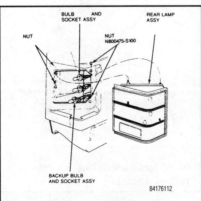

Fig. 87 Rear turn signal/brake/parking light assembly removal—Grand Marquis/Colony Park wagon

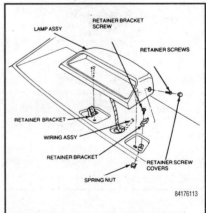

Fig. 88 High-mount brake light removal—1989–91 sedan

4. From the bottom of the light, remove the bulb and socket assembly by twisting counterclockwise.

5. Installation is the reverse of the removal procedure.

1993–94 VEHICLES

♦ See Figure 90

1. Remove the 2 screws retaining the light to the adjustable attaching brackets.
2. Lift up the light and disconnect the wiring connector.
3. Remove the 2 screws and adjustable attaching brackets from the replacement light. The brackets from the old light can be reused.
4. If the bulb needs to be replaced, pull the bulb out of the socket and install a new one.
5. Installation is the reverse of the removal procedure.

STATION WAGON

♦ See Figure 91

1. Remove the 2 screws from the light assembly.
2. Pull the light rearward and remove from the tailgate moulding.
3. Disengage the wiring harness strain relief clip by pulling straight out from the light assembly.
4. Remove the bulb and socket assembly by gently twisting and pulling straight out of the light assembly.
5. Installation is the reverse of the removal procedure.

Dome Light

♦ See Figures 92 and 93

1. If equipped with standard dome light, remove the lens by squeezing it inward to release the locking tabs.

2. If equipped with combination dome/map light, remove the lens using a small thin-bladed prybar to release the locking tabs.
3. Pull the bulb from the socket.
4. Installation is the reverse of the removal procedure.

Cargo Light

STATION WAGON

♦ See Figure 94

1. Carefully pry the end of the lens that is furthest away from the switch down and away from the light housing.
2. Pull the bulb from its socket.
3. Installation is the reverse of the removal procedure.

License Plate Lights

1. On 1989–91 sedan, raise the trunk lid. With the trunk lid open, twist the light socket approximately 1/8 turn counterclockwise and pull the socket and bulb assembly from the light housing.
2. On 1989–91 station wagon, remove the 2 screws retaining the light assembly to the tailgate. Pull the light assembly from the tailgate, grasp and twist the light socket approximately 1/8 turn counterclockwise and pull the socket and bulb assembly from the light housing.
3. On 1992–94 vehicles, use a Phillips head screwdriver to remove the 2 plastic rivets retaining the light assembly to the rear bumper. With a small prybar, remove the rivet retainer and pull the light assembly from the bumper. Grasp and twist the light socket approximately 1/8 turn counterclockwise and pull the socket and bulb assembly from the light housing.
4. Installation is the reverse of the removal procedure.

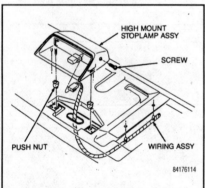

Fig. 89 High-mount brake light removal—1992 vehicles

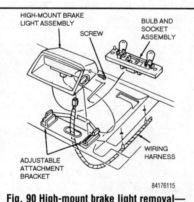
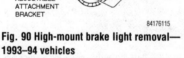

Fig. 90 High-mount brake light removal—1993–94 vehicles

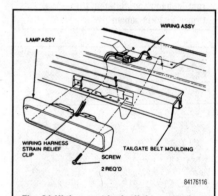

Fig. 91 High-mount brake light removal—station wagon

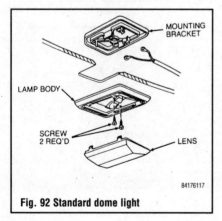

Fig. 92 Standard dome light

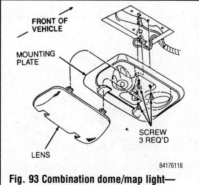
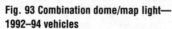

Fig. 93 Combination dome/map light—1992–94 vehicles

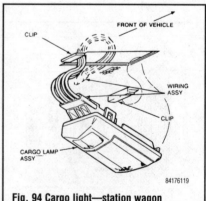

Fig. 94 Cargo light—station wagon

CIRCUIT PROTECTION

Fuses

▶ **See Figures 95, 96, 97 and 98**

All vehicles are equipped with a fuse panel located on the left side of the lower instrument panel. In addition, 1992–94 vehicles are equipped with a combination fuse/relay panel called the "power distribution box" which is located in the right front of the engine compartment.

REPLACEMENT

1. Locate the fuse panel and remove the cover, if necessary.
2. Look through the clear side of the fuse in question, to see if the metal wire inside is separated. If the wire is separated, the fuse is blown and must be replaced.

3. Remove the fuse by pulling it from its cavity; no special tools are required.
4. Replace the blown fuse only with one having the same amp rating for that particular circuit. Push the fuse straight in until the fuse seats fully in the cavity.

Fusible Links

▶ **See Figure 99**

Fuse links are used to protect the main wiring harness and selected branches from complete burn-out, should a short circuit or electrical overload occur. A fuse link is a short length of insulated wire, integral with the engine compartment wiring harness. It is several wire gauges smaller than the circuit it protects and generally located in-line directly from the positive terminal of the battery.

Fig. 95 Fuse panel location—1992 Crown Victoria shown

Fig. 96 Removing the cover from the fuse panel—1992 Crown Victoria shown

Fig. 97 Removing the cover from the power distribution box

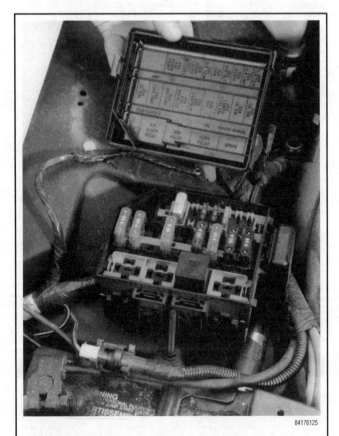

Fig. 98 View of the contents of the power distribution box

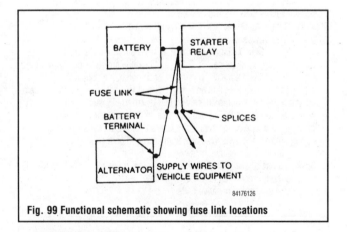

Fig. 99 Functional schematic showing fuse link locations

Production fuse links are color coded as follows:
- Gray: 12 gauge
- Dark Green: 14 gauge
- Black: 16 gauge
- Brown: 18 gauge
- Dark Blue: 20 gauge

When a heavy current flows, such as when a booster battery is connected incorrectly or when a short to ground occurs in the wiring harness, the fuse link burns out and protects the alternator or wiring.

A burned out fuse link may have bare wire ends protruding from the insulation, or it may have only expanded or bubbled insulation with illegible identification. When it is hard to determine if the fuse link is burned out, perform the continuity test:

1. Make sure the battery is okay, then turn on the headlights or an accessory. If the headlights or accessory do not work, the fuse link is probably burned out.

2. If equipped with more than one fuse link, use the same procedure as in Step 1 to test each link separately.

3. To test the fuse link that protects the alternator, make sure the battery is okay, then check with a voltmeter for voltage at the BAT terminal of the alternator. No voltage indicates that the fuse link is probably burned out.

REPLACEMENT

▶ **See Figures 100, 101 and 102**

When replacing a fuse link, always make sure the replacement fuse link is a duplicate of the one removed with respect to gauge, length and insulation. Original equipment and original equipment specification replacement fuse links have insulation that is flame proof. Do not fabricate a fuse link from ordinary wire because the insulation may not be flame proof.

If a circuit protected by a fuse link becomes inoperative, inspect for a blown fuse link. If the fuse link wire insulation is burned or opened, disconnect the feed as close as possible behind the splice in the harness. If the damaged fuse link is between 2 splices (weld points in the harness), cut out the damaged portion as close as possible to the weld points.

Replace the fuse link as follows:

1. To service a 2-link group when only one link has blown and the other link is not damaged, proceed as follows:

a. Disconnect the negative battery cable.

b. Cut out the blown fusible link (2 places).

c. Position the correct eyelet type service fusible link with the bare end to the correct size wire connector and crimp to the wire ends.

d. Heat the splice insulation until the tubing shrinks and adhesive flows from each end of the connector.

e. Connect the negative battery cable.

2. To service a fuse link in a multi-feed or single circuit, proceed as follows:

a. Disconnect the negative battery cable.

b. Determine which circuit is damaged, its location and the cause of the open fuse link. If the damaged fuse link is one of 3 fed by a common number 10 or 12 gauge feed wire, determine the specific affected circuit.

c. Cut the damaged fuse link from the wiring harness and discard. If the fuse link is one of 3 circuits fed by a single feed wire, cut it out of the harness at each splice end and discard.

d. Obtain the proper fuse link and butt connectors for attaching the fuse link to the harness.

e. Strip ⁵⁄₁₆ in. (7.6mm) of insulation from the wire ends and insert into the proper size wire connector. Crimp and heat the splice insulation until the tubing shrinks and adhesive flows from each end of the connector.

f. To replace a fuse link on a single circuit in a harness, cut out the damaged portion. Strip approximately ½ in. (12.7mm) of insulation from the 2 wire ends and attach the correct size fuse link to each wire end with the proper gauge wire connectors. Crimp and heat the splice insulation until the tubing shrinks and adhesive flows from each end of the connector.

g. Connect the negative battery cable.

3. To service a fuse link with an eyelet terminal on one end, such as the charging circuit, proceed as follows:

a. Disconnect the negative battery cable.

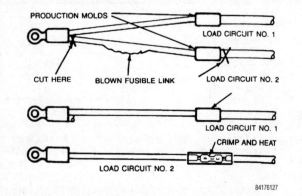

Fig. 100 Fusible link replacement in a 2-link group when only one link has blown

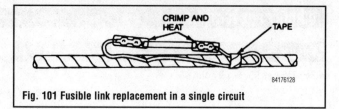

Fig. 101 Fusible link replacement in a single circuit

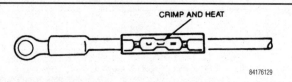

Fig. 102 Fusible link repair using the eyelet terminal fuse link of the specified gauge for attachment to a circuit wire end.

b. Cut off the fuse link behind the weld, strip approximately ½ in. (12.7mm) of insulation from the cut end, and attach the appropriate new eyelet fuse link to the cut stripped wire with the proper size connector.

c. Crimp and heat the splice insulation until the tubing shrinks and adhesive flows from each end of the connector.

d. Connect the negative battery cable.

➥Do not mistake a resistor wire for a fuse link. The resistor wire is generally longer and has print stating "Resistor—do not cut or splice."When attaching a No. 16, 18 or 20 gauge fuse link to a heavy gauge wire, always double the stripped wire end of the fuse link before inserting and crimping it into the wire connector for positive wire retention.

Circuit Breakers

Circuit breakers are used on certain electrical components requiring high amperage. The advantage of the circuit breaker is its ability to open and close the electrical circuit as the load demands, rather than the necessity of a part replacement. The following circuit breakers are used:

• **Windshield Wiper Circuit**—one 8.25 amp circuit breaker located on the fuse panel.

• **Power Windows**—one 20 amp circuit breaker located on the fuse panel on 1989 two-door vehicles, two 20 amp circuit breakers on all other 1989 vehicles, 1 located on the fuse panel and 1 at the starter relay.

• **Power Windows and Tailgate Power Window Switch**—one 20 amp circuit breaker located on the fuse panel on 1990–91 vehicles.

• **Power Windows and Trunk Lid Release**—one 20 amp circuit breaker located on the fuse panel on 1992–94 vehicles.

• **Headlight and High Beam**—one 22 amp circuit breaker incorporated in the lighting switch.

• **Power Seats and Door Locks**—one 30 amp circuit breaker located on the fuse panel on 1988–91 vehicles, located in the power distribution box on 1992–94 vehicles.

REPLACEMENT

Those circuit breakers that are fuse panel mounted are replaced as follows:

1. Locate the fuse panel and remove the cover, if necessary.

2. Remove the circuit breaker by pulling it from its cavity; no special tools are required.

3. Replace the circuit breaker only with one having the same amp rating for that particular circuit. Push the circuit breaker straight in until it seats fully in the cavity.

Flashers

REPLACEMENT

The turn signal and emergency flashers are attached to the fuse panel. They are replaced in the same manner as the fuses and circuit breakers.

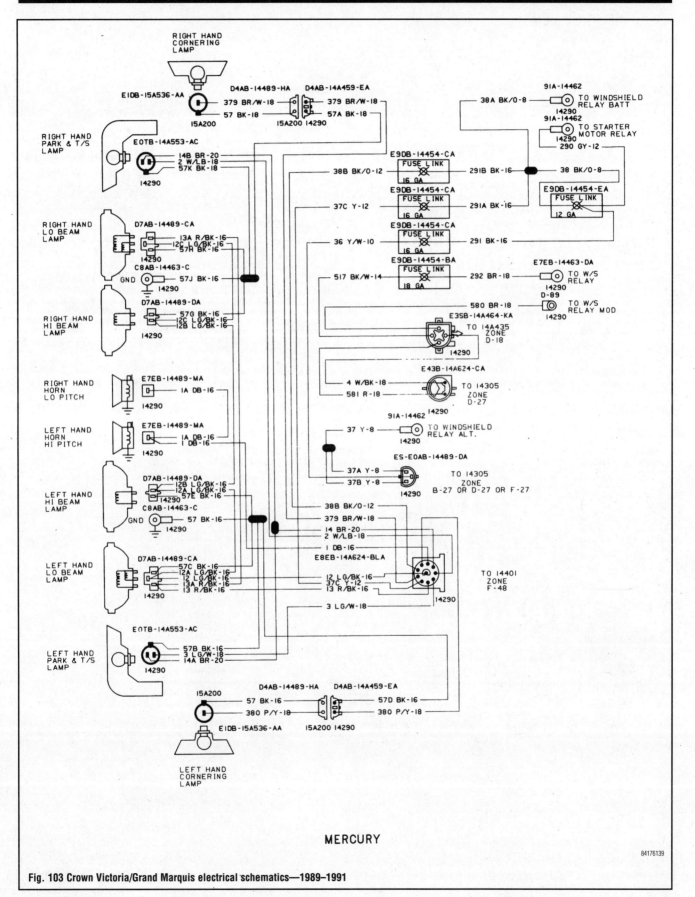

MERCURY

84176139

Fig. 103 Crown Victoria/Grand Marquis electrical schematics—1989–1991

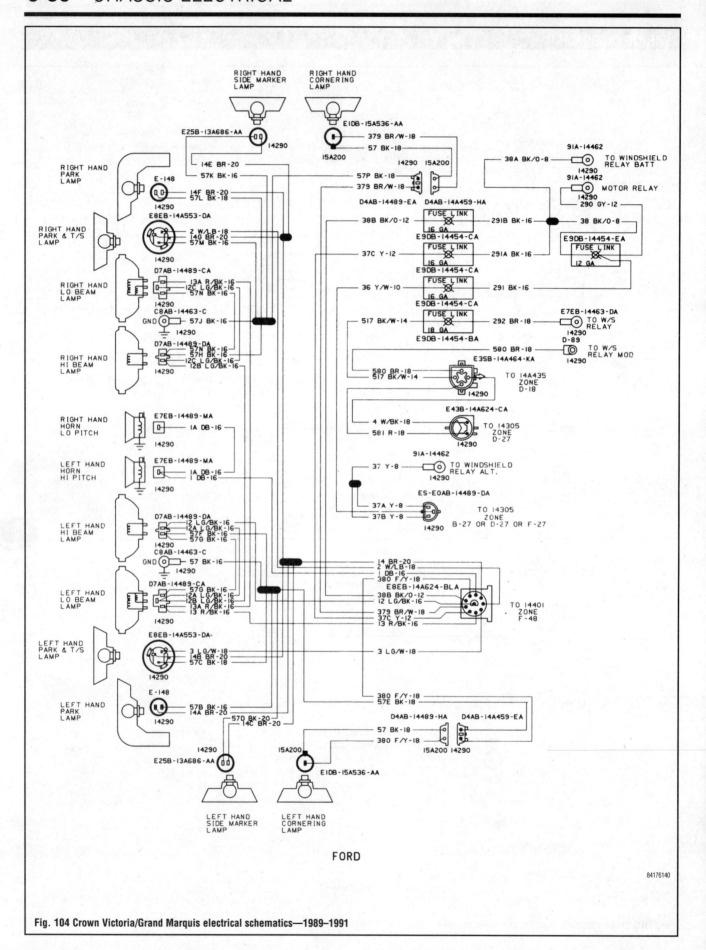

Fig. 104 Crown Victoria/Grand Marquis electrical schematics—1989–1991

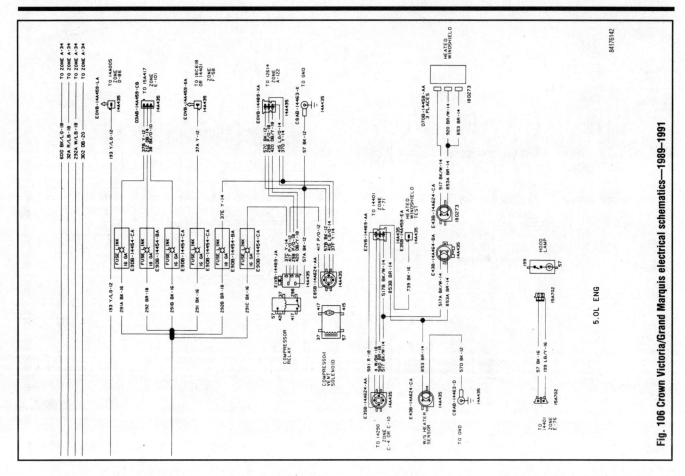

Fig. 106 Crown Victoria/Grand Marquis electrical schematics—1989-1991

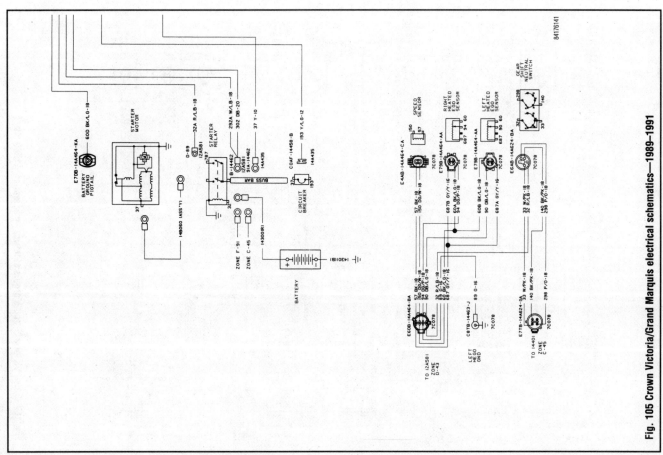

Fig. 105 Crown Victoria/Grand Marquis electrical schematics—1989-1991

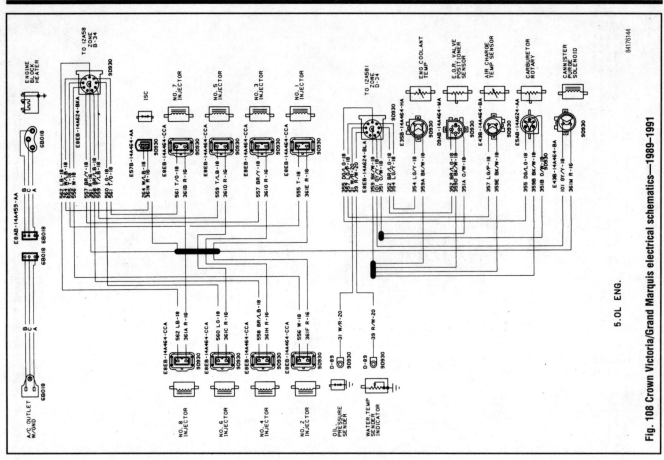

Fig. 108 Crown Victoria/Grand Marquis electrical schematics—1989-1991

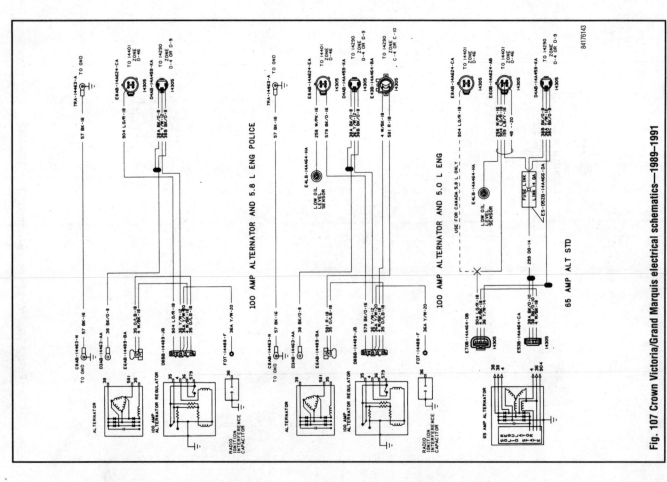

Fig. 107 Crown Victoria/Grand Marquis electrical schematics—1989-1991

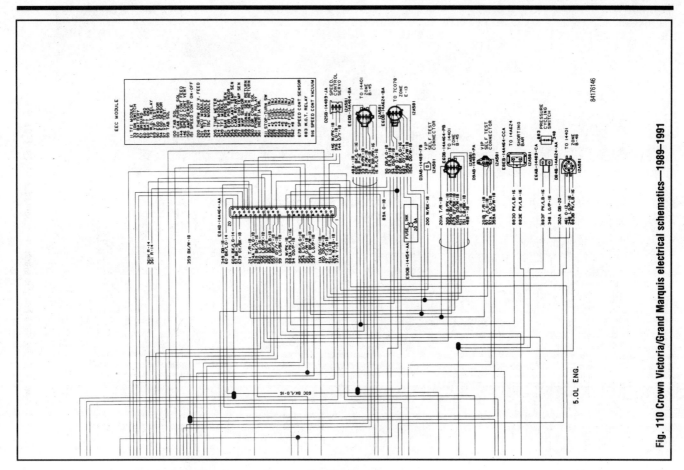

Fig. 110 Crown Victoria/Grand Marquis electrical schematics—1989–1991

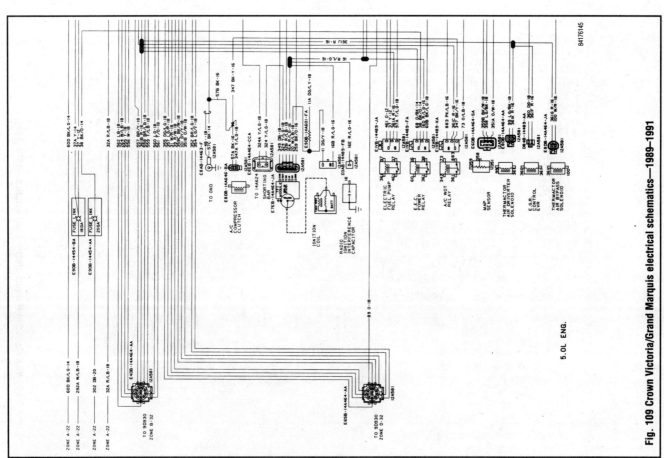

Fig. 109 Crown Victoria/Grand Marquis electrical schematics—1989–1991

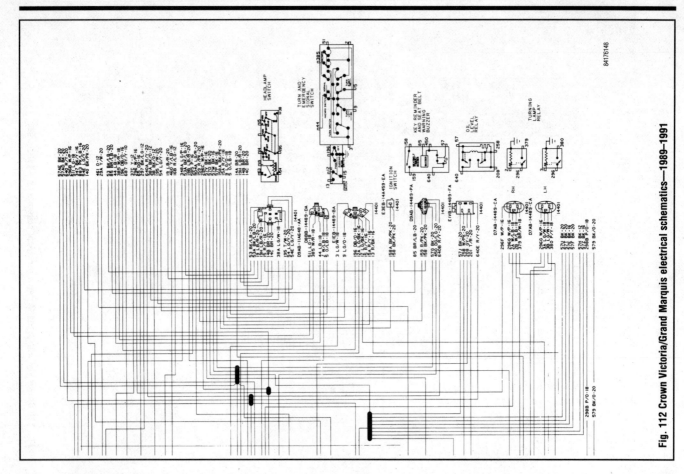

Fig. 112 Crown Victoria/Grand Marquis electrical schematics—1989–1991

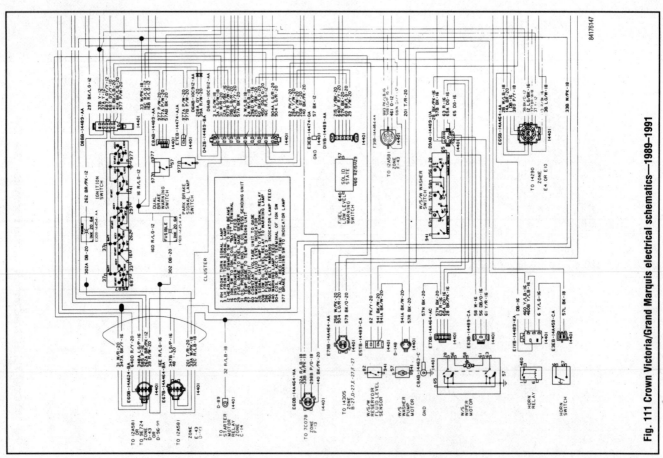

Fig. 111 Crown Victoria/Grand Marquis electrical schematics—1989–1991

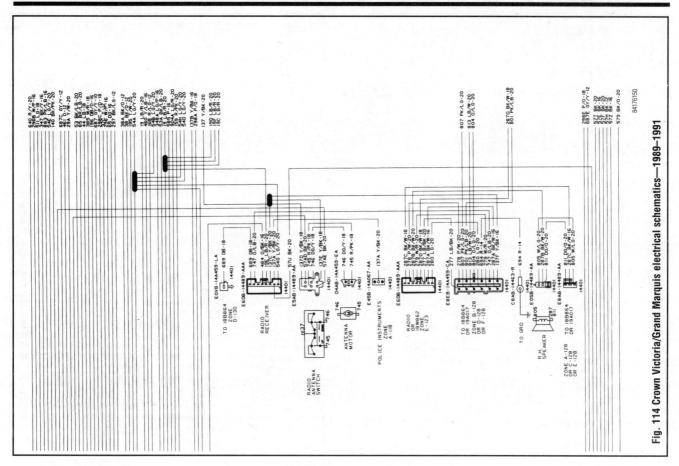

Fig. 114 Crown Victoria/Grand Marquis electrical schematics—1989–1991

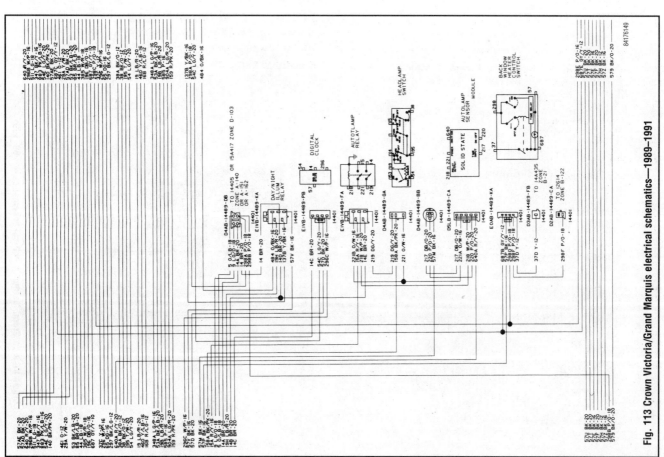

Fig. 113 Crown Victoria/Grand Marquis electrical schematics—1989–1991

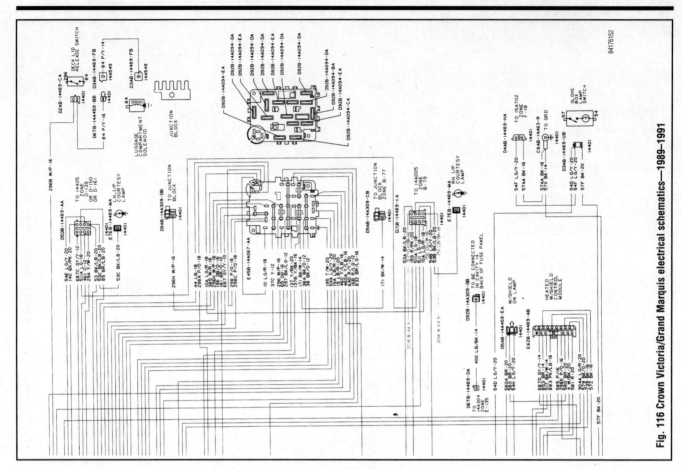

Fig. 116 Crown Victoria/Grand Marquis electrical schematics—1989–1991

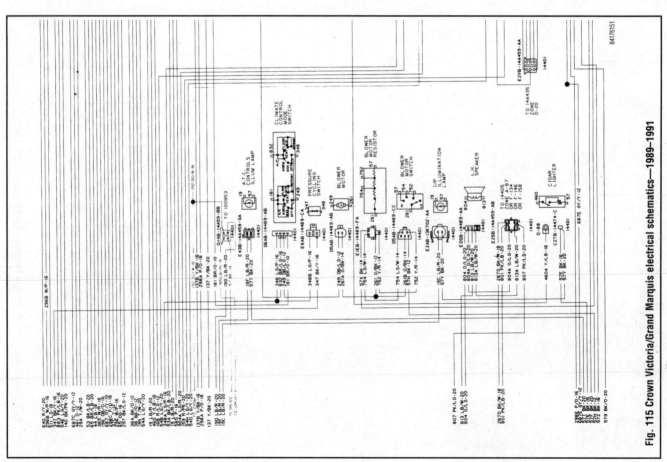

Fig. 115 Crown Victoria/Grand Marquis electrical schematics—1989–1991

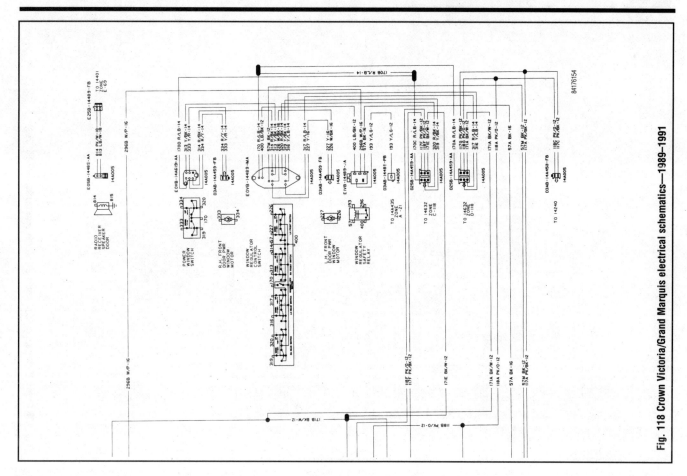

Fig. 118 Crown Victoria/Grand Marquis electrical schematics—1989–1991

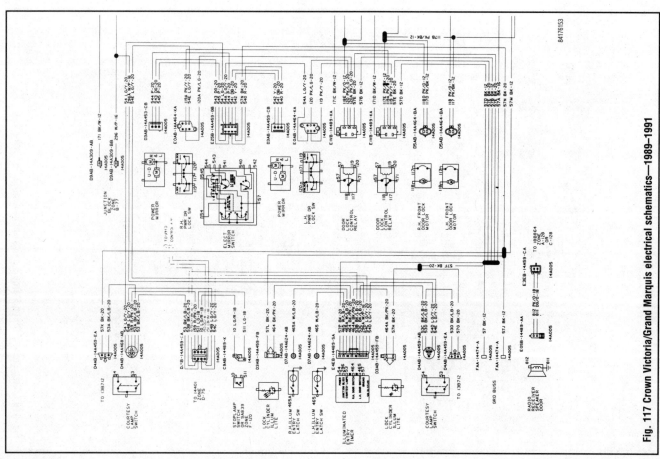

Fig. 117 Crown Victoria/Grand Marquis electrical schematics—1989–1991

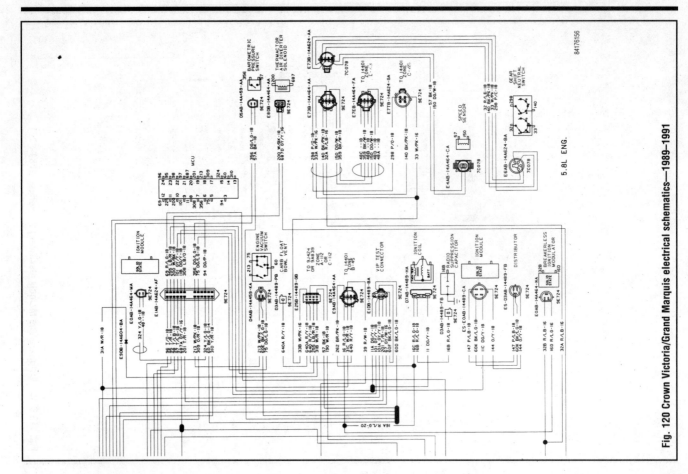

Fig. 120 Crown Victoria/Grand Marquis electrical schematics—1989–1991

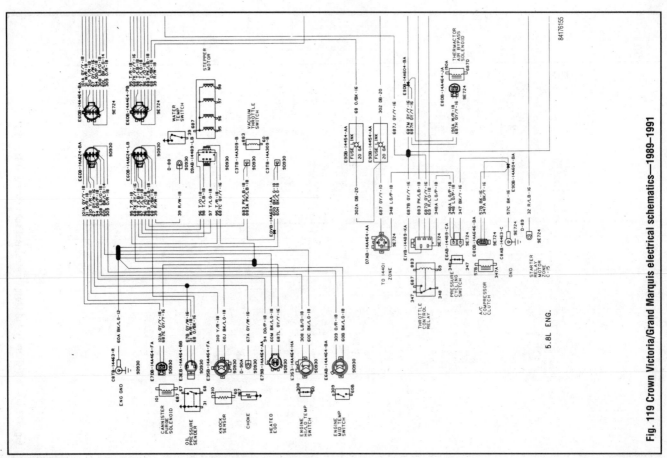

Fig. 119 Crown Victoria/Grand Marquis electrical schematics—1989–1991

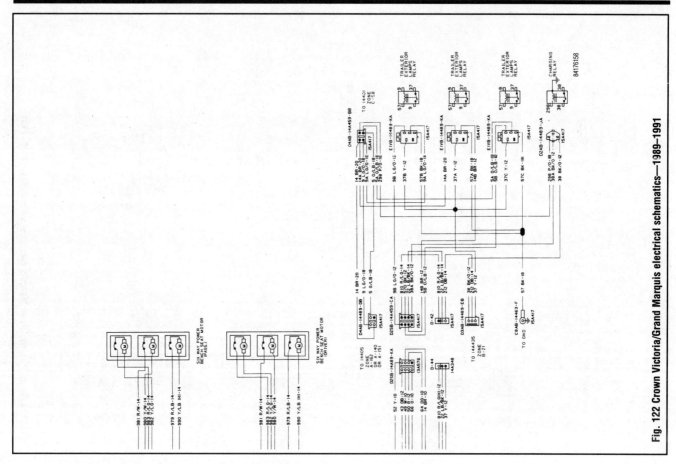

Fig. 122 Crown Victoria/Grand Marquis electrical schematics—1989–1991

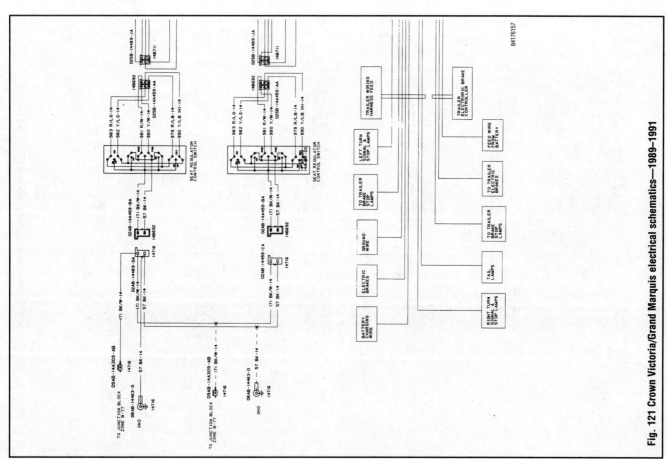

Fig. 121 Crown Victoria/Grand Marquis electrical schematics—1989–1991

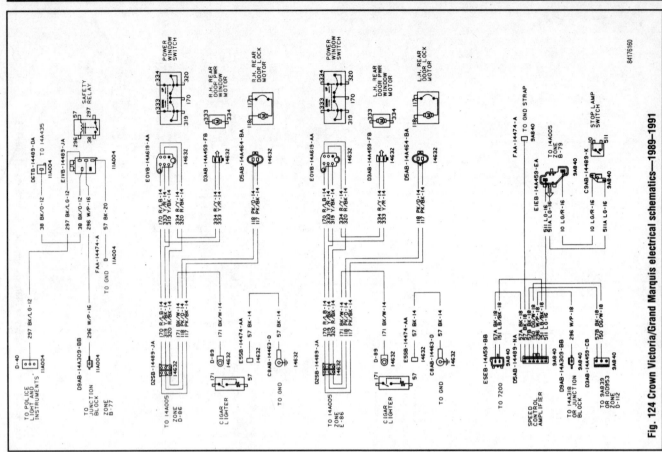

Fig. 124 Crown Victoria/Grand Marquis electrical schematics—1989–1991

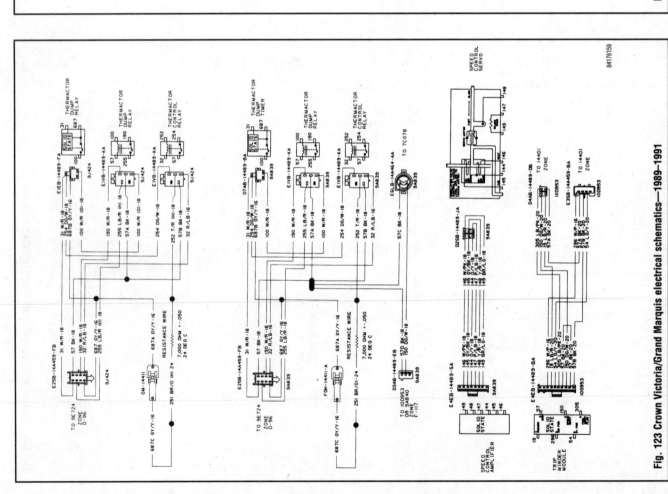

Fig. 123 Crown Victoria/Grand Marquis electrical schematics—1989–1991

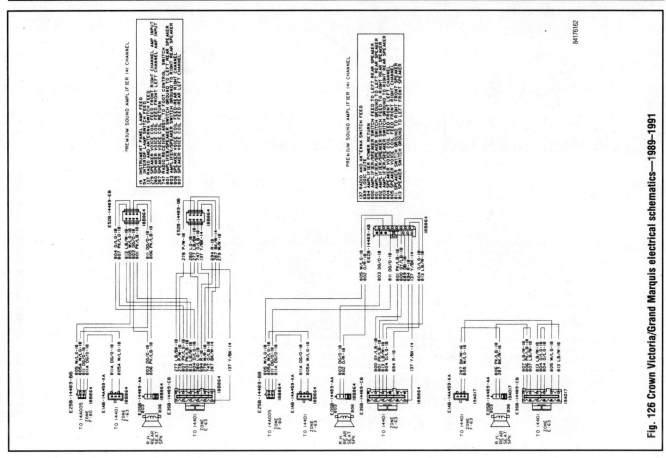

Fig. 126 Crown Victoria/Grand Marquis electrical schematics—1989–1991

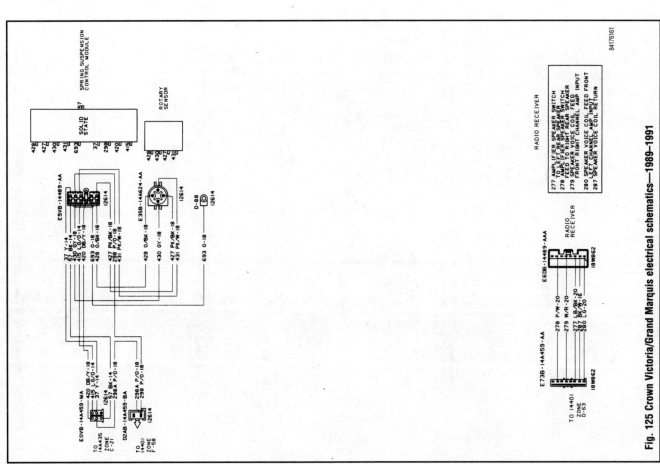

Fig. 125 Crown Victoria/Grand Marquis electrical schematics—1989–1991

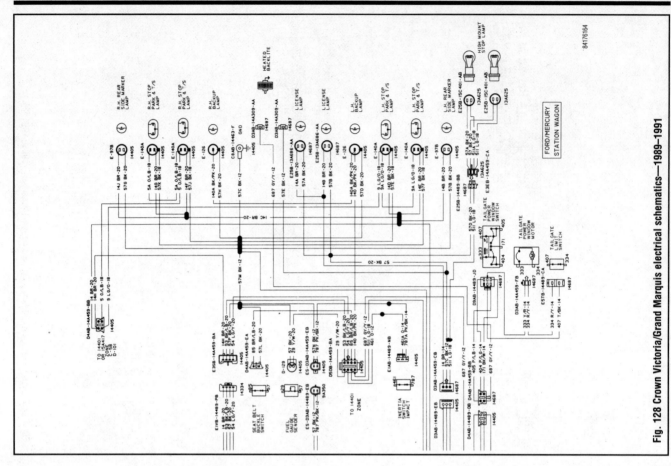

Fig. 128 Crown Victoria/Grand Marquis electrical schematics—1989-1991

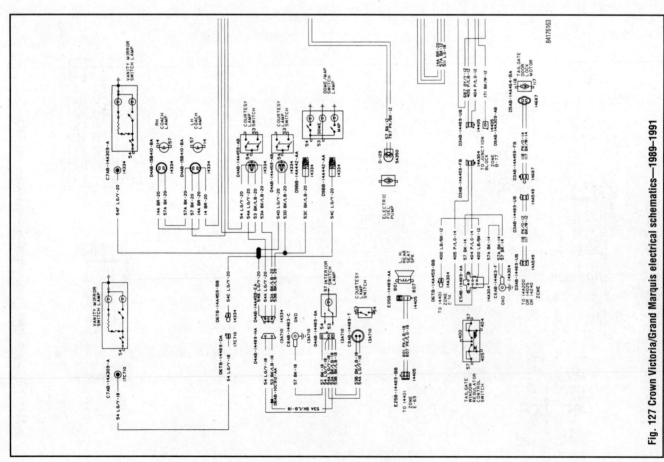

Fig. 127 Crown Victoria/Grand Marquis electrical schematics—1989-1991

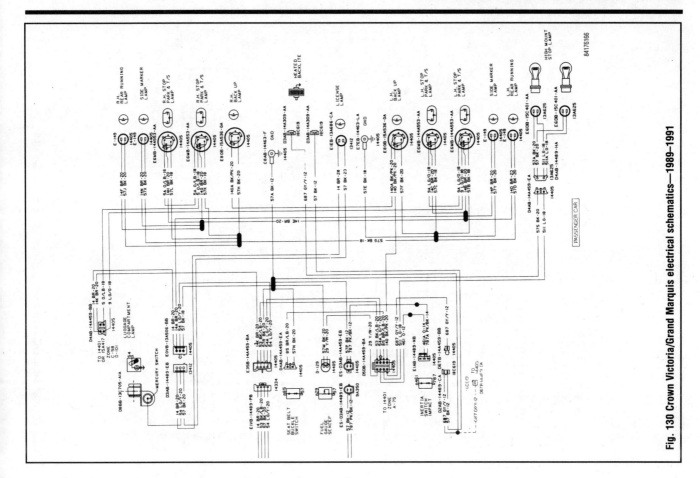

Fig. 130 Crown Victoria/Grand Marquis electrical schematics—1989–1991

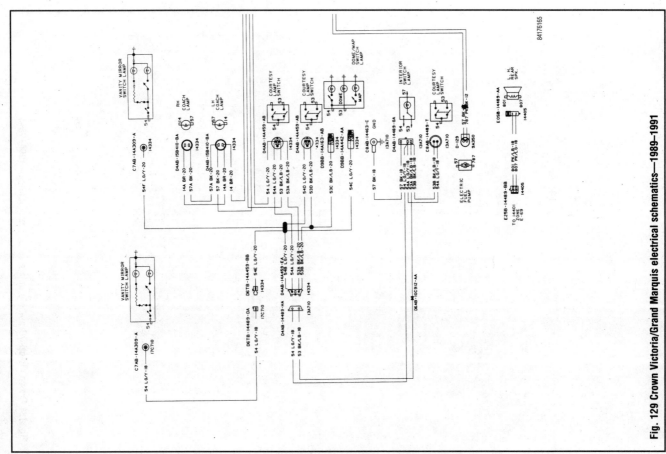

Fig. 129 Crown Victoria/Grand Marquis electrical schematics—1989–1991

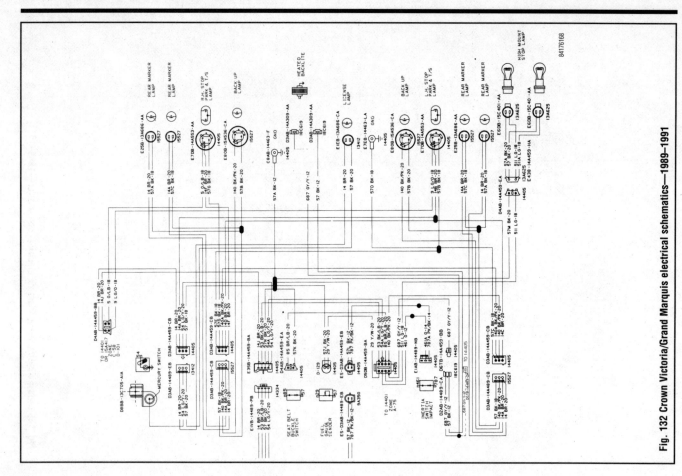

Fig. 132 Crown Victoria/Grand Marquis electrical schematics—1989–1991

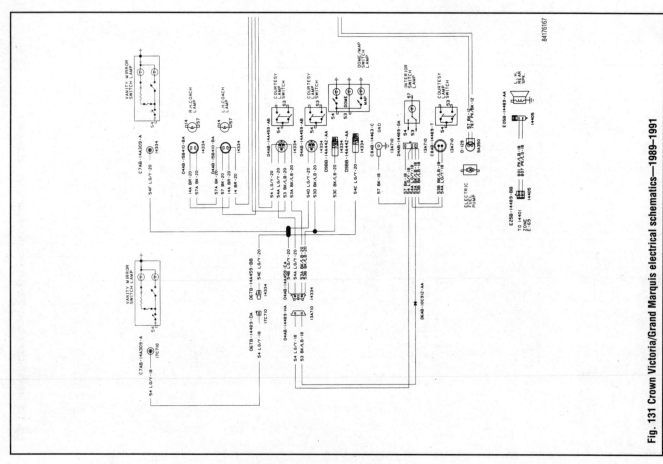

Fig. 131 Crown Victoria/Grand Marquis electrical schematics—1989–1991

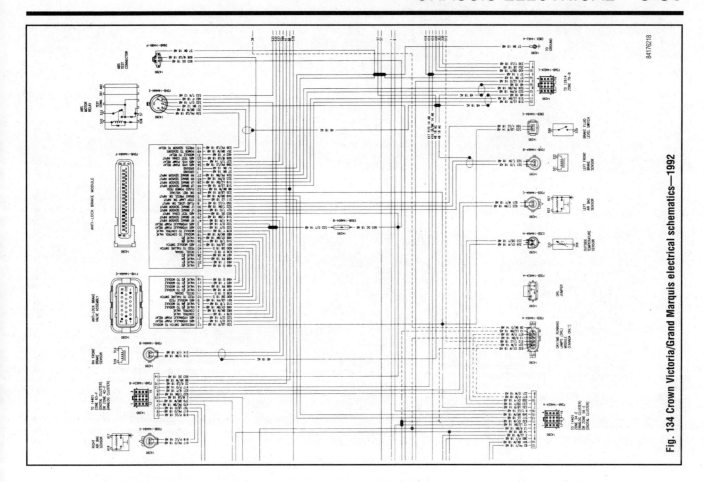

Fig. 134 Crown Victoria/Grand Marquis electrical schematics—1992

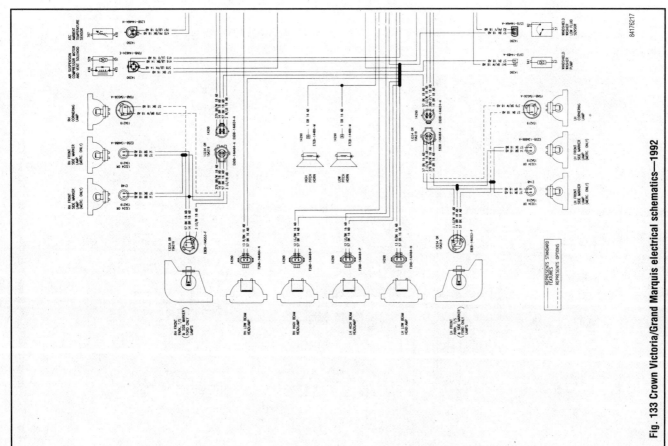

Fig. 133 Crown Victoria/Grand Marquis electrical schematics—1992

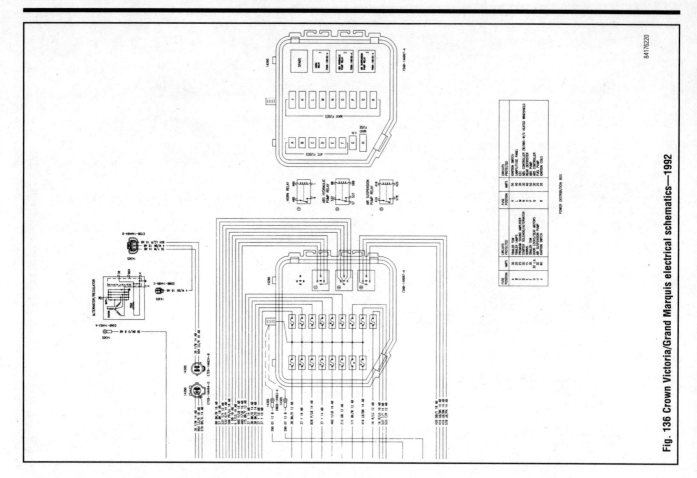

Fig. 136 Crown Victoria/Grand Marquis electrical schematics—1992

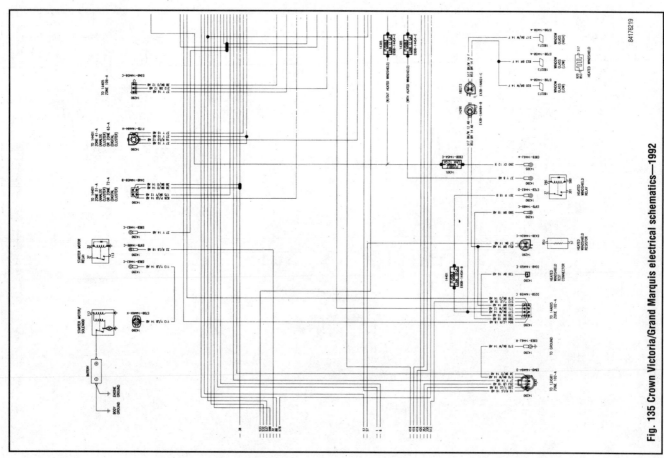

Fig. 135 Crown Victoria/Grand Marquis electrical schematics—1992

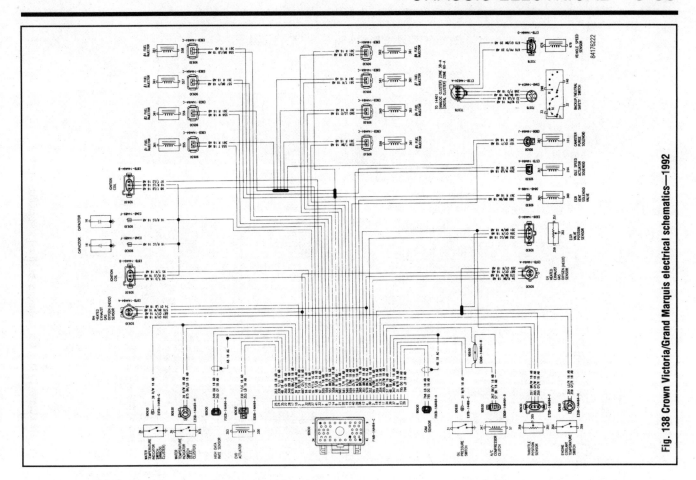

Fig. 138 Crown Victoria/Grand Marquis electrical schematics—1992

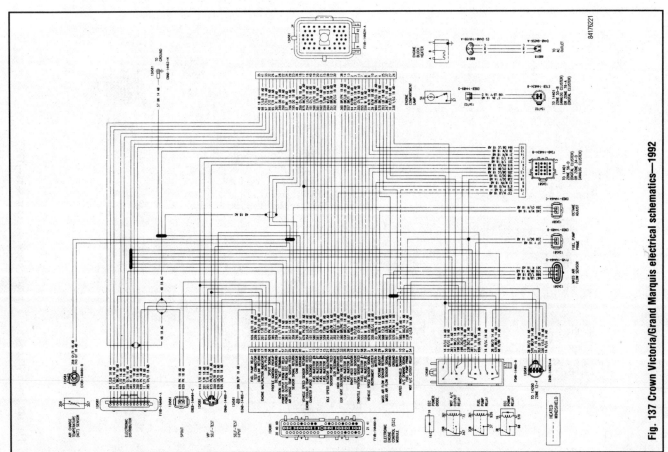

Fig. 137 Crown Victoria/Grand Marquis electrical schematics—1992

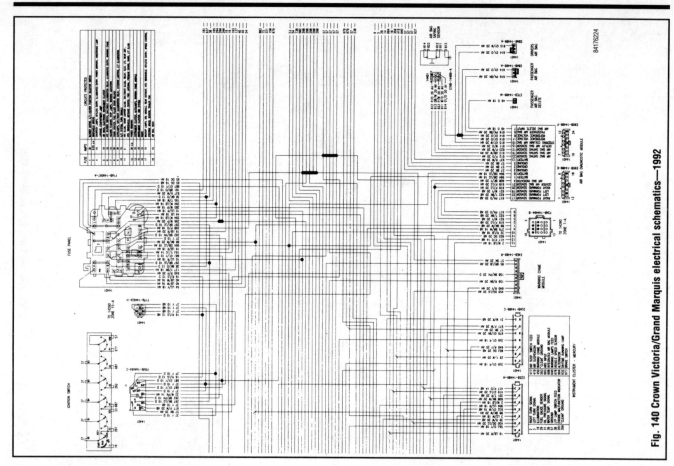

Fig. 140 Crown Victoria/Grand Marquis electrical schematics—1992

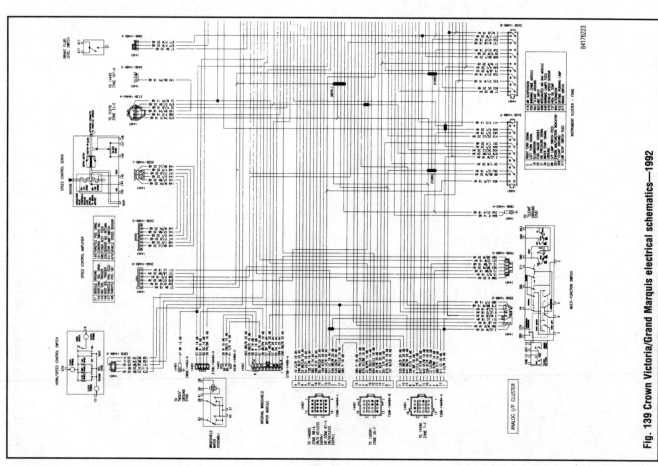

Fig. 139 Crown Victoria/Grand Marquis electrical schematics—1992

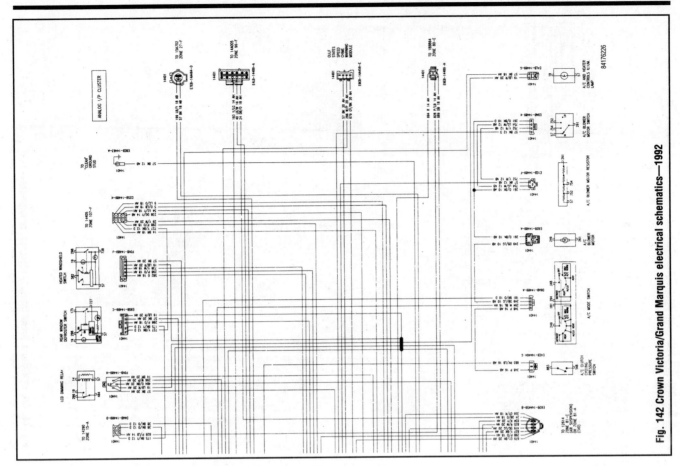

Fig. 142 Crown Victoria/Grand Marquis electrical schematics—1992

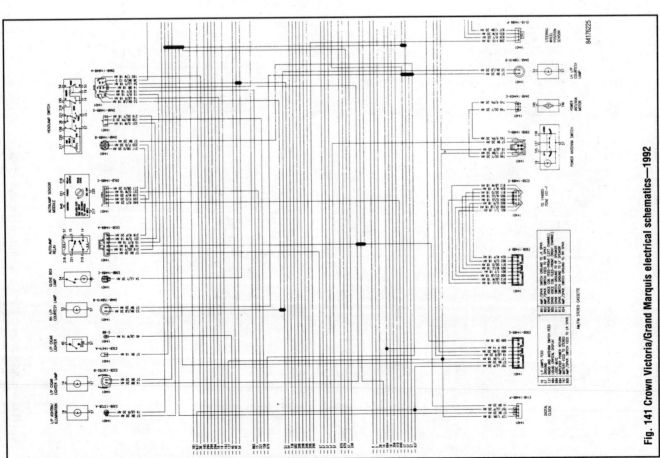

Fig. 141 Crown Victoria/Grand Marquis electrical schematics—1992

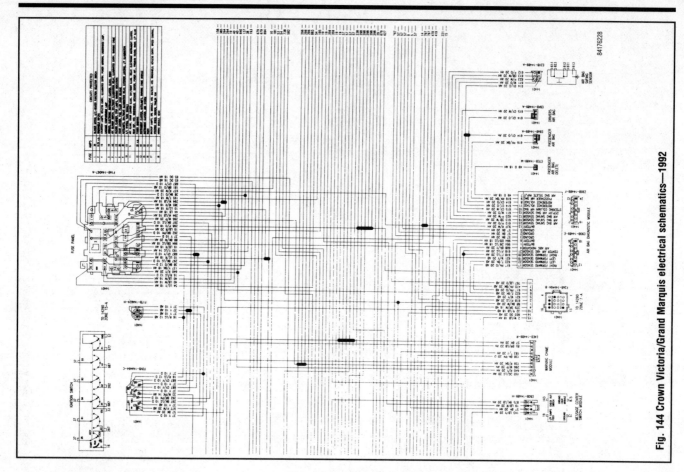

Fig. 144 Crown Victoria/Grand Marquis electrical schematics—1992

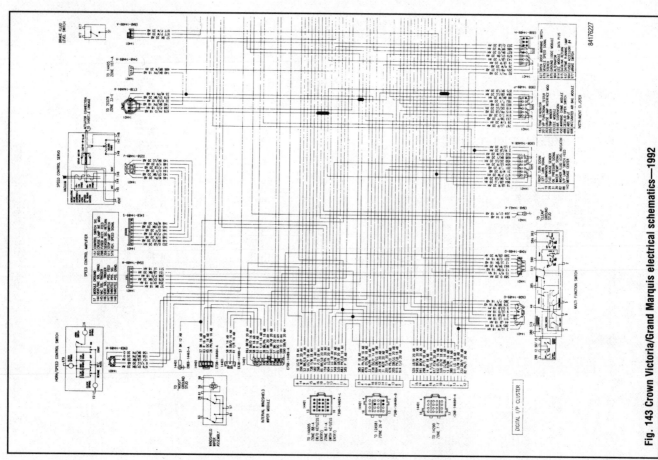

Fig. 143 Crown Victoria/Grand Marquis electrical schematics—1992

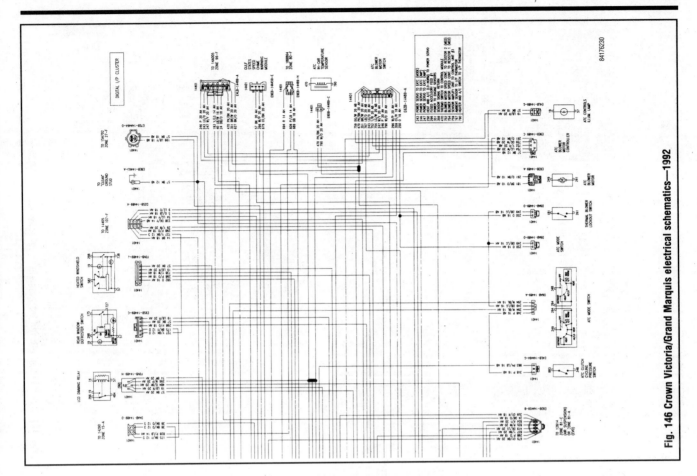

Fig. 146 Crown Victoria/Grand Marquis electrical schematics—1992

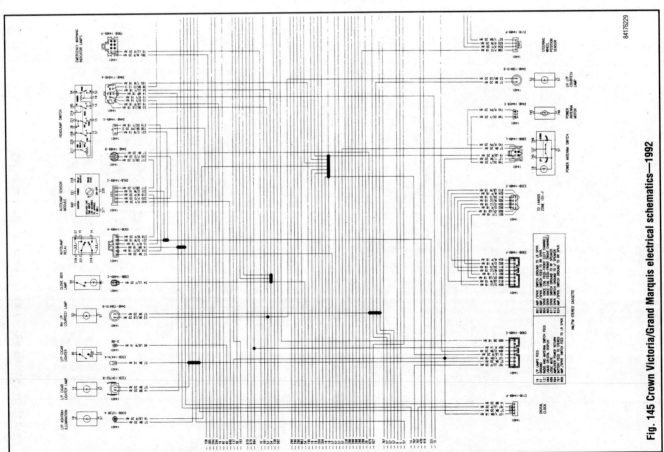

Fig. 145 Crown Victoria/Grand Marquis electrical schematics—1992

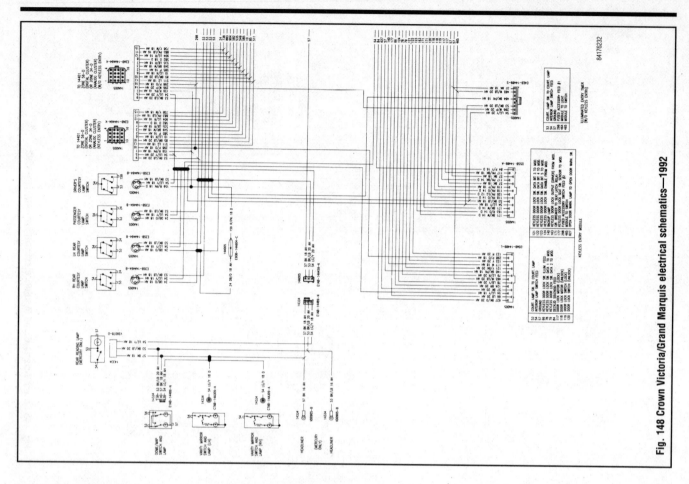

Fig. 148 Crown Victoria/Grand Marquis electrical schematics—1992

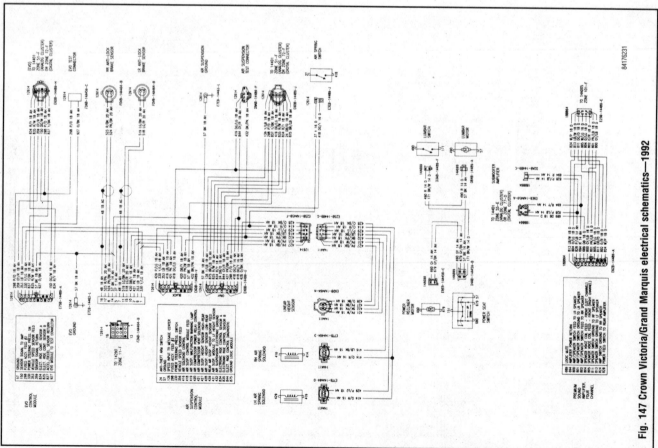

Fig. 147 Crown Victoria/Grand Marquis electrical schematics—1992

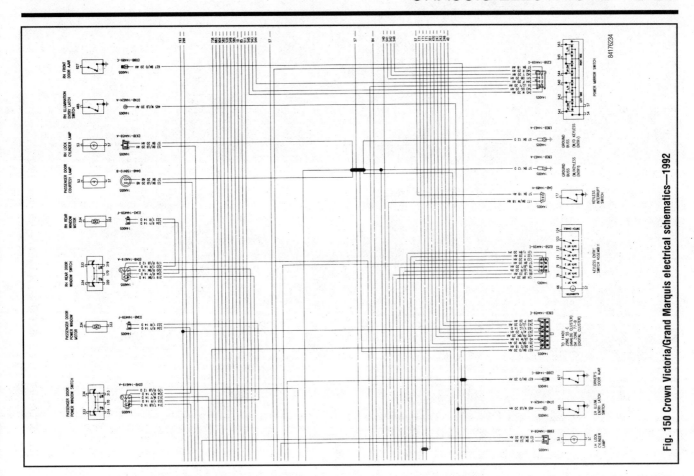

Fig. 150 Crown Victoria/Grand Marquis electrical schematics—1992

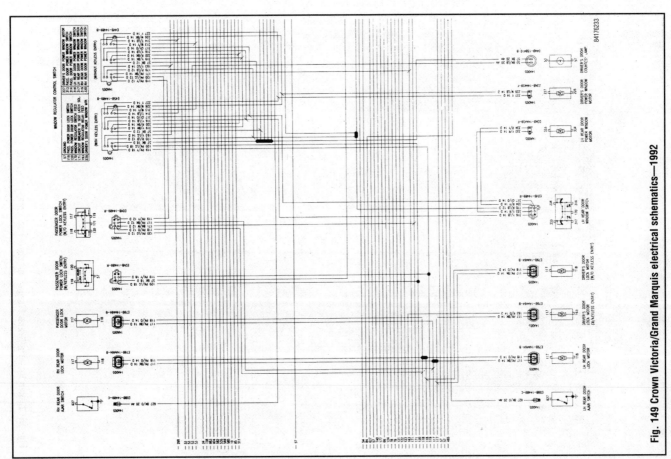

Fig. 149 Crown Victoria/Grand Marquis electrical schematics—1992

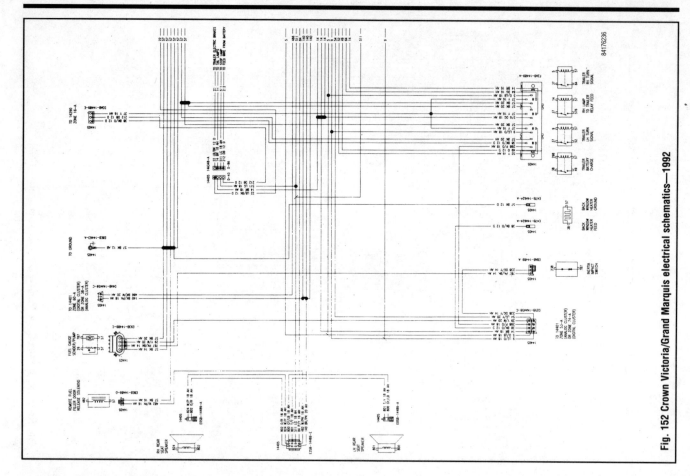

Fig. 152 Crown Victoria/Grand Marquis electrical schematics—1992

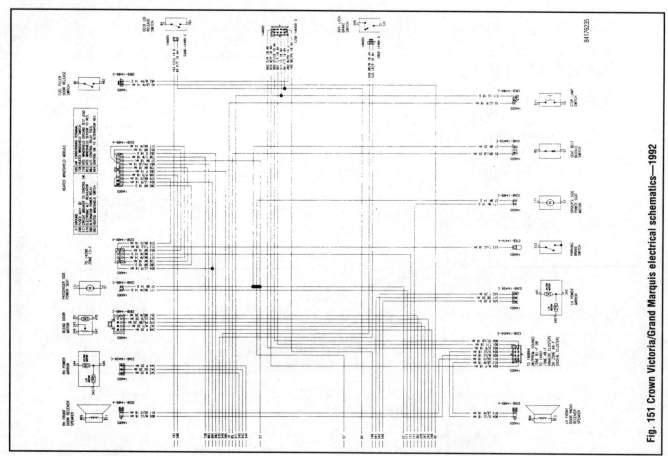

Fig. 151 Crown Victoria/Grand Marquis electrical schematics—1992

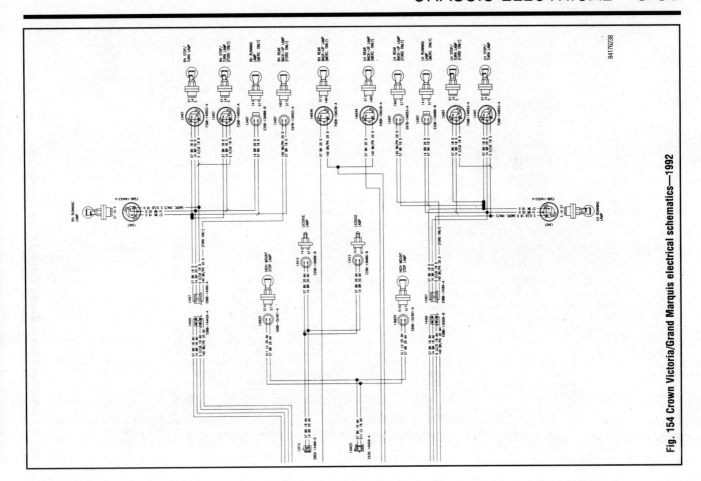

Fig. 154 Crown Victoria/Grand Marquis electrical schematics—1992

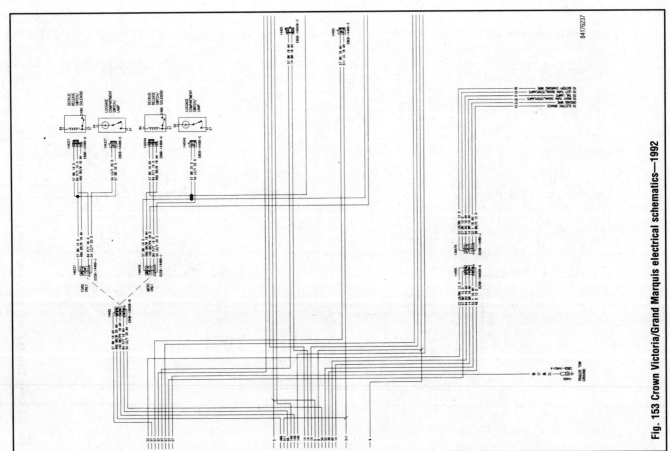

Fig. 153 Crown Victoria/Grand Marquis electrical schematics—1992

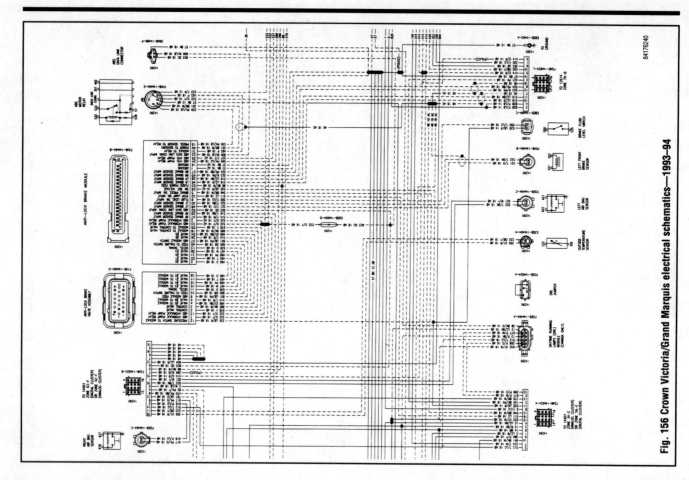

Fig. 156 Crown Victoria/Grand Marquis electrical schematics—1993-94

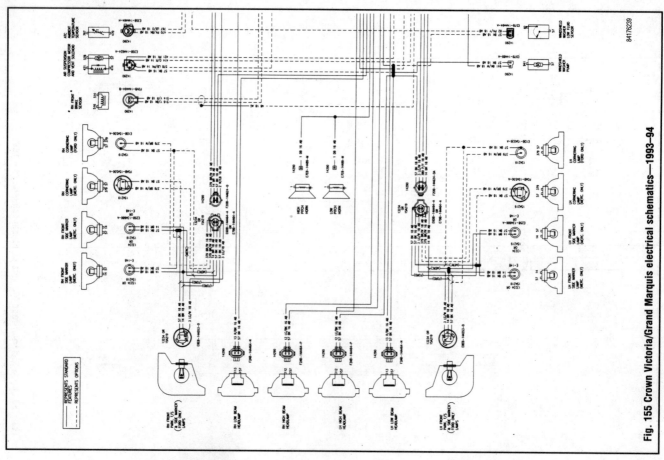

Fig. 155 Crown Victoria/Grand Marquis electrical schematics—1993-94

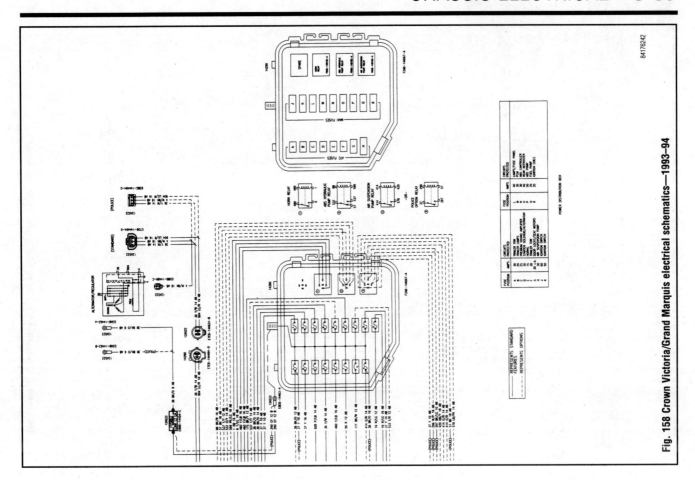

Fig. 158 Crown Victoria/Grand Marquis electrical schematics—1993-94

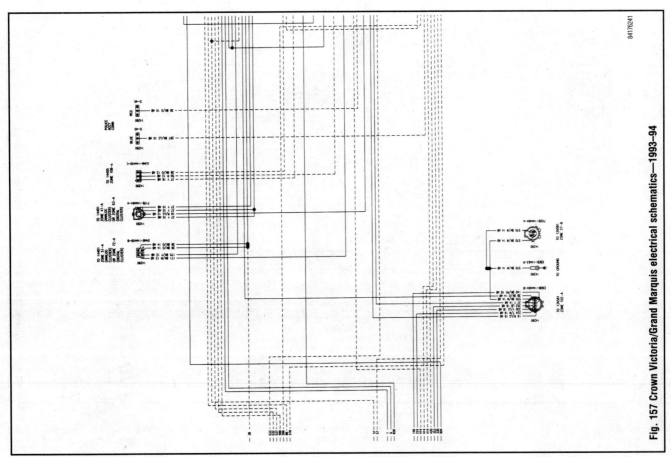

Fig. 157 Crown Victoria/Grand Marquis electrical schematics—1993-94

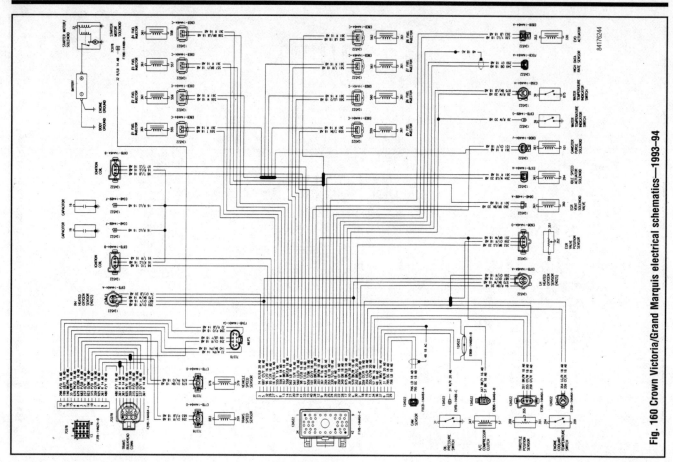

Fig. 160 Crown Victoria/Grand Marquis electrical schematics—1993-94

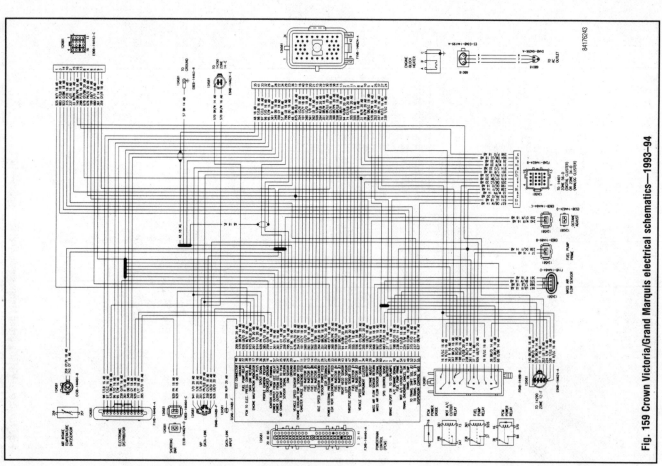

Fig. 159 Crown Victoria/Grand Marquis electrical schematics—1993-94

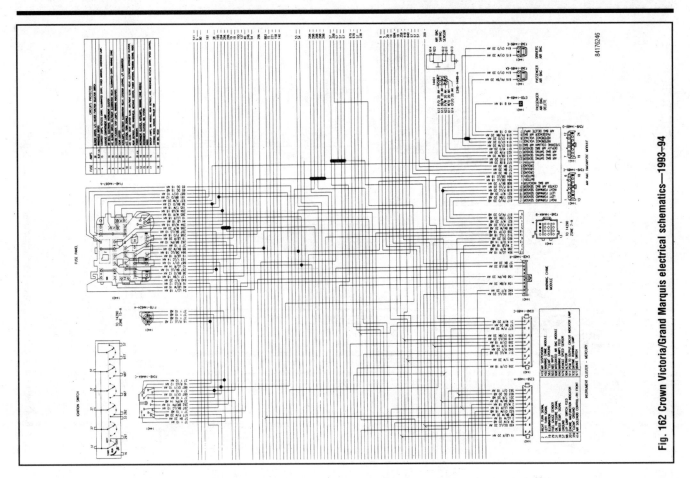

Fig. 162 Crown Victoria/Grand Marquis electrical schematics—1993–94

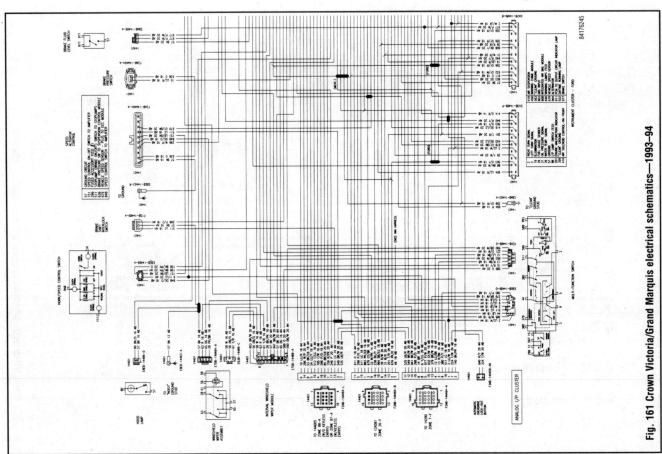

Fig. 161 Crown Victoria/Grand Marquis electrical schematics—1993–94

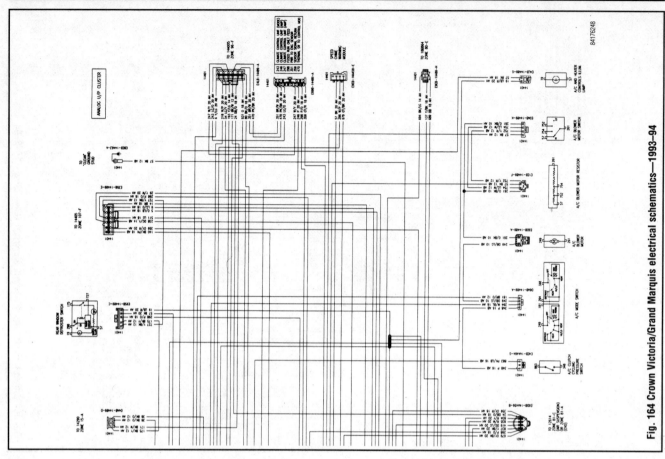

Fig. 164 Crown Victoria/Grand Marquis electrical schematics—1993–94

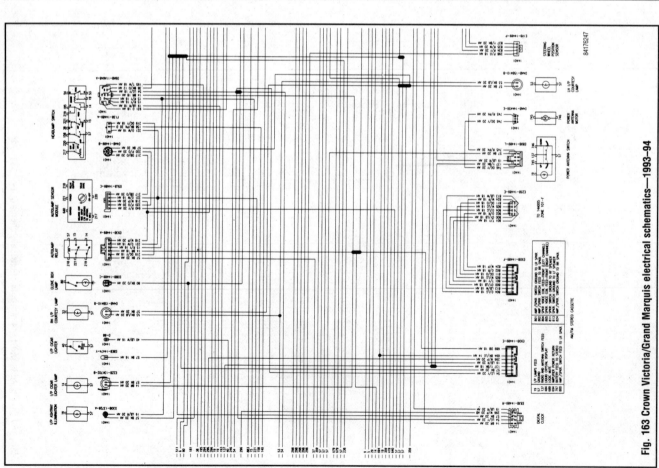

Fig. 163 Crown Victoria/Grand Marquis electrical schematics—1993–94

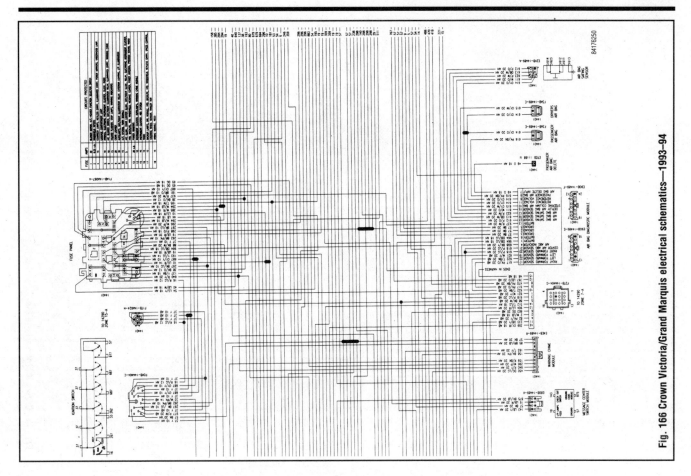

Fig. 166 Crown Victoria/Grand Marquis electrical schematics—1993–94

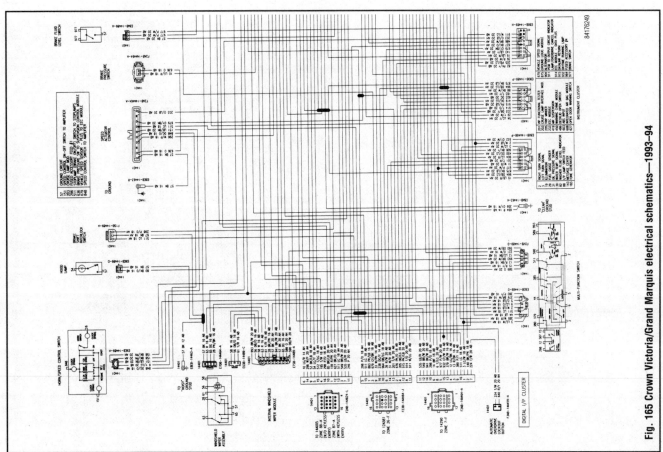

Fig. 165 Crown Victoria/Grand Marquis electrical schematics—1993–94

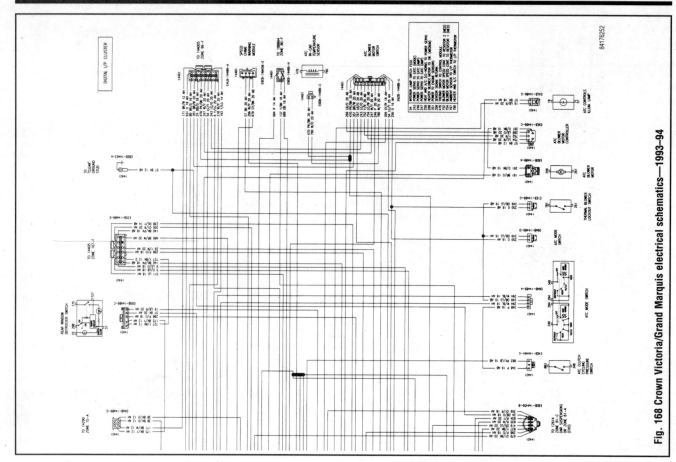

Fig. 168 Crown Victoria/Grand Marquis electrical schematics—1993–94

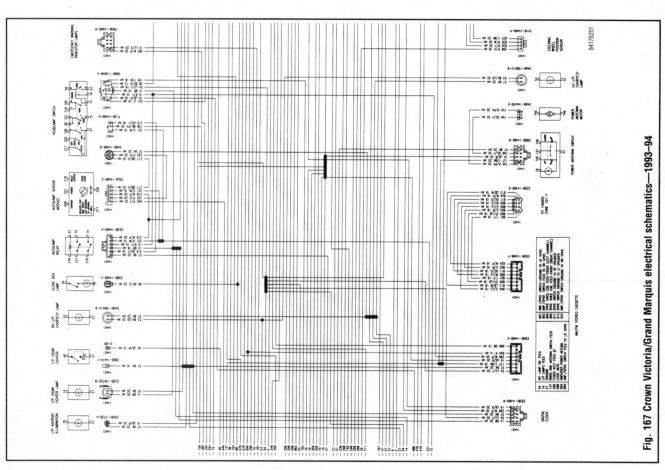

Fig. 167 Crown Victoria/Grand Marquis electrical schematics—1993–94

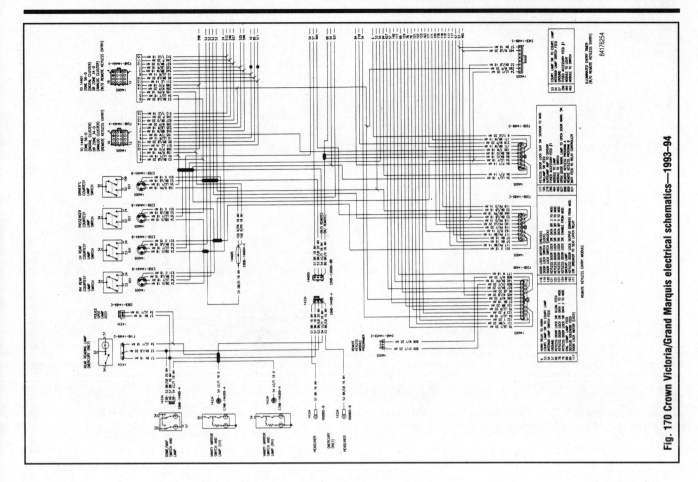

Fig. 170 Crown Victoria/Grand Marquis electrical schematics—1993–94

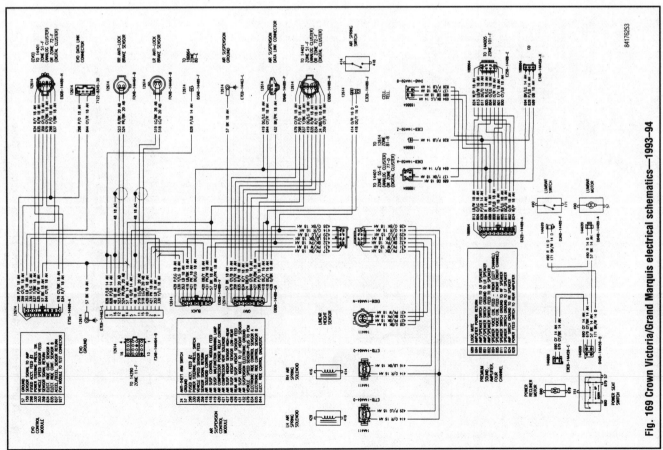

Fig. 169 Crown Victoria/Grand Marquis electrical schematics—1993–94

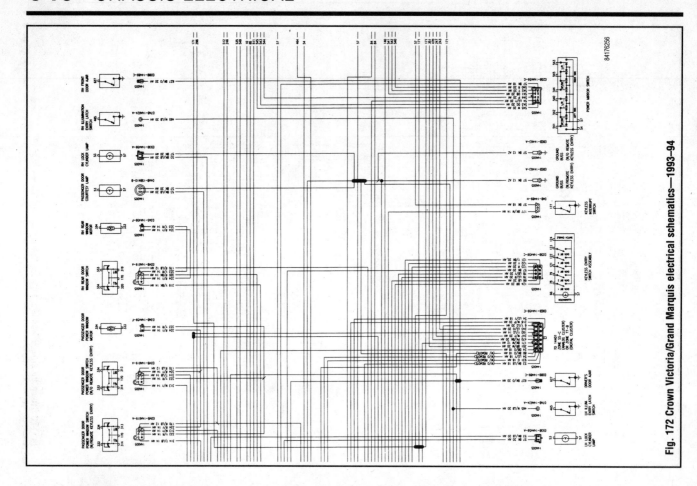

Fig. 172 Crown Victoria/Grand Marquis electrical schematics—1993–94

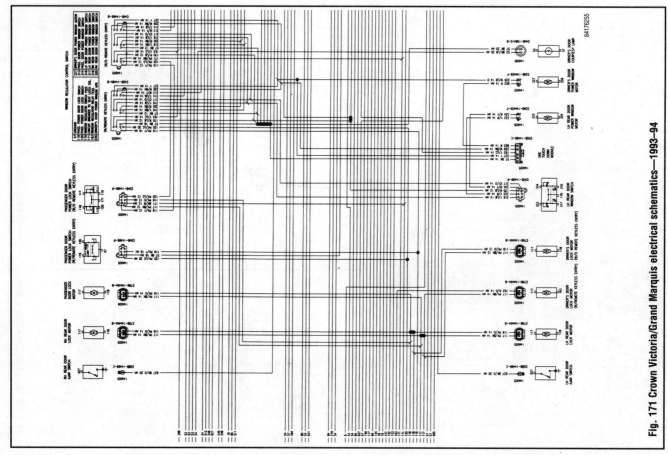

Fig. 171 Crown Victoria/Grand Marquis electrical schematics—1993–94

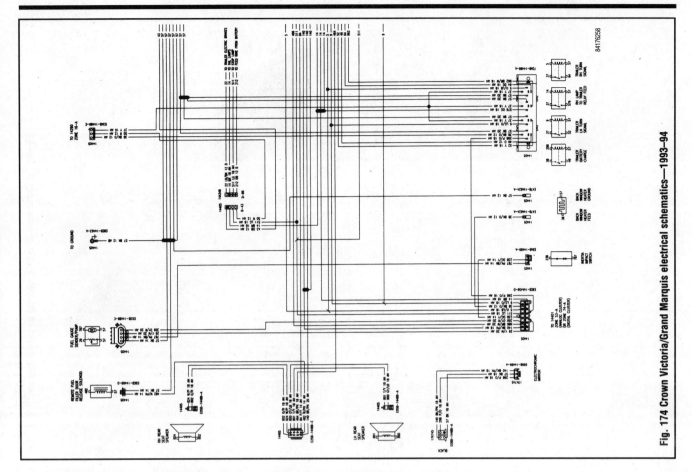

Fig. 174 Crown Victoria/Grand Marquis electrical schematics—1993–94

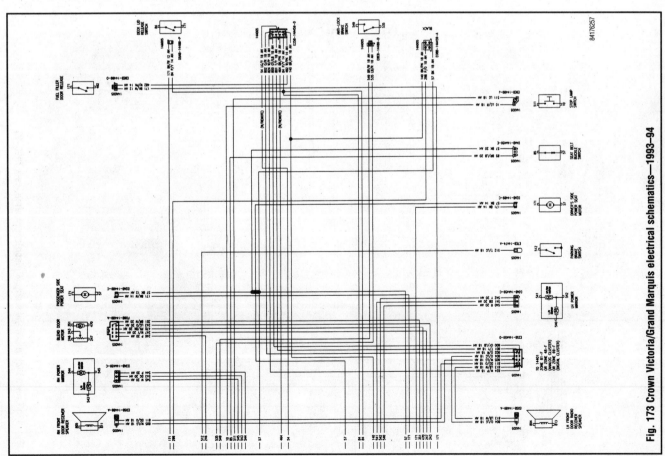

Fig. 173 Crown Victoria/Grand Marquis electrical schematics—1993–94

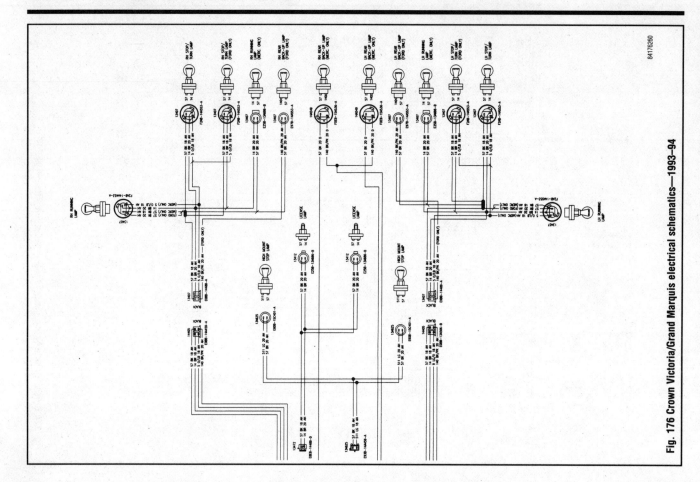

Fig. 176 Crown Victoria/Grand Marquis electrical schematics—1993–94

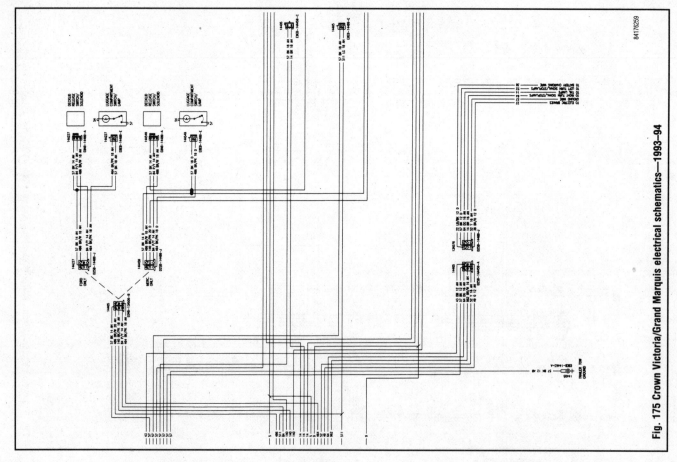

Fig. 175 Crown Victoria/Grand Marquis electrical schematics—1993–94

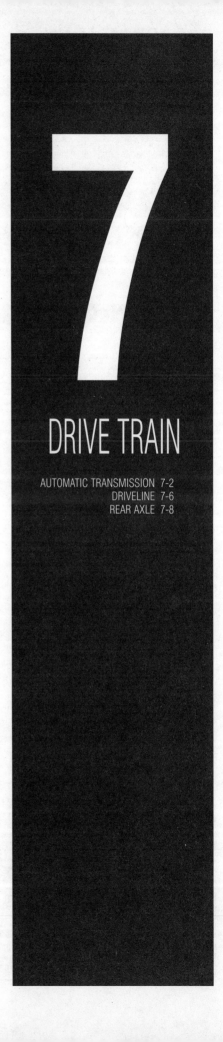

7

DRIVE TRAIN

AUTOMATIC TRANSMISSION

Identification

All vehicles are equipped with a 4-speed automatic overdrive transmission. In February 1992, an electronically controlled version (AODE) of the transmission was introduced, replacing the previous (AOD) version. The newer design transmission features electronic control of shift timing, shift feel and torque converter clutch by the Powertrain Control Module (PCM).

For transmission identification information, see Section 1.

Fluid Pan

For automatic transmission fluid pan removal and installation, and filter service procedures, refer to the automatic transmission pan and filter service procedure in Section 1.

Adjustments

SHIFT LINKAGE

1989 Vehicles

▶ See Figure 1

1. Place the selector lever in the **OVERDRIVE** position, tight against the overdrive stop. An 8 lb. weight should be hung on the selector lever to ensure the lever remains against the overdrive stop during the linkage adjustment.
2. Loosen the shift rod adjusting bolt.
3. Shift the transmission into **OVERDRIVE** by pushing the column shift rod downward to the lowest position and pulling up 3 detents.
4. Make sure the selector lever has not moved from the overdrive stop. Tighten the bolt to 14–23 ft. lbs. (19–31 Nm).
5. Check the transmission operation for all selector lever detent positions.

1990–92 Vehicles

▶ See Figure 2

1. Loosen the adjusting stud nut at the transmission shift lever.
2. From the passenger compartment, place the steering column selector lever in **OVERDRIVE** and hold the selector lever in position by placing a 3 lb. weight (8 lb. weight on 1990 vehicles) on the lever.
3. Rotate the transmission manual lever clockwise to low and return it 2 detent positions counterclockwise to the **OVERDRIVE** position.
4. Align the flats of the adjusting stud with the flats of the cable slot and install the cable on the stud.

➡Do not push or pull on the rod while assembling the rod to the stud.

5. Tighten the adjusting stud nut and washer assembly to 10–18 ft. lbs. (13–25 Nm).
6. Check the shift lever for proper operation.

1993–94 Vehicles

▶ See Figures 3 and 4

1. Place the shift lever in the **OVERDRIVE** position. Hang a 3 lb. weight on the shift lever to make sure it is firmly located on the OVERDRIVE detent.
2. Use a small prybar in the slot of the slide adjuster to open the adjuster.
3. Move the transmission manual shift lever to the **OVERDRIVE** position, second detent from the most rearward position.
4. Push the slide adjuster closed.
5. Check the operation of the transmission in each selector lever position. Make sure the neutral safety switch is functioning properly.

SHIFT INDICATOR CABLE

▶ See Figure 5

1. Remove the instrument panel lower trim panel.
2. Place the steering column selector lever in the **OVERDRIVE** position and hold the lever in position by placing a 3 lb. weight (8 lb. weight on 1989–1990 vehicles) on the lever.
3. Rotate the adjustment screw located on the right side of the column to align the indicator within the letter "O" on the standard cluster adjustment.
4. If equipped with the electronic cluster, align the indicator so that both calibration dots are white when parallel to the steering column centerline.
5. Cycle the shift lever through all of the positions and check that the transmission range indicator covers the proper letter or number in each position.
6. Install the instrument panel lower trim panel.

THROTTLE VALVE LINKAGE

Automatic Overdrive (AOD) Transmission

4.6L AND 5.0L ENGINES

▶ See Figures 6, 7, 8 and 9

1. Set the parking brake and place the shift selector in **N**.
2. Remove the air cleaner cover and inlet tube from the throttle body inlet to access the throttle lever and cable.

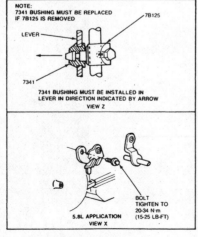

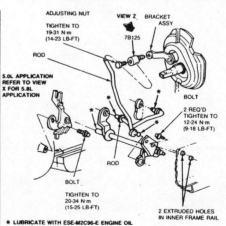

Fig. 1 Automatic transmission shift linkage—1989 vehicles

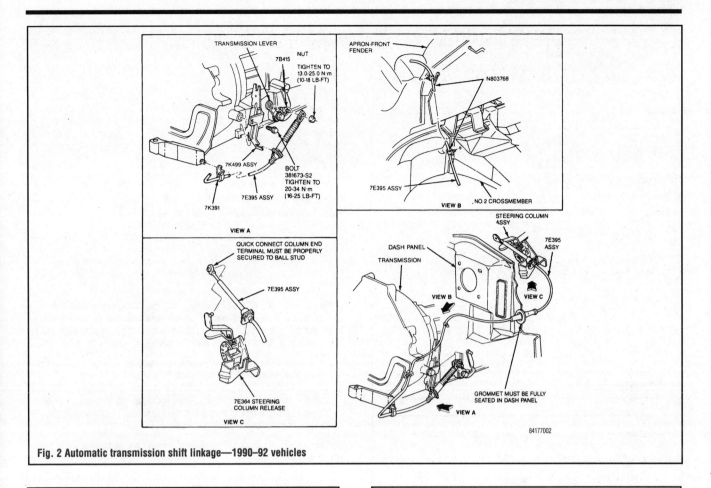

Fig. 2 Automatic transmission shift linkage—1990–92 vehicles

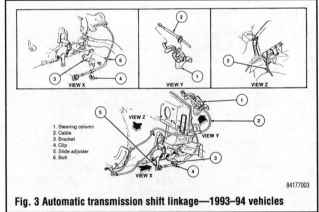

Fig. 3 Automatic transmission shift linkage—1993–94 vehicles

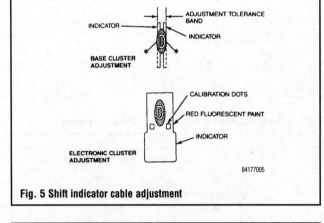

Fig. 5 Shift indicator cable adjustment

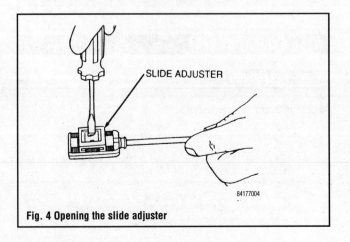

Fig. 4 Opening the slide adjuster

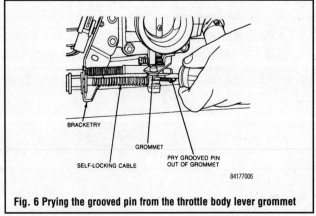

Fig. 6 Prying the grooved pin from the throttle body lever grommet

3. Using a small prybar, pry the grooved pin on the cable assembly out of the grommet on the throttle body lever. Push out the white locking tab.

4. Check the plastic block with pin and tab; it should slide freely on the notched rod. If not, the white tab may not be pushed out far enough.

5. While holding the throttle lever firmly against the idle stop, push the grooved pin into the grommet on the throttle lever as far as it will go.

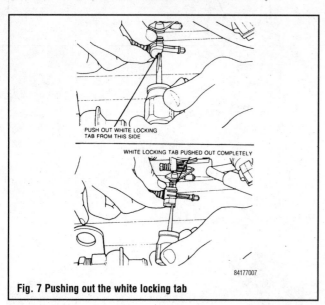

Fig. 7 Pushing out the white locking tab

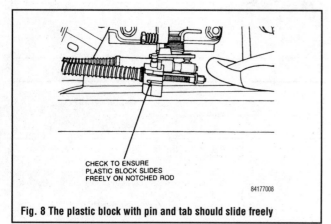

Fig. 8 The plastic block with pin and tab should slide freely

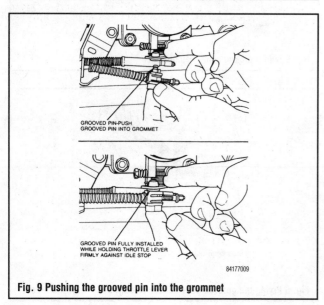

Fig. 9 Pushing the grooved pin into the grommet

6. Make sure the throttle lever does not move while pushing the pin into the grommet.

7. Install the air cleaner cover and inlet tube.

5.8L ENGINE

Before any engine throttle valve linkage adjustments can be made, the throttle lever at the carburetor must be positioned at its minimum idle stop. Make sure the engine idle speed is set to specification, then shut the engine off and remove the air cleaner. De-cam the fast idle cam on the carburetor so the throttle lever is against the idle stop or throttle solenoid positioner stop. Adjust the linkage as follows:

1. Adjust the linkage at the carburetor as follows:

a. Make sure the carburetor is set at the minimum idle stop. Set the parking brake and place the transmission in **N**.

➡ **The transmission selector lever must be in N.**

b. Back out the linkage lever adjusting screw all the way, until the screw end is flush with the lever face.

c. Turn in the adjusting screw until a thin shim (0.005 in. maximum), or piece of writing paper fits snugly between the end of the screw and throttle lever.

➡ **To eliminate the effect of friction, push the linkage lever forward (tending to close the gap) and release before checking the clearance between the end of the screw and throttle lever. Do not apply any load on the levers with tools or hands while checking the gap.**

d. Turn in the adjusting screw an additional 3 turns. Three turns are preferred, however one turn is permissible if screw travel is limited.

e. If it is not possible to turn in the adjusting screw at least one additional turn or if there was insufficient screw adjusting capacity to obtain an initial gap in Step b, go to Step 2 and adjust the rod linkage at the transmission.

2. Adjust the linkage at the transmission as follows:

➡ **The rod linkage must be adjusted whenever a new throttle valve control rod is installed.**

a. Set the linkage lever adjustment screw at approximately mid-range.

b. If a new throttle valve control rod is being installed, connect the rod to the linkage lever at the carburetor.

➡ **The following Steps involve working in close proximity to the exhaust system. Make sure the exhaust system is allowed to cool before proceeding further.**

c. Raise and safely support the vehicle.

d. Loosen the bolt on the sliding trunnion block on the throttle valve control rod. Remove any corrosion from the control rod and free up the trunnion block so it slides freely on the control rod.

e. Push up on the lower end of the control rod to make sure the linkage lever at the carburetor is firmly against the throttle lever. Release the force on the rod; the rod must stay up.

f. Firmly push the throttle valve control lever on the transmission up against its internal stop. Tighten the bolt on the trunnion block. Do not relax force on the lever until the bolt is tightened.

g. Lower the vehicle and verify that the throttle lever is still against the minimum idle stop or throttle solenoid positioner stop. If not, repeat the linkage adjustment at the transmission.

Neutral Safety Switch

REMOVAL & INSTALLATION

Automatic Overdrive Transmission

The neutral safety switch is located on the transmission case above the manual lever.

1. Set the parking brake.
2. Place the selector lever in the manual **L** position.
3. Remove the air cleaner assembly.
4. Disconnect the negative battery cable.
5. Disconnect the neutral safety switch electrical harness from the switch by lifting the harness straight up off the switch without side-to-side motion.

6. Reach in the area of the left hand dash panel, using a 24 inch extension, universal adapter and socket tool T74P–77247–A or equivalent, and remove the neutral safety switch and O-ring.

➡**Use of different tools could crush or puncture the walls of the switch.**

To install:

7. Install the neutral safety switch and new O-ring using socket tool T74P–77247–A or equivalent.
8. Tighten the switch to 8–11 ft. lbs. (11–15 Nm).
9. Connect the neutral safety switch to the wiring harness.
10. Connect the negative battery cable.
11. Check that the vehicle starts in the **N** or **P** position.

Shift Linkage

REMOVAL & INSTALLATION

1989 Vehicles

➡**The automatic transmission linkage system uses urethane plastic grommets to connect the various rods and levers. Whenever a rod is disconnected from a grommet-type connector, the old grommet must be removed and a new one installed.**

1. Raise and safely support the vehicle.
2. Remove the bolts attaching the linkage at the transmission, frame rail and column shift lever. Remove the linkage.
3. Wherever linkage has been removed from a grommet, remove the grommet using grommet removal tool T84P–7341–A or equivalent.

To install:

4. Adjust the stop on grommet installation tool T84P–7341–B or equivalent, to ½ in. (12.7mm). Coat the outside of the new grommet with lubricant.
5. Position the grommet on the lever and install it using the installation tool. Turn the screw on the tool to force the grommet into position. Turn the grommet several times to make sure it is seated in the lever.
6. Install and connect the shift linkage. Tighten the linkage-to-frame rail bolts to 9–18 ft. lbs. (12–24 Nm). Tighten the linkage bracket-to-transmission bolt to 15–25 ft. lbs. (20–34 Nm).
7. Lower the vehicle.
8. Adjust the shift linkage as described in this Section, then tighten the shift rod adjusting bolt to 14–23 ft. lbs. (19–31 Nm).

1990–94 Vehicles

▶ **See Figure 10**

1. Working under the instrument panel, remove the shift cable plastic terminal from the column selector lever pivot ball by prying with a small prybar between the cable plastic terminal and selector lever.
2. Remove the shift control cable and retaining bracket from the steering column.
3. Remove the cable from the retaining bracket by unlocking the lock tab and sliding the cable out of the bracket.
4. Raise and safely support the vehicle.
5. On 1990–92 vehicles, loosen the transmission adjusting stud nut and remove the slotted terminal from the stud. On 1993–94 vehicles, remove the slide adjuster from the manual shift lever pivot ball by prying with a small prybar between the slide adjuster and manual shift lever.
6. Remove the cable from the routing clips at the transmission housing and frame rail. Lower the vehicle.
7. From the engine compartment, unseat the cable grommet from the dash panel and pull the cable from the passenger compartment.

To install:

8. From the engine compartment, feed the plastic terminal end of the cable through the dash panel opening.
9. From the passenger compartment, pull the rubber grommet on the shift cable into the dash panel opening and seat it securely.
10. Install the shift cable into the steering column retaining bracket. Make sure the locking tab is fully seated.
11. Install the shift cable and retaining bracket assembly to the steering column casting.

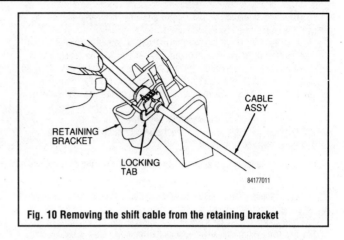

Fig. 10 Removing the shift cable from the retaining bracket

12. Apply a small amount of grease to the column selector lever pivot ball, then attach the cable plastic terminal to the pivot ball.
13. From the engine compartment, route the shift cable in the fender apron routing clip.
14. Raise and safely support the vehicle.
15. Install the cable in the frame rail and transmission routing clips, and the transmission bracket. Make sure the locking tab is fully seated.
16. Adjust the shift cable as described in this Section.
17. Lower the vehicle.

Extension Housing Seal

REMOVAL & INSTALLATION

1. Raise and safely support the vehicle.
2. Remove the driveshaft according to the procedure in this Section.
3. Carefully remove the seal, using a suitable seal removal tool.
4. Inspect the sealing surface of the driveshaft yoke for scoring or damage. If scored or damaged, the yoke must be replaced.
5. Inspect the seal bore in the extension housing for burrs or damage. Burrs can be removed with crocus cloth.

To install:

6. Install the seal in the housing using a suitable seal installer; the seal should be firmly seated in the bore.
7. Coat the inside diameter of the rubber portion of the seal with grease.
8. Install the driveshaft as described in this Section.
9. Lower the vehicle. Operate the vehicle and check for leaks.

Transmission

REMOVAL & INSTALLATION

1. Disconnect the negative battery cable. Raise the vehicle and support safely.
2. Drain the fluid from the transmission by removing all oil pan bolts except the 2 at the front. Loosen the 2 at the front and drop the oil pan at the rear to allow the fluid to drain into a container. When drained, reinstall a few of the bolts to hold the pan in place.
3. Remove the converter bottom cover and remove the converter drain plug, to allow the converter to drain. After the converter has drained, reinstall the drain plug and tighten. Remove the converter to flywheel nuts by turning the converter to expose the nuts.

➡**Crank the engine over with a wrench on the crankshaft pulley attaching bolt.**

4. Mark the position of the driveshaft on the rear axle flange and remove the driveshaft. Install a suitable plug in the transmission extension housing to prevent fluid leakage.
5. Disconnect the starter cable and remove the starter. Disconnect the wiring from the neutral safety switch.

6. Remove the mount-to-crossmember and crossmember-to-frame bolts. Remove the mount-to-transmission bolts.

7. On 1989 vehicles, disconnect the manual rod from the transmission manual lever using grommet removal tool T84P-7341-A or equivalent. On 1990-94 vehicles, disconnect the shift cable from the transmission. If equipped, disconnect the throttle valve cable from the transmission throttle valve lever.

8. On 1993-94 vehicles, disconnect the wiring connectors to the wiring harness.

9. Remove the bellcrank bracket from the converter housing.

10. Position a suitable jack and raise the transmission. Remove the transmission mount and crossmember.

➡️**It may be necessary to disconnect or remove interfering exhaust system components.**

11. Lower the transmission to gain access to the oil cooler lines. Disconnect the oil cooler lines from the transmission.

12. If equipped, disconnect the speedometer cable from the extension housing.

13. Remove the transmission dipstick tube-to-engine block retaining bolt and remove the tube and dipstick from the transmission.

14. Secure the transmission to the jack with a chain and remove the transmission-to-engine bolts.

15. Carefully pull the transmission and converter assembly rearward and lower them from the vehicle.

To install:

16. Tighten the converter drain plug to 21-23 ft. lbs. (28-30 Nm).

17. If removed, position the converter on the transmission and rotate into position to make sure the drive flats are fully engaged in the pump gear.

➡️**Lubricate the pilot with chassis grease.**

18. Raise the converter and transmission assembly. Rotate the converter until the studs and drain plug are in alignment with the holes in the flywheel. Align the orange balancing marks on the converter stud and flywheel bolt hole if balancing marks are present.

19. Move the converter and transmission assembly forward into position, being careful not to damage the flywheel and converter pilot.

➡️**The converter face must rest squarely against the flywheel. This indicates that the converter pilot is not binding in the engine crankshaft. To ensure the converter is properly seated, grasp a converter stud. It should move freely back and forth in the flywheel hole. If the converter will not move, the transmission must be removed and the converter repositioned so the impeller hub is properly engaged in the pump gear.**

20. Install the transmission-to-engine attaching bolts. Tighten the bolts to 40-50 ft. lbs. (55-68 Nm).

21. Remove the safety chain from around the transmission.

22. Install a new O-ring on the lower end of the transmission dipstick tube and install the tube to the transmission case.

23. If equipped, connect the speedometer cable to the transmission case.

24. Connect the oil cooler lines to the right side of the transmission case.

25. Position the crossmember on the side supports. Position the rear mount on the crossmember and install the attaching bolt/nut.

26. Secure the engine rear support to the transmission extension housing.

27. Install any exhaust system components, if removed.

28. Lower the transmission and remove the jack.

29. Secure the crossmember to the side supports with the attaching bolts.

30. If equipped, connect the throttle valve linkage to the throttle valve lever. On 1993-94 vehicles, connect the wiring harness connectors.

31. On 1989 vehicles, connect the manual linkage rod to the transmission manual lever using grommet installation tool T84P-7341-B or equivalent. On 1990-94 vehicles, connect the shift cable.

32. Install the converter to flywheel attaching nuts and tighten to 20-34 ft. lbs. (27-46 Nm). Install the converter housing cover.

33. Secure the starter motor in place and connect all electrical connections.

34. Install the driveshaft, aligning the marks that were made during removal.

35. Install the transmission fluid pan bolts and tighten, evenly, to 107-119 inch lbs. (12-13.5 Nm).

36. Lower the vehicle. Fill the transmission with the proper type and quantity of fluid, start the engine and check the transmission for leakage. Adjust the linkage as required.

DRIVELINE

Driveshaft and U-Joints

REMOVAL & INSTALLATION

1. Raise and safely support the vehicle. Mark the position of the driveshaft yoke on the axle companion flange so they can be reassembled in the same way to maintain balance.

2. Remove the flange bolts and disconnect the driveshaft from the axle companion flange.

3. Allow the rear of the driveshaft to drop down slightly. Pull the driveshaft and slip yoke rearward until the yoke just clears the transmission extension housing seal. Mark the position of the slip yoke in relation to the transmission output shaft, then remove the driveshaft.

4. Plug the transmission to prevent fluid leakage.

To install:

5. Lubricate the yoke splines with suitable grease. Remove the plug from the transmission and inspect the extension housing seal; replace if necessary.

6. Align the slip yoke and output shaft with the marks made at removal and install the yoke into the transmission extension housing. Be careful not to bottom the slip yoke hard against the transmission seal.

7. Rotate the axle flange, as necessary, to align the marks made during removal. Install the driveshaft yoke to the axle flange. Install the bolts and tighten to 71-95 ft. lbs. (95-130 Nm).

U-JOINT REPLACEMENT

▶ **See Figures 11, 12, 13, 14 and 15**

1. Remove the driveshaft from the vehicle and place it in a vise, being careful not to damage it. Mark the position of the yokes in relation to the driveshaft tube, so they can be reinstalled the same way.

2. Remove the snaprings which retain the bearing cups in the yokes and in both ends of the driveshaft.

3. Remove the driveshaft tube from the vise and position the U-joint in the vise with a socket smaller than the bearing cup on one side and a socket larger than the bearing cup on the other side.

4. Slowly tighten the jaws of the vise so that the smaller socket forces the U-joint spider and the opposite bearing cup out of the driveshaft and into the larger socket.

5. Remove the U-joint from the vise and remove the socket from over the bearing cup. The bearing cup should be forced out of the driveshaft enough to grip and remove with pliers.

6. Drive the spider in the opposite direction in the same manner as in Step 4 in order to make the opposite bearing cup accessible, and pull it free with pliers. Use this procedure to remove all bearing cups from both U-joints.

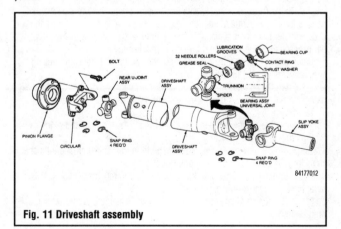

84177012

Fig. 11 Driveshaft assembly

Fig. 12 Removing the bearing cup

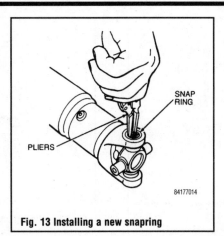

Fig. 13 Installing a new snapring

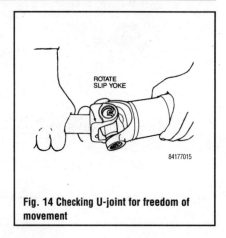

Fig. 14 Checking U-joint for freedom of movement

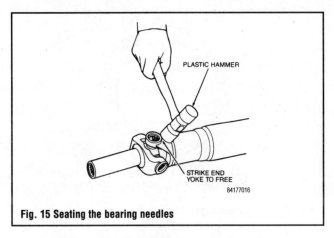

Fig. 15 Seating the bearing needles

7. After removing the bearing cups, remove the spiders from the driveshaft and yokes.

8. Thoroughly clean all dirt and foreign material from the yoke areas of the driveshaft and yokes.

9. Start a new bearing cup into the yoke of the driveshaft. Install the new spider in the driveshaft yoke and bearing. Position the yoke in the vise. Slowly close the vise, pressing the bearing cup into the yoke. Use the smaller socket to press the cup in far enough so that the retaining snapring can be installed.

10. Open the vise and start a new bearing cup in the opposite hole. Press the bearing cup into the yoke in the same manner as in Step 9. Make sure the spider assembly is in line with the bearing cup as it is pressed in.

✻✻✻ WARNING

It is very easy to damage or misalign the needle rollers in the bearing cup if the spider assembly is not kept in line with the bearing cup during assembly. If the U-joint binds easily and/or the bearing cup cannot be pressed in far enough to install the snapring, one or more needle rollers has probably been knocked to the bottom of the cup. Remove the bearing cup, reposition the needle rollers and reinstall.

11. Install all remaining U-joint cups in the same manner. When installing the slip yoke and rear yoke, make sure the marks align that were made during removal. Make sure all snaprings are properly installed.

12. Check the U-joints for freedom of movement. If binding has resulted from misalignment during assembly, a sharp rap on the yoked with a brass or plastic hammer will seat the bearing cups. Take care to support the shaft end and do not strike the bearing cups during this procedure. Make sure the U-joints are free to rotate easily without binding before installing the driveshaft.

13. If supplied, install the grease fittings in the U-joints.

14. Install the driveshaft. Grease the new U-joints if they are equipped with grease fittings.

DRIVESHAFT BALANCING

◆ See Figures 16, 17, 18 and 19

Driveline vibration or shudder, felt mainly on acceleration, coasting or under engine braking, can be caused, among other things, by improper driveshaft installation or imbalance. If driveshaft vibration is suspected, proceed as follows:

1. Raise and safely support the vehicle.

2. Remove the rear wheel and tire assemblies and the rear drum or rotor assemblies.

3. Mark the position of the driveshaft to the rear axle companion flange.

4. Mark one hole position on the driveshaft yoke at the rear of the driveshaft with the letter A and the 8 circular axle flange holes (starting with the mating hole with driveshaft position A) from one through eight. Position A1 is considered the original index position.

5. Disconnect the driveshaft from the rear axle flange and re-index 180 degrees at axle position A5. Check for vibration at road test speed. If vibration is still present, evaluate positions A3 and A7.

6. If further improvement is desired, evaluate the remaining positions that are located between the best of the 2 previous positions, A3 and A7. If the vehicle tests okay at any point during this procedure, do not proceed further.

7. If re-indexing at the axle is unsuccessful, disconnect the driveshaft and re-index 180 degrees at the transmission output shaft only. Reconnect the driveshaft and check for vibration at road test speed. If the vehicle tests okay, do not proceed further.

➡**While the driveshaft is removed from the vehicle, manipulate the U-joints in each direction of rotation. If the U-joint feels stiff or has a notchy, gritty feel in any direction, replace the U-joints.**

8. If re-indexing at both the axle and transmission is unsuccessful, mark the rear of the driveshaft in 4 equal parts and number than 1, 2, 3 and 4. Install a screw-type hose clamp with the screw at position 1.

9. Check for vibration at road test speed. Rotate the clamp to each of the other 3 positions and check for vibration.

10. If the vibration is worse in all positions, go to Step 15. If the vibration is better in any one position, go to Step 11. If the vibration is better in any two positions, rotate the clamp screw to a mid-point between the two positions.

11. Install another clamp, with the screw in the same position as the first clamp. Check for vibration at road test speed.

12. If the vibration is acceptable, do not proceed further, the problem is corrected. If the vibration is the same, or worse, go to Step 13.

13. Rotate the screws of the clamps equally away from each other about ½ in. Check for vibration at road test speed.

14. If the vibration is acceptable, do not proceed further, the problem is corrected. If the vibration is not acceptable, go to Step 15.

15. Install the drum or rotor assemblies and wheel and tire assemblies. Road test the vehicle; vibration felt when the car is raised may be acceptable during a road test.

16. If the vibration is acceptable, the problem is corrected. If the vibration is not acceptable, investigate other driveline components: wheels, tires, axle bearings, etc.

➡**If the vibration was corrected with the addition of clamps, the clamps will be left on the driveshaft permanently. Check the clamp clearance after installation to prevent any contact with the floorpan or other parts.**

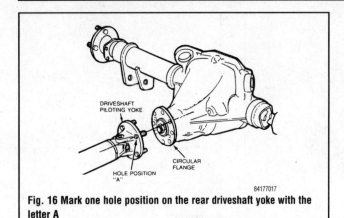

Fig. 16 Mark one hole position on the rear driveshaft yoke with the letter A

Fig. 18 Installing another hose clamp on the driveshaft

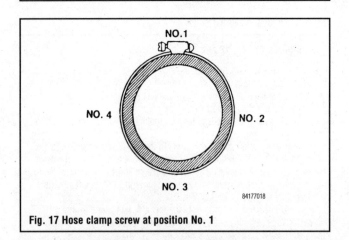

Fig. 17 Hose clamp screw at position No. 1

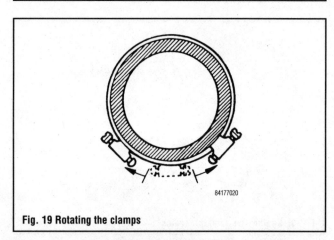

Fig. 19 Rotating the clamps

REAR AXLE

Identification

All vehicles are equipped with an integral carrier solid rear axle. An identification tag is attached to the differential case cover. The tag contains information pertaining to the manufacturing plant, inerchangeability, build date, ring gear diameter and axle ratio. For further rear axle identification information, see Section 1.

Determining Axle Ratio

The drive axle is said to have a certain ratio. This number (usually a whole number and a decimal fraction) is actually a comparison of the number of gear teeth on the ring gear and the pinion gear. For example, a 4.11 rear means that theoretically, there are 4.11 teeth on the ring gear and one tooth on the pinion gear or, put another way, the driveshaft must turn 4.11 times to turn the wheels once. Actually, on a 4.11 rear, there might be 37 teeth on the ring gear and 9 teeth on the pinion gear. By dividing the number of teeth on the pinion gear into the number of teeth on the ring gear, the numerical axle ratio (4.11) is obtained. This also provides a good method of ascertaining exactly what axle ratio one is dealing with.

Another method of determining gear ratio is to jack up and support the car so that both rear wheels are off of the ground. Make a chalk mark on the rear wheel and the driveshaft. Put the transmission in neutral. Turn the rear wheel one complete turn and count the number of turns that the driveshaft makes. The number of turns that the driveshaft makes in one complete revolution of the rear wheel is an approximation of the rear axle ratio.

Axle Shaft, Bearing and Seal

REMOVAL & INSTALLATION

▶ **See Figures 20 thru 26**

1. Raise and safely support the vehicle. Remove the wheel and tire assembly and remove the brake drum or brake rotor.
2. If equipped, remove the anti-lock brake speed sensor.
3. Clean all dirt from the area of the carrier cover. Drain the axle lubricant by removing the housing cover.
4. Remove the differential pinion shaft lock bolt and differential pinion shaft.
5. Push the flanged end of axle shafts toward the center of the vehicle and remove the C-lock from the button end of the axle shaft. Remove the axle shaft from the housing, being careful not to damage the anti-lock brake sensor ring, if equipped.
6. Insert wheel bearing and seal replacer tool T85L−1225−AH or equivalent, in the bore and position it behind the bearing so the tangs on the tool engage the bearing outer race. Remove the bearing and seal as a unit using an impact slide hammer.
   To install:
7. Lubricate the new bearing with rear axle lubricant. Install the bearing into the housing bore using a suitable bearing installer.
8. Install a new axle seal using a seal installer.

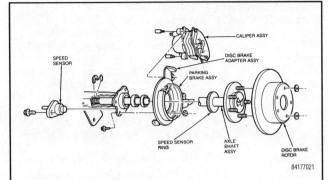

Fig. 20 Axle shaft, bearing, seal and related components—1992–94 vehicles with anti-lock brakes

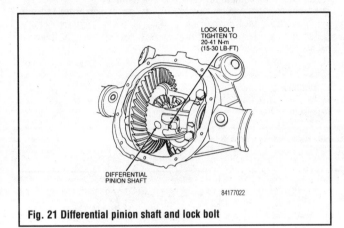

Fig. 21 Differential pinion shaft and lock bolt

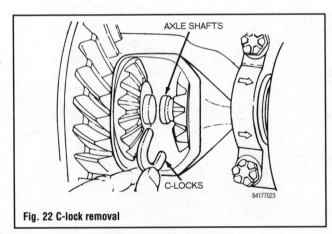

Fig. 22 C-lock removal

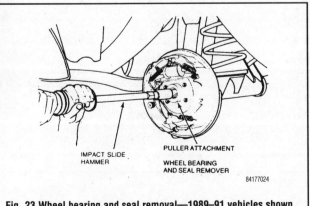

Fig. 23 Wheel bearing and seal removal—1989–91 vehicles shown

➡**Check for the presence of an axle shaft O-ring on the spline end of the shaft and install, if not present.**

9. Carefully slide the axle shaft into the axle housing, without damaging the bearing/seal assembly or anti-lock brake sensor ring, if equipped. Start the splines into the side gear and push firmly until the button end of the axle shaft can be seen in the differential case.

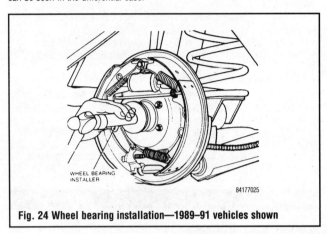

Fig. 24 Wheel bearing installation—1989–91 vehicles shown

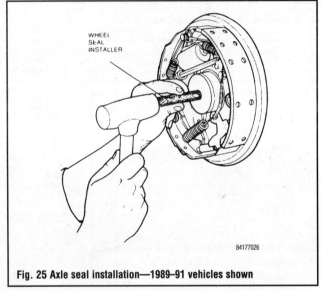

Fig. 25 Axle seal installation—1989–91 vehicles shown

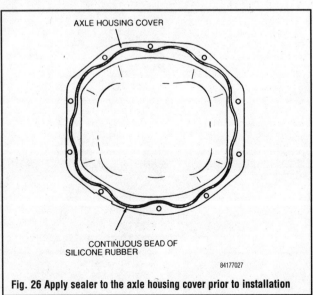

Fig. 26 Apply sealer to the axle housing cover prior to installation

10. Install the C-lock on the button end of the axle shaft splines, then push the shaft outboard until the shaft splines engage and the C-lock seats in the counterbore of the differential side gear.

11. Insert the differential pinion shaft through the case and pinion gears, aligning the hole in the shaft with the lock bolt hole. Apply locking compound to the lock bolt and install in the case and pinion shaft. Tighten to 15–30 ft. lbs. (20–41 Nm).

12. Cover the inside of the differential case with a shop rag and clean the machined surface of the carrier and cover. Remove the shop rag.

13. Apply a 1/8–3/16 in. wide bead of silicone sealer to the cover and install on the carrier. Tighten the bolts in a crisscross pattern. Final torque the cover retaining bolts to 28–35 ft. lbs. (38–47 Nm).

14. Add rear axle lubricant to the carrier to a level 1/4–7/16 in. below the bottom of the fill hole. If equipped with limited slip differential, add friction modifier C8AZ–19B564–A or equivalent. Install the filler plug and tighten to 15–30 ft. lbs. (20–41 Nm).

15. Install the anti-lock brake speed sensor, if equipped. Tighten the retaining bolt to 40–60 inch lbs. (4.5–6.8 Nm).

16. Install the brake calipers and rotors or the brake drums, as required. Install the wheel and tire assembly and lower the vehicle.

Pinion Seal

REMOVAL & INSTALLATION

▶ See Figures 27, 28, 29, 30 and 31

1. Raise and safely support the vehicle. Remove the wheel and tire assemblies and remove the brake drums or brake rotors.

2. Mark the position of the driveshaft yoke on the axle companion flange so they may be reassembled in the same way to maintain balance.

3. Disconnect the driveshaft from the rear axle companion flange, remove the driveshaft and remove the driveshaft from the extension housing. Plug the extension housing to prevent leakage.

4. Install an inch pound torque wrench on the pinion nut and record the torque required to maintain rotation of the pinion through several revolutions.

5. While holding the companion flange with holder tool T78P–4851–A or equivalent, remove the pinion nut.

6. Clean the area around the oil seal and place a drain pan under the seal.

7. Mark the companion flange in relation to the pinion shaft so the flange can be installed in the same position.

8. Remove the rear axle companion flange using tool T65L–4851–B or equivalent.

✳✳ WARNING

Never strike the companion flange with a hammer.

9. Position a small prybar under the flange of the pinion seal and carefully strike with a hammer to wedge the prybar between the seal flange and differential housing.

10. Pry up on the metal flange of the pinion seal. Install gripping pliers and strike with a hammer until the pinion seal is removed.

To install:

11. Clean the oil seal seat surface and install the seal in the carrier using seal replacer tool T79P–4676–A or equivalent. Apply grease to the lips of the seal.

12. Check the companion flange and pinion shaft splines for burrs. If burrs are evident, remove them using crocus cloth.

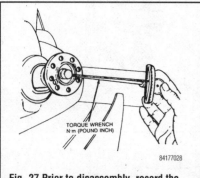

Fig. 27 Prior to disassembly, record the torque required to maintain pinion rotation through several revolutions

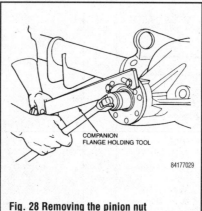

Fig. 28 Removing the pinion nut

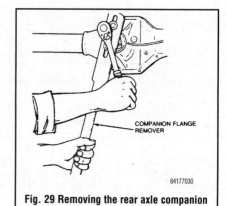

Fig. 29 Removing the rear axle companion flange

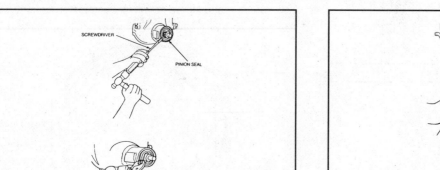
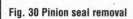

Fig. 30 Pinion seal removal

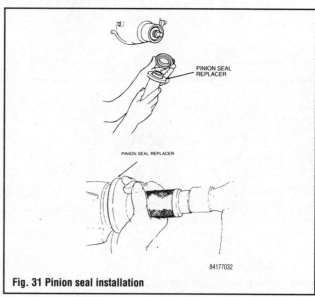

Fig. 31 Pinion seal installation

13. Apply a small amount of lubricant to the companion flange splines, align the marks on the flange and and the pinion shaft and install the flange.

14. Install a new nut on the pinion shaft and apply lubricant on the washer side of the nut.

15. Hold the flange with the holder tool while tightening the nut. Rotate the pinion occasionally to ensure proper seating. Take frequent pinion bearing torque preload readings until the original recorded preload reading is obtained.

16. If the original recorded preload is less than 8–14 inch lbs. (0.9–1.6 Nm), then tighten the nut until the rotational torque of to 8–14 inch lbs. (0.9–1.6 Nm) is obtained. If the original preload is higher than 8–14 inch lbs. (0.9–1.6 Nm), tighten to the original recorded preload.

➡**Under no circumstances should the pinion nut be backed off to reduce preload. If reduced preload is required, a new collapsible pinion spacer and pinion nut must be installed.**

17. Remove the plug from the transmission extension housing and install the front end of the driveshaft on the transmission output shaft.

18. Connect the rear end of the driveshaft to the axle companion flange, aligning the scribe marks. Tighten the 4 bolts to 71–95 ft. lbs. (95–130 Nm).

19. Add lubricant to the axle until it is ¼–⁷⁄₁₆ in. below the bottom of the fill hole with the axle in operating position. If equipped with limited slip differential, add friction modifier C8AZ–19B564–A or equivalent. Make sure the axle vent is not plugged with debris.

20. Install the brake drums or rotors. Install the wheel and tire assemblies and lower the vehicle.

21. Operate the vehicle and check for leaks.

Axle Housing

REMOVAL & INSTALLATION

▶ **See Figure 32**

1. Raise and safely support the vehicle. Position safety stands under the rear frame crossmember.

2. Remove the cover and drain the axle lubricant.

3. Remove the wheel and tire assemblies. Remove the brake drums or brake rotors.

4. If equipped, remove the anti-lock brake speed sensors.

5. Remove the lock bolt from the differential pinion shaft and remove the shaft.

6. Push the axle shafts inward to remove the C-locks and remove the axle shafts.

7. If equipped with drum brakes, remove the 4 retaining nuts from each backing plate and wire the backing plate to the underbody.

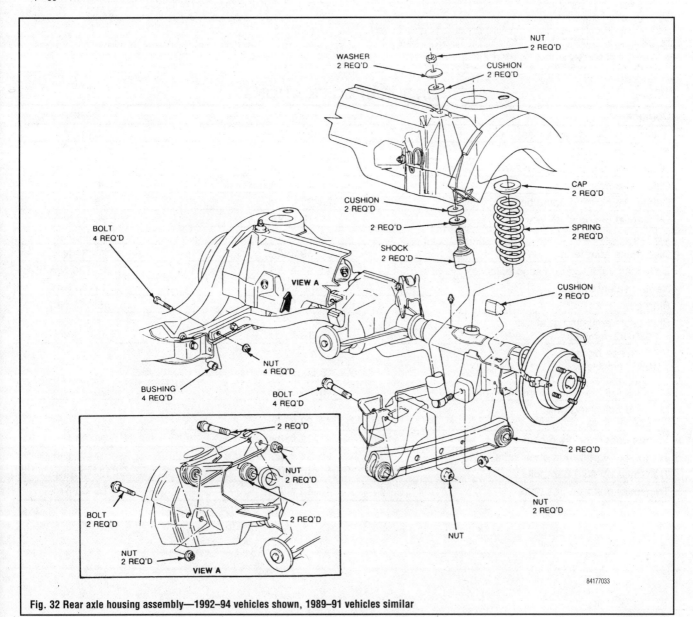

Fig. 32 Rear axle housing assembly—1992–94 vehicles shown, 1989–91 vehicles similar

8. If equipped with disc brakes, remove the disc brake adapter bracket, bolts and J-nuts. Remove the 4 retaining nuts from each adapter and wire the adapters to the underbody.

9. Mark the position of the driveshaft yoke on the axle companion flange. Disconnect the driveshaft at the companion flange and wire it to the underbody.

10. Support the axle housing with jackstands. Disengage the brake line from the clips that retain the line to the axle housing.

11. Disconnect the vent from the rear axle housing.

12. If equipped with air springs, remove them according to the procedure in Section 8.

13. Disconnect the lower shock absorber studs from the mounting brackets on the axle housing.

14. Remove the nuts and bolts and disconnect the upper arms from the mountings on the axle housing ear brackets.

15. Lower the axle housing assembly until the springs are released and lift out the springs.

16. Remove the nuts and bolts and disconnect the suspension lower arms at the axle housing.

17. Lower the axle housing and remove it from the vehicle.

To install:

18. Position the axle housing under the vehicle and raise the axle with a hoist or jack. Connect the lower suspension arms to their mounting brackets on the axle housing. Do not tighten the bolts and nuts at this time.

19. Reposition the rear springs.

20. Raise the housing into position.

21. Connect the upper arms to the mounting ears on the housing. Tighten the nuts and bolts to 103–133 ft. lbs. (140–180 Nm). Tighten the lower arm bolts and nuts to 103–133 ft. lbs. (140–180 Nm).

22. Install the axle vent and install the brake line to the clips that retain the line to the axle housing. Secure the brake junction block to the housing cast boss.

23. Connect the air spring lines as described in Section 8.

24. If equipped with drum brakes, install the brake backing plates on the axle housing flanges. If equipped with disc brakes, install the disc brake adapters and tighten the nuts to 20–29 ft. lbs. (27–40 Nm). Install the disc brake adapter brackets, bolts and J-nuts. Tighten to 20–39 ft. lbs. (27–54 Nm).

25. Connect the lower shock absorber studs to the mounting bracket on the axle housing.

26. Connect the driveshaft to the companion flange and tighten the bolts and nuts to 70–95 ft. lbs. (95–130 Nm).

27. Slide the rear axle shafts into the housing until the splines enter the side gear. Push the axle shafts inward and install the C-lock at the end of each shaft spline. Pull the shafts outboard until the C-lock enters the recess in the side gears.

28. Install the pinion shaft. Apply locking compound to the pinion shaft lock bolt. Install and tighten to 15–30 ft. lbs. (20–41 Nm).

29. Install the rear brake drums or disc brake rotors and calipers.

30. Install the anti-lock brake speed sensor, if equipped.

31. Install the rear carrier cover using new silicone sealer. Tighten to 28–35 ft. lbs. (38–47 Nm).

32. Add rear axle lubricant to the carrier to a level ¼–⁷⁄₁₆ in. below the bottom of the fill hole. If equipped with limited slip, add friction modifier C8AZ-19B564-A or equivalent. Install the filler plug and tighten to 15–30 ft. lbs. (20–41 Nm).

33. Install the wheel and tire assemblies and lower the vehicle. Road test.

TORQUE SPECIFICATIONS

Component	U.S.	Metric
Anti-lock brake speed sensor	40–60 inch lbs.	4.5–6.8 Nm
Control arm-to-axle bolts	103–133 ft. lbs.	140–180 Nm
Differential bearing caps	70–85 ft. lbs.	95–115 Nm
Differential filler plug	15–30 ft. lbs.	20–41 Nm
Differential housing cover bolts	28–35 ft. lbs.	38–47 Nm
Differential pinion shaft lock bolt	15–30 ft. lbs.	20–41 Nm
Disc brake adapter nuts	20–29 ft. lbs.	27–40 Nm
Disc brake adapter bracket bolts	20–39 ft. lbs.	27–54 Nm
Driveshaft yoke-to-axle flange bolts	71–95 ft. lbs.	95–130 Nm
Neutral safety switch	8–11 ft. lbs.	11–15 Nm
Ring gear bolts	70–85 ft. lbs.	95–115 Nm
Shift cable adjusting stud nut 1990–92 vehicles	10–18 ft. lbs.	13–25 Nm
Shift linkage bolts 1989 vehicles Linkage-to-frame rail Linkage bracket-to-transmiission	 9–18 ft. lbs. 15–25 ft. lbs.	 12–24 Nm 20–34 Nm
Shift rod adjustiing bolt 1989 vehicles	14–23 ft. lbs.	19–31 Nm
Torque converter drain plug	21–23 ft. lbs.	28–30 Nm
Torque converter-to-flywheel nuts	20–34 ft. lbs.	27–46 Nm
Transmission fluid pan bolts	107–119 inch lbs.	12–13.5 Nm
Transmission-to-engine bolts	40–50 ft. lbs.	55–68 Nm

84177069

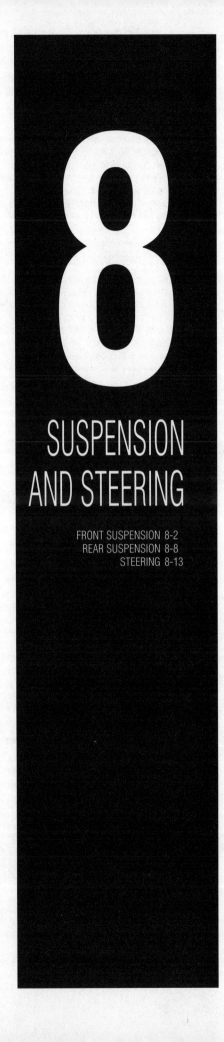

8

SUSPENSION
AND STEERING

FRONT SUSPENSION

♦ **See Figures 1 and 2**

All vehicles are equipped with independent front suspension. Each wheel is independently connected to the frame by a steering knuckle, ball joints and upper and lower control arms. Coil springs are mounted between the spring housings on the frame and the lower control arms. Ride control is provided by shock absorbers mounted inside the coil springs and attached to the lower control arms by bolts. The upper end of each shock absorber extends through the spring housing and is attached to the frame by rubber grommets, grommet retainers and a nut.

Front suspension side roll is controlled by a spring steel stabilizer bar mounted in rubber bushings and attached to the frame by brackets. The stabilizer bar ends are connected by links to the lower control arms or spindles.

Each upper control arm is attached to a cross-shaft through rubber bushings. The cross-shaft is bolted to the frame. A ball joint is riveted or bolted to the outer end of the control arm, and attached to the spindle by a castellated nut retained with a cotter pin, or by a pinch bolt and nut.

The inner ends of the lower control arms have pressed-in bushings. The lower control arms are attached to the frame by bolts passing through the bushings. The lower ball joint is pressed into the lower control arm and is attached to the spindle by a castellated nut retained with a cotter pin.

➡**All suspension fasteners are important attaching parts in that they could affect the performance of vital parts and systems, and/or could result in major service expense. Any part must be replaced with one of the same part number or with an exact equivalent part if replacement becomes necessary. Do not use a replacement part of lesser quality or substitute design. Torque values must be used as specified during assembly to ensure proper part retention.**

Coil Springs

REMOVAL & INSTALLATION

♦ **See Figures 3, 4 and 5**

1. Raise and safely support the vehicle. Remove the wheel and tire assembly.
2. On 1989–91 vehicles, disconnect the stabilizer bar link from the lower arm.
3. Remove the shock absorber. Remove the steering link from the pitman arm.
4. Using spring compressor tool D78P–5310–A or equivalent, install 1 plate with the pivot ball seat facing downward into the coils of the spring. Rotate the plate, so it is flush with the upper surface of the lower arm.
5. Install the other plate with the pivot ball seat facing upward into the coils of the spring. Insert the upper ball nut through the coils of the spring, so the nut rests in the upper plate.
6. Insert the compression rod into the opening in the lower arm, through the upper and lower plate and upper ball nut. Insert the securing pin through the upper ball nut and compression rod.

➡**This pin can only be inserted 1 way into the upper ball nut because of a stepped hole design.**

7. With the upper ball nut secured, turn the upper plate so it walks up the coil until it contacts the upper spring seat. Then back off ½ turn.
8. Install the lower ball nut and thrust washer on the compression rod and screw on the forcing nut. Tighten the forcing nut until the spring is compressed enough so it is free in its seat.
9. Remove the 2 lower arm pivot bolts, disengage the lower arm from the frame crossmember and remove the spring.
10. If a new spring is to be installed, perform the following:
   a. Mark the position of the upper and lower plates on the spring with chalk.
   b. With an assistant, compress a new spring for installation and measure the compressed length and the amount of curvature of the old spring.
11. Loosen the forcing nut to relieve the spring tension and remove the tools from the spring.

To install:

12. Assemble the spring compressor and locate in the same position as indicated in Step 10a.

13. Before compressing the coil spring, make sure the upper ball nut securing the pin is inserted properly.
14. Compress the coil spring until the spring height reaches the dimension obtained in Step 10b.
15. Position the coil spring assembly into the lower arm and reverse the removal procedure.

Shock Absorbers

REMOVAL & INSTALLATION

❊❊ CAUTION

All vehicles except police applications are equipped with gas-pressurized shock absorbers which will extend unassisted. Do not apply heat or flame to the shock absorber tube.

1. Remove the nut, washer and bushing from the upper end of the shock absorber.
2. Raise and safely support the vehicle by the frame rails allowing the front wheels to hang.
3. Remove the 2 bolts securing the shock absorber to the lower control arm and remove the shock absorber.

To install:

4. Prior to installation, purge a new shock of air by repeatedly extending it in its normal position and compressing it while inverted.
5. Install a new bushing and washer on the top of the shock absorber and position the unit inside the front spring. Install the 2 lower attaching bolts and torque them to 13–16 ft. lbs. (17–23 Nm).
6. Lower the vehicle.
7. Place a new bushing and washer on the shock absorber top stud and install a new attaching nut. Tighten to 26 ft. lbs. (41 Nm).

TESTING

1. Remove the shock absorber from the vehicle.
2. Extend the shock absorber fully while it is right side up, as installed in the vehicle. Then turn it upside down and fully compress it. Repeat this procedure at least 3 times to make sure any trapped air has been expelled.
3. Place the shock absorber right side up in a vise and hand stroke the shock absorber. Check the shock absorber insulators for damage and wear.
4. If the shock absorber is properly primed, in its installed position, and there is a lag or a skip occurring near mid-stroke of the shaft reverse travel direction, the shock absorber must be replaced.
5. Replace the shock absorber if there is any seizing during the shaft full travel, except at either end of the travel.
6. Replace the shock absorber if upon the shaft fast, reverse stroke, there is any noise encountered other than a faint swish, such as a clicking sound.
7. If there are excessive fluid leaks, and the shock absorber action remains erratic after purging air, replace the shock absorber.

Upper Ball Joint

INSPECTION

♦ **See Figure 6**

1. Raise the vehicle and place floor jacks beneath the lower control arms.
2. Make sure the front wheel bearings are properly adjusted.
3. Inspect the lower ball joint and replace the lower control arm assembly, if required.
4. Have an assistant grasp the bottom of the tire and move the wheel in and out.
5. As the wheel is being moved, observe the upper control arm where the spindle attaches to it. Any movement between the upper part of the spindle and the upper control arm indicates a bad ball joint which must be replaced.

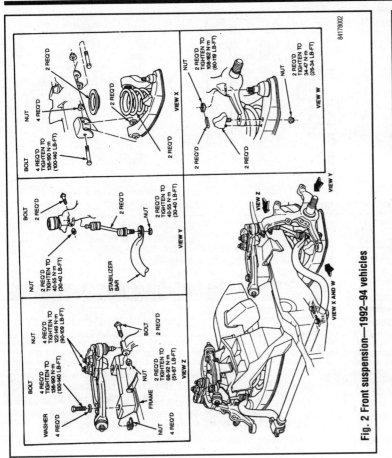

Fig. 2 Front suspension—1992–94 vehicles

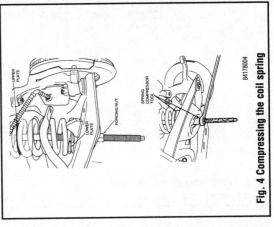

Fig. 4 Compressing the coil spring

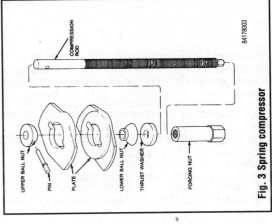

Fig. 3 Spring compressor

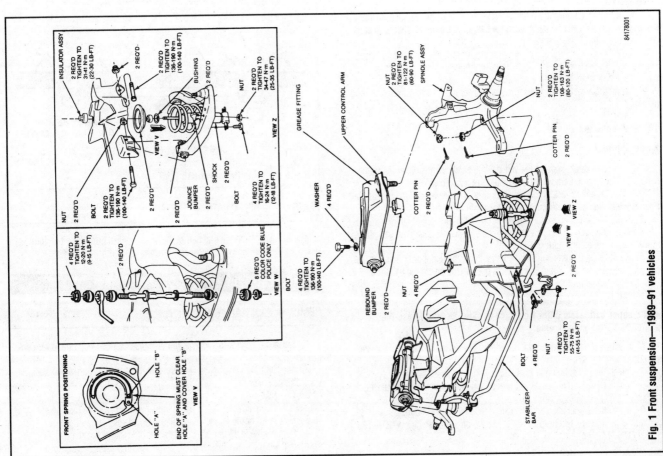

Fig. 1 Front suspension—1989–91 vehicles

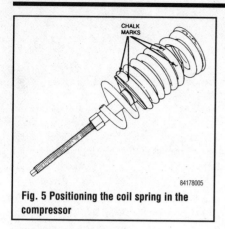

Fig. 5 Positioning the coil spring in the compressor

84178005

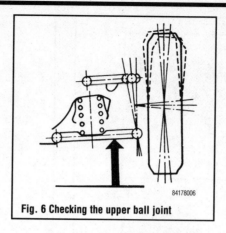

Fig. 6 Checking the upper ball joint

84178006

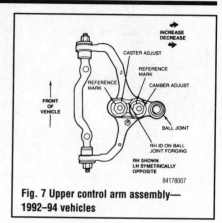

Fig. 7 Upper control arm assembly—1992–94 vehicles

84178007

REMOVAL & INSTALLATION

1989–91 Vehicles

➥Ford Motor Company recommends replacement of the upper control arm and ball joint as an assembly. However, aftermarket replacement parts are available, which can be installed using the following procedure.

1. Raise the vehicle and support on frame points so the front wheels fall to their full down position. Remove the wheel and tire assembly.
2. Drill a ⅛ in. hole completely through each ball joint attaching rivet.
3. Using a large chisel, cut off the head of each rivet and drive them from the arm.
4. Place a jack under the lower arm and raise to compress the coil spring.
5. Remove the cotter pin and attaching nut from the ball joint stud.
6. Using a ball joint removal tool, loosen the ball joint stud from the spindle and remove the ball joint from the arm.

To install:

7. Clean all metal burrs from the arm and install the new ball joint, using the service part nuts and bolts to attach the ball joint. Do not attempt to rivet the ball joint once it has been removed.
8. Install the ball joint stud into the spindle. Tighten the ball joint-to-upper spindle nut to 60–90 ft. lbs. (81–122 Nm). Continue to tighten until the slot for the cotter pin is aligned. Install a new cotter pin.
9. Install the wheel and tire assembly and lower the vehicle. Check front end alignment.

1992–94 Vehicles

♦ See Figure 7

1. Raise and safely support the vehicle with safety stands under the frame behind the lower arm. Remove the wheel and tire assembly.
2. Position a floor jack under the lower arm at the lower ball joint area. The floor jack will support the spring load on the lower arm.
3. Remove the retaining nut and pinch bolt from the upper ball joint stud.
4. Mark the position of the alignment cams. When replacing the ball joint this will approximate the current alignment.
5. Remove the 2 nuts retaining the ball joint to the upper arm. Remove the ball joint and spread the slot with a suitable prybar to separate the ball joint stud from the spindle.

To install:

➥The upper ball joints differ from side to side. Be sure to use the proper ball joint on each side.

6. Position the ball joint on the upper arm and insert the ball stud into the spindle.
7. Install the pinch bolt and retaining nut. Tighten to 67 ft. lbs. (92 Nm).
8. Install the alignment cams to the approximate position at removal. If not marked, install in neutral position.
9. Install the 2 nuts attaching the ball joint to the arm. Hold the cams and tighten the nuts to 90–109 ft. lbs. (122–149 Nm) on 1992 vehicles or 107–129 ft. lbs. (145–175 Nm) on 1993–94 vehicles.

10. Remove the floor jack from the lower arm and install the wheel and tire assembly. Remove the safety stands and lower the vehicle.
11. Check and adjust the front end alignment.

Lower Ball Joint

INSPECTION

♦ See Figure 8

1. Support the vehicle in normal driving position with ball joints loaded.
2. Wipe the grease fitting and ball joint cover checking surface clean. The checking surface is the round boss into which the grease fitting is threaded.
3. The checking surface should project outside the cover. If the checking surface is inside the cover, replace the lower control arm assembly.

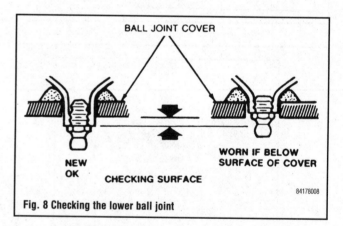

Fig. 8 Checking the lower ball joint

84178008

REMOVAL & INSTALLATION

The ball joint is an integral part of the lower control arm. If the ball joint is defective, the entire lower control arm must be replaced.

Stabilizer Bar

REMOVAL & INSTALLATION

1. Raise the front of the vehicle and place jackstands under the lower control arms.
2. On 1989–91 vehicles, remove the link nuts and disconnect the stabilizer bar from the links.
3. On 1992–94 vehicles, remove the retaining nuts from the pinch bolts at the spindles. Spread the slots in the spindles with a prybar to free the ball studs. Be careful not to damage the ball joint stud seal.
4. Remove the stabilizer bar brackets from the frame and remove the stabilizer bar. If worn, cut the insulators from the stabilizer bar.

5. On 1992–94 vehicles, remove the retaining nuts from the ball joint studs at the end of the bar. Use removal tool 3290–D or equivalent to separate the links from the ends of the stabilizer bar.

To install:

6. Coat the necessary parts of the stabilizer bar with rubber lubricant. Slide new insulators onto the stabilizer bar.

7. On 1992–94 vehicles, install the ball joint links into the ends of the bar with the retaining nuts. Tighten to 30–40 ft. lbs. (40–55 Nm).

8. On 1989–91 vehicles, attach the ends of the stabilizer bar to the lower control arm with new nuts and links. Tighten the nuts to 9–15 ft. lbs. (12–20 Nm). Install the insulator brackets and tighten the bolts to 14–26 ft. lbs. (19–35 Nm).

9. On 1992–94 vehicles, position the bar under the vehicle and engage the upper ball joint links to the spindles. Install the insulator brackets with the retaining nuts. Tighten the pinch bolts and nuts at the spindles to 30–40 ft. lbs. (40–55 Nm) Tighten the bracket-to-frame nuts to 44–59 ft. lbs. (59–81 Nm).

Upper Control Arm

REMOVAL & INSTALLATION

1989–91 Vehicles

1. Raise and safely support the vehicle on safety stands positioned on the frame just behind the lower arm. Remove the wheel and tire assembly.

2. Remove the cotter pin from the upper ball joint stud nut. Loosen the nut a few turns but do not remove.

3. Install ball joint press T57P–3006–B or equivalent, between the upper and lower ball joint studs with the adapter screw on top.

➡This tool should be seated firmly against the ends of both studs, not against the nuts or lower stud cotter pin.

4. With a wrench, turn the adapter screw until the tool places the stud under compression. Tap the spindle near the upper stud with a hammer to loosen the stud in the spindle.

➡Do not loosen the stud from the spindle with tool pressure only. Do not contact the boot seal with the hammer.

5. Remove the tool from between the ball joint studs and place a floor jack under the lower arm.

6. Remove the upper arm attaching bolts and the upper arm.

To install:

7. Transfer the rebound bumper from the old arm to the new arm, or replace the bumper if worn or damaged.

8. Position the upper arm shaft to the frame bracket. Install the 2 attaching bolts and washers. Tighten to 100–140 ft. lbs. (136–190 Nm).

9. Connect the upper ball joint stud to the spindle and install the attaching nut. Tighten the nut to 60–90 ft. lbs. (81–122 Nm). Continue to tighten the nut until the slot for the cotter pin is aligned. Install a new cotter pin.

10. Install the wheel and tire assembly and lower the vehicle. Check the front end alignment.

1992–94 Vehicles

1. Raise and safely support the vehicle on safety stands positioned on the frame just behind the lower arm.

2. Remove the wheel and tire assembly and position a floor jack under the lower arm.

3. Remove the retaining nut from the upper ball joint stud to spindle pinch bolt. Tap the pinch bolt to remove from the spindle.

4. Using a suitable prybar, spread the slot to allow the ball joint stud to release out of the spindle.

5. Remove the upper arm retaining bolts and the upper arm.

To install:

6. Transfer the rebound bumper from the old arm to the new arm, or replace the bumper if worn or damaged.

7. Use reference marks from the camber and caster cams as initial settings.

8. Position the upper arm shaft to the frame bracket. Install the 2 retaining bolts and washers. Position the arm in the center of the slot adjustment range and tighten to 100–140 ft. lbs.

9. Connect the upper ball joint stud to the spindle and install the retaining pinch bolt and nut. Tighten the nut to 67 ft. lbs. (92 Nm).

10. Install the wheel and tire assembly and lower the vehicle. Check the front end alignment.

CONTROL ARM BUSHING REPLACEMENT

▶ **See Figures 9 and 10**

1. Remove the upper control arm from the vehicle.

2. Remove the nuts and washers from both ends of the control arm shaft. Discard the nuts.

3. Press the bushings from the control arm and shaft using C-clamp tool T74P–3044–A1 or equivalent, and its adapters.

4. Position the shaft and new bushings to the upper control arm. Use the C-clamp tool and adapters to press the new bushings into place.

5. Make sure the control arm shaft is positioned so the serrated side contacts the frame.

6. Install an inner washer, rear bushing only, and 2 outer washers with new nuts on each end of the shaft. Tighten the nuts to 85–100 ft. lbs. (115–136 Nm).

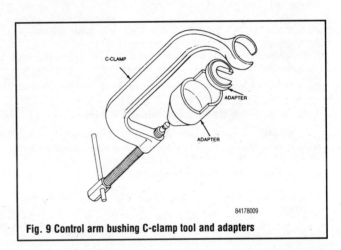

Fig. 9 Control arm bushing C-clamp tool and adapters

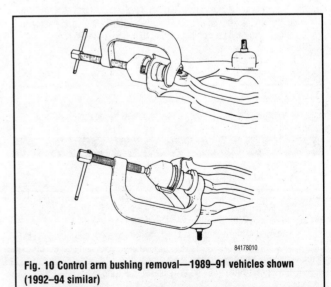

Fig. 10 Control arm bushing removal—1989–91 vehicles shown (1992–94 similar)

Lower Control Arm

REMOVAL & INSTALLATION

1. Raise the front of the vehicle and position safety stands on the frame behind the lower control arms. Remove the wheel and tire assembly.

2. Remove the brake caliper and suspend with a length of wire; do not let the caliper hang by the brake hose. Remove the brake rotor and dust shield. Remove the anti-lock brake sensor, if equipped.

3. Remove the jounce bumper; inspect and save for installation if in good condition. Remove the shock absorber.

4. On 1989–91 vehicles, disconnect the stabilizer link from the lower arm.

5. Disconnect the steering center link from the pitman arm.

6. Remove the cotter pin and loosen the lower ball joint stud nut 1–2 turns.

➡**Do not remove the nut at this time.**

7. On 1989–91 vehicles, install a suitable ball joint press tool to place the ball joint stud under compression. With the stud under compression, tap the spindle sharply with a hammer to loosen the stud in the spindle. Remove the ball joint press tool.

8. On 1992–94 vehicles, tap the spindle boss sharply to relieve the stud pressure. Tap the spindle sharply, near the lower stud, with a hammer to loosen the stud in the spindle.

9. Place a floor jack under the lower arm. Remove the coil spring as described in this Section.

10. Remove the ball joint nut and remove the lower control arm.

To install:

11. Position the arm assembly ball joint stud into the spindle and install the nut. Tighten to 80–120 ft. lbs. (108–163 Nm). Continue to tighten until the slot for the cotter pin is aligned. Install a new cotter pin.

12. Position the coil spring into the upper spring pocket and raise the lower arm, aligning the holes in the arm with the holes in the crossmember. Install the bolts and nuts with the washer installed on the front bushing. Do not tighten at this time.

➡**Make sure the pigtail of the lower coil of the spring is in the proper location of the seat on the lower arm, between the 2 holes.**

13. Remove the spring compressor tool.

14. Connect the steering center link at the pitman arm and install the nut. Tighten to 44–46 ft. lbs. (59–63 Nm). Continue to tighten until the slot for the cotter pin is aligned. Install a new cotter pin.

15. Install the shock absorber and the jounce bumper.

16. Install the dust shield, rotor and caliper. Install the anti-lock brake sensor, if equipped.

17. On 1989–91 vehicles, position the stabilizer link to the lower control arm and install the link, bushing and retaining nut. Tighten to 9–15 ft. lbs. (12–20 Nm).

18. Install the wheel and tire assembly and lower the vehicle. With the vehicle supported on the wheels and tires at normal curb height, tighten the lower control arm-to-crossmember bolts to 109–140 ft. lbs. (148–190 Nm).

19. Check the front end alignment.

CONTROL ARM BUSHING REPLACEMENT

The control arm bushings are integral with the lower control arm. If the bushings are defective, the entire lower control arm must be replaced.

Spindle

REMOVAL & INSTALLATION

1. Raise the front of the vehicle and position safety stands on the frame behind the lower control arms. Remove the wheel and tire assembly.

2. Remove the brake caliper and suspend with a length of wire; do not let the caliper hang by the brake hose. Remove the brake rotor and dust shield. Remove the anti-lock brake sensor, if equipped.

3. Disconnect the tie rod end from the spindle using removal tool 3290–D or equivalent.

4. On 1989–91 vehicles, proceed as follows:

a. Remove and discard the cotter pins from both ball joint studs and loosen the stud nuts 1–2 turns. Do not remove the nuts at this time.

b. Position a suitable ball joint press tool between the upper and lower ball joint studs. Turn the tool with a wrench until the tool places the studs under compression.

c. Using a hammer, sharply hit the spindle near the studs to loosen the studs from the spindle.

5. On 1992–94 vehicles, proceed as follows:

a. Remove and discard the cotter pin from the lower ball joint stud and loosen the stud nut 1–2 turns. Do not remove the nut at this time.

b. Using a hammer, sharply hit the spindle near the stud to loosen the stud from the spindle.

c. Remove the pinch bolts from the upper ball joint and stabilizer link ball joint at the spindle.

6. Position a floor jack under the lower control arm at the lower ball joint area, and raise the jack to support the lower arm.

➡**The jack will support the spring load on the lower control arm.**

7. On 1989–91 vehicles, remove the upper and lower ball joint stud nuts and remove the spindle.

8. On 1992–94 vehicles, remove the lower ball joint stud nut. Pry the slots with a suitable prybar at the upper ball joint and link ball joint to separate from the spindle. Remove the spindle.

To install:

9. On 1992–94 vehicles, position the spindle on the stabilizer bar upper ball joint stud. Install the pinch bolt and loosely install the nut.

10. Position the spindle on the lower ball joint stud and install the stud nut. Tighten the nut to 80–119 ft. lbs. (108–162 Nm). Continue to tighten the nut until a slot for the cotter pin is aligned. Install a new cotter pin.

11. Raise the lower arm and guide the upper ball joint stud into the spindle.

12. On 1989–91 vehicles, install the upper ball joint stud nut and tighten to 60–90 ft. lbs. (81–122 Nm). Continue to tighten the nut until a slot for the cotter pin is aligned. Install a new cotter pin.

13. On 1992–94 vehicles, install the upper ball joint stud pinch bolt and nut. Tighten the nut to 67 ft. lbs. (92 Nm). Tighten the stabilizer link to spindle pinch bolt nut to 30–50 ft. lbs. (40–55 Nm).

14. Connect the tie rod end to the spindle. Install the nut and tighten to 43–46 ft. lbs. (59–63 Nm). Continue to tighten the nut until the slot for the cotter pin is aligned and install a new cotter pin.

15. Install the brake dust shield, caliper, rotor and anti-lock brake sensor, if equipped.

16. Install the wheel and tire assembly and lower the vehicle.

17. Check the front end alignment.

Front Wheel Bearings

REPLACEMENT

1989–91 Vehicles

Because these vehicles use non-sealed bearings, they should be periodically removed, cleaned, inspected and repacked. If replacement becomes necessary, the same procedures are used to install the new bearings, the only difference being that new races must be installed in the hubs before the new bearings are used. This is done to assure proper bearing life. For details on removing, cleaning and repacking the bearings, please refer to Section 1 of this manual.

1992–94 Vehicles

◆ **See Figures 11, 12 and 13**

1. Raise and safely support the vehicle. Remove the wheel and tire assembly.

2. Remove and discard the grease cap from the hub.

3. Remove the brake caliper. Suspend the caliper with a length of wire; do not let it hang from the brake hose.

4. Remove the rotor. If the factory installed push on nuts are installed, remove them first.

5. Remove and discard the wheel hub nut.

6. Remove the hub and bearing assembly.

To install:

7. Install the hub and bearing assembly. Install a new wheel hub nut and tighten to 189–254 ft. lbs. (255–345 Nm).

8. Install the rotor and push on nuts, if equipped. Install a new grease cap.

9. Install the brake caliper.

10. Install the wheel and tire assembly and lower the vehicle.

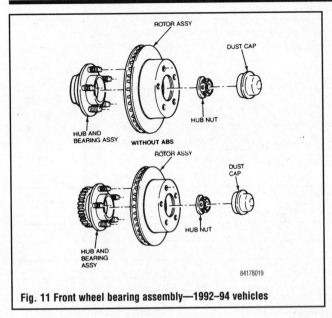

Fig. 11 Front wheel bearing assembly—1992–94 vehicles

Front End Alignment

CASTER

♦ **See Figures 14 and 15**

Caster is the forward or rearward tilt of the top of the front wheel spindle. If the top of the spindle tilts to the rear, caster is positive. If the top of the spindle tilts to the front, caster is negative.

On 1989–91 vehicles, caster adjustment is made using special tools that are inserted into holes in the frame. The upper control arm shaft retaining bolts are then loosened and the tools are used to act on the control arm shaft to make the caster adjustment.

On 1992–94 vehicles, caster adjustment is made using the adjustment cam located on the upper control arm.

CAMBER

♦ **See Figures 15 and 16**

Camber is the amount the centerline of the wheel is tilted inward or outward from the true vertical. If a wheel tilts outward away from the vehicle, camber is positive. If the top of a wheel tilts inward toward the vehicle, camber is negative.

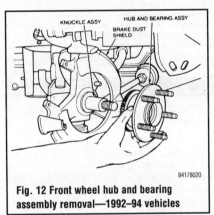

Fig. 12 Front wheel hub and bearing assembly removal—1992–94 vehicles

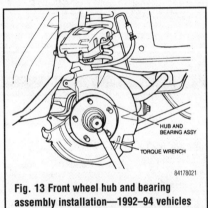

Fig. 13 Front wheel hub and bearing assembly installation—1992–94 vehicles

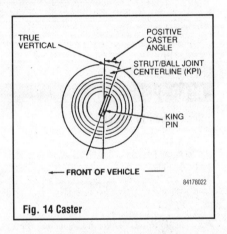

Fig. 14 Caster

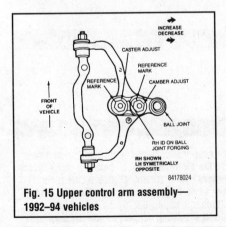

Fig. 15 Upper control arm assembly—1992–94 vehicles

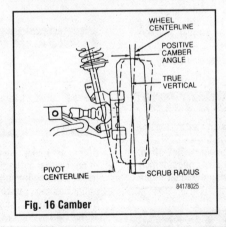

Fig. 16 Camber

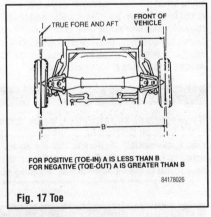

Fig. 17 Toe

On 1989–91 vehicles, camber adjustment is made using the same tools described under caster. On 1992–94 vehicles, camber is adjusted using the other adjustment cam on the upper control arm.

TOE-IN

♦ **See Figures 17 and 18**

With the front wheels in the straight-ahead position, measure the distance between the extreme front and also between the extreme rear of both front wheels. The difference between the 2 distances is the toe-in or toe-

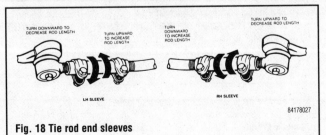

Fig. 18 Tie rod end sleeves

out. Toe is only adjusted after the caster and camber is checked and adjusted.

Toe-in adjustment is made by turning the threaded sleeves connecting the inner and outer tie rod ends. Toe should be checked with the engine running, so the power steering control valve will be in the center (neutral) position, if equipped, and the steering wheel locked in place with a steering wheel holder.

WHEEL ALIGNMENT

| Year | Model | Caster | | Camber | | Toe-in (in.) | Steering Axis Inclination (deg.) |
		Range (deg.)	Preferred Setting (deg.)	Range (deg.)	Preferred Setting (deg.)		
1989	Crown Victoria	2½P–4½P	3½P	1¼N–¼P	½N	1/16	11
	Grand Marquis	2½P–4½P	3½P	1¼N–¼P	½N	1/16	11
1990	Crown Victoria	2½P–4½P	3½P	1¼N–¼P	½N	1/16	11
	Grand Marquis	2½P–4½P	3½P	1¼N–¼P	½N	1/16	11
1991	Crown Victoria	2½P–4½P	3½P	1¼N–¼P	½N	1/16	11
	Grand Marquis	2½P–4½P	3½P	1¼N–¼P	½N	1/16	11
1992	Crown Victoria	4¾P–6¼P	5½P	1¼N–¼P	½N	1/16	11
	Grand Marquis	4¾P–6¼P	5½P	1¼N–¼P	½N	1/16	11
1993 -94	Crown Victoria	4¾P–6¼P	5½P	1¼N–¼P	½N	1/16	11
	Grand Marquis	4¾P–6¼P	5½P	1¼N–¼P	½N	1/16	11

N—Negative
P—Positive

84178R03

REAR SUSPENSION

▶ **See Figures 19 and 20**

The rear axle is suspended from the vehicle frame by 2 upper and 2 lower control arms. Two coil or air springs are connected between the rear axle and the frame. Ride control is provided by 2 shock absorbers mounted between the coil springs upper seats and brackets welded to the axle tube.

In addition, some vehicles are equipped with a stabilizer bar to control side roll.

➡**All suspension fasteners are important attaching parts in that they could affect the performance of vital parts and systems, and/or could result in major service expense. Any part must be replaced with one of the same part number or with an exact equivalent part if replacement becomes necessary. Do not use a replacement part of lesser quality or substitute design. Torque values must be used as specified during assembly to ensure proper part retention.**

✳✳ CAUTION

If equipped with air suspension, the air suspension switch, located in the trunk on the right-hand trim panel, must be turned OFF before raising the vehicle. Failure to turn the air suspension switch off may result in unexpected inflation or deflation of the air springs, which may result in the vehicle shifting, possibly causing personal injury.

Coil Springs

REMOVAL & INSTALLATION

1. Raise and safely support the vehicle. Place jack stands under the frame side rails.
2. Support the rear axle housing.
3. Remove the rear stabilizer bar, if equipped.
4. Disconnect the lower studs of both rear shock absorbers from the mounting brackets on the axle tube.
5. Unsnap the right parking brake cable from the right upper arm retainer before lowering the axle.

6. Lower the axle housing until the coil springs are released. Remove the springs and insulators.
   To install:
7. Position the spring in the upper and lower seats with an insulator between the upper end of the spring and frame seat.
8. Raise the axle and connect the shock absorbers to the mounting brackets. Install new retaining nuts and tighten to 56–76 ft. lbs. (77–103 Nm).
9. Snap the right parking cable into the upper arm retainer. Install the stabilizer bar, if equipped.
10. Remove the support from the rear axle housing and lower the vehicle.

Air Springs

REMOVAL & INSTALLATION

▶ **See Figures 21 thru 31**

✳✳ CAUTION

Before servicing any air suspension component, disconnect power to the system by turning the air suspension switch OFF or by disconnecting the negative battery cable. Do not remove an air spring under any circumstances when there is pressure in the air spring. Do not remove any components supporting an air spring without either exhausting the air or providing support for the air spring.

1. Turn the air suspension switch **OFF**.
2. Raise and safely support the vehicle on the frame. The suspension must be fully down with no load.
3. Remove the heat shield, as required. Remove the spring retainer clip.
4. Remove the air spring solenoid as follows:
   a. Disconnect the electrical connector and then disconnect the air line.
   b. Remove the solenoid clip.
   c. Rotate the solenoid counterclockwise to the first stop.
   d. Pull the solenoid straight out slowly to the second stop to bleed air from the system.

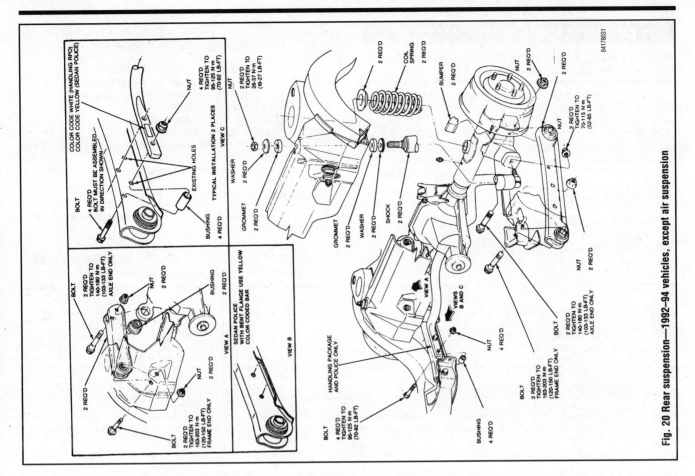

Fig. 20 Rear suspension—1992-94 vehicles, except air suspension

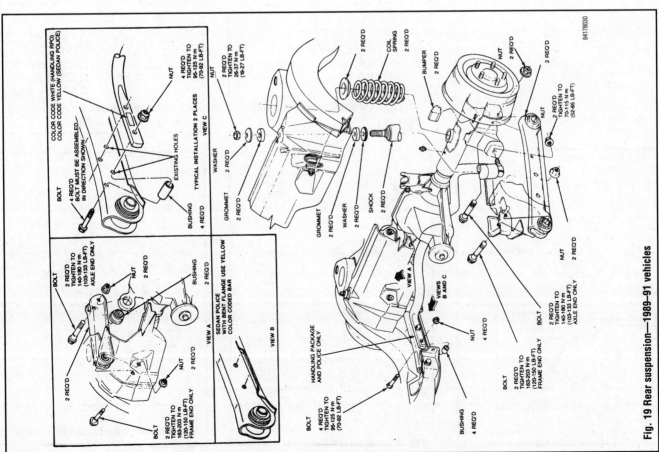

Fig. 19 Rear suspension—1989-91 vehicles

✳✳ CAUTION

Do not fully release the solenoid until the air is completely bled from the air spring or personal injury may result.

e. After the air is fully bled from the system, rotate counterclockwise to the third stop and remove the solenoid from the solenoid housing. Remove the large O-ring from the solenoid housing.

5. Remove the spring piston-to-axle spring seat as follows:

a. Insert air spring removal tool T90P–5310–A or equivalent, between the axle tube and the spring seat on the forward side of the axle.

b. Position the tool so its flat end rests on the piston knob. Push downward, forcing the piston and retainer clip off the axle spring seat.

6. Remove the air spring.

To install:

7. Install the air spring solenoid as follows:

a. Check the solenoid O-rings for cuts or abrasion. Replace the O-rings as required. Lightly grease the O-ring area of the solenoid and the larger solenoid housing O-ring with silicone dielectric compound.

b. Insert the solenoid into the air spring end cap and rotate clockwise to the third stop, push in to the second stop, then rotate clockwise to the first stop.

c. Install the solenoid clip. Inspect the wire harness connector and ensure the rubber gasket is in place at the bottom of the connector cavity.

8. Install the air spring into the frame spring seat, taking care to keep the solenoid air and electrical connections clean and free of damage.

9. Connect the push on spring retainer clip to the knob of the spring cap from the top side of the frame spring seat.

10. Connect the air line and electrical connector to the solenoid. Install the heat shield to frame spring seat, if required.

11. Align the air spring piston to axle seats. Squeeze to increase pressure and push downward on the piston, snapping the piston to axle seat at rebound and supported by the shock absorber.

➡**The air springs may be damaged if the suspension is allowed to compress before the spring is inflated.**

12. Refill the air spring as follows:

a. Turn the air suspension switch **ON**. The ignition switch must be **ON**

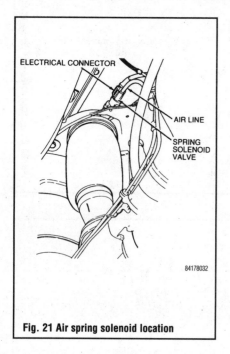

Fig. 21 Air spring solenoid location

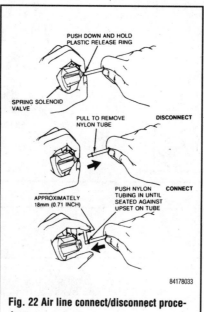

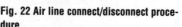

Fig. 22 Air line connect/disconnect procedure

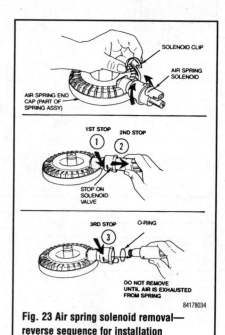

Fig. 23 Air spring solenoid removal—reverse sequence for installation

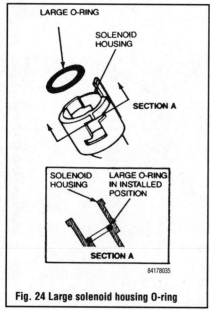

Fig. 24 Large solenoid housing O-ring

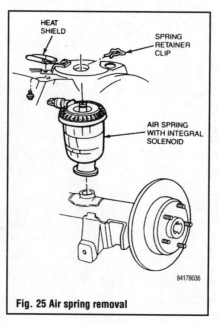

Fig. 25 Air spring removal

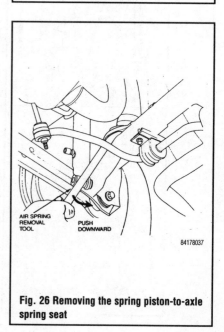

Fig. 26 Removing the spring piston-to-axle spring seat

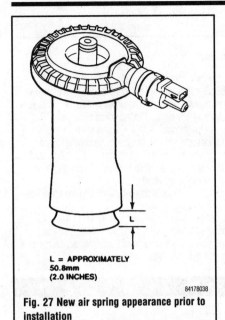

Fig. 27 New air spring appearance prior to installation

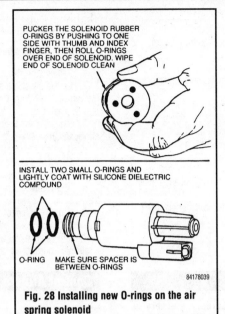

Fig. 28 Installing new O-rings on the air spring solenoid

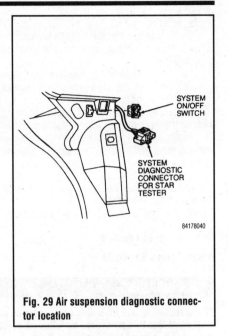

Fig. 29 Air suspension diagnostic connector location

Code	Description
23	Vent Rear
26	Compress Rear
31	Cycle Compressor On and Off Repeatedly
32	Cycle Vent Solenoid Valve Open and Closed Repeatedly
33	Cycle Spring Solenoid Valves Open and Closed Repeatedly

Fig. 30 Air suspension codes

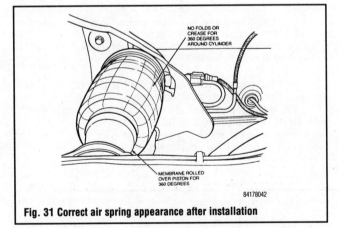

Fig. 31 Correct air spring appearance after installation

and the engine running or a battery charger must be connected to the battery to reduce battery drain.

b. Fold back or remove the right luggage compartment trim panel and connect SUPER STAR II tester 007–0041–A or equivalent to the air suspension diagnostic connector, which is located near the air suspension switch.

c. Set the tester to EEC-IV/MCU mode. Also set the tester to FAST mode. Release the tester button to the HOLD (up) position and turn the tester **ON**.

d. Depress the tester button to TEST (down) position. A Code 10 will be displayed. Within 2 minutes a Code 13 will be displayed. After Code 13 is displayed, release the tester button to HOLD (up) position, wait 5 seconds and depress the tester button to TEST (down) position. Ignore any codes displayed.

e. Release the tester button to the HOLD (up) position. Wait at least 20 seconds, then depress the tester button to TEST (down) position. Within 10 seconds, the codes will be displayed in the order shown.

f. Within 4 seconds after Code 26 is displayed, release the tester button to the HOLD (up) position. Waiting longer than 4 seconds may result in Functional Test 31 being entered. The compressor will fill the air springs with air as long as the tester button is in the HOLD (up) position. To stop filling the air springs, depress the tester button to the TEST (down) position.

➡It is possible to overheat the compressor during this operation. If the compressor overheats, the self-resetting circuit breaker in the compressor will open and remain open for about 15 minutes. This allows the compressor to cool down.

g. To exit Functional Test 26, disconnect the tester and turn the ignition switch OFF.

13. Lower the vehicle.

Shock Absorbers

REMOVAL & INSTALLATION

Without Automatic Leveling

◆ See Figure 32

❊❊ CAUTION

All vehicles except police applications are equipped with gas-pressurized shock absorbers which will extend unassisted. Do not apply heat or flame to the shock absorber tube.

1. If equipped with air suspension, turn the air suspension switch **OFF**.
2. Raise and safely support the vehicle. Make sure the rear axle is supported.
3. To assist in removing the upper attachment on shock absorbers using a plastic dust tube, place and open end wrench on the hex stamped into the dust tube's metal cap. For shock absorbers with a steel dust tube, simply grasp the tube to prevent stud rotation when loosening the retaining nut.
4. Remove the shock absorber retaining nut, washer and insulator from the stud on the upper side of the frame. Discard the nut. Compress the shock to clear the hole in the frame and remove the inner insulator and washer from the upper retaining stud.
5. Remove the self-locking retaining nut and disconnect the shock absorber lower stud from the mounting bracket on the rear axle.

To install:

6. Prime the new shock absorber as follows:

   a. With the shock absorber right side up (as installed in the vehicle), extend it fully.

   b. Turn the shock upside down and fully compress it.

   c. Repeat the previous 2 steps at least 3 times to make sure any trapped air has been expelled.

7. Place the inner washer and insulator on the upper retaining stud and position the shock absorber with the stud through the hole in the frame.

8. While holding the shock absorber in position, install the outer insulator, washer and a new stud nut on the upper side of the frame. Tighten the nut to 25 ft. lbs. (34 Nm).

9. Extend the shock absorber and place the lower stud in the mounting bracket hole on the rear axle housing. Install a new self-locking nut and tighten to 56–76 ft. lbs. (77–103 Nm).

10. Lower the vehicle and, if equipped, turn the air suspension switch **ON**.

With Automatic Leveling

♦ **See Figures 33 and 34**

✳✳ WARNING

When removing and installing rear air shock absorbers, it is very important that this procedure be followed exactly. Failure to do so may result in damaged shock absorbers.

1. Make sure the ignition switch is in the **OFF** position.

2. Disconnect the height sensor connector link before allowing the rear axle to hang free.

3. Raise and safely support the vehicle so the suspension arms hang free. The rear shock absorbers will vent air through the compressor and a hissing noise will be heard. When the noise stops, the air lines can be disconnected. A residual pressure of 8–24 psi will remain in the air lines.

4. Disconnect the air line by pushing in on the retainer ring(s) and pulling the line(s) out.

5. Remove the top retaining nut, washer and bushing.

6. Remove the bottom retaining nut and washer. Remove the shock absorber.

To install:

7. Position the shock absorber and install the bottom retaining washer and nut. Tighten to 52–85 ft. lbs. (70–115 Nm).

8. Install the top bushing, washer and retaining nut. Tighten to 14–26 ft. lbs. (19–35 Nm).

➥**Check the rubber sleeve on the shock absorber to be sure it is not wrapped up. To assist in identifying wrap-up during installation, a white stripe is on the rubber sleeve and on the shock absorber body. The stripes should align. To correct a wrap-up condition, loosen the upper shock retaining nut and turn the shock to align the stripes. Retighten the retaining nut.**

9. Connect the air line to the shock absorber by pushing in on the retainer ring and installing the air line.

10. Connect the height sensor connecting link and lower the vehicle.

TESTING

Except Air Shock Absorbers

1. Remove the shock absorber from the vehicle.

2. Extend the shock absorber fully while it is right side up, as installed in the vehicle. Then turn it upside down and fully compress it. Repeat this procedure at least 3 times to make sure any trapped air has been expelled.

3. Place the shock absorber right side up in a vise and hand stroke the shock absorber. Check the shock absorber insulators for damage and wear.

4. If the shock absorber is properly primed, in its installed position, and there is a lag or a skip occurring near mid-stroke of the shaft reverse travel direction, the shock absorber must be replaced.

5. Replace the shock absorber if there is any seizing during the shaft full travel, except at either end of the travel.

6. Replace the shock absorber if upon the shaft fast, reverse stroke, there is any noise encountered other than a faint swish, such as a clicking sound.

7. If there are excessive fluid leaks, and the shock absorber action remains erratic after purging air, replace the shock absorber.

Control Arms

REMOVAL & INSTALLATION

Upper Control Arm

➥**If one upper control arm requires replacement, also replace the upper control arm on the other side of the vehicle. If both upper arms are to be replaced, remove and install one at a time to prevent the axle from rolling or slipping sideways. If both upper control arms and both lower control arms are to be removed at the same time, remove both coil or air springs, as detailed in this Section.**

1. If equipped, turn the air suspension switch **OFF**.

2. Raise the vehicle and support the frame side rails with jack stands.

3. Support the rear axle under the differential pinion nose as wheel as under the axle.

4. Unsnap the parking brake cable from the upper arm retainer. If equipped, disconnect the height sensor from the ball stud on the left upper control arm.

5. Remove and discard the nut and bolt retaining the upper arm to the axle housing. Disconnect the arm from the housing.

6. Remove and discard the nut and bolt retaining the upper arm to the frame bracket and remove the arm.

To install:

7. Hold the upper arm in place on the front arm bracket and install a new retaining bolt and self-locking nut. Do not tighten at this time.

8. Secure the upper arm to the axle housing with new retaining bolts and nuts. The bolts must be pointed toward the front of the vehicle.

9. Raise the suspension with a jack until the upper arm rear pivot hole is in position with the hole in the axle bushing. Install a new pivot bolt and nut with the nut facing inboard.

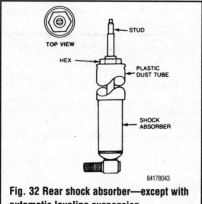

Fig. 32 Rear shock absorber—except with automatic leveling suspension

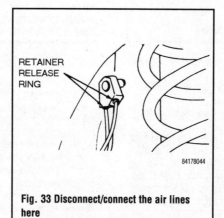

Fig. 33 Disconnect/connect the air lines here

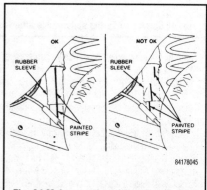

Fig. 34 Make sure the rubber sleeve on the air shock absorber is not wrapped up

10. Tighten the upper arm-to-axle pivot bolts to 103–132 ft. lbs. (140–180 Nm) and upper arm-to-frame pivot bolts to 119–149 ft. lbs. (162–203 Nm).

11. Snap the parking brake cable into the upper arm retainer. Connect the height sensor to the ball stud on the left upper arm, if equipped.

12. Remove the supports from the frame and axle and lower the vehicle. If equipped, turn the air suspension switch **ON**.

Lower Control Arm

➡If one lower control arm requires replacement, also replace the lower control arm on the other side of the vehicle. If both upper control arms and both lower control arms are to be removed at the same time, remove both coil or air springs, as detailed in this Section.

1. If equipped, turn the air suspension switch **OFF**.
2. Mark the rear shock absorber tube relative to the protective sleeve with the vehicle in the normal ride height position.
3. Raise the vehicle and support the frame side rails with jack stands. Allow the axle housing to hang with the shock absorbers fully extended to relieve spring pressure.
4. Remove the stabilizer bar, if equipped.
5. Support the axle with jack stands under the differential pinion nose as well as under the axle.
6. Remove and discard the lower arm pivot bolts and nuts and remove the lower arm.

To install:
7. Position the lower arm to the frame bracket and axle. Install new bolts and nuts with the nuts facing outboard.
8. Raise the axle to the normal ride height position, compressing the shock absorbers to the marks made during the removal procedure. Tighten the lower arm-to-axle pivot bolt to 103–132 ft. lbs. (140–180 Nm) and lower arm-to-frame pivot bolt to 119–149 ft. lbs. (162–203 Nm).

9. Install the stabilizer bar, if equipped.
10. Remove the jack stands and lower the vehicle. If equipped, turn the air suspension switch **ON**.

Stabilizer Bar

REMOVAL & INSTALLATION

1. If equipped, turn the air suspension switch **OFF**.
2. Raise the vehicle and support the frame side rails with jack stands. Allow the axle housing to hang with the shock absorbers fully extended.
3. On 1989–91 vehicles, remove the bolts, nuts and spacers retaining the stabilizer bar to the lower control arms and remove the stabilizer bar. Discard the bolts and nuts.
4. On 1992–94 vehicles, disconnect the stabilizer bar arms from the links. Remove the bolts and brackets retaining the stabilizer bar to the rear axle and remove the stabilizer bar.

To install:
5. On 1989–91 vehicles, align the 4 holes in the stabilizer bar with the holes in the lower control arms. Install the color coded end of the bar on the right side of the vehicle. Install 4 new bolts and nuts and the existing spacers. Tighten to 70–92 ft. lbs. (95–125 Nm).
6. On 1992–94 vehicles, install 2 brackets onto the stabilizer bar insulators and hook both brackets into the T-slot of the rear axle bracket. Install the retaining bolts and tighten to 16–21 ft. lbs. (21–29 Nm). Connect the stabilizer bar eyes to the links using insulators, nuts and washers. Tighten to 13–17 ft. lbs. (17–23 Nm).
7. Remove the jack stands and lower the vehicle. If equipped, turn the air suspension switch **ON**.

STEERING

Steering Wheel

REMOVAL & INSTALLATION

1989 Vehicles

1. Disconnect the negative battery cable.
2. Remove the horn pad and cover assembly. Disconnect the horn electrical connector.
3. Disconnect the cruise control switch electrical connector, if equipped.
4. Remove and discard the steering wheel bolt. Remove the steering wheel using a suitable puller. .

➡Do not use a knock-off type steering wheel puller or strike the retaining bolt with a hammer. This could cause damage to the steering shaft bearing.

To install:
5. Align the index marks on the steering wheel and shaft and install the steering wheel.
6. Install a new steering wheel retaining bolt and tighten to 30–35 ft. lbs. (41–47 Nm).
7. Connect the cruise control electrical connector, if equipped.
8. Connect the horn electrical connector and install the horn pad and cover.
9. Connect the negative battery cable.

1990–94 Vehicles

▶ See Figures 35 and 36

✳✳ CAUTION

The air bag system must be disarmed, before working on the system. Failure to do so may result in deployment of the air bag and possible personal injury.

1. Center the front wheels in the straight-ahead position.
2. Properly disarm the air bag system; see the procedure in Section 6.
3. Remove the 4 air bag module retaining nuts and lift the module off the steering wheel. Disconnect the air bag wire harness from the air bag module and remove the module from the steering wheel.

✳✳ CAUTION

When carrying a live air bag, make sure the bag and trim cover are pointed away from the body. In the unlikely event of an accidental deployment, the bag will then deploy with minimal chance of injury. When placing a live air bag on a bench or other surface, always face the bag and trim cover up, away from the surface. This will reduce the motion of the module if it is accidently deployed.

4. Disconnect the cruise control wire harness from the steering wheel, if equipped.
5. Remove and discard the steering wheel bolt. Remove the steering wheel using a suitable puller. Route the contact assembly wire harness through the steering wheel as the wheel is lifted off the shaft.

➡Do not use a knock-off type steering wheel puller or strike the retaining bolt with a hammer. This could cause damage to the steering shaft bearing.

To install:
6. Make sure the front wheels are in the straight-ahead position.
7. Route the contact assembly wire harness through the steering wheel opening at the 3 o'clock position and install the steering wheel on the steering shaft. The steering wheel and shaft alignment marks should be aligned. Make sure the air bag contact wire is not pinched.
8. Install a new steering wheel retaining bolt and tighten to 23–33 ft. lbs. (31–45 Nm).
9. If equipped, connect the cruise control wire harness to the wheel and snap the connector assembly into the steering wheel clip. Make sure the wiring does not get trapped between the steering wheel and contact assembly.

10. Connect the air bag wire harness to the air bag module and install the module to the steering wheel. Tighten the module retaining nuts to 24–32 inch lbs. (2.7–3.7 Nm).

11. Enable the air bag system according to the procedure in Section 6.

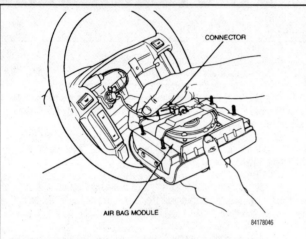

Fig. 35 Removing the air bag module from the steering wheel

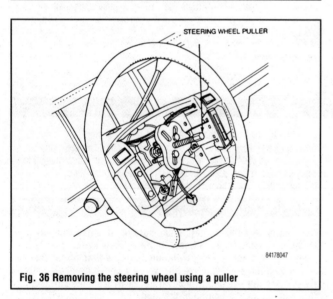

Fig. 36 Removing the steering wheel using a puller

Combination Switch

The combination switch incorporates the turn signal, dimmer and windshield wiper switch functions on 1990–94 vehicles. The combination switch incorporates only the turn signal and dimmer function on 1989 vehicles. For windshield wiper switch removal and installation on 1989 vehicles, refer to the procedure in this Section.

REMOVAL & INSTALLATION

1989 Vehicles

▶ **See Figure 37**

1. Disconnect the negative battery cable.
2. Remove the switch lever by grasping and pulling straight out.
3. Remove the steering column cover retaining screws and remove the cover.
4. Remove the shroud retaining screws and remove the shroud.
5. With the wiring connectors exposed, carefully lift the connector retainer tabs and disconnect the connectors.
6. Remove the switch retaining screws and lift up the switch assembly.
7. Installation is the reverse of the removal procedure.

1990–94 Vehicles

▶ **See Figure 38**

1. Disconnect the negative battery cable.
2. If equipped with tilt column, move to the lowest position and remove the tilt lever.
3. Remove the ignition lock cylinder; refer to the procedure in this Section.
4. Remove the shroud screws and remove the upper and lower shrouds.

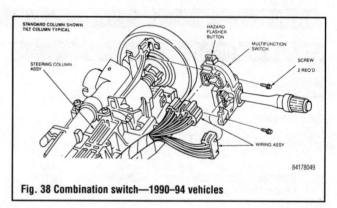

Fig. 38 Combination switch—1990–94 vehicles

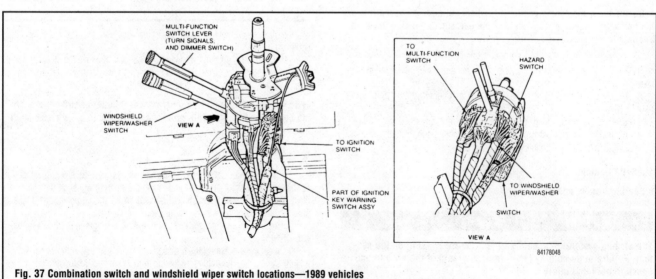

Fig. 37 Combination switch and windshield wiper switch locations—1989 vehicles

5. Remove the 2 self-tapping screws attaching the combination switch to the steering column casting and remove the switch.

6. Remove the wiring harness retainer and disconnect the 2 electrical connectors.

7. Installation is the reverse of the removal procedure.

Windshield Wiper Switch

REMOVAL & INSTALLATION

1989 Vehicles

1. Disconnect the negative battery cable.
2. Remove the split steering column cover retaining screws.
3. Separate the halves and remove the wiper switch retaining screws.
4. Disconnect the electrical connector and remove the wiper switch.
5. The installation of the wiper switch is the reverse of the removal procedure.

Ignition Switch

REMOVAL & INSTALLATION

1. Disconnect the negative battery cable.
2. On 1989 vehicles with tilt column, remove the upper extension shroud by unsnapping the shroud from the retaining clip at the 9 o'clock position.
3. Remove the steering column shroud by removing the attaching screws. On 1990–94 vehicles, remove the tilt lever, if equipped.
4. On 1990–94 vehicles, remove the instrument panel lower steering column cover.
5. Disconnect the electrical connector from the ignition switch.
6. Rotate the ignition key lock cylinder to the **RUN** position.
7. Remove the 2 screws attaching the ignition switch.
8. Disengage the ignition switch from the actuator pin and remove the switch.
    To install:
9. Adjust the new ignition switch by sliding the carrier to the **RUN** position.
10. Check to ensure that the ignition key lock cylinder is in the **RUN** position. The **RUN** position is achieved by rotating the key lock cylinder approximately 90 degrees from the **LOCK** position.
11. Install the ignition switch onto the actuator pin.
12. Align the switch mounting holes and install the attaching screws. Tighten the screws to 50–69 inch lbs. (5.6–7.9 Nm).
13. Connect the electrical connector to the ignition switch.
14. Connect the negative battery cable. Check the ignition switch for proper function in **START** and **ACC** positions. Make sure the column is locked in the **LOCK** position.
15. Install the remaining components in the reverse order of removal.

Ignition Lock Cylinder

REMOVAL & INSTALLATION

Functional Lock

▶ **See Figure 39**

The following procedure is for vehicles with functioning lock cylinders. Ignition keys are available for these vehicles or the ignition key numbers are known and the proper key can be made.

1. Disconnect the negative battery cable. If equipped, properly disarm the air bag system; refer to Section 6.
2. On 1989 vehicles, remove the trim shroud halves by removing the attaching screws. Remove the electrical connector from the key warning switch.
3. Turn the ignition to the **RUN** position.
4. Place a ⅛ in. diameter wire pin or small drift punch in the hole in the casting surrounding the lock cylinder and depress the retaining pin while pulling out on the lock cylinder to remove it from the column housing.

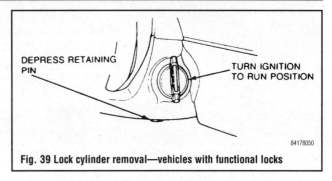

Fig. 39 Lock cylinder removal—vehicles with functional locks

To install:
5. To install the lock cylinder, turn it to the **RUN** position and depress the retaining pin. Insert the lock cylinder into its housing in the lock cylinder casting.
6. Make sure the cylinder is fully seated and aligned in the interlocking washer before turning the key to the **OFF** position. This action will permit the cylinder retaining pin to extend into the hole in the lock cylinder housing.
7. Using the ignition key, rotate the cylinder to ensure the correct mechanical operation in all positions.
8. Check for proper start in **P** or **N**. Also make sure the start circuit cannot be actuated in **D** or **R** positions and that the column is locked in the **LOCK** position.
9. Connect the key warning buzzer electrical connector and install the trim shrouds, if required.

Non-Functional Lock

The following procedure is for vehicles with non-functioning locks. On these vehicles, the lock cylinder cannot be rotated due to a lost or broken key, the key number is not known, or the lock cylinder cap is damaged and/or broken, preventing the lock cylinder from rotating.

1. Disconnect the negative battery cable. If equipped, properly disarm the air bag system; refer to Section 6.
2. Remove the steering wheel; refer to the procedure in this Section.
3. On 1989 vehicles, remove the trim shroud halves by removing the attaching screws. Remove the electrical connector from the key warning switch.
4. On 1989–90 vehicles, drill out the retaining pin using a ⅛ in. diameter drill, being careful not to drill deeper than ½ in. Position a chisel at the base of the ignition lock cylinder. Strike the chisel with sharp blows, using a hammer, to break the cap away from the lock cylinder.
5. On 1991–94 vehicles, use channel lock or vise grip type pliers to twist the lock cylinder cap until it separates from the lock cylinder.
6. Drill approximately 1¾ in. down the middle of the ignition key slot, using a ⅜ in. diameter drill bit, until the lock cylinder breaks loose from the breakaway base of the lock cylinder. Remove the lock cylinder and drill shavings from the lock cylinder housing.
7. Remove the snapring or retainer, washer and steering column lock gear. Thoroughly clean all drill shavings and other foreign materials from the casting.
8. Inspect the lock cylinder housing for damage and replace, as necessary.
    To install:
9. Install the ignition lock cylinder and check for smooth operation.
10. Connect the electrical connector to the key warning switch and install the trim shrouds, if necessary.
11. Install the steering wheel and connect the negative battery cable.

Steering Linkage

▶ **See Figure 40**

REMOVAL & INSTALLATION

Pitman Arm

▶ **See Figure 41**

1. Position the front wheels in the straight-ahead position. Raise and safely support the vehicle.

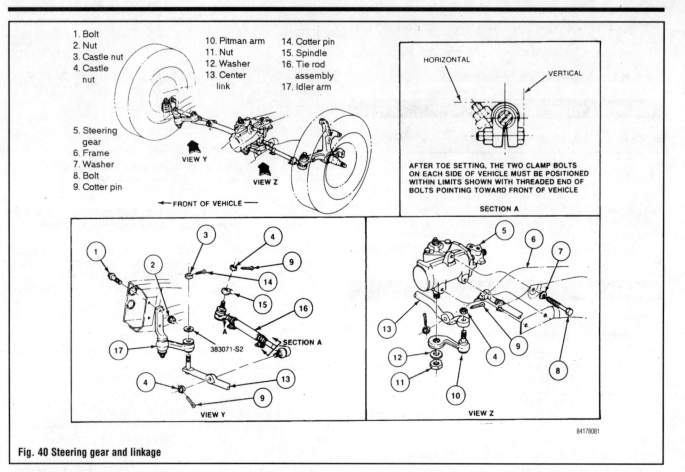

Fig. 40 Steering gear and linkage

2. Remove and discard the cotter pin from the castellated nut that attaches the center link to the pitman arm. Remove the castellated nut.

3. Disconnect the center link from the pitman arm using removal tool 3290–D or equivalent.

4. Remove the pitman arm retaining nut and lockwasher

5. Make sure the front wheel are in the straight-ahead position. Remove the pitman arm from the steering gear sector shaft using pitman arm puller T64P–3590–F or equivalent.

To install:

6. With the front wheels in the straight-ahead position, place the pitman arm, pointing it rearward, on the sector shaft. Align the blind tooth on the pitman arm with the blind tooth on the steering gear sector shaft.

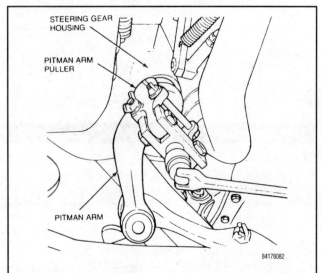

Fig. 41 Removing the pitman arm from the steering gear sector shaft

7. Install the nut and lockwasher and tighten to 233–250 ft. lbs. (316–338 Nm).

8. Install the center link on the pitman arm and install the castellated nut. Tighten the nut to 43–47 ft. lbs. (59–63 Nm) and install a new cotter pin.

➡ **If, after the nut has been torqued, the nut castellations and stud hole do not align for cotter pin installation, tighten the nut further until the cotter pin can be installed. Never back off the nut.**

Idler Arm

1. Raise and safely support the vehicle.

2. Remove the cotter pin, nut and washer retaining the center link to the idler arm. Discard the cotter pin.

3. Remove the center link from the idler arm.

4. Remove the bolts and nuts holding the idler arm to the frame and remove the idler arm.

To install:

5. Install the idler arm to the frame with the bolts and nuts. Tighten to 85–97 ft. lbs. (115–132 Nm).

6. Place the idler arm and front wheels in the straight-ahead position to maintain steering wheel alignment and prevent bushing damage.

7. Install the center link nut and washer and tighten to 43–47 ft. lbs. (59–63 Nm). Install a new cotter pin.

➡ **If, after the nut has been torqued, the nut castellations and stud hole do not align for cotter pin installation, tighten the nut further until the cotter pin can be installed. Never back off the nut.**

Center Link

1. Raise and safely support the vehicle.

2. Remove the cotter pins and nuts that attach the inner tie rod ends to the center link. Discard the cotter pins.

3. Disconnect the inner tie rod ends from the center link using removal tool 3290–D or equivalent.

4. Remove the cotter pin and nut that retains the pitman arm to the center link. Disconnect the pitman arm from the center link using removal tool 3290–D or equivalent.

5. Remove the cotter pin and nut retaining the idler arm to the center link and remove the center link. Discard the cotter pin.

To install:

6. Position the center link to the pitman arm and idler arm and loosely install the nuts. Place the idler arm and front wheels in the straight-ahead position to maintain steering wheel alignment and prevent bushing damage. Tighten the nuts to 43–47 ft. lbs. (59–63 Nm) and install new cotter pins.

➡**If, after the nut has been torqued, the nut castellations and stud hole do not align for cotter pin installation, tighten the nut further until the cotter pin can be installed. Never back off the nut.**

7. Install the tie rode ends on the center link and tighten the nuts to 43–47 ft. lbs. (59–63 Nm). Install new cotter pins.

8. Lower the vehicle. Check the toe and adjust, if necessary.

Tie Rod Ends

▶ **See Figure 42**

1. Raise and support the vehicle safely.
2. Remove the cotter pin and nut from the tie rod end ball stud.
3. Loosen the tie rod adjusting sleeve clamp bolts and remove the rod end from the spindle arm or center link, using removal tool 3290–D or equivalent.
4. Remove the tie rod end from the sleeve, counting the exact number of turns required to do so. Discard all parts removed from the sleeve.

To install:

5. Install the new tie rod end into the sleeve, using the exact number of turns it took to remove the old one. Install the tie rod end ball stud into the spindle arm or center link.
6. Install the stud nut. Tighten to 43–47 ft. lbs. (59–63 Nm) and install a new cotter pin.

➡**If, after the nut has been torqued, the nut castellations and stud hole do not align for cotter pin installation, tighten the nut further until the cotter pin can be installed. Never back off the nut.**

7. Check the toe and adjust if necessary. Loosen the clamps from the sleeve and oil the sleeve, clamps, bolts and nuts. Position the adjusting sleeve clamps as shown in the figure, then tighten the clamp nuts to 20–22 ft. lbs. (27–29 Nm).

Power Steering Gear

ADJUSTMENTS

Meshload

▶ **See Figure 43**

Should excessive steering lash be encountered, a meshload adjustment may be required. Adjust the total-over-center position load to eliminate excessive lash between the sector and rack teeth as follows:

1. Disconnect the pitman arm from the sector shaft.
2. Disconnect the fluid return line at the reservoir. Cap the reservoir return line pipe.
3. Place the end of the return line in a clean container and turn the steering wheel from left stop to right stop several times to discharge the fluid from the gear.
4. Turn the steering wheel to 45 degrees from the left stop.
5. Using an inch pound torque wrench on the steering wheel nut, determine the torque required to rotate the shaft slowly approximately ¼ turn from the 45 degree position. If equipped with tilt column, place the steering wheel in the center tilt position.
6. Turn the steering wheel back to center and determine the torque required to rotate the shaft back and forth across the center position. If the reading is not to specification, loosen the nut and turn the adjuster screw until the reading is to specification. Tighten the wheel nut while holding the screw in place.
7. Check the readings and replace the pitman arm and steering wheel hub cover.
8. Connect the fluid return line to the reservoir and fill the reservoir. Check the belt tension and adjust, if necessary.

REMOVAL & INSTALLATION

▶ **See Figure 44**

1. Disconnect the negative battery cable.
2. Remove the stone shield.
3. Tag the pressure and return lines so they may be reassembled in their original positions.
4. Disconnect the pressure and return lines from the steering gear. Plug the lines and ports in the gear to prevent the entry of dirt.
5. Remove the clamp bolts retaining the flexible coupling to the steering gear.
6. Raise and safely support the vehicle. Remove the nut from the sector shaft.
7. Remove the pitman arm from the sector shaft with pitman arm removal tool T64P–3590–F or equivalent. Remove the tool from the pitman arm.

✳✳ WARNING

Do not damage the seals and/or gear housing. Do not use a non-approved tool such as a pickle fork.

8. Support the steering gear and remove the steering gear retaining bolts.
9. Work the gear free of the flex coupling and remove the gear.
10. If the flex coupling did not come off with the gear, lift it off the shaft.

To install:

11. Turn the steering wheel to the straight-ahead position.
12. Center the steering gear input shaft with the indexing flat facing downward on 1989–91 vehicles. On 1992–94 vehicles, center the steering gear input shaft with the centerline of the 2 indexing flats at 4 o'clock.
13. Slide the steering gear input shaft into the flex coupling and into place on the frame side rail. Install the retaining bolts and tighten to 50–65 ft. lbs. (68–88 Nm).
14. Make sure the wheels are in the straight-ahead position. Install the pitman arm on the sector shaft and install the lockwasher and nut. Tighten the nut to 233–250 ft. lbs. (316–338 Nm).

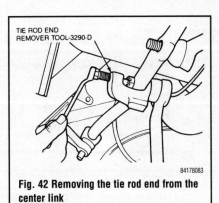

Fig. 42 Removing the tie rod end from the center link

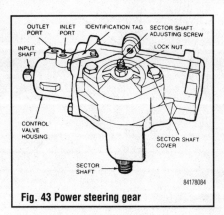

Fig. 43 Power steering gear

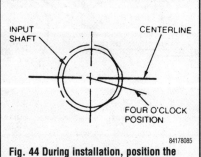

Fig. 44 During installation, position the steering gear input shaft as shown on 1992–94 vehicles

15. Move the flex coupling into place on the steering gear input shaft. Install the retaining bolt and tighten to 20–30 ft. lbs. (27–41 Nm).

16. Connect the pressure and return lines to the steering gear and tighten the lines. Fill the reservoir and turn the steering wheel from stop-to-stop to distribute the fluid. Check the fluid level and add fluid, if necessary.

17. Start the engine and turn the steering wheel from left to right. Check for leaks. Install the stone shield.

Power Steering Pump

REMOVAL & INSTALLATION

♦ **See Figures 45 and 46**

1. Disconnect the negative battery cable.
2. Disconnect the fluid return hose at the pump and drain the fluid into a container.
3. Remove the pressure hose from the pump and, if necessary, drain the fluid into a container. Do not remove the fitting from the pump.
4. Disconnect the belt from the pulley. On 5.0L and 5.8L engines, use pulley removal tool T69L–10300–B or equivalent, to remove the pulley.
5. Remove the mounting bolts and remove the pump.

To install:

6. On 5.0L and 5.8L engines, place the pump on the mounting bracket and install the bolts at the front of the pump. Tighten to 30–45 ft. lbs. (40–62 Nm).
7. On 4.6L engine, place the pump on the mounting bosses of the engine block and install the bolts at the side of the pump. Tighten to 15–22 ft. lbs. (20–30 Nm).
8. On 5.0L and 5.8L engines, install the pump pulley using pulley replacer tool T65P–3A733–C or equivalent.
9. Place the belt on the pump pulley and adjust the tension, if necessary.
10. Install the pressure hose to the pump fitting. Tighten the tube nut with a tube nut wrench rather than with an open-end wrench. Tighten to 20–25 ft. lbs. (27–34 Nm) on 1989–91 vehicles or 35–45 ft. lbs. (47–60 Nm) on 1992–94 vehicles.

➡Do not overtighten this fitting. Swivel and/or end play of the fitting is normal and does not indicate a loose fitting. Over-tightening the tube nut can collapse the tube nut wall, resulting in a leak and requiring replacement of the entire pressure hose assembly. Use of an open-end wrench to tighten the nut can deform the tube nut hex which may result in improper torque and may make further servicing of the system difficult.

11. Connect the return hose to the pump and tighten the clamp. Fill the reservoir with the proper type and quantity of fluid. Bleed the air from the system.

BLEEDING

1. Disconnect the ignition coil. Raise and safely support the vehicle so the front wheels are off the floor.
2. Fill the power steering fluid reservoir.
3. Crank the engine with the starter and add fluid until the level remains constant.
4. While cranking the engine, rotate the steering wheel from lock-to-lock.

➡The front wheels must be off the floor during lock-to-lock rotation of the steering wheel.

5. Check the fluid level and add fluid, if necessary.
6. Connect the ignition coil wire. Start the engine and allow it to run for several minutes.
7. Rotate the steering wheel from lock-to-lock.
8. Shut off the engine and check the fluid level. Add fluid, if necessary.
9. If air is still present in the system, purge the system of air using power steering pump air evacuator tool 021–00014 or equivalent, as follows:

a. Make sure the power steering pump reservoir is full to the COLD FULL mark on the dipstick or to just above the minimum indication on the reservoir.

b. Tightly insert the rubber stopper of the air evacuator assembly into the pump reservoir fill neck.

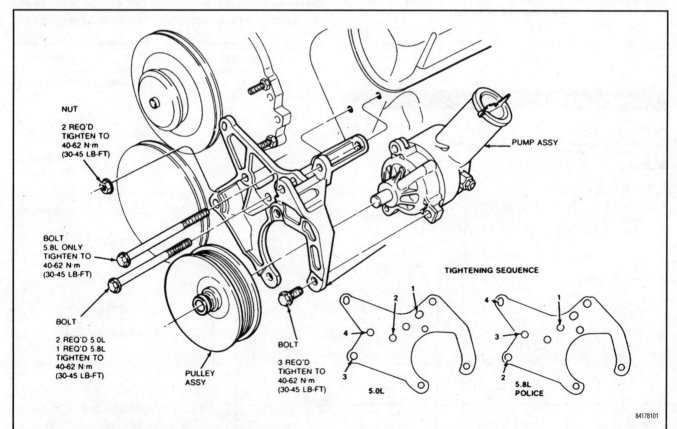

Fig. 45 Power steering pump—5.0L and 5.8L engines

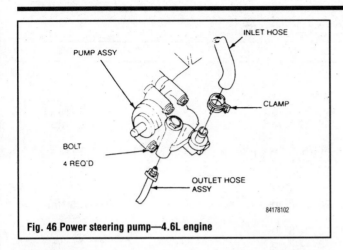

Fig. 46 Power steering pump—4.6L engine

c. Apply 15 in. Hg maximum vacuum on the pump reservoir for a minimum of 3 minutes with the engine idling. As air purges from the system, vacuum will fall off. Maintain adequate vacuum with the vacuum source.

d. Release the vacuum and remove the vacuum source. Fill the reservoir to the COLD FULL mark or to just above the minimum indication on the reservoir.

e. With the engine idling, apply 15 in. Hg vacuum to the pump reservoir. Slowly cycle the steering wheel from lock-to-lock every 30 seconds for approximately 5 minutes. Do not hold the steering wheel on the stops while cycling. Maintain adequate vacuum with the vacuum source as the air purges.

f. Release the vacuum and remove the vacuum source. Add fluid, if necessary.

g. Start the engine and cycle the steering wheel. Check for oil leaks at all connections. In severe cases of aeration, it may be necessary to repeat Steps 9b–9f.

TORQUE SPECIFICATIONS

Component	U.S.	Metric
Air bag clockspring contact screws	18–26 inch lbs.	2–3 Nm
Air bag module nuts		
1990	35–53 inch lbs.	4–6 Nm
1991–94	24–32 inch lbs.	2.7–3.7 Nm
Center link-to-idler arm nut	43–47 ft. lbs.	59–63 Nm
Center link-to-pitman arm nut	43–47 ft. lbs.	59–63 Nm
Combination switch screws	18–26 inch lbs.	2–3 Nm
Control arms		
Front		
Lower arm-to-crossmember bolts	109–140 ft. lbs.	148–190 Nm
Upper arm shaft nuts	85–100 ft. lbs.	115–136 Nm
Upper arm-to-frame bolts	100–140 ft. lbs.	136–190 Nm
Rear		
Lower arm-to-axle bolt	103–132 ft. lbs.	140–180 Nm
Lower arm-to-frame bolt	119–149 ft. lbs.	162–203 Nm
Upper arm-to-axle bolt	103–132 ft. lbs.	140–180 Nm
Upper arm-to-frame bolt	119–149 ft. lbs.	162–203 Nm
Front wheel hub nut		
1992–94 vehicles	189–254 ft. lbs.	255–345 Nm
Idler arm-to-frame bolts	85–97 ft. lbs.	115–132 Nm
Ignition switch screws	50–69 inch lbs.	5.6–7.9 Nm
Lower ball joint-to-spindle nut	80–120 ft. lbs.	108–163 Nm
Pitman arm nut	233–250 ft. lbs.	316–338 Nm
Power steering pressure hose nut		
1989–91	20–25 ft. lbs.	27–34 Nm
1992–94	35–45 ft. lbs.	47–60 Nm
Power steering pump bolts		
4.6L engine	15–22 ft. lbs.	20–30 Nm
5.0L and 5.8L engines	30–45 ft. lbs.	40–62 Nm
Shock Absorbers		
Front		
Lower bolts	13–16 ft. lbs.	17–23 Nm
Upper nut	26 ft. lbs.	41 Nm
Rear		
Lower nut		
Air shock absorber	52–85 ft. lbs.	70–115 Nm
Except air shock absorber	56–76 ft. lbs.	77–103 Nm
Upper nut	25 ft. lbs.	34 Nm

84178R5A

TORQUE SPECIFICATIONS

Component	U.S.	Metric
Stabilizer bar		
Front		
Bracket bolts/nuts		
1989–91	14–26 ft. lbs.	19–35 Nm
1992–94	44–59 ft. lbs.	59–81 Nm
Link nuts		
1989–91	9–15 ft. lbs.	12–20 Nm
1992–94	30–40 ft. lbs.	40–55 Nm
Rear		
1989–91		
Bar-to-lower arm bolts	70–92 ft. lbs.	95–125 Nm
1992–94		
Bar-to-axle bracket bolts	16–21 ft. lbs.	21–29 Nm
Link nuts	13–17 ft. lbs.	17–23 Nm
Steering column		
Flex coupling pinch bolt		
1990–94	31–41 ft. lbs.	40–56 Nm
Lock housing and pivot bolts		
1990–94	14–20 ft. lbs.	20–28 Nm
Lower bearing screws		
1990–94	5–8 ft. lbs.	7–11 Nm
Lower steering shaft bolt		
1989	35–45 ft. lbs.	48–61 Nm
1990–94	31–41 ft. lbs.	40–56 Nm
Support bracket nuts		
1989	20–37 ft. lbs.	27–50 Nm
1990–94	9–14 ft. lbs.	13–19 Nm
Steering gear flex coupling bolt	20–30 ft. lbs.	27–41 Nm
Steering gear sector shaft cover bolts	55–70 ft. lbs.	75–95 Nm
Steering gear-to-frame bolts	50–65 ft. lbs.	68–88 Nm
Steering gear valve housing bolts	30–45 ft. lbs.	40–60 Nm
Steering wheel bolt		
1989	30–35 ft. lbs.	41–47 Nm
1990–94	23–33 ft. lbs.	31–45 Nm
Tie rod end nut	43–47 ft. lbs.	59–63 Nm
Tie rod end sleeve clamp nut	20–22 ft. lbs.	27–29 Nm
Upper ball joint pinch bolt		
1992–94	67 ft. lbs.	92 Nm
Upper ball joint-to-control arm nuts		
1992	90–109 ft. lbs.	122–149 Nm
1993–94	107–129 ft. lbs.	145–175 Nm
Upper ball joint-to-spindle nut		
1989–91	60–90 ft. lbs.	81–122 Nm

84178R6A

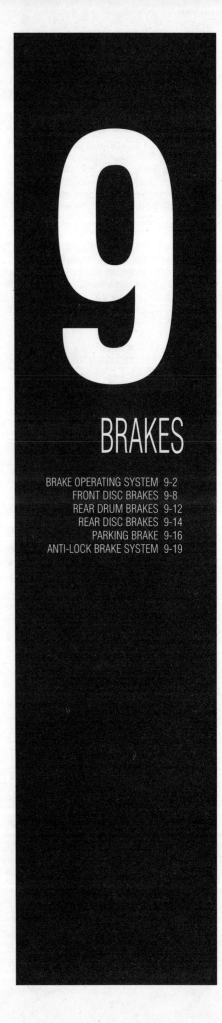

9

BRAKES

BRAKE OPERATING SYSTEM

General Information

All vehicles are equipped with front disc brakes. 1989–91 vehicles are equipped with drum brakes at the rear while 1992–94 vehicles are equipped with rear disc brakes. An Anti-lock Brake System (ABS) with Traction Assist (TA) is optional equipment on 1992–94 vehicles.

The front disc brake system consists of hydraulically actuated single-piston sliding caliper assemblies with inner and outer brake pads, acting on ventilated cast iron rotors. The rotors are attached to the front hubs, which are attached to and rotate on the front spindles.

The rear disc brake system is similar in design to the front, except the rear rotors are mounted to the rear axle shaft flanges.

The rear drum brakes use internal, hydraulically actuated, expanding brake shoes that are applied against a rotating cast iron brake drum. The brake drum is mounted to the rear axle shaft flange.

The pedal actuated brake hydraulic system consists of the power brake booster, master cylinder, pressure control valve and brake lines and hoses. On all 1989–91 vehicles and 1992–94 vehicles without anti-lock brakes, the dual hydraulic system is split front to rear. Both front brakes comprise one circuit and both rear brakes the other circuit. On 1992–94 vehicles with anti-lock brakes, the dual hydraulic system is diagonally split with the left front and right rear comprising one circuit and the right front and left rear, the other circuit.

The optional anti-lock brake system with traction control prevents wheel lockup by automatically modulating the brake pressure during an emergency stop. Without wheel lockup, the driver can maintain steering control and stop the vehicle in the shortest possible distance under most conditions.

Traction control reduces wheel spin on slippery or loose surfaces. During acceleration, if one or both rear wheels lose traction and begin to spin, the traction control system will rapidly apply and release the appropriate rear brake to reduce wheel spin and assist traction.

The anti-lock brake/traction control system consists of the vacuum booster and master cylinder assembly, hydraulic control unit, electronic control unit, wheel sensors and a pedal travel switch.

Adjustments

DRUM BRAKES

▶ **See Figure 1**

The drum brakes are self-adjusting and need manual adjustment only after the brake shoes have been replaced or when the length of the adjusting screw has been changed while performing another brake service operation. Manual adjustment is made with the drums removed, using a brake adjustment gauge and the following procedure.

When adjusting the brake shoes, check the parking brake cables for proper adjustment. Makes sure the link operates freely with the brake shoes centered on the backing plate.

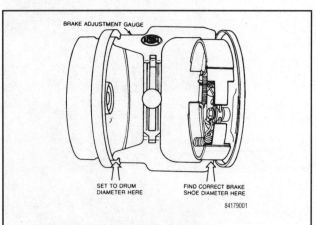

Fig. 1 Using the brake shoe adjustment gauge

➡**Make sure the upper ends of the brake shoes are seated on the anchor pin. The parking brake link should have 0.005–0.025 in. (0.127–0.64mm) end-play after overcoming the load of the parking brake link anti-rattle spring.**

1. Install brake adjustment gauge D81L–1103–A or equivalent, on the brake drum to determine the inside diameter of the drum.

2. Position the adjustment gauge on the brake shoes. Hold the automatic adjusting lever out of the way and rotate the adjustment screw until the brake shoe diameter fits the gauge.

➡**Make sure the adjustment screw rotates freely. If necessary, lubricate the screw threads with suitable grease.**

3. Rotate the brake adjustment gauge around the brake shoes to be sure of the setting.

4. Install the brake drums and wheel and tire assemblies. Lower the vehicle.

5. Apply the brakes several times with moderate pressure while backing up, moving the vehicle forward after each stop.

6. After adjustment, check brake operation by making several stops from varying forward speeds.

Brake Light Switch

REMOVAL & INSTALLATION

1. Disconnect the negative battery cable.

2. Disconnect the electrical connector at the switch. The locking tab on the connector must be lifted before the connector can be removed.

3. Remove the hairpin retainer, slide the brake light switch, the pushrod and the nylon washers and bushings away from the pedal and remove the switch.

➡**Since the switch side plate nearest the brake pedal is slotted, it is not necessary to remove the brake master cylinder pushrod and 1 washer from the brake pedal pin.**

To install:

4. Position the switch so the U-shaped side is nearest the pedal and directly over/under the pin. Then slide the switch down/up trapping the master cylinder pushrod and black bushing between the switch side plates. Push the switch and pushrod assembly firmly toward the brake pedal arm. Assemble the outside white plastic washer to the pin and install the hairpin retainer to trap the whole assembly.

5. Assemble the wire harness connector to the switch. Check the switch for proper operation.

➡**The brake light switch wire harness must be long enough to travel with the switch during full pedal stroke. If wire length is insufficient, reroute the harness or service, as required.**

Brake Pedal

REMOVAL & INSTALLATION

1. Disconnect the negative battery cable.

2. Disconnect the brake light switch electrical connector from the switch.

3. Loosen the booster retaining nuts approximately ¼ in. (6.35mm) at the pedal support. Remove the pushrod retainer and nylon washer. Slide the brake light switch outboard along the brake pedal pin just far enough for the outer hole of the switch frame to clear the pin. Remove the switch by sliding it downward. Remove the black brake light switch bushing from the pushrod.

4. Slide the pushrod and nylon washer, if equipped, off the pedal pin.

5. Remove the locknut and then remove the pivot bolt, brake pedal, pivot spacer and bushings from the pedal support.

To install:

6. Apply a light coating of SAE 10W-40 engine oil to the bushings. Locate the bushings and pivot spacer in the brake pedal hub.

7. Position the brake pedal assembly in the pedal support and install the pivot bolt. Install the locknut and tighten to 10–20 ft. lbs. (14–27 Nm).

8. Install the inner nylon washer, if equipped, the master cylinder pushrod and the black brake light switch bushing on the brake pedal pin. Position the brake light switch so it straddles the pushrod with the slot on the pedal pin and the switch outer frame hole just clearing the pin. Slide the switch upward onto the pin and pushrod. Slide the assembly inboard toward the brake pedal arm. Install the outer nylon washer and the pushrod retainer. Lock the retainer securely.

9. Tighten the booster retaining nuts to 21 ft. lbs. (29 Nm).

10. Connect the brake light switch electrical connector and connect the negative battery cable.

Master Cylinder

REMOVAL & INSTALLATION

▶ **See Figure 2**

1. Disconnect the negative battery cable.

2. If equipped with anti-lock brakes, depress the brake pedal several times to exhaust all vacuum in the system.

3. Remove the brake lines from the primary and secondary outlet ports of the master cylinder.

4. On vehicles without anti-lock brakes, disconnect the brake warning indicator switch connector. On vehicles with anti-lock brakes, remove the electrical connector bracket retaining nut and disconnect the fluid level indicator electrical connector.

5. If equipped with anti-lock brakes, disconnect the Hydraulic Control Unit (HCU) supply hose at the master cylinder and secure in a position to prevent loss of brake fluid.

6. Remove the nuts attaching master cylinder to the brake booster assembly.

7. Slide the master cylinder forward and upward from the vehicle.

To install:

8. If equipped with anti-lock brakes, install a new seal in the groove in the master cylinder mounting face.

9. Install the master cylinder on the booster studs and install the mounting nuts. Tighten the nuts to 21 ft. lbs. (21–29 Nm).

10. Install short lengths of brake line in the master cylinder outlet ports and position them so they point back into the reservoir and the ends of the lines are submerged in brake fluid.

11. Fill the reservoir with brake fluid and cover the reservoir with a shop towel.

✳✳ WARNING

Do not allow brake fluid to spill on the vehicle's finish; it will remove the paint. In case of a spill, flush the area with water.

12. Pump the brakes until clear, bubble-free fluid comes out of both brake lines.

13. Remove the short brake lines and connect the vehicle brake lines to the master cylinder. Bleed each brake line at the master cylinder using the following procedure:

a. Have an assistant pump the brake pedal 10 times and then hold firm pressure on the pedal.

b. Position a shop towel under the rear most brake line fitting. Loosen the fitting with a tubing wrench until a stream of brake fluid comes out. Have the assistant maintain pressure on the brake pedal until the brake line fitting is tightened again.

c. Repeat this operation until clear, bubble free fluid comes out from around the brake line fitting.

d. Repeat this bleeding operation at the front brake line fitting.

➡ **On some vehicles, the master cylinder is equipped with a bleeder fitting. In these cases, the master cylinder can be bled in the same manner as a caliper or wheel cylinder. Refer to Bleeding in this Section.**

14. If equipped, attach the HCU supply hose to the master cylinder.

15. Connect the brake warning indicator switch connector or the fluid level indicator electrical connector, as required. Install the electrical connector bracket and retaining nut, if equipped.

16. Bleed the system. Fill the master cylinder reservoir to the proper level.

17. Operate the brakes several times, then check for external hydraulic leaks.

Power Brake Booster

REMOVAL & INSTALLATION

Without ABS

▶ **See Figure 3**

1. Disconnect the negative battery cable.

2. Remove the master cylinder from the booster and move it aside without disconnecting the brake lines. Be careful not to kink the brake lines.

3. Disconnect the manifold vacuum hose from the booster check valve.

4. Working inside the vehicle below the instrument panel, remove the brake light switch connector. Remove the switch retaining pin and slide the switch off the brake pedal pin just far enough for the outer arm to clear the pin, then remove the switch. Be careful not to damage the switch.

5. Remove the booster-to-dash panel attaching nuts.

6. Slide the booster pushrod, nylon washers, if equipped, and bushing off the brake pedal pin. Slide the pushrod out from the engine side of the dash panel and remove the booster.

To install:

7. Place the booster in position on the dash panel.

8. Working inside the vehicle, Install the inner nylon washer, if equipped, booster pushrod and bushing on the brake pedal pin. Install the booster-to-dash panel attaching nuts and tighten to 21 ft. lbs. (29 Nm).

9. Position the brake light switch so it straddles the booster pushrod with the switch slot toward the pedal blade and the hole just clearing the pin. Be careful not to bend or deform the switch.

10. Install the nylon washer on the pin, and secure all parts to the pin with the hairpin retainer. Make sure the retainer is fully installed and locked over the pedal pin. Connect the brake light switch electrical connector.

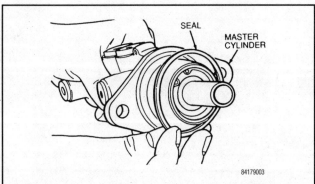

Fig. 2 Installing a new seal in the groove in the master cylinder mounting face—vehicles with ABS

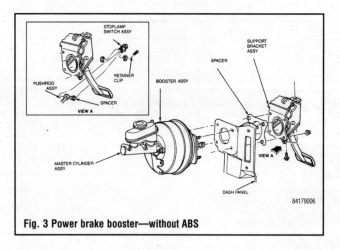

Fig. 3 Power brake booster—without ABS

11. Connect the manifold vacuum hose to the booster check valve using a hose clamp.

12. Install the master cylinder and tighten the nuts to 21 ft. lbs. (29 Nm).

13. Connect the negative battery cable. Start the engine and check power brake operation.

With ABS

▶ See Figure 4

1. Disconnect the negative battery cable.

2. Pump the brake pedal until all vacuum is removed from the booster. This will prevent the O-ring from being sucked into the booster during disassembly.

3. Remove the electrical connector bracket retaining nut from the master cylinder stud and disconnect the connector.

4. Working in the engine compartment, remove the cruise control actuator cable and cruise control servo; refer to Section 6.

5. Disconnect the manifold vacuum hose from the booster check valve.

6. Disconnect the fluid level indicator electrical connector from the master cylinder reservoir cap.

7. Disconnect the brake lines from the master cylinder outlet ports and remove the Hydraulic Control Unit (HCU) supply hose. Plug the ports and reservoir feed to prevent brake fluid from leaking onto paint and wiring.

8. Working inside the passenger compartment, disconnect the brake light switch electrical connector from the switch. Disengage the pedal position switch from the stud.

9. Remove the hairpin retainer and outer nylon washer from the pedal pin. Slide the brake light switch off the pedal just far enough for the arm to clear the pin. Remove the switch, being careful not to damage it during removal.

10. Remove the booster-to-dash panel attaching nuts. Slide the bushing and booster pushrod off the brake pedal pin.

11. From inside the engine compartment, move the booster forward until the booster studs clear the dash panel. Remove the booster/master cylinder assembly and place it on a clean bench.

12. Remove the master cylinder-to-booster nuts and slide the master cylinder away from the booster.

To install:

13. Make sure the O-ring is in place in the groove on the master cylinder, then slide the master cylinder onto the booster studs. Install the nuts and tighten to 21 ft. lbs. (29 Nm).

14. Position the booster/master cylinder assembly on the dash.

15. Working inside the passenger compartment, install the booster pushrod and bushing on the brake pedal pin. Install the booster-to-dash panel nuts and tighten to 21 ft. lbs. (29 Nm).

16. Position the brake light switch so it straddles the booster pushrod with the switch slot toward the pedal blade and the hole just clearing the pin. Slide the switch completely onto the pin. Be careful not to bend or deform the switch.

17. Install the nylon washer on the pin, and secure all parts to the pin with the hairpin retainer. Make sure the retainer is fully installed and locked over the pedal pin. Connect the brake light switch electrical connector.

18. Install and adjust the pedal travel switch as explained in this Section.

19. Install the cruise control servo and cruise control actuator cable; refer to Section 6.

20. Connect the brake lines to the master cylinder and attach the low pressure hose to the reservoir.

21. Connect the manifold vacuum hose to the booster check valve and the electrical connector to the master cylinder reservoir cap.

22. Connect the electrical connector and install the retaining bracket and nut.

23. Connect the negative battery cable. Bleed the brake system.

ADJUSTMENT

Without ABS

▶ See Figures 5, 6 and 7

The power brake booster has an adjustable pushrod (output rod) that is used to compensate for dimensional variations in an assembled booster. The pushrod length is adjusted after each booster power unit has been assembled in production. A properly adjusted pushrod that remains assembled to the booster with which it was matched in production should never require adjustment.

A booster that is suspected of having an improper pushrod length will indicate either of the following:

• A pushrod that is too long will prevent the master cylinder piston from completely releasing hydraulic pressure, eventually causing the brakes to drag.

• A pushrod that is too short will increase brake pedal travel and cause a groaning noise to come from the booster.

If necessary, booster pushrod length can be verified using the following procedure. It will be necessary to fabricate a gauge of the dimensions shown in Figs. 8 or 9.

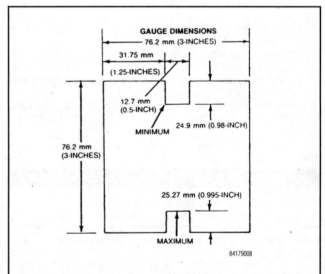

Fig. 5 Dimensions for booster pushrod length gauge—1989 vehicles

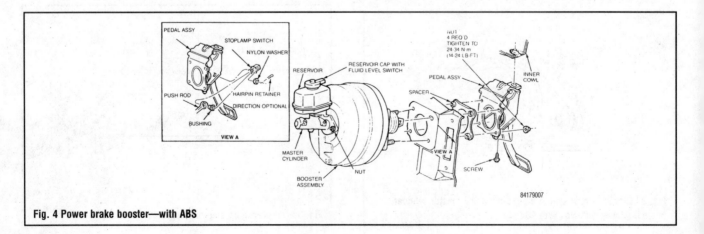

Fig. 4 Power brake booster—with ABS

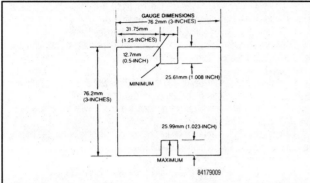

Fig. 6 Dimensions for booster pushrod length gauge—1990–94 vehicles

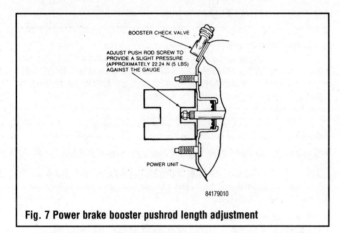

Fig. 7 Power brake booster pushrod length adjustment

1. Without disconnecting the brake lines, disconnect the master cylinder and position it away from the booster. The master cylinder must be supported to prevent damaging the brake lines.

2. With the engine running, gauge and adjust the pushrod length from the knurled area. A force of approximately 5 lbs. applied to the pushrod with the gauge will ensure that the pushrod is seated within the power unit.

3. Install the master cylinder on the booster. Gradually alternate tightening the attaching nuts to 21 ft. lbs. (29 Nm).

➡Do not adjust the pushrod too long or brake drag could result.

With ABS

The booster pushrod (output rod) is not adjustable. The pushrod length is set during assembly. A properly set pushrod that remains within the assembled booster after it was assembled in production, should never require service.

A booster that is suspected of having an improper set pushrod length will indicate either of the following:

• A pushrod that is too long will prevent the master cylinder piston from completely releasing hydraulic pressure and causing the brakes to drag.

• A pushrod that is too short will increase brake pedal travel and cause a clunk or groaning noise to come from the booster.

If necessary, booster pushrod length can be verified with a depth micrometer using the following procedure:

1. With the engine OFF, depress the brake pedal several times to deplete the vacuum in the brake booster.

2. Without disconnecting the brake lines, disconnect the master cylinder and position it away from the booster. The master cylinder must be supported to prevent damaging the brake lines.

3. Measure the pushrod length while a force of approximately 5 lbs. is applied to the pushrod end. The correct pushrod dimension is 1.11 in. plus or minus 0.01 in. (28.3mm plus or minus 0.3mm) as measured from the master cylinder mounting surface.

4. If the pushrod dimension is correct, install the master cylinder on the booster and alternately tighten the attaching nuts to 21 ft. lbs. (29 Nm).

5. If the pushrod dimension is incorrect, the booster must be replaced.

Valves

All vehicles are equipped with a brake pressure control valve. On vehicles with anti-lock brakes, the valve assembly consists of twin brake proportioning valves, which proportion the pressure to both rear brakes, individually. On vehicles without anti-lock brakes, pressure control is installed into the master cylinder, and proportions pressure to the rear brake circuit through a junction block on the frame. When the brake pedal is applied, the full rear brake fluid pressure passes through the proportioning valves to the rear brake system until the valve split point is reached. Above it split point, the proportioning valves begin to reduce the hydraulic pressure to the rear brakes, creating a balanced braking condition between the front and rear wheels.

A metering valve is used on 1989 vehicles and 1990–91 vehicles equipped with the 5.8L engine. The metering valve limits the hydraulic pressure to the front disc brakes until a predetermined front hydraulic pressure has been reached.

REMOVAL & INSTALLATION

Brake Pressure Control Valve

◆ See Figure 8

WITH ABS

1. Disconnect the brake inlet lines and the rear lines from the brake control valve assembly.

2. Remove the screw retaining the control valve assembly to the frame and remove the brake control valve.

To install:

3. Position the control valve on the frame and secure with the retaining screw.

4. Connect the rear brake outlet lines to the control valve assembly and tighten the line nuts to 10–18 ft. lbs. (14–24 Nm).

5. Connect the inlet lines to the control valve assembly and tighten the line nuts to 10–18 ft. lbs. (14–24 Nm).

6. Bleed the brake system.

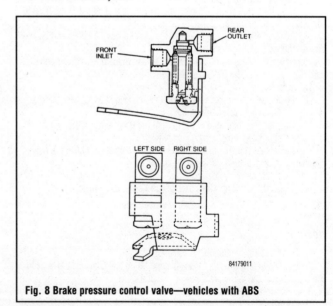

Fig. 8 Brake pressure control valve—vehicles with ABS

Metering Valve

◆ See Figure 9

1. Disconnect the front brake system inlet line and the left and right front brake outlet lines from the metering valve.

2. Remove the screw retaining the metering valve to the frame and remove the metering valve from the vehicle.

To install:

3. Position the metering valve on the frame and secure with the retaining screw. Tighten the screw to 7–11 ft. lbs. (10–14 Nm).

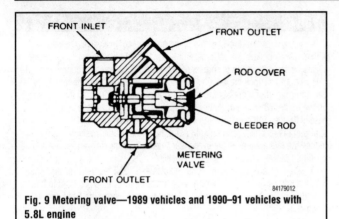

FRONT INLET — FRONT OUTLET

ROD COVER

BLEEDER ROD

METERING VALVE

FRONT OUTLET

84179012

Fig. 9 Metering valve—1989 vehicles and 1990–91 vehicles with 5.8L engine

4. Connect the front brake outlet lines to the metering valve assembly and tighten the line nuts to 10–18 ft. lbs. (14–24 Nm).

5. Connect the front brake inlet line to the metering valve assembly and tighten the line nut to 10–18 ft. lbs. (14–24 Nm).

6. Bleed the brake system.

➡**If the brake system is pressure bled, the metering valve bleeder rod must be pushed in.**

Brake Hoses

REMOVAL & INSTALLATION

Front

1. Raise and safely support the vehicle.
2. Remove the wheel and tire assembly.
3. Using a tubing wrench, loosen the line fitting that connects the hose to the brake line at the frame bracket. Plug the brake line.
4. Remove the horseshoe-shaped retaining clip from the hose and bracket and disengage the hose from the bracket.
5. Remove the hollow bolt retaining the hose to the brake caliper and discard the sealing washers. Remove the brake hose.
   To install:
6. Install the hose to the caliper with the hollow bolt and 2 new sealing washers. Tighten the hollow bolt to 30 ft. lbs. (41 Nm).
7. Position the upper end of the hose in the frame bracket and install the horseshoe clip. Make sure the hose is not twisted.
8. Remove the plug from the brake line and connect the line to the hose. Tighten the fitting to 10–18 ft. lbs. (13–24 Nm).
9. Bleed the brake system.
10. Install the wheel and tire assembly and lower the vehicle.

Rear

1989–91

1. Raise and safely support the vehicle.
2. Using a tubing wrench, loosen the line fitting that connects the hose to the brake line at the frame bracket. Plug the brake line.
3. Disconnect the hose from the rear axle junction block.
   To install:
4. Secure the brake hose to the junction block.
5. Position the upper end of the hose in the frame bracket and install the horseshoe clip. Make sure the hose is not twisted.
6. Remove the plug from the brake line and connect the line to the hose. Tighten the fitting to 10–18 ft. lbs. (13–24 Nm).
7. Bleed the brake system and lower the vehicle.

1992–94

1. Raise and safely support the vehicle.
2. Remove the wheel and tire assembly.

3. Using a tubing wrench, loosen the line fitting that connects the hose to the brake line at the frame bracket. Plug the brake line.
4. Remove the bolt attaching the hose bracket to the frame.
5. Remove the hollow bolt retaining the hose to the brake caliper and discard the sealing washers. Remove the brake hose.
   To install:
6. Install the hose to the caliper with the hollow bolt and 2 new sealing washers. Tighten the hollow bolt to 30–40 ft. lbs. (41–54 Nm).
7. Position the hose bracket to the frame and secure with the bolt. Make sure the hose is not twisted.
8. Remove the plug from the brake line and connect the line to the hose. Tighten the fitting to 10–18 ft. lbs. (13–24 Nm).
9. Bleed the brake system.
10. Install the wheel and tire assembly and lower the vehicle.

Brake Lines

REMOVAL & INSTALLATION

1. Raise and safely support the vehicle.
2. Remove the necessary components to gain access to the brake line.
3. Disconnect the brake line fittings ate each end of the line to be replaced.
4. Disconnect the line from any retaining clips and remove the line from the vehicle.
   To install:
5. Try to obtain a replacement line that is the same length as the line that was removed. If the line is longer, you will have to cut it and flare the end.

➡**Use only brake line tubing approved for automotive use.**

6. Use a suitable tubing bender to make the necessary bends in the line. Work slowly and carefully; try to make the bends look as close as possible to those on the line being replaced.

➡**When bending the brake line, be careful not to kink or crack the line. If the brake line becomes kinked or cracked, it must be replaced.**

7. Before installing the brake line, flush it with brake cleaner to remove any dirt or foreign material.
8. Install the line into the vehicle. Be sure to attach the line to the retaining clips, as necessary. Make sure the replacement brake line does not contact any components that could rub the line and cause a leak.
9. Connect the brake line fittings and tighten to 10–18 ft. lbs. (13–24 Nm).
10. Bleed the brake system.
11. Install any removed components and lower the vehicle.

BRAKE LINE FLARING

▶ **See Figures 10 and 11**

Use only brake line tubing approved for automotive use; never use copper tubing. Whenever possible, try to work with brake lines that are already cut to the length needed. These lines are available at most auto parts stores and have machine made flares, the quality of which is hard to duplicate with most of the available inexpensive flaring kits.

When the brakes are applied, there is a great amount of pressure developed in the hydraulic system. An improperly formed flare can leak with resultant loss of stopping power. If you have never formed a double-flare, take time to familiarize yourself with the flaring kit; practice forming double-flares on scrap tubing until you are satisfied with the results.

The following procedure applies to most commercially available double-flaring kits. If these instructions differ in any way from those in your kit, follow the instructions in the kit.

1. Cut the brake line to the necessary length using a tubing cutter.
2. Square the end of the tube with a file and chamfer the edges.
3. Insert the tube into the proper size hole in the bar until the end of the tube sticks out the thickness of the single flare adapter. Tighten the bar wing nuts tightly so the tube cannot move.
4. Place the single flare adapter into the tube and slide the bar into the yoke.
5. Position the yoke screw over the single flare adapter and tighten it until the bar is locked in the yoke. Continue tightening the yoke screw until the adapter bottoms on the bar. This should form the single flare.

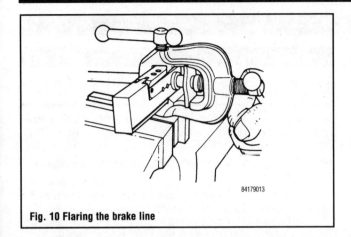

Fig. 10 Flaring the brake line

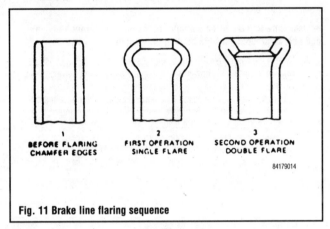

Fig. 11 Brake line flaring sequence

Fig. 12 Bleeding the right front brake caliper

➡Make sure the tube is not forced out of the hole in the bar during the single flare operation. If it is, the single flare will not be formed properly and the procedure must be repeated from Step 1.

6. Loosen the yoke screw and remove the single flare adapter.

7. Position the yoke screw over the tube and tighten until the taper contacts the single flare and the bar is locked in the yoke. Continue tightening to form the double flare.

➡Make sure the tube is not forced out of the hole in the bar during the double flare operation. If it is, the double flare will not be formed properly and the procedure must be repeated from Step 1.

8. Loosen the screw and remove the bar from the yoke. Remove the tube from the bar.

9. Check the flare for cracks or uneven flaring. If the flare is not perfect, cut it off and begin again at Step 1.

Bleeding

WITHOUT ABS

▶ See Figure 12

1. Clean all dirt from the master cylinder filler cap.

2. If the master cylinder is known or suspected to have air in the bore, it must be bled before any of the wheel cylinders or calipers. To bleed the master cylinder, position a shop towel under the primary (rear) outlet fitting and loosen the fitting approximately ¾ turn. Have an assistant depress the brake pedal slowly through it's full travel. Close the outlet fitting and let the pedal return slowly to the fully released position. Wait 5 seconds and then repeat the operation until all air bubbles disappear.

3. Repeat Step 2 with the secondary (front) outlet fitting.

➡On some vehicles, the master cylinder is equipped with a bleeder fitting. In these cases, the master cylinder can be bled in the same manner as a caliper or wheel cylinder. Refer to Bleeding in this Section.

4. Continue to bleed the brake system by removing the rubber dust cap from the wheel cylinder bleeder fitting or caliper fitting at the right-hand rear of the vehicle. Place a suitable box wrench on the bleeder fitting and attach a rubber drain tube to the fitting. The end of the tube should fit snugly around the bleeder fitting. Submerge the other end of the tube in a container partially filled with clean brake fluid and loosen the fitting ¾ turn.

5. Have an assistant push the brake pedal down slowly through it's full travel. Close the bleeder fitting and allow the pedal to slowly return to it's full release position. Wait 5 seconds and repeat the procedure until no bubbles appear at the submerged end of the bleeder tube. Secure the bleeder fitting and remove the bleeder tube. Install the rubber dust cap on the bleeder fitting.

6. Repeat the procedure in Steps 4 and 5 in the following sequence: left rear, right front, left front. Refill the master cylinder reservoir after each wheel cylinder or caliper has been bled and install the master cylinder cover and gasket. When brake bleeding is completed, the fluid level should be filled to the maximum level indicated on the reservoir.

➡Never reuse brake fluid that has been drained from the hydraulic system or has been allowed to stand in an open container for an extended period of time.

7. Always make sure the disc brake pistons are returned to their normal positions by depressing the brake pedal several times until normal pedal travel is established. If the pedal feels spongy, repeat the bleeding procedure.

WITH ABS

Refer to the procedure under Anti-lock Brake System, in this Section.

FRONT DISC BRAKES

Brake Pads

REMOVAL & INSTALLATION

▶ **See Figures 13 thru 19**

1. Remove and discard half the brake fluid from the master cylinder. Properly dispose of the used brake fluid.
2. Raise and safely support vehicle. Remove the front wheel and tire assemblies.
3. Remove the caliper locating pins and remove the caliper from the anchor plate and rotor, but do not disconnect the brake hose.
4. Remove the outer brake pad from the caliper assembly and remove the inner brake pad from the caliper piston.
5. Inspect the disc brake rotor for scoring and wear. Replace or machine, as necessary.
6. Suspend the caliper inside the fender housing with a length of wire. Do not let the caliper hang by the brake hose.

To install:

7. Use a large C-clamp and wood block to push the caliper piston back into its bore.

8. Install new locating pin insulators in the caliper housing, using a fabricated tool as shown in Figure. Check to see if both insulator flanges straddle the housing holes.

➡ **Do not attempt to install the rubber insulators with a sharp edged tool.**

9. Install the inner brake pad in the caliper piston. Be careful not to bend the pad clips in the piston, or distortion and rattles can result.
10. Install the outer brake pad, making sure the clips are properly seated. The outer pads are marked Left-Hand (LH) and Right-Hand (RH) and must be installed in the proper caliper.

➡ **Make sure that the large diameter of the pins are through the outer pad hole to prevent possible binding or bending.**

11. Install the caliper over the rotor with the outer brake pad against the rotor's braking surface. This prevents pinching the piston boot between the inner brake pad and the piston.
12. Lubricate the caliper locating pins and the inside of the locating pin insulators with silicone dielectric grease. Install the caliper locating pins and thread them into the spindle/anchor plate assembly by hand.
13. Tighten the caliper locating pins to 45–65 ft. lbs. (61–88 Nm).
14. Install the wheel and tire assembly. Lower the vehicle.
15. Pump the brake pedal prior to moving the vehicle to seat the brake pads. Refill the master cylinder.
16. Road test the vehicle.

Fig. 13 Front disc brake caliper

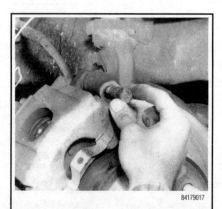

Fig. 14 Removing the caliper locating pin

Fig. 15 Removing the front brake caliper

Fig. 16 Removing the outer brake pad

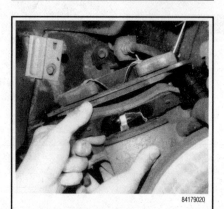

Fig. 17 Removing the inner brake pad

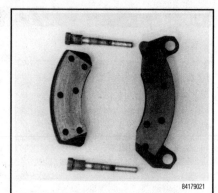

Fig. 18 Inner and outer brake pads and caliper locating pins

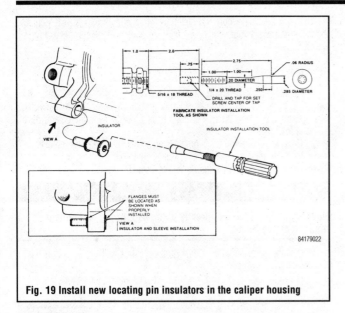

Fig. 19 Install new locating pin insulators in the caliper housing

INSPECTION

▶ **See Figure 20**

Inspect the disc brake pads for oil or grease contamination, abnormal wear or cracking, and for deterioration or damage due to heat. Check the thickness of the pads; the minimum allowable thickness is ⅛ in. Always replace the brake pads in axle sets; never replace just one pad of a brake assembly.

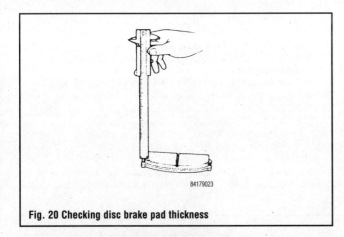

Fig. 20 Checking disc brake pad thickness

Brake Caliper

REMOVAL & INSTALLATION

▶ **See Figure 21**

1. Raise and safely support the vehicle. Remove the front wheel and tire assembly.
2. Loosen the brake line fitting that connects the brake hose to the brake line at the frame bracket. Plug the brake line. Remove the retaining clip from the hose and bracket and disengage the hose from the bracket.
3. Remove the hollow bolt attaching the brake hose to the caliper and remove the brake hose. Discard the sealing washers.
4. Remove the caliper locating pins and remove the caliper. If removing both calipers, mark the right and left sides so they may be reinstalled correctly.
   To install:
5. Install the caliper over the rotor with the outer brake pad against the rotor's braking surface. This prevents pinching the piston boot between the inner brake pad and the piston.

6. Lubricate the locating pins and the inside of the locating pin insulators with silicone dielectric grease. Install the caliper locating pins and thread them into the spindle/anchor plate assembly by hand.
7. Tighten the caliper locating pins to 45–65 ft. lbs. (61–88 Nm).
8. Install new sealing washers on each side of the brake hose fitting outlet and install the hollow bolt, through the hose fitting and into the caliper. Tighten the bolt to 30 ft. lbs. (41 Nm).
9. Position the other end of the brake hose in the bracket and install the retaining clip. Make sure the hose is not twisted.
10. Remove the plug from the brake line, connect the brake line to the brake hose and tighten the fitting nut to 10–18 ft. lbs. (13–24 Nm).
11. Bleed the brake system, install the wheel and tire assembly and lower the vehicle.
12. Apply the brake pedal several times before moving the vehicle, to position the brake pads.
13. Road test the vehicle.

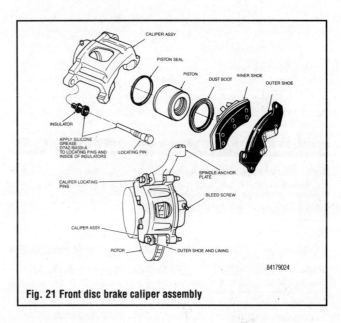

Fig. 21 Front disc brake caliper assembly

OVERHAUL

▶ **See Figures 21, 22 and 23**

Disassembly

1. Remove the front disc brake caliper from the vehicle and place it on a bench.
2. Remove the brake pads from the caliper.
3. Place shop towels between the caliper piston and the caliper bridge to cushion the piston's impact. Using an air nozzle, apply air pressure to the

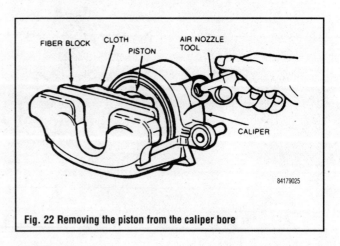

Fig. 22 Removing the piston from the caliper bore

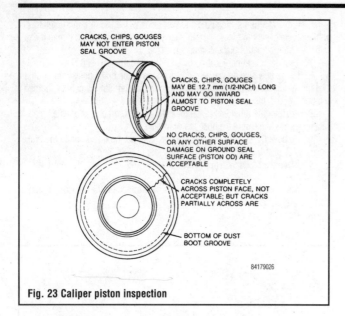

CRACKS, CHIPS, GOUGES MAY NOT ENTER PISTON SEAL GROOVE

CRACKS, CHIPS, GOUGES MAY BE 12.7 mm (1/2-INCH) LONG AND MAY GO INWARD ALMOST TO PISTON SEAL GROOVE

NO CRACKS, CHIPS, GOUGES, OR ANY OTHER SURFACE DAMAGE ON GROUND SEAL SURFACE (PISTON OD) ARE ACCEPTABLE

CRACKS COMPLETELY ACROSS PISTON FACE, NOT ACCEPTABLE; BUT CRACKS PARTIALLY ACROSS ARE

BOTTOM OF DUST BOOT GROOVE

84179026

Fig. 23 Caliper piston inspection

caliper fluid port to blow the piston out of its bore. If the piston is seized and cannot be forced from the caliper, tap lightly around the piston while applying air pressure.

✳✳ CAUTION

Apply only enough air pressure to ease the piston out of the caliper. Excessive pressure can force the piston out of the caliper bore with enough force to cause personal injury. Never attempt to catch the piston by hand as it comes out of the bore.

✳✳ WARNING

Do not use a screwdriver or prybar to pry the piston out of the bore; damage to the piston may result.

  4. Remove the dust boot from the caliper.
  5. Remove and discard the rubber piston seal from the caliper bore.

Cleaning and Inspection

  1. Clean all metal parts with isopropyl alcohol, then clean out and dry the grooves and passageways with compressed air. Make sure the caliper bore and component parts are thoroughly clean.

  2. Check the caliper bore and piston for damage or excessive wear. Replace the piston if it is pitted or scored, or on Police vehicles if the chrome plating is worn off.

Assembly

  1. Apply a film of clean brake fluid to a new caliper piston seal and install it in the caliper bore. Make sure the seal is firmly seated in the groove and not twisted.
  2. Install a new dust boot by setting the flange squarely in the outer groove of the caliper bore.
  3. Coat the piston with brake fluid. Using a C-clamp and a wood block, install the piston into the caliper bore. Make sure the piston is not cocked. Spread the dust boot over the piston as it is installed.

✳✳ WARNING

Never apply the C-clamp directly to the caliper piston; damage to the piston may result.

  4. Seat the dust boot in the piston groove. Make sure the dust boot is tight in the boot groove on the piston.
  5. Install the disc brake pads and install the caliper on the vehicle.

Disc Brake Rotor

REMOVAL & INSTALLATION

1989–91 Vehicles

▶ See Figure 24

  1. Raise and safely support the vehicle.
  2. Remove the wheel and tire assembly.
  3. Remove the caliper from the spindle and rotor, but do not disconnect the brake hose. Suspend the caliper inside the fender housing with a length of wire. Do not let the caliper hang by the brake hose.
  4. Remove the grease cap from the hub and remove the cotter pin, nut retainer and adjusting nut.
  5. Grasp the hub/rotor assembly and pull it out far enough to loosen the washer and outer wheel bearing. Push the hub/rotor assembly back onto the spindle and remove the washer and outer wheel bearing.
  6. Remove the hub/rotor assembly from the spindle.
  7. Inspect the rotor for scoring and wear. Replace or machine as necessary. If machining, observe the minimum thickness specification.
  To install:
  8. If the rotor is being replaced, remove the protective coating from the new rotor with brake cleaner. Pack a new set of bearings with high-temperature

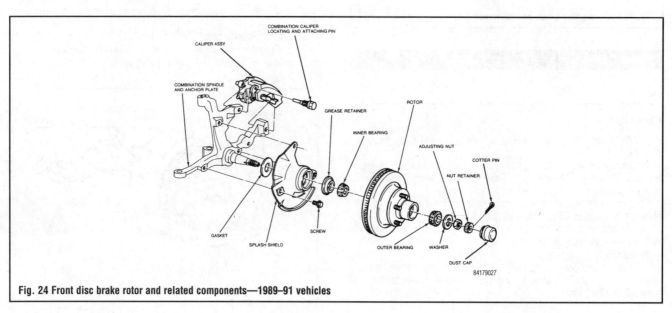

COMBINATION CALIPER LOCATING AND ATTACHING PIN

CALIPER ASSY

COMBINATION SPINDLE AND ANCHOR PLATE

GREASE RETAINER

INNER BEARING

ROTOR

ADJUSTING NUT

COTTER PIN

NUT RETAINER

GASKET

SCREW

SPLASH SHIELD

OUTER BEARING

WASHER

DUST CAP

84179027

Fig. 24 Front disc brake rotor and related components—1989–91 vehicles

wheel bearing grease and install the inner roller bearing in the inner cup. Pack grease lightly between the lips of a new seal and install the seal, using a seal installer.

9. If the original rotor is being installed, make sure the grease in the hub is clean and adequate, the inner bearing and grease seal are lubricated and in good condition, and the rotor braking surfaces are clean.

10. Install the hub/rotor assembly on the spindle. Keep the assembly centered on the spindle to prevent damage to the grease seal or spindle threads.

11. Install the outer wheel bearing, washer and adjusting nut. Adjust the wheel bearings according to the procedure in Section 8, then install the nut retainer, cotter pin and grease cap.

12. Install the caliper and the wheel and tire assembly. Lower the vehicle.

13. Apply the brake pedal several times before moving the vehicle, to position the brake pads.

1992–94 Vehicles

▶ See Figure 25

1. Raise and safely support the vehicle.
2. Remove the wheel and tire assembly.
3. Remove the caliper from the spindle and rotor, but do not disconnect the brake hose. Suspend the caliper inside the fender housing with a length of wire. Do not let the caliper hang by the brake hose.
4. Remove the rotor retaining push nuts, if equipped, and remove the rotor from the hub.
5. Inspect the rotor for scoring and wear. Replace or machine as necessary. If machining, observe the minimum thickness specification.

To install:

6. If the rotor is being replaced, remove the protective coating from the new rotor with brake cleaner. If the original rotor is being installed, make sure the braking surfaces are clean.
7. Install the rotor on the hub.
8. Install the caliper and the wheel and tire assembly. Lower the vehicle.

9. Apply the brake pedal several times before moving the vehicle, to position the brake pads.

INSPECTION

Check the disc brake rotor for scoring, cracks or other damage. Check the minimum thickness and rotor runout.

A brake pulsation that is present during brake application is caused by either foreign material build-up or contamination on the rotor braking surface or uneven rotor thickness. If there is a foreign material build-up or contamination found on the rotor or lining surfaces, hand sand the linings and rotors. Uneven rotor thickness (thickness variation) may be caused by: excessive runout, caliper drag or the abrasive action of the brake lining. If brake pulsation is present, attempt stopping the vehicle with the transmission in the NEUTRAL position. If the pulsation is gone, the drivetrain should be inspected. If the pulsation remains, inspect the brakes.

Check the rotor thickness using a micrometer or calipers. The brake rotor minimum thickness must not be less than 0.972 in. on 1989–91 vehicles or 0.974 in. on 1992–94 vehicles.

Rotor runout can be checked using a dial indicator. Mount the indicator to the spindle or upper control arm and position the indicator foot on the center of the braking surface. Rotate the rotor to check the runout. On 1992–94 vehicles, make sure there is no rust or foreign material between the rotor and hub face. Hold the rotor to the hub by inverting the lugnuts and tightening them to 85–105 ft. lbs. (115–142 Nm). Rotor runout must not exceed 0.003 in.

If rotor runout exceeds specification on 1989–91 vehicles, machine the rotor if it will not be below the minimum thickness specification after machining. On 1992–94 vehicles, the rotor can be repositioned on the hub to obtain the lowest possible runout. If runout remains excessive, remove the rotor and check the hub runout. Replace the hub if hub runout exceeds 0.002 in. If after replacing the hub, rotor runout remains excessive, machine the rotor if it will not be below the minimum thickness specification after machining.

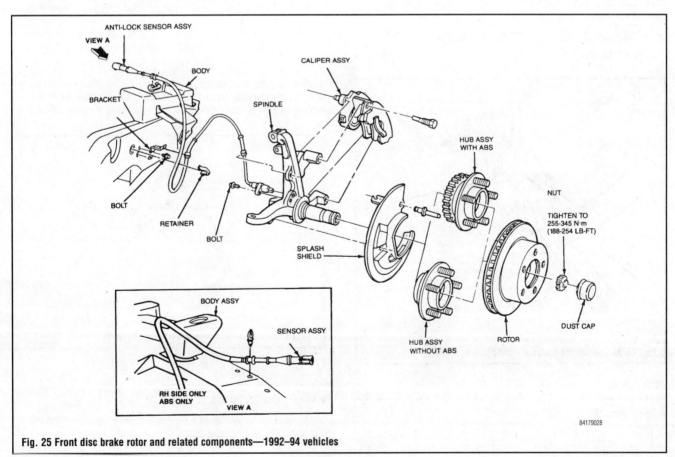

84179028

Fig. 25 Front disc brake rotor and related components—1992–94 vehicles

REAR DRUM BRAKES

✳✳ CAUTION

Brake shoes contain asbestos, which has been determined to be a cancer causing agent. Never clean the brake surfaces with compressed air! Avoid inhaling any dust from any brake surface! When cleaning brake surfaces, use a commercially available brake cleaning fluid.

Brake Drums

REMOVAL & INSTALLATION

♦ **See Figure 26**

1. Raise and safely support the vehicle.
2. Remove the wheel and tire assembly.
3. Remove the drum retaining nuts, if equipped, and remove the brake drum.

➡ **If the drum will not come off, pry the rubber plug from the backing plate. Insert a narrow rod through the hole in the backing plate and disengage the adjusting lever from the adjusting screw. While holding the adjustment lever away from the screw, back off the adjusting screw with a brake adjusting tool. Be careful not damage the notches in the adjusting screw or the self-adjusting mechanism will not function properly.**

4. Inspect the brake drum for scoring and wear. Replace or machine as necessary. If machining, observe the maximum diameter specification.

To install:
5. If a new drum is being installed, remove the protective coating from the drum using brake cleaner. Sand the drum lightly and wipe with a cloth soaked in denatured alcohol.
6. Adjust the brake shoes according to the procedure in this Section.
7. Install the brake drum and the wheel and tire assembly.
8. Lower the vehicle.

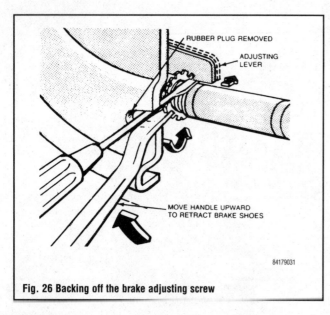

Fig. 26 Backing off the brake adjusting screw

INSPECTION

♦ **See Figure 27**

Clean all grease, brake fluid and other contaminants from the brake drum using brake cleaner. Visually check the drum for scoring, cracks or other damage.

Measure the diameter of the drum using a suitable micrometer. Measure the diameter at various points around the circumference of the drum and at the bot-

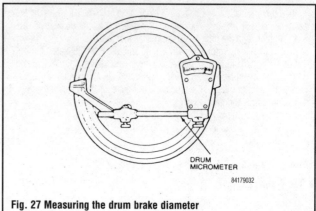

Fig. 27 Measuring the drum brake diameter

tom of the deepest groove, to determine if the drum can be machined or must be replaced.

If the braking surface diameter is worn in excess of the maximum diameter, the drum must be replaced.

Brake Shoes

INSPECTION

♦ **See Figure 28**

Inspect the brake shoes for peeling, cracking or extremely uneven wear on the lining. Check the lining thickness using calipers. If the brake lining is damaged or worn within $\frac{1}{32}$ in. of the rivet heads on riveted linings, the shoes must be replaced. The shoes must also be replaced if the linings are contaminated with brake fluid or grease. Always replace brake shoes in axle sets. Never replace just one shoe of a brake assembly.

Check the condition of the brake shoes, brake springs and drums for signs of overheating. If the shoes have a slight blue coloring, indicating overheating, the brake springs should be replaced. Overheated springs lose their tension and could allow the new shoes to drag and wear prematurely, if not replaced.

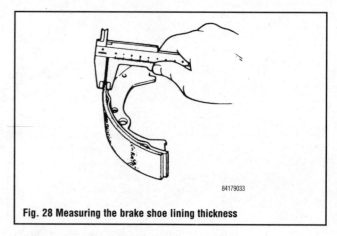

Fig. 28 Measuring the brake shoe lining thickness

REMOVAL & INSTALLATION

♦ **See Figures 29, 30 and 31**

1. Raise and safely support the vehicle. Remove the rear wheel and tire assemblies. Remove the brake drum.
2. Remove the shoe-to-anchor springs and unhook the cable eye from the anchor pin. Remove the anchor pin plate.
3. Remove the shoe hold-down springs, shoes, adjusting screw, pivot nut, socket and automatic adjustment parts.

4. Remove the parking brake link, spring and retainer. Disconnect the parking brake cable from the parking brake lever.

5. After removing the rear brake secondary shoe, disassemble the parking brake lever from the shoe by removing the retaining clip and spring washer.

To install:

6. Before installing the rear brake shoes, assemble the parking brake lever to the secondary shoe and secure it with the spring washer and retaining clip.

7. Apply a light coating of caliper slide grease at the points where the brake shoes contact the backing plate. Be careful not to get any lubricant on the brake linings.

8. Position the brake shoes on the backing plate. The primary shoe with the short lining faces the front of the vehicle, the secondary shoe with the long lining, to the rear. Secure the assembly with the hold-down springs. Install the parking brake link, spring and retainer. Back-off the parking brake adjustment, then connect the parking brake cable to the parking brake lever.

9. Install the anchor pin plate on the anchor pin. Place the cable eye over the anchor pin with the crimped side toward the drum. Install the primary shoe-to-anchor spring.

10. Install the cable guide on the secondary shoe web with the flanged hole fitted into the hole in the secondary shoe web. Thread the cable around the cable guide groove.

➡**The cable must be positioned in the groove and not between the guide and the shoe web.**

11. Install the secondary shoe-to-anchor spring. Make sure the cable eye is not cocked or binding on the anchor pin when installed. All parts should be flat on the anchor pin.

12. Apply a thin coat of lubricant to the threads and the socket end of the adjusting screw. Turn the adjusting screw into the adjusting pivot nut to the limit of the threads, then back-off ½ turn.

➡**Make sure the socket end of the adjusting screw is stamped with an R or L, indicating the right or left side of the vehicle. The adjusting screw assemblies must be installed on the correct side for proper brake shoe adjustment.**

13. Place the adjusting socket on the screw and install the assembly between the shoe ends with the adjusting screw toothed wheel nearest the secondary shoe.

14. Hook the cable hook into the hole in the adjusting lever. The adjusting levers are stamped with an **R** or **L** to indicate their installation on the right or left side.

15. Position the hooked end of the adjuster spring completely into the large hole in the primary shoe web. Connect the loop end of the spring to the adjuster lever hole.

16. Pull the adjuster lever, cable and automatic adjuster spring down and toward the rear, engaging the pivot hook in the large hole of the secondary shoe web.

17. After installation, check the action of the adjuster by pulling the cable between the cable guide and the adjuster lever toward the secondary shoe web, far enough to lift the lever past a tooth on the adjusting screw wheel. The lever should snap into position behind the next tooth, and the release of the cable should cause the adjuster spring to return the lever to its original position. This return action of the lever will turn the adjusting screw one tooth.

18. If pulling the cable does not produce the action described in Step 17, or if the lever action is sluggish instead of positive and sharp, check the position of the lever on the adjusting screw toothed wheel.

19. With the brake in a vertical position (anchor at the top), the lever should contact the adjusting wheel 3/16 in. plus or minus 1/32 in. above the centerline of the screw. If the contact point is below this centerline, the lever will not lock on the teeth in the adjusting screw wheel, and the screw will not be turned.

20. Adjust the brake shoes as explained in this Section, then proceed as follows to determine the cause of this condition:

    a. Make sure that the upper or anchor pin end of the cable is pulled toward the cable guide as far as possible and that the end fitting is pointing toward the cable guide.

    b. Check the cable end fittings. The cable should completely fill or extend slightly beyond the crimped section of the fittings. If it does not meet this specification, possible damage is indicated and the cable assembly should be replaced.

    c. Check the cable length. Measure from the inside edge of the hook to the far edge of the anchor hole. The cable length for 11 in. brakes is 11 1/8 in. plus or minus 1/64 in.

    d. Check the cable guide for damage. The cable groove should be parallel to the shoe web, and the body of the guide should lie flat against the web. Replace the guide if it shows damage.

    e. Check the pivot hook on the lever. The hook surfaces should be square with the body of the lever for proper pivoting. Replace the lever if the hook shows damage.

    f. Make sure that the adjusting screw socket is properly seated in the notch in the shoe web.

21. Make sure the upper ends of the brake shoes are seated against the anchor pin and the shoes are centered on the backing plate. If they are not

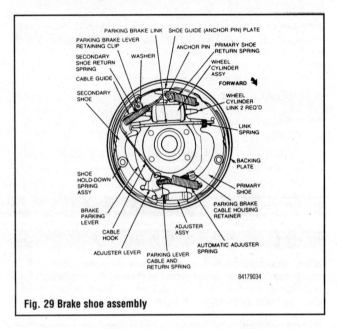

Fig. 29 Brake shoe assembly

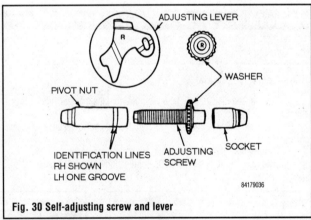

Fig. 30 Self-adjusting screw and lever

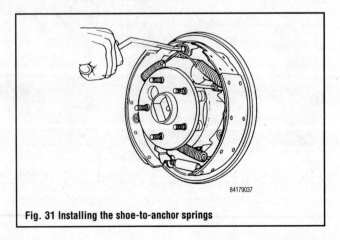

Fig. 31 Installing the shoe-to-anchor springs

seated, back-off the parking brake system adjustment to obtain 0.005–0.025 in. play after overcoming the load of the parking brake link spring.

➡**Whenever the brake shoes are removed, the parking brake cable adjustment should be checked.**

22. Make sure the brake shoes are properly adjusted, then install the brake drum and wheel and tire assemblies and lower the vehicle.

23. Apply the brakes several times while backing up the vehicle. After each stop, the vehicle must be moved forward.

24. Check brake operation by making several stops from varying forward speeds.

Wheel Cylinders

INSPECTION

Carefully pull the lower edges of the wheel cylinder boots away from the cylinders to see if the interior of the cylinder is wet with brake fluid. Excessive fluid at this point indicates leakage past the piston cups and a need for wheel cylinder replacement.

➡**A slight amount of fluid is nearly always present and acts as a lubricant for the piston.**

REAR DISC BRAKES

✳✳ CAUTION

Brake pads contain asbestos, which has been determined to be a cancer causing agent. Never clean the brake surfaces with compressed air! Avoid inhaling any dust from any brake surface! When cleaning brake surfaces, use a commercially available brake cleaning fluid.

Brake Pads

REMOVAL & INSTALLATION

▸ **See Figures 32, 33 and 34**

1. Remove and discard half the brake fluid from the master cylinder. Properly dispose of the used brake fluid.

2. Raise and safely support vehicle. Remove the rear wheel and tire assemblies.

3. Remove the caliper locating pins. Lift the caliper off the rotor and anchor plate using a rotating motion. Do not disconnect the brake hose.

REMOVAL & INSTALLATION

1. Raise and safely support the vehicle.

2. Remove the wheel and tire assembly and the brake drum.

3. Remove the brake shoe assembly.

4. Disconnect the brake line from the wheel cylinder at the backing plate. The line will separate from the wheel cylinder when the wheel cylinder is removed from the backing plate.

5. Remove the wheel cylinder attaching bolts and remove the wheel cylinder.

➡**Be careful to prevent brake fluid from contacting the brake shoe linings or they must be replaced.**

To install:

6. Wipe the end of the brake line to remove any foreign matter before making connections.

7. Position the wheel cylinder on the backing plate and finger-tighten the brake line to the wheel cylinder.

8. Install the wheel cylinder attaching bolts and tighten to 10–20 ft. lbs. (14–28 Nm).

9. Tighten the brake line fitting nut to 10–18 ft. lbs. (13–24 Nm).

10. Install the links in the ends of the wheel cylinder and install the brake shoe assembly.

11. Adjust the brakes and install the brake drum. Bleed the brake system.

12. Install the wheel and tire assembly and lower the vehicle.

✳✳ WARNING

Do not pry directly against the plastic piston or damage to the piston will occur.

4. Remove the inner and outer brake pads.

5. Inspect the disc brake rotor for scoring and wear. Replace or machine, as necessary.

6. Suspend the caliper inside the fender housing with a length of wire. Do not let the caliper hang by the brake hose.

To install:

7. Use a large C-clamp and wood block to push the caliper piston back into its bore.

✳✳ WARNING

Never apply the C-clamp directly to the plastic caliper piston; damage to the piston may result.

8. Remove all rust buildup from the inside of the caliper legs (outer pad contact area).

84179039
Fig. 32 Rear disc brake assembly

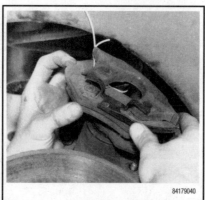
84179040
Fig. 33 Removing the outer brake pad

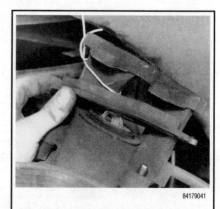
84179041
Fig. 34 Removing the inner brake pad

9. Install the inner brake pad, then the outer brake pad, making sure the clips are properly seated.

10. Position the caliper above the rotor with the anti-rattle spring located on the lower adapter support arm. Install the caliper over the rotor with a rotating motion. Make sure the inner pad is properly positioned.

11. Insert the caliper locating pins and thread them in by hand. Tighten them to 19–26 ft. lbs. (26–35 Nm).

12. Install the wheel and tire assembly and lower the vehicle.

13. Pump the brake pedal prior to moving the vehicle to seat the brake pads. Refill the master cylinder.

14. Road test the vehicle.

INSPECTION

▶ See Figure 35

Inspect the disc brake pads for oil or grease contamination, abnormal wear or cracking, and for deterioration or damage due to heat. Check the thickness of the pads; the minimum allowable thickness is 0.123 in. Always replace the brake pads in axle sets; never replace just one pad of a brake assembly.

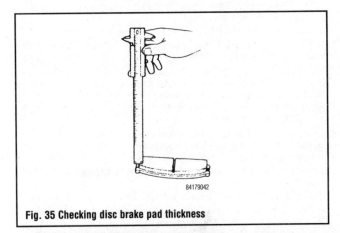

Fig. 35 Checking disc brake pad thickness

Brake Caliper

REMOVAL & INSTALLATION

▶ See Figures 36 and 37

1. Raise and safely support the vehicle. Remove the rear wheel and tire assembly.

2. Remove the brake fitting retaining bolt from the caliper and disconnect the flexible brake hose from the caliper. Plug the hose and the caliper fitting.

3. Remove the caliper locating pins. Lift the caliper off the rotor and anchor plate using a rotating motion.

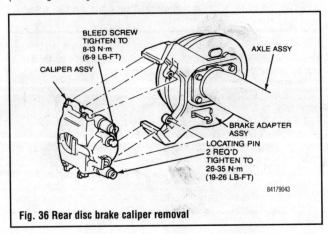

Fig. 36 Rear disc brake caliper removal

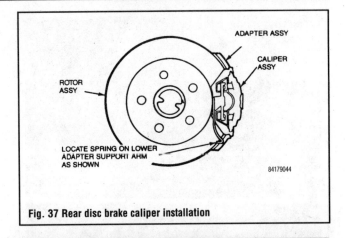

Fig. 37 Rear disc brake caliper installation

✱✱ WARNING

Do not pry directly against the plastic piston or damage to the piston will occur.

To install:

4. Position the caliper assembly above the rotor with the anti-rattle spring located on the lower adapter support arm. Install the caliper over the rotor with a rotating motion. Make sure the inner pad is properly positioned.

5. Install the caliper locating pins and start them in the threads by hand. Tighten them to 19–26 ft. lbs. (26–35 Nm).

6. Install the brake hose on the caliper with a new gasket on each side of the fitting outlet. Insert the retaining bolt and tighten to 30–40 ft. lbs. (40–54 Nm).

7. Bleed the brake system, install the wheel and tire assembly and lower the vehicle.

8. Pump the brake pedal prior to moving the vehicle to position the linings.

9. Road test the vehicle.

OVERHAUL

The rear disc brake calipers are overhauled using the same procedure as the front disc brake calipers. For details, please refer to that procedure located earlier in this section.

Disc Brake Rotor

REMOVAL & INSTALLATION

▶ See Figures 38, 39 and 40

1. Raise and safely support the vehicle. Remove the wheel and tire assembly.

2. Remove the caliper, but do not disconnect the brake hose. Suspend the caliper inside the fender housing with a length of wire. Do not let the caliper hang by the brake hose.

3. Remove the rotor retaining push nuts and remove the rotor from the hub.

➡If additional force is required to remove the rotor, apply penetrating oil to the rotor/flange mating surface. Install a suitable 3-jaw puller and remove the rotor. If excessive force must be used during rotor removal, the rotor should be checked for lateral runout before reinstallation.

4. Inspect the rotor for scoring and wear. Replace or machine as necessary. If machining, observe the minimum thickness specification.
   To install:

5. If the rotor is being replaced, remove the protective coating from the new rotor with brake cleaner. If the original rotor is being installed, make sure the rotor braking and mounting surfaces are clean.

6. Install the rotor. The pushnuts do not have to be reinstalled.

7. Install the caliper and the wheel and tire assembly. Lower the vehicle.

8. Pump the brake pedal to position the brake pads, before moving the vehicle.

9. Road test the vehicle.

Fig. 38 Suspend the caliper inside the fender housing with a length of wire; do not let the caliper hang by the brake hose

Fig. 39 Removing the push nuts

Fig. 40 Removing the rear disc brake rotor

INSPECTION

Check the disc brake rotor for scoring, cracks or other damage. Check the minimum thickness and rotor runout.

A brake pulsation that is present during brake application is caused by either foreign material build-up or contamination on the rotor braking surface or uneven rotor thickness. If there is a foreign material build-up or contamination found on the rotor or lining surfaces, hand sand the linings and rotors. Uneven rotor thickness (thickness variation) may be caused by: excessive runout, caliper drag or the abrasive action of the brake lining. If brake pulsation is present, attempt stopping the vehicle with the transmission in the NEUTRAL position. If the pulsation is gone, the drivetrain should be inspected. If the pulsation remains, inspect the brakes.

Check the rotor thickness using a micrometer or calipers. The brake rotor minimum thickness must not be less than 0.44 in.

Rotor runout can be checked using a dial indicator. Mount the indicator to the brake adapter and position the indicator foot on the center of the braking surface. Rotate the rotor to check the runout. Make sure there is no rust or foreign material between the rotor and axle flange. Hold the rotor to the axle flange by inverting the lugnuts and tightening them to 85–105 ft. lbs. (115–142 Nm). Rotor runout must not exceed 0.003 in.

If rotor runout exceeds specification, the rotor can be repositioned on the axle flange to obtain the lowest possible runout. If runout remains excessive, machine the rotor if it will not be below the minimum thickness specification after machining.

PARKING BRAKE

Cables

♦ See Figure 41

REMOVAL & INSTALLATION

Front Cable

♦ See Figures 42, 43 and 44

1. Raise and safely support the vehicle. On 1989 vehicles, loosen the adjusting nut at the adjuster.
2. Disconnect the cable from the intermediate for 1989 or rear for 1990–94 cable connector located along the left side frame rail.
3. Use a 13mm box end wrench to depress the retaining tabs and remove the conduit retainer from the frame. Remove screw holding the plastic inner fender apron to the frame, at the rear of the fender panel.
4. Pull back the fender apron. If equipped, remove the spring clip retainer that holds the parking brake cable to the frame.
5. Pull the cable through the frame and let it hang in the wheel housing. Lower the vehicle.
6. Inside the passenger compartment, remove the sound deadener cover from the cable at the dash panel.
7. On 1989 vehicles, remove the spring retainer and cable end from the clevis at the parking brake control.

8. On 1990–94 vehicles, pull the cable until the parking brake control take up spring tang is at full clockwise position. Fabricate a tool from metal of the dimensions shown in the illustration, then use it to retain the reel spring and disconnect the cable from the take up reel.

✳✳ CAUTION

Keep fingers away from the reel mechanism while the fabricated tool is in place.

9. Using a 13mm box end wrench, depress the retaining tabs and remove the conduit from the control assembly. Push the cable down through the dash panel and remove cable from inside the wheel housing.
To install:
10. Start the cable through the opening in the dash panel inside the passenger compartment.
11. On 1989 vehicles, connect the end of the cable to the parking brake control clevis and secure it with a spring clip. On 1990–94 vehicles, connect the end of the cable to the parking brake control take up reel.
12. Press the tabbed conduit retainer into the parking brake control and install the sound deadener cover patch at the dash panel.
13. Raise and safely support the vehicle. Insert the cable through the frame member toward the rear of the vehicle. Press the tabbed conduit retainer into the frame hole.

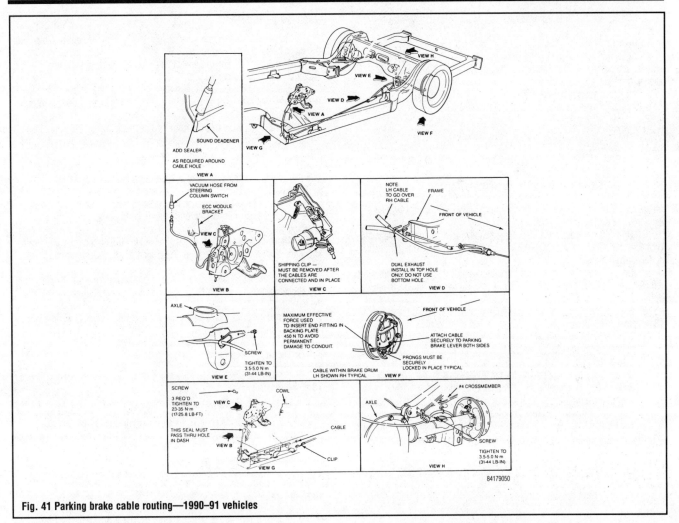

Fig. 41 Parking brake cable routing—1990–91 vehicles

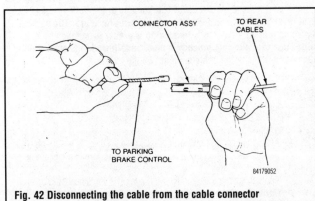

Fig. 42 Disconnecting the cable from the cable connector

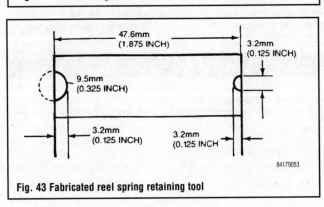

Fig. 43 Fabricated reel spring retaining tool

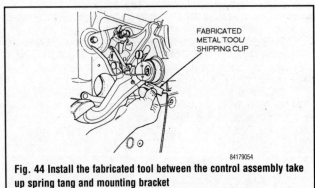

Fig. 44 Install the fabricated tool between the control assembly take up spring tang and mounting bracket

14. On 1989 vehicles, install the cable-to-frame spring clip retainer behind the fender apron and connect the front cable to the intermediate cable connector on the left side frame rail.

15. On 1990–94 vehicles, connect the control cable to the rear cable connector on the left side frame rail and use pliers to remove the fabricated tool used to retain the take up reel.

16. Lower the vehicle. On 1989 vehicles, adjust the parking brake. On 1990–94 vehicles, check parking brake operation.

Intermediate Cable

1989 VEHICLES

1. Raise and safely support the vehicle. Loosen the cable adjusting nut.
2. Disconnect the parking brake release spring at the frame.

3. Disconnect the cable from the cable connectors and remove it from the vehicle.

To install:

4. Attach the intermediate cable to the front and rear cable connectors. Make sure the rearward end of the cable goes through the release spring before attaching the cable to the connector.

5. Attach the release spring to the frame.

6. Adjust the parking brake and lower the vehicle.

Rear Cables

1989–91 VEHICLES

1. Raise and safely support the vehicle. On 1990–91 vehicles, disconnect the control cable from the rear cable at the connector.

2. On 1989 vehicles, disconnect the parking brake release spring at the frame. On 1990–91 vehicles with dual exhaust, disconnect the parking brake cable retainer spring at the frame.

3. On 1989 vehicles, disconnect the left cable from the intermediate cable connector. On 1990–91 vehicles, disconnect the left cable from the right cable at the adjuster bracket.

4. On 1989 vehicles, use a 13mm box end wrench to depress the tabs and remove the left conduit retainer from the rod adjuster. Remove the cable retainer from the left lower arm.

5. Release the right cable tabbed conduit retainer from the frame, using a 13mm box end wrench.

6. On 1989 vehicles, remove the clip retaining the right cable to the frame crossmember. Remove the cable retainer from the right lower arm and disconnect the cable from the retainer on the right upper arm.

7. On 1990–91 vehicles, remove the cable retainer from the left shock bracket and disconnect the cable from the retainer on the crossmember and upper control arm clip.

8. Remove the wheel and tire assemblies and the brake drums.

9. Working on the wheel side of the rear brake, remove the brake automatic adjuster spring. Compress the prongs on the parking brake cable so they can pass through the hole in the backing plate. Pull the cable retainer through the hole.

10. With the tension off the cable spring at the parking brake lever, lift the cable end out of the slot in the lever. Remove the cable through the backing plate hole.

To install:

11. Position the cables approximately in their installed position. Insert enough of the parking brake cable through the backing plate hole, so the cable end can be attached to the parking brake lever on the rear brake shoe.

12. Pull the excess slack from the cable wire inside the brake, and push the cable conduit through the backing plate hole until the retainer prongs expand. The prongs must be securely locked in place. Install the automatic brake adjuster spring.

13. Install the brake drums and wheel and tire assemblies.

14. On 1989 vehicles, attach the right cable to the right upper and lower arms, frame crossmember and through the frame bracket using the existing retaining clips. Press the tabbed retainer into the crossmember hole until it is securely locked into place.

15. On 1990–91 vehicles, attach the right cable to the crossmember retainer hook and through the upper control arm clip. Press the tabbed retainer into the crossmember hole until it is securely locked into place.

16. On 1989 vehicles, attach the left cable to the left lower arm with the retainer, and route the cable toward the front of the vehicle. Be sure to route the cable over the right cable. Install the left cable through the flanged hole in the adjuster and press the tabbed retainer into place.

17. On 1990–91 vehicles, attach the left cable to the drum backing plate and route the cable toward the front of the vehicle under the right cable between the stabilizer bar stud and shock. Connect the right cable end to the equalizer bracket (part of the left cable).

18. On 1989 vehicles, connect the left cable end to the connector at the intermediate cable. Insert the threaded rod of the right cable through the 2 holes in the adjuster. Loosely attach the adjuster nut.

19. On 1989 vehicles, install the cable release springs to the frame attaching hole and adjust the parking brake. On 1990–91 vehicles, connect the rear cable connector to the control cable.

20. Lower the vehicle. On 1990–91 vehicles, check the operation of the parking brake control.

1992–94 VEHICLES

1. Raise and safely support the vehicle. Disconnect the control cable from the rear cable at the connector.

2. Disconnect the parking brake cable retainer spring at the frame, if equipped with dual exhaust.

3. Disconnect the left cable from the right cable at the adjuster bracket. Release the right cable tabbed conduit retainer from the frame, using a 13mm box end wrench.

4. Remove the cable retainer from the left shock bracket, the wire retainer on the left axle bracket and disconnect the cable from the retainer on the right axle tube by removing the bolt and retainer.

5. Remove the cable retaining E-clip and cable eyelet from the brake lever. Pull the cable out of the disc brake adapter boss. Remove the cables.

To install:

6. Insert the brake cable through the mounting boss and connect it to the lever.

7. Push the cable conduit through the mounting boss and install the retaining clip.

8. Attach the right cable to the axle retaining clip, through the wire retainer and left shock absorber plastic loop. Press the tabbed retainer into the crossmember hole until locked into place.

9. Route the left cable under the right cable between the stabilizer bar stud and shock absorber. Connect the right cable end to the equalizer bracket (part of the left cable).

10. Connect the rear cable connector to the control cable. Lower the vehicle and check parking brake operation.

ADJUSTMENT

1989 Vehicles

1. Make sure the parking brake is fully released.

2. Place the transmission in **N**. Raise and safely support the vehicle.

3. Tighten the adjusting nut against the cable equalizer, causing a rear wheel brake drag. Loosen the adjusting nut until the rear brakes are fully released. There should be no brake drag.

4. Lower the vehicle and check the operation of the parking brake.

1990–94 Vehicles

➡**The following procedure is to be used only if a new parking brake control assembly is installed. All components of the parking brake system must be installed prior to the adjustment procedure. The parking brake control with automatic tensioning is preset by means of a shipping clip. The following procedure must be followed in sequence and must be done with the vehicle weight on the axle.**

1. Verify removal of the shipping clip. The take up reel will apply tension to the system.

2. Depress the parking brake control to the 8th notch.

3. Push the parking brake control pedal to release.

4. Check function as follows:

   a. Apply the parking brake with a full stroke, to the 9th or 10th notch.

   b. Release the parking brake by shifting the vehicle into a forward gear with the engine running. The control must release.

   c. Apply the parking brake with a full stroke, to the 9th or 10th notch.

   d. Manually release the parking brake with the push to release feature.

➡**With the control in the OFF position, the rear brakes must not drag. Check for movement of the rear cables from their conduits when the intermediate cable is deflected with a force of 10–15 lbs.**

Brake Shoes

REMOVAL & INSTALLATION

1992–94 Vehicles

▶ **See Figures 45 and 46**

1. Raise and safely support the vehicle.

2. Remove the rear axle shaft; refer to Section 7.

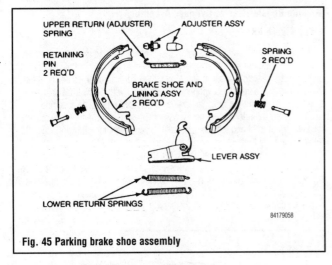

Fig. 45 Parking brake shoe assembly

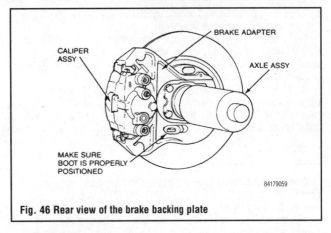

Fig. 46 Rear view of the brake backing plate

3. Disconnect the brake cable from the lever.

4. Remove the brake shoe retaining springs and pins.

5. Set the adjuster assembly to the shortest length. Pull the shoes away from the backing plate slightly and spread them enough to remove the adjuster assembly.

6. Remove the upper return (adjuster) spring.

7. Lift the shoes over the support and remove the shoes and actuating lever as an assembly. Make sure the lever does not damage the boot or pull the boot out of position.

8. Disassemble the shoes, lever and springs.

To install:

9. Install the lower return springs and actuating lever to the brake shoes.

10. Make sure the boot is properly positioned in the backing plate. Install the shoes by first inserting the lever through the boot, then lowering the shoes into position.

11. Install the upper return (adjuster) spring and install the adjuster assembly.

12. Install the brake shoe retaining springs and pins.

13. Connect the brake cable to the lever.

14. Install the rear axle shaft.

15. Center the brake shoes on the backing plate. Using an 8 in. micrometer or calipers, gauge the brake shoes to the dimensions shown in Fig. 60.

ANTI-LOCK BRAKE SYSTEM

General Description

♦ **See Figure 47**

The Anti-lock Brake System (ABS) with Traction Assist (TA) prevents wheel lockup by automatically modulating the brake pressure during an emergency stop. Each brake is controlled separately. The brake pedal force required to engage the anti-lock function may vary with the road surface conditions. A dry surface requires a higher force, while a slippery surface requires much less force.

During ABS operation, the driver will feel a pulsation in the brake pedal, accompanied by a slight up and down movement in the pedal height and a

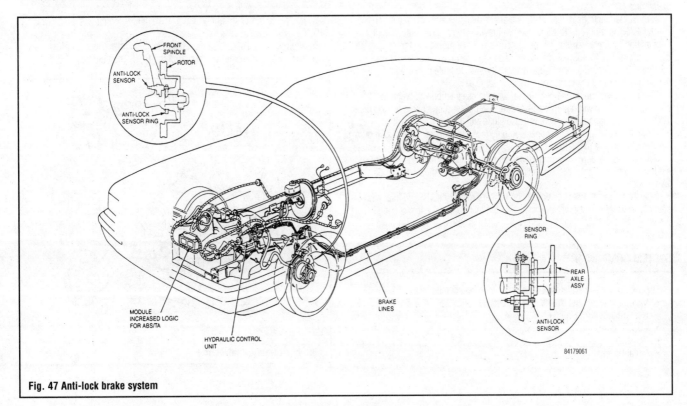

Fig. 47 Anti-lock brake system

clicking sound. The pedal effort and feel during non-ABS braking are similar to that of a conventional power brake system.

The TA system senses wheel spin upon acceleration, turns on the Hydraulic Control Unit (HCU) pump and applies fluid pressure to the appropriate rear wheel. Two additional isolation valves in the HCU will also close to permit fluid to flow only to the rear wheels.

The TA system will only function up to 25 mph. The system also monitors TA usage to avoid overheating the rear brakes. If the system does sense brake overheating, the ABS module will inhibit TA operation until the rear brakes are permitted to cool down.

SYSTEM OPERATION

When the brakes are applied, fluid is forced from the master cylinder outlet ports to the Hydraulic Control Unit (HCU) inlet ports. This pressure is transmitted through 4 normally open solenoid valves contained inside the HCU, then through the outlet ports of the HCU to each wheel. The primary (rear) circuit of the master cylinder feeds the right front and left rear brakes. The secondary (front) circuit of the master cylinder feeds the left front and right rear brakes. If the ABS module senses that a wheel is about to lock, based on wheel speed sensor data, it pulses the normally open solenoid valve to close, for that circuit. This prevents any more fluid from entering that circuit. The ABS module then looks at the sensor signal from the affected wheel again. If that wheel is still decelerating, it opens the normally closed solenoid valve for that circuit. This dumps any pressure that is trapped between the normally open valve and the caliper back to the reservoir. Once the affected wheel comes back up to speed, the ABS module returns the valves to their normal condition allowing fluid flow to the affected brake.

The ABS module monitors the electromechanical components of the system. Malfunction of the anti-lock brake system will cause the ABS module to shut off or inhibit the system. However, normal power assisted braking remains. Malfunctions are indicated by 1 or 2 warning lamps inside the vehicle. Hydraulic fluid loss in the HCU reservoir will also disable the anti-lock system.

The 4 wheel anti-lock brake system is self monitoring. When the ignition switch is placed in the **RUN** position, the ABS module will perform a preliminary self-check on the anti-lock electrical system indicated by a 3–4 second illumination of the amber CHECK ANTI-LOCK BRAKE lamp in the instrument cluster. During vehicle operation, including normal and anti-lock braking, the ABS module monitors all electrical anti-lock functions and some hydraulic operations.

In most malfunctions of the anti-lock brake system, the amber CHECK ANTI-LOCK BRAKE and/or red BRAKE lamp(s) will be illuminated. The sequence of illumination for these warning lamps combined with the problem symptoms, can determine the appropriate diagnostic tests to perform. However, most malfunctions are recorded as a coded number in the ABS module memory and assist in pinpointing the component needing service.

During acceleration, if one or both rear wheels lose traction and begin to spin, the TA system will rapidly apply and release the appropriate rear brake(s). The accompanying isolation valve will also close and the ABS pump will run. The isolation valve allows brake operation only to the rear brake of the circuit by closing off pressure to the front brake.

If the brakes are applied during TA operation, the ABS module receives a signal from the brake light switch or the pressure switch and automatically stops TA cycling.

If the TA system is used continually on slippery roads, the ABS module may shut off the system to prevent overheating of the rear brakes. System cycling is monitored by the ABS module and the information is stored in the keep-alive memory.

SYSTEM COMPONENTS

The anti-lock brake system consists of the following components:
- Vacuum booster and master cylinder assembly
- Hydraulic Control Unit (HCU)
- ABS module
- Wheel sensors
- Pedal travel switch

Vacuum Booster/Master Cylinder Assembly

◆ See Figure 48

The diaphragm-type brake booster is self-contained and is mounted on the engine compartment side of the dash panel. The vacuum brake booster uses engine intake manifold vacuum and atmospheric pressure for it's power. If the brake booster is damaged or inoperative, replace it with a new booster. The brake booster, excluding the check valve, is serviced only as an assembly.

The master cylinder is a tandem master cylinder. The primary (rear) circuit feeds the right front and left rear brakes. The secondary circuit (front) feeds the left front and right rear brakes. It is serviced as a complete assembly.

The master cylinder reservoir is a clear translucent plastic container with 3 main chambers. An integral fluid level switch is part of the reservoir cap assembly, with 1 electrical connector pointing rearward for wire harness connection. A low pressure hose is attached to the reservoir which feeds brake fluid to the hydraulic control unit reservoir. The reservoir and cap are serviced separately.

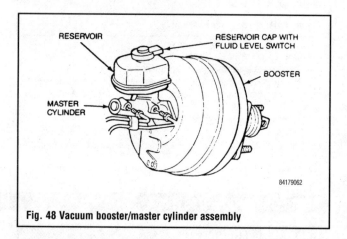

Fig. 48 Vacuum booster/master cylinder assembly

Hydraulic Control Unit

◆ See Figures 49 and 50

The Hydraulic Control Unit (HCU) is located in the front of the engine compartment on the left side below the air cleaner. The HCU consists of a valve body, pump and motor assembly, and a brake fluid reservoir with fluid level indicator.

During normal braking, fluid from the master cylinder enters the HCU through 2 inlet ports located at the rear of the HCU. The fluid then passes

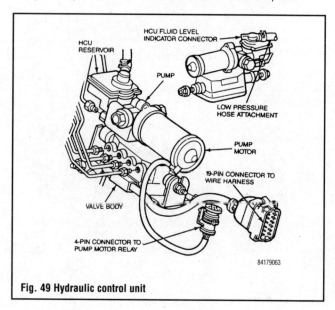

Fig. 49 Hydraulic control unit

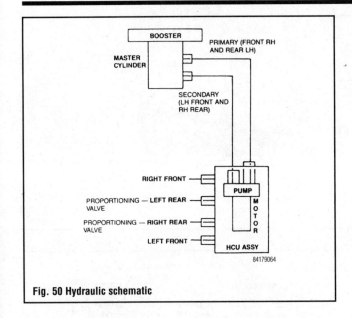

Fig. 50 Hydraulic schematic

through 4 normally open inlet valves, one to each wheel. If the ABS module senses that a wheel is about to lock, the ABS module pulses the appropriate inlet valve which closes that valve. This prevents any more fluid from entering the affected brake. The ABS module then looks at that wheel again. If it is still decelerating, the ABS module opens the normally closed outlet valve which decreases the pressure trapped in the line.

The traction assist valve body contains 2 isolation valves for Traction Assist (TA) function, one for the primary circuit and one for the secondary circuit. The isolation valves close during traction assist operation to prevent front brake application.

The valve body, pump and motor, and reservoir are serviced separately. Other than seals and gaskets, no internal parts can be serviced.

ABS Module

♦ **See Figure 51**

The ABS module is located in the engine compartment on a bracket that is attached to the radiator support.

The ABS module is an on-board, self-test, non-repairable unit consisting of 2 microprocessors and the necessary circuitry for their operation. These microprocessors are programmed identically. The ABS module monitors system operation during normal driving as well as during anti-lock braking and traction assist cycling.

Under normal driving conditions, the microprocessors produce short test pulses to the solenoid valves that check the electrical system without any mechanical reaction. Impending wheel lock conditions trigger signals from the ABS module that open and close the appropriate solenoid valves. This results

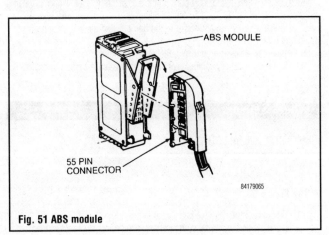

Fig. 51 ABS module

in moderate pulsations in the brake pedal. If brake pedal travel exceeds a preset dimension determined by the pedal travel switch setting, the ABS module will send a signal to the pump to turn on and provide high pressure to the brake system. When the pump starts to run, a gradual rise in pedal height will be noticed. This rise will continue until the pedal travel switch closes and the pump will shut off until the pedal travel exceeds the travel switch setting again. During normal braking, the brake pedal feel will be identical to a standard brake system.

During traction assist operation, the ABS module will close the appropriate isolation valves and operate the pump. If the brakes are applied during cycling, the system will automatically shut off. The ABS module monitors traction assist usage and will shut off the traction assist features to prevent overheating of the rear brakes. If the system shuts off, there is a cool down period required before it becomes functional again. This cool down period varies depending on brake usage during the cool down period. Anti-lock braking is still fully functional during the cool down period.

Most malfunctions which occur to the anti-lock brake system and the traction assist will be stored as a coded number in the keep-alive memory of the ABS module. The codes can be retrieved by following the on-board self-test procedures.

Pedal Travel Switch

The pedal travel switch monitors brake pedal travel and sends this information to the ABS module through the wire harness. The switch adjustment is critical to pedal feel during ABS cycling.

The switch is mounted to the dump valve adapter bracket and to the ABS adapter bracket mounted inside the brake pedal support.

The switch is normally closed. When brake pedal travel exceeds the switch setting during an anti-lock stop, the electronic controller senses that the switch is open and grounds the pump motor relay coil. This energizes the relay and turns the pump motor ON. When the pump motor is running, the master cylinder is filled with high pressure brake fluid and the brake pedal will be pushed up until the switch closes. When the switch closes, the pump is turned OFF and the pedal will drop some with each ABS control cycle until the travel switch opens again and the pump is turned ON. This minimizes pedal feedback during ABS cycling.

If the pedal travel switch is not adjusted properly or is not electrically connected, it will result in objectionable pedal feel during ABS stops. Most problems with the switch or its installation will result in the pump running during the entire ABS stop. The pedal will become very firm, pushing the driver's foot up to an unusually high position.

Wheel Sensors

♦ **See Figure 52**

The anti-lock brake system uses 4 sets of variable-reluctance sensors and toothed speed indicator rings to determine the rotational speed of each wheel. The sensors operate on the magnetic induction principal. As the teeth on the speed indicator ring rotate past the stationary sensor, a signal proportional to the speed of the rotation is generated and sent to the ABS module through a coaxial cable and shielded wiring harness.

The front sensors are attached to the suspension knuckles and the speed indicator rings are pressed onto the front hubs. The rear sensors are attached to the rear brake adapters and the speed indicator rings are pressed onto the rear axle shafts.

ABS Module

REMOVAL & INSTALLATION

♦ **See Figure 53**

1. Disconnect the negative battery cable.
2. Locate the ABS module at the left front side of the radiator support.
3. Disconnect the 55-pin connector from the ABS module. Unlock the connector by pulling up the lever completely. Move the end of the connector away from the ABS module until all terminals are clear, then pull the connector up and out of the slots in the ABS module.

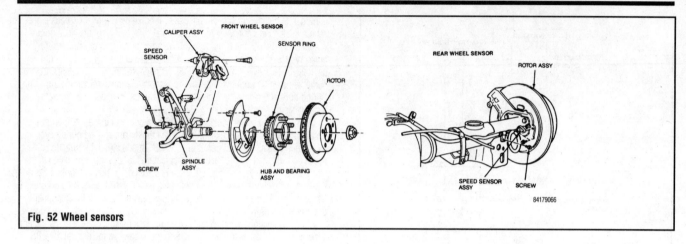

Fig. 52 Wheel sensors

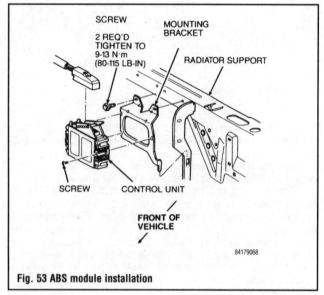

Fig. 53 ABS module installation

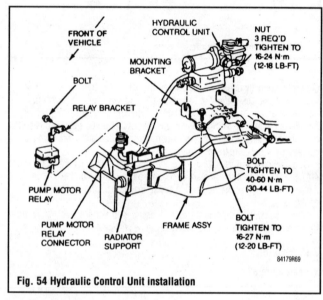

Fig. 54 Hydraulic Control Unit installation

4. Remove the 3 screws attaching the ABS module to the mounting bracket and remove the ABS module.

To install:

5. Align the ABS module with the bracket so that the lever is facing the drivers side of the vehicle. If all 3 mounting holes in the ABS module do not line up with the holes in the mounting bracket, the ABS module is incorrectly aligned with the bracket. Install the 3 attaching screws and tighten to 40–60 inch lbs. (4.5–6.8 Nm).

6. Connect the 55-pin connector by installing the bottom part of the connector into the slots in the ABS module and pushing the top portion of the connector into the ABS module. Then, pull the locking lever completely down to ensure proper installation.

7. Connect the negative battery cable.

Hydraulic Control Unit (HCU)

REMOVAL & INSTALLATION

♦ **See Figure 54**

1. Disconnect the negative battery cable and remove the air cleaner and air outlet tube.

2. Disconnect the 19-pin connector from the HCU to the wire harness and disconnect the 4-pin connector from the HCU to the pump motor relay.

3. Remove the 2 lines from the inlet ports and the 4 lines from the outlet ports of the HCU. Plug each port to prevent brake fluid from spilling onto the paint and wiring.

4. Remove the 3 nuts retaining the HCU assembly to the mounting bracket and remove the assembly from the vehicle.

➡**The nut on the front of the HCU also retains the relay mounting bracket.**

To install:

5. Position the HCU assembly into the mounting bracket. Install the 3 retaining nuts and tighten to 12–18 ft. lbs. (16–24 Nm). Make sure the ABS pump motor relay bracket is retained by the front bracket nut.

6. Connect 4 lines to the outlet ports on the side of the HCU and 2 lines to the inlet ports on the rear of the HCU and tighten the fittings to 10–18 ft. lbs. (14–24 Nm).

7. Connect the 19-pin connector to the harness and the 4-pin connector to the pump motor relay.

8. Install the air cleaner and air outlet tube.

9. Connect the battery cables, properly bleed the brake system and check for fluid leaks.

Wheel Sensors

REMOVAL & INSTALLATION

Front

♦ **See Figure 55**

1. Disconnect the negative battery cable.

2. From inside the engine compartment, disconnect the sensor assembly 2-pin connector from the wiring harness.

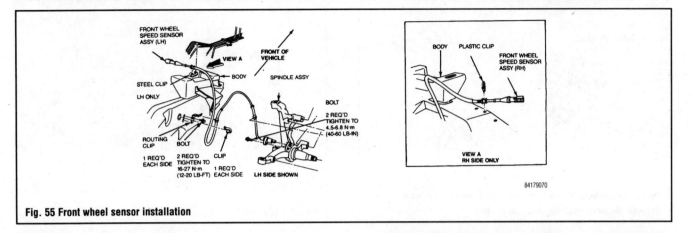

Fig. 55 Front wheel sensor installation

3. Remove the steel routing clip attaching the sensor wire to the tube bundle on the left sensor or remove the plastic routing clip attaching the sensor wire to the frame on the right sensor.

4. Remove the rubber coated spring steel clip holding the sensor wire to the frame.

5. Remove the sensor wire from the steel routing clip on the frame and from the dust shield.

6. Remove the sensor attaching bolt from the front spindle and slide the sensor out of the mounting hole.

To install:

7. Install the sensor into the mounting hole in the front spindle and attach with the mounting bolt. Tighten the bolt to 40–60 inch lbs. (4.5–6.8 Nm).

8. Insert the sensor routing grommets into the dust shield and the steel bracket on the frame. Route the wire into the engine compartment.

9. Install the rubber coated steel clip that holds the sensor wire to the frame into the hole in the frame.

10. Install the steel clip that holds the sensor wire to the tube bundle on the left side or the plastic clip that holds the sensor to the frame on the right side.

11. Connect the 2-pin connector to the wire harness and connect the negative battery cable.

Rear

1. Disconnect the negative battery cable.

2. From inside the luggage compartment, disconnect the 2-pin sensor connector from the wiring harness and push the sensor wire through the hole in the floor.

3. Raise and safely support the vehicle. Remove the sensor wire from the routing bracket located on top of the rear axle carrier housing and remove the steel clip holding the sensor wire and brake line against the axle housing.

4. Remove the screw from the clip holding the sensor wire and brake line to the bracket on the axle.

5. Remove the sensor attaching bolt from the rear adapter and remove the sensor.

To install:

6. Insert the sensor into the rear adapter plate and tighten the sensor attaching bolt to 40–60 inch lbs. (4.5–6.8 Nm).

7. Attach the clip holding the sensor and brake line to the bracket on the axle housing and secure with the screw. Tighten to 40–60 inch lbs. (4.5–6.8 Nm).

8. Install the steel clip around the axle tube that holds the sensor wire and brake line against the axle tube and push the spool-shaped grommet into the clip located on top of the axle carrier housing.

9. Push the sensor wire connector up through the hole in the floor and seat the large round grommet into the hole.

10. Connect the sensor 2-pin connector to the wiring harness inside the luggage compartment. Connect the negative battery cable.

Toothed Indicator Rings

REMOVAL & INSTALLATION

Front

♦ **See Figure 56**

1. Raise and safely support the vehicle.

2. Remove the wheel and tire assembly.

3. Remove the caliper, rotor and hub assemblies.

4. Remove the indicator ring from the hub using a suitable 3-jaw puller.

To install:

5. Support the center of the hub so that the wheel studs do not rest on the work surface.

6. Position the new ring on the hub making sure the ring is not cocked. Place a flat plate on top of the ring and press until it is flush with the top of the hub.

7. Install the hub, rotor and caliper assemblies.

8. Install the wheel and tire assembly and lower the vehicle.

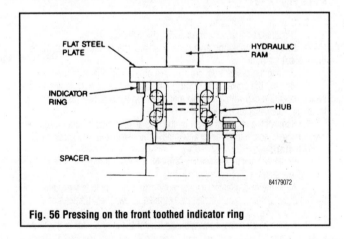

Fig. 56 Pressing on the front toothed indicator ring

Rear

♦ **See Figure 57**

1. Raise and safely support the vehicle.

2. Remove the wheel and tire assembly.

3. Remove the rear axle shaft; refer to Section 7.

4. Using a thin blade cold chisel between the indicator ring and axle flange, strike the chisel evenly around the flange forcing the indicator ring off its journal.

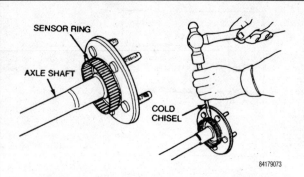

Fig. 57 Removing the rear toothed indicator ring—be careful not to damage the wheel bearing and seal journal

※ **WARNING**

Be extremely careful not to scratch or nick the wheel bearing and seal journal.

To install:

5. Remove any burrs or nicks from the sensor ring journal.
6. Position sensor ring installation tool T89P–20202–A, or equivalent on a press with the pilot ring facing down.
7. Place the new sensor ring over the installation tool.
8. Insert the axle shaft through the tool and place pinion bearing cup replacer tool T85T–4616–AH over the end of the axle shaft.
9. Press the axle shaft until the axle shaft bottoms out on the axle flange.
10. Install the axle shaft into the rear axle.
11. Install the wheel and tire assembly and lower the vehicle.

Pedal Travel Switch

REMOVAL & INSTALLATION

▶ **See Figure 58**

1. Disconnect the negative battery cable.
2. Disconnect the wire harness lead at the switch connector.
3. Using a suitable tool, pry the connector locator out of the holes in the brake pedal support.
4. Unsnap the switch hook from the pin on the ABS adapter bracket.
5. Holding the brake pedal down to gain access, squeeze the tabs on the switch mounting clip with a suitable tool and push the clip through the hole in the dump valve adapter bracket.
6. Remove the rearmost screw on the ABS adapter bracket and loosen the second screw. Rotate the bracket and remove the switch and wire assembly.
To install:
7. Route the switch wire harness through the lower triangular hole in the brake pedal support.
8. Align the ABS adapter bracket with the mounting hole in the sidewall of the brake pedal support and install the rearmost screw. Then, tighten both bracket mounting screws.
9. Install the electrical connector and locator to the right side of the brake pedal support.
10. Holding the brake pedal down, insert the switch mounting clip into the hole in the dump valve adapter bracket and push firmly until a click is heard.
11. Rotate the switch and check that the mounting clip ears are fully engaged.
12. Adjust the switch and connect the negative battery cable.

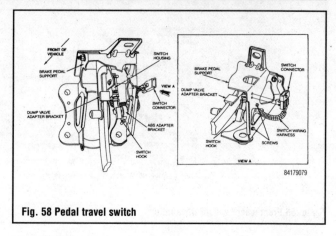

Fig. 58 Pedal travel switch

ADJUSTMENT

Any time the switch is unhooked from the pin for any reason, the following adjustment procedure should be performed to ensure correct switch adjustment.

1. Push the switch plunger fully into the switch housing. This zeroes out the switch adjustment so that it can be automatically reset to the correct dimension.
2. Slowly pull the arm back out of the switch housing past the detent point.

➡**At this point it should be impossible to reattach the arm to the pin unless the brake pedal is forced down.**

3. To complete the adjustment, depress the brake pedal until the switch hook can be snapped onto the pin. Snap the hook onto the pin and pull the brake pedal back up to its normal at rest position. This automatically sets the switch to the proper adjustment.

Filling and Bleeding

The brake fluid level in the master cylinder reservoir should be between 0.16 in. (4mm) below the MAX line on the side of the reservoir and the MAX line. If the brake fluid is low, the red BRAKE lamp will illuminate. To add brake fluid, clean and remove the cap and pour clean brake fluid into the top of the reservoir, filling to specification. If brake fluid has to be added often, check all hydraulic connections for leaks.

The anti-lock brake system must be bled in 2 steps, as follows:

1. The master cylinder and hydraulic control unit must be bled using the anti-lock brake breakout box/bleeding adapter tool T90P–50–ALA, or equivalent. If this procedure is not followed, air will be trapped in the HCU, which will eventually lead to a spongy brake pedal. To bleed the master cylinder and HCU:

a. Disconnect the 55-pin plug from the ABS module and install the anti-lock brake breakout/bleeding adapter to the wire harness 55-pin plug.
b. Place the bleed/harness switch in the **BLEED** position.
c. Turn the ignition switch **ON**. At this point the red OFF light should turn ON.
d. Push the motor button on the adapter down. This starts the pump motor. The red OFF light will turn **OFF** and the green ON light will turn **ON**. The pump motor will run for 60 seconds once the motor button is pushed. If the pump motor is to be turned **OFF** for any reason before the 60 seconds has elapsed, push the abort button.
e. After 20 seconds of pump motor operation, push and hold the valve button down. Hold the valve button for 20 seconds, then release.
f. The pump motor will continue to run for an additional 20 seconds after the valve button is released.

2. The brake lines can now be bled in the conventional manner. Bleed in the following sequence:
   a. Right rear.
   b. Left front.
   c. Left rear.
   d. Right front.

Diagnosis and Testing

SERVICE PRECAUTIONS

• Use caution when disassembling any hydraulic components as the system will contain residual pressure.
• Cover the area around the component to be removed with a shop cloth to catch any brake fluid spray.
• Do not allow brake fluid to come in contact with painted surfaces.
• Follow all procedures for diagnosis in the prescribed order given.
• Certain components within the anti-lock braking system are not intended to be serviced or repaired. Only those components with removal and installation procedures should be serviced.
• Do not use rubber hoses or other parts not specifically specified for the rear anti-lock braking system. When using repair kits, replace all parts included in the kit. Partial or incorrect repair may lead to functional problems.
• Lubricate rubber parts with clean, fresh brake fluid to ease assembly. Do not use lubricated shop air to clean parts; damage to rubber components may result.
• Use only brake fluid from an unopened container. Use of suspect or contaminated brake fluid can reduce system performance and/or durability.
• A clean repair area is essential. Perform repairs after components have been thoroughly cleaned. Do not allow components to come into contact with any substance containing mineral oil; this includes used shop rags.
• The control unit is a microprocessor similar to other computer units in the vehicle. Insure that the ignition switch is **OFF** before removing or installing controller harnesses. Avoid static electricity discharge at or near the controller.
• Never disconnect any electrical connection or the battery with the ignition switch **ON**.
• Always wear a grounded wrist strap when servicing any control module or component with solid-state circuits.
• Leave new components and modules in the shipping package until ready to install them.
• To avoid static discharge, always touch a vehicle ground after sliding across a vehicle seat or walking across carpeted or vinyl floors.

WARNING LAMP FUNCTIONS

The anti-lock brake system uses 2 warning lamps to alert the driver of malfunctions in the system.

The red BRAKE warning lamp will come on for only 2 reasons: If the brake fluid level in the master cylinder reservoir falls below the level which is predetermined by the Fluid Level Switch (FLS), or if the parking brake is applied.

The amber CHECK ANTI-LOCK BRAKE warning lamp will come on for numerous reasons. It warns the driver that the ABS and Traction Assist have been turned off due to a problem that exists in the system. Normal power-assisted braking remains but the wheels can lock during a panic stop while the lamp is on. Certain procedures must be followed to find the fault in this situation.

Make sure that the diagnostic procedures are followed step-by-step in order, as indicated.

✸✸ WARNING

Following the wrong sequence or bypassing steps will lead to unnecessary replacement of parts and/or incorrect resolution of the symptom.

The diagnostic procedure consists of 4 sections:
1. Pre-test checks
2. On-board tests
3. Quick-test checks
4. Warning lamp symptom chart
5. Diagnostic tests

PRE-TEST CHECKS

1. Make sure that the parking brake is fully released. If the parking brake is applied, the BRAKE lamp will be illuminated.
2. Check brake fluid levels.

➡**If the brake fluid level is low in the master cylinder reservoir, the red BRAKE lamp will illuminate. If the brake fluid level in the hydraulic control unit reservoir is low, the amber CHECK ANTI-LOCK BRAKE lamp will be illuminated.**

3. Make sure that the following connectors are connected and the terminals are secure in the connectors:
• 55-pin connector of the computer module
• 19-pin connector of the HCU valve body
• 4-pin and 7-pin connectors of the pump motor relay
• 4-pin connector of the solid state pump motor relay
• 3-pin connector of the master cylinder reservoir
• 2-pin connector of the HCU reservoir
• 5-pin connector of the main power relay
• 2-pin connector of each wheel speed sensor
• 2-pin connector of the pedal travel switch
• 2-pin connector of the stoplamp switch.
4. Make sure that all fuses and diodes are not damaged.
5. Make sure that the battery is fully charged and all connections are clean and tight.
6. Check the ground connections for the anti-lock system which are located near the computer module and pump motor relay.

ON-BOARD TESTS

The anti-lock brake/traction assist system electronic control module is capable of performing a self-test using SUPER STAR II tester 007–00041, or equivalent. If the SUPER STAR II tester is not available, the anti-lock Quick-Test check sheet should be used.

The anti-lock brake/traction assist control module monitors system operation and can store all defined service codes in its memory. It is important to understand that the ABS module cannot recognize some failures, therefore if a problem exists and no service codes are stored by the ABS module, other diagnostic steps must be followed.

The module cannot store a service code if there is no power to the module. This fault can be found by using the quick check sheet.

If a component failure exists while performing the self test, a code 18, 19 or 20 series code will override any other stored code and will not allow other codes to be output. If the failure is intermittent or if the code was left in the ABS module due to improper erasing procedures, the code will be output during the self-test including any other stored codes.

READING CODES

STAR Tester Connection and Battery Check

♦ See Figure 59

1. Turn the ignition switch to the **OFF** position.
2. Locate the SUPER STAR II tester connector in the engine compartment on the right shock tower.
3. Connect the SUPER STAR II tester connector to the vehicle connector.

➡**Only 1 multi-pin connector is used.**

4. Turn **ON** the power switch on the right side of the SUPER STAR II tester. A steady 00 or blank screen will appear to signify that the tester is ready to start the self-test and receive service codes.

➡**If the message LO BAT appears in the upper left corner of the read-out display and stays on, replace the tester's 9-volt battery before continuing with the self-test. The message LO BAT will appear momentarily when the power switch is turned OFF.**

5. With the ignition still **OFF**, push the self-test button in the center of the SUPER STAR II tester.
6. Push the self-test button again. This deactivates the self-test sequence.

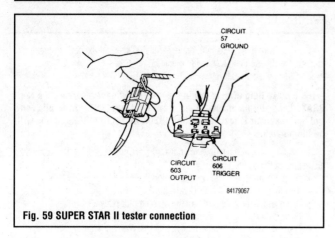

CIRCUIT 57 GROUND

CIRCUIT 603 OUTPUT

CIRCUIT 606 TRIGGER

84179067

Fig. 59 SUPER STAR II tester connection

7. If the tester passes the above test (00 or blank screen with button in TEST position), proceed with the on-board self-test procedure. If any service codes appear during the self-test, the proper pinpoint test to perform will be listed in the trouble code index.

Self-Test Procedure

The anti-lock brake/traction assist system has self-diagnostic capabilities, however, the module as received from manufacturing is equipped with a stored error—Code 61. This will affect the service procedure.

The stored codes can be retrieved from the ABS module in the following manner:

1. Connect the SUPER STAR II tester to the connector located in the engine compartment.
2. Turn **ON** the tester and latch the button down in the **TEST** position.
3. Turn the ignition switch to the **RUN** position.
4. Read the first code output, after approximately 15 seconds the next code will be output. Leave the button latched until all codes are output.

➡**Make sure that all codes are written down.**

The diagnostic procedure should be as follows, providing that the CHECK ANTI-LOCK BRAKE lamp stays on all the time or flashes intermittently.

➡**If the BRAKE warning lamp is on or intermittently comes on, use the warning lamp symptom chart.**

5. If the first code received is 18, 19 or in the 20's and no other code is received, service the indicated component. No other codes can be output if an 18, 19 or 20 series fault code exists. After servicing the indicated 18, 19 or 20 series code, repeat the procedure for retrieving error codes.

➡**If there are more codes stored in the ABS module memory, no codes will erase until all codes have been output by the tester, all faults have been serviced and the vehicle is driven about 25 mph. This means that if an 18, 19 or 20's code originally existed and was serviced, it can be ignored when running the self-test the second time.**

6. If a Code 61 is received and no other faults are received, service the indicated Code 61 fault.
7. If no code or only a Code 10 is received, use the anti-lock quick check sheet, since some fault possibilities are not recognized and retained in the ABS module memory.

Code Listings

- **11** ABS Module
- **17** Reference Voltage
- **18** Isolation Valve No. 1
- **19** Isolation Valve No. 2
- **22** LH Front Inlet Valve or Reference Voltage
- **23** LH Front Outlet Valve
- **24** RH Front Inlet Valve
- **25** RH Front Outlet Valve
- **26** RH Rear Inlet Valve
- **27** RH Rear Outlet Valve
- **28** LH Rear Inlet Valve
- **29** LH Rear Outlet Valve
- **31** LH Front Sensor
- **32** RH Front Sensor
- **33** RH Rear Sensor
- **34** LH Rear Sensor
- **35** LH Front Sensor
- **36** RH Front Sensor
- **37** RH Rear Sensor
- **38** LH Rear Sensor
- **41** LH Front Sensor
- **42** RH Front Sensor
- **43** RH Rear Sensor
- **44** LH Rear Sensor
- **51** LH Front Outlet Valve
- **52** RH Front Outlet Valve
- **53** RH Rear Outlet Valve
- **54** RH Rear Outlet Valve
- **55** LH Front Sensor
- **56** RH Front Sensor
- **57** RH Rear Sensor
- **58** LH Rear Sensor
- **61** FLS Circuits
- **62** Travel Switch
- **63** Pump Motor Speed Sensor
- **64** Pump Motor Pressure
- **66** Pressure Switch
- **67** Pump Motor Relay
- **71** LH Front Sensor
- **72** RH Front Sensor
- **73** RH Rear Sensor
- **74** LH Rear Sensor
- **75** LH Front Sensor
- **76** RH Front Sensor
- **77** RH Rear Sensor
- **78** LH Rear Sensor

CLEARING CODES

1. The original error codes in the ABS module from the assembly plant will erase automatically if everything is in working order and the vehicle is driven about 25 mph.
2. All error codes must be output, all faults corrected, anti-lock lamp off and the vehicle driven about 25 mph, before the memory will clear.

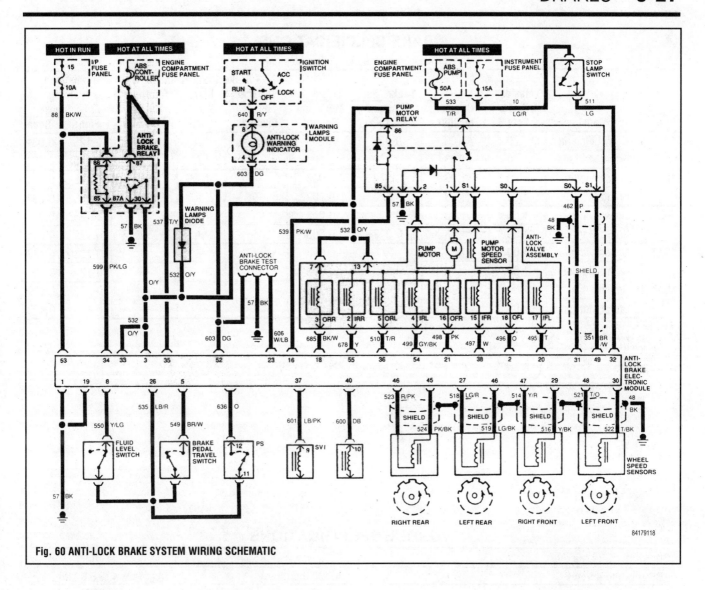

Fig. 60 ANTI-LOCK BRAKE SYSTEM WIRING SCHEMATIC

BRAKE SPECIFICATIONS

All measurements in inches unless noted.

Year	Model	Master Cylinder Bore	Brake Disc			Brake Drum Diameter			Minimum Lining Thickness	
			Original Thickness	Minimum Thickness	Maximum Runout	Original Inside Diameter	Max. Wear Limit	Maximum Machine Diameter	Front	Rear
1989	Crown Victoria	1.00	1.03	0.972	0.003	①	NA	②	0.125	0.031
	Grand Marquis	1.00	1.03	0.972	0.003	①	NA	②	0.125	0.031
1990	Crown Victoria	1.00	1.03	0.972	0.003	①	NA	②	0.125	0.031
	Grand Marquis	1.00	1.03	0.972	0.003	①	NA	②	0.125	0.031
1991	Crown Victoria	1.00	1.03	0.972	0.003	①	NA	②	0.125	0.031
	Grand Marquis	1.00	1.03	0.972	0.003	①	NA	②	0.125	0.031
1992	Crown Victoria	1.00	③	④	0.003	—	—	—	0.125	0.123
	Grand Marquis	1.00	③	④	0.003	—	—	—	0.125	0.123
1993 -94	Crown Victoria	1.00	③	④	0.003	—	—	—	0.125	0.123
	Grand Marquis	1.00	③	④	0.003	—	—	—	0.125	0.123

NA—Not available
① Sedan except Police, Taxi and Trailer tow:
   10.000
   Station Wagon, Police, Taxi and Trailer tow:
   11.030
② Sedan except Police, Taxi and Trailer tow:
   10.060
   Station Wagon, Police, Taxi and Trailer tow:
   11.090
③ Front: 1.03
   Rear: 0.50
④ Front: 0.974
   Rear: 0.44

84179R83

TORQUE SPECIFICATIONS

Component	U.S.	Metric
ABS module screws	40–60 inch lbs.	4.5–6.8 Nm
Brake booster mounting nuts	21 ft. lbs.	29 Nm
Brake hose-to-caliper bolt	30 ft. lbs.	41 Nm
Brake line fitting nuts	10–18 ft. lbs.	14–24 Nm
Brake pedal pivot bolt	10–20 ft. lbs.	14–27 Nm
Caliper locating pins Front caliper Rear caliper	45–65 ft. lbs. 19–26 ft. lbs.	61–88 Nm 26–35 Nm
Control assembly bolts 1989	17–26 ft. lbs.	23–35 Nm
Drum brake backing plate bolts	20–39 ft. lbs.	28–54 Nm
Hydraulic control unit nuts	12–18 ft. lbs.	16–24 Nm
Master cylinder mounting nuts	21 ft. lbs.	29 Nm
Master cylinder stop bolt	9–35 inch lbs.	1–4 Nm
Metering valve screw	7–11 ft. lbs.	10–14 Nm
Pressure control valve Without ABS	10–18 ft. lbs.	14–24 Nm
Wheel cylinder bolts	10–20 ft. lbs.	14–28 Nm
Wheel sensor bolts	40–60 inch lbs.	4.5–6.8 Nm

84179082

10

BODY AND TRIM

EXTERIOR

Doors

REMOVAL & INSTALLATION

➡**Two people are needed to remove and install the doors.**

1. Disconnect the negative battery cable.
2. Disconnect the necessary wiring connectors.
3. With an assistant supporting the door, remove the hinge retaining bolts and remove the door.

➡**If you are using a jack or similar tool to support the door, be careful not to damage the paint.**

4. If the door is to be replaced, transfer the following components to the new door if in usable condition: trim panel, watershield, outside mouldings, clips, window regulators and door latch components.

   To install:

5. With an assistant positioning the door, install and partially tighten the hinge bolts.
6. Align the door and tighten the bolts to 19–25 ft. lbs. (25–35 Nm).
7. Connect the necessary wiring connectors and connect the negative battery cable.

ADJUSTMENT

Door Hinges

▶ **See Figures 1 and 2**

The door hinges provide sufficient adjustment to correct most door misalignment conditions. The holes of the hinge and/or the hinge attaching points are enlarged or elongated to provide for hinge and door alignment.

➡**Do not cover up a poor door alignment with a latch striker adjustment.**

1. Refer to the figures to determine which hinge bolts must be loosened to move the door in the desired direction.
2. Loosen the hinge bolts just enough to permit movement of the door with a padded prybar.
3. Move the door the estimated necessary distance, then tighten the hinge bolts to 19–25 ft. lbs. (25–35 Nm). Check the door fit to make sure there is no bind or interference with the adjacent panel.
4. Repeat the operation until the desired fit is obtained. Check the striker plate alignment for proper door closing.

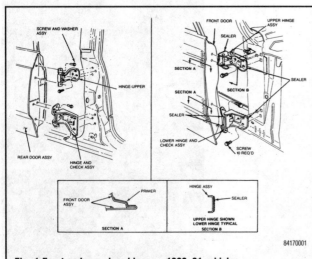

Fig. 1 Front and rear door hinges—1989–91 vehicles

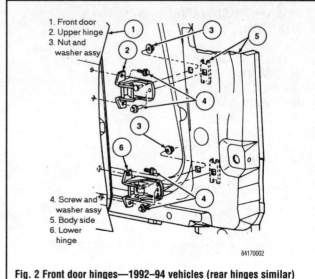

Fig. 2 Front door hinges—1992–94 vehicles (rear hinges similar)

Door Latch Striker

▶ **See Figure 3**

The latch striker should be shimmed to get the clearance between the striker and the latch. To check this clearance, clean the latch jaws and the striker area. Apply a thin layer of dark grease to the striker. As the door is opened and closed, a measurable pattern will result on the latch striker. Use a maximum of 2 shims on 1989–90 vehicles or one shim on 1991–94 vehicles, under the striker. Use Torx® drive bit set D79P–2100–T or equivalent, to loosen and tighten the latch striker to 25–32 ft. lbs. (35–45 Nm).

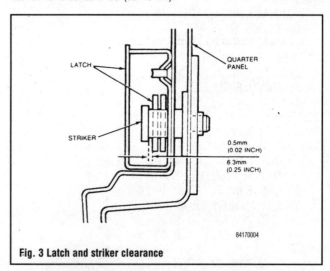

Fig. 3 Latch and striker clearance

Hood

REMOVAL & INSTALLATION

1. Open and support the hood. Mark the position of the hood hinges on the hood.
2. Protect the body with covers to prevent damage to the paint.
3. With the help of an assistant, remove the 2 bolts attaching each hinge to the hood, being careful not to let the hood slip when the bolts are removed.
4. Remove the hood from the vehicle.

To install:

5. With the help of an assistant, position the hood on its hinges and install the attaching bolts. Remove the body covers.

6. Adjust the hood for an even fit between the fenders and a flush fit with the front of the fenders.

7. Adjust the hood latch, if necessary.

ALIGNMENT

Hood Alignment

♦ **See Figure 4**

The hood can be adjusted fore-and-aft and side-to-side by loosening the hood-to-hinge retaining bolts and repositioning the hood. To raise or lower the hood, loosen the hinge-to-fender reinforcement retaining bolts and raise or lower the hinge as necessary.

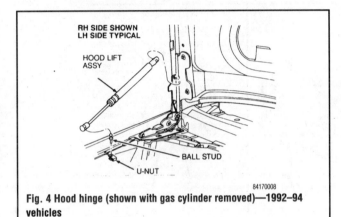

RH SIDE SHOWN
LH SIDE TYPICAL

HOOD LIFT
ASSY

BALL STUD

U-NUT

84170008

Fig. 4 Hood hinge (shown with gas cylinder removed)—1992–94 vehicles

Hood Latch

➡**Before adjusting the hood latch mechanism, make sure the hood is properly aligned.**

1. Loosen the hood latch attaching bolts until they are just loose enough to move the latch.

2. Move the latch side-to-side to align it with the opening in the hood inner panel.

3. Loosen the locknuts on the 2 hood bumpers and lower the bumpers.

4. Move the hood latch up or down as required to obtain a flush fit between the top of the hood and fenders when an upward pressure is applied to the front of the hood. Tighten the hood latch attaching screws to 7–10 ft. lbs. (9–14 Nm).

5. Raise the 2 hood bumpers to eliminate any looseness at the front of the hood when closed. Tighten the hood bumper locknuts.

6. Open and close the hood several times, to check operation.

Trunk Lid

REMOVAL & INSTALLATION

♦ **See Figure 5**

1. Open the trunk lid. Mark the position of the trunk lid relative to the trunk lid hinges.

2. Protect the body with covers to prevent damage to the paint.

3. With the help of an assistant, remove the 2 bolts attaching each hinge to the trunk lid, being careful not to let the trunk lid slip when the bolts are removed.

4. Remove the trunk lid from the vehicle.

To install:

5. With the help of an assistant, position the trunk lid on its hinges and install the attaching bolts. Remove the body covers.

6. Adjust the trunk lid's position in the trunk lid opening.

7. Adjust the trunk lid latch and/or striker, if necessary.

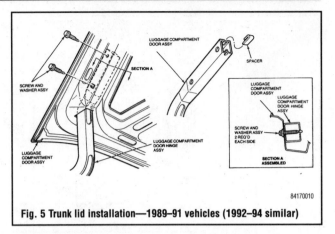

LUGGAGE COMPARTMENT
DOOR ASSY

SECTION A

SPACER

SCREW AND
WASHER ASSY

LUGGAGE
COMPARTMENT
DOOR ASSY

LUGGAGE
COMPARTMENT
DOOR HINGE
ASSY

LUGGAGE
COMPARTMENT
DOOR ASSY

LUGGAGE COMPARTMENT
DOOR HINGE
ASSY

SCREW AND
WASHER ASSY
2 REQ'D
EACH SIDE

SECTION A
ASSEMBLED

84170010

Fig. 5 Trunk lid installation—1989–91 vehicles (1992–94 similar)

ALIGNMENT

Trunk Lid Alignment

The trunk lid can be shifted fore-and-aft by loosening the hinge-to-trunk lid retaining screws. The up and down adjustment is made by loosening the hinge-to-trunk lid retaining screws and raising or lowering the trunk lid.

The trunk lid should be adjusted for an even and parallel fit with the trunk lid opening. The trunk lid should also be adjusted up and down for a flush fit with the surrounding panels. Be careful not to damage the trunk lid or surrounding body panels.

Trunk Lid Latch/Striker

➡**The latch assembly is fixed and not adjustable on all vehicles except 1989–91 Grand Marquis. Any latch adjustment must be made at the striker.**

EXCEPT 1989–91 GRAND MARQUIS

Before adjusting the striker, open and close the trunk lid to double-check the striker alignment. On 1992–94 Crown Victoria, remove the scuff plate striker covering before attempting any striker adjustment.

Loosen the 2 screw and washer assemblies and adjust the striker by moving up and down or from side-to-side as necessary. Tighten the screw and washer assemblies to 7–10 ft. lbs. (9–14 Nm).

➡**Do not try to correct a poor trunk lid alignment with a latch striker adjustment.**

1989–91 GRAND MARQUIS

The striker can be adjusted up and down and the latch can be adjusted side-to-side. Before adjusting the trunk lid make sure the trunk lid is properly aligned. To adjust the striker, loosen the retaining screws, move the striker as required to enter the latch assembly without deflecting the trunk lid sideways, and tighten the retaining screws. Move the striker plate up or down as necessary to provide proper trunk lid seal between the trunk lid and the lower back panel.

Tailgate

REMOVAL & INSTALLATION

♦ **See Figure 6**

1. Disconnect the negative battery cable.

2. Open the tailgate as a drop gate and place a support under the tailgate.

➡**Be careful not to damage the paint.**

3. Remove the tailgate inside trim panel and access cover.

4. Remove the torsion bar retainer bracket.

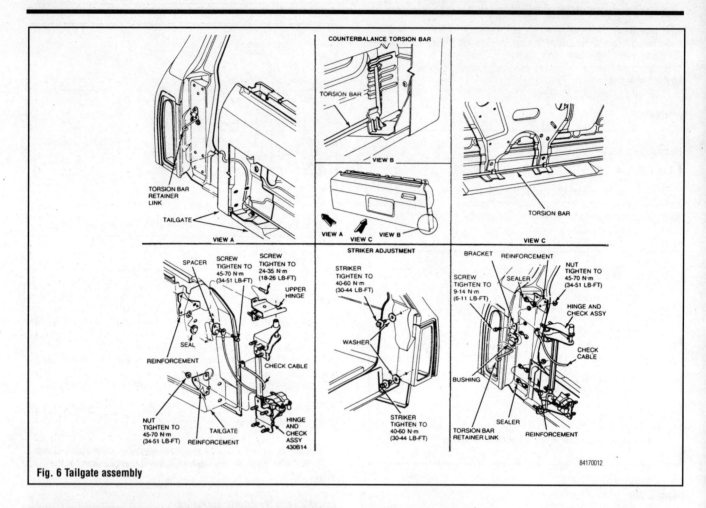

Fig. 6 Tailgate assembly

Be careful when working with the torsion bar. The bar is under tension in the installed position.

5. Raise the tailgate glass and latch the upper tailgate latch by hand. Make sure the glass is supported.
6. Remove the wiring harness from the tailgate.
7. Mark the location of the hinge to the tailgate and remove the nuts attaching the hinge to the tailgate.
8. Actuate the outside handle to disengage the lower latch and remove the tailgate.
9. Installation is the reverse of the removal procedure.

ALIGNMENT

Upper Latch-to-Lower Latch Link

Place the tailgate latches in the closed (latched) position. Disconnect the upper latch-to-lower latch link from the lower latch. Adjust the upper latch-to-lower latch link to engage with the lower latch (no load on the link).

To check the adjustment, the upper latch must not close when the lower latch is in the open position. The upper and lower latches must open at approximately the same time when the outside handle is operated.

Upper Hinge and Latch Release Link

Remove the tailgate inside trim panel and access cover. Disengage the upper hinge release link from the lock release control assembly. Position the adjuster on the upper hinge release link to engage the lever on the lock release control assembly with no load on the link. Assemble the link to the control assembly.

Check the adjustment as follows:
1. The power window regulator must not operate when the latch release control is in the released position.
2. The inside release handle must not operate when the window is down and the upper latch is locked by either the key or the inside push button.

Tailgate Striker

Fore-and-aft and up and down adjustment of the strikers is accomplished by means of square holes in the pillar, backed by floating tapping plates. Lateral adjustment is accomplished by adding or removing shims.

Upper Key Cylinder to Latch Link

Remove the tailgate inside trim panel and access cover. Disengage the key cylinder link from the key cylinder. If the door cannot be unlocked or the window cannot be lowered, shorten the rod by turning the adjuster deeper into the threaded portion of the rod. If the door cannot be locked or the window cannot be raised, lengthen the rod by turning the adjuster. Assemble the adjusted link to the key cylinder lever.

The door must lock and unlock and the window must open and close when properly adjusted.

Outside Handle to Latch Link

Remove the tailgate inside trim panel and access cover. Disengage the outside handle link at the handle. Close the upper latch. Position the adjuster on the handle lever with no load on the link.

➡ **If the release rod is adjusted too long, the tailgate will not lock.**

Adjustment is correct if the tailgate can be opened as a door, and the door locks and unlocks properly.

Tailgate

♦ See Figure 7

Visually inspect the lever position to the upper left-hand hinge on the tailgate to determine whether or not the lever is fully seated in the correct design position. If the lever is only partially seated, the following adjustment must be made:

1. Open the tailgate as a drop gate.
2. Remove the tailgate inside handle assembly and trim panel.
3. Close the upper right-hand latch on the tailgate.
4. Disconnect the upper hinge link rod retainer clip from the lock release control assembly.
5. With the upper hinge release link rod in the normal position, turn the adjuster on the threaded end of the rod so that it can be aligned and easily inserted into the lock release control assembly lever.
6. Lock the retainer clip assembly over the threaded rod and loosely install the inside handle.
7. Open the upper right-hand latch on the tailgate.
8. Operate the tailgate as a gate to make sure the gate is not binding and the latches lock and unlock properly.
9. Operate the tailgate as a door to make sure that it opens and closes without disengagement. The door must lock and unlock and the window must open and close when properly adjusted.
10. Adjust the hinge or striker, as necessary. Install the trim panel.

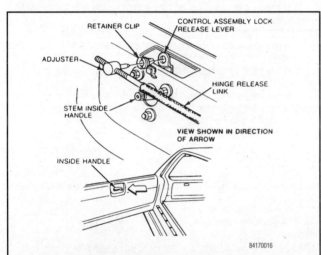

Fig. 7 Disconnect the hinge release rod from the control assembly lock. Release the lever and let the release rod set in the normal standing position. Align the retainer and adjuster to easily set into the control assembly lock. Release the lever as shown

Bumpers

REMOVAL & INSTALLATION

1989–91 Vehicles

FRONT

♦ See Figure 8

1. Remove the stone deflector attaching springs from the lower outboard ends of the bumper.
2. Remove the 6 nuts (3 on each side) attaching the reinforcement to the isolator.

> ❋❋ **WARNING**
>
> **Never apply heat to the bumper energy absorbers. Heat could cause the material inside the absorbers to expand and flow out of the absorbers or crack the metal housing. Always remove the absorbers before making body frame service near them.**

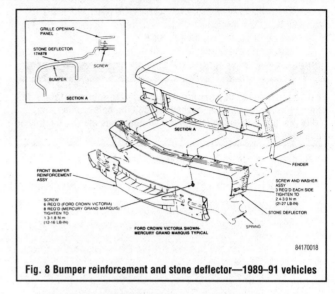

Fig. 8 Bumper reinforcement and stone deflector—1989–91 vehicles

3. Remove the bumper assembly from the vehicle.
4. Remove the bumper guards (one nut and one screw) on each side and the license plate bracket, if equipped, screws prior to removal of the reinforcement from the bumper.
5. Remove the 8 hex-head bolts at the top and 4 hex-head bolts at the bottom and remove the reinforcement from the bumper.
6. Remove the bumper pads, if equipped.

> ❋❋ **WARNING**
>
> **Avoid damaging the bumper pads—Squeeze the retaining tabs with pliers until the tabs can be pushed through the holes in the bumper. If this procedure is not followed, the bumper pads may be destroyed upon removal.**

7. If required, remove the body-mounted stone deflector.

To install:

8. If a new bumper is being installed, remove the protective wax coating from the replacement bumper.
9. Install the body-mounted stone deflector, if removed.
10. Install the 3 bumper pads, if equipped.
11. Install the bumper guards.
12. Install the bumper reinforcement to the bumper. Tighten the 12 bolts to 17–25 ft. lbs. (22–34 Nm).
13. Install the license plate bracket, if equipped.
14. Position the bumper assembly to the vehicle, position the spacers and install the retaining nuts. Do not tighten the nuts at this time.
15. Adjust the bumper vertical and side-to-side position until the bumper meets the stone deflector (no gap). Adjust the fore-and-aft positions to obtain desired body clearances. Use spacers for fore-and-aft adjustment, as required. Tighten the isolator-to-reinforcement nuts to 22–31 ft. lbs. (30–42 Nm). Check the bumper-to-ground height.
16. Install the stone deflector retaining springs at the lower outboard ends of the bumper.

REAR—SEDAN

♦ See Figure 9

1. Remove the stone deflector attaching springs from the lower outboard ends of the bumper.
2. Remove the 4 nuts from each side that attach the reinforcement to the isolator and remove the bumper assembly.

> ❋❋ **WARNING**
>
> **Never apply heat to the bumper energy absorbers. Heat could cause the material inside the absorbers to expand and flow out of the absorbers or crack the metal housing. Always remove the absorbers before making body frame service near them.**

3. Remove the 15 screws and 2 nuts attaching the bumper bar to the reinforcement and remove the reinforcement.

4. Remove the bumper guards, if equipped.

5. Remove the bumper pads, if equipped.

✳✳ WARNING

Avoid damaging the bumper pads—Squeeze the retaining tabs with pliers until the tabs can be pushed through the holes in the bumper. If this procedure is not followed, the bumper pads may be destroyed upon removal.

6. If required, remove the body-mounted stone deflector.

To install:

7. If a new bumper is being installed, remove the protective wax coating from the replacement bumper.

8. Install the body-mounted stone deflector, if removed.

9. Install the bumper pads to the bumper, if equipped. Install the bumper guard, if equipped.

10. Install the bumper reinforcement to the bumper and tighten the screws to 17–25 ft. lbs. (22–34 Nm).

11. Install 2 bumper reinforcement-to-bumper attaching nuts and tighten to 17–23 ft. lbs. (23–31 Nm).

12. Position the bumper assembly to the vehicle, install the spacer and secure with the attaching nuts. Do not tighten at this time.

13. Adjust the bumper vertical and side-to-side position until the bumper meets the stone deflector (no gap). Adjust the fore-and-aft positions to obtain desired body clearances. Use spacers for fore-and-aft adjustment, as required. Tighten the isolator-to-reinforcement nuts to 22–31 ft. lbs. (30–42 Nm). Check the bumper-to-ground height.

14. Install the stone deflector attaching springs at the lower outboard ends of the bumper.

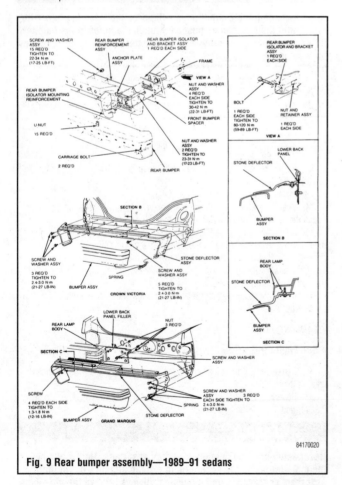

Fig. 9 Rear bumper assembly—1989–91 sedans

REAR—STATION WAGON

♦ **See Figure 10**

1. Remove the 6 bolts attaching the bumper assembly to the isolators, and remove the bumper assembly.

✳✳ WARNING

Never apply heat to the bumper energy absorbers. Heat could cause the material inside the absorbers to expand and flow out of the absorbers or crack the metal housing. Always remove the absorbers before making body frame service near them.

2. Remove the 12 screws attaching the bumper to the reinforcement and deflector, and remove the reinforcement.

3. Remove the 4 screws attaching the bumper-mounted stone deflector, and remove the stone deflector.

4. Remove the bumper guards, if equipped.

5. Remove the bumper pads, if equipped.

✳✳ WARNING

Avoid damaging the bumper pads—Squeeze the retaining tabs with pliers until the tabs can be pushed through the holes in the bumper. If this procedure is not followed, the bumper pads may be destroyed upon removal.

6. If required, remove the body-mounted end stone deflectors.

To install:

7. If a new bumper is being installed, remove the protective wax coating from the replacement bumper.

8. Install the bumper guards, if equipped. Install the bumper pads, if equipped.

9. Position the bumper-mounted stone deflector to the bumper and install the 4 screws.

10. Position the right and left bumper reinforcement to the bumper and stone deflector. Install 6 screws to each side and tighten to 17–25 ft. lbs. (22–34 Nm).

11. Attach the end deflectors to the quarter panel, if removed, before installing the bumper to the body.

12. Position the bumper assembly to the vehicle with the insulators and spacers in place and install the isolator-to-reinforcement bolts. Do not tighten at this time.

13. Adjust the bumper height so that the distance from the top edge to the ground meets the specification in the appropriate illustration. Then, adjust the bumper for desired body clearance. Tighten the isolator-to-reinforcement bolts to 35–50 ft. lbs. (47–68 Nm).

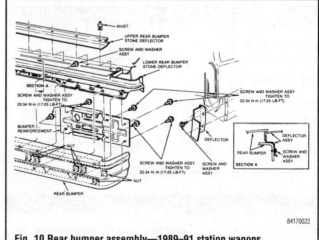

Fig. 10 Rear bumper assembly—1989–91 station wagons

1992–94 Vehicles

FRONT

▶ **See Figures 11 and 12**

1. Remove the side marker lights; refer to Section 6.
2. On Grand Marquis, remove the parking light/turn signal light from the bumper cover.
3. Remove the 2 retaining screw and washer assemblies at the upper outboard end of the bumper cover and the 2 retaining screws at the outboard vertical of the bumper cover to fender assembly.
4. Remove the 6 retaining screws at the wheel opening flange from the bumper cover to fender assembly.
5. Remove the 2 retaining screws and washers attaching the bumper cover and fender assemblies at the lower surface.
6. Remove the 4 retaining screws and washers attaching the bumper cover and radiator support at the lower surface.
7. Remove the front license plate bracket, if equipped. Drill out the rivets and transfer the bracket if replacing the bumper cover.
8. Disengage the retention tabs on the bumper cover surface from the grille opening panel. Push up on the tabs, pull the cover forward and remove the bumper cover.
9. Remove the 6 retaining nuts and remove the bumper from the isolators.
10. Installation is the reverse of the removal procedure. Tighten the bumper-to-isolator nuts to 33–51 ft. lbs. (45–70 Nm). Observe the bumper to ground distance specifications.

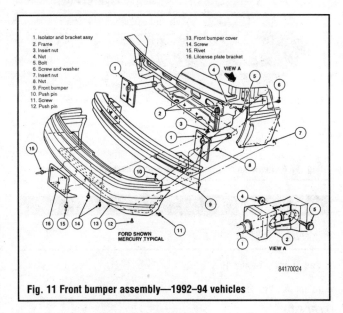

1. Isolator and bracket assy
2. Frame
3. Insert nut
4. Nut
5. Bolt
6. Screw and washer
7. Insert nut
8. Nut
9. Front bumper
10. Push pin
11. Screw
12. Push pin
13. Front bumper cover
14. Screw
15. Rivet
16. License plate bracket

VIEW A

FORD SHOWN
MERCURY TYPICAL

VIEW A

84170024

Fig. 11 Front bumper assembly—1992–94 vehicles

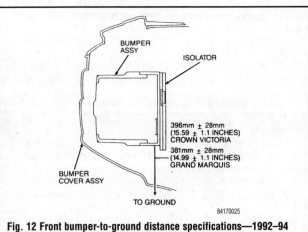

BUMPER ASSY

ISOLATOR

396mm ± 28mm
(15.59 ± 1.1 INCHES)
CROWN VICTORIA

381mm ± 28mm
(14.99 ± 1.1 INCHES)
GRAND MARQUIS

BUMPER COVER ASSY

TO GROUND

84170025

Fig. 12 Front bumper-to-ground distance specifications—1992–94 vehicles

REAR

▶ **See Figures 13 and 14**

1. Drill out the rivets and remove the license plate bracket.
2. Remove the 6 retaining screws from the bumper cover to wheel opening flange.
3. Remove the 10 push pins attaching the bottom of the bumper cover to the quarter panel and bumper.
4. Working inside the trunk, remove the 12 retaining nuts attaching the bumper cover to the body and remove the bumper cover.
5. Remove the 6 nuts attaching the bumper to the isolator and remove the bumper.
6. Installation is the reverse of the removal procedure. Tighten the bumper-to-isolator nuts to 33–51 ft. lbs. (45–70 Nm). Observe the bumper to ground distance specifications.

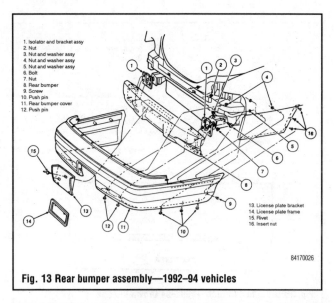

1. Isolator and bracket assy
2. Nut
3. Nut and washer assy
4. Nut and washer assy
5. Nut and washer assy
6. Bolt
7. Nut
8. Rear bumper
9. Screw
10. Push pin
11. Rear bumper cover
12. Push pin
13. License plate bracket
14. License plate frame
15. Rivet
16. Insert nut

84170026

Fig. 13 Rear bumper assembly—1992–94 vehicles

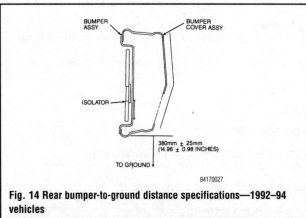

BUMPER ASSY

BUMPER COVER ASSY

ISOLATOR

380mm ± 25mm
(14.96 ± 0.98 INCHES)

TO GROUND

84170027

Fig. 14 Rear bumper-to-ground distance specifications—1992–94 vehicles

Grille

REMOVAL & INSTALLATION

Crown Victoria

1989–91

1. Remove the headlight doors.
2. Remove the 4 screws from the front of the grille.
3. Remove the locking tabs from the grille opening panel and remove the grille.

To install:

4. Insert the locking tabs into the grille opening panel.
5. Install the 4 screws in the front of the grille.
6. Install the headlight doors.

→**There is no grille removal and installation procedure for 1992 vehicles, as this model year did not feature a grille.**

1993–94

▶ **See Figure 15**

1. Open the hood.
2. Working behind the grille opening panel, use a small flat blade prybar to depress the barbs on the 7 retainers across the top of the grille.
3. Release the 2 retainers at the bottom of the grille and remove the grille from the vehicle.

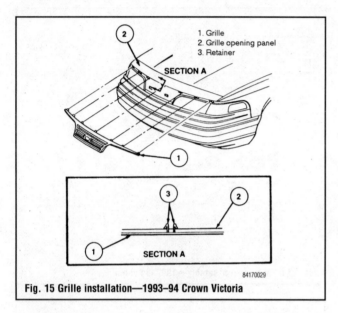

1. Grille
2. Grille opening panel
3. Retainer

Fig. 15 Grille installation—1993–94 Crown Victoria

To install:

4. Line up the 7 retainers across the top of the grille to the holes in the grille opening panel.
5. Carefully insert the retainers and push in until fully seated.
6. Push in the bottom of the grille to snap in the bottom 2 retainers.

Grand Marquis

1989–91

→ **See Figure 16**

1. Depress the grille's 6 snap-in tabs with a flat blade tool.
2. Pull the tabs out of the grille opening panel and remove the grille.

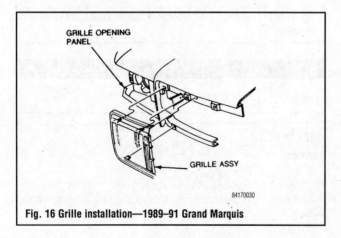

Fig. 16 Grille installation—1989–91 Grand Marquis

To install:

3. Align the snap-in tbs with the slots in the grille opening panel.
4. Firmly press the tabs into the slots in the grille opening panel.

1992–94

▶ **See Figure 17**

1. Remove the sight shield.
2. Remove the side marker lights; refer to Section 6.
3. Remove the headlights; refer to Section 6.
4. Remove the 11 retaining nuts and 4 screws retaining the grille opening panel moulding assembly and remove as one piece.
5. Remove the 4 retaining bolts and remove the grille.

To install:

6. Install the grille and secure with the 4 retaining bolts.
7. Install the grille opening panel moulding assembly and secure with the nuts and screws.
8. Install the headlights and the side marker lights.
9. Install the sight shield.

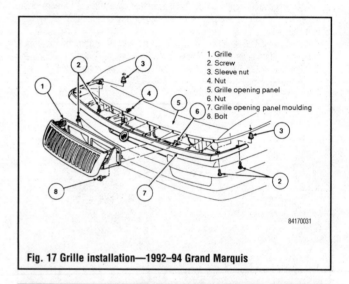

1. Grille
2. Screw
3. Sleeve nut
4. Nut
5. Grille opening panel
6. Nut
7. Grille opening panel moulding
8. Bolt

Fig. 17 Grille installation—1992–94 Grand Marquis

Outside Mirrors

REMOVAL & INSTALLATION

▶ **See Figures 18 and 19**

Manual Mirrors

LEFT SIDE

1. Loosen the bezel setscrew (standard trim) or remove the retaining nut (deluxe trim) to allow door trim panel removal.
2. Remove the door trim panel and watershield; refer to the procedure in this Section.
3. Remove the 2 ring clips, if equipped with vent windows, or 4 ring clips, if not equipped with vent windows, that position and retain the mirror cable inside the door.
4. Remove the 2 screws retaining the mirror to the door outer panel. Carefully remove the mirror and control cable from the door.

To install:

5. Carefully guide the mirror actuator and cable through the hole in the door outer panel. Install the 2 screws that hold the mirror assembly on the door outer panel and tighten securely.
6. Properly position the control cable and retain with the ring clips.
7. After inserting the control lever through the holes in the watershield and trim panel armrest, install the door trim panel and watershield.
8. Secure the control lever in the bezel (standard trim) with its setscrew or in the trim panel armrest (deluxe trim) with the large nut.
9. Check mirror operation.

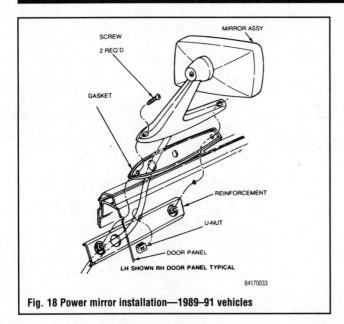

Fig. 18 Power mirror installation—1989–91 vehicles

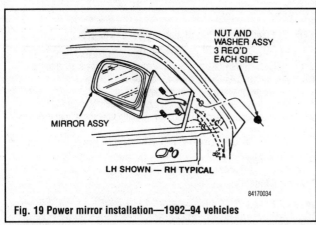

Fig. 19 Power mirror installation—1992–94 vehicles

RIGHT SIDE

1. Remove the large nut retaining the control lever in the instrument panel.
2. Push the control lever through the hole and disengage the 3 plastic cable guides located along the lower backside of the instrument panel.
3. Push out the A-pillar plug and pull the cable through the hole.
4. Remove the door trim panel and watershield; refer to the procedure in this Section.
5. From inside the door, remove the door grommet. Carefully pull the cable and rubber plug(s) through the hole in the face of the door inner panel and through the support strap.
6. Remove the 2 screws that retain the mirror to the door outer panel. Carefully remove the mirror and control cable from the door.
   To install:
7. Carefully guide the control lever and cable through the hole in the door outer panel. Install the 2 screws that hold the mirror assembly on the door outer panel and tighten securely.
8. Position the cable inside the door and through the support strap.
9. Insert the control lever and cable through the hole in the door inner panel and carefully seat the rubber plug.
10. Insert the control lever and cable through the hole in the door hinge and carefully seat the rubber plug.
11. Position the cable along the lower backside of the instrument panel and engage the 3 plastic cable guides.
12. Push the control lever through the hole in the instrument panel and secure with the large nut.
13. Check mirror operation.

Power Mirrors

1989–91 VEHICLES

1. Disconnect the negative battery cable.
2. Remove the interior door handle.
3. Remove the door trim panel; refer to the procedure in this Section.
4. On the left door, remove the bezel from the power mirror control switch.
5. Remove the switch housing from the armrest and disconnect all electrical connectors.
6. Using a putty knife or similar tool, pry the trim panel retaining clips from the door inner panel and remove the panel.
7. Disconnect the mirror wiring connectors and remove the necessary wiring guides.
8. Remove the 2 mirror retaining screws and remove the mirror, guiding the wiring and connectors through the hole in the door.
   To install:
9. Guide the wiring and connectors through the hole in the door. Install the mirror on the door and secure with the retaining screws.
10. Position and install the wiring guides. Connect the mirror wiring connectors.
11. Install the door trim panel.
12. Connect all electrical connectors to the switch housing and install the switch housing on the armrest.
13. On the left door, install the bezel nut to the power mirror control switch.
14. Install the interior door handle.
15. Connect the negative battery cable and check mirror operation.

1992–94 VEHICLES

1. Disconnect the negative battery cable.
2. Remove the door trim panel; refer to the procedure in this Section.
3. Remove the push pin from the mirror access hole cover. Remove the screw under the push pin and remove the access hole cover.
4. Disconnect the mirror wiring connectors and remove the necessary wiring guides.
5. Remove the 3 mirror retaining nuts and remove the mirror, guiding the wiring and connectors through the hole in the door.
   To install:
6. Guide the wiring and connectors through the hole in the door. Install the mirror on the door and secure with the retaining nuts.
7. Position and install the wiring guides. Connect the mirror wiring connectors.
8. Install the mirror access hole cover. Install the retaining screw and push pin.
9. Install the door trim panel.
10. Connect all electrical connectors to the switch housing and install the switch housing on the armrest.
11. On the left door, install the bezel nut to the power mirror control switch.
12. Connect the negative battery cable and check mirror operation.

Antenna

REMOVAL & INSTALLATION

Fixed Antenna

1989 VEHICLES

▶ **See Figure 20**

1. Disconnect the negative battery cable.
2. Remove the antenna mast.
3. Remove the base cap from the antenna base and remove the base attaching screws.
4. Remove the radio from the instrument panel and unplug the antenna lead.
5. Pull the antenna lead through the dash from the engine compartment.
6. Pull the antenna base and cable assembly up through the antenna hole in the fender after removing the cable from the retaining clips on the heater and air conditioner hoses.

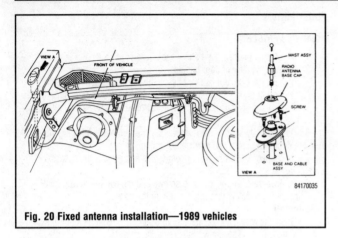

Fig. 20 Fixed antenna installation—1989 vehicles

To install:

7. Insert the antenna lead into the fender hole.
8. Install the base-to-fender attaching screws and install the base cap.
9. Install the antenna mast into the base.
10. Pass the cable through the locator clips on the heater and air conditioner hoses.
11. Route the antenna cable through the dash panel from the engine compartment. Seat the grommet by pulling the cable from inside the passenger compartment.
12. Connect the antenna lead to the radio and install the radio in the instrument panel.
13. Connect the negative battery cable.

1990–91 VEHICLES

1. Disconnect the negative battery cable.
2. Remove the antenna mast.
3. Remove the base cap from the antenna base and remove the base attaching screws.
4. Unplug the antenna lead from the antenna cable extension at the right end of the instrument panel under the glove compartment door.
5. Pull the antenna lead through the "A" pillar from the underside of the fender.
6. Pull the antenna base and cable assembly up through the antenna hole in the fender.

To install:

7. Insert the antenna lead into the fender hole.
8. Install the base-to-fender attaching screws and install the base cap.
9. Install the antenna mast into the base.
10. Route the antenna cable through the hole in the "A" pillar from the underside of the fender. Seat the grommet by pulling the cable from inside the passenger compartment.
11. Connect the antenna lead to the cable extension located at the right end of the instrument panel.
12. Connect the negative battery cable.

1992–94 VEHICLES

♦ See Figure 21

1. Disconnect the negative battery cable.
2. Remove the antenna mast.
3. Remove the antenna nut and stanchion from the top of the fender.
4. Unplug the antenna lead from the antenna cable extension at the right end of the instrument panel under the glove compartment door.
5. Pull the antenna lead through the "A" pillar from the underside of the fender.
6. Remove the screw retaining the bottom of the antenna bracket to the fender.
7. Lower the antenna base, bracket and cable assembly from the underside of the fender.

To install:

8. Install the antenna assembly through the bottom of the fender.
9. Install the stanchion and nut and tighten the nut to 50–70 inch lbs. (5.7–8.0 Nm).

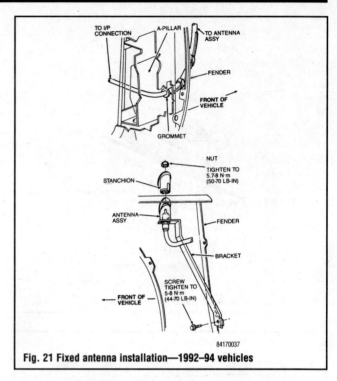

Fig. 21 Fixed antenna installation—1992–94 vehicles

10. Install the screw retaining the bottom of the antenna bracket to the fender and tighten to 44–70 inch lbs. (5–8 Nm).
11. Install the antenna mast into the base.
12. Route the antenna cable through the hole in the "A" pillar from the underside of the fender. Seat the grommet by pulling the cable from inside the passenger compartment.
13. Connect the antenna lead to the cable extension located at the right end of the instrument panel.
14. Connect the negative battery cable.

Power Antenna

1989 VEHICLES

♦ See Figure 22

1. Disconnect the negative battery cable.
2. Lower the antenna inside the engine compartment and disconnect the antenna lead from the power antenna near the right-hand plastic fender apron. Disconnect the antenna motor wires from the antenna overlay wire assembly connector.
3. Remove the antenna nut and chrome trim stanchion.
4. Remove the fender attaching bolts from the right fender to partially loosen the fender from the vehicle and to gain access to the antenna.
5. Remove the power antenna support bracket bolt and remove the power antenna.

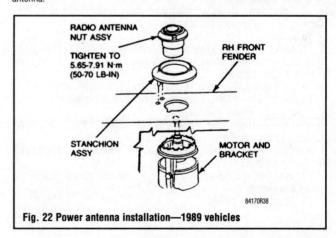

Fig. 22 Power antenna installation—1989 vehicles

6. Position the power antenna to the right-hand fender hole. Install the stanchion and nut and tighten to 50–70 inch lbs. (5.7–8.0 Nm).

7. Install the support bracket mounting nut and tighten to 44–70 inch lbs. (5–8 Nm).

8. Install the right fender mounting bolts.

9. Connect the antenna lead and tighten to 18–27 inch lbs. (2–3 Nm). Connect the antenna motor wires from the antenna overlay wire assembly connector in the engine compartment.

10. Connect the negative battery cable.

1990–94 VEHICLES

1. Disconnect the negative battery cable.

2. Lower the antenna inside the engine compartment and disconnect the antenna lead and power connector located in the passenger compartment on the right cowl side (antenna connection attached at right end on instrument panel). Pull the antenna and power lead through the "A" pillar from the underside of the fender.

3. Remove the antenna nut and chrome trim stanchion.

4. Remove the power antenna support bracket screw and remove the power antenna.

To install:

5. Position the power antenna to the right-hand fender hole. Install the stanchion and nut and tighten to 50–70 inch lbs. (5.7–8.0 Nm) on 1990–91 vehicles or 31–44 inch lbs. (3.5–5.0 Nm) on 1992–94 vehicles.

6. Install the support bracket retaining screw and tighten to 44–70 inch lbs. (5–8 Nm) on 1990–91 vehicles or 12–15 inch lbs. (1.3–1.7 Nm) on 1992–94 vehicles.

7. Route the antenna cable and power lead through the hole in the "A" pillar from the underside of the fender. Seat the grommet by pulling the cable from inside the passenger compartment.

8. Connect the antenna lead and power lead at the right cowl side inside the passenger compartment. Connect the negative battery cable.

Fenders

REMOVAL & INSTALLATION

▶ **See Figures 23 and 24**

1. Remove the front panel assembly and bumper; refer to the procedure in this Section.

2. Remove the battery if removing the right fender.

3. Remove the one cowl seal assembly-to-fender retaining screw.

4. Remove the hood; refer to the procedure in this Section.

5. Remove the 2 fender-to-radiator support panel upper brace retaining screws and remove the brace.

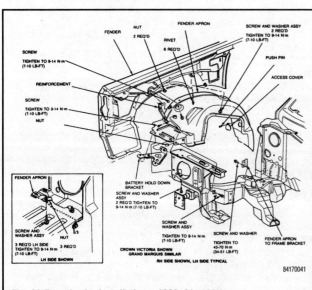

Fig. 23 Front fender installation—1989–91 vehicles

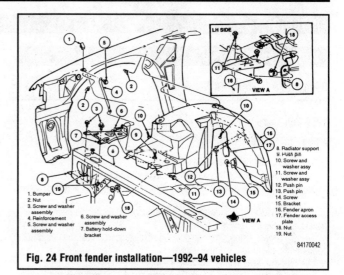

Fig. 24 Front fender installation—1992–94 vehicles

6. Remove the one fender apron-to-frame retaining screw (inside the wheel opening).

7. Remove the access cover retained by one push pin inside the rear of the fender apron and remove the center fender-to-cowl retaining screw (inside the access opening). If equipped, remove the one push pin retaining the apron to the fender (next to the access opening).

8. Remove the fender-to-radiator support panel retaining screws.

9. Remove the screws (3 left side or one right side) retaining the fender apron to the radiator support panel.

10. If removing the right fender, remove the 2 nuts and screws retaining the battery hold-down bracket to the fender and radiator support panel.

11. Remove the 3 upper and 2 lower fender-to-cowl retaining screws.

12. Remove the fender.

13. If the apron is to be removed, remove the 2 screws inside the top of the apron. On 1989–91 vehicles, drill out the 6 rivets at the wheel opening.

14. On the right fender, remove the 2 fender-to-battery hold-down bracket reinforcement brace screws and remove the brace.

15. Remove the apron.

To install:

16. Position the apron in the fender and install the 2 screws inside the top of the apron. Tighten to 7–10 ft. lbs. (9–14 Nm).

17. Position the fender-to-battery hold-down bracket reinforcement brace and install the 2 screws. Tighten to 7–10 ft. lbs. (9–14 Nm).

18. On 1989–91 vehicles, install 6 new rivets at the wheel opening.

19. Position the fender to the vehicle and install the 3 upper fender-to-cowl retaining screws. Tighten the 2 screws entering the cowl top to 25–38 ft. lbs. (34–51 Nm). Tighten the one screw entering the fender through the front of the hood hinge to 17–25 ft. lbs. (22–34 Nm).

20. Install the 2 lower fender-to-cowl retaining screws. Tighten to 7–10 ft. lbs. (9–14 Nm) on 1989–91 vehicles or 17–25 ft. lbs. (22–34 Nm) on 1992–94 vehicles.

21. Install the 2 battery support/hold-down bracket-to-fender apron nuts and screws. Tighten the screws to 7–10 ft. lbs. (9–14 Nm) and nuts to 5–8 ft. lbs. (7–11 Nm).

22. Install the screws retaining the fender apron to the radiator support panel and tighten to 7–10 ft. lbs. (9–14 Nm).

23. Install the fender-to-radiator support panel screws and tighten to 7–10 ft. lbs. (9–14 Nm).

24. Install the center fender-to-cowl screw through the access hole and tighten to 7–10 ft. lbs. (9–14 Nm). Install the access hole cover with the push pin retainer.

25. Install the fender apron-to-frame retaining screw and tighten to 7–10 ft. lbs. (9–14 Nm).

26. Position the fender-to-radiator support panel upper brace and tighten the retaining screws to 7–10 ft. lbs. (9–14 Nm).

27. Install the one cowl seal assembly-to-fender retaining screw.

28. Check the fit of the fender to the door and hood and position as required.

29. Install the hood.

30. Install the battery, if removed.

31. Install the front panel assembly and bumper.

Instrument Panel

REMOVAL & INSTALLATION

1989 Vehicles

▶ **See Figures 25 and 26**

1. Disconnect the negative battery cable.
2. Remove the 2 screws attaching the instrument panel pad to the instrument panel at each defroster opening. Be careful not to drop the screws into the defroster openings.
3. Remove the one screw attaching each outboard end of the instrument panel pad to the instrument panel.
4. On Crown Victoria, remove one pad attaching screw near the upper right corner of the glove compartment door.
5. Remove the 5 screws attaching the lower edge of the instrument panel pad to the instrument panel. Pull the instrument panel pad rearward and remove it from the vehicle.
6. Remove the 2 screws attaching the steering column opening cover to the instrument panel and remove the cover.
7. Loosen the right and left front door sill plate screws, then remove the right and left cowl side trim panels.
8. Disconnect the wiring harnesses from the steering column at the multiple connectors.

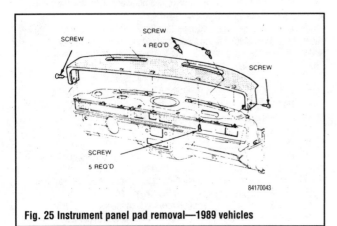

Fig. 25 Instrument panel pad removal—1989 vehicles

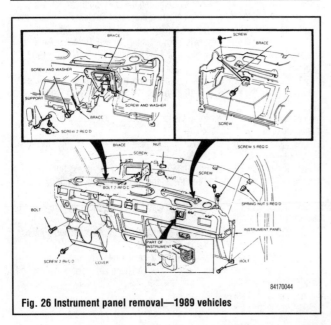

Fig. 26 Instrument panel removal—1989 vehicles

9. Disconnect the transmission selector indicator from the steering column.
10. Remove the nuts and washers attaching the steering column to the instrument panel brace and lay the steering column down on the seat.
11. Remove the one screw attaching the lower flange brace to the lower flange of the instrument panel just to the right of the steering column opening.
12. Remove the one screw attaching the instrument panel support to the lower edge of the instrument panel below the A/C-heater control assembly.
13. Disconnect the speedometer cable from the speedometer by pushing the cable retainer sideways and pulling the cable from the speedometer.
14. Remove the glove compartment from the instrument panel.
15. Disconnect the temperature control cable from the plenum and disconnect the vacuum jumper harness at the vacuum multiple connector located above the floor air distribution duct.
16. Disconnect the antenna cable from the radio, if equipped.
17. Remove the 5 screws attaching the top of the instrument panel to the cowl at the windshield opening.
18. Remove the one bolt attaching each lower end of the instrument panel to the cowl side (A-pillar).
19. Cover the steering column and seat with a protective cover and lay the instrument panel on the seat, disconnecting any wiring or other connections as necessary to allow the instrument panel to lay on the seat.

To install:

20. Position the instrument panel near the cowl and connect any wiring or other connections that were disconnected in Step 19.
21. Install one bolt attaching each lower end of the instrument panel to the cowl side (A-pillar).
22. Install 5 screws to attach the top of the instrument panel to the cowl panel at the windshield opening.
23. Connect the antenna cable to the radio, if equipped.
24. Connect the vacuum jumper harness (from the control assembly) to the plenum vacuum harness at the vacuum multiple connector located above the floor air distribution duct.
25. Connect and adjust the temperature control cable to the temperature blend door. See Section 6.
26. Connect the speedometer cable to the speedometer.
27. Install one screw to attach the instrument panel support to the lower edge of the instrument panel below the A/C-heater control assembly.
28. Install one screw to attach the lower flange brace to the lower flange of the instrument panel just to the right of the steering column opening.
29. Install the glove compartment and check the arms.
30. Install the right and left cowl side trim panels and tighten the door sill plate attaching screws.
31. Position the steering column to the instrument panel brace and install the retaining nuts and washers.
32. Connect the transmission indicator to the steering column.
33. Connect the wire harnesses to the steering column at the multiple connectors. Install the steering column opening cover.
34. Position the instrument panel pad to the instrument panel and install the 5 screws along the lower edge of the pad.
35. Install one screw to attach each outboard end of the pad to the instrument panel.
36. On Crown Victoria, install one pad attaching screw near the upper right corner of the glove compartment door.
37. Install 2 instrument panel pad attaching screws at each defroster opening. Be careful not to drop the screws into the defroster opening.
38. Connect the negative battery cable. Check operation of all instruments, lights, controls and the A/C-heater system.

1990–91 Vehicles

▶ **See Figures 27 thru 34**

1. Position the front wheels in the straight-ahead position.
2. Disconnect the negative battery cable. Properly disarm the air bag system; see Section 6.
3. Remove the right and left mouldings from the instrument panel by pulling up and snapping out of the retainers.
4. Remove the right and left lower insulator panels from the instrument panel.

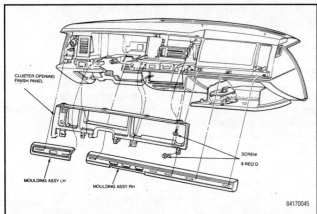

Fig. 27 Instrument panel mouldings and cluster opening finish panel—1990–91 vehicles

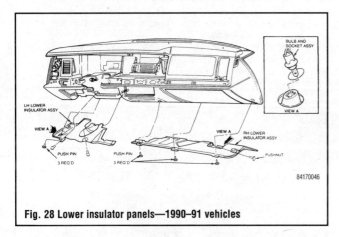

Fig. 28 Lower insulator panels—1990–91 vehicles

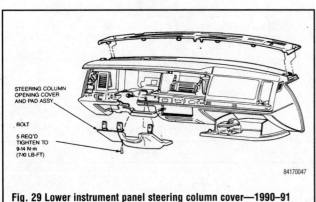

Fig. 29 Lower instrument panel steering column cover—1990–91 vehicles

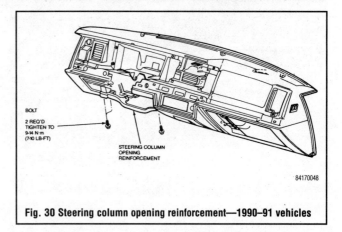

Fig. 30 Steering column opening reinforcement—1990–91 vehicles

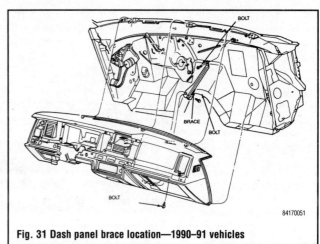

Fig. 31 Dash panel brace location—1990–91 vehicles

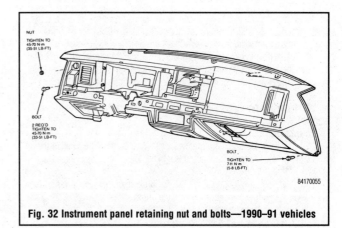

Fig. 32 Instrument panel retaining nut and bolts—1990–91 vehicles

5. Remove the 5 bolts retaining the lower instrument panel steering column cover and remove the cover.

6. Remove the 2 bolts and reinforcement from under the steering column.

7. Remove the ignition lock cylinder; refer to Section 8.

8. Remove the tilt lever and the upper and lower steering column shrouds.

9. Disconnect the wiring from the steering column switches and the transmission range selector cable from the column.

➡ **Do not rotate the steering column shaft.**

10. Place a cover on the front seat to protect it from damage. Remove the 4 nuts retaining the steering column to the instrument panel and lower the column on the front seat.

11. Install the lock cylinder to make sure the steering column shaft does not turn.

12. Open the glove compartment door and depress the sides inward. Lower the glove compartment assembly toward the floor.

13. Through the left side of the glove compartment opening, remove the 2 bolts retaining the instrument panel to the dash panel brace. Through the top of the glove compartment opening, remove the one bolt retaining the brace to the instrument panel.

14. Remove the right and left cowl trim panels.

15. Disconnect the wires of the main wire loom from the engine compartment on both the right and left sides. Disengage the rubber grommets from the dash panel, then feed the wire loom through the hole in the dash panel into the passenger compartment.

16. Disconnect the wires from the instrument panel at the right and left cowl sides.

17. Remove the one bolt and nut retaining the instrument panel to the left side and the one bolt retaining the instrument panel to the right side.

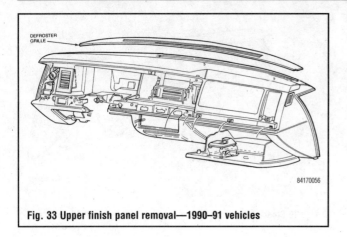

Fig. 33 Upper finish panel removal—1990–91 vehicles

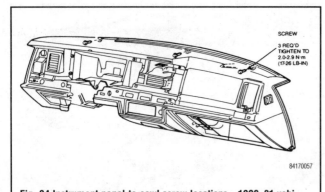

Fig. 34 Instrument panel-to-cowl screw locations—1990–91 vehicles

18. Pull up to unsnap the upper finish panel and remove the upper finish panel.

19. Using the steering column and glove compartment openings, and by reaching under the instrument panel, disconnect all electrical connections, vacuum hoses, demister hose, heater-A/C vacuum lines and radio antenna.

20. Close the glove compartment door and support the instrument panel. Remove the 3 screws retaining the top of the instrument panel to the cowl top and disconnect any remaining wires. Remove the instrument panel from the vehicle.

21. If the instrument panel is being replaced, transfer all parts to the new panel.

To install:

22. Carefully position the instrument panel in the vehicle and install the 3 screws retaining the top of the instrument panel to the cowl top. Tighten to 17–26 inch lbs. (2.0–2.9 Nm).

23. Open the glove compartment door and depress the sides inward. Lower the glove compartment assembly toward the floor.

24. Connect the radio antenna and all electrical connections and vacuum lines that were disconnected in Step 19.

25. Install the upper finish panel.

26. Install the bolt retaining the instrument panel to the right side and tighten to 16–25 ft. lbs. (22–34 Nm). Install the bolt and nut retaining the instrument panel on the left side and tighten to 33–51 ft. lbs. (45–70 Nm).

27. Connect the instrument panel wires at the right and left cowl sides.

28. Feed the main wire loom through the hole in the dash panel into the engine compartment. Secure the rubber grommets in the dash panel. Connect the main wire loom wires on the right and left sides.

29. Install the right and left cowl trim panels.

30. Install the bolts retaining the instrument panel to the dash panel brace. Close the glove compartment door.

31. Remove the lock cylinder from the steering column. Raise the column into position and install the 4 retaining nuts. Tighten to 15–25 ft. lbs. (21–34 Nm).

32. Connect the transmission range selector cable to the steering column and the wiring to the steering column switches.

33. Install the steering column shrouds and the tilt lever. Install the ignition lock cylinder.

34. Install the reinforcement under the steering column and tighten the bolts to 7–10 ft. lbs. (9–14 Nm).

35. Install the lower instrument panel steering column cover and tighten the bolts to 7–10 ft. lbs. (9–14 Nm).

36. Install the lower insulator panels and the instrument panel mouldings.

37. Connect the negative battery cable and properly enable the air bag system. Check operation of all instruments, lights, controls and the A/C-heater system. Check the air bag indicator operation.

1992–94 Vehicles

▶ See Figures 35, 36 and 37

1. Position the front wheels in the straight-ahead position.

2. Disconnect the negative battery cable. Properly disarm the air bag system; see Section 6.

3. Remove the right and left mouldings from the instrument panel by pulling up and snapping out of the retainers.

4. Remove the right and left lower insulator panels from the instrument panel.

5. Remove the 5 bolts retaining the lower instrument panel steering column cover and remove the cover.

6. Remove the 2 bolts and reinforcement from under the steering column.

7. Pull up to unsnap the upper finish panel and remove the upper finish panel.

8. Remove the ignition lock cylinder; refer to Section 8.

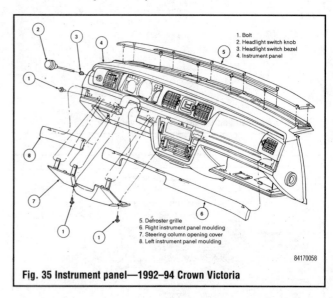

Fig. 35 Instrument panel—1992–94 Crown Victoria

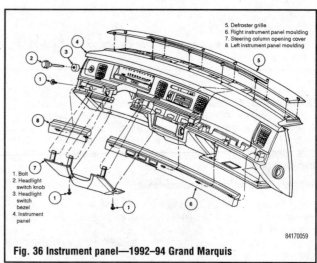

Fig. 36 Instrument panel—1992–94 Grand Marquis

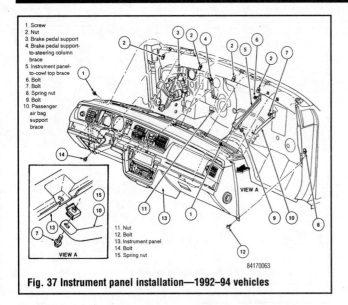

1. Screw
2. Nut
3. Brake pedal support
4. Brake pedal support-to-steering column brace
5. Instrument panel-to-cowl top brace
6. Bolt
7. Bolt
8. Spring nut
9. Bolt
10. Passenger air bag support brace

VIEW A

11. Nut
12. Bolt
13. Instrument panel
14. Bolt
15. Spring nut

VIEW A

84170063

Fig. 37 Instrument panel installation—1992–94 vehicles

9. Remove the tilt lever and the upper and lower steering column shrouds.

10. Disconnect the wiring from the steering column switches and the transmission range selector cable from the column.

➡**Do not rotate the steering column shaft.**

11. Place a cover on the front seat to protect it from damage. Remove the 4 nuts retaining the steering column to the instrument panel and lower the column on the front seat.

12. Install the lock cylinder to make sure the steering column shaft does not turn.

13. Open the glove compartment door and depress the sides inward. Lower the glove compartment assembly toward the floor.

14. Through the left side of the glove compartment opening, remove the 2 bolts retaining the instrument panel to the dash panel brace.

15. Remove the right and left cowl trim panels.

16. Disconnect the wires of the main wire loom from the engine compartment on both the right and left sides. Disengage the rubber grommets from the dash panel, then feed the wire loom through the hole in the dash panel into the passenger compartment.

17. Disconnect the wires from the instrument panel at the right and left cowl sides.

18. Remove the 2 lower bolts retaining the instrument panel to the A-pillar.

19. Using the steering column and glove compartment openings, and by reaching under the instrument panel, disconnect all electrical connections, vacuum hoses, demister hose, heater-A/C vacuum lines and radio antenna.

20. Close the glove compartment door and support the instrument panel. Remove the 5 screws retaining the top of the instrument panel to the cowl top and disconnect any remaining wires. Remove the instrument panel from the vehicle.

21. If the instrument panel is being replaced, transfer all parts to the new panel.

To install:

22. Carefully position the instrument panel in the vehicle and install the 5 screws retaining the top of the instrument panel to the cowl top. Tighten to 17–26 inch lbs. (2.0–2.9 Nm).

23. Open the glove compartment door and depress the sides inward. Lower the glove compartment assembly toward the floor.

24. Connect the radio antenna and all electrical connections and vacuum lines that were disconnected in Step 19.

25. Install the 2 lower bolts retaining the instrument panel to the A-pillar and tighten to 17–25 ft. lbs. (22–34 Nm).

26. Connect the instrument panel wires at the right and left cowl sides.

27. Feed the main wire loom through the hole in the dash panel into the engine compartment. Secure the rubber grommets in the dash panel. Connect the main wire loom wires on the right and left sides.

28. Install the right and left cowl trim panels.

29. Install the bolts retaining the instrument panel to the dash panel brace. Close the glove compartment door.

30. Remove the lock cylinder from the steering column. Raise the column into position and install the 4 retaining nuts. Tighten to 15–25 ft. lbs. (21–34 Nm).

31. Connect the transmission range selector cable to the steering column and the wiring to the steering column switches.

32. Install the steering column shrouds and the tilt lever. Install the ignition lock cylinder.

33. Install the upper finish panel.

34. Install the reinforcement under the steering column and tighten the bolts to 7–10 ft. lbs. (9–14 Nm).

35. Install the lower instrument panel steering column cover and tighten the bolts to 7–10 ft. lbs. (9–14 Nm).

36. Install the lower insulator panels and the instrument panel mouldings.

37. Connect the negative battery cable and properly enable the air bag system. Check operation of all instruments, lights, controls and the A/C-heater system. Check the air bag indicator operation.

Door Panels

REMOVAL & INSTALLATION

1989–91 Vehicles

▶ **See Figures 38 and 39**

1. Disconnect the negative battery cable.

2. On 1990–91 vehicles, remove the speaker grille.

3. Remove the retaining screws from the door inside handle cup. If equipped with armrest courtesy lamps, remove the lens, detach the bulb and wiring assembly from the pull cup and remove the pull cup.

4. Working through the pull cup opening, disconnect the remote lock rod from the lock knob.

5. Remove the retaining screw and the remote mirror bezel nut from the power window regulator housing switch plate, if equipped. Raise the plate to expose the window switch and power door lock switch and disconnect the switches.

6. Remove the retaining screws from the armrest finish panel. Remove the retaining screws from the armrest and remove the armrest.

7. Using a suitable trim pad removal tool, carefully pry the trim panel plastic push pin retainers from the door inner panel.

➡**Do not use the trim panel to pry the clips from the door inner panel. Replace any bent, damaged or missing push pins.**

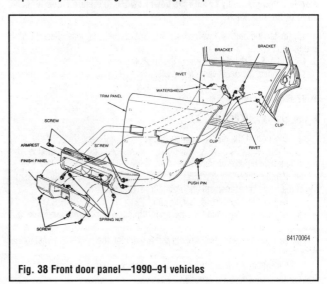

BRACKET
BRACKET
RIVET
WATERSHIELD
TRIM PANEL
CLIP
SCREW
CLIP
RIVET
ARMREST
SCREW
FINISH PANEL
PUSH PIN
SPRING NUT
SCREW

84170064

Fig. 38 Front door panel—1990–91 vehicles

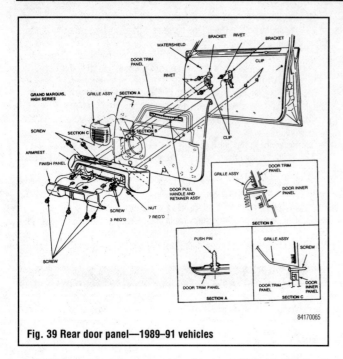

Fig. 39 Rear door panel—1989–91 vehicles

8. Disconnect the radio speaker wiring, if equipped. Remove the trim panel and watershield.

To install:

9. If the door panel is to be replaced, transfer the plastic push pins to the new panel. Make sure that the watershield is positioned correctly to the door sheet metal. Remove the door pull handle from the old panel and transfer to the new one.

10. Position the door panel loosely to the door belt opening and route the wiring harness through the appropriate access holes in the panel. Connect the radio speaker, if equipped.

11. Align the plastic push pins on the door panel to the holes in the door sheet metal and press the pins into place.

12. Install the armrest and route the window regulator, remote mirror cable and power lock harness through the access hole. Install the armrest finish panel.

13. Install the power window regulator switch plate housing to the armrest connecting the power window switch, power door lock switch and remote mirror bezel nut, if equipped, prior to securing the retainer screw.

14. Connect the lock remote rod to the lock knob retainer boss.

➡**Make sure that the remote rod is fully seated into the retainer boss, then function manually or with the power switch to ensure smooth operation of the lock knob.**

15. Install the bulb and wiring assembly. Install the lamp lens, if equipped, and the pull cup.

16. On 1990–91 vehicles, install the speaker grille.

17. Connect the negative battery cable.

1992–94 Vehicles

▶ **See Figures 40 and 41**

1. Disconnect the negative battery cable.

2. If removing the driver's door panel, remove the nut from the outside rearview mirror control switch.

3. Remove the window regulator switch housing by gently prying up, starting at the front. Disconnect all connectors from the switch housing.

4. Remove the door inside handle cup.

5. Remove the push pin from the door trim panel upper front extension and remove the screw.

6. Remove the lower self-tapping screw retaining the door trim panel to the door inner panel.

7. On Grand Marquis, pry up the screw covers from the door pull handle and remove the screws and handle.

8. Lift the door panel upward and snap out the panel. Disconnect the necessary wire harnesses and remove the panel.

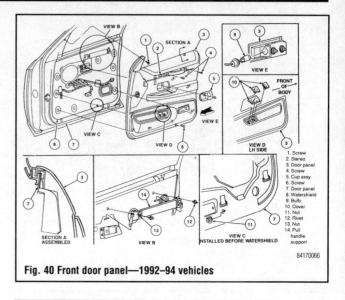

Fig. 40 Front door panel—1992–94 vehicles

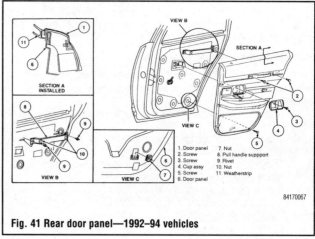

Fig. 41 Rear door panel—1992–94 vehicles

To install:

9. Connect the wire harnesses to the door panel, as necessary.

10. Install the door panel by pushing in and down until it snaps into place.

11. Install all self-tapping screws retaining the door trim panel to the door inner panel.

12. On Grand Marquis, install the door pull handle, tighten the screws and install the screw covers.

13. Install the push pin covering screw on the panel upper front extension.

14. Install the inside door handle cup.

15. Install the window regulator switch housing and install the nut on the outside rearview mirror control switch, if removed.

16. Connect the negative battery cable.

Headliner

REMOVAL & INSTALLATION

1989–91 Vehicles

▶ **See Figure 42**

1. Remove the sun visors and the visor arm clip.

2. Remove the assist handles and coat hooks, if equipped.

3. Remove the upper screw and loosen the lower screws that retain the center body pillar inside the finish panel to the body side assembly.

4. Remove the roof side rail mouldings.

5. Remove the upper screws and loosen the lower screws retaining the windshield side garnish mouldings.

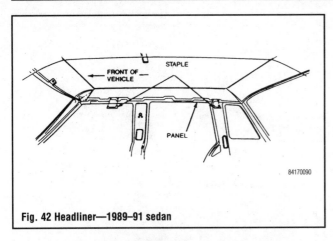

Fig. 42 Headliner—1989–91 sedan

6. Remove the windshield upper garnish moulding.
7. Remove the bolt retaining the shoulder belt to the floor.
8. On Station wagons, if equipped, remove the seat belt anchor bolt from the roof area.
9. Remove the rear window upper garnish mouldings and side garnish mouldings.
10. Remove the package tray trim panel and the roof side panels.
11. Remove the dome light.
12. Adjust the front seats full forward.
13. Shift the headliner all the way to one side, allowing it to be removed. Bend the opposite side flap inboard to remove. Remove the headliner through either rear door.
14. Installation is the reverse of the removal procedure.

1992–94 Vehicles

▶ **See Figure 43**

1. Disconnect the negative battery cable.
2. Remove the sun visors and assist handles from the mounting base retainers.

➡**Do not remove the screws from the sun visors or grab handles.**

3. Using a suitable tool, pry all the mounting clips and mounting base inserts from the sheet metal mounting brackets around the edge of the headliner.
4. Remove the map light assembly from the mounting bracket and disconnect the wiring. Do not remove the mounting bracket from the windshield header.
5. Remove the reading light assemblies from the C-pillars and disconnect the wiring. Do not remove the mounting brackets from the C-pillars.
6. Carefully pull down the front of the headliner and disconnect the headliner wiring harness from the main wiring harness.
7. Remove the trim mouldings from the A, B and C-pillars.
8. Disengage the weatherstrips from the top half of all door openings.

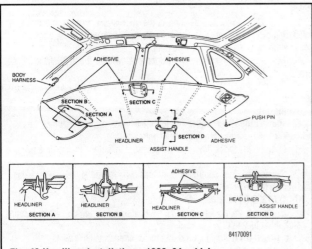

Fig. 43 Headliner installation—1992–94 vehicles

9. Remove the front seat assembly; refer to the procedure in this Section.
10. Pull down the sides of the headliner above the door openings to expose the adhesive beads. Using a hot knife or wide-blade putty knife, cut the adhesive beads lengthwise across the headliner.

➡**The headliner is now free to be removed from the vehicle. It may be necessary to fold the headliner in half to facilitate removal.**

11. Remove the headliner through the right front door.
12. Clean the remaining adhesive from the roof sheet metal. Remove any remaining mounting bases or retaining clips from the roof sheet metal.
To install:
13. Carefully position the new headliner in the vehicle with the fabric side down. Let the headliner rest on the floor.
14. Apply adhesive F1VY–19562–A or equivalent, across the headliner at the positions shown in the figure, using a hand-held adhesive gun.
15. With the help of an assistant on the other side, raise the headliner into position.

❊❊ WARNING

Be careful when lifting the headliner into position, to prevent getting adhesive on the steering wheel and other interior components.

16. Align the visor base inserts with the openings in the headliner. Press the visors into position by snapping the visor pins into the roof mounting holes.
17. Tighten the outboard visor mounting screws.
18. Position the assist handles into the roof rail openings and press the retainers into place.
19. Position the rear light mounting base into the sheet metal mounting bracket and snap the base into place.
20. Pull the headliner down at the windshield header and connect the headliner harness connector to the body harness connector.
21. Position the map light into the mounting base and snap into place.
22. Insert the visor locating hooks into the mounting brackets and install the retaining screws.
23. Tighten the grab handle retaining screws. Insert the assist handle end tabs into the handle depressions.
24. Install the A, B and C-pillar trim mouldings.
25. Install the front seat.
26. Connect the negative battery cable. Check the operation of all lights removed and check power seat operation, if equipped.

Door Locks

REMOVAL & INSTALLATION

Front Door Latch

▶ **See Figures 44 and 45**

1. Remove the door trim panel and the watershield.
2. Mark the location of the rear run lower retaining bolt and remove the bolt.
3. Disconnect the outside release rod.
4. Check all rod connections. Correct any misconnected or loose connections and check operation before replacing parts.
5. Disconnect the rods from the latch. The remote link and the latch-to-lock cylinder rod cannot be removed because of the rod's end configuration.
6. Remove the lock cylinder rod from the lock cylinder lever.
7. Remove the power actuator, power rod and clip, if equipped.
8. Remove the door latch remote control.
9. Remove the latch assembly retaining screws. Disconnect the door indicator switch wire, if equipped, and remove the latch from the door.
10. Remove the anti-theft shield from the latch.
11. Remove the remote link, the latch-to-lock cylinder rods, and the door indicator switch from the latch where applicable.
To install:
12. Install new rod retaining clips and grommets in the new latch assembly, using the removed latch as a guide.
13. Position the door indicator switch to the latch and install the attaching screw. Install the anti-theft shield to the latch.

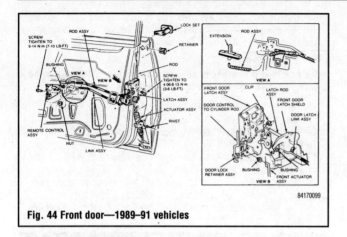

Fig. 44 Front door—1989–91 vehicles

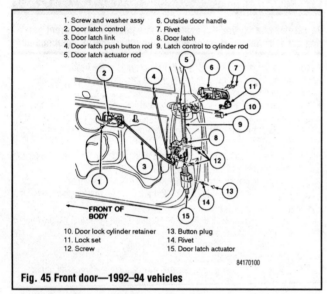

1. Screw and washer assy
2. Door latch control
3. Door latch link
4. Door latch push button rod
5. Door latch actuator rod
6. Outside door handle
7. Rivet
8. Door latch
9. Latch control to cylinder rod

FRONT OF BODY

10. Door lock cylinder retainer
11. Lock set
12. Screw
13. Button plug
14. Rivet
15. Door latch actuator

84170100

Fig. 45 Front door—1992–94 vehicles

14. Install the remote link and the latch-to-lock cylinder rod.
15. Position the latch in the door and connect the wire to the door indicator switch. Install the latch and retaining screws with the anti-theft shield. Tighten to 3–6 ft. lbs. (4–8 Nm).
16. Install the door latch remote control.
17. Connect the latch-to-lock cylinder rod to the lock cylinder lever, manual lock rod and power lock rod, if equipped.
18. Connect the outside release rod to the latch and check latch operation.
19. Install the rear run lower attaching bolt in the original position.
20. Install the door trim panel and watershield.

Rear Door Latch

♦ **See Figure 46**

1. Remove the door trim panel and watershield.
2. Disconnect the door latch actuating rod from the latch assembly.
3. Remove the rear door latch bellcrank.
4. Remove the door latch remote control. Disconnect the power lock rod, if equipped.
5. Remove the 3 latch assembly retaining screws. Disconnect the wire from the door indicator switch, if equipped, and remove the latch assembly from the door.
6. Remove the door indicator switch from the latch assembly and remove the 2 link assemblies from the latch.
To install:
7. Install new clips and grommets in the new latch assembly, using the removed latch as a guide.
8. Install the door indicator switch on the latch assembly.
9. Install the 2 link assemblies into the lower lever grommets.

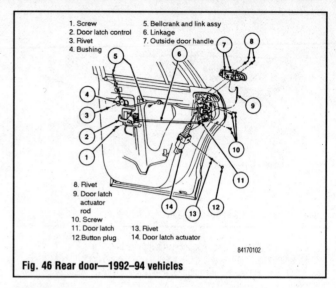

1. Screw
2. Door latch control
3. Rivet
4. Bushing
5. Bellcrank and link assy
6. Linkage
7. Outside door handle
8. Rivet
9. Door latch actuator rod
10. Screw
11. Door latch
12. Button plug
13. Rivet
14. Door latch actuator

84170102

Fig. 46 Rear door—1992–94 vehicles

10. Connect the power lock rod, if equipped.
11. Position the latch assembly on the door and connect the wire to the door indicator switch, if equipped. Install the 3 retaining screws and tighten to 3–6 ft. lbs. (4–8 Nm).
12. Connect the door latch actuating rod to the latch assembly.
13. Install the door latch bellcrank and remote control.
14. Check latch operation, then install the door panel and watershield.

Door Latch Remote Control

1. Remove the door trim panel and watershield.
2. Remove the retaining screw and disengage the attaching tab.
3. Rotate the remote control clockwise on the right door or counterclockwise on the left door while moving it forward to disconnect the remote control from the remote control rod and the door.
To install:
4. Install a new rod end bushing to the remote control if the remote control is being replaced.
5. Position the remote control to the door inner panel with the remote control rod started into the remote control bushing. Rotate the remote control ¼ turn onto the remote rod (counterclockwise on the right door or clockwise on the left door).
6. Engage the tab on the remote control into the slot on the inner panel and install the retaining screw. Check remote control and latch operation.
7. Install the trim panel and watershield.

Door Lock Cylinder

1. Remove the trim panel and position the watershield away from the access holes.
2. On 1992-94 vehicles, disconnect the door latch actuator rod from the latch. Remove the 2 rivets retaining the outside door handle to the door and remove the handle and rod from the door.
3. Disconnect the lock control-to-door lock cylinder rod at the lock cylinder arm.
4. Remove the door lock cylinder retainer and remove the lock cylinder from the door.
To install:
5. Transfer the lock cylinder arm to the new lock cylinder. Replace the rod retainer if it shows any signs of wear or warpage.
6. Position the lock cylinder in the door and install the lock cylinder retainer.
7. Connect the lock control-to-door lock cylinder rod at the lock cylinder and secure the retainer.
8. On 1992-94 vehicles, proceed as follows:
   a. Transfer the actuator rod to a new outside door handle plastic bushing slot, if the handle is to replaced.
   b. Insert the handle and rod into the door and install 2 rivets.
   c. Connect the door latch actuator rod to the door latch.

d. Check the operation of the outside door handle and the door latch.

9. Carefully position the watershield to the inner panel and install the door panel.

Power Door Lock Actuator Motor

1989–91 VEHICLES

1. Disconnect the negative battery cable.
2. Remove the door trim panel and watershield.
3. Disconnect the actuator motor link from the door latch.
4. Remove the pop-rivet attaching the motor to the door.
5. Disconnect the wiring connector and remove the actuator motor.

To install:

6. Connect the wiring connector to the actuator motor.
7. Position the motor in the door and secure with a pop-rivet.
8. Connect the actuator motor link to the door latch.

➡**Be careful that the actuator's boot does not twist during installation. The pop-rivet must be installed so the bracket base is tight to the inner panel.**

9. Install the watershield and door panel. Connect the negative battery cable.

1992–94 VEHICLES

1. Disconnect the negative battery cable.
2. Remove the door trim panel and watershield.
3. Remove the pop-rivet attaching the motor to the door.
4. Disconnect the wiring connector and remove the actuator motor.
5. Remove the door latch and disconnect the actuator motor link from the door latch.
6. Remove the actuator motor.

To install:

7. Connect the actuator motor link to the door latch.
8. Position the motor in the door and secure with a pop-rivet.

➡**The pop-rivet must be installed so the bracket base is tight to the inner panel.**

9. Connect the wiring connector to the actuator motor.
10. Install the watershield and door panel. Connect the negative battery cable.

Power Door Lock Switch

1989–91 VEHICLES

1. Disconnect the negative battery cable.
2. Remove the inside handle cup and press down on the lock rod to disengage the rod from the snapring and knob.
3. Remove the attaching screw and switch housing from the armrest.
4. Remove the 2 screws attaching the connector to the switch housing.
5. Carefully pry the switch from the connector using a suitable tool. Be careful not to damage the electrical contact pins.
6. Installation is the reverse of the removal procedure. Position the switch to the connector and carefully press into place.

1992–94 VEHICLES

▶ **See Figure 47**

1. Disconnect the negative battery cable.
2. If removing the driver's door switch, remove the nut from the outside rearview mirror control switch.
3. Gently pry up the front portion of the switch housing.
4. Gently pry up the sides and rear of the switch housing from the armrest cavity.
5. Remove the 2 screws retaining the connector to the switch housing.
6. Carefully pry the switch from the connector using a suitable tool. Be careful not to damage the electrical contact pins.
7. Installation is the reverse of the removal procedure. Position the switch to the connector and carefully press into place.

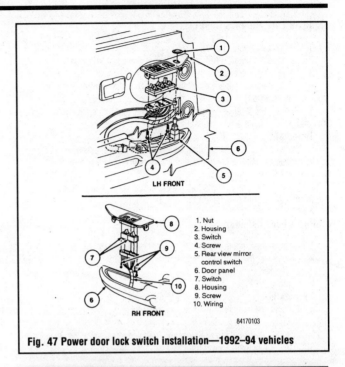

1. Nut
2. Housing
3. Switch
4. Screw
5. Rear view mirror control switch
6. Door panel
7. Switch
8. Housing
9. Screw
10. Wiring

84170103

Fig. 47 Power door lock switch installation—1992–94 vehicles

Tailgate Lock

REMOVAL & INSTALLATION

Tailgate Upper Latch

1. Remove the tailgate trim panel and access cover.
2. Disconnect the power lock actuator link from the latch, if equipped.
3. Disconnect the 3 links with double 90 degree ends from the clips on the other end of the link. Disconnect the center control to upper latch link at the latch end.
4. Rotate the push-button rod out of the bushing in the latch lever.
5. Disconnect the wire connector from the power window switch and limit switch.
6. Remove the 3 latch retaining screws and remove the latch.

To install:

7. Transfer the rods and clips to the new latch. Make sure the rods and clips are inserted into the same side of the lever.
8. Position the latch in the tailgate and install the 3 retaining screws, taking care to position all rods. Tighten to 4–7 ft. lbs. (5–9 Nm).
9. Connect the rods to the connecting components. Connect the center control to the upper latch link.
10. Connect the wiring connectors to the power window switch and limit switch. Connect the power lock actuator, if equipped.
11. Install the access cover and trim panel on the tailgate

Tailgate Lower Latch

1. Remove the interior trim panel and access cover from the tailgate.
2. Disconnect the latch actuator link from the lower latch.
3. Remove the 3 lower latch retaining screws and remove the lower latch from the tailgate.

To install:

4. Install a new retainer clip in the lower latch.
5. Position the lower latch to the tailgate and install the 3 retaining screws. Tighten to 4–7 ft. lbs. (5–9 Nm).
6. Adjust and connect the latch actuator link to the lower latch. Adjust the lower latch striker, if necessary.
7. Install the access panel and trim panel on the tailgate.

Tailgate Lock Release Control

1. Remove the inside handle.
2. Remove the interior trim panel and access cover from the tailgate.
3. Raise the tailgate glass.
4. Disconnect the upper hinge release link and latch control rod from the lock release control.
5. Remove the 3 release control retaining nuts and rotate the control assembly off the latch release link assembly.

To install:

6. Install new clips and bushings onto the new control assembly.
7. Rotate the release control onto the upper latch link. Position the tailgate and install the 3 retaining nuts.
8. Connect the other 2 rods to the lock release control and adjust.
9. Install the trim panel and the inside handle.

Tailgate Lock Cylinder

1. Remove the tailgate inside trim panel and the access hole cover.
2. Disconnect the latch release link and remove the latch rod assembly from the lock cylinder.
3. Remove the lock cylinder.

To install:

4. Transfer the retainer to the new lock cylinder and insert the lock cylinder into the tailgate.
5. Install the lock cylinder retainer and the latch release link into the clip.
6. Install the tailgate access hole cover and the trim panel.

Tailgate Lock Actuator

1. Disconnect the negative battery cable.
2. Remove the tailgate trim panel and watershield.
3. Remove the rivet retaining the lock actuator rod from the latch.
4. Disconnect the wiring connector and remove the actuator.

To install:

5. Connect the wiring connector to the actuator.
6. Connect the lock actuator rod to the latch and assemble to the tailgate inner panel. Install the watershield and trim panel.

➡Be careful that the actuator boot does not twist during installation. The pop-rivet must be installed so the bracket base is tight to the inner panel.

Door Glass

REMOVAL & INSTALLATION

1989–91 Vehicles

FRONT DOOR

♦ **See Figure 48**

1. Remove the door trim panel and watershield.
2. Raise the glass to gain access to the 3 glass bracket retaining rivets. Position a suitable block support between the door outer panel and the glass bracket to stabilize the glass during glass removal.
3. Remove the center pin of each rivet with a drift punch. Drill out the remainder of the rivet with a ¼ in. diameter drill, being careful not to enlarge the rivet attachment.

❊❊ WARNING

Do not attempt to pry the rivets out as damage to the glass bracket and glass spacer retainer could result.

4. Remove the glass.

To install:

5. Install the spacer and retainer assemblies into the glass retention holes. Make sure each assembly is securely fastened.
6. Insert the glass into the door between the door belt weatherstrips.
7. Position the regulator arm slide assembly into the C-channel of the glass bracket.
8. Position the glass to the glass bracket and install three ¼ in. blind rivets. Three ¼ in.-20 bolt, washer and nut assemblies can also be used to attach

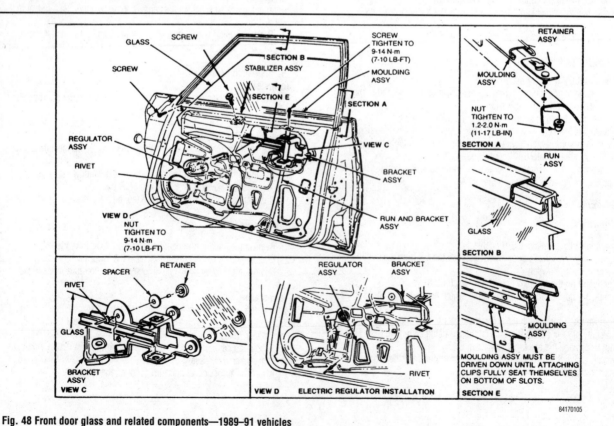

Fig. 48 Front door glass and related components—1989–91 vehicles

84170105

the glass to the glass bracket. Tighten the bolt and nut to 3–5 ft. lbs. (4–7 Nm).

9. If necessary, loosen the upper and lower retaining screws on the run and bracket assembly to position the glass in the door frame.

10. Install the door trim panel and watershield.

REAR DOOR

▶ **See Figure 49**

1. Remove the door trim panel and watershield.

2. Remove the glass-to-glass bracket retaining rivets. Remove the center pin from the rivets with a drift punch and drill the head from each rivet with a ¼ in. diameter drill. Lower the glass approximately 6 in. and let it rest in the door well.

3. Remove the door window glass inner stabilizer retaining screw and remove the stabilizer assembly.

4. Remove the retainer and division bar glass run attaching screw and washer assembly at the bottom.

5. Remove the screw and washer assembly at the top of the division bar at the door frame. Tilt the division bar and main glass forward and remove the weather-strip from the top of the door frame.

6. Remove the stationary vent glass and weather-strip from the door frame.

7. Position the retainer, division bar and main glass in the upright position. Pull the main glass and division bar above and outside the door frame. Swing the glass and division bar assemblies 90 degrees from the door frame and work the glass and division bar upward and out of the door channel between the belt mouldings.

To install:

➡ **The rear door glass, rear door window glass channel, division bar glass run, and retainer and division bar assembly are preassembled prior to installation.**

8. Install the glass channel to the glass using glass Everseal tape or equivalent, 0.065 in. (1.65mm) thick **x** 1¾ in. (44.45mm) wide **x** 17 ¾ in.

(450.85mm) long. Be sure to align the notches in the glass to the cutouts within the glass channel. Clear tape from channel for installing glass guides.

9. Install 2 nylon guides into the glass channel slots and snap the mylar flocked glass run over the glass channel.

10. Lubricate the inside section of the retainer and division bar assembly with silicone lubricant. Place the retainer and division bar assembly over the nylon guides and slide over the glass channel.

11. Install the run assembly into the door frame (front and top of door). Leave the last 6 in. (152mm) of run assembly next to the division bar hanging loose out of the door frame.

12. While holding the rear door glass, retainer and division bar 90 degrees from the door, insert the retainer and division bar between the door belt weather-strip. Swing the glass inboard to the belt and install loosely in the door channel. The upper front corner of the glass should touch the beltline in this position.

➡**Lubricate the belt and vent weatherstrips with silicone lubricant or soapy solution for easier installation.**

13. Subassemble fixed rear window glass and weather-strip and install firmly into the rear of the door frame.

14. Set the main glass and retainer and division bar into position and install the top screw and washer assembly. Make sure that the sealer at the screw head covers the hole for a tight seal.

15. Install the loose 6 in. of run assembly into the door frame and division bar. Install the remaining flocked run into the frame.

16. Install the retainer and division bar retaining screw.

17. Install the window glass inner stabilizer assembly with the retaining screw.

18. Install 2 glass-to-glass bracket rivets or use ¼ in.-20 **x** 1 bolts and nuts. Tighten the bolts to no more than 3–5 ft. lbs. (4–7 Nm).

19. Install the retainer assembly rear door glass. Run the front lower (front guide) with the upper bracket locked into the frame and loosely attach the bottom bracket to the front face of the door (hinge face) with the screw and washer assembly. Install the flocked run into the front guide. Lower the glass to make sure there is no binding. Tighten the screw and washer assembly.

20. Install the door watershield and trim panel.

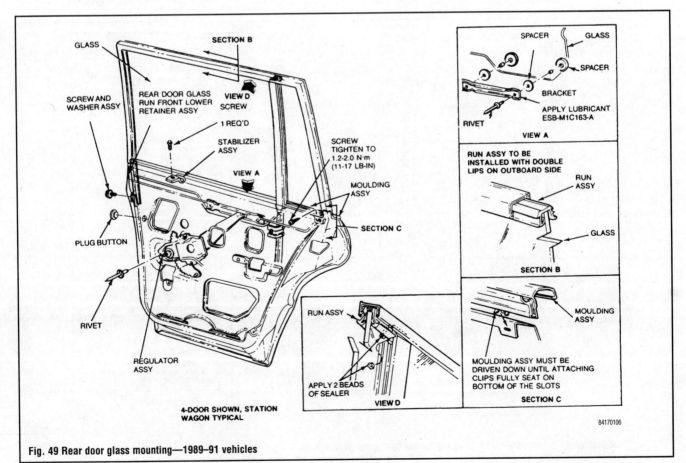

Fig. 49 Rear door glass mounting—1989–91 vehicles

84170106

1992–94 Vehicles

▶ **See Figure 50**

1. Remove the door trim panel and watershield.
2. Loosen the glass run retainer retaining screw and position the retainer forward.
3. Lower the glass to gain access to the 2 glass bracket rivets. Position a suitable block support between the door outer panel and the glass bracket to stabilize the glass during rivet removal.
4. Remove the center pins from the rivets using a drift punch. Drill out the remainder of the rivets using a ¼ in. diameter drill.

✳✳ WARNING

Do not attempt to pry out the rivets as damage to the glass could result.

5. Remove the glass.

To install:

6. Insert the glass into the door between the outer belt weather-strip and inner panel.
7. Position the glass into the door frame and lower the window to align with the regulator bracket.
8. Install two ¼ in. blind rivets. Two ¼-20 **x** 1 in. screw, washer and nut assemblies can also be used. Tighten the screws to no more than 7–10 ft. lbs. (9–14 Nm).
9. Adjust the door glass as follows:
   a. Loosen, but do not remove, the upper regulator retaining nuts.
   b. Raise the glass to the full-up position and tighten the nuts to 7–10 ft. lbs. (9–14 Nm).
   c. Loosen, but do not remove, the front glass run retainer bolt.
   d. Lower the glass to the full down position and tighten the run retainer bolt to 7–10 ft. lbs. (9–14 Nm).
10. Install the door trim panel and watershield.

Door Window Regulator

REMOVAL & INSTALLATION

1989–91 Vehicles

FRONT DOOR

1. Remove the door trim panel and watershield. Support the glass in the full-up position.
2. Disconnect the power window motor wiring connector, if equipped.
3. Remove the center pin from the regulator retaining rivets (3 rivets on manual window, 4 rivets on power window) with a drift punch. Using a ¼ in. diameter drill, drill out the remainder of the rivet, being careful not to enlarge the sheet metal retaining holes.

✳✳ CAUTION

If the regulator counterbalance spring must be removed or replaced for any reason, make sure that the regulator arms are in a fixed position prior to removal to prevent possible injury during C-spring unwind.

4. Disengage the regulator arm slide from the glass bracket C-channel and remove the regulator from the door.

To install:

5. Position the regulator in the door and insert the square slide into the glass bracket C-channel.
6. Position the regulator to the retaining holes in the door inner panel. Install 3 (manual window) or 4 (power window) ¼ in. blind rivets. Three (manual window) or 4 (power window) ¼ in.-20 **x** ½ in. screw and washer assemblies and ¼ in.-20 nut and washer assemblies can also be used.
7. Connect the power window wiring connector, if equipped.
8. Cycle the regulator to check for proper operation.
9. Install the door trim panel and watershield.

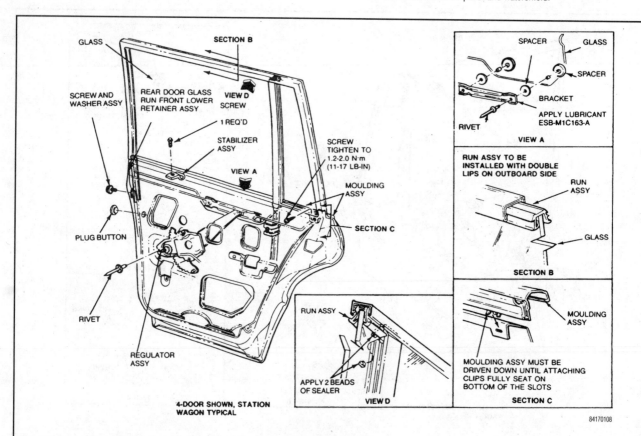

Fig. 50 Front door glass installation—1992–94 vehicles (rear door glass similar)

84170108

REAR DOOR

1. Remove the door trim panel and watershield.
2. Remove the 3 retaining rivets (manual) or 4 rivets (power). Remove the center pin from the rivets with a drift punch. Drill out the head of the rivet using a ¼ in. diameter drill. Be careful not to enlarge the sheet metal holes during drilling.
3. Remove the regulator arm roller from the glass bracket channel and remove the regulator from the door.

To install:

4. Lubricate the window regulator rollers, shafts and the entire length of the roller guides with multi-purpose grease.
5. Install the regulator into the access hole in the inner panel.
6. Position the regulator arm roller into the glass bracket channel.
7. Install the rivets attaching the regulator to the door inner panel. Three (manual window) or 4 (power window) ¼ in.-20 **x** ½ in. screw and washer assemblies and ¼ in.-20 nut and washer assemblies can also be used.
8. Install the watershield and door trim panel.

1992–94 Vehicles

OPERATIONAL WINDOW

1. Remove the door trim panel and watershield.
2. Remove the door glass.
3. Disconnect the power window motor wiring connector.
4. Remove the two ¼ in. rivets attaching the lower bracket of the regulator to the inner panel. Use a drift punch to knock out the center pins, then drill out the remainder of the rivet with a ¼ in. diameter drill. Be careful not to enlarge the sheet metal holes in the door inner panel.
5. Remove the 3 motor retaining screws from inside the door to remove the motor from the bracket assembly.
6. Remove the 2 upper regulator retaining nuts and remove the regulator from the door.

To install:

7. Apply an even coating of multi-purpose grease to the window regulator rollers, shafts and the entire length of the roller guides.
8. Install the regulator into the access hole in the inner panel.
9. Position the regulator using the upper regulator studs and tabs on the motor mounting bracket.
10. Install the rivets attaching the regulator to the door inner panel. Two ¼ in.-20 **x** ½ in. screw and washer assemblies and ¼ in.-20 nut and washer assemblies can also be used.
11. Install the 2 upper regulator retaining nuts. Install the motor, being careful not to overtighten the screws.
12. Install and adjust the door glass.
13. Install the watershield and door trim panel.

DOWN AND INOPERABLE WINDOW

1. Disconnect the negative battery cable.
2. Remove the door trim panel and watershield.
3. Remove the motor retaining screws through the holes.

✸✸ WARNING

Be careful not to strike or scratch the glass, as it could break.

4. Remove the motor assembly from the drum housing.
5. Raise the glass to the full-up position by hand and secure with a clamp.
6. Remove the regulator as outlined in the previous procedure.

To install:

7. Install the regulator as described in the previous procedure.
8. Assemble the motor drive assembly to the drum housing. Align the mounting holes in the motor with the holes in the drum housing.
9. Align the motor drive assembly to the mounting bracket.
10. Install the 3 retaining screws to the mounting bracket and tighten to 50–60 inch lbs. (5.6–6.8 Nm).
11. Connect the motor wire to the harness.
12. Connect the negative battery cable. Remove the clamp and check window operation.
13. Install the watershield and door trim panel.

Power Window Motor

REMOVAL & INSTALLATION

1989–91 Vehicles

▶ **See Figures 51 and 52**

1. Open the door and raise the window to the full-up position, if possible.
2. Disconnect the negative battery cable.
3. Remove the door trim panel and watershield. Disconnect the power window motor wiring.
4. Check inside the door to make sure that electrical wires are not in-line of the holes to be drilled. Using a ½ in. drill bit, drill three ½ in. diameter holes in the door inner panel. Use the drill dimples in the door panel to locate the holes.

✸✸ CAUTION

Prior to motor assembly removal, make sure that the regulator arm is in a fixed position to prevent counterbalance spring unwind.

5. Remove the 3 window motor mounting bolts.
6. Push the motor toward the outside sheet metal to disengage the motor assembly from the regulator gear. If the window is down, push against the motor with a suitable tool through the drilled access holes. After the motor is disengaged, pull the window up.
7. Remove the motor from inside the door.

To install:

8. Position the motor and drive to the regulator and install the 3 screws snug—not tight.
9. Install the plug button in the lower access hole drilled into the door and paint body color. This hole will not be covered up by the door trim panel. Install

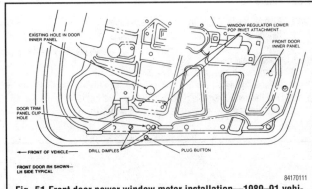

Fig. 51 Front door power window motor installation—1989–91 vehicles

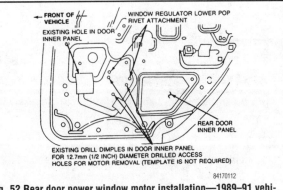

Fig. 52 Rear door power window motor installation—1989–91 vehicles

2 pieces of pressure sensitive waterproof tape approximately 1 in. square to seal the upper access holes covered by the door trim panel.

10. Connect the motor wires at the connector and cycle the glass to ensure gear engagement. After the gears are engaged, tighten the 3 motor and drive retaining screws to 50–84 inch lbs. (5.6–9.6 Nm).

11. Install the watershield and door trim panel.

12. Connect the negative battery cable. Check the window for proper operation.

➡ **Make sure that all drain holes at the bottom of the doors are open to prevent water accumulation over the motors.**

1992–94 Vehicles

1. Disconnect the negative battery cable.
2. Remove the door trim panel and watershield.
3. Disconnect the motor wires at the multiple connector.
4. Remove the motor retaining screws using Torx® drive bit set D79P–2100–T or equivalent, and separate the motor from the bracket and cable drum housing.
5. Remove the motor from inside the door.

To install:

6. Position the motor and drive to the cable drum housing and motor mounting bracket. Install the 3 motor screws and tighten to 50–60 inch lbs. (5.6–6.8 Nm).
7. Connect the power window motor wiring and negative battery cable. Check window operation.
8. Install the watershield and door trim panel.

Tailgate Window Motor

REMOVAL & INSTALLATION

◆ **See Figure 53**

1. Remove the tailgate trim panel and watershield.
2. Remove the tailgate inner panel lower access cover.
3. Lower the tailgate to the DOWN position and raise the glass until the glass brackets are accessible.
4. Disconnect the negative battery cable.
5. Remove the center pin from the glass-to-glass bracket rivets with a drift punch. Drill the heads from the rivets with a ¼ in. drill and remove the rivets.
6. Disconnect the wires from the rear window defroster terminals, if equipped.

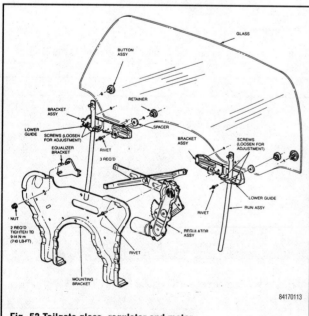

Fig. 53 Tailgate glass, regulator and motor

7. Slide the glass from the tailgate.
8. Remove the glass brackets from the regulator arm rollers and equalizer bracket.
9. Disconnect the motor wires at the connector.
10. Remove both run assemblies.
11. Remove the 4 regulator attaching rivets and remove the regulator from the tailgate.
12. Drill a ⁵⁄₁₆ in. hole through the regulator sector gear and regulator plate. Install a ¼ in. bolt and nut through the hole to prevent the sector gear from moving when the motor and drive assembly is removed from the regulator.
13. Remove the motor and drive from the regulator.

To install:

14. Install the motor and drive to the regulator.
15. Position the regulator in the tailgate and install ¼ in. blind rivets or ¼ in.-20 **x** 1 in. bolts and ¼ in.-20 nuts. Tighten the bolts to no more than 3–5 ft. lbs. (4–7 Nm).
16. Install both run assemblies to the tailgate.
17. Connect the motor wires at the connector.
18. Install the glass brackets on the regulator arm rollers and equalizer bracket.
19. Position the glass into the tailgate and glass brackets. Make sure the spacers are placed between the glass and the glass bracket.
20. Install ¼ in.-20 **x** 1 in. bolts and ¼ in.-20 nuts or blind rivets to attach the glass bracket to the glass. Tighten the bolts to no more than 3–5 ft. lbs. (4–7 Nm).
21. Adjust the glass as follows:

   a. Full-up position: The glass should be properly positioned within the glass opening to ensure a good seal with the weather-strip. The top edge of the glass should be parallel to the top of the glass opening when the glass is closed. To adjust, loosen each upper stop bracket attaching nut and check the glass fit. If the glass does not fit properly, loosen the equalizer bracket nuts and move the glass until the top edge of the glass is parallel to the glass opening. Tighten the equalizer bracket nuts. After the glass has been positioned in the opening, move the upper stop brackets down firmly against the stops and tighten the attaching nuts.

   b. Side-to-side position: Loosen the 2 lower left-hand guide-to-bracket attaching screws. Move the glass from side-to-side as necessary to obtain a good glass overlap with the weather-strip on each side of the glass. Tighten the guide attaching screws after adjustment.

   c. In and out tilt: The top edge of the glass can be tilted in or out to obtain a good seal against the weather-strip. To adjust, loosen the guide-to-bracket and lower run attaching screws. Move the run in or out as necessary to move the glass top edge against the weather-strip to obtain a good seal. Tighten the attaching screws after a good seal is obtained.

22. Connect the wires to the rear window defroster terminals, if equipped.
23. Install the tailgate inner panel lower access cover and the watershield and tailgate trim panel.

Windshield and Fixed Glass

REMOVAL & INSTALLATION

If your windshield, or other fixed window, is cracked or chipped, you may decide to replace it with a new one yourself. However, there are two main reasons why replacement windshields and other window glass should be installed only by a professional automotive glass technician: safety and cost.

The most important reason a professional should install automotive glass is for safety. The glass in the vehicle, especially the windshield, is designed with safety in mind in case of a collision. The windshield is specially manufactured from two panes of specially-tempered glass with a thin layer of transparent plastic between them. This construction allows the glass to "give" in the event that a part of your body hits the windshield during the collision, and prevents the glass from shattering, which could cause lacerations, blinding and other harm to passengers of the vehicle. The other fixed windows are designed to be tempered so that if they break during a collision, they shatter in such a way that there are no large pointed glass pieces. The professional automotive glass technician knows how to install the glass in a vehicle so that it will function optimally during a collision. Without the proper experience, knowledge and tools, installing a piece of automotive glass yourself could lead to additional harm if an accident should ever occur.

Cost is also a factor when deciding to install automotive glass yourself. Performing this could cost you much more than a professional may charge for the same job. Since the windshield is designed to break under stress, an often life saving characteristic, windshields tend to break VERY easily when an inexperienced person attempts to install one. Do-it-yourselfers buying two, three or even four windshields from a salvage yard because they have broken them during installation are common stories. Also, since the automotive glass is designed to prevent the outside elements from entering your vehicle, improper installation can lead to water and air leaks. Annoying whining noises at highway speeds from air leaks or inside body panel rusting from water leaks can add to your stress level and subtract from your wallet. After buying two or three windshields, installing them and ending up with a leak that produces a noise while driving and water damage during rainstorms, the cost of having a professional do it correctly the first time may be much more alluring. We here at Chilton, therefore, advise that you have a professional automotive glass technician service any broken glass on your vehicle.

WINDSHIELD CHIP REPAIR

▶ **See Figures 54 and 55**

➡**Check with your state and local authorities on the laws for state safety inspection. Some states or municipalities may not allow chip repair as a viable option for correcting stone damage to your windshield.**

Although severely cracked or damaged windshields must be replaced, there is something that you can do to prolong or even prevent the need for replacement of a chipped windshield. There are many companies which offer windshield chip repair products, such as Loctite's® Bullseye™ windshield repair kit. These kits usually consist of a syringe, pedestal and a sealing adhesive. The syringe is mounted on the pedestal and is used to create a vacuum which pulls the plastic layer against the glass. This helps make the chip transparent. The adhesive is then injected which seals the chip and helps to prevent further stress cracks from developing

➡**Always follow the specific manufacturer's instructions.**

Inside Rear View Mirror

REMOVAL & INSTALLATION

Mirror

1989–91 VEHICLES

▶ **See Figure 56**

1. Loosen the mirror-to-mounting bracket setscrew.
2. Remove the mirror by sliding upward and away from the mounting bracket.

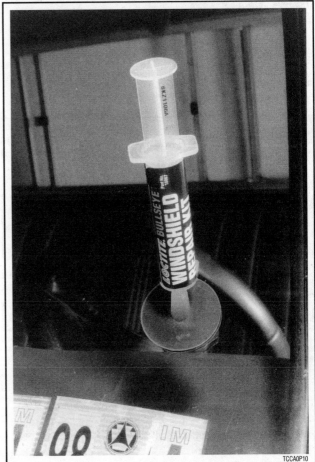

Fig. 55 Most kits use a self-stick applicator and syringe to inject the adhesive into the chip or crack

3. Installation is the reverse of the removal procedure. Tighten the setscrew to 10–20 inch lbs. (1.1–2.3 Nm).

1992 VEHICLES

1. Insert a small, flat screwdriver into the slot until the spring is contacted.
2. Remove the mirror by pushing on the spring with the screwdriver while sliding the mirror upward and away from the mounting bracket.
3. Installation is the reverse of the removal procedure.

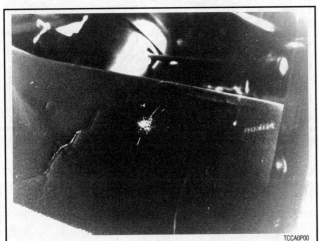

Fig. 54 Small chips on your windshield can be fixed with an after-market repair kit, such as the one from Loctite®

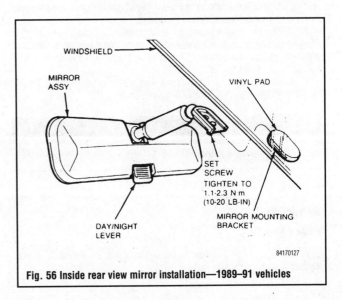

Fig. 56 Inside rear view mirror installation—1989–91 vehicles

▶ **See Figure 57**

1. While firmly holding the mirror, insert inside mirror removal tool T91T–17700–A or equivalent, into the slot until the button is contacted.
2. Remove the mirror by pushing the mirror upward and away from the mounting bracket.
3. Installation is the reverse of the removal procedure.

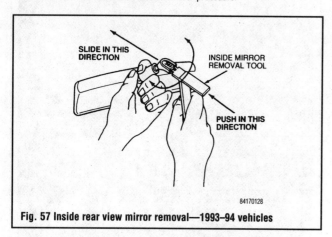

Fig. 57 Inside rear view mirror removal—1993–94 vehicles

Mirror Mounting Bracket

➡It will be necessary to obtain rear view mirror adhesive kit D9AZ–19554–CA or equivalent, for the following procedure.

1. If the bracket vinyl pad remains on the windshield, apply low heat from a suitable heat gun until the vinyl softens. Peel the vinyl off the windshield and discard.

To install:

2. Make sure the glass, bracket and rear view mirror adhesive kit are at least at room temperature, 65–75°F (18.3–23.9°C).
3. Locate and mark the mirror mounting bracket location on the outside surface of the windshield.
4. Thoroughly clean the bonding surfaces of the glass and bracket to remove old adhesive. Use mild abrasive cleaner on the glass and fine sandpaper on the bracket to lightly roughen the surface. Wipe clean with an alcohol moistened cloth.
5. Crush the accelerator vial (part of the rear view mirror adhesive kit) and apply the accelerator to the bonding surface of the bracket and windshield. Let dry for 3 minutes.
6. Apply 2 drops of rear view mirror adhesive to the mounting surface of the bracket. Using a clean toothpick or wooden match, quickly spread the adhesive evenly over the mounting surface of the bracket.
7. Quickly position the mounting bracket on the windshield. The ⅜ in. (9.5mm) circular depression in the bracket must be toward the bottom edge and toward the inside of the passenger compartment. Press the bracket firmly against the windshield for one minute.
8. Allow the bond to set for 5 minutes. Remove any excess bonding material from the windshield with an alcohol dampened cloth.

Seats

REMOVAL & INSTALLATION

Front

MANUAL SEAT

▶ **See Figure 58**

1. Remove the insulator retaining rivets, if equipped, and the insulators from the front and rear of the seat tracks.

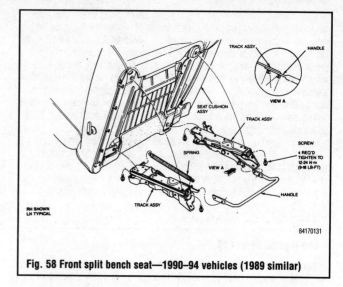

Fig. 58 Front split bench seat—1990–94 vehicles (1989 similar)

2. Remove the seat track retaining screws and nuts from inside the vehicle. Move the seat full-forward to release the assist spring and lift the seat and seat track assembly from the vehicle.

➡Be careful when handling the seat and track assembly. Dropping the assembly or sitting on a seat not secured in the vehicle may result in damaged components.

3. Installation is the reverse of the removal procedure.

POWER SEAT

▶ **See Figures 59, 60 and 61**

1. Disconnect the negative battery cable.
2. Remove the access covers from the lower shields, if equipped, or insulators, if equipped, to expose the nuts and washers and/or bolts.
3. Remove the nuts and washers and/or bolts retaining the seat track to the floorpan.
4. Lift the seat up enough to disconnect the seat harness connector and disconnect the connector.
5. On 1989 vehicles, remove the bolt(s) attaching the seat belts to the floor.
6. Remove the seat and track assembly from the vehicle.
7. Installation is the reverse of the removal procedure.

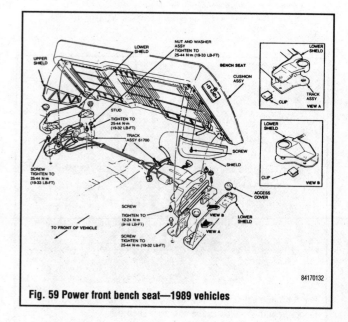

Fig. 59 Power front bench seat—1989 vehicles

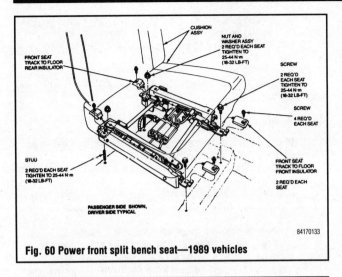

Fig. 60 Power front split bench seat—1989 vehicles

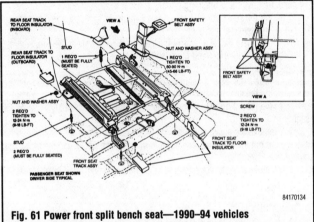

Fig. 61 Power front split bench seat—1990–94 vehicles

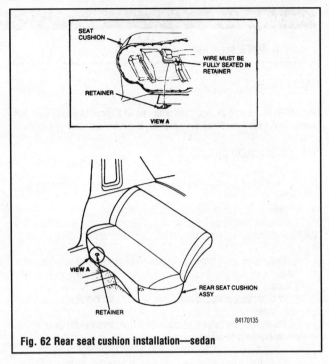

Fig. 62 Rear seat cushion installation—sedan

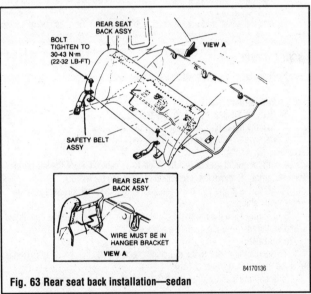

Fig. 63 Rear seat back installation—sedan

Rear

SEDAN

▶ See Figures 62 and 63

1. Apply knee pressure to the lower front portion of the rear seat cushion. Push rearward to disengage the seat cushion from the retainer brackets.
2. Remove the outer seat belt and seat back lower retaining screws.
3. Grasp the seat back at the bottom and lift up to disengage the hanger wire from the retainer brackets.
4. Remove the seat back from the vehicle.

To install:

5. Position the seat back into the vehicle so that the hanger wire is engaged with the retaining brackets.
6. Install the outer seat belt and seat back lower retainer screws. Tighten to 22–32 ft. lbs. (30–43 Nm).
7. Position the seat cushion into the vehicle. Apply knee pressure to the lower portion of the seat cushion, pushing rearward and down to lock the cushion into position.
8. Check the rear seat cushion to make sure it is secured into the floor retainer.

STATION WAGON—SECOND SEAT

1. Apply knee pressure to the lower front portion of the seat cushion. Push rearward to disengage the seat cushion from the retainer brackets and remove the cushion from the vehicle.
2. Remove the 3 screws attaching the seat back to the seat back floor panel.
3. Pull the bottom of the seat back forward and lift the seat back off the seat back floor panel.

To install:

4. Position the seat back to the seat back floor panel and secure with the attaching screws. Tighten the screws to 31–61 inch lbs. (3.5–7.0 Nm).

5. Position the seat cushion into the vehicle. Apply knee pressure to the lower portion of the seat cushion, pushing rearward and down to lock the cushion into position.
6. Check the seat cushion to make sure it is secured into the floor retainer.

STATION WAGON—AUXILIARY SEAT

1. Remove the 2 lower retaining screws securing the rear seat back to the folding floor.
2. Lift up and disengage the upper clips of the rear seat back from the top of the folding floor.
3. Disengage the seat cushion latch and remove the seat cushion from the vehicle.

To install:

4. Position the rear seat cushion into the vehicle and engage the seat cushion pin and latch.
5. Center the seat back on the folding floor and push down, engaging the upper clips of the back to the top of the folding floor.
6. Install 2 screws at the lower edge of the auxiliary load floor panel and tighten to 7–10 ft. lbs. (9–14 Nm).

Power Seat Motor

REMOVAL & INSTALLATION

1989 Vehicles

→1989 vehicles can be equipped with one of 2 types of power seat systems. One uses a rack and pinion drive, the other a screw-type drive.

RACK AND PINION DRIVE

1. Disconnect the negative battery cable.
2. Remove the seat and track assembly from the vehicle; refer to the procedure in this Section.
3. Remove the 3 motor-to-mounting bracket attaching bolts.
4. Remove the clamps retaining the drive cables to the seat tracks. Open the wire retaining straps and remove the motor and cables from the seat track.
5. Remove the cable retaining brackets and remove the drive cables from the motor.

To install:

6. Position the cables and retaining brackets to the motor and install the retaining screws.
7. Position the cables to the seat tracks and the motor to the mounting bracket. Install the 3 motor-to-mounting bracket bolts.
8. Install the clamps retaining the drive cables to the seat tracks.
9. Insert the motor wire in the wire straps and connect the wire at the connector.
10. Install the seat and track assembly in the vehicle. Connect the negative battery cable.

SCREW DRIVE

1. Disconnect the negative battery cable.
2. Remove the seat and track assembly from the vehicle; refer to the procedure in this Section.
3. Remove the seat track from the seat cushion.
4. Identify the cables and their respective locations.
5. Remove the nut from the stabilizer rod and remove the motor bracket screw.
6. Lift the motor and deflect the 3 left-hand cables toward the left-hand track assembly. Remove the 3 left-hand cables from the motor.
7. Move the motor along the stabilizer rod to the right, disengaging the right-hand cables.
8. Lift and slide the motor off of the stabilizer rod. Remove the 2 locknuts retaining the motor to the mounting bracket.

To install:

9. Secure the motor to the mounting bracket using the 2 locknuts. Tighten to 8–10 inch lbs. (0.91–1.12 Nm).
10. Insert the stabilizer rod through the motor and lower the motor into place.
11. Position the 3 left-hand drive cables to the motor. Fully engage the square ends of the cables into the motor armature.
12. Align the right-hand drive cable ends with the motor armature.
13. With the 3 left-hand cables engaged in the motor, lift the motor and

insert the right-hand cable into the motor, being sure to fully engage the square end of the cable into the motor armature. Lower the motor into place.
14. Install the screw retaining the motor bracket to the seat track and tighten to 53–70 inch lbs. (6–8 Nm).
15. Install the nut retaining the motor to the stabilizer rod.
16. Install the seat and track assembly in the vehicle. Connect the negative battery cable.

1990–94 Vehicles

1. While the seat is still in the vehicle, remove the rear Torx® head motor retaining screw from the track assembly.
2. Run the seat motor to align the gear with the notches in the track assembly.
3. Remove the seat and track assembly. Remove the seat back as follows:
   a. Remove the recliner release lever handle, bezel and spacer, if equipped.
   b. Remove the seat back release knob and bezel, if equipped.
   c. Pull back the rear outboard cushion trim cover at the carpet and remove the push pin from the frame. Remove the 2 rear (one upper and one lower) hog rings to expose the lower recliner latch or 4-door recliner lock out plate. Remove the 2 retaining bolts and cable retainer, if equipped.
   d. Lift the seat back upward and pull outboard to disengage the center hinge. Remove the seat back.
4. Disconnect the seat control from the track assembly at the connectors.
5. Remove the upper and lower shield(s) from the outboard side of the seat cushion, if equipped.
6. Remove the 4 bolts retaining each track to the seat frame. Remove the nut retaining the seat belt buckle to the track and remove the center occupant belt from the mounting slot. Remove the track and motor assembly from the seat.
7. Remove the assist springs.
8. Tap out the roll pins retaining the inner track assembly to the motor and outer track assembly.
9. Remove the 2 motor retaining nuts and remaining Torx® head screw.
10. Carefully separate the motor from the seat track assembly. Remove the drive cross shaft.

To install:

11. Position the motor to the seat track assembly. Make sure the guide is in place around the gear.
12. Install the motor retaining nuts and front Torx® head screw.
13. Assemble the inner track assembly and drive cross shaft to the outer track and motor assembly. Install the roll pins. Make sure the tracks are aligned in proper position.
14. Install the assist springs.
15. Position the track and motor assembly to the seat cushion.
16. Install the 4 track-to-cushion retaining bolts. Install the center occupant belt through the mounting slot and install the seat belt buckle and retaining nut to the track.
17. Install the upper and lower shield(s) to the outboard seat cushion, if equipped.
18. Connect the seat control to the track assembly at the connectors.
19. Install the seat back in the reverse order of removal.
20. Install the seat in the vehicle.
21. Position the seat to allow the rear Torx® head screw to be installed.
22. Check the seat for proper operation.

TORQUE SPECIFICATIONS

Component	U.S.	Metric
Auxiliary load floor panel screws Station wagon	7–10 ft. lbs.	9–14 Nm
Battery support-to-fender apron nuts	5–8 ft. lbs.	7–11 Nm
Battery support-to-fender apron screws	7–10 ft. lbs.	9–14 Nm
Bumper reinforcement bolts	17–25 ft. lbs.	22–34 Nm
Bumper reinforcement nuts	17–23 ft. lbs.	23–31 Nm
Bumper-to-isolator nuts 1992–94	33–51 ft. lbs.	45–70 Nm
Center fender-to-cowl screw	7–10 ft. lbs.	9–14 Nm
Door glass bracket bolts/nuts 1989–91	3–5 ft. lbs.	4–7 Nm
1992–94	7–10 ft. lbs.	9–14 Nm
Door hinge bolts	19–25 ft. lbs.	25–35 Nm
Door latch screws	3–6 ft. lbs.	4–8 Nm
Door latch striker	25–32 ft. lbs.	35–45 Nm
Fender apron-to-fender screws	7–10 ft. lbs.	9–14 Nm
Fender apron-to-frame screw	7–10 ft. lbs.	9–14 Nm
Fender apron-to-radiator support screws	7–10 ft. lbs.	9–14 Nm
Fender-to-battery hold-down bracket screws	7–10 ft. lbs.	9–14 Nm
Fender-to-radiator support brace screws	7–10 ft. lbs.	9–14 Nm
Fixed antenna bracket screw 1992–94	44–70 inch lbs.	5–8 Nm
Fixed antenna nut 1992–94	50–70 inch lbs.	5.7–8.0 Nm
Hood latch screws	7–10 ft. lbs.	9–14 Nm
Inside rear view mirror setscrew 1989–91	10–20 inch lbs.	1.1–2.3 Nm
Instrument panel left side retaining bolt/ nut 1990–91	33–51 ft. lbs.	45–70 Nm
Instrument panel right side retaining bolt 1990–91	16–25 ft. lbs.	22–34 Nm
Instrument panel steering column cover bolts 1990–91	7–10 ft. lbs.	9–14 Nm
Instrument panel-to-A-pillar bolts 1992–94	17–25 ft. lbs.	22–34 Nm
Instrument panel-to-cowl top screws 1990–94	17–26 inch lbs.	2.0–2.9 Nm

84170R53

TORQUE SPECIFICATIONS

Component	U.S.	Metric
Isolator-to-reinforcement nuts	22–31 ft. lbs.	30–42 Nm
Lower fender-to-cowl screws		
1989–91	7–10 ft. lbs.	9–14 Nm
1992–94	17–25 ft. lbs.	22–34 Nm
Power antenna bracket nut		
1989–91	44–70 inch lbs.	5–8 Nm
1992–94	12–15 inch lbs.	1.3–1.7 Nm
Power antenna nut		
1989–91	50–70 inch lbs.	5.7–8.0 Nm
1992–94	31–44 inch lbs.	3.5–5.0 Nm
Power window motor screws		
1989–91	50–84 inch lbs.	5.6–9.6 Nm
1992–94	50–60 inch lbs.	5.6–6.8 Nm
Seat belt anchor bolts	23–29 ft. lbs.	30–40 Nm
Second seat back-to-floor panel screws		
Station wagon	31–61 inch lbs.	3.5–7.0 Nm
Steering column reinforcement bolts		
1990–94	7–10 ft. lbs.	9–14 Nm
Steering column retaining nuts		
1990–94	15–25 ft. lbs.	21–34 Nm
Tailgate glass bracket bolts/nuts	3–5 ft. lbs.	4–7 Nm
Tailgate latch screws	4–7 ft. lbs.	5–9 Nm
Trunk lid latch striker screws	7–10 ft. lbs.	9–14 Nm
Upper fender-to-cowl screws		
At cowl top	25–38 ft. lbs.	34–51 Nm
At hood hinge	17–25 ft. lbs.	22–34 Nm

84170R54

GLOSSARY

AIR/FUEL RATIO: The ratio of air-to-gasoline by weight in the fuel mixture drawn into the engine.

AIR INJECTION: One method of reducing harmful exhaust emissions by injecting air into each of the exhaust ports of an engine. The fresh air entering the hot exhaust manifold causes any remaining fuel to be burned before it can exit the tailpipe.

ALTERNATOR: A device used for converting mechanical energy into electrical energy.

AMMETER: An instrument, calibrated in amperes, used to measure the flow of an electrical current in a circuit. Ammeters are always connected in series with the circuit being tested.

AMPERE: The rate of flow of electrical current present when one volt of electrical pressure is applied against one ohm of electrical resistance.

ANALOG COMPUTER: Any microprocessor that uses similar (analogous) electrical signals to make its calculations.

ARMATURE: A laminated, soft iron core wrapped by a wire that converts electrical energy to mechanical energy as in a motor or relay. When rotated in a magnetic field, it changes mechanical energy into electrical energy as in a generator.

ATMOSPHERIC PRESSURE: The pressure on the Earth's surface caused by the weight of the air in the atmosphere. At sea level, this pressure is 14.7 psi at 32°F (101 kPa at 0°C).

ATOMIZATION: The breaking down of a liquid into a fine mist that can be suspended in air.

AXIAL PLAY: Movement parallel to a shaft or bearing bore.

BACKFIRE: The sudden combustion of gases in the intake or exhaust system that results in a loud explosion.

BACKLASH: The clearance or play between two parts, such as meshed gears.

BACKPRESSURE: Restrictions in the exhaust system that slow the exit of exhaust gases from the combustion chamber.

BAKELITE: A heat resistant, plastic insulator material commonly used in printed circuit boards and transistorized components.

BALL BEARING: A bearing made up of hardened inner and outer races between which hardened steel balls roll.

BALLAST RESISTOR: A resistor in the primary ignition circuit that lowers voltage after the engine is started to reduce wear on ignition components.

BEARING: A friction reducing, supportive device usually located between a stationary part and a moving part.

BIMETAL TEMPERATURE SENSOR: Any sensor or switch made of two dissimilar types of metal that bend when heated or cooled due to the different expansion rates of the alloys. These types of sensors usually function as an on/off switch.

BLOWBY: Combustion gases, composed of water vapor and unburned fuel, that leak past the piston rings into the crankcase during normal engine operation. These gases are removed by the PCV system to prevent the buildup of harmful acids in the crankcase.

BRAKE PAD: A brake shoe and lining assembly used with disc brakes.

BRAKE SHOE: The backing for the brake lining. The term is, however, usually applied to the assembly of the brake backing and lining.

BUSHING: A liner, usually removable, for a bearing; an anti-friction liner used in place of a bearing.

CALIPER: A hydraulically activated device in a disc brake system, which is mounted straddling the brake rotor (disc). The caliper contains at least one piston and two brake pads. Hydraulic pressure on the piston(s) forces the pads against the rotor.

CAMSHAFT: A shaft in the engine on which are the lobes (cams) which operate the valves. The camshaft is driven by the crankshaft, via a belt, chain or gears, at one half the crankshaft speed.

CAPACITOR: A device which stores an electrical charge.

CARBON MONOXIDE (CO): A colorless, odorless gas given off as a normal byproduct of combustion. It is poisonous and extremely dangerous in confined areas, building up slowly to toxic levels without warning if adequate ventilation is not available.

CARBURETOR: A device, usually mounted on the intake manifold of an engine, which mixes the air and fuel in the proper proportion to allow even combustion.

CATALYTIC CONVERTER: A device installed in the exhaust system, like a muffler, that converts harmful byproducts of combustion into carbon dioxide and water vapor by means of a heat-producing chemical reaction.

CENTRIFUGAL ADVANCE: A mechanical method of advancing the spark timing by using flyweights in the distributor that react to centrifugal force generated by the distributor shaft rotation.

CHECK VALVE: Any one-way valve installed to permit the flow of air, fuel or vacuum in one direction only.

CHOKE: A device, usually a moveable valve, placed in the intake path of a carburetor to restrict the flow of air.

CIRCUIT: Any unbroken path through which an electrical current can flow. Also used to describe fuel flow in some instances.

CIRCUIT BREAKER: A switch which protects an electrical circuit from overload by opening the circuit when the current flow exceeds a predetermined level. Some circuit breakers must be reset manually, while most reset automatically.

COIL (IGNITION): A transformer in the ignition circuit which steps up the voltage provided to the spark plugs.

COMBINATION MANIFOLD: An assembly which includes both the intake and exhaust manifolds in one casting.

COMBINATION VALVE: A device used in some fuel systems that routes fuel vapors to a charcoal storage canister instead of venting them into the atmosphere. The valve relieves fuel tank pressure and allows fresh air into the tank as the fuel level drops to prevent a vapor lock situation.

COMPRESSION RATIO: The comparison of the total volume of the cylinder and combustion chamber with the piston at BDC and the piston at TDC.

CONDENSER: 1. An electrical device which acts to store an electrical charge, preventing voltage surges. 2. A radiator-like device in the air conditioning system in which refrigerant gas condenses into a liquid, giving off heat.

CONDUCTOR: Any material through which an electrical current can be transmitted easily.

CONTINUITY: Continuous or complete circuit. Can be checked with an ohmmeter.

COUNTERSHAFT: An intermediate shaft which is rotated by a mainshaft and transmits, in turn, that rotation to a working part.

CRANKCASE: The lower part of an engine in which the crankshaft and related parts operate.

CRANKSHAFT: The main driving shaft of an engine which receives reciprocating motion from the pistons and converts it to rotary motion.

CYLINDER: In an engine, the round hole in the engine block in which the piston(s) ride.

CYLINDER BLOCK: The main structural member of an engine in which is found the cylinders, crankshaft and other principal parts.

CYLINDER HEAD: The detachable portion of the engine, usually fastened to the top of the cylinder block and containing all or most of the combustion chambers. On overhead valve engines, it contains the valves and their operating parts. On overhead cam engines, it contains the camshaft as well.

DEAD CENTER: The extreme top or bottom of the piston stroke.

DETONATION: An unwanted explosion of the air/fuel mixture in the combustion chamber caused by excess heat and compression, advanced timing, or an overly lean mixture. Also referred to as "ping".

DIAPHRAGM: A thin, flexible wall separating two cavities, such as in a vacuum advance unit.

DIESELING: A condition in which hot spots in the combustion chamber cause the engine to run on after the key is turned off.

DIFFERENTIAL: A geared assembly which allows the transmission of motion between drive axles, giving one axle the ability to turn faster than the other.

DIODE: An electrical device that will allow current to flow in one direction only.

DISC BRAKE: A hydraulic braking assembly consisting of a brake disc, or rotor, mounted on an axle, and a caliper assembly containing, usually two brake pads which are activated by hydraulic pressure. The pads are forced against the sides of the disc, creating friction which slows the vehicle.

DISTRIBUTOR: A mechanically driven device on an engine which is responsible for electrically firing the spark plug at a predetermined point of the piston stroke.

DOWEL PIN: A pin, inserted in mating holes in two different parts allowing those parts to maintain a fixed relationship.

DRUM BRAKE: A braking system which consists of two brake shoes and one or two wheel cylinders, mounted on a fixed backing plate, and a brake drum, mounted on an axle, which revolves around the assembly.

DWELL: The rate, measured in degrees of shaft rotation, at which an electrical circuit cycles on and off.

ELECTRONIC CONTROL UNIT (ECU): Ignition module, module, amplifier or igniter. See Module for definition.

ELECTRONIC IGNITION: A system in which the timing and firing of the spark plugs is controlled by an electronic control unit, usually called a module. These systems have no points or condenser.

END-PLAY: The measured amount of axial movement in a shaft.

ENGINE: A device that converts heat into mechanical energy.

EXHAUST MANIFOLD: A set of cast passages or pipes which conduct exhaust gases from the engine.

FEELER GAUGE: A blade, usually metal, or precisely predetermined thickness, used to measure the clearance between two parts.

FIRING ORDER: The order in which combustion occurs in the cylinders of an engine. Also the order in which spark is distributed to the plugs by the distributor.

FLOODING: The presence of too much fuel in the intake manifold and combustion chamber which prevents the air/fuel mixture from firing, thereby causing a no-start situation.

FLYWHEEL: A disc shaped part bolted to the rear end of the crankshaft. Around the outer perimeter is affixed the ring gear. The starter drive engages the ring gear, turning the flywheel, which rotates the crankshaft, imparting the initial starting motion to the engine.

FOOT POUND (ft. lbs. or sometimes, ft.lb.): The amount of energy or work needed to raise an item weighing one pound, a distance of one foot.

FUSE: A protective device in a circuit which prevents circuit overload by breaking the circuit when a specific amperage is present. The device is constructed around a strip or wire of a lower amperage rating than the circuit it is designed to protect. When an amperage higher than that stamped on the fuse is present in the circuit, the strip or wire melts, opening the circuit.

GEAR RATIO: The ratio between the number of teeth on meshing gears.

GENERATOR: A device which converts mechanical energy into electrical energy.

HEAT RANGE: The measure of a spark plug's ability to dissipate heat from its firing end. The higher the heat range, the hotter the plug fires.

HUB: The center part of a wheel or gear.

HYDROCARBON (HC): Any chemical compound made up of hydrogen and carbon. A major pollutant formed by the engine as a byproduct of combustion.

HYDROMETER: An instrument used to measure the specific gravity of a solution.

INCH POUND (inch lbs.; sometimes in.lb. or in. lbs.): One twelfth of a foot pound.

INDUCTION: A means of transferring electrical energy in the form of a magnetic field. Principle used in the ignition coil to increase voltage.

INJECTOR: A device which receives metered fuel under relatively low pressure and is activated to inject the fuel into the engine under relatively high pressure at a predetermined time.

INPUT SHAFT: The shaft to which torque is applied, usually carrying the driving gear or gears.

INTAKE MANIFOLD: A casting of passages or pipes used to conduct air or a fuel/air mixture to the cylinders.

JOURNAL: The bearing surface within which a shaft operates.

KEY: A small block usually fitted in a notch between a shaft and a hub to prevent slippage of the two parts.

MANIFOLD: A casting of passages or set of pipes which connect the cylinders to an inlet or outlet source.

MANIFOLD VACUUM: Low pressure in an engine intake manifold formed just below the throttle plates. Manifold vacuum is highest at idle and drops under acceleration.

MASTER CYLINDER: The primary fluid pressurizing device in a hydraulic system. In automotive use, it is found in brake and hydraulic clutch systems and is pedal activated, either directly or, in a power brake system, through the power booster.

MODULE: Electronic control unit, amplifier or igniter of solid state or integrated design which controls the current flow in the ignition primary circuit based on input from the pick-up coil. When the module opens the primary circuit, high secondary voltage is induced in the coil.

NEEDLE BEARING: A bearing which consists of a number (usually a large number) of long, thin rollers.

OHM: (Ω) The unit used to measure the resistance of conductor-to-electrical flow. One ohm is the amount of resistance that limits current flow to one ampere in a circuit with one volt of pressure.

OHMMETER: An instrument used for measuring the resistance, in ohms, in an electrical circuit.

OUTPUT SHAFT: The shaft which transmits torque from a device, such as a transmission.

OVERDRIVE: A gear assembly which produces more shaft revolutions than that transmitted to it.

OVERHEAD CAMSHAFT (OHC): An engine configuration in which the camshaft is mounted on top of the cylinder head and operates the valve either directly or by means of rocker arms.

OVERHEAD VALVE (OHV): An engine configuration in which all of the valves are located in the cylinder head and the camshaft is located in the cylinder block. The camshaft operates the valves via lifters and pushrods.

OXIDES OF NITROGEN (NOx): Chemical compounds of nitrogen produced as a byproduct of combustion. They combine with hydrocarbons to produce smog.

OXYGEN SENSOR: Use with the feedback system to sense the presence of oxygen in the exhaust gas and signal the computer which can reference the voltage signal to an air/fuel ratio.

PINION: The smaller of two meshing gears.

PISTON RING: An open-ended ring with fits into a groove on the outer diameter of the piston. Its chief function is to form a seal between the piston and cylinder wall. Most automotive pistons have three rings: two for compression sealing; one for oil sealing.

PRELOAD: A predetermined load placed on a bearing during assembly or by adjustment.

PRIMARY CIRCUIT: the low voltage side of the ignition system which consists of the ignition switch, ballast resistor or resistance wire, bypass, coil, electronic control unit and pick-up coil as well as the connecting wires and harnesses.

PRESS FIT: The mating of two parts under pressure, due to the inner diameter of one being smaller than the outer diameter of the other, or vice versa; an interference fit.

RACE: The surface on the inner or outer ring of a bearing on which the balls, needles or rollers move.

REGULATOR: A device which maintains the amperage and/or voltage levels of a circuit at predetermined values.

RELAY: A switch which automatically opens and/or closes a circuit.

RESISTANCE: The opposition to the flow of current through a circuit or electrical device, and is measured in ohms. Resistance is equal to the voltage divided by the amperage.

RESISTOR: A device, usually made of wire, which offers a preset amount of resistance in an electrical circuit.

RING GEAR: The name given to a ring-shaped gear attached to a differential case, or affixed to a flywheel or as part of a planetary gear set.

ROLLER BEARING: A bearing made up of hardened inner and outer races between which hardened steel rollers move.

ROTOR: 1. The disc-shaped part of a disc brake assembly, upon which the brake pads bear; also called, brake disc. 2. The device mounted atop the distributor shaft, which passes current to the distributor cap tower contacts.

SECONDARY CIRCUIT: The high voltage side of the ignition system, usually above 20,000 volts. The secondary includes the ignition coil, coil wire, distributor cap and rotor, spark plug wires and spark plugs.

SENDING UNIT: A mechanical, electrical, hydraulic or electro-magnetic device which transmits information to a gauge.

SENSOR: Any device designed to measure engine operating conditions or ambient pressures and temperatures. Usually electronic in nature and designed to send a voltage signal to an on-board computer, some sensors may operate as a simple on/off switch or they may provide a variable voltage signal (like a potentiometer) as conditions or measured parameters change.

SHIM: Spacers of precise, predetermined thickness used between parts to establish a proper working relationship.

SLAVE CYLINDER: In automotive use, a device in the hydraulic clutch system which is activated by hydraulic force, disengaging the clutch.

SOLENOID: A coil used to produce a magnetic field, the effect of which is to produce work.

SPARK PLUG: A device screwed into the combustion chamber of a spark ignition engine. The basic construction is a conductive core inside of a ceramic insulator, mounted in an outer conductive base. An electrical charge from the spark plug wire travels along the conductive core and jumps a preset air gap to a grounding point or points at the end of the conductive base. The resultant spark ignites the fuel/air mixture in the combustion chamber.

SPLINES: Ridges machined or cast onto the outer diameter of a shaft or inner diameter of a bore to enable parts to mate without rotation.

TACHOMETER: A device used to measure the rotary speed of an engine, shaft, gear, etc., usually in rotations per minute.

THERMOSTAT: A valve, located in the cooling system of an engine, which is closed when cold and opens gradually in response to engine heating, controlling the temperature of the coolant and rate of coolant flow.

TOP DEAD CENTER (TDC): The point at which the piston reaches the top of its travel on the compression stroke.

TORQUE: The twisting force applied to an object.

TORQUE CONVERTER: A turbine used to transmit power from a driving member to a driven member via hydraulic action, providing changes in drive ratio and torque. In automotive use, it links the driveplate at the rear of the engine to the automatic transmission.

TRANSDUCER: A device used to change a force into an electrical signal.

TRANSISTOR: A semi-conductor component which can be actuated by a small voltage to perform an electrical switching function.

TUNE-UP: A regular maintenance function, usually associated with the replacement and adjustment of parts and components in the electrical and fuel systems of a vehicle for the purpose of attaining optimum performance.

TURBOCHARGER: An exhaust driven pump which compresses intake air and forces it into the combustion chambers at higher than atmospheric pressures. The increased air pressure allows more fuel to be burned and results in increased horsepower being produced.

VACUUM ADVANCE: A device which advances the ignition timing in response to increased engine vacuum.

VACUUM GAUGE: An instrument used to measure the presence of vacuum in a chamber.

VALVE: A device which control the pressure, direction of flow or rate of flow of a liquid or gas.

VALVE CLEARANCE: The measured gap between the end of the valve stem and the rocker arm, cam lobe or follower that activates the valve.

VISCOSITY: The rating of a liquid's internal resistance to flow.

VOLTMETER: An instrument used for measuring electrical force in units called volts. Voltmeters are always connected parallel with the circuit being tested.

WHEEL CYLINDER: Found in the automotive drum brake assembly, it is a device, actuated by hydraulic pressure, which, through internal pistons, pushes the brake shoes outward against the drums.

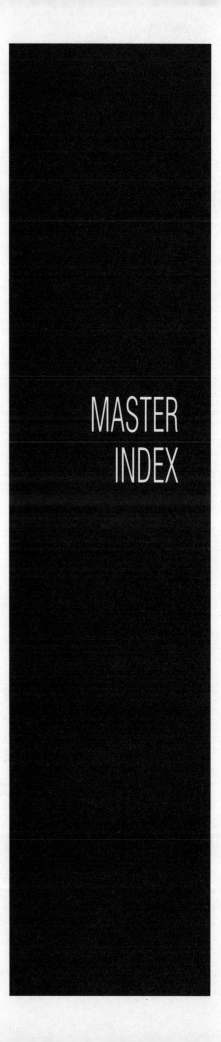

MASTER
INDEX